**LaunchPad**   **launchpadworks.com**

At Macmillan Education, we are committed to providing online resources that meet the needs of instructors and students in powerful yet simple ways. LaunchPad, our course space, offers our trusted content and student-friendly approach, organized for easy assignability in a simple user interface.

- **Interactive e-Book:** The e-book for *Ways of the World* comes with powerful study tools, multimedia content, and easy customization for instructors. Students can search, highlight, and bookmark, making it easier to study.

- **LearningCurve:** Game-like adaptive quizzing motivates students to engage with their course, and reporting tools help teachers identify the needs of their students.

- **Easy to Start:** Pre-built, curated units are easy to assign or adapt with additional material, such as readings, videos, quizzes, discussion groups, and more.

LaunchPad also provides access to a gradebook that offers a window into students' performance — either individually or as a whole. Use LaunchPad on its own or integrate it with your school's learning management system so your class is always on the same page.

To learn more about LaunchPad for *Ways of the World* or to request access, go to **launchpadworks.com**. If your book came packaged with an access card to LaunchPad, follow the card's login instructions.

Ways of the World

A Brief Global History
with Sources

Ways of the World
A Brief Global History
with Sources

ROBERT W. STRAYER

The College at Brockport: State University of New York

ERIC W. NELSON

Missouri State University

THIRD EDITION

Bedford/St.Martin's
A Macmillan Education Imprint

Boston • New York

For Evelyn Rhiannon with Love

For Bedford/St. Martin's

*Vice President, Editorial, Macmillan Higher
  Education Humanities:* Edwin Hill

Publisher for History: Michael Rosenberg

Director of Development for History: Jane Knetzger

Senior Developmental Editor: Leah R. Strauss

Senior Production Editor: Christina M. Horn

Senior Production Supervisor: Dennis J. Conroy

Executive Marketing Manager: Sandra McGuire

Media Editor: Jennifer Jovin

Associate Editor: Tess Fletcher

Production Assistant: Erica Zhang

Copy Editor: Jennifer Brett Greenstein

Indexer: Leoni Z. McVey

Cartography: Mapping Specialists, Ltd.

Photo Researcher: Bruce Carson

Director of Rights and Permissions: Hilary Newman

Senior Art Director: Anna Palchik

Text Design: Joyce Weston

Cover Design: William Boardman

Composition: Jouve

Printing and Binding: C.O.S. Printers Pte Ltd

Manufactured in Singapore.

0   9   8   7
f   e   d   c

For information, write: Bedford/St. Martin's, 75 Arlington Street, Boston, MA 02116
  (617-399-4000)

ISBN 978-1-4576-9991-7 (Combined Edition)
ISBN 978-1-319-01841-2 (Volume 1)
ISBN 978-1-319-01844-3 (Loose-leaf Edition, Volume 1)
ISBN 978-1-319-01842-9 (Volume 2)
ISBN 978-1-319-01845-0 (Loose-leaf Edition, Volume 2)

Preface

Why This Book This Way

Publishing this third edition of *Ways of the World* feels to me, its original author, a little like sending a child off to college or into the world. This familiar but changed and enhanced book is, I hope, more mature than it was at its birth in the first edition or in its growing-up years in the second. Much of this maturing of *Ways of the World* derives from its recent acquisition of a coauthor, Eric Nelson, a professor of history at Missouri State University, where he teaches world history and early modern European history. With a D.Phil. from the University of Oxford, Eric has written several books about sectarian conflict and religious peacemaking in early modern France. And he is known as an enormously popular and skilled teacher, winning numerous awards, including the CASE/Carnegie Endowment for the Advancement of Teaching Professor of the Year in Missouri Award for 2012. Furthermore, he has become a national leader in online course design and pedagogy. More personally, Eric has been a delight to work with as we have collaborated in every dimension of preparing *Ways of the World* for its third edition. So henceforth and with great pleasure, the authorial "I" becomes a "we."

Over the years following its initial appearance in 2008, *Ways of the World* has changed, or "grown up," in other ways as well. Most substantially, since 2010 it has become not simply a textbook but also a "docutext" or sourcebook, containing chapter-based sets of written and visual primary sources. Reflected in the subtitle of the book, *A Brief Global History with Sources*, this addition has provided a "laboratory" experience located within the textbook, enabling students to engage directly with the evidence of documents and images—in short to "do history" even as they are reading history. Following the narrative portion of each chapter is a set of primary sources, either documentary or visual. Each collection is organized around a particular theme, issue, or question that derives from the chapter narrative. As the title of these features suggests, they enable students to "**work with evidence**" and thus begin to understand the craft of historians as well as their conclusions. They include brief headnotes that provide context for the sources, and they are accompanied by a series of probing Doing History questions appropriate for in-class discussion and writing assignments.

Furthermore, the organization of the narrative has been tightened and its content enhanced by integrating both the gender and the environmental material more fully. Coverage of particular areas of the world, such as Southeast Asia, Latin America, and Pacific Oceania, has been strengthened. And the book has more often highlighted individual people and particular events, which sometimes get lost in the broad sweep of world history. Finally, *Ways of the World* has acquired a very substantial electronic and online presence with a considerable array of pedagogical and learning aids.

Despite these changes, *Ways of the World* is also recognizably the same book that it was in earlier versions—it has the same narrative brevity, the same big picture focus, the same thematic and comparative structure, the same clear and accessible writing, and the same musing or reflective tone. All of this has attracted for *Ways of the World* a remarkable, and somewhat surprising, audience. Even before this third edition appeared, the book had been adopted by world history instructors at over 600 colleges and universities, and more than 275,000 students have used the book.

Tools for the Digital Age

Because the teaching of history is changing rapidly, we are pleased to offer online novel interactive complements to the new edition of *Ways of the World* via Bedford's learning platform, known as **LaunchPad**. Available for packaging with the book, LaunchPad's course space and interactive e-book are ready to use as is, or can be edited and customized with your own material and assigned right away. Developed with extensive feedback from history instructors and students, LaunchPad includes the complete narrative e-book, as well as abundant primary documents, assignments, and activities. Key learning outcomes are addressed via formative and summative assessment, short-answer and essay questions, multiple-choice quizzing, and **LearningCurve**, an adaptive learning tool designed to get students to read before they come to class. With LearningCurve, students move through the narrative text at their own pace and accumulate points as they go, in a game-like fashion. Feedback for incorrect responses explains why the answer is incorrect and directs students back to the text to review before they attempt to answer the question again. The end result is a better understanding of the key elements of the text.

In addition to LearningCurve, we are delighted to offer 23 new online **primary source projects called Thinking through Sources**, one for each chapter of the book. These features, available only in LaunchPad, extend and substantially amplify the Working with Evidence source projects provided in the print book and also available in LaunchPad. They explore in greater depth a central theme from each chapter, and they integrate both documentary and visual sources. Most importantly, these LaunchPad features are uniquely surrounded by a distinctive and sophisticated pedagogy of self-grading exercises. Featuring immediate substantive feedback for each rejoinder, these exercises help students learn even when they select the wrong answer. More broadly, such exercises guide students in assessing their understanding of the sources, in organizing those sources for use in an essay, and in drawing useful conclusions from them. In this interactive learning environment, students will enhance their ability to build arguments and to practice histori-cal reasoning. Thus this LaunchPad pedagogy does for skill development what LearningCurve does for content mastery and reading comprehension.

More specifically, a short **quiz after each source** offers students the oppor-tunity to check their understanding of materials that often derive from quite distant times and places. Some questions focus on audience, purpose, point of view, limi-tations, or context, while others challenge students to draw conclusions about the source or to compare one source with another. Immediate substantive feedback for each rejoinder and the opportunity to try again create an active learning environ-ment where students are rewarded for reaching the correct answer through their own process of exploration.

Two activities at the end of each Thinking through Sources exercise ask stu-dents to make supportable inferences and draw appropriate conclusions from sources with reference to a **Guiding Question**. In the **Organize the Evidence activity**, students identify which sources provide evidence for a topic that would potentially compose part of an answer to the guiding question. In the **Draw Conclusions from the Evidence activity**, students assess whether a specific piece of evidence drawn from the sources supports or challenges a conclusion related to the guiding question. Collectively these assignments create an active learning environment where reading with a purpose is reinforced by immediate feedback and support. The guiding question provides a foundation for in-class activities or a summative writing assignment.

These guiding questions challenge students to assess what the sources collec-tively reveal, drawing on documents and images alike. The Thinking through Sources feature linked to Chapter 5, for instance, presents a range of sources deal-ing with expressions of patriarchy in the Mediterranean, Indian, and Chinese civi-lizations. Its guiding question asks students to compare them, while its Organize the Evidence activity invites students to identify in turn those sources that shed light on marriage, the confinement of women, the authority of men, and opposi-tion to patriarchal norms. The feature related to Chapter 21 offers both written and visual sources probing the nature of the Stalinist phenomenon with a guiding ques-tion that asks students to identify various postures—both positive and critical—toward it. The Draw Conclusions from the Evidence activity attached to this feature challenges students to identify whether specific pieces of evidence drawn from the sources support particular conclusions: that some individuals found oppor-tunities for personal advancement in Stalin's Soviet Union; that socialist ideals and values were betrayed during his rule; and that the Soviet Union accomplished some of the fundamental goals of Stalinism.

In a further set of features available only in LaunchPad, the text's narrative is enhanced through **Author Preview Videos (with Bob Strayer)**, which imagina-tively introduce each chapter, and **Another Voice Podcasts (with Eric Nelson)**, which enrich the treatment of particular issues and sometimes gently argue with the narrative text. Both the videos and the podcasts make extensive use of visuals.

LaunchPad also provides a simple, user-friendly platform for individual instructors to add their own voice, materials, and assignments to the text, guiding their students' learning outside of the traditional classroom setting.

Available with training and support, LaunchPad can help take history teaching and learning into a new era. To learn more about the benefits of Learning-Curve and LaunchPad and the different versions to package with LaunchPad, visit **macmillanhighered.com/strayersources/catalog** and see the Versions and Supplements section on page xix.

What Else Is New in the Third Edition?

In addition to the new online Thinking through Sources exercises and Eric Nelson's Another Voice Podcasts described above, further substantive changes to this third edition include the following:

- A much-enhanced treatment of **environmental issues** in world history throughout the book, including a more thorough account of environmentalism and climate change during the past century.
- A more frequent and thorough **inclusion of Pacific Oceania** within the narrative, especially in Chapter 6, where it takes its rightful place as a distinctive cultural region alongside other such regions in Africa and the Americas.
- A new feature called **Zooming In** calls attention twice in each chapter to particular people, places, and events, situating them in a larger global context. It incorporates many of the biographical "portraits" from the second edition, while adding many new examples as well. These include the remarkable archeological sites of Göbekli Tepe and Caral, the Buddhist "university" of Nalanda, an account of the camel, tales of the Islamic folk character Mullah Nasruddin, the Ottoman devshirme, the Russian Decembrists, the Cuban Revolution, the civil war in Mozambique, and many more.
- The **map program** in the book has been revised and strengthened.
- The **source-based features** in the print book (Working with Evidence) include a number of new entries such as Australian Dreamtime stories in Chapter 1 and conflicting views of Islam and women's dress in Chapter 22. An entirely new feature in Chapter 3 probes outsiders' accounts of Persia and Egypt, the Germanic peoples of Central Europe, and the Xiongnu living to the north of China. And in Chapter 17, students will now encounter a variety of socialist voices from an industrializing Europe.

Promoting Active Learning

As all instructors know, students can often "do the assignment" or read the required chapter and yet have little understanding of it when they come to class. The problem, frequently, is passive studying—a quick once-over, perhaps some highlighting of the text—but little sustained involvement with the material. A central peda-gogical problem in all teaching is how to encourage more active, engaged styles of learning. We want to enable students to manipulate the information of the book, using its ideas and data to answer questions, to make comparisons, to draw conclu-sions, to criticize assumptions, and to infer implications that are not explicitly dis-closed in the text itself.

Ways of the World seeks to promote active learning in various ways. Most obvi-ously, the source-based features in the book itself (Working with Evidence) and those housed separately on LaunchPad (Thinking through Sources) invite students to engage actively with documents and images alike, assisted by abundant ques-tions to guide that engagement. The wrap-around pedagogy that accompanies the Thinking through Sources activities virtually ensures active learning, if it is required by instructors. So do the LearningCurve quizzes that help students actively rehearse what they have read and foster a deeper understanding and retention of the material.

Another active learning element involves motivation. A **contemporary vignette** opens each chapter with a story that links the past and the present to show the continuing resonance of history in the lives of contemporary people. Chapter 6, for example, begins by describing the inauguration in 2010 of Bolivian president Evo Morales at an impressive ceremony at Tiwanaku, the center of an ancient Andean empire, and emphasizing the continuing importance of this ancient civili-zation in Bolivian culture. At the end of each chapter, a short **Reflections** section raises provocative, sometimes quasi-philosophical, questions about the craft of the historian and the unfolding of the human story. We hope these brief essays provide an incentive for our students' own pondering and grist for the mill of vigorous class discussions.

A further technique for encouraging active learning lies in the provision of frequent contextual markers. Student readers need to know where they are going and where they have been. Thus part-opening **Big Picture essays** preview what follows in the subsequent chapters. A **chapter outline** opens each chapter, while **A Map of Time** provides a chronological overview of major events and pro-cesses. In addition, a **Seeking the Main Point** question helps students focus on the main theme of the chapter. Each chapter also has at least one **Summing Up So Far** question that invites students to reflect on what they have learned to that point in the chapter. **Snapshot boxes** present succinct glimpses of particular themes, regions, or time periods, adding some trees to the forest of world history. A **list of terms** at the end of each chapter invites students to check their grasp of the mate-rial. As usual with books published by Bedford/St. Martin's, a **rich illustration program** enhances the narrative.

Active learning means approaching the text with something to look for, rather than simply dutifully completing the assignment. *Ways of the World* provides such cues in abundance. A series of **questions in the margins**, labeled "change," "comparison," or "connection," allows students to read the adjacent material with a clear purpose in mind. **Big Picture Questions** at the end of each chapter deal with matters not directly addressed in the text. Instead, they provide opportunities for integration, comparison, analysis, and sometimes speculation.

What's in a Title?

The title of a book should evoke something of its character and outlook. The main title *Ways of the World* is intended to suggest at least three dimensions of the text.

The first is **diversity** or **variation**, for the "ways of the world," or the ways of being human in the world, have been many and constantly changing. This book seeks to embrace the global experience of humankind in its vast diversity, while noticing the changing location of particular centers of innovation and wider influence.

Second, the title *Ways of the World* invokes major **panoramas**, **patterns**, or **pathways** in world history, as opposed to highly detailed narratives. Many world history instructors have found that students often feel overwhelmed by the sheer quantity of information that a course in global history can require of them. In the narrative sections of this book, the larger patterns or the "big pictures" of world history appear in the foreground on center stage, while the still-plentiful details, data, and facts occupy the background, serving in supporting roles.

A third implication of the book's title lies in a certain **reflective** or **musing quality** of *Ways of the World*, which appears especially in the Big Picture essays that introduce each part of the book and in a Reflections section at the end of each chapter. These features of the book offer many opportunities for pondering larger questions. The Reflections section in Chapter 4, for example, explores how historians and religious believers sometimes rub each other the wrong way, while that of Chapter 12 probes the role of chance and coincidence in world history. The Chapter 21 Reflections asks whether historians should make judgments about the societies they study and whether it is possible to avoid doing so. The Big Picture introductions to Parts Three and Six raise questions about periodization, while that of Part Five explores how historians might avoid Eurocentrism when considering an era when Europe was increasingly central in world history. None of these issues can be easily or permanently resolved, but the opportunity to contemplate them is among the great gifts that the study of history offers us.

The Dilemma of World History: Inclusivity and Coherence

The great virtue of world history lies in its inclusivity, for its subject matter is the human species itself. No one is excluded, and all may find a place within the grand narrative of the human journey. But that virtue is also the source of world history's greatest difficulty—telling a coherent story. How can we meaningfully present the planet's many and distinct peoples and their intersections with one another in the confines of a single book or a single term? What prevents that telling from bogging down in the endless detail of various civilizations or cultures, from losing the forest for the trees, from implying that history is just "one damned thing after another"?

Less Can Be More

From the beginning, *Ways of the World* set out to cope with this fundamental conundrum of world history—the tension between inclusion and coherence—in several ways. The first is the relative brevity of the narrative. This means leaving some things out or treating them more succinctly than some instructors might expect. But it also means that the textbook need not overwhelm students or dominate the course. It allows for more creativity from instructors in constructing their own world history courses, giving them the opportunity to mix and match text, sources, and other materials in distinctive ways. Coherence is facilitated as well by a themes and cases approach to world history. Most chapters are organized in terms of broad themes that are illustrated with a limited number of specific examples.

The Centrality of Context: Change, Comparison, Connection

A further aid to achieving coherence amid the fragmenting possibilities of inclusion lies in maintaining the centrality of context, for in world history nothing stands alone. Those of us who practice world history as teachers or textbook authors are seldom specialists in the particulars of what we study and teach. Rather, we are "specialists of the whole," seeking to find the richest, most suggestive, and most meaningful contexts in which to embed those particulars. Our task, fundamentally, is to teach contextual thinking.

To aid in this task, *Ways of the World* repeatedly highlights three such contexts, what I call the "**three Cs**" of world history: **change/continuity**, **comparison**, and **connection**. The first "C" emphasizes large-scale **change**, both within and especially across major regions of the world. Examples include the peopling of the planet, the breakthrough to agriculture, the emergence of "civilization," the rise of universal religions, the changing shape of the Islamic world, the linking of Eastern and Western hemispheres in the wake of Columbus's voyages, the Industrial Revolution, the rise and fall of world communism, and the acceleration of globalization during the twentieth century. The flip side of change, of course, is continuity, implying a focus on what persists over long periods of time. And so *Ways of the World* seeks to juxtapose these contrasting elements of human experience. While civilizations have changed dramatically over time, some of their essential features—cities, states, patriarchy, and class inequality, for example—have long endured.

The second "C" involves frequent **comparison**, a technique of integration through juxtaposition, bringing several regions or cultures into our field of vision at the same time. It encourages reflection both on the common elements of the human experience and on its many variations. Such comparisons are pervasive throughout the book, informing both the chapter narratives and many of the docutext features. *Ways of the World* explicitly examines the difference, for example, between the Agricultural Revolution in the Eastern and Western hemispheres; between the beginnings of Buddhism and the early history of Christianity and Islam; between patriarchy in Athens and in Sparta; between European and Asian empires of the early modern era; between the Chinese and the Japanese response to European intrusion; between the Russian and Chinese revolutions; and many more. Many of the primary source features are also broadly comparative or cross-cultural. For example, a document-based feature in Chapter 11 explores percep-tions of the Mongols from the perspective of Persians, Russians, Europeans, and the Mongols themselves. Likewise, an image-based feature in Chapter 15 uses art and architecture to examine various expressions of Christianity in Reformation Europe, colonial Bolivia, seventeenth-century China, and Mughal India.

The final "C" emphasizes **connection**, networks of communication and exchange that increasingly shaped the character of the societies that participated in them. For world historians, cross-cultural interaction becomes one of the major motors of historical transformation. Such connections are addressed in nearly every chapter and in many docutext features. Examples include the clash of the ancient Greeks and the Persians; the long-distance commercial networks that linked the Afro-Eurasian world; the numerous cross-cultural encounters spawned by the spread of Islam; the trans-hemispheric Columbian exchange of the early modern era; and the growth of a genuinely global economy.

Organizing World History: Time, Place, and Theme

All historical writing occurs at the intersection of time, place, and theme. **Time** is the matrix in which history takes shape, allowing us to chart the changes and the continuities of human experience. **Place** recognizes variation and distinctiveness among societies and cultures as well as the importance of the environmental set-ting in which history unfolds. **Theme** reflects the need to write or teach about one thing at a time—the creation of empires, gender identity, the development of religious traditions, or cross-cultural trade, for example—even while exploring the linkages among them. Organizing a world history textbook involves balancing these three principles of organization in a flexible format that can accommodate a variety of teaching approaches and curricular strategies. In doing so, we have also drawn on our own sense of "what works" in the classroom and on best practice in the field.

This book addresses the question of time or chronology by dividing world history into six major periods. Each of these six "parts" begins with a **Big Picture essay** that introduces the general patterns of a particular period and raises questions about the problems historians face in periodizing the human past.

Part One (to 500 B.C.E.) deals in two chapters with beginnings—of human migration and social construction from the Paleolithic era through the Agricultural Revolution and the development of the First Civilizations. These chapters pursue such important themes on a global scale, illustrating them with regional examples treated comparatively.

Part Two examines the millennium of second-wave civilizations (500 B.C.E.– 500 C.E.) and employs the thematic principle in exploring the major civilizations of Eurasia (Chinese, Indian, Persian, and Mediterranean), with separate chapters focusing on their empires (Chapter 3), their religious and cultural traditions (Chapter 4), and their social organization (Chapter 5). These Afro-Eurasian chapters are followed by a single chapter (Chapter 6) that examines regionally the second-wave era in sub-Saharan Africa, the Americas, and Pacific Oceania.

Part Three, embracing the thousand years between 500 and 1500 C.E., reflects a mix of theme and place. Chapter 7 focuses topically on commercial networks across the world, while Chapters 8, 9, and 10 deal regionally with the Chinese, Islamic, and Christian worlds respectively. Chapter 11 treats pastoral societies as a broad theme and the Mongols as the most dramatic illustration of their impact on the larger stage of world history. Chapter 12, which bridges the two volumes of the book, presents an around-the-world tour in the fifteenth century, which serves both to conclude Volume 1 and to open Volume 2.

Part Four considers the early modern era (1450–1750) and treats each of its three chapters thematically. Chapter 13 compares European and Asian empires; Chapter 14 lays out the major patterns of global commerce and their consequences; and Chapter 15 focuses on cultural patterns, including the globalization of Christianity and the rise of modern science.

Part Five takes up the era of maximum European influence in the world, from 1750 to 1914. It charts the emergence of distinctively modern societies, devoting separate chapters to the Atlantic revolutions (Chapter 16) and the Industrial Revolution (Chapter 17). Chapters 18 and 19 focus on the growing impact of those European societies on the rest of humankind—first on the world of formal colonies and then on the still-independent states of China, the Ottoman Empire, and Japan.

Part Six, which looks at the most recent century (1914–2015), is perhaps the most problematic for world historians, given the abundance of data and the absence of time to sort out what is fundamental and what is peripheral. Its four chapters explore themes of global significance. Chapter 20 focuses on the descent of Europe into war, depression, and the Holocaust, and the global outcomes of this collapse. Chapter 21 examines global communism—its birth in revolution, its efforts to create socialist societies, its role in the cold war, and its abandonment by the end of the twentieth century. Chapter 22 turns the spotlight on the African, Asian, and Latin American majority of the world's inhabitants, describing their exit from formal colonial rule and their emergence on the world stage as the developing countries. Chapter 23 concludes this account of the human journey by assessing the economic, environmental, and cultural dimensions of what we know as globalization.

"It Takes a Village"

In any enterprise of significance, "it takes a village," as they say. Bringing *Ways of the World* to life in this new edition, it seems, has occupied the energies of several villages. Among the privileges and delights of writing and revising this book has been the opportunity to interact with our fellow villagers.

We are grateful to the community of fellow historians who contributed their expertise to this revision. Carter Findley, Humanities Distinguished Professor at Ohio State University, carefully read the sections of the book dealing with the Islamic world, offering us very useful guidance. Gregory Cushman from the University of Kansas provided us with an extraordinarily detailed analysis of places where our coverage of environmental issues might be strengthened. He also gave us a similarly comprehensive review of our Latin American and Pacific Oceania material. We also extend a special thanks to Stanley Burstein, emeritus at California State University–Los Angeles, who has been a wonderfully helpful mentor on all matters ancient, and to Edward Gutting and Suzanne Sturn for original translations of particular documents. We are grateful for their contributions.

The largest of these communities consists of the many people who read earlier editions and made suggestions for improvement. We offer our thanks to the following reviewers: Maria S. Arbelaez, University of Nebraska–Omaha; Veronica L. Bale, Mira Costa College; Christopher Bellitto, Kean University; Monica Bord-Lamberty, Northwood High School; Ralph Croizier, University of Victoria; Edward Dandrow, University of Central Florida; Peter L. de Rosa, Bridgewater State University; Amy Forss, Metropolitan Community College; Denis Gainty, Georgia State University; Steven A. Glazer, Graceland University; Sue Gronewald, Kean University; Andrew Hamilton, Viterbo University; J. Laurence Hare, University of Arkansas; Michael Hinckley, Northern Kentucky University; Bram Hubbell, Friends Seminary; Ronald Huch, Eastern Kentucky University; Elizabeth Hyde, Kean University; Mark Lentz, University of Louisiana–Lafayette; Kate McGrath, Central Connecticut State University; C. Brid Nicholson, Kean University; Donna Patch, Westside High School; Jonathan T. Reynolds, Northern Kentucky University; James Sabathne, Hononegah High School; Christopher Sleeper, Mira Costa College; Ira Spar, Ramapo College and Metropolitan Museum of Art; Kristen Strobel, Lexington High School; Michael Vann, Sacramento State University; Peter Winn, Tufts University; and Judith Zinsser, Miami University of Ohio.

We extend our thanks to the contributors to the supplements: Lisa Tran, California State University–Fullerton; Michael Vann, Sacramento State University; and John Reisbord. We would also like to offer a special thanks to Mike Fisher and Eric Taylor for their time and expertise producing the Another Voice Podcasts.

The Bedford village has been a second community sustaining this enterprise and the one most directly responsible for the book's third edition. It would be difficult for any author to imagine a more supportive and professional publishing team. Our chief point of contact with the Bedford village has been Leah Strauss, our development editor. She has coordinated the immensely complex task of assembling a new edition of the book and has done so with great professional care, with timely responses to our many queries, and with sensitivity to the needs and feelings of authors, even when she found it necessary to decline our suggestions.

Others on the team have also exhibited that lovely combination of personal kindness and professional competence that is so characteristic of the Bedford way. Editorial director Edwin Hill and publisher Michael Rosenberg have kept an eye on the project amid many duties. Jane Knetzger, director of development, provided overall guidance as well as the necessary resources. Christina Horn, our production editor, managed the process of turning a manuscript into a published book and did so with both grace and efficiency. Operating behind the scenes in the Bedford village, a series of highly competent and always supportive people have shepherded this revised edition along its way. Photo researcher Bruce Carson identified and acquired the many images that grace this new edition of *Ways of the World* and did so with a keen eye and courtesy. Copy editor Jennifer Brett Greenstein polished the prose and sorted out our many inconsistent usages with a seasoned and perceptive eye. Sandra McGuire has overseen the marketing process, while Bedford's sales representatives have reintroduced the book to the academic world. Jen Jovin supervised the development of ancillary materials to support the book, and William Boardman ably coordinated research for the lovely covers that mark *Ways of the World*. Eve Lehman conducted the always-difficult negotiations surrounding permissions with more equanimity than we could have imagined. And our editorial assistant Tess Fletcher handled the thousand and one details of this process so well that we were hardly aware that they were being handled.

Yet another "village" that contributed much to *Ways of the World* is the group of distinguished scholars and teachers who worked with Robert Strayer on an earlier world history text, *The Making of the Modern World*, published by St. Martin's Press (1988, 1995). They include Sandria Freitag, Edwin Hirschmann, Donald Holsinger, James Horn, Robert Marks, Joe Moore, Lynn Parsons, and Robert Smith. That collective effort resembled participation in an extended seminar, from which I benefited immensely. Their ideas and insights have shaped my own understanding of world history in many ways and greatly enriched *Ways of the World*.

A final and much smaller community sustained this project and its authors. It is that most intimate of villages that we know as a marriage. Sharing that village with me (Robert Strayer) is my wife, Suzanne Sturn. It is her work to bring ideas and people to life onstage, even as I try to do so between these covers. She knows how I feel about her love and support, and no one else needs to. And across the street, I (Eric Nelson) would also like to thank two new residents of this village: my wife, Alice Victoria, and our little girl, Evelyn Rhiannon, to whom this new edition is dedicated. Without their patience and support, I could not have become part of such an interesting journey.

To all of our fellow villagers, we offer deep thanks for an immensely rewarding experience. We are grateful beyond measure.

Robert Strayer, La Selva Beach, California, Summer 2015
Eric Nelson, Springfield, Missouri, Summer 2015

Versions and Supplements

Adopters of *Ways of the World* and their students have access to abundant print and digital resources and tools, including documents, assessment and presentation materials, the acclaimed Bedford Series in History and Culture volumes, and much more. The LaunchPad course space provides access to the narrative with all assignment and assessment opportunities at the ready. See below for more information, visit the book's catalog site at **macmillanhighered.com/strayersources /catalog**, or contact your local Bedford/St. Martin's sales representative.

Get the Right Version for Your Class

To accommodate different course lengths and course budgets, *Ways of the World* is available in several different formats, including 3-hole-punched loose-leaf Budget Books versions and low-priced PDF e-books. And for the best value of all, package a new print book with LaunchPad at no additional charge to get the best each format offers—a print version for easy portability and reading with a LaunchPad interactive e-book and course space with loads of additional assignment and assessment options.

- **Combined Volume** (Chapters 1–23): available in paperback and e-book formats and in LaunchPad
- **Volume 1, Through the Fifteenth Century** (Chapters 1–12): available in paperback, loose-leaf, and e-book formats and in LaunchPad
- **Volume 2, Since the Fifteenth Century** (Chapters 12–23): available in paperback, loose-leaf, and e-book formats and in LaunchPad

As noted below, any of these volumes can be packaged with additional titles for a discount. To get ISBNs for discount packages, see the online catalog at **macmillanhighered.com/strayersources/catalog** or contact your Bedford/St. Martin's representative.

LaunchPad Assign LaunchPad—an Assessment-Ready Interactive E-book and Course Space

Available for discount purchase on its own or for packaging with new books at no additional charge, LaunchPad is a breakthrough solution for today's courses. Intuitive and easy to use for students and instructors alike, LaunchPad is ready to use as is and can be edited, customized with your own material, and assigned in seconds. *LaunchPad for Ways of the World* provides Bedford/St. Martin's high-quality content all in one place, including the full interactive e-book plus LearningCurve formative quizzing; guided reading activities designed to help students read actively for key concepts; additional primary sources, with auto-graded source-based questions to build skill development; images; videos; chapter summative quizzes; and more.

Through a wealth of formative and summative assessments, including the adaptive learning program of LearningCurve (see the full description below), students gain confidence and get into their reading before class. In addition to LearningCurve, we are delighted to offer new online primary source projects called Thinking through Sources, one for each chapter of *Ways of the World*. These features, available only in LaunchPad, explore in greater depth a central theme from each chapter and, most importantly, are uniquely surrounded by a distinctive and sophisticated pedagogy of self-grading exercises. Featuring immediate substantive feedback for each rejoinder, these exercises help students learn even when they select the wrong answer. These exercises guide students in assessing their understanding of the sources, in organizing those sources for use in an essay, and in drawing useful conclusions from them. In this interactive learning environment, students will enhance their ability to build arguments and to practice historical reasoning. Thus this LaunchPad pedagogy does for skill development what LearningCurve does for content mastery and reading comprehension.

LaunchPad easily integrates with course management systems, and with fast ways to build assignments, rearrange chapters, and add new pages, sections, or links, it lets teachers build the courses they want to teach and hold students accountable. For more information, visit **launchpadworks.com**, or to arrange a demo, contact us at **history@macmillanhighered.com**.

LearningCurve Assign LearningCurve So Your Students Come to Class Prepared

Students using LaunchPad receive access to LearningCurve for *Ways of the World*. Assigning LearningCurve in place of reading quizzes is easy for instructors, and the reporting features help instructors track overall class trends and spot topics that are giving students trouble so they can adjust their lectures and class activities. This online learning tool is popular with students because it was designed to help them rehearse content at their own pace in a nonthreatening, game-like environment. The feedback for wrong answers provides instructional coaching and sends students back to the book for review. Students answer as many questions as necessary to reach a target score, with repeated chances to revisit material they haven't mastered. When LearningCurve is assigned, students come to class better prepared.

Take Advantage of Instructor Resources

Bedford/St. Martin's has developed a rich array of teaching resources for this book and for this course. They range from lecture and presentation materials and assessment tools to course management options. Most can be found in LaunchPad or can be downloaded or ordered at **macmillanhighered.com/strayersources/catalog**.

Bedford Coursepack for Blackboard, Canvas, D2L, or Moodle. We can help you integrate our rich content into your course management system. Registered instructors can download coursepacks that include our popular free resources and book-specific content for *Ways of the World*. Visit **macmillanhighered.com/cms** to find your version or download your coursepack.

Instructor's Resource Manual. The instructor's manual offers both experienced and first-time instructors tools presenting textbook material in engaging ways. It includes content learning objectives, annotated chapter outlines, and strategies for teaching with the textbook, plus suggestions on how to get the most out of LearningCurve and a survival guide for first-time teaching assistants.

Guide to Changing Editions. Designed to facilitate an instructor's transition from the previous edition of *Ways of the World* to this new edition, this guide presents an overview of major changes as well as of changes in each chapter.

Online Test Bank. The test bank includes a mix of fresh, carefully crafted multiple-choice, matching, short-answer, and essay questions for each chapter. All questions appear in Microsoft Word format and in easy-to-use test bank software that allows instructors to add, edit, re-sequence, and print questions and answers. Instructors can also export questions into a variety of course management systems.

The Bedford Lecture Kit: **Lecture Outlines, Maps, and Images.** Be effective and save time with *The Bedford Lecture Kit*. These presentation materials are downloadable individually from the Instructor Resources tab at **macmillanhighered .com/strayersources/catalog**. They include fully customizable multimedia presentations built around chapter outlines that are embedded with maps, figures, and images from the textbook and are supplemented by more detailed instructor notes on key points and concepts.

Package and Save Your Students Money

For information on free packages and discounts up to 50%, visit **macmillanhighered .com/strayersources/catalog**, or contact your local Bedford/St. Martin's sales representative. The products that follow all qualify for discount packaging.

The Bedford Series in History and Culture. More than 100 titles in this highly praised series combine first-rate scholarship, historical narrative, and important primary documents for undergraduate courses. Each book is brief, inexpensive, and focused on a specific topic or period. For a complete list of titles, visit **bedford stmartins.com/history/series**.

Rand McNally Atlas of World History. This collection of almost 70 full-color maps illustrates the eras and civilizations in world history from the emergence of human societies to the present.

The Bedford Glossary for World History. This handy supplement for the survey course gives students historically contextualized definitions for hundreds of terms — from *abolitionism* to *Zoroastrianism* — that they will encounter in lectures, reading, and exams.

World History Matters: A Student Guide to World History Online. Based on the popular "World History Matters" Web site produced by the Center for History and New Media, this unique resource, edited by Kristin Lehner (The Johns Hopkins University), Kelly Schrum (George Mason University), and T. Mills Kelly (George Mason University), combines reviews of 150 of the most useful and reliable world history Web sites with an introduction that guides students in locating, evaluating, and correctly citing online sources.

Trade Books. Titles published by sister companies Hill and Wang; Farrar, Straus and Giroux; Henry Holt and Company; St. Martin's Press; Picador; and Palgrave Macmillan are available at a 50% discount when packaged with Bedford/St. Martin's textbooks. For more information, visit **macmillanhighered.com/tradeup**.

A Pocket Guide to Writing in History. This portable and affordable reference tool by Mary Lynn Rampolla provides reading, writing, and research advice useful to students in all history courses. Concise yet comprehensive advice on approaching typical history assignments, developing critical reading skills, writing effective history papers, conducting research, using and documenting sources, and avoiding plagiarism — enhanced with practical tips and examples throughout — has made this slim reference a best seller.

A Student's Guide to History. This complete guide to success in any history course provides the practical help students need to be successful. In addition to introducing students to the nature of the discipline, author Jules Benjamin teaches a wide range of skills from preparing for exams to approaching common writing assignments, and explains the research and documentation process with plentiful examples.

Brief Contents

Contents

---

photo: © De Agostini Picture Library/age fotostock

XXV

2   First Civilizations: Cities, States, and Unequal Societies, 3500 B.C.E.–500 B.C.E.   59

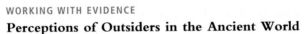

photo: © Peter M. Wilson/
Alamy

PART THREE   An Age of Accelerating Connections, 500–1500

7 Commerce and Culture, 500–1500

photos: From the *"Maqamat" of Abu Mohammed el Qasim ibn Ali Hariri* (1054–1122), 1237/© BnF, Dist. RMN–Grand Palais/ Art Resource, NY; From the Psalter of Charles the Bold, 15th century/Victoria & Albert Museum, London, UK/ Bridgeman Images

11 Pastoral Peoples on the Global Stage: The Mongol Moment, 1200–1500   457

12   The Worlds of the Fifteenth Century   499

PART FOUR   The Early Modern World, 1450–1750

13 Political Transformations: Empires and Encounters, 1450–1750

PART FIVE   The European Moment in World History, 1750–1914

---

16 Atlantic Revolutions, Global Echoes, 1750–1914

photo: Musée de la Ville de
Paris, Musée Carnavalet, Paris,
France/© RMN–Grand Palais/
Art Resource, NY

17 Revolutions of Industrialization, 1750–1914

photo: Vivian's copper foundry,
Swansea, Wales, engraving by
Durand-Brager/Bibliothèque des
Arts décoratifs, Paris, France/
Gianni Dagli Orti/The Art Archive
at Art Resource, NY

18 Colonial Encounters in Asia, Africa, and Oceania, 1750–1950

19 Empires in Collision: Europe, the Middle East, and East Asia, 1800–1914

PART SIX   The Most Recent Century, 1914–2015

20   Collapse at the Center: World War, Depression, and the Rebalancing of Global Power, 1914–1970s

photo: Library of Congress, Prints and Photographs Division, LC-USZC4-2119

photo: Private Collection/RIA
Novosti/Bridgeman Images

Maps

Big Picture Maps

Chapter Maps

Features

Zooming In

Snapshot

Thinking through Sources

Primary Source Exercises Available Only in LaunchPad

For more information, visit **macmillanhighered.com/strayersources/catalog** or contact your Bedford/St. Martin's representative.

Working with Evidence

At the end of each chapter of *Ways of the World* is a set of primary sources called **Working with Evidence** that represent the kind of evidence that historians use in drawing their conclusions about the past. In addition, there are primary source activities surrounded by a distinctive and sophisticated pedagogy of self-grading exercises called **Thinking through Sources** available only in LaunchPad, the interactive course space for this book. (For more information about LaunchPad, visit **launchpadworks.com**, or to arrange a demo, contact us at **history@macmillan .com**.) Some of the primary sources are written—inscriptions, letters, diaries, law codes, official records, sacred texts, and much more. Others are visual—paintings, sculptures, engravings, photographs, posters, cartoons, buildings, and artifacts. Collectively they provide an opportunity for you to practice the work of historians in a kind of guided "history laboratory." In working with this evidence, you are "doing history," much as students conducting lab experiments in chemistry or biology courses are "doing science."

Since each feature explores a theme of the chapter, the chapter narrative itself provides a broad context for analyzing these sources. Furthermore, brief introductions to each feature and to each document or image offer more specific context or background information, while questions provide specific elements to look for as you examine each source. Other more integrative questions offer a focus for using those sources together to probe larger historical issues. What follows are a few more specific suggestions for assessing these raw materials of history.

Working with Written Sources

Written sources or documents are the most common type of primary source that historians use. Analysis of documents usually begins with the basics:

- Who wrote the document?
- When and where was it written?
- What type of document is it (for example, a letter to a friend, a political decree, an exposition of a religious teaching)?

Sometimes the document itself will provide answers to these questions. On other occasions, you may need to rely on the introductions.

Once these basics have been established, a historian is then likely to consider several further questions, which situate the document in its particular historical context:

- Why was the document written, for what audience, and under what circumstances?

- What point of view does it reflect? What other views or opinions is the document arguing against?

Inspiration and intention are crucial factors that shape the form and content of a source. For instance, one might examine a document differently depending on whether it was composed for a private or a public readership, or whether it was intended to be read by a small elite or a wider audience.

Still another level of analysis seeks to elicit useful information from the document.

- What material in the document is believable, and what is not?
- What might historians learn from this document?
- What can the document tell us about the individual who produced it and the society from which he or she came?

In all of this, historical imagination is essential. Informed by knowledge of the context and the content of the document, your imagination will help you read it through the eyes of its author and its audience. You should ask yourself: how might this document have been understood at the time it was written? But in using your imagination, you must take care not to read into the documents your own assumptions and understandings. It is a delicate balance, a kind of dance that historians constantly undertake. Even documents that contain material that historians find unbelievable can be useful, for we seek not only to know what actually happened in the past but also to grasp the world as the people who lived that past understood it. And so historians sometimes speak about reading documents "against the grain," looking for meanings that the author might not have intended to convey.

While each source must be read and understood individually, historians typically draw their strongest conclusions when they analyze a number of such sources together. The document features in *Ways of the World* are designed to explore sets of primary sources that address a central theme of the chapter by drawing on several related texts. In the documents for Chapter 11, for example, you can reflect on the Mongol Empire by reading several accounts written by Mongols themselves and several others composed by Russian or Persian victims of Mongol aggression. And in Chapter 22, you will encounter a debate among Muslims about the relationship between their faith and the modern world, with positions ranging from those that advocate the removal of Islam from public life to those that seek to embed Islamic law in the social and cultural fabric of their countries.

Working with Visual Sources

Visual sources derive from the material culture of the past—religious icons or paintings that add to our understanding of belief systems, a family portrait that provides insight into presentations of self in a particular time and place, a building or sculpture that reveals how power and authority were displayed in a specific empire. These kinds of evidence represent another category of primary source material that historians can use to re-create and understand the past. But such visual sources can be even more difficult to interpret than written documents. The ideas that animated the creators of particular images or artifacts are often not obvious. Nor are the meanings they conveyed to those who viewed or used them. The lovely images from the Indus River valley civilization contained in the visual sources feature for Chapter 2, for example, remain enigmatic although still engaging to twenty-first-century viewers.

Despite the difficulties of interpretation, visual sources can provide insights not offered by written documents. Various images of the Buddha shown in Chapter 4 effectively illustrate how the faith that he initiated changed as it spread beyond India to other parts of Asia. And the posters from Mao Zedong's China in Chapter 21 convey an immediate emotional sense about the meanings attached to communism at the time, at least to its supporters. Indeed, for preliterate societies, such as those described in Chapter 1, archeological and artistic evidence is almost all that remains of their history.

To use visual sources, we must try as best we can to see these pieces of evidence through the eyes of the societies that produced them and to decode the symbols and other features that imbue them with meaning. Thus context is, if anything, even more crucial for analyzing visual evidence than it is for documents. Understanding scenes from the life of Muhammad, featured in Chapter 9, depends heavily on some knowledge of Islamic history and culture. And the images in Chapter 16, illustrating various perceptions of the French Revolution, require some grasp of the unfolding of that enormous upheaval.

A set of basic questions, similar to those you would ask about a written document, provides a starting point for analyzing visual sources:

- When and where was the image or artifact created?
- Who made the image or artifact? Who paid for or commissioned it? For what audience(s) was it intended?
- Where was the image or artifact originally displayed or used?

Having established this basic information about the image or artifact, you may simply want to describe it, as if to someone who had never seen it before.

- If the source is an image, who or what is depicted? What activities are shown? How might you describe the positioning of figures, their clothing, hairstyles, and other visual cues?
- If the source is an object or building, how would you describe its major features?

Finally, you will want to take a stab at more interpretive issues, making use of what you know about the context in which the visual source was created.

- What likely purpose or function did the image or artifact serve?
- What message(s) does it seek to convey?

- How could it be interpreted differently depending on who viewed or used it?
- What are the meanings of any symbols or other abstract features in the visual source?
- What can the image or artifact tell us about the society that produced it and the time period in which it was created?

Beyond analyzing particular images or objects, you will be invited to draw conclusions from sets of related visual sources that address a central theme in the chapter. What can you learn, for example, about the life of Chinese elites from the visual sources in Chapter 8? And what do the images in the Working with Evidence feature of Chapter 15 disclose about the reception of Christianity in various cultural settings?

Primary sources—documentary and visual alike—are the foundation for all historical accounts. To read only secondary sources, such as textbooks or articles, is to miss much of the flavor and texture of history as it was actually experienced by people in the past. But immersing yourself in the documents and visual sources presented here allows you to catch a glimpse of the messiness, the ambiguity, the heartaches, and the achievements of history as it was lived.

Using these sources effectively, however, is no easy task. In fact, the work of historians might well be compared with that of Sisyphus, the ancient Greek king who, having offended the gods, was condemned to eternally roll a large rock up a mountain, only to have it ceaselessly fall back down. Like Sisyphus, historians work at a mission that can never be completely successful—to recapture the past before it is lost forever in the mists of time and fading memory. The evidence available is always partial and fragmentary. Historians and students of history alike are limited and fallible, for we operate often at a great distance—in both time and culture—from those we are studying. And we rarely agree on important matters, divided as we are by sex, nationality, religion, race, and values, all of which shape our understandings of the past.

Despite these challenges, scholars and students alike have long found their revisiting of the past a compelling project—intensely interesting, personally meaningful, and even fun—particularly when working with "primary" or "original" sources, which are the building blocks of all historical accounts. Such sources are windows into the lives of our ancestors, though these windows are often smudged and foggy. We hope that working with the evidence contained in these sources will enrich your own life as you listen in on multiple conversations from the past, eavesdropping, as it were, on our ancestors.

Prologue

From Cosmic History to Human History

History books in general, and world history textbooks in particular, share something in common with those Russian nested dolls in which a series of carved figures fit inside one another. In much the same fashion, all historical accounts take place within some larger context, as stories within stories unfold. Individual biographies and histories of local communities, particularly modern ones, occur within the context of one nation or another. Nations often find a place in some more encompassing civilization, such as the Islamic world or the West, or in a regional or continental context such as Southeast Asia, Latin America, or Africa. And those civilizational or regional histories in turn take on richer meaning when they are understood within the even broader story of world history, which embraces humankind as a whole.

Change

What have been the major turning points in the pre-human phases of "big history"?

In recent decades, some world historians have begun to situate that remarkable story of the human journey in the much larger framework of both cosmic and planetary history, an approach that has come to be called "big history." It is really the "history of everything" from the big bang to the present, and it extends over the enormous, almost unimaginable timescale of some 13.7 billion years, the current rough estimate of the age of the universe.[1]

The History of the Universe

To make this vast expanse of time even remotely comprehensible, some scholars have depicted the history of the cosmos as if it were a single calendar year (see Snapshot). On that cosmic calendar, most of the action took place in the first few milliseconds of January 1. As astronomers, physicists, and chemists tell it, the universe that we know began in an eruption of inconceivable power and heat. Out of that explosion of creation emerged matter, energy, gravity, electromagnetism, and the "strong" and "weak" forces that govern the behavior of atomic nuclei. As gravity pulled the rapidly expanding cosmic gases into increasingly dense masses, stars formed, with the first ones lighting up around 1 to 2 billion years after the big bang, or the end of January to mid-February on the cosmic calendar.

Hundreds of billions of stars followed, each with its own history, though following common patterns. They emerge, flourish for a time, and then collapse and die. In their final stages, they sometimes generate supernovae, black holes, and pulsars—phenomena at least as fantastic as the most exotic of earlier creation stories. Within the stars, enormous nuclear reactions gave rise to the elements that are

SNAPSHOT   The History of the Universe as a Cosmic Calendar[2]

Big bang	January 1	13.7 billion years ago
Stars and galaxies begin to form	End of January / mid-February	12 billion years ago
Milky Way galaxy forms	March / early April	10 billion years ago
Origin of the solar system	September 9	4.7 billion years ago
Formation of the earth	September 15	4.5 billion years ago
Earliest life on earth	Late September / early October	4 billion years ago
Oxygen forms on earth	December 1	1.3 billion years ago
First worms	December 16	658 million years ago
First fish, first vertebrates	December 19	534 million years ago
First reptiles, first trees	December 23	370 million years ago
Age of dinosaurs	December 24–28	329–164 million years ago
First human-like creatures	December 31 (late evening)	2.7 million years ago
First agriculture	December 31: 11:59:35	12,000 years ago
Birth of the Buddha / Greek civilization	December 31: 11:59:55	2,500 years ago
Birth of Jesus	December 31: 11:59:56	2,000 years ago
Aztec and Inca empires	December 31: 11:59:59	500 years ago

reflected in the periodic table known to all students of chemistry. Over eons, these stars came together in galaxies, such as our own Milky Way, which probably emerged in March or early April, and in even larger structures called groups, clusters, and superclusters. Adding to the strangeness of our picture of the cosmos is the recent and controversial notion that perhaps 90 percent or more of the total mass of the universe is invisible to us, consisting of a mysterious and mathematically predicted substance known to scholars only as "dark matter."

The contemplation of cosmic history has prompted profound religious or philosophical questions about the meaning of human life. For some, it has engendered a sense of great insignificance in the face of cosmic vastness. In disputing the earth- and human-centered view of the cosmos, long held by the Catholic Church, the eighteenth-century French thinker Voltaire wrote: "This little globe, nothing more than a point, rolls in space like so many other globes; we are lost in this immensity."[3] Nonetheless, human consciousness and our awareness of the mystery of this immeasurable universe render us unique and generate for many people feelings of awe, gratitude, and humility that are almost religious. As tiny but knowing observers of this majestic cosmos, we have found ourselves living in a grander home than ever we knew before.

The History of a Planet

For most of us, one star, our own sun, is far more important than all the others, despite its quite ordinary standing among the billions of stars in the universe and its somewhat remote location on the outer edge of the Milky Way galaxy. Circling that star is a series of planets, formed of leftover materials from the sun's birth. One of those planets, the third from the sun and the fifth largest, is home to all of us. Human history—our history—takes place not only on the earth but also as part of the planet's history.

That history began with the emergence of the entire solar system about two-thirds of the way through the history of the universe, some 4.7 billion years ago, or early September on the cosmic calendar. Geologists have learned a great deal about the history of the earth: the formation of its rocks and atmosphere; the movement of its continents; the collision of the tectonic plates that make up its crust; and the constant changes of its landscape as mountains formed, volcanoes erupted, and erosion transformed the surface of the planet. All of this has been happening for more than 4 billion years and continues still.

The most remarkable feature of the earth's history—and so far as we know unrepeated elsewhere—was the emergence of life from the chemical soup of the early planet. It happened rather quickly, only about 600 million years after the earth itself took shape, or late September on the cosmic calendar. Then for some 3 billion years, life remained at the level of microscopic single-celled organisms. According to biologists, the many species of larger multicelled creatures—all of the flowers, shrubs, and trees as well as all of the animals of land, sea, and air—have evolved in an explosive proliferation of life-forms over the past 600 million years, or since mid-December on the cosmic calendar. The history of life on earth has, however, been periodically punctuated by massive die-offs, at least five of them, in which very large numbers of animal or plant species have perished. The most widespread of these "extinction events," known to scholars as the Permian mass extinction, occurred around 250 million years ago and eliminated some 96 percent of living species on the planet. That catastrophic diminution of life-forms on the planet has been associated with massive volcanic eruptions, the release of huge quantities of carbon dioxide and methane into the atmosphere, and a degree of global warming that came close to extinguishing all life on the planet. Much later, around 65 million years ago, another such extinction event decimated about 75 percent of plant and animal species, including what was left of the dinosaurs. It too, some scientists believe, involved another wave of volcanic eruptions and drastic climate change, exacerbated this time by the impact of a huge asteroid, perhaps six miles in diameter, which landed near the Yucatán peninsula off the coast of southern Mexico. Many scholars believe we are currently in the midst of a sixth extinction event, driven, like the others, by major climate change, but which, unlike the others, is the product of human actions.

So life on earth has been and remains both fragile and resilient. Within these conditions, every species has had a history as its members struggled to find resources, cope with changing environments, and deal with competitors. Egocentric creatures that we are, however, human beings have usually focused their history books and history courses entirely on a single species—our own, *Homo sapiens*, humankind. On the cosmic calendar, *Homo sapiens* is an upstart primate whose entire history occurred in the last few minutes of December 31. Almost all of what we normally study in history courses—agriculture, writing, civilizations, empires, industrialization—took place in the very last minute of that cosmic year. The entire history of the United States occurred in the last second.

Yet during that very brief time, humankind has had a career more remarkable and arguably more consequential for the planet than any other species. At the heart of human uniqueness lies our amazing capacity for accumulating knowledge and skills. Other animals learn, of course, but for the most part they learn the same things over and over again. Twenty-first-century chimpanzees in the wild master the same skills as their ancestors did a million years ago. But the exceptional communication abilities provided by human language allow us to learn from one another, to express that learning in abstract symbols, and then to pass it on, cumulatively, to future generations. Thus we have moved from stone axes to lasers, from spears to nuclear weapons, from "talking drums" to the Internet, from grass huts to the pyramids of Egypt, the Taj Mahal of India, and the skyscrapers of modern cities.

This extraordinary ability has translated into a human impact on the earth that is unprecedented among all living species.[4] Human populations have multiplied far more extensively and have come to occupy a far greater range of environments than has any other large animal. Through our ingenious technologies, we have appropriated for ourselves, according to recent calculations, some 25 to 40 percent of the solar energy that enters the food chain. We have recently gained access to the stored solar energy of coal, gas, and oil, all of which have been many millions of years in the making, and we have the capacity to deplete these resources in a few hundred or a few thousand years. Other forms of life have felt the impact of human activity, as numerous extinct or threatened species testify. Human beings have even affected the atmosphere and the oceans as carbon dioxide and other emissions of the industrial age have warmed the climate of the planet in ways that broadly resemble the conditions that triggered earlier extinction events. Thus human history has been, and remains, of great significance, not for ourselves alone, but also for the earth itself and for the many other living creatures with which we share it.

The History of the Human Species . . . in a Single Paragraph

The history of our species has occupied roughly the last 250,000 years, conventionally divided into three major phases, based on the kind of technology that was most widely practiced. The enormously long Paleolithic age, with its gathering and hunting way of life, accounts for 95 percent or more of the time that humans have occupied the planet. People utilizing a stone-age Paleolithic technology initially settled every major landmass on the earth and constructed the first human societies (see Chapter 1). Then beginning about 12,000 years ago with the first Agricultural Revolution, the domestication of plants and animals increasingly became the primary means of sustaining human life and societies. In giving rise to agricultural villages and chiefdoms, to pastoral communities depending on their herds of animals, and to state- and city-based civilizations, this agrarian way of life changed virtually everything and fundamentally reshaped human societies and their relationship to the natural order. Finally, around 1750 a quite sudden spurt in the rate of technological change, which we know as the Industrial Revolution, began to take hold. That vast increase in productivity, wealth, and human control over nature once again transformed almost every aspect of human life and gave rise to new kinds of societies that we call "modern."

Here then, in a single paragraph, is the history of humankind—the Paleolithic era, the agricultural era, and, most recently and briefly, the modern industrial era. Clearly this is a big picture perspective, based on the notion that the human species as a whole has a history that transcends any of its particular and distinctive cultures. That perspective—known variously as planetary, global, or world history—has become increasingly prominent among those who study the past. Why should this be so?

Why World History?

Not long ago—in the mid-twentieth century, for example—virtually all college-level history courses were organized in terms of particular civilizations or nations. In the United States, courses such as Western Civilization or some version of American History served to introduce students to the study of the past. Since then, however, a set of profound changes has pushed much of the historical profession in a different direction.

Change

Why has world history achieved an increasingly prominent place in American education in recent decades?

The world wars of the twentieth century, revealing as they did the horrendous consequences of unchecked nationalism, persuaded some historians that a broader view of the past might contribute to a sense of global citizenship. Economic and cultural globalization has highlighted both the interdependence of the world's peoples and their very unequal positions within that world. Moreover, we are aware as never before that our problems—whether they involve economic well-being, global warming, disease, or terrorism—respect no national boundaries. To many thoughtful people, a global present seemed to call for a global past. Furthermore, as colonial empires shrank and new nations asserted themselves on the world stage, these peoples also insisted that their histories be accorded equivalent treatment with those of Europe and North America. An explosion of new knowledge about the histories of Asia, Africa, and pre-Columbian America erupted from the research of scholars around the world. All of this has generated a "world history movement," reflected in college and high school curricula, in numerous conferences and specialized studies, and in a proliferation of textbooks, of which this is one.

This world history movement has attempted to create a global understanding of the human past that highlights broad patterns cutting across particular civilizations and countries, while acknowledging in an inclusive fashion the distinctive histories of its many peoples. This is, to put it mildly, a tall order. How is it possible to encompass within a single book or course the separate stories of the world's various peoples? Surely it must be something more than just recounting the history of one civilization or culture after another. How can we distill a common history of humankind as a whole from the distinct trajectories of particular peoples? Because no world history book or course can cover everything, what criteria should we use for deciding what to include and what to leave out? Such questions have ensured no end of controversy among students, teachers, and scholars of world history, making it one of the most exciting fields of historical inquiry.

Change, Comparison, and Connection: The Three Cs of World History

Despite much debate and argument, one thing is reasonably clear: in world history, nothing stands alone. Every event, every historical figure, every culture, society, or civilization gains significance from its inclusion in some larger context. Most world historians would probably agree on three such contexts that define their field of study. Each of those contexts confronts a particular problem in our understanding of the past.

The first context in which the particulars of world history can be situated is that of **change** over time. In world history, it is the "big picture" changes—those that affect large segments of humankind—that are of greatest interest. How did the transition from a gathering and hunting economy to one based on agriculture take place? How did cities, empires, and civilizations take shape in various parts of the world? What lay behind the emergence of a new balance of global power after 1500, one that featured the growing prominence of Europe on the world stage? What generated the amazing transformations of the "revolution of modernity" in recent centuries? How did the lives of women change as a result of industrialization?

A focus on change provides an antidote to a persistent tendency of human thinking that historians call "essentialism." A more common term is "stereotyping." It refers to our inclination to define particular groups of people with an unchanging or essential set of characteristics. Women are nurturing; peasants are conservative;

Americans are aggressive; Hindus are religious. Serious students of history soon become aware that every significant category of people contains endless divisions and conflicts and that those human communities are constantly in flux. Peasants may often accept the status quo, except of course when they rebel, as they frequently have. Americans have experienced periods of isolationism and withdrawal from the world as well as times of aggressive engagement with it. Things change.

But some things persist, even if they also change. We should not allow an emphasis on change to blind us to the continuities of human experience. A recognizably Chinese state has operated for more than 2,000 years. Slavery and patriarchy persisted as human institutions for thousands of years until they were challenged in recent centuries, and in various forms they exist still. The teachings of Buddhism, Christianity, and Islam have endured for centuries, though with endless variations and transformations.

A second major context that operates constantly in world history books and courses is that of **comparison**. Whatever else it may be, world history is a comparative discipline, seeking to identify similarities and differences in the experience of the world's peoples. What is the difference between the development of agriculture in the Middle East and in Mesoamerica? Was the experience of women largely the same in all patriarchal societies? What did the Roman Empire and Han dynasty China have in common? Why did the Industrial Revolution and a modern way of life evolve first in Western Europe rather than somewhere else? What distinguished the French, Russian, and Chinese revolutions from one another? What different postures toward modernity emerged within the Islamic world? Describing and, if possible, explaining such similarities and differences are among the major tasks of world history. Comparison, then, is a recurring theme in this book, with expressions in every chapter.

Comparison has proven an effective tool in efforts to counteract Eurocentrism, the notion that Europeans or people of European descent have long been the primary movers and shakers of the historical process. That notion arose in recent centuries when Europeans were in fact the major source of innovation in the world and did for a time exercise something close to world domination. This temporary preeminence decisively shaped the way Europeans thought and wrote about their own histories and those of other people. In their own eyes, Europeans alone were progressive people, thanks to some cultural or racial superiority. Everyone else was to some degree stagnant, backward, savage, or barbarian. The unusual power of Europeans allowed them for a time to act on those beliefs and to convey such ways of thinking to much of the world. But comparative world history sets European achievements in a global and historical context, helping us to sort out what was distinctive about the development of Europe and what similarities it bore to other major regions of the world. Puncturing the pretensions of Eurocentrism has been high on the agenda of world history.

A third context that informs world history involves the interactions, encounters, and **connections** among different and often distant peoples. World history is less about what happened within particular civilizations or cultures than about the processes and outcomes of their meetings with one another. Focusing on cross-cultural connections—whether those of conflict or more peaceful exchange—represents an effort to counteract a habit of thinking about particular peoples, states, or cultures as self-contained or isolated communities. Despite the historical emergence of many separate and distinct societies, none of them developed alone. Each was embedded in a network of relationships with both near and more distant peoples.

Moreover, these cross-cultural connections did not begin with Columbus. The Chinese, for example, interacted continuously with the nomadic peoples on their northern border; generated technologies that diffused across all of Eurasia; transmitted elements of their culture to Japan, Korea, and Vietnam; and assimilated a foreign religious tradition, Buddhism, which had originated in India. Though clearly distinctive, China was not a self-contained or isolated civilization.

The growing depth and significance of such cross-cultural relationships, known now as globalization, has been a distinguishing feature of the modern era. The voyages of Columbus brought the peoples of the Eastern and Western hemispheres into sustained contact for the first time with enormous global consequences. Several centuries later, Europeans took advantage of their industrial power to bring much of the world temporarily under their control. The new technologies of the twentieth century have intertwined the economies, societies, and cultures of the world's peoples more tightly than ever before. During the past five centuries, the encounter with strangers, or at least with their ideas and practices, was everywhere among the most powerful motors of change in human societies. Thus world history remains always alert to the networks, webs, and cross-cultural encounters in which particular civilizations or peoples were enmeshed.

Changes, comparisons, and connections—all of them operating on a global scale—represent three contexts or frameworks that can help us bring some coherence to the multiple and complex stories of world history. They will recur repeatedly in the pages that follow.

A final observation about this account of world history: *Ways of the World*, like all other world history textbooks, is radically unbalanced in terms of coverage. The first chapter, for example, takes on some 95 percent of the human story, well over 200,000 years of our history. By contrast, the last century alone occupies four entire chapters. In fact, the six major sections of the book deal with progressively shorter time periods, in progressively greater detail. This imbalance owes much to the relative scarcity of information about earlier periods of our history. But it also reflects a certain "present mindedness," for we look to history, always, to make sense of our current needs and circumstances. And in doing so, we often assume that more recent events have a greater significance for our own lives in the here and now than those that occurred in more distant times. Whether you agree with this assumption or not, you will have occasion to ponder it as you consider the many and various "ways of the world" that have emerged in the course of the human journey and as you contemplate their relevance for your own journey.

Second Thoughts

What's the Significance?

big history, lvi

cosmic calendar, lvi

the three Cs, lxi

comparative world history, lxii

Big Picture Questions

1. How do modern notions of the immense size and age of the universe affect your understanding of human history?
2. What examples of comparison, connection, and change in world history would you like to explore further as your course unfolds?
3. In what larger contexts might you place your own life history?

Next Steps: For Further Study

David Christian, Cynthia Stokes Brown, and Craig Benjamin, *Big History: Between Nothing and Everything* (2013). A thoughtful survey of the emerging field of "big history" by three of its leading practitioners.

Ross E. Dunn, ed., *The New World History: A Teacher's Companion* (2000). A collection of articles dealing with the teaching of world history.

Patrick Manning, *Navigating World History: Historians Create a Global Past* (2003). An up-to-date overview of the growth of world history, the field's achievements, and the debates within it.

J. R. McNeill and William H. McNeill, *The Human Web: A Bird's-Eye View of World History* (2003). An approach to world history that emphasizes the changing webs of connection among human communities.

Heidi Roupp, ed., *Teaching World History in the Twenty-First Century: A Resource Book* (2010). A practical resource book for the teaching of world history.

"World History Matters," http://worldhistorymatters.org/. A point of entry to many world history Web sites, featuring numerous images and essays.

Ways of the World

A Brief Global History
with Sources

PART ONE

FIRST THINGS FIRST

Beginnings in History
to 500 B.C.E.

Contents

TURNING POINTS IN EARLY WORLD HISTORY

Human beings have long been inveterate storytellers. Those who created our myths, legends, fairy tales, oral traditions, family sagas, and more have sought to distill meaning from experience, to explain why things turned out as they did, and to provide guidance for individuals and communities. Much the same might be said of modern historians. They too tell stories—about individuals, communities, nations, and, in the case of world history, of humankind as a whole. Those stories seek to illuminate the past, to provide context for the present, and, very tentatively, to offer some indication about possible futures. All tellers of stories—ancient and modern alike—have to decide at what point to begin their accounts and what major turning points in those narratives to highlight. For world historians seeking to tell the story of "all under Heaven," as the Chinese put it, four major "beginnings," each of them an extended historical process, have charted the initial stages of the human journey.

The Emergence of Humankind

Ever since Charles Darwin, most scholars have come to view human beginnings in the context of biological change on the planet. In considering this enormous process, we operate on a timescale quite different from the billions of years that mark the history of the universe and of the earth. According to archeologists and anthropologists, the evolutionary line of descent leading to *Homo sapiens* diverged from that leading to chimpanzees, our closest primate relatives, some 5 million to 6 million years ago, and it happened in eastern and southern Africa. There, perhaps twenty or thirty different species emerged, all of them members of the Homininae (or hominid) family of human-like creatures. What they all shared was bipedalism, the ability to walk upright on two legs. In 1976, the archeologist Mary Leakey uncovered in what is now Tanzania a series of footprints of three such hominid individuals, preserved in cooling volcanic ash about 3.5 million years ago. Two of them walked side by side, perhaps holding hands.

Over time, these hominid species changed. Their brains grew larger, as evidenced by the size of their skulls. About 2.3 million years ago, a hominid creature known as *Homo habilis* began to make and use simple stone tools. Others

3

started to eat meat, at least occasionally. By 1 million years ago, some hominid species, especially *Homo erectus*, began to migrate out of Africa, and their remains have been found in various parts of Eurasia. This species is also associated with the first controlled use of fire.

Eventually all of these earlier hominid species died out, except one: *Homo sapiens*, ourselves. With a remarkable capacity for symbolic language that permitted the accumulation and transmission of learning, we too emerged first in Africa and quite recently, probably no more than 250,000 years ago (although specialists constantly debate these matters). For a long time, all of the small number of *Homo sapiens* lived in Africa, but sometime after 100,000 years ago, they too began to migrate out of Africa onto the Eurasian landmass, then to Australia, and ultimately into the Western Hemisphere and the Pacific islands. The great experiment of human history had begun.

The Globalization of Humankind

Today, every significant landmass on earth is occupied by human beings, but it was not always so. A mere half million years ago our species did not exist, and only 100,000 years ago that species was limited to Africa and numbered, some scholars believe, fewer than 10,000 individuals. These ancient ancestors of ours, rather small in stature and not fast on foot, were armed with a very limited technology of stone tools with which to confront the multiple dangers of the natural world. But then, in perhaps the most amazing tale in all of human history, they moved from this very modest and geographically limited role in the scheme of things to a worldwide and increasingly dominant presence. What kinds of societies, technologies, and understandings of the world accompanied, and perhaps facilitated, this globalization of humankind?

The phase of human history during which these initial migrations took place is known to scholars as the Paleolithic era. The word "Paleolithic" literally means the "old stone age," but it refers more generally to a food-collecting or gathering, hunting, and fishing way of life, before agriculture allowed people to grow food or raise animals deliberately. Paleolithic cultures operated within natural ecosystems, while creatively manipulating the productive capacities of those systems to sustain individual lives and societies. Lasting until roughly 11,000 years ago, and in many places much longer, the Paleolithic era represents over 95 percent of the time that human beings have inhabited the earth, although it accounts for only about 12 percent of the total number of people who have lived on the planet. It was during this time that *Homo sapiens* colonized the world, making themselves at home in every environmental setting, from the frigid Arctic to the rain forests of Central Africa and Brazil, in mountains, deserts, and plains. It was an amazing achievement, accomplished by no other large species. Accompanying this global migration were slow changes in the technological tool kits of early humankind as well as early attempts to impose meaning on the world through art, ritual, religion, and stories. Although often neglected by historians and history textbooks, this long period of the human experience merits greater attention and is the focus of the initial sections of Chapter 1.

The Revolution of Farming and Herding

In 2014, almost all of the world's 7.2 billion people lived from the food grown on farms and gardens and from domesticated animals raised for their meat, milk, or eggs. But before 11,000 years ago, no one survived in this fashion. Then, repeatedly and fairly rapidly, at least in world history terms, human communities in parts of the Middle East, Asia, Africa, and the Americas began the laborious process of domesticating animals and selecting seeds to be planted. This momentous accomplishment represents another "first" in the human story. After countless millennia of relying on the gathering of wild foods and the hunting of wild animals, why and how did human societies begin to practice farming and animal husbandry? What changes to human life did this new technology bring with it?

This food-producing revolution, also considered in Chapter 1, surely marks the single most significant and enduring transformation of the human condition and of human relationships to the natural world. Now our species learned to exploit and manipulate particular organisms, both plant and animal, even as we created new and simplified ecosystems. The entire period from the beginning of agriculture to the Industrial Revolution around 1750 might be considered a single phase of the human story—the age of agriculture—calculated now on a timescale of millennia or centuries rather than the more extended periods of earlier eras. Although the age of agriculture was far shorter than the immense Paleolithic era that preceded it, farming and raising animals allowed for a substantial increase in human numbers and over many centuries an enduring transformation of the environment. Forests were felled, arid lands irrigated, meadows plowed, and mountains terraced. Increasingly, the landscape reflected human intentions and actions.

In the various beginnings of food production lay the foundations for some of the most enduring divisions within the larger human community. Much depended on the luck of the draw—on the climate and soils, on the various wild plants and animals that were available for domestication. Everywhere communities worked within their environments to develop a consistent supply of food. Some relied primarily on single crops, while others cultivated several crops that collectively met their needs. Root crops such as potatoes were prominent in the Andes, while tree crops such as bananas were important in Africa and grain crops such as wheat, rice, or corn prevailed elsewhere. Many communities engaged heavily in small or large animal husbandry, but others, especially in the Americas, did not. In some regions, people embraced agriculture on a full-time basis, but many more agricultural communities, at least initially, continued to rely in part on gathering, hunting, or fishing for their dietary needs. These various approaches led to a spectrum of settlement patterns from sedentary villages to fully nomadic communities, and many in between. In general, the most mobile of these societies were those of pastoralists, who depended heavily on their herds of domesticated animals for survival. Such communities, which usually thrived in more arid environments where farming was difficult, had to move frequently, often in regular seasonal patterns, to secure productive pasturelands for their animals. However, not all were fully nomadic, because in some regions pastoralists were able to combine permanent settlements with seasonal migration of animals to grazing areas. Thus the Agricultural Revolution fostered a wide variety of adaptations to the natural environment and an equally wide range of social organizations.

The Turning Point of Civilization

The most prominent and powerful human communities to emerge from this Agricultural Revolution were those often designated as "civilizations," more complex societies that were based in bustling cities and governed by formal states. Virtually all of the world's people now live in such societies, so that states and cities have come to seem almost natural. In world history terms, however, their appearance is a rather recent phenomenon. Not until several thousand years *after* the beginning of agriculture did the first cities and states emerge, around 3500 B.C.E. Well after 1000 C.E., substantial numbers of people still lived in communities without any state or urban structures. Nonetheless, people living in state- and city-based societies or civilizations have long constituted the most powerful and innovative human communities on the planet. They gave rise to empires of increasing size, to enduring cultural and religious traditions, to new technologies, to sharper class and gender inequalities, to new conceptions of masculinity and femininity, and to large-scale warfare.

For all these reasons, civilizations have featured prominently in accounts of world history, sometimes crowding out the stories of other kinds of human communities. The earliest civilizations, which emerged in at least seven separate locations between 3500 and 500 B.C.E., have long fascinated professional historians and lovers of history everywhere. What was their relationship to the Agricultural Revolution? What new ways of living did they bring to the experience of humankind? These are the questions that inform Chapter 2.

Time and World History

Reckoning time is central to all historical study, for history is essentially the story of change over time. Recently it has become standard in the Western world to refer to dates prior to the birth of Christ as B.C.E. (before the Common Era), replacing the earlier B.C. (before Christ) usage. This convention is an effort to become less Christian-centered and Eurocentric in our use of language, although the chronology remains linked to the birth of Jesus. Similarly, the time following the birth of Christ is referred to as C.E. (the Common Era) rather than A.D. (*Anno Domini*, Latin for "year of the Lord"). Dates in the more distant past are designated in this book as BP ("before the present," by which scholars mean 1950, the dawn of the nuclear age) or simply as so many "years ago." Of course, these conventions are only some of the many ways that human societies have charted time, and they reflect the global dominance of Europeans in recent centuries. But the Chinese frequently dated important events in terms of the reign of particular emperors, while Muslims created a new calendar beginning with Year 1, marking Muhammad's forced relocation from Mecca to Medina in 622 C.E. As with so much else, the maps of time that we construct reflect the cultures in which we have been born and the historical experience of our societies.

World history frequently deals with very long periods of time, often encompassing many millennia or centuries in a single paragraph or even in a single sentence. Such quick summaries may sometimes seem to flatten the texture of historical experience, minimizing the immense complexities and variations of human life and dismissing the rich and distinctive flavor of individual lives. Yet this very drawback of world history permits its greatest contribution to our understanding—perspective, context, a big picture framework in which we can situate the particular events, societies, and individual experiences that constitute the historical record. Such a panoramic outlook on the past allows us to discern patterns and trends that may be invisible from the viewpoint of a local community or a single nation. In the narrative that follows, there will be plenty of particulars—events, places, people—but always embedded in some larger setting that enriches their significance.

MAPPING PART ONE

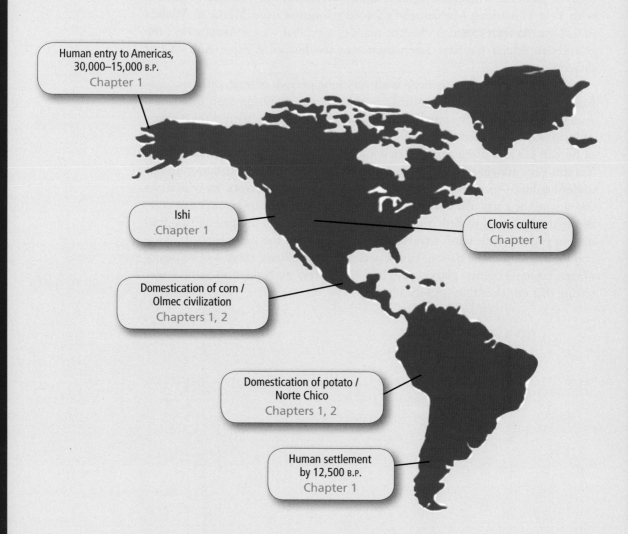

Human entry to Americas,
30,000–15,000 B.P.
Chapter 1

Ishi
Chapter 1

Clovis culture
Chapter 1

Domestication of corn /
Olmec civilization
Chapters 1, 2

Domestication of potato /
Norte Chico
Chapters 1, 2

Human settlement
by 12,500 B.P.
Chapter 1

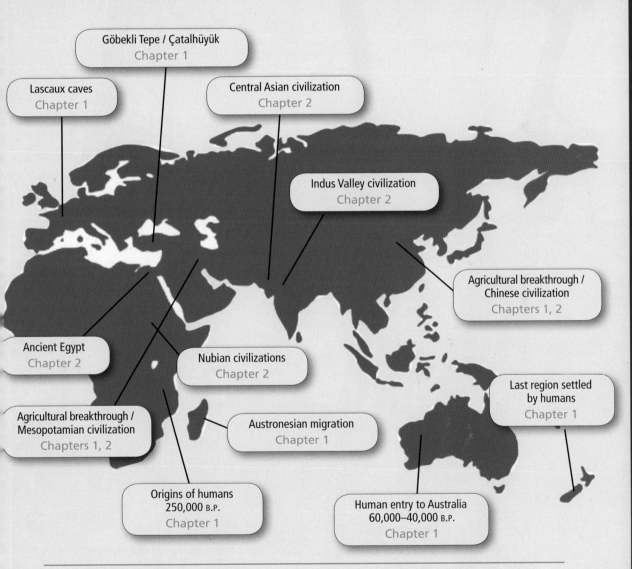

Göbekli Tepe / Çatalhüyük
Chapter 1

Lascaux caves
Chapter 1

Central Asian civilization
Chapter 2

Indus Valley civilization
Chapter 2

Agricultural breakthrough /
Chinese civilization
Chapters 1, 2

Ancient Egypt
Chapter 2

Nubian civilizations
Chapter 2

Last region settled
by humans
Chapter 1

Agricultural breakthrough /
Mesopotamian civilization
Chapters 1, 2

Austronesian migration
Chapter 1

Origins of humans
250,000 B.P.
Chapter 1

Human entry to Australia
60,000–40,000 B.P.
Chapter 1

9

CHAPTER 1

First Peoples; First Farmers

Most of History in a Single Chapter
to 4000 B.C.E.

"We do not want cattle, just wild animals to hunt and water that we can drink."[1] That was the view of Gudo Mahiya, a prominent member of the Hadza people of northern Tanzania, when he was questioned in 1997 about his interest in a settled life of farming and cattle raising. The Hadza represent one of the very last peoples on earth to continue a way of life that was universal among humankind until 10,000 to 12,000 years ago. In 2014, only about 1,300 Hadza survived, and of these just several hundred still made a living by hunting game, collecting honey, digging up roots, and gathering berries and fruit. Those few lived in quickly assembled grass huts located in small mobile camps averaging eighteen people and moved frequently around their remote region, following animal migrations. Almost certainly, their way of life is doomed, as farmers, cattle herders, governments, missionaries, and now tourists push them toward extinction. The likely disappearance of their culture is among the final chapters of a very long story in which gathering, hunting, and fishing peoples have been unsuccessfully on the defensive against more numerous and powerful neighbors for 10,000 years.

Nonetheless, that way of life sustained humankind for more than 95 percent of the time that our species has inhabited the earth. During countless centuries, human beings successfully adapted to a wide variety of environments without benefit of deliberate farming or animal husbandry. Instead, our early ancestors wrested a livelihood by gathering wild foods such as berries, nuts, roots, and grain; by scavenging dead animals; by hunting live animals; and by

Paleolithic Art The rock art of gathering and hunting peoples has been found in Africa, Europe, Australia, and elsewhere. This image from the San people of southern Africa represents aspects of their outer life in the form of wild animals and hunters with bows as well as the inner life of their shamans during a trance, reflected in the elongated figures with both human and animal features.

fishing. Known to scholars as "gathering and hunting" peoples, they were foragers or food collectors rather than food producers. Because they used stone rather than metal tools, they also have been labeled "Paleolithic," or "Old Stone Age," peoples.

Then, around 12,000 years ago, an enormous transformation began to unfold as a few human societies—in Eurasia, Africa, and the Americas alike—started to practice the deliberate cultivation of plants and the domestication of animals. This Agricultural or Neolithic (New Stone Age) Revolution marked a technological breakthrough of immense significance, with implications for every aspect of human life. This chapter, then, dealing with the long Paleolithic era and the initial transition to an agricultural way of life, represents most of human history—everything, in fact, before the advent of urban-based civilizations, which began around 5,500 years ago.

And yet history courses and history books often neglect this long phase of the human journey and instead choose to begin the story with the early civilizations of Egypt, Mesopotamia, China, and elsewhere. Some historians identify "real history" with writing and so dismiss the Paleolithic and Neolithic eras as largely unknowable because their peoples did not write. Others, impressed with the rapid pace of change in human affairs in more recent times, assume that nothing much of real significance happened during the long Paleolithic era—and that no change meant no history.

But does it make sense to ignore the first 200,000 years or more of human experience? Although written records are absent, scholars have learned a great deal about Paleolithic and Neolithic peoples through their material remains: stones and bones, fossilized seeds, rock paintings and engravings, and much more. Archeologists, biologists, botanists, demographers, linguists, and anthropologists have contributed much to our growing understanding of gathering and hunting peoples and early agricultural societies. Furthermore, the achievements of Paleolithic peoples—the initial settlement of the planet, the creation of the earliest human societies, the beginnings of reflection on the great questions of life and death—surely deserve our attention. And the breakthrough to agriculture arguably represents the single most profound transformation of human life in all of history. The changes wrought by our early ancestors, though far slower than those of more recent times, were extraordinarily rapid in comparison to the transformation experienced by any other species. Those changes were almost entirely cultural or learned, rather than the product of biological evolution, and they provided the foundation on which all subsequent human history was constructed. Our grasp of the human past is incomplete—massively so—if we choose to disregard the Paleolithic and Neolithic eras.

SEEKING THE MAIN POINT

What arguments does this chapter make for paying serious attention to human history before the coming of "civilization"?

Out of Africa: First Migrations

The first 150,000 years or more of human experience was an exclusively African story. Around 200,000 to 250,000 years ago, in the grasslands of eastern and southern Africa, *Homo sapiens* first emerged, following in the footsteps of many other hominid or human-like species before it. Time and climate have erased much of the record

A MAP OF TIME   (All dates B.P.: Before the Present)

250,000–200,000	Earliest *Homo sapiens* in Africa
100,000–60,000	Beginnings of migration out of Africa
70,000	Human entry into eastern Asia
60,000–40,000	Human entry into Australia (first use of boats)
45,000	Human entry into Europe
30,000	Extinction of large mammals in Australia
30,000–15,000	Human entry into the Americas
30,000–17,000	Cave art in Europe
25,000	Extinction of Neanderthals
16,000–10,000	End of last Ice Age (global warming)
12,000–10,000	Earliest agricultural revolutions
11,000	Extinction of large mammals in North America
After 8,000	First chiefdoms in Mesopotamia
6,000–5,000	Beginning of domestication of corn in southern Mexico
3,500–1,000	Austronesian migration to Pacific islands and Madagascar
1,000–800	Human entry into New Zealand (last major region to receive human settlers)

of these early people, and Africa has witnessed much less archeological research than have other parts of the world. Nonetheless, scholars have turned up evidence of distinctly human behavior in Africa long before its appearance elsewhere. Africa, almost certainly, was the place where the "human revolution" occurred, where "culture," defined as learned or invented ways of living, became more important than biology in shaping behavior.

What kinds of uniquely human activity show up in the early African record?[2] In the first place, human beings began to inhabit new environments within Africa — forests and deserts — where no hominids had lived before. Accompanying these movements of people were technological innovations of various kinds: stone blades and points fastened to shafts replaced the earlier hand axes; tools made from bones appeared, and so did grindstones. Evidence of hunting and fishing, not just the scavenging of dead animals, marks a new phase in human food collection. Settlements were planned around the seasonal movement of game and fish. Patterns of exchange over a distance of almost 200 miles indicate larger networks of human communication. The use of body ornaments, beads, and pigments such as ochre as well as possible planned burials suggests the kind of social and symbolic behavior that has characterized human activity ever since. The earliest evidence for this kind of human activity comes from the Blombos Cave in South Africa, where excavations in 2008 uncovered a workshop for the processing of ochre dating to around 100,000 years ago, well before such behavior surfaced elsewhere in the world.

Then, sometime between 100,000 and 60,000 years ago, human beings began their long trek out of Africa and into Eurasia, Australia, the Americas, and, much later, the islands of the Pacific (see Map 1.1). In occupying the planet, members of our species accomplished the remarkable feat of learning to live in virtually every environmental setting on earth, something that no other large animal had done; and they did it with only stone tools and a gathering and hunting technology to aid them. Furthermore, much of this long journey occurred during the difficult climatic conditions of the last Ice Age (at its peak around 20,000 years ago), when thick ice sheets covered much of the Northern Hemisphere. The Ice Age did give these outward-bound human beings one advantage, however: the amount of water frozen in northern glaciers lowered sea levels around the planet, creating land bridges among various regions that were separated after the glaciers melted. Britain was then joined to Europe; eastern Siberia was connected to Alaska; and parts of what is now Indonesia were linked to mainland Southeast Asia.

Into Eurasia

Human migration out of Africa led first to the Middle East and from there westward into Europe about 45,000 years ago and eastward into Asia. Among the most carefully researched areas of early human settlement in Eurasia are those in southern France and northern Spain. Colder Ice Age climates around 20,000 years ago apparently pushed more northerly European peoples southward into warmer regions. There they altered their hunting habits, focusing on reindeer and horses, and developed new technologies such as spear throwers and perhaps the bow and arrow as well as many different kinds of stone tools. Most remarkably, they also left a record of their world in hundreds of cave paintings, depicting bulls, horses, and other animals, brilliantly portrayed in colors of red, yellow, brown, and black. Images of human beings, impressions of human hands, and various abstract designs sometimes accompanied the cave paintings.

■ **Change**
What was the sequence of human migration across the planet?

Farther east, archeologists have uncovered still other remarkable Paleolithic adaptations to Ice Age conditions. Across the vast plains of Central Europe, Ukraine, and Russia, new technologies emerged, including bone needles, multilayered clothing, weaving, nets, storage pits, baskets, and pottery. Partially underground dwellings constructed from the bones and tusks of mammoths compensated for the absence of caves and rock shelters. All of this suggests that some of these people had lived in more permanent settlements, at least temporarily abandoning their nomadic journeys. Associated with these Eastern European peoples were numerous female figurines, the oldest of which was uncovered in 2008 in Germany and dated to at least 35,000 years ago. Carved from stone, antlers, mammoth tusks, or, occasionally, baked clay, these so-called Venus figurines depict the female form, often with exaggerated breasts, buttocks, hips, and stomachs. Similar figurines have been found all across Eurasia, raising any number of controversial questions. Does their widespread distribution suggest a network of human communication and cultural diffusion over a wide area? If so, did they move from west to east or vice versa? What do they mean in terms of women's roles and status in Paleolithic societies?

Into Australia

Early human migration to Australia, perhaps 60,000 years ago, came from Indonesia and involved another first in human affairs—the use of boats. Over time, people settled in most regions of this huge continent, though quite sparsely. Scholars estimate the population of Australia at about 300,000 in 1788, when the first Europeans arrived. Over tens of thousands of years, the

Australian Rock Art
This Australian rock painting utilized the distinctive Aboriginal X-ray style, showing the internal bones and organs. The largest and main figure at the top is a Creation Ancestor known as Namondjok. To the right is Namarrgon, or Lightning Man, who generates the tremendous lightning storms that occur during the rainy season. The arc around his body represents the lightning, while the axes on his head, elbow, and feet are used to split the dark clouds, creating thunder and lightning. The female figure beneath Namondjok is Barrginj, the wife of Lightning Man, while the people below her, elaborately dressed, are perhaps on their way to a ceremony. (Aboriginal rock painting from the Kakadu National Park/Werner Forman Archive/Bridgeman Images)

peoples of Australia developed perhaps 250 languages; learned to collect a wide variety of bulbs, tubers, roots, seeds, and cereal grasses; and became proficient hunters of large and small animals, as well as birds, fish, and other marine life. A relatively simple technology, appropriate to a gathering and hunting economy, sustained Australia's Aboriginal people into modern times. When outsiders arrived in the late eighteenth century, Aboriginals still practiced that ancient way of life, despite the presence of agriculture in nearby New Guinea.

Accompanying Aboriginals' technological simplicity and traditionalism was the development of an elaborate and complex outlook on the world, known as the Dreamtime. (See Working with Evidence, page 49, for more on the Dreamtime.) Expressed in endless stories, in extended ceremonies, and in the evocative rock art of the continent's peoples, the Dreamtime recounted the beginning of things: how ancestral beings crisscrossed the land, creating its rivers, hills, rocks, and waterholes; how various peoples came to inhabit the land; and how they related to animals and to one another. In this view of the world, everything in the natural order was a vibration, an echo, a footprint of these ancient happenings, which linked the current inhabitants intimately to particular places and to timeless events in the past.

The journeys of the Dreamtime's ancestral beings reflect the networks of migration, communication, and exchange that linked the continent's many Paleolithic

Map 1.1   The Global Dispersion of Humankind

With origins in Africa perhaps 250,000 years ago, members of our species (*Homo sapiens*) have migrated to every environmental setting on the planet over the past 100,000 years.

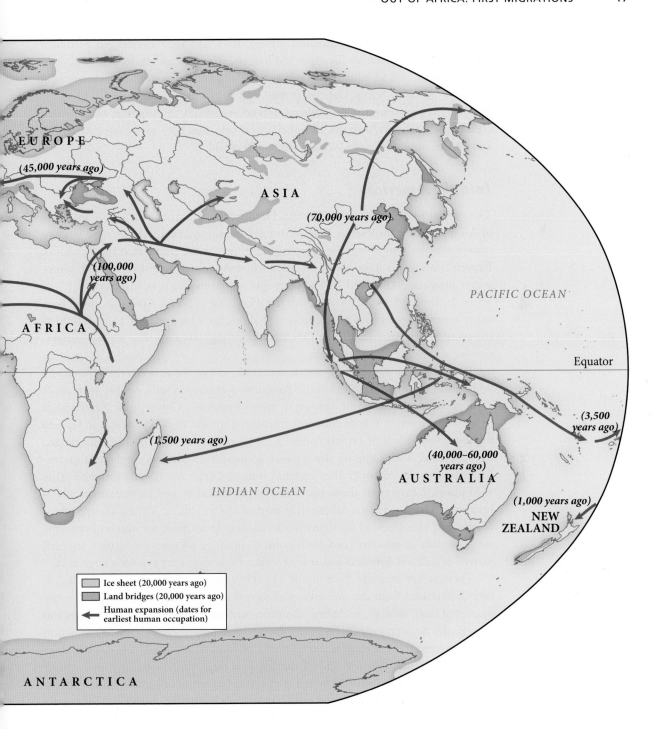

peoples. Far from living as isolated groups, they had long exchanged particular stones, pigments, materials for ropes and baskets, wood for spears, feathers and shells for ornaments, and an addictive psychoactive drug known as *pituri* over distances of hundreds of miles. Songs, dances, stories, and rituals likewise circulated. Precisely how far back in time these networks extend is difficult to pinpoint, but it seems clear that Paleolithic Australia, like ancient Europe, was both many separate worlds and, at the same time, one loosely connected world.

Into the Americas

The earliest settlement of the Western Hemisphere occurred much later than that of Australia, for it took some time for human beings to penetrate the frigid lands of eastern Siberia, which was the jumping-off point for the move into the Americas. Experts continue to argue about precisely when the first migrations occurred (somewhere between 30,000 and 15,000 years ago), about the route of migration (by land across the Bering Strait or by sea down the west coast of North America), about how many separate migrations took place, and about how long it took to penetrate to the tip of South America. Some DNA evidence suggests a possible separate migration by sea from Pacific Polynesia.

Whenever the earliest migrations occurred, one of the first clearly defined and widespread cultural traditions in the Americas is associated with people who made a distinctive projectile point, known to archeologists as a Clovis point. Scattered all over North America, Clovis culture first emerged around 13,000 years ago and spread rapidly across much of North America. Scattered bands of Clovis people ranged over this huge area, camping along rivers, springs, and waterholes, where large animals congregated. Although they certainly hunted smaller animals and gathered many wild plants, Clovis men show up in the archeological record most dramatically as hunters of very large mammals, such as mammoths and bison. Killing a single mammoth could provide food for many weeks or, in cold weather, for much of the winter. The wide distribution of Clovis point technology suggests yet again a regional pattern of cultural diffusion and at least indirect communication over a large area.

Then, rather abruptly, by roughly 11,000 years ago, all trace of the Clovis culture disappeared from the archeological record at about the same time that many species of large animals, including the mammoth and several species of horses and camels, also became extinct. Did the Clovis people hunt these animals to extinction and then vanish themselves as their source of food disappeared? Or did the drier climate that came with the end of the Ice Age cause this megafaunal extinction? Experts disagree, but what happened next was the creation of a much greater diversity of cultures as people adapted to this new situation in various ways. Hunters on the Great Plains continued to pursue bison, which largely avoided the fate of the mammoths. Others learned to live in the desert, taking advantage of seasonal plants and smaller animals, while those who lived near the sea, lakes, or streams drew on local fish and birds. Many peoples of the Americas retained their gathering and hunting way of life into modern times, while others became farmers and, in a few favored regions, later developed cities and large-scale states.

Into the Pacific

The last phase of the great human migration to the ends of the earth took place in the Pacific Ocean and was distinctive in many ways. In the first place, it occurred quite recently, jumping off only about 3,500 years ago from the Bismarck and Solomon Islands near New Guinea as well as from the islands of the Philippines. It was everywhere a waterborne migration, making use of oceangoing canoes and remarkable navigational skills, and it happened very quickly and over a huge area of the planet. Speaking Austronesian languages that trace back to southern China, these oceanic voyagers had settled every habitable piece of land in the Pacific basin within about 2,500 years. Other Austronesians had sailed west from Indonesia across the Indian Ocean to settle the island of Madagascar off the coast of eastern Africa. This extraordinary process of expansion made the Austronesian family of languages the most geographically widespread in the world and Austronesian trading net-works, reaching some 5,000 miles from western Indonesia to the mid-Pacific, the most extensive. With the occupation of Aotearoa (New Zealand) and Rapa Nui (Easter Island) around 1000 to 1200 C.E., the initial human settlement of the planet was finally complete (see Map 1.2).

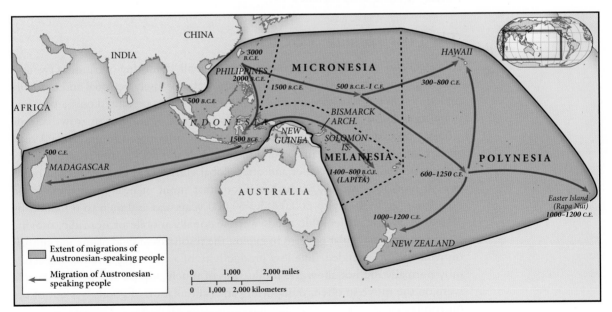

Map 1.2   Migration of Austronesian-Speaking People
People speaking Austronesian languages completed the human settlement of the earth quite recently as they settled the islands of the vast Pacific and penetrated the Indian Ocean to Madagascar, off the coast of southeast Africa.

■ Comparison

How did Austronesian migrations differ from other early patterns of human movement?

In contrast with all of the other initial migrations, these Pacific voyages were undertaken by agricultural people who carried both domesticated plants and animals in their canoes. Both men and women made these journeys, suggesting a deliberate intention to colonize new lands. Virtually everywhere they went, two developments followed. One was the creation of highly stratified societies or chiefdoms, of which ancient Hawaiian society is a prime example. In Hawaii, an elite class of chiefs with political and military power ruled over a mass of commoners. The other development involved a profound ecological impact of this initial intrusion into a pristine environment: extensive deforestation and the quick extinction of many species of animals, especially large flightless birds such as the *moa* of New Zealand, which largely vanished within a century of human arrival. (See Chapter 6, pages 258–62, for more on the historical development of Pacific Oceania.)

The Ways We Were

During their long journeys across the earth, Paleolithic people created a multitude of separate and distinct societies, each with its own history, culture, language, identity, stories, and rituals, but the limitations of a gathering and hunting technology using stone tools imposed some commonalities on these ancient people. Based on the archeological record and on observations of gathering and hunting peoples that still existed in recent centuries, scholars have sketched out some of the common features of these early societies.

The First Human Societies

Above all else, these Paleolithic societies were small, consisting of bands of twenty-five to fifty people, in which all relationships were intensely personal and normally understood in terms of kinship. The available technology permitted only a very low population density and ensured an extremely slow rate of population growth. Some scholars speculate that this growth was dramatically interrupted around 70,000 years ago by an enormous volcanic eruption on the island of Sumatra in present-day Indonesia, resulting in a cooler and drier global climate and causing human numbers to drop to some 10,000 or less. From that point of near extinction, world population grew slowly to 500,000 by 30,000 years ago and then to 6 million by 10,000 years ago.[3] Paleolithic bands were seasonally mobile or nomadic, moving frequently and in regular patterns to exploit the resources of wild plants and animals on which they depended. The low productivity of a gathering and hunting economy normally did not allow the production of much surplus, and because people were on the move so often, transporting an accumulation of goods was out of the question.

All of this resulted in highly egalitarian societies, lacking the many inequalities of wealth and power that came later with agricultural and urban life. With no formal chiefs, kings, bureaucrats, soldiers, nobles, or priests, Paleolithic men and women were perhaps freer of human tyranny and oppression than any subsequent kind of human society, even if they were more constrained by the forces of nature. Without specialists, most people possessed the same set of skills, although male and female tasks often differed sharply. The male role as hunter, especially of big game, perhaps gave rise to one of the first criteria of masculine identity: success in killing large animals.

Relationships between women and men usually were far more equal than in later societies. As the primary food gatherers, women provided the bulk of the family's sustenance. One study of the San people, a surviving gathering and hunting society in southern Africa, found that plants, normally gathered by women, provided 70 percent of the diet, while meat, hunted by men, accounted for just 30 percent. This division of labor underpinned what anthropologist Richard Lee called "relative equality between the sexes with no-one having the upper hand." Among the San, teenagers engaged quite freely in sex play, and the concept of female virginity was apparently unknown, as were rape, wife beating, and the sexual double standard. Although polygamy was permitted, most marriages were in fact monogamous because women strongly resisted sharing a husband with another wife. Frequent divorce among very young couples allowed women to leave unsatisfactory marriages easily. Lee found that longer-term marriages seemed to be generally fulfilling and stable. Both men and women expected a satisfying sexual relationship, and both occasionally took lovers, although discreetly.[4]

When the British navigator and explorer Captain James Cook first encountered the gathering and hunting peoples of Australia in 1770, he described them, perhaps a little enviously, in this way:

> They live in a Tranquillity which is not disturb'd by the Inequality of Conditions: The Earth and sea of their own accord furnishes them with all things necessary for life, they covet not Magnificent houses, Household-stuff. . . . In short they seem'd to set no value upon any thing we gave them. . . . They think themselves provided with all the necessarys of Life.[5]

The Europeans who settled permanently among such people some twenty years later, however, found a society in which physical competition among men was expressed in frequent one-on-one combat and in formalized but bloody battles. It also meant recurrent, public, and quite brutal

■ Change
In what ways did a gathering and hunting economy shape other aspects of Paleolithic societies?

Native Australians
A small number of Aboriginal Australians maintained their gathering and hunting way of life well into the twentieth century. Here an older woman shows two young boys how to dig for honey ants, a popular food. (© Bill Bachman/Alamy)

beatings of wives by their husbands.[6] And some Aboriginal myths sought to explain how men achieved power over women. Among the San, frequent arguments about the distribution of meat or the laziness or stinginess of particular people generated conflict, as did rivalries among men over women. Richard Lee identified twenty-two murders that had occurred between 1920 and 1955 and several cases in which the community came together to conduct an execution of particularly disruptive individuals. More generally, recent studies have found that in Paleolithic societies some 15 percent of deaths occurred through violence at the hands of other people, a rate far higher than in later civilizations, where violence was largely monopolized by the state.[7] Although sometimes romanticized by outsiders, the relative equality of Paleolithic societies did not always ensure a utopia of social harmony.

Like all other human cultures, Paleolithic societies had rules and structures. A gender-based division of labor usually cast men as hunters and women as gatherers. Values emphasizing reciprocal sharing of goods resulted in clearly defined rules about distributing the meat from an animal kill. Various rules about incest and adultery governed sexual behavior, while understandings about who could hunt or gather in particular territories regulated economic activity. Leaders arose as needed to organize a task such as a hunt, but without conferring permanent power on individuals.

Economy and the Environment

For a long time, modern people viewed their gathering and hunting ancestors as primitive and impoverished, barely eking out a living from the land. In more recent decades, anthropologists studying contemporary Paleolithic societies—those that survived into the twentieth century—began to paint a different picture. They noted that gathering and hunting people frequently worked fewer hours to meet their material needs than did people in agricultural or industrial societies and so had more leisure time. One scholar referred to them as "the original affluent society," not because they had so much but because they wanted or needed so little.[8] Nonetheless, life expectancy was low, probably little more than thirty-five years on average. Life in the wild was surely dangerous, and dependency on the vagaries of nature rendered it insecure as well.

But Paleolithic people also acted to alter the natural environment substantially. The use of deliberately set fires to encourage the growth of particular plants certainly changed the landscape and in Australia led to the proliferation of fire-resistant eucalyptus trees at the expense of other plant species. In many ecosystems, especially small ones like Pacific islands, the arrival of humans resulted in the rapid extinction of some native plants and animals. Other hominid, or human-like, species, such as the Neanderthals in Europe or "Flores man," discovered in 2003 in Indonesia, also perished after living side by side with *Homo sapiens* for millennia.

Whether their disappearance occurred through massacre, interbreeding, peaceful competition, or something unrelated to the human presence, ultimately they did not survive the rise of humankind. Thus the biological environment inhabited by gathering and hunting peoples was not wholly natural but was shaped in part by their own hands.

The Realm of the Spirit

The religious or spiritual dimension of Paleolithic culture has been hard to pin down, because bones and stones tell us little about what people thought, art is subject to many interpretations, and the experience of contemporary gathering and hunting peoples may not reflect the distant past. Clear evidence exists, however, for a rich interior life. The presence of rock art deep inside caves and far from living spaces suggests a "ceremonial space" separate from ordinary life. The extended rituals of contemporary Australian Aboriginals, which sometimes last for weeks, confirm this impression, as do numerous and elaborate burial sites found throughout the world. No full-time religious specialists or priests led these ceremonies, but part-time shamans (people believed to be especially skilled at dealing with the spirit world) emerged as the need arose. Such people sometimes entered an altered state of consciousness or a trance while performing the ceremonies, often with the aid of psychoactive drugs.

Precisely how Paleolithic people understood the nonmaterial world is hard to reconstruct, and speculation abounds. Linguistic evidence from ancient Africa suggests a variety of understandings: some Paleolithic societies were apparently monotheistic; others saw several levels of supernatural beings, including a creator deity, various territorial spirits, and the spirits of dead ancestors; still others believed in an impersonal force suffused throughout the natural order that could be accessed by shamans during a trance dance.[9] The prevalence of Venus figurines and other symbols all across Europe has convinced some, but not all, scholars that Paleolithic religious thought had a strongly feminine dimension, embodied in a Great Goddess and concerned with the regeneration and renewal of life.[10] Many gathering and hunting peoples likely developed a cyclical view of time derived from recurring natural cycles: sunrise and sunset; changing seasons; the phases of the moon; patterns of female fertility—birth, menstruation, pregnancy, new birth—and, of course, life, death, and new life. These understandings of the cosmos, which saw endlessly repeated patterns of regeneration and disintegration, differed from later Western views, which saw time moving in a straight line toward some predetermined goal. Nor did Paleolithic people make sharp distinctions between the material and spiritual worlds, for they understood that animals, rocks, trees, mountains, and much more were animated by spirit or possessed souls of their own. Earlier scholars sometimes dubbed such views as "animistic" and regarded them as "primitive" or "simple" in comparison to later literate religions. More recent

The Willendorf Venus
Less than four and a half inches in height and dating to about 25,000 years ago, this female figure, which was found near the town of Willendorf in Austria, has become the most famous of the many Venus figurines. Certain features— the absence of both face and feet, the coils of hair around her head, the prominence of her breasts and sexual organs—have prompted much speculation among scholars about the significance of these intriguing carvings. (Naturhistorisches Museum, Vienna, Austria/ Ali Meyer/Bridgeman Images)

SNAPSHOT   Paleolithic Era in Perspective

	Paleolithic Era (from 10,000 to 250,000 years ago)	Agricultural Era (from 200 to 10,000 years ago)	Modern Industrial Era (since 1800)
Duration of each era, as a percentage of 250,000 years[11]	96%	4%	0.08%
Percentage of people who lived, out of 80 billion total	12%	68%	20%
Percentage of years lived in each era (reflects changing life expectancies)	9%	62%	29%

accounts generally avoid the term, preferring to focus on the specifics of particular religious traditions rather than some overall evolutionary scheme.

Settling Down: The Great Transition

Though glacially slow by contemporary standards, changes in Paleolithic cultures occurred over time as people moved into new environments, as populations grew, as climates altered, and as different human groups interacted with one another. For example, all over the Afro-Eurasian world after 25,000 years ago, a tendency toward the miniaturization of stone tools is evident, analogous perhaps to the miniaturization of electronic components in the twentieth century. Known as micro-blades, these smaller and more refined spear points, arrowheads, knives, and scrapers were carefully struck from larger cores and often mounted in antler, bone, or wooden handles. Another important change in the strategies of Paleolithic people involved the collection of wild grains, which represented a major addition to the food supply beyond the use of roots, berries, and nuts. This innovation originated in northeastern Africa around 16,000 years ago.

But the most striking and significant change in the lives of Paleolithic peoples occurred as the last Ice Age came to an end between 16,000 and 10,000 years ago. What followed was a general global warming, though one with periodic fluctuations and cold snaps. Unlike the contemporary global warming, generated by human activity and especially the burning of fossil fuels, this ancient warming phase was a wholly natural phenomenon, part of a long cycle of repeated heating and cooling characteristic of the earth's climatic history. Plants and animals that had struggled

■ **Change**
Why did some Paleolithic peoples abandon earlier, more nomadic ways and begin to live a more settled life?

in the Ice Age climate now flourished and increased their range, providing a much richer and more diverse environment for many human societies. Under these improved conditions, human populations grew, and some previously nomadic gathering and hunting communities, but not all of them, found it possible to settle down and live in more permanent settlements or villages. These societies were becoming both larger and more complex, and it was less possible to simply move away if trouble struck. Settlement also meant that households could store and accumulate goods to a greater degree than previously. Because some people were more energetic, more talented, or luckier than others, the thin edge of inequality gradually began to wear away the egalitarianism of Paleolithic communities.

Changes along these lines emerged in many places. Paleolithic societies in Japan, known as Jomon, settled down in villages by the sea, where they greatly expanded the number of animals, both land and marine, that they consumed. They also created some of the world's first pottery, along with dugout canoes, paddles, bows, bowls, and tool handles, all made from wood. A similar pattern of permanent settlement, a broader range of food sources, and specialized technologies is evident in parts of Scandinavia, Southeast Asia, North America, and the Middle East between 12,000 and 4,000 years ago. In Labrador, longhouses accommodating 100 people appear in the archeological record. Far more elaborate burial sites in many places testify to the growing complexity of human communities and the kinship systems that bound them together. Separate cemeteries for dogs suggest that humankind's best friend was also our first domesticated animal friend. Some of the most stunning and unexpected achievements of such sedentary Paleolithic people come from the archeological complex of Göbekli Tepe (goh-BEHK-lee TEH-peh) in southeastern Turkey, described more fully in the Zooming In feature on page 26.

Studies of more recent gathering and hunting societies, which were able to settle permanently in particular resource-rich areas, show marked differences from their more nomadic counterparts. Among the Chumash of southern California, for example, early Spanish settlers found peoples who had developed substantial and permanent structures accommodating up to seventy persons; hereditary political elites; elements of a market economy, including the use of money and private ownership of some property; and the beginnings of class distinctions.

This process of settling down among gathering and hunting peoples—and the changes that followed from it—marked a major turn in human history, away from countless millennia of nomadic journeys by very small communities. It also provided the setting within which the next great transition would occur. Growing numbers of men and women, living in settled communities, placed a much greater demand on the environment than did small bands of people on the move. Therefore, it is perhaps not surprising that among the innovations that emerged in some of these more complex gathering and hunting societies was yet another way for increasing the food supply—agriculture.

SUMMING UP SO FAR

How do you understand the significance of the long Paleolithic era in the larger context of world history?

Göbekli Tepe: Monumental Construction before Agriculture

Perhaps the most stunning archeological discovery of recent decades comes from the site known as Göbekli Tepe, or "potbelly hill," in southeastern Turkey, which has been under excavation since the mid-1990s. Dating to almost 12,000 years ago, this twenty-five-acre complex currently consists of about 200 massive limestone pillars, some as tall as eighteen feet and weighing as much as fifty tons. Carved in a T shape, perhaps to represent human beings with arms outstretched, they were arranged in a set of walled circles or rings. Five such circles have been unearthed so far, with another twenty or so awaiting excavation. Gracefully carved wild animals—gazelles, snakes, boars, foxes, lions, scorpions, vultures—decorate the pillars. Göbekli Tepe was probably a ceremonial or religious site, for little evidence of long-term human habitation has been found. Dubbed "the world's oldest temple," it likely attracted worshippers or pilgrims from many miles around and

Göbekli Tepe.

may well have served as a place of ritual burials, although no actual graves have yet been found.

The most amazing feature of Göbekli Tepe involves those who constructed it, for they were clearly gathering and hunting peoples, living at least part of the year in settled villages. No evidence of agriculture or domesticated animals has emerged. Rather, the tens of thousands of animal bone fragments found at the site suggest that those who built the complex dined on wild gazelles, pigs, sheep, deer, vultures, and ducks, as well as wild plants native to the area. Thus Göbekli Tepe represents a kind of monumental construction long associated only with agricultural societies and civilizations, forcing scholars to rethink their understanding of the late Paleolithic era.

Breakthroughs to Agriculture

The chief feature of the long Paleolithic era—and the first human process to operate on a global scale—was the initial settlement of the earth. Then, beginning around 12,000 years ago, a second global pattern began to unfold—agriculture. The terms "Neolithic (New Stone Age) Revolution" and "Agricultural Revolution" both refer to the deliberate cultivation of particular plants as well as the taming and breeding of particular animals. Thus a whole new way of life gradually replaced the earlier practices of gathering and hunting in most parts of the world. Although it took place over centuries and millennia, the coming of agriculture represented a genuinely revolutionary transformation of human life all across the planet and provided the foundation for almost everything that followed: growing populations, settled villages, animal-borne diseases, horse-drawn chariot warfare, cities, states, empires, civilizations, writing, literature, and much more.

How did such pre-agricultural peoples with only the simplest of stone tools carve, transport, and erect such enormous structures? What kind of social organization facilitated their remarkable achievement? What did this complex mean to those who created it? Since stones and bones tell us little about these matters, many mysteries remain.

Although Göbekli Tepe was the product of pre-agricultural peoples, the process of its construction may well have played a role in the breakthrough to farming in this region. Klaus Schmidt, the chief archeologist at the site for many years, argued that the need for food to supply those who built and maintained this massive religious complex may well have triggered the development of agriculture in the area. Certainly, some of the earliest domesticated wheat has been located just twenty miles away and at roughly the same date. If this connection holds, it suggests that the

Carved lion on a stone pillar at Göbekli Tepe.

human impulse to worship collectively played a significant role in generating the epic transformation of the Agricultural Revolution.

Scholars have long believed that large-scale construction, settled village life, and institutional religion were generated by agricultural societies. The finds at Göbekli Tepe and elsewhere now suggest that these achievements may have figured in the creation of those farming communities. Perhaps they were precursors to agriculture rather than products of it.

Questions: In what ways has Göbekli Tepe forced historians to rethink earlier views? How does this archeological discovery affect your own understanding of the Paleolithic era?

photo: © Vincent J. Musi/National Geographic Society/Corbis

Among the most revolutionary aspects of the age of agriculture was a new relationship between humankind and other living things, for now men and women were not simply using what they found in nature but actively changing nature as well. They were consciously "directing" the process of evolution. The actions of farmers in the Americas, for example, transformed corn from a plant with a cob of an inch or so to one measuring about six inches by 1500. Later efforts more than doubled that length. Farmers everywhere stamped the landscape with a human imprint in the form of fields with boundaries, terraced hillsides, irrigation ditches, and canals. Animals too were transformed as selective breeding produced sheep that grew more wool, cows that gave more milk, and chickens that laid more eggs than their wild counterparts.

This was "domestication"—the taming, and the changing, of nature for the benefit of humankind—but it created a new kind of mutual dependence. Many domesticated plants and animals could no longer survive in the wild and relied on human action or protection to reproduce successfully. Similarly, farmers and herders became dependent on their domesticated plants and animals, for as their populations grew, those larger numbers could no longer sustain themselves in the older gathering, hunting, and fishing fashion. From an outside point of view, it might well seem that corn and cows had tamed human beings, using people to ensure their own survival and growth as a species, as much as the other way around. In many agricultural communities, however, gathering, hunting, and fishing did not quickly disappear, but long continued to supplement agriculture and animal husbandry as food sources. Even in modern industrial societies, hunting continues as a sport, gathering wild mushrooms and berries persists as an enjoyable pastime, and fishing for both profit and pleasure remains a widespread activity. In such ways, the original human style of living resonates still, even in the twenty-first century.

A further revolutionary aspect of the agricultural age is summed up in the term "intensification." It means getting more for less, in this case more food and resources—far more—from a much smaller area of land than was possible with a gathering and hunting technology. More food meant more people. Growing populations in turn required an even more intensive exploitation of the environment. And so was launched the continuing human effort to "subdue the earth" and to "have dominion over it," as the biblical story in Genesis recorded God's command to Adam and Eve.

Common Patterns

Perhaps the most extraordinary feature of the Neolithic or Agricultural Revolution was that it occurred, separately and independently, in many widely scattered parts of the world: the Fertile Crescent of Southwest Asia, several places in sub-Saharan Africa, China, Southeast Asia, New Guinea, Mesoamerica, the Andes, and eastern North America (see Map 1.3). Even more remarkably, all of this took place at roughly the same time (at least as measured by the 250,000-year span of human history on the planet)—between 12,000 and 4,000 years ago. These facts have generated many questions with which historians have long struggled. Why was the Agricultural Revolution so late in the history of humankind? What was unique about the period after 10,000 B.C.E. that may have triggered or facilitated this vast upheaval? In what different ways did the Agricultural Revolution take shape in its various locations? How did it spread from its several points of origin to the rest of the earth? And what impact did it have on the making of human societies?

It is no accident that the Agricultural Revolution coincided with the end of the last Ice Age, a process of global warming that began some 16,000 years ago. By about 11,000 years ago, the Ice Age was over, and climatic conditions similar to those of our own time generally prevailed. This was but the latest of some twenty-

■ **Change**
What accounts for the emergence of agriculture after countless millennia of human life without it?

five periods of glaciation and warming that have occurred over the past several million years of the earth's history and that are caused by minor periodic changes in the earth's orbit around the sun. The end of the last Ice Age, however, coincided with the migration of *Homo sapiens* across the planet and created new conditions that made agriculture more possible in some areas, even as rising sea levels inundated other regions (see Map 1.1). Combined perhaps with active hunting by human societies, climate change in some places helped to push into extinction various species of large mammals on which Paleolithic people had depended, thus adding to the pressure to find new food sources. The warmer, wetter, and more stable conditions, particularly in the tropical and temperate regions of the earth, also permitted the flourishing of more wild plants, especially cereal grasses, which were the ancestors of many domesticated crops. What climate change took away with one hand, it apparently gave back with the other.

Over their long history, gathering and hunting peoples had already developed a deep knowledge of the natural world and, in some cases, the ability to manage it actively. They had learned to make use of a large number of plants and to hunt and eat both small and large animals, creating what archeologists call a "broad-spectrum diet." In the Middle East, people had developed sickles for cutting newly available wild grain, baskets to carry it, mortars and pestles to remove the husk, and storage pits to preserve it. Peoples of the Amazon and elsewhere had learned to cut back some plants to encourage the growth of their favorites. Native Australians had built elaborate traps in which they could capture, store, and harvest large numbers of eels.

In hindsight, much of this looks like a kind of preparation for agriculture. Because women in particular had long been intimately associated with collecting wild plants, they were the likely innovators who led the way to deliberate farming, with men perhaps taking the lead in domesticating animals. Clearly the knowledge and technology necessary for agriculture were part of a longer process involving more intense human exploitation of the earth. Nowhere was agriculture an overnight invention.

Using such technologies, and benefiting from the global warming at the end of the last Ice Age, gathering and hunting peoples in various resource-rich areas were able to settle down and establish more permanent villages, abandoning their nomadic ways and more intensively exploiting the local area. In settling down, however, they found themselves now required to support growing populations. Evidence for increasing human numbers around the world during this period of global warming has persuaded some scholars that agriculture was a response to the need for additional food, perhaps even a "food crisis." Such conditions surely motivated people to experiment and to innovate in an effort to increase the food supply. Clearly, many of the breakthroughs to agriculture occurred only *after* gathering and hunting peoples had already grown substantially in numbers and had established a sedentary way of life.

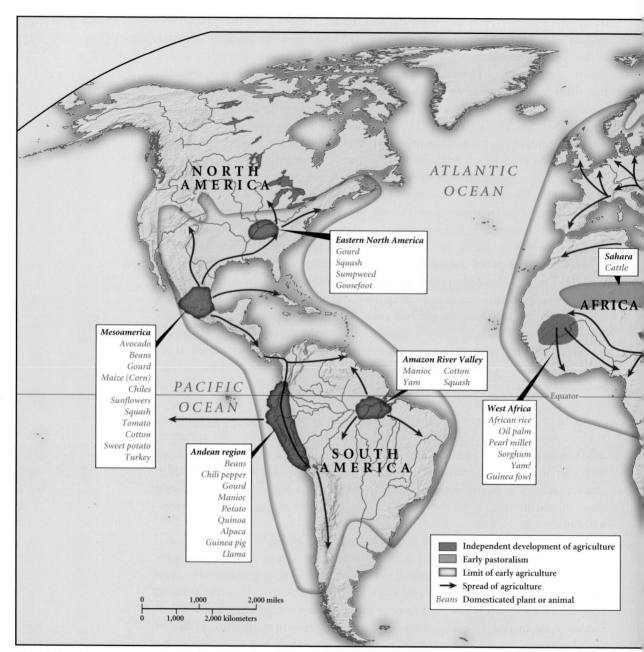

Map 1.3   The Global Spread of Agriculture and Pastoralism

From ten or more separate points of origin, agriculture spread to adjacent areas, eventually encompassing almost all of the world's peoples.

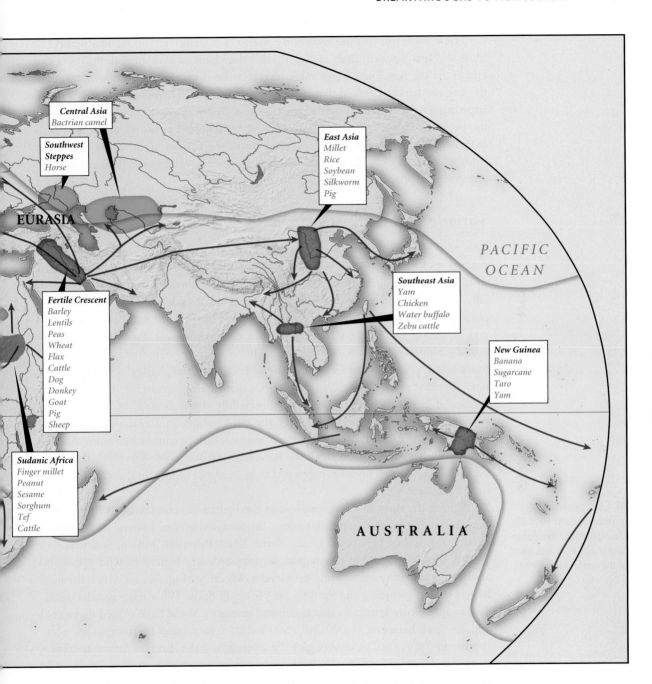

Central Asia
Bactrian camel

*Southwest
Steppes*
Horse

EURASIA

East Asia
Millet
Rice
Soybean
Silkworm
Pig

Fertile Crescent
Barley
Lentils
Peas
Wheat
Flax
Cattle
Dog
Donkey
Goat
Pig
Sheep

Southeast Asia
Yam
Chicken
Water buffalo
Zebu cattle

New Guinea
Banana
Sugarcane
Taro
Yam

Sudanic Africa
Finger millet
Peanut
Sesame
Sorghum
Tef
Cattle

*PACIFIC
OCEAN*

AUSTRALIA

These were some of the common patterns that facilitated the Agricultural Revolution. New opportunities appeared with the changed climatic conditions at the end of the Ice Age. New knowledge and technology emerged as human communities explored and exploited that changed environment. The disappearance of many large mammals, growing populations, newly settled ways of life, and fluctuations in the process of global warming—all of these represented pressures or incentives to increase food production and thus to minimize the risks of life in a new era. From some combination of these opportunities and incentives emerged the profoundly transforming process of the Agricultural Revolution.

Variations

This new way of life initially operated everywhere with a simple technology—the digging stick or hoe. Plows were developed much later. But the several transitions to this hoe-based agriculture, commonly known as horticulture, varied considerably, depending on what plants and animals were available locally. For example, potatoes were found in the Andes region, but not in Africa or Asia; wheat and wild pigs existed in the Fertile Crescent, but not in the Americas. Furthermore, of the world's 200,000 plant species, only several hundred have been domesticated, and in more recent centuries just five of these—wheat, corn, rice, barley, and sorghum— have supplied more than half of the calories that sustain human life. Only fourteen species of large mammals have been successfully domesticated, of which sheep, pigs, goats, cattle, and horses have been the most important. Because they are stubborn, nervous, solitary, or finicky, many animals simply cannot be readily domesticated. Thus the kind of Agricultural Revolution that unfolded in particular places depended very much on what happened to be available locally; in short, it depended on sheer luck.

■ Comparison

In what different ways did the Agricultural Revolution take shape in various parts of the world?

Among the most favored areas—and the first to experience a full Agricultural Revolution—was the Fertile Crescent, an area sometimes known as Southwest Asia, consisting of present-day Iraq, Syria, Israel/Palestine, Jordan, and southern Turkey (see Map 1.4). In this region, an extraordinary variety of wild plants and animals capable of domestication provided a rich array of species on which the now largely settled gathering and hunting people could draw. What triggered the transition to agriculture remains a much-debated question. Some have argued that a cold and dry spell between 11,000 and 9500 B.C.E., a very rapid but temporary interruption in the general process of global warming, was the stimulus for the transition to farming. Larger settled populations, now threatened with the loss of the wild plants and animals on which they had come to depend, found a solution in domestication, either during or soon after this cold and dry period passed. Figs were apparently the first cultivated crop, dating to about 9400 B.C.E. In the millennium or so that followed, wheat, barley, rye, peas, lentils, sheep, goats, pigs, and cattle all came under human control, providing the foundation for the world's first agricultural societies.

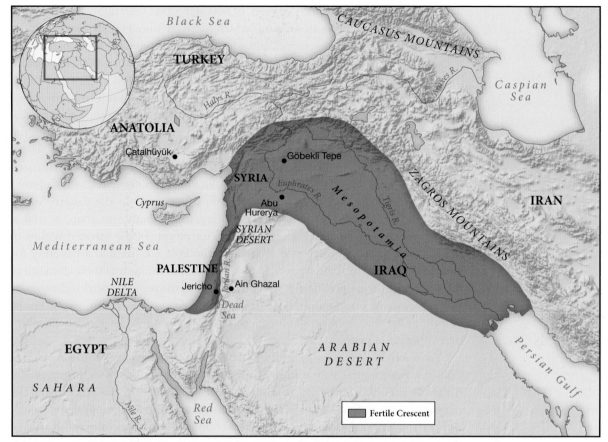

Map 1.4   The Fertile Crescent

Located in what is now called the Middle East, the Fertile Crescent was the site of many significant processes in early world history, including a major breakthrough to agriculture and later the development of one of the First Civilizations.

Archeological evidence suggests that the transition to a fully agricultural way of life in parts of this region took place quite quickly, within as few as 500 years. Signs of that transformation included large increases in the size of settlements, which now housed as many as several thousand people. In these agricultural settings, archeologists have found major innovations: the use of sun-dried mud bricks; the appearance of monuments or shrine-like buildings; displays of cattle skulls; more elaborate human burials, including the removal of the skull; and more sophisticated tools, such as sickles, polished axes, and awls. From this point on, global climate remained remarkably stable, when compared to sharp variations of earlier times, which proved to be a great advantage for settled life and agricultural development.

At roughly the same time, or perhaps a bit later, another process of domestication was unfolding on the African continent in the eastern part of what is now the

Sahara in present-day Sudan. Between 10,000 and 5,000 years ago, scholars tell us that there was no desert in this region, which received more rainfall than currently, had extensive grassland vegetation, and was "relatively hospitable to human life."[12] It seems likely that cattle were domesticated in this region about 1,000 years before they were separately brought under human control in the Middle East and India. At about the same time, the donkey was also domesticated in northeastern Africa near the Red Sea and spread from there into Southwest Asia, even as the practice of raising sheep and goats moved in the other direction. In terms of farming, the African pattern again was somewhat different. Unlike the Fertile Crescent, where a number of plants were domesticated in a small area, sub-Saharan Africa witnessed the emergence of several widely scattered farming practices. Sorghum, which grows well in arid conditions, was the first grain to be "tamed" in the eastern Sahara region. In the highlands of Ethiopia, teff, a tiny, highly nutritious grain, as well as enset, a relative of the banana, came under cultivation. In the forested region of West Africa, yams, oil palm trees, okra, and the kola nut (used as a flavoring for cola drinks) emerged as important crops. The scattered location of these domestications generated a less productive agriculture than in the more favored and compact Fertile Crescent, but a number of African domesticates—sorghum, castor beans, gourds, millet, the donkey—subsequently spread to enrich the agricultural practices of Eurasian peoples.

Yet another pattern of agricultural development took shape in the Americas. Like the Agricultural Revolution in Africa, the domestication of plants in the Americas occurred separately in a number of locations—in the coastal Andean regions of western South America, in Mesoamerica, in the Mississippi River valley, and perhaps in the Amazon basin. Surely the most distinctive common feature of these regions was the relative absence of animals that could be domesticated. Of the fourteen major species of large mammals that have been brought under human control, just two, the llama and alpaca, existed in the Western Hemisphere, and only in the Andes region, where they proved enormously useful for food, fiber, and transportation. Without goats, sheep, pigs, cattle, or horses, the peoples of the Americas lacked sources of protein, manure (for fertilizer), and power (to draw plows or pull carts, for example) that were widely available to societies in the Afro-Eurasian world. Because they could not depend on domesticated animals for meat, many agricultural peoples in the Americas relied more on hunting and fishing than did peoples in the Eastern Hemisphere. Europe too lacked most of the animals that could be readily domesticated, but it was geographically closer to areas that had them and so could borrow from neighboring regions. Farmers in the Americas could not.

While the Americas lacked the cereal grains that were widely available in Afro-Eurasia, they had maize or corn, first domesticated in southern Mexico by 4000 to 3000 B.C.E. Unlike the cereal grains of the Fertile Crescent, which closely resemble their wild predecessors, the ancestor of corn, a mountain grass called teosinte (tee-

The Statues of Ain Ghazal
Among the largest of the early agricultural settlements investigated by archeologists is that of Ain Ghazal, located in the modern state of Jordan. Inhabited from about 7200 to 5000 B.C.E., in its prime it was home to some 3,000 people, who lived in multi-roomed stone houses; cultivated barley, wheat, peas, beans, and lentils; and herded domesticated goats. These remarkable statues, around three feet tall and made of limestone plaster applied to a core of bundled reeds, were among the most startling finds at that site. Did they represent heroes, gods, goddesses, or ordinary people? No one really knows. (Courtesy, Department of Antiquities of Jordan [DoA]/Photo by John Tsantesi, Courtesy, Dr. Gary O. Rollefson)

uh-SIHN-tee), looks nothing like what we now know as corn or maize. Thousands of years of selective adaptation were required to develop a sufficiently large cob and number of kernels to sustain a productive agriculture, an achievement that one geneticist has called "arguably man's first, and perhaps his greatest, feat of genetic engineering."[13] Thus while Middle Eastern societies quite rapidly replaced their gathering and hunting economy with agriculture, that process took several thousand years in Mesoamerica. Beyond maize, Native American farmers domesticated squash, beans, potatoes, sunflowers, quinoa, pigweed, and goosefoot, which were harvested on a large scale.

Another difference in the unfolding of the Agricultural Revolution lay in the north/south orientation of the Americas, which required agricultural practices to move through, and adapt to, quite distinct climatic and vegetation zones if they were to spread. The east/west axis of North Africa / Eurasia meant that agricultural innovations could spread more rapidly because they were entering roughly similar environments. Thus corn, beans, and squash, which were first domesticated in Mesoamerica, took several thousand years to travel the few hundred miles from their Mexican homeland to the southwestern United States and another thousand years or more to arrive in eastern North America. The llama, guinea pig, quinoa, and potato, which were domesticated in the Andean highlands, never reached Mesoamerica.

The Globalization of Agriculture

■ Connection

In what ways did agriculture spread? Where and why was it sometimes resisted?

From the various places where it originated, agriculture spread gradually to much of the rest of the earth, although for a long time it coexisted with gathering and hunting ways of life, even as it eroded and diminished those cultures. Broadly speaking, this extension of farming occurred in two ways. The first, known as diffusion, refers to the gradual spread of agricultural techniques, and perhaps of the plants and animals themselves, but without the extensive movement of agricultural people. Neighboring groups exchanged ideas and products in a down-the-line pattern of communication. A second process involved the slow colonization or migration of agricultural peoples as growing populations pushed them outward. Often this meant the conquest, absorption, or displacement of the earlier gatherers and hunters, along with the spread of the languages and cultures of the migrating farmers. In many places, both processes took place.

Triumph and Resistance

Some combination of diffusion and migration underpinned the spread of agriculture to new regions, and the adoption of farming practices was at times accompanied by the spread of languages as well. For instance, between 6500 and 4000 B.C.E. the agricultural package of Southwest Asia spread into Europe, Central Asia, Egypt, and North Africa. In the case of Europe, the adoption of agriculture was accompanied by the spread into the region of Indo-European languages, which had originated further east in Anatolia or, as some scholars suggest, in the area north of the Black and Caspian Seas. In a similar process, the Chinese farming system moved into Southeast Asia and elsewhere, and with it a number of related language families developed. India received agricultural influences from the Middle East, Africa, and China alike. Within Africa, the development of agricultural societies in the southern half of the continent is associated with the migration of peoples speaking one or another of the some 400 Bantu languages. Beginning from what is now southern Nigeria or Cameroon around 3000 B.C.E., Bantu-speaking people moved east and south over the next several millennia, taking with them their agricultural, cattle-raising, and, later, ironworking skills, as well as their languages. The Bantus generally absorbed, killed, or drove away the indigenous Paleolithic peoples or exposed them to animal-borne diseases to which they had no immunities. A similar process brought agricultural Austronesian-speaking people, who originated in southern China, to the Philippine and Indonesian islands, with similar consequences for their earlier inhabitants. Later, Austronesian speakers carried agriculture to the uninhabited islands of the Pacific and to Madagascar off the coast of southeastern Africa (see Map 1.2, page 19).

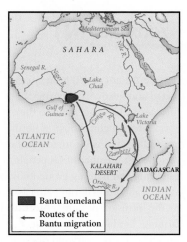

Bantu Migrations

The globalization of agriculture was a prolonged process, lasting 10,000 years or more after its first emergence in the Fertile Crescent, but it did not take hold everywhere. The Agricultural Revolution in highland New Guinea, for example, generated a number of domesticated plants including yams, taro, bananas, and sugarcane. But while these spread to parts of Island Southeast Asia, they did not pass to the nearby peoples of Australia, who remained steadfastly committed to gathering and hunting ways of life. The people of the west coast of North America, arctic regions, and southwestern Africa also maintained their gathering and hunting economies into the modern era. A very few, such as the Hadza, described at the beginning of this chapter, practice it still in vanishing numbers.

Some of those who resisted the swelling tide of agriculture lived in areas unsuitable to farming, such as harsh desert or arctic environments; others lived in regions of particular natural abundance, so they felt little need for agriculture. Such societies found it easier to resist agriculture if they were not in the direct line of advancing, more powerful farming people. But many of the remaining gathering and hunting peoples knew about agricultural practices from nearby neighbors, suggesting that they quite deliberately chose to resist it in favor of the freer life of their Paleolithic ancestors.

Nonetheless, by the beginning of the Common Era, the global spread of agriculture had reduced gathering and hunting peoples to a small and dwindling minority of humankind. If that process meant "progress" in certain ways, it also claimed many victims as the relentlessly expanding agricultural frontier slowly destroyed gathering and hunting societies. Whether this process occurred through the peaceful diffusion of new technologies, through intermarriage, through disease, or through the violent displacement of earlier peoples, the steady erosion of this ancient way of life has been a persistent thread of the human story over the past 10,000 years. The final chapters of that long story are being written in our own times. (See Zooming In, page 38, for a recent example of this process.) After the Agricultural Revolution, the future, almost everywhere, lay with the farmers and herders and with the distinctive societies that they created.

The Culture of Agriculture

What did that future look like? In what ways did societies based on the domestication of plants and animals differ from those rooted in a gathering and hunting economy? In the first place, the Agricultural Revolution led to an increase in

■ **Change**
What changes did the Agricultural Revolution bring in its wake?

Ishi, the Last of His People

Ishi.

In late August of 1911, an emaciated and nearly naked man, about fifty years old, staggered into the corral of a slaughterhouse in northern California. As it turned out, he was the last member of his people, a gathering and hunting group known as the Yahi, pushed into extinction by the intrusion of more powerful farming, herding, and "civilized" societies. It was a very old story, played out for over 10,000 years since the Agricultural Revolution placed Paleolithic cultures on the defensive, inexorably eroding their presence on the earth. The tragic story of this individual allows us to put a human face on that enormous and largely unrecorded process.

Within a few days, this bedraggled and no doubt bewildered man was taken into the care of several anthropologists from the University of California, who brought him to a museum in San Francisco, where he lived until his death from tuberculosis in 1916.

They called him Ishi, which means "person" in his native language, because he was unwilling to provide them with his own given name. In his culture, it was highly inappropriate to reveal one's name, especially to strangers.

In the mid-nineteenth century, the Yahi consisted of about 300 to 400 people living in a rugged and mountainous area of northern California. There they hunted, fished, gathered acorns, and otherwise provided for themselves in a fashion familiar to gathering and hunting peoples the world over. But the 1849 California gold rush brought a massive influx of American settlers, miners, and farmers that quickly pushed the Yahi to the edge of extinction. Yahi raiding and resistance was met by massacres at the hands of local militias and vigilantes, who were only too glad to "clean up the Indians," killing and scalping

photo: Courtesy of The Bancroft Library, University of California, Berkeley

human population, as the greater productivity of agriculture was able to support much larger numbers. An early agricultural settlement uncovered near Jericho in present-day Israel probably had 2,000 people, a vast increase in the size of human communities compared to much smaller Paleolithic bands. On a global level, scholars estimate that the world's population was about 6 million around 10,000 years ago, before the Agricultural Revolution got under way, and shot up to some 50 million by 5,000 years ago and 250 million by the beginning of the Common Era. Here was the real beginning of the human dominance over other forms of life on the planet.

That dominance was reflected in major environmental transformations. In a growing number of places, forests and grasslands became cultivated fields and grazing lands. Human selection modified the genetic composition of numerous plants and animals. In parts of the Middle East, within a thousand years after the beginning of settled agricultural life, some villages were abandoned when soil erosion and

hundreds. One such massacre in 1865 likely killed Ishi's father, while the young Ishi, his mother, and a few others escaped.

By 1870, Ishi's community had dwindled to fifteen or sixteen people, who lived in an even more inaccessible region of their homeland. In these desperate circumstances, traditional gender roles blurred, even as they undertook great efforts to conceal their presence. To avoid making footprints when traveling, they jumped from rock to rock; they ground acorns on smooth stones rather than on more obvious hollowed-out rocks and carefully camouflaged their thatched dwellings and camp-fires. By 1894, this tiny Yahi community numbered only five people: Ishi, his mother, his sister or cousin, and an older man and woman.

Then in 1908, a group of American surveyors came across a naked Ishi harpooning fish in the river, and a few days later they found the tiny settlement that sheltered the remaining Yahi. Only Ishi's aged mother was present, hidden under a pile of skins and rags. They did not harm her, but they took away every movable item—tools, food, baskets, bows and arrows—as souvenirs. Ishi returned to carry his mother away and she soon died. He never saw his sister/cousin or the others again. For some time, then, Ishi lived absolutely alone, until he stumbled into the slaughterhouse on August 29, 1911, his hair burned short in a Yahi sign of mourning.

In his new home in the museum, Ishi became something of a media sensation, willingly demonstrating his skills for visitors—starting a fire and fashioning tools and weapons of stone and bone, but refusing to make baskets, because it was women's work. Actively cooperating with anthropologists who sought to document the culture of his people, he took them on a hunt one summer, teaching them how to track and kill deer and to process the meat on the spot. All who met him remarked on his gentleness and kindness, his love of company, his delight in children, and his fondness for laughing and joking. Alfred Kroeber, the primary anthropologist involved with Ishi, observed, "He was the most patient man I ever knew . . . without trace of self-pity or of bitterness to dull the purity of his cheerful enduringness."[14]

Questions: What accounts for the ability of Ishi's people to survive into the twentieth century? What emotional or moral posture toward Ishi's life seems most appropriate? What perspective does it lend to the larger story of the gradual erosion of gathering and hunting societies the world over?

deforestation led to declining crop yields, which could not support mounting populations. The advent of more intensive agriculture associated with city-based civilizations only heightened this human impact on the landscape.

Human life too changed dramatically in farming communities, and not necessarily for the better. Farming involved hard work and more of it than in many earlier gathering and hunting societies. The remains of early agricultural people show some deterioration in health—more tooth decay, malnutrition, and anemia; a shorter physical stature; and diminished life expectancy. Living close to animals subjected humans to new diseases—smallpox, flu, measles, chicken pox, malaria, tuberculosis, rabies—while living in larger communities generated epidemics for the first time in human history. Furthermore, relying on a small number of plants or animals rendered early agricultural societies vulnerable to famine, in case of crop failure, drought, or other catastrophes. The advent of agriculture bore costs as well as benefits.

Agriculture also imposed constraints on human communities. Some Paleolithic people had settled in permanent villages, but most agricultural people did so, as farming usually required a settled life. A good example of an early agricultural settlement comes from northern China, one of the original independent sources of agriculture, where the domestication of rice, millet, pigs, and chickens gave rise to settled communities by about 7,000 years ago. In 1953, workers digging the foundation for a factory uncovered the remains of an ancient village, now called Banpo, near the present-day city of Xian. Millet, pigs, and dogs had been domesticated, but diets were supplemented with wild plants, animals, and fish. Some forty-five houses covered with thatch laid over wooden beams provided homes to perhaps 500 people. More than 200 storage pits permitted the accumulation of grain, and six kilns and pottery wheels enabled the production of various pots, vases, and dishes, many decorated with geometric designs and human and animal images. A large central space suggests an area for public religious or political activity, and a trench surrounding the village indicates some common effort to defend the community.

Early agricultural villages such as Banpo reveal another feature of the age of agriculture—an explosion of technological innovation. Mobile Paleolithic peoples had little use for pots, but such vessels were essential for settled societies, and their creation and elaboration accompanied agriculture everywhere. So too did the weaving of textiles, made possible by collecting the fibers of domesticated plants (cotton and flax, for example) and raising animals such as sheep. Evidence for the invention of looms of several kinds dates back to 7,000 years ago, and textiles, some elaborately decorated, show up in Peru, Switzerland, China, and Egypt. Like agriculture itself, weaving was a technology in which women were probably the primary innovators. It was a task that was compatible with child-rearing responsibilities, which virtually all human societies assigned primarily to women. Another technology associated with the Agricultural Revolution was metallurgy. The working of gold and copper, then bronze, and, later, iron became part of the jewelry-, tool-, and weapon-making skill set of humankind. The long "stone age" of human technological history was coming to an end, and the age of metals was beginning.

Nok Culture

The agricultural and iron-using Nok culture of northern Nigeria in West Africa generated a remarkable artistic tradition of terra-cotta, or fired-clay, figures depicting animals and, especially, people. This one dates to somewhere between 600 B.C.E. and 600 C.E. Some scholars have dubbed this and many similar Nok sculptures "thinkers." Does it seem more likely that this notion reflects a present-day sensibility or that it is an insight into the mentality of the ancient artist who created the image? (Musée du Quai Branly/Scala/Art Resource, NY)

A further set of technological changes, beginning around 4000 B.C.E., has been labeled the "secondary products revolution."[15] These technological innovations involved new uses for domesticated animals, beyond their meat and hides. Agricultural people in parts of Europe, Asia, and Africa learned to milk their animals, to harvest their wool, and to enrich the soil with their manure. Even more important, they learned to ride horses and camels and to hitch various animals to plows and carts. Because these animals did not exist in the Americas, this revolutionary new source of power and transportation was available only in the Eastern Hemisphere.

Finally, the Agricultural Revolution presented to humankind the gift of wine and beer, often a blessing, sometimes a curse. As barley, wheat, rice, and grapes were domesticated, their potential for generating alcoholic beverages soon became apparent. Evidence for wine making in the mountains of present-day northwestern Iran dates to around 5400 B.C.E., though its expense rendered it an elite beverage for millennia. Chinese wine making can be traced to around 4000 B.C.E. Drunken debauchery and carousing among the aristocracy prompted an unsuccessful effort by one Chinese ruler around 1046 B.C.E. to outlaw the beverage. The precise origins of beer are unclear, but its use was already quite widespread in the Middle East by 4000 B.C.E., when a pictogram on a seal from Mesopotamia showed two figures using straws to drink beer from a large pottery jar. Regarded as a gift from the gods, beer, like bread, was understood in Mesopotamia as something that could turn a savage into a fully human and civilized person.[16] In the Americas, an alcoholic beverage known as *chicha* had been produced from maize, manioc, honey, and various fruits from ancient times and was the drink of choice in the Inca court.

Social Variation in the Age of Agriculture

The resources generated by the Agricultural Revolution opened up vast new possibilities for the construction of human societies, but they led to no single or common outcome. Differences in the natural environment, the encounter with strangers, and, sometimes, deliberate choices gave rise to several distinct kinds of societies early on in the age of agriculture, all of which have endured into modern times.

Pastoral Societies

One variation of great significance grew out of the difference between the domestication of plants and the domestication of animals. Many societies made use of both, but in regions where farming was difficult or impossible—arctic tundra, certain grasslands, and deserts—some people came to depend far more extensively on their animals, such as sheep, goats, cattle, horses, camels, or reindeer. Animal husbandry was a "distinct form of food-producing economy," relying on the products of animals.[17] Those animals could turn grass or waste products into meat, fiber, hides, and milk; they were useful for transport and warfare; and they could walk to market. Known as herders, pastoralists, or nomads, peoples largely dependent on their

■ **Comparison**
What different kinds of societies emerged out of the Agricultural Revolution?

The Domestication of Animals
Although farming often gets top billing in discussions of the Neolithic Revolution, the raising of animals was equally important, for they provided meat, pulling power, transportation (in the case of horses and camels), and manure. Animal husbandry also made possible pastoral societies, which were largely dependent on their domesticated animals. This rock art painting from the Sahara (now southeastern Algeria) dates to somewhere around 4000 B.C.E. and depicts an early pastoral community. The white ovals represent a group of huts. (Fresco from Tassili n'Ager, Algeria, Henri Lhote Collection/Musée de l'Homme, Paris, France/Erich Lessing/Art Resource, NY)

domesticated animals emerged most prominently in Central Asia, the Arabian Peninsula, the Sahara, and parts of eastern and southern Africa. What they had in common was mobility, for they moved seasonally as they followed the changing patterns of the vegetation necessary as pasture for their animals. Some lived a nomadic existence of constant seasonal movement, but for others it was possible to combine permanent settlements in lowland areas and the movement of animals to more mountainous pasturelands in the summer.

The particular animals central to pastoral economies differed from region to region. The domestication of horses by 4000 B.C.E. and the mastery of horseback-riding skills several thousand years later enabled the growth of pastoral peoples all across the steppes of Central Asia by the first millennium B.C.E. Although organized primarily in kinship-based clans or tribes, these nomads periodically created powerful military confederations, which played a major role in the history of Eurasia for thousands of years. In the Inner Asian, Arabian, and Saharan deserts, domesticated camels made possible the human occupation of forbidding environments. (See Zooming In: The Arabian Camel, Chapter 7, page 302.) The grasslands south of the Sahara and in parts of eastern Africa supported cattle-raising pastoralists. In the Americas, llamas and alpacas were tremendously important in the economy of Andean civilizations, but only in a few pockets in the Andes did human communities rely as heavily on their domesticated animals as did the pastoral peoples of the Afro-Eurasian world.

The relationship between nomadic herders and their farming neighbors has been one of the enduring themes of Afro-Eurasian history. Frequently, it was a relationship of conflict, as pastoral peoples, unable to produce their own agricultural products, were attracted to the wealth and sophistication of agrarian societies and sought access to their richer grazing lands as well as their food crops and manufactured products. The biblical story of the deadly rivalry between two brothers—Cain, a "tiller of the ground," and Abel, a "keeper of sheep"—reflects this ancient conflict, which persisted well into modern times. But not all was conflict between pastoral and agricultural peoples. The more peaceful exchange of technologies, ideas, products, and people across the ecological frontier of pastoral and agricultural societies also served to enrich and to change both sides. In the chapters that follow, we will encounter pastoral societies repeatedly, particularly as they interact with neighboring agricultural and "civilized" peoples.

Within pastoral communities, the relative equality of men and women, characteristic of most Paleolithic societies, persisted, perhaps because women's work was so essential. Women were centrally involved in milking animals, in processing that milk, and in producing textiles such as felt, which was widely used in Central Asia for tents, beds, rugs, and clothing. Among the Saka pastoralists in what is now Azerbaijan, women rode horses and participated in battles along with men. A number of archeological sites around the Black Sea have revealed high-status women buried with armor, swords, daggers, and arrows. In the Xinjiang region of western China, still other women were buried with the apparatus of healers and shamans, strongly suggesting an important female role in religious life.

Agricultural Village Societies

For thousands of years, people practiced agriculture using digging sticks or hoes, rather than plows, and even after plows came into use, many societies continued with hoe-based or horticultural farming. Most such hoe-based agricultural peoples lived in settled villages such as those of Banpo or Jericho, but to varying degrees they continued to augment their agricultural livelihood with gathering, hunting, and fishing. They also retained much of the social and gender equality of gathering and hunting communities, as they continued to do without kings, chiefs, bureaucrats, or aristocracies.

An example of this type of social order can be found at Çatalhüyük (cha-TAHL-hoo-YOOK), a very early agricultural village in southern Turkey, which flourished between 7400 and 6000 B.C.E. A careful excavation of the site revealed a population of several thousand people who buried their dead under their houses and then filled the houses with dirt and built new ones on top, layer upon layer. No streets divided the houses, which were constructed adjacent to one another. People moved about the village on adjoining rooftops, from which they entered their homes. Despite the presence of many specialized crafts, few signs of inherited social inequality have surfaced. Nor is there any indication of male or female dominance, although men were more closely associated with hunting wild animals and women with plants and agriculture. "Both men and women," concludes one scholar, "could carry out a series of roles and enjoy a range of positions, from making tools to grinding grain and baking to heading a household."[18]

In many horticultural villages, women's critical role as farmers as well as their work in the spinning and weaving of textiles no doubt contributed to a social position of relative equality with men. Some such societies traced their descent through the female line and practiced marriage patterns in which men left their homes to live with their wives' families. Archeologist Marija Gimbutas has highlighted the prevalence of female imagery in the art of early agricultural societies in Europe and

Anatolia, which has suggested to her a widespread cult of the Goddess, focused on "the mystery of birth, death and the renewal of life."[19] But early agriculture did not produce identical gender systems everywhere. Some societies practiced patrilineal descent and required a woman to live in the household of her husband. Grave sites in early Eastern European farming communities reveal fewer adult females than males, indicating perhaps the practice of female infanticide. Some early written evidence from China suggests a long-term preference for male children. These variations in practice suggest that gender roles were likely determined more by cultural preference than by any biological need for a sexual division of labor and power.

In all of their diversity, many village-based agricultural societies flourished well into the modern era, usually organizing themselves in terms of kinship groups or lineages, which incorporated large numbers of people well beyond the immediate or extended family. Such a system provided the framework within which large numbers of people could make and enforce rules, maintain order, and settle disputes without going to war. In short, the lineage system performed the functions of government, but without the formal apparatus of government, and thus did not require kings or queens, chiefs, or permanent officials associated with a state organization. Despite their democratic qualities and the absence of centralized authority, village-based lineage societies sometimes developed modest social and economic inequalities. Elders could exploit the labor of junior members of the community and sought particularly to control women's reproductive powers, which were essential for the growth of the lineage. People with special knowledge, skills, or experience could achieve higher status and greater influence. Among the Igbo of southern Nigeria well into the twentieth century, "title societies" enabled men and women of wealth and character to earn a series of increasingly prestigious "titles" that set them apart from other members of their community, although these honors could not be inherited. Lineages also sought to expand their numbers, and hence their prestige and power, by incorporating war captives or migrants in subordinate positions, sometimes as slaves.

Given the frequent oppressiveness of organized political power in human history, agricultural village societies represent an intriguing alternative to the states, kingdoms, and empires so often highlighted in the historical record. They pioneered the human settlement of vast areas; adapted to a variety of environments; maintained a substantial degree of social and gender equality; created numerous cultural, artistic, and religious traditions; and interacted continuously with their neighbors.

Chiefdoms

In other places, agricultural village societies came to be organized politically as chiefdoms, in which inherited positions of power and privilege introduced a more distinct element of inequality, but unlike later kings, chiefs could seldom use force

Cahokia
Pictured here in an artist's reconstruction, Cahokia (near St. Louis, Missouri) was the center of an important agricultural chiefdom around 1100 C.E. See Chapter 6 for details. (Cahokia Mounds State Historic Site, Illinois. Painting by Lloyd K. Townsend)

to compel the obedience of their subjects. Instead, chiefs relied on their generosity or gift giving, their ritual status, or their personal charisma to persuade their followers. The earliest such chiefdoms seem to have emerged in the Tigris-Euphrates river valley called Mesopotamia (present-day Iraq), sometime after 6000 B.C.E., when temple priests may have organized irrigation systems and controlled trade with nearby societies.

Many chiefdoms followed in all parts of the world, and the more recent ones have been much studied by anthropologists. For example, chiefdoms emerged everywhere in the Pacific islands, which had been colonized by agricultural Polynesian peoples. Chiefs usually derived from a senior lineage, tracing their descent to the first son of an imagined ancestor. With both religious and secular functions, chiefs led important rituals and ceremonies, organized the community for warfare, directed its economic life, and sought to resolve internal conflicts. They collected tribute from commoners in the form of food, manufactured goods, and raw materials. These items in turn were redistributed to warriors, craftsmen, religious specialists, and other subordinates, while chiefs kept enough to maintain their prestigious positions and imposing lifestyle. In North America as well, a remarkable series of chiefdoms emerged in the eastern woodlands, where an extensive array of large earthen mounds testify to the organizational capacity of these early societies. The largest of them, known as Cahokia, flourished around 1100 C.E.

Thus the Agricultural Revolution radically transformed both the trajectory of the human journey and the evolution of life on the planet. This epic process granted to one species, *Homo sapiens*, a growing power over many other species of plants and animals and made possible an increase in human numbers far beyond what a gathering and hunting economy could support.

But if agriculture provided humankind with the power to dominate nature, it also, increasingly, enabled some people to dominate others. This was not immediately apparent, and for several thousand years, and much longer in some places, agricultural villages and pastoral communities retained elements of the social equality that had characterized Paleolithic life. Slowly, though, many of the resources released by the Agricultural Revolution accumulated in the hands of a few. Rich and poor, chiefs and commoners, landowners and dependent peasants, rulers and subjects, dominant men and subordinate women, slaves and free people—these distinctions, so common in the record of world history, took shape most extensively in highly productive agricultural settings, which generated a substantial economic surplus. There the endless elaboration of such differences, for better or worse, became a major feature of those distinctive agricultural societies known to us as "civilizations."

The distinctions that historians make among various kinds of human communities—gathering and hunting peoples, pastoral societies, agricultural village communities, chiefdoms, civilizations—do not represent hard-and-fast differences, but lie on a continuum. Many gathering and hunting societies were nomadic, but some became sedentary; many agricultural and pastoral peoples continued to enrich their diets with foods hunted, gathered, or fished; the line between chiefdoms and civilizations is not always obvious. Such terms are useful for identifying variations in human history, but lived experience is usually messier and less clear than our tidy concepts.

SUMMING UP SO FAR

What was revolutionary about the Agricultural Revolution?

REFLECTIONS

The Uses of the Paleolithic

Even when it is about the distant past, history is also about those who tell it in the present. We search the past, always, for our own purposes. For example, modern people were long inclined to view their Paleolithic or gathering and hunting ancestors as primitive or superstitious, unable to exercise control over nature, and ignorant of its workings. Such a view was, of course, a kind of self-congratulation, designed to highlight the "progress" of modern humankind. It was a way of saying, "Look how far we have come."

In more recent decades, however, growing numbers of people, disillusioned with modernity, have looked to the Paleolithic era for material with which to criticize, rather than celebrate, contemporary life. Feminists have found in gathering and hunting peoples a much more gender-equal society and religious thinking that featured the divine feminine, qualities that encouragingly suggested that patriarchy was neither inevitable nor eternal. Environmentalists have sometimes identified peoples in the distant past who were uniquely in tune with the natural environment rather than seeking to dominate it. Some nutritionists have advocated a "Paleolithic diet" of wild plants and animals as well suited to our physiology. Critics of modern materialism and competitive capitalism have been delighted to discover societies in which values of sharing and equality predominated over those of accumulation and hierarchy. Still others have asked, in light of the long Paleolithic era, whether the explosive population and economic growth of recent centuries should be considered normal or natural. Perhaps they are better seen as extraordinary, possibly even pathological. All of these uses of the Paleolithic have been a way of asking, "What have we lost in the mad rush to modernity, and how can we recover it?"

Both those who look with disdain on Paleolithic "backwardness" and those who praise, often quite romantically, its simplicity and equality seek to use these ancient people for their own purposes. In our efforts to puzzle out the past, all of us—historians and students of history very much included—stand somewhere. None of us can be entirely detached when we view the past, but this is not necessarily a matter for regret. What we may lose in objectivity, we gain in passionate involvement with the historical record and with the many men and women who have inhabited it. Despite its remoteness from us in time and manner of living, the Paleolithic era resonates still in the twenty-first century, reminding us of our kinship with these distant people and the significance of that kinship to finding our own way in a very different world.

Second Thoughts

What's the Significance?

Venus figurines, 14; 23

Dreamtime, 15

Clovis culture, 18

megafaunal extinction, 18

Austronesian migrations, 19

"the original affluent society," 22

shamans, 23

trance dance, 23

Paleolithic settling down, 24

Göbekli Tepe, 25

Fertile Crescent, 28; 32

teosinte, 34

diffusion, 36

Bantu migration, 37

Ishi, 38

Banpo, 40

"secondary products revolution," 41

pastoral societies, 41

Çatalhüyük, 43

chiefdoms, 44

Big Picture Questions

1. In what ways did various Paleolithic societies differ from one another, and how did they change over time?

2. The Agricultural Revolution marked a decisive and progressive turning point in human history. What evidence might you offer to support this claim, and how might you argue against it?

3. How did early agricultural societies differ from those of the Paleolithic era?

4. Was the Agricultural Revolution inevitable? Why did it occur so late in the story of humankind?

5. In what different ways did human beings relate to the natural world during the early and long phases of our history explored in the chapter?

Next Steps: For Further Study

Elizabeth Wayland Barber, *Women's Work: The First 20,000 Years* (1994). Explores the role of women in early technological development, particularly textile making.

Peter Bellwood, *First Farmers: The Origins of Agricultural Societies* (2005). An up-to-date account of the Agricultural Revolution, considered on a global basis.

David Christian, *This Fleeting World: A Short History of Humanity* (2008). A lovely essay by a leading world historian, which condenses parts of his earlier *Maps of Time* (2004).

Steven Mithen, *After the Ice: A Global Human History, 20,000–5000 B.C.* (2004). An imaginative tour of world archeological sites during the Agricultural Revolution.

Lauren Ristvet, *In the Beginning* (2007). A brief account of human evolution, Paleolithic life, the origins of agriculture, and the First Civilizations, informed by recent archeological discoveries.

Fred Spier, *Big History and the Future of Humanity* (2011). An effort to place human history in the context of cosmic, geological, and biological history with a focus on the growth of complexity.

Mark B. Tauger, *Agriculture in World History* (2011). An overview of the origins and significance of farming on a global scale.

"The Agricultural Revolution," http://www.youtube.com/watch?v=Yocja_N5s1I. An eleven-minute animated survey from John Green's *Crash Course World History* series.

"Prehistoric Art," http://witcombe.sbc.edu/ARTHprehistoric.html#general. An art history Web site with a wealth of links to Paleolithic art around the world.

Stories of the Australian Dreamtime

The Aboriginal, or native, peoples of Australia have lived on their island/continent for tens of thousands of years, and until the arrival of Europeans in the late eighteenth century, they practiced a gathering and hunting way of life. These peoples have persisted into the twenty-first century as a small minority in modern Australia, and a dwindling few of them still practice their ancient culture. Over an enormously long period of time, these peoples developed an elaborate body of myths, legends, and stories that gave expression to an Aboriginal cosmology, or understanding of the world. Known collectively as the Dreamtime, these stories served to anchor the landscape and its human and animal inhabitants to distant events and mythical ancestors.

In this cosmology, long before humans appeared, ancestral beings emerged from the earth and traversed the land. Their places of emergence became waterholes or caves; their journeys gave rise to rivers and gorges; trees grew where their digging sticks were stuck in the ground; plants arose from their footsteps. In Aboriginal thinking, the numerous rock paintings that dot the landscape were not the product of human hands but the continuing presence, image, or shadow of these ancestral beings.

A contemporary Aboriginal artist, Semon Deeb, explains:

> Around the beginning the Ancestral Beings rose from the folds of the earth and stretching up to the scorching sun they called, "I am!" As each Ancestor sang out their name, "I am Snake," "I am Honey Ant," they created the most sacred of their songs. Slowly they began to move across the barren land naming all things and thus bringing them into being. Their words forming verses as the Ancestors walked about, they sang mountains, rivers and deserts into existence. Wherever they went, their songs remained, creating a web of Songlines over the Country. As they travelled the Ancestors hunted, ate, made love, sang and danced leaving a trail of Dreaming along the songlines. Finally at the end of their journey the Ancestral Beings sang "back into" the earth where they can be seen as land formations, sleeping.[20]

Transmitted orally and changing over time, numerous Dreamtime stories have been collected and set down in writing over the past two centuries. The tales presented here illustrate these Aboriginal efforts to give meaning and shape to their experience.

Source 1.1
Understanding Creation

People everywhere have sought to understand the beginnings of things and through doing so to frame human life in some larger and more meaningful context. In this and other stories from Australia, creation occurred in the Dreamtime, or the "time before time," when ancient ancestral beings brought into existence the latent possibilities of a world that was frozen or asleep. Then they disappeared when their work was finished. But they remained present in the sun, moon, and stars, in the features of the landscape, in the animals of the world, or in paintings on the walls of rock faces.

- How might you compare this creation story with the biblical account in Genesis?

- How much of a difference does it make that both male and female figures participated in creation?

- What is the relationship between Yhi and Baiame in creating and sustaining the world? Do they play equal roles, or is one superior to the other?

- In what ways are human beings and other living creatures made aware of their connection to the spirit world?

Yhi Brings Life to the World
(oral tradition recorded in twentieth century)

In the beginning the world lay quiet, in utter darkness. There was no vegetation, no living or moving thing on the bare bones of the mountains. No wind blew across the peaks. There was no sound to break the silence.

The world was not dead. It was asleep, waiting for the soft touch of life and light. Undead things lay asleep in icy caverns in the mountains. Somewhere in the immensity of space Yhi [a sun goddess of light and creation] stirred in her sleep, waiting for the whisper of Baiame, the Great Spirit [a creator deity, Sky Father], to come to her.

Then the whisper came, the whisper that woke the world. Sleep fell away from the goddess like a garment falling to her feet. Her eyes opened and the darkness was dispelled by their shining. . . .

The Nullarbor Plain was bathed in a radiance that revealed its sterile wastes.

Yhi floated down to earth and began a pilgrimage that took her far to the west, to the east, to north, and south. Where her feet rested on the ground, there the earth leaped in ecstasy. Grass, shrubs, trees, and flowers sprang from it, lifting themselves towards the radiant source of light. Yhi's tracks crossed and recrossed until the whole earth was clothed with vegetation.

Her first joyous task completed, Yhi, the sun goddess, rested on the Nullarbor Plain, looked around her, and knew that the Great Spirit was pleased with the result of her labour.

"The work of creation is well begun," Baiame said, "but it has only begun. The world is full of beauty, but it needs dancing life to fulfill its destiny. Take your light into the caverns of earth and see what will happen."

Yhi rose and made her way into the gloomy spaces beneath the surface. There were no seeds there to spring to life at her touch. Harsh shadows lurked behind the light. Evil spirits shouted, "No, no, no," until the caverns vibrated with voices that boomed and echoed in the darkness. The shadows softened. Twinkling points of light sparkled in an opal mist. Dim forms stirred restlessly.

"Sleep, sleep, sleep," the evil spirits wailed, but the shapes had been waiting for the caressing warmth of the sun goddess. Filmy wings opened, bodies raised themselves on long legs. . . . Soon Yhi was surrounded by myriads of insects, creeping, flying, swarming from every dark corner. . . . They followed her out into the world, into the sunshine, into the embrace of the waiting grass and leaves and flowers. . . . There was work for the insects to do in the world, and time for play, and time to adore the goddess.

"Caves in the mountains, the eternal ice," whispered Baiame. Yhi sped up the hill slopes. . . . She disappeared into the caverns, chilled by the black ice that hung from the roofs and walls. . . . [There her light awakened snakes, reptiles, birds, and many other animals.] Birds and animals gathered round her, singing in their own voices, racing down the slopes, choosing homes for themselves, drinking in a new world of light, colour, sound, and movement.

"It is good. My world is alive," Baiame said.

Yhi took his hand and called in a golden voice to all the things she had brought to life. "This is the land of Baiame. It is yours forever, to enjoy. Baiame is the Great Spirit. He will guard you and listen to your requests. I have nearly finished my work, so you must listen to my words."

"I shall send you the seasons of summer and winter—summer with warmth which ripens fruit ready for eating, winter for sleeping while the cold winds sweep through the world and blow away the refuse of summer. These are changes that I shall send you . . . , the creatures of my love. Soon I shall leave you and live far above in the sky. When you die your bodies will remain here, but your spirits will come to live with me."

She rose from the earth and dwindled to a ball of light in the sky, and sank slowly behind the western hills. All living things sorrowed, and their hearts were filled with fear, for with the departure of Yhi darkness rushed back into the world.

Long hours passed, and sorrow was soothed by sleep. Suddenly there was a twittering of birds, for the wakeful ones had seen a glimmer of light in the east. It grew stronger and more birds joined in until there came a full-throated chorus as Yhi appeared in splendour and flooded the plains with the morning light.

One by one the birds and animals woke up, as they have done every morning since the first dawn. After the first shock of darkness they knew that day would succeed night, that there would always be a new sunrise and sunset, giving hours of daylight for work and play, and night for sleeping.

The river spirit and the lake spirit grieve most of all when Yhi sinks to rest. They long for her warmth and light. They mount up into the sky, striving with all their might to reach the sun goddess. Yhi smiles on them and they dissolve into drops of water which fall back upon the earth as rain and dew, freshening the grass and the flowers and bringing new life.

One last deed remained to be done, because the dark hours of night were frightening for some of the creatures. Yhi sent the Morning Star to herald her coming each day. Then, feeling sorry for the star in her loneliness, she gave her Bahloo, the Moon, for her husband. A sigh of satisfaction arose from the earth when the white moon sailed majestically across the sky, giving birth to myriads of stars, making a new glory in the heavens.

Source: "Yhi Brings Life to the World," in A. W. Reed, *Aboriginal Stories of Australia* (Chatsworth, New South Wales: New Holland Publishers, 1980), 11–14.

Source 1.2
Understanding the Significance of Animals

The platypus is a semi-aquatic mammal that lays eggs, has fur, and sports a duck-like bill, a beaver-like tail, and otter-like feet. A spur on its rear foot delivers poisonous venom. Aboriginal Australians have long revered this rather strange and eclectic creature and have considered killing it taboo. A widely told story explains Aboriginal thinking about the platypus. Here is one version of that story.

- To what social problems might this story respond? What social meaning might it carry for a land of many small societies and interacting peoples?

- Does this tale bear something of universal human wisdom, or is it a more distinctly Aboriginal Australian story?

The Platypus
(oral tradition recorded in twentieth century)

In the Dreamtime all the creatures on earth thought that they belonged to the most important group of creatures. Each group had their own special meetings. . . . The animals thought that they were the most special because they had fur on their bodies and could run across the land. The birds thought that they were even more special because they could fly and lay eggs. And the water creatures thought that they were even more special still because they could swim and explore all the water-ways on earth and because "there is more water than land anyway," they said.

But then someone in each group remembered that shy Platypus belong to no group at all and each one of them resolved to ask Platypus to join their own Very Special Group. . . . [In response to each of these requests,] Platypus asked them to come back after he had thought about their offer.

Now Platypus asked his friends and family whose group he should join, but no one could help him. . . . After thinking hard about it for some time, Platypus called all the animals and bird and water creatures to his place. They all gathered around, all wondering which group Platypus would join. Platypus came out of his home, climbed a log and

when all the creatures were quiet, Platypus spoke. "Thank you all for coming today. I have decided not to join any group at all."

All the creatures were shocked. "You have to join someone's group," they cried.

"Please listen," said Platypus patiently. "Everyone is special in their own special way, and I don't have to join any group to prove that. After all, I have a bit of animal in me because of my fur and because I like running across the land, but I have a bit of bird in me too, because my wife lays eggs and we both have beaks. And if that's not enough, I also have a bit of water creature in me because my home is near the water's edge, and I like swimming and exploring the underwater world. So you see, I don't have to join any special group to be special. But it's not only me—every one of us has something that makes us special in our own very special way."

All the creatures agreed and from that time onwards, Platypus has been considered very wise and very special indeed.

Source: Pauline McLeod, *Aboriginal Art and Stories* (Carlingford, New South Wales: Intechnics, 1994), http://trove.nla.gov.au/work /11650463?q&versionId=45880979.

Source 1.3
Understanding Men and Women

No theme in human history and human interactions is more universal than the relationship of men and women. Many Aboriginal stories seek to justify the superiority of men, while hinting at the possibility of an earlier time when women had the upper hand and implying that they might challenge male authority once again.

- What does this story suggest about the relationships between women and men? Does it support or undermine notions of gender equality among Paleolithic peoples?

- What was the source of Mutjinga's power? How does the story explain her abuse of that power?

- What aspects of a gathering and hunting way of life are reflected in this tale? What elements of Dreamtime cosmology appear in the story?

The Man–Eater: The Mutjinga Myth
(oral tradition recorded in twentieth century)

In the Dreamtime, in the land of the Murinbata people, a great river flowed from the hills through a wide plain to the sea. As it is today, the land then was rich with much fish and game. From the river rose at one place a series of high hills, where lived an old woman named Mutjinga, a woman of power. She it was who called the invisible spirits to her side with secret incantations that none other knew. She was a *kirman*, leader of the ceremonies in which the people sang and danced the exploits of the totemic beings so their spirits would be pleased and would bring food in its season and many children for the people. In those days, all the things in the world had both a physical form that could be touched, seen, and felt, and a spirit form, which was invisible. When living things died, their spirits went to a secret cave where they remained until it was time for them to be born again. Mutjinga was caretaker of this cave. Only she knew where it was. In the cave, she kept the sacred totems to which the spirits returned.

Mutjinga could speak with the spirits. Because she had this power, she could do many things which the men could not. She could send the spirits to frighten away game, to waylay people at night, or to cause a child to be born without life. The men feared the power of Mutjinga and did not consort with her. They called upon her to lead their dances and teach them songs, but none came to sit by her fire.

Mutjinga became lonely and sent for her young granddaughter to keep her company. Mutjinga and the girl gathered bulbs and nuts and caught small game, but Mutjinga found no satisfaction in this food, for she craved the flesh of men. . . .

[*The story then recounts how Mutjinga dug a hole and covered it with branches in order to trap unsuspecting hunters. Magically turning herself into a goanna (a lizard), she appeared to hunters, led them to their deaths in the hole, and then ate them. This fate befell even the younger brother of her granddaughter, despite the girl's unsuccessful efforts to save him. He too was killed and partially eaten, while Mutjinga kept the rest of his body in a nearby stream.*]

The next morning, the little girl was at her early chores when she saw two men coming up the hillside. As she watched, recognition lit her face and she turned toward Mutjinga.

"It is my father and brother who come. Please do not harm them," she implored.

"I crave their flesh. If you trick me again I shall eat you, as well as your father and brother," Mutjinga warned. "This time I shall wait beside you until the men appear so you cannot deceive me."

The men approached the fire, paid their respects to the old woman, and greeted the child warmly. "Daughter, have you seen your brother who came hunting this way yesterday?" the father asked.

Mutjinga hastened to reply for the child. "No, we have not seen him," she said. "It is too bad, for nearby are many goanna holes. There is a large goanna right there," and she pointed to the hole where she kept the club.

"I thirst. First give me water," said the father.

"There is cold water in the stream," the little girl told him as she pointed down the hill.

The two men walked through the bush to the stream. As the father bent to drink, he saw the leg of his elder son, which Mutjinga had weighted down in the water with a large rock. At once he understood.

"The old woman will kill us unless we kill her first," he said to his younger son, and the two men returned to the fire.

"The goanna went into the tall grass," Mutjinga told them when they appeared. "Leave your spears and light a fire to burn the grass. This will drive the goanna out, and when it runs toward its hole, you can kill it with your spears."

The men went to fire the grass. As soon as they were out of sight, the father said, "Son, climb this tree and watch the old woman closely. She works powerful magic."

This the son did, and he saw Mutjinga speak the magic words. She repeated them twice. He watched as the woman and the girl changed into goannas. From the limb of the tree, he observed the larger goanna chase the smaller one into the bush. Soon great billows of smoke were rising from the burning grass. The small goanna scuttled from the bush, its companion nipping at its heels. They ran past the hunters and disappeared down the hole.

"Get the spears," the father commanded and ran toward the hole. Just as the son returned, spears in hand, the ground beneath the father gave way and he plunged through. Waiting at the bottom was Mutjinga, club raised for the kill. But the son hurled his spear and Mutjinga fell bleeding to the ground.

The father seized her roughly. "Say the magic words that will release my daughter or we shall kill you," he threatened.

Painfully Mutjinga did as she was bidden. The daughter changed into her human form and the two men and the girl climbed from the hole.

"Daughter, show us the secret cave where the spirits are hidden," said the father, "and teach us the magic words you have learned from the old woman. We shall take the spirits to another place, and we shall have the power."

And so it was. The father took the totems from that place and hid them in another cave. He became the *kirman*, the song leader, and he taught the people the sacred dances and ceremonies. To him they brought their problems and he judged between them when they quarreled. And to this day, the men have kept the power.

Source: Louis A. Allen, *Time Before Morning* (New York: Thomas Y. Crowell, 1975), 145–48.

Source 1.4

Understanding Death

Death marks the end of a life, but an awareness of death shapes much of the living of our lives. And so humans everywhere have sought to understand death, with an eye perhaps to avoiding or delaying it. In the Australian Dreamtime, the immortal ancestor Purukapali was responsible for the introduction of death into the world. The story that follows is one version of this event.

■ How does this story account for the entry of death into human life?

■ What responses to death are suggested in the story?

■ Does such a story carry any meaning to modern people of the twenty-first century?

How Death Came: The Purukapali Myth
(oral tradition recorded in twentieth century)

In the pleasant land of the Tiwi people, Purukapali lived with his wife, Bima, and their infant son, Djinini. This was in the earliest days when spirits became men and death had not yet come to the earth. In their camp also lived Purukapali's younger brother, Tjapara, strong and handsome. Many times the brothers stalked wallaby together, but most often it was Purukapali who carried game into the camp and received the women's praise.

Tjapara had no wife and he hungered for Bima. One morning after the brothers had returned from the hunt, Bima rose and placed the sleeping Djinini beside her husband, who was skinning a slain wallaby.

"I go find yams," she said. "Guard the child. He will sleep now and will have my milk when I return."

She picked up a net bag and walked off into the bush. Tjapara watched her swinging hips and said, "I saw shellfish at the shore. I will go gather them," and he strode off toward the beach, leaving Purukapali with the sleeping child.

As soon as he was well out of sight, Tjapara quickly circled back through the bush and came upon Bima as she bent over her digging stick. Softly he crept upon her and clasped her from behind.

"Lie with me," he urged.

Only a moment did the wife of Purukapali resist. Then the long hours slipped quickly by. In the camp the child cried for his mother's milk. Still the couple tarried. From the camp came the faint voice of Purukapali calling his wife. Bima started to rise, but Tjapara was still eager. "Soon," he said and pulled her toward him.

Now the Sun Woman carried her torch to the horizon and the shadows grew long. Again the voice of Purukapali sounded, angry and stricken. Bima rose to answer, but Tjapara placed his hand over her mouth.

"We must go bathe, or Purukapali will know we have lain together," he said.

The two went to a hidden cove and entered the water. They played together in the coolness and ate some crabs they found near the shore. This was Tjapara's favorite food. But Purukapali's angry voice again reached their hearing. The frightened Bima took her net bag and hurried to camp. She found Djinini on the grass, cold and still. Death had come to him in the early darkness. Bima lifted the child and pressed him to her breast.

Now Purukapali turned on his wife. "He was hungry. He cried for you and you did not come. Now he is gone from us and will not return," said the father, and he wrested the dead infant from Bima's arms.

Bima began to moan and beat her breast. "I am a bad woman, for I let my son die," she cried.

Hearing this, great anger came to Purukapali. Still holding his dead son, he turned on Bima and began to beat her with his freed hand. As she bent before his blows, Tjapara stepped from the bush and thrust himself between the couple.

"Give the child to me, brother, and I will bring him back to life in three days," he said.

But Bima lashed out at Tjapara in despair. "You killed him!" she accused, "for you would not let me go."

Now did Purukapali understand. Still holding fast to the child, he picked up a forked fighting stick and attacked. "You, too, shall die!" he screamed at his brother.

Tjapara refused to run and begged again for the child. But Purukapali threw the stick in response and struck his brother in the eye. "You will die as the baby died," he shouted. In his excitement, Purukapali dropped the lifeless body of Djinini.

Half blinded, Tjapara fought back. Soon the two men were locked in combat. Blood gushed from Tjapara's gouged eye and from the gashes on his face. He began to weaken.

Now Bima picked up Djinini and held him out to her husband. "Take the child you loved so dearly," she pleaded. "Do not kill your brother."

Her plea went unheard as Purukapali again hurled his killing stick. Tjapara fled to a tall tree and frantically began to climb. When he reached the top limb, he let out a great shout and leaped into the sky, rising higher and higher until he reached the moon.

Purukapali returned to camp and took Djinini's body in his arms. "I shall die with my son," he announced to the Tiwi people. "And all who now live also shall die."

Then he danced the first ceremony of death and sang of the events that led to it. "This shall be your pukamani ceremony," he decreed, "and you shall dance it to remember those who die." Purukapali wrapped his son in paperbark, walked backward into the sea, and disappeared. As he sank beneath the surface, a whirlpool formed which marks the spot to this day.

Bima lived on, but grief soon made her haggard and old. She too wandered about the camp, complaining in a shrill voice until she, too, died. Her spirit lived on as the curlew bird, which still flits and cries mournfully about the beaches.

Tjapara became the Moon Man. He can be seen in the night sky, his face marked by the bruises and wounds that Purukapali inflicted. He still feels Purukapali at his heels, for he never ceases his restless journey. Hungry from his travels, he gorges on crabmeat, growing rounder and fatter each day until he has feasted so much he falls sick. His wasting body is the waning moon. Each month he dies, but after three days he comes back to life and begins his journey once again. His loneliness is over, for he has found many wives, the planets, who accompany him on his journey across the sky.

So death comes to the people of earth, the Tiwi say, but always life returns.

Source: Louis A. Allen, *Time Before Morning* (New York: Thomas Y. Crowell Company, 1975), 215–19.

Stories of the Australian Dreamtime

1. **Considering human commonality and diversity:** The study of world history highlights both the common humanity of people from all times and places as well as the vast differences that have separated particular cultures from one another. How might these texts serve to illustrate both of these perspectives?

2. **Linking documents and text narrative:** How do these documents support or amplify the narrative account of the Paleolithic era in Chapter 1? How might they challenge or contradict that narrative?

3. **Considering the relationship of technology and culture:** How might the gathering and hunting technology of these Australian peoples have shaped their cultural understandings as expressed in these sources? In what ways might cultural expression, as a product of human imagination, have developed independently of their technology? Does it make sense to evaluate technology as more or less "advanced"? Should culture be assessed in the same way?

4. **Pondering relevance:** How might these stories from a very different time and place speak to us in the modern world of the twenty-first century? Or are they only of historical interest?

5. **Thinking about sources:** How does the fact that these stories were only committed to writing over the past two centuries affect their usefulness as historical sources?

CHAPTER 2

First Civilizations

Cities, States, and Unequal Societies
3500 B.C.E.–500 B.C.E.

"Sometimes the weight of civilization can be overwhelming. The fast pace . . . the burdens of relationships . . . the political strife . . . the technological complexity—it's enough to make you dream of escaping to a simpler life more in touch with nature."[1] Found on the Web site of an organization called Mother Nature Network, this expression of discontent with modernity reflects the perspectives of the back-to-the-land movement that began in the mid-1960s as an alternative to the pervasive materialism of modern life. Growing numbers of urban dwellers, perhaps as many as a million in North America, exchanged their busy city lives for a few acres of rural land and a very different way of living.

This urge to "escape from civilization" has long been a central feature in modern life. It found expression in Henry David Thoreau's musings on his sojourn at Walden Pond. It is also a major theme in Mark Twain's famous novel *The Adventures of Huckleberry Finn,* in which the restless and rebellious Huck resists all efforts to "sivilize" him by fleeing to the freedom of life on the river. In addition, it is a large part of the "cowboy" image in American culture, and it permeates environmentalist efforts to protect the remaining wilderness areas of the country. Nor has this impulse been limited to modern societies and the Western world. The ancient Chinese teachers of Daoism likewise urged their followers to abandon the structured and demanding world of urban and civilized life and to immerse themselves in the eternal patterns of the natural order. It is a strange paradox that we count the creation of civilizations among the major

Raherka and Mersankh Writing was among the defining features of civilizations almost everywhere. In ancient Egyptian civilization, the scribes who possessed this skill enjoyed both social prestige and political influence. This famous statue shows Raherka, an "inspector of the scribes" during Egypt's Fifth Dynasty (ca. 2350 B.C.E.), in an affectionate pose with his wife, Mersankh.

achievements of humankind and yet people within them have often sought to escape the constraints, artificiality, hierarchies, and other discontents of civilized living.

So what exactly are these civilizations that have generated such ambivalent responses among their inhabitants? When, where, and how did they first arise in human history? What changes did they bring to the people who lived within them? Why might some people criticize or seek to escape from them?

As historians commonly use the term, "civilization" represents a new and particular type of human society, made possible by the immense productivity of the Agricultural Revolution. Such societies encompassed far larger populations than any earlier form of human community and for the first time concentrated some of those people in sizable cities. Both within and beyond these cities, people were organized and controlled by states whose leaders could use force to compel obedience. Profound differences in economic function, skill, wealth, and status sharply divided the people of civilizations, making them far less equal and subject to much greater oppression than had been the case in earlier Paleolithic communities, agricultural villages, pastoral societies, or chiefdoms. Pyramids, temples, palaces, elaborate sculptures, written literature, and complex calendars, as well as more elaborate class and gender hierarchies, slavery, and large-scale warfare—all of these have been among the cultural products of civilization.

SEEKING THE MAIN POINT

What distinguished "civilizations" from earlier Paleolithic and Neolithic societies?

Something New: The Emergence of Civilizations

Like agriculture, civilization was a global phenomenon, showing up independently in seven major locations scattered around the world during the several millennia after 3500 B.C.E. and in a number of other smaller expressions as well (see Map 2.1). In the long run of human history, these civilizations—small breakthroughs to a new way of life—gradually absorbed, overran, or displaced people practicing other ways of living. Over the next 5,000 years, civilization, as a unique kind of human community, gradually encompassed ever-larger numbers of people and extended over ever-larger territories, even as particular civilizations rose, fell, revived, and changed.

Introducing the First Civilizations

■ Change
When and where did the First Civilizations emerge?

The earliest of these civilizations emerged around 3500 B.C.E. to 3000 B.C.E. in three places. One was the "cradle" of Middle Eastern civilization, expressed in the many and competing city-states of Sumer in southern Mesopotamia (located in present-day Iraq). Much studied by archeologists and historians, Sumerian civilization likely gave rise to the world's earliest written language, which was used initially by officials to record the goods received by various temples. Almost simultaneously, the Nile River valley in northeastern Africa witnessed the emergence

A MAP OF TIME   (All dates B.C.E.)

3500–3000	Beginnings of Mesopotamian, Egyptian, and Norte Chico civilizations
3400–3200	Nubian kingdom of Ta-Seti
3200–2350	Period of independent Sumerian city-states
2663–2195	Old Kingdom Egypt (high point of pharaoh's power and pyramid building)
2200–2000	Beginnings of Chinese, Indus Valley, and Central Asian (Oxus) civilizations
2070–1600	Xia dynasty in China (traditionally seen as first dynasty of Chinese history)
After 2000	*Epic of Gilgamesh* compiled
1900–1500	Babylonian Empire
1792–1750	Reign of Hammurabi
1700	Abandonment of Indus Valley cities
1550–1064	New Kingdom Egypt
1200	Beginnings of Olmec civilization
760–660	Kush conquest of Egypt
586	Babylonian conquest of Judah
By 500	Egypt and Mesopotamia incorporated into Persian Empire

of Egyptian civilization, famous for its pharaohs and pyramids, as well as a separate civilization known as Nubia, farther south along the Nile. Unlike the city-states of Sumer, Egyptian civilization took shape as a unified territorial state in which cities were rather less prominent. Later in this chapter, we will compare these two First Civilizations in greater detail.

Less well known and only recently investigated by scholars was a third early civilization that was developing along the central coast of Peru from roughly 3000 B.C.E. to 1800 B.C.E., at about the same time as the civilizations of Egypt and Sumer. This desert region received very little rainfall, but it was punctuated by dozens of rivers that brought the snowmelt of the adjacent Andes Mountains to the Pacific Ocean. Along a thirty-mile stretch of that coast and in the nearby interior, a series of some twenty-five urban centers emerged in an area known as Norte Chico, the largest of which was Caral, in the Supe River valley. (See Zooming In: Caral, a City of Norte Chico, page 64.)

Norte Chico was a distinctive civilization in many ways. Its cities were smaller than those of Mesopotamia and show less evidence of economic specialization. The

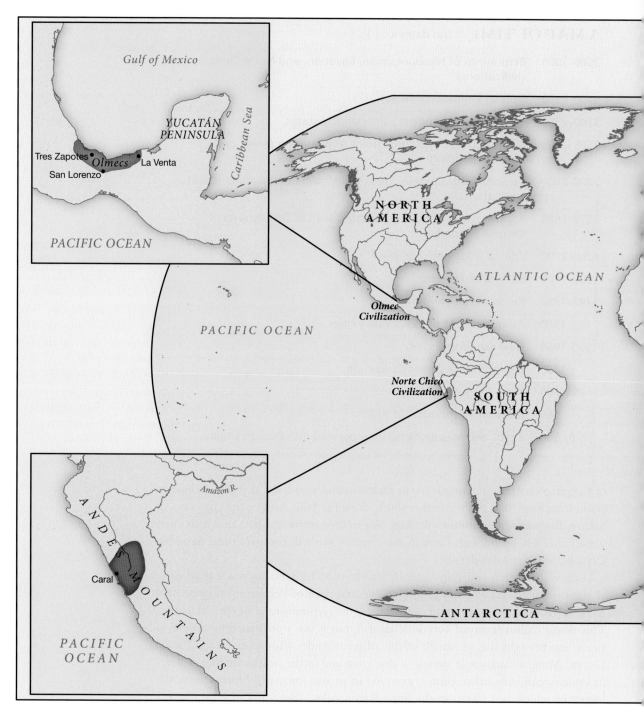

Map 2.1   First Civilizations

Seven First Civilizations emerged independently in locations scattered across the planet, all within a few thousand years, from 3500 to 1000 B.C.E.

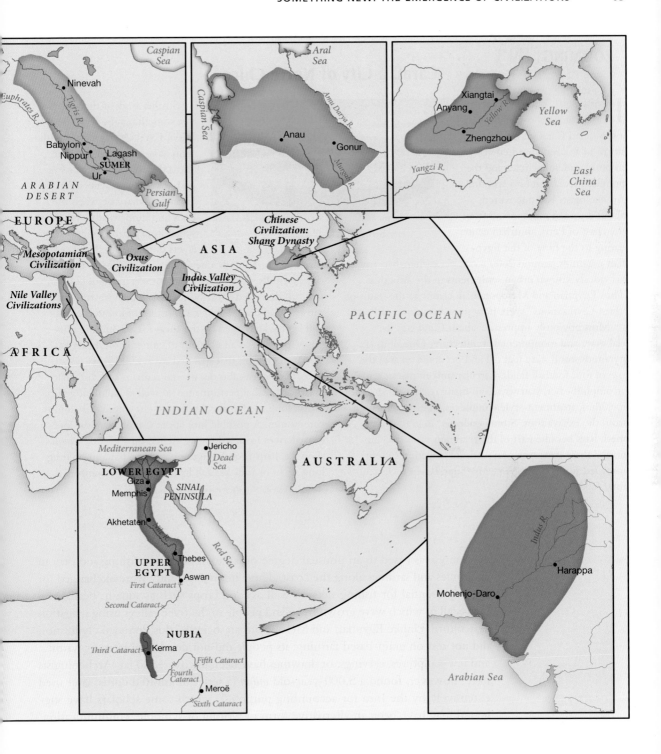

Caral, a City of Norte Chico

In early 2001, published reports of archeological excavations at a site called Caral set off a firestorm of amazed commentary in both academic circles and the popular media. And no wonder! Archeologists had uncovered, about fourteen miles inland from the coast of Peru, an urban center dating to the time of the Egyptian pyramids, around 2600 B.C.E., far earlier than any previously known urban settlements in the Americas. Thus Egyptian and Mesopotamian claims to the status of "First Civilizations" were now joined by those of Peru.

Stonework at Caral.

Most obviously impressive about Caral was its elaborate and monumental architecture. One of its six pyramids stood sixty feet tall and occupied an area the size of four football fields. Circular sunken plazas, temples, an amphitheater, stairways, and many residential spaces, including apartment-style complexes, likewise emerged from the excavations. Stones collected in grass-woven mesh bags became part of the retaining walls that supported these structures. An intricate irrigation system funneled water from the nearby Supe River to agricultural fields.

Smaller finds at the site convey something about ordinary life in Caral. A clay figure with long hair, a colorful costume, and a decorative necklace suggested a shaman, who served as an intermediary between the gods and humans at Caral. The skeleton of a baby, wrapped in layers of fine cloth, had been carefully buried with a necklace of stone beads. Dozens of beautifully carved flutes and cornets made of condor, pelican, deer, and llama bones revealed an instrumental musical tradition. A *quipu*, consisting of knotted cords and later widely used by the Incas for accounting purposes, pointed to an element of cultural continuity in the Andes region that spanned over 4,000 years.

Archeologists also discovered remains of plants that enhanced sexual performance, as well as hallucinogenic drugs, long used in the Andes and elsewhere in religious ceremonies. A possible hint about Caral's religious outlook derives from a drawing etched on a gourd, which shows a sharp-toothed figure wearing a hat and holding long sticks or rods in each hand. It clearly resembles

photo: © Peruvian National Institute/epa/Corbis

economy was based to an unusual degree on an extremely rich fishing industry in anchovies and sardines along the coast. These items apparently were exchanged for cotton, essential for fishing nets, as well as food crops such as squash, beans, and guava, all of which were grown by inland people in the river valleys using irrigation agriculture. Unlike Egyptian and Mesopotamian societies, this Peruvian civilization did not rest on grain-based farming; its people did not develop pottery or writing; and few sculptures, carvings, or drawings have been uncovered so far. Archeologists have, however, found a 5,000-year-old *quipu* (a series of knotted cords, later used extensively by the Inca for accounting purposes), which some scholars have suggested may have been an alternative form of writing or symbolic communication. Furthermore, the cities of Norte Chico lacked defensive walls, and archeologists have discovered little evidence of warfare, such as burned buildings and mutilated corpses. Norte Chico apparently "lighted a cultural fire" in the Andes and estab-

the Staff God prevalent in later Andean civilizations. And the remains of a young man found in a ceremonial place suggest the possibility of human sacrifice.

Nor was Caral an isolated instance of urban living. More than twenty other related sites in the river valleys of the area make up what scholars are now calling the Norte Chico civilization. Caral and other inland cities had close relationships with coastal communities, exchanging their agricultural products such as cotton, beans, squash, and sweet potatoes for sardines and anchovies, whose bones have been found in abundance in Caral. Goods from as far away as present-day Ecuador, the high Andes, and rain forests that lay to the east suggest a network of wider relationships.

But what was missing from Caral has proved equally intriguing. Grain-based agriculture, pottery, metallurgy, and writing—all features of urban life in Egypt and Mesopotamia—were noticeably absent in Caral. Do we therefore need to revisit the criteria for defining a "First Civilization"? Warfare too apparently played little role in Caral, as no walls, fortresses, weapons, or signs of violent

The bone flutes found at Caral.

destruction have appeared in the archeological record. Does this mean that Caral uniquely enjoyed "a thousand years of peace," as one of the lead excavators suggested? Was trade rather than warfare the stimulus to creating a complex society? Perhaps so, but it is early in the study of this distinctive civilization. We may want to remember that Maya civilization was once viewed as a peaceful society of stargazing people devoted to religious and intellectual pursuits, until scholars discovered unmistakable evidence for bloodletting rituals and violent conflict among its various city-states. The past may not change, but our understanding of it is in constant flux.

Questions: In what ways do recent discoveries at Caral invite reconsideration of Andean civilization and of the history of the earliest civilizations generally? What do you find most surprising about Caral?

photo: © George Steinmetz/Corbis

lished a pattern for the many Andean civilizations that followed—Chavín, Moche, Wari, Tiwanaku, and Inca.[2]

Somewhat later, at least four additional First Civilizations made their appearance. In the Indus and Saraswati river valleys of what is now Pakistan, a remarkable civilization arose during the third millennium B.C.E. By 2000 B.C.E., it embraced a far larger area than Mesopotamia, Egypt, or coastal Peru and was expressed primarily in its elaborately planned cities. All across this huge area, common patterns prevailed: standardized weights, measures, architectural styles, even the size of bricks. As elsewhere, irrigated agriculture provided the economic foundation for the civilization, and a written language, thus far undeciphered, provides evidence of a literate culture for the few.

Unlike its Middle Eastern counterparts, the Indus Valley civilization apparently generated no palaces, temples, elaborate graves, kings, or warrior classes. In short, the archeological evidence provides little indication of a political hierarchy or centralized state. This absence of evidence has sent scholars scrambling to provide an explanation for the obvious specialization, coordination, and complexity that the Indus Valley civilization exhibited. A series of small republics, rule by priests, an early form of the caste system—all of these have been suggested as alternative mechanisms of integration in this first South Asian civilization. Although no one knows for sure, the possibility that the Indus Valley may have housed a sophisticated civilization without a corresponding state has excited the imagination of scholars. (See Working with Evidence: Indus Valley Civilization, page 91.)

Whatever its organization, the local environmental impact of the Indus Valley civilization, as in many others, was heavy and eventually undermined its ecological foundations. Repeated irrigation increased the amount of salt in the soil and lowered crop yields. The making of mud bricks, dried in ovens, required an enormous amount of wood for fuel, generating large-scale deforestation and soil erosion. Thus environmental degradation contributed significantly to the abandonment of these magnificent cities by about 1700 B.C.E. Thereafter, they were largely forgotten, until their rediscovery by archeologists in the twentieth century. Nonetheless, many features of this early civilization—ceremonial bathing, ritual burning, yoga positions, bulls and elephants as religious symbols, styles of clothing and jewelry—continued to nourish the later civilization of the Indian subcontinent. In fact they persist into the present.[3]

The early civilization of China, dating to perhaps 2200 B.C.E., was very different from that of the Indus Valley. The ideal—if not always the reality—of a centralized state was evident from the days of the Xia (shyah) dynasty (2070–1600 B.C.E.), whose legendary monarch Wu organized flood control projects that "mastered the waters and made them to flow in great channels." Subsequent dynasties—the Shang (1600–1046 B.C.E.) and the Zhou (JOH) (1046–771 B.C.E.)—substantially enlarged the Chinese state, erected lavish tombs for their rulers, and buried thousands of human sacrificial victims to accompany them in the next world. By the Zhou dynasty, a distinctive Chinese political ideology had emerged, featuring a ruler, known as the Son of Heaven. This monarch served as an intermediary between heaven and earth and ruled by the Mandate of Heaven only so long as he governed with benevolence and maintained social harmony among his people. An early form of written Chinese has been discovered on numerous oracle bones, which were intended to predict

Shang Dynasty Bronze
This bronze tiger, created around 1100 B.C.E., illustrates Chinese skill in working with bronze and the mythological or religious significance of the tiger as a messenger between heaven and the human world. (© Asian Art & Archeology, Inc./Corbis)

the future and to assist China's rulers in the task of governing. Like Egypt, China has experienced an impressive continuity of identity as a distinct civilization from its earliest expression into modern times.

Central Asia was the site of yet another First Civilization. In the Oxus or Amu Darya river valley and nearby desert oases (what is now northern Afghanistan and southern Turkmenistan), a quite distinctive and separate civilization took shape very quickly after 2200 B.C.E. Within two centuries, a number of substantial fortified centers had emerged, containing residential compounds, artisan workshops, and temples, all surrounded by impressive walls and gates. Economically based on irrigation agriculture and stock raising, this Central Asian or Oxus civilization had a distinctive cultural style, expressed in its architecture, ceramics, burial techniques, seals, and more, though it did not develop a literate culture. Evidence for an aristocratic social hierarchy comes from depictions of gods and men in widely differing dress performing various functions from eating at a banquet to driving chariots to carrying heavy burdens. Visitors to this civilization would have found occasional goods from China, India, and Mesopotamia, as well as products from pastoral nomads of the steppe land and the forest dwellers of Siberia. According to a leading historian, this Central Asian civilization was the focal point of a "Eurasian-wide system of intellectual and commercial exchange."[4] Compared to Egyptian and Mesopotamian civilizations, however, it had a relatively brief history, for by 1700 B.C.E., it had faded away as a civilization, at about the same time as a similar fate befell its Indus Valley counterpart. Its cities were abandoned and apparently forgotten until their resurrection by archeologists in the twentieth century. And yet its influence persisted, as elements of this civilization's cultural style show up much later in Iran, India, and the eastern Mediterranean world.

A final First Civilization, known as the Olmec, took shape around 1200 B.C.E. along the coast of the Gulf of Mexico near present-day Veracruz in southern Mexico. Based on an agricultural economy of maize, beans, and squash, Olmec cities arose from a series of competing chiefdoms and became ceremonial centers filled with elaborately decorated temples, altars, pyramids, and tombs of rulers. The most famous artistic legacy of the Olmecs lay in some seventeen colossal basalt heads, weighing twenty tons or more. Recent discoveries suggest that the Olmecs may well have created the first written language in the Americas by about 900 B.C.E. Sometimes regarded as the "mother civilization" of Mesoamerica, Olmec civilization generated cultural patterns—mound building, artistic styles, urban planning, a game played with a rubber ball, ritual sacrifice, and bloodletting by rulers—that spread widely throughout the region and influenced subsequent civilizations, such as the Maya and Teotihuacán.

Beyond these seven First Civilizations, other smaller civilizations also flourished. Lying south of Egypt in the Nile Valley, an early Nubian civilization (3400–3200 B.C.E.) known as Ta-Seti was clearly distinctive and independent of its northern neighbor, although Nubia was later involved in a long and often contentious relationship with Egypt. Likewise in China, a large city known as Sanxingdui, rich in bronze sculptures and much else, arose separately but at the same time as the more well-known Shang dynasty. As a new form of human society, civilization was beginning its long march toward encompassing almost all of humankind by the twentieth century. At the time, however, these breakthroughs to new forms of culture and society were small islands of innovation in a sea of people living in much older ways.

The Question of Origins

The first question that historians ask about almost everything is "How did it get started?" Scholars of all kinds—archeologists, anthropologists, sociologists, and historians—have been arguing about the origins of civilization for a very long time, with no end in sight. Amid all the controversy, one thing seems reasonably clear: civilizations had their roots in the Agricultural Revolution. That is the reason they appeared so late in the human story, for only an agricultural technology permitted human communities to produce sufficient surplus to support large populations and the specialized or elite minorities who did not themselves produce food. But not all agricultural societies or chiefdoms developed into civilizations, so something else must have been involved. It is the search for this "something else" that has provoked such great debate among scholars.

■ **Change**

What accounts for the initial breakthroughs to civilization?

Some historians have emphasized the need to organize large-scale irrigation projects as a stimulus for the earliest civilizations, but archeologists have found that the more complex water control systems appeared long after states and civilizations had already been established. Alternatively, perhaps states responded to the human need for order as larger and more diverse populations grew up in particular localities. Others have suggested that states were useful in protecting the privileges of favored groups. Warfare and trade have figured in still other explanations for the rise of civilizations. Geography surely played a role as well, for civilizations often took shape in biologically rich and productive environments such as wetlands, estuaries, and river basins. Anthropologist Robert Carneiro combined several of these factors in a thoughtful approach to the question.[5] He argued that a growing density of population, producing more congested and competitive societies, was a fundamental motor of change, especially in areas where rich agricultural land was limited, either by geography (oceans, deserts, mountains) or by powerful neighboring societies. Such settings provided incentives for innovations, such as irrigation or plows that could produce more food, because opportunities for territorial expansion were not readily available. But circumscribed environments with dense populations also generated intense competition among rival groups, which led to repeated warfare. A strong and highly organized state was a decided advantage in such competition. Because losers could not easily flee to new lands, they were absorbed into the winner's society as a lower class. Successful leaders of the winning side emerged as elites with an enlarged base of land, a class of subordinated workers, and a powerful state at their disposal—in short, a civilization.

Although such a process was relatively rapid by world history standards, it took many generations, centuries, or perhaps millennia to evolve. It was, of course, an unconscious undertaking in which the participants had little sense of the long-term outcome as they coped with the practical problems of life on a day-to-day basis. What is surprising, though, is the rough similarity of the outcome in many widely separated places from about 3500 B.C.E. to the beginning of the Common Era.

However they got started (and much about this is still guesswork), the First Civilizations, once established, represented a very different kind of human society than anything that came before. All of them were based on highly productive agricultural economies. Various forms of irrigation, drainage, terracing, and flood control enabled these early civilizations to tap the food-producing potential of their regions more intensively. All across the Afro-Eurasian hemisphere, though not in the Americas, animal-drawn plows and metalworking greatly enhanced the productivity of farming. Ritual sacrifice, sometimes including people, accompanied the growth of civilization, and the new rulers normally served as high priests, their right to rule legitimated by association with the sacred.

An Urban Revolution

It was the resources from agriculture that made possible one of the most distinctive features of the First Civilizations—cities. What would an agricultural villager have made of Uruk, ancient Mesopotamia's largest city? Uruk had walls more than twenty feet tall and a population around 50,000 in the third millennium B.C.E. The city's center, visible for miles around, was a stepped pyramid, or ziggurat, topped with a temple (see the photo on page 77). Inside the city, this village visitor would have found other temples as well, serving as centers of ritual performance and as places for the redistribution of stored food. Numerous craftspeople labored as masons, copper workers, and weavers and in many other specialties, while bureaucrats helped administer the city. It was, surely, a "vibrant, noisy, smelly, sometimes bewildering and dangerous, but also exciting place."[6] Here is how the *Epic of Gilgamesh*, Mesopotamia's ancient epic poem, describes the city:

Come then, Enkidu, to ramparted Uruk,
Where fellows are resplendent in holiday clothing,
Where every day is set for celebration,
Where harps and drums are played.
And the harlots too, they are fairest of form,
Rich in beauty, full of delights,
Even the great gods are kept from sleeping at night.[7]

Equally impressive to a village visitor would have been the city of Mohenjo Daro (moe-hen-joe DAHR-oh), which flourished along the banks of the Indus River around 2000 B.C.E. With a population of perhaps 40,000, Mohenjo Daro and

■ Change
What was the role of cities in the early civilizations?

Mohenjo Daro

Flourishing around 2000 B.C.E., Mohenjo Daro was by far the largest city of the Indus Valley civilization, covering more than 600 acres. This photograph shows a small part of that city as it has been uncovered by archeologists during the past century. The large watertight tank or pool, shown in the foreground, probably offered bathers an opportunity for ritual purification. (View of the Great Bath/Luca Tettoni/Bridgeman Images)

its sister city of Harappa featured large, richly built houses of two or three stories, complete with indoor plumbing, luxurious bathrooms, and private wells. Streets were laid out in a grid-like pattern, and beneath the streets ran a complex sewage system. Workers lived in row upon row of standardized two-room houses. Grand public buildings, including what seems to be a huge public bath, graced the city, while an enormous citadel was surrounded by a brick wall some forty-five feet high.

Even larger, though considerably later, was the Mesoamerican city of Teotihuacán (tay-uh-tee-wah-KAHN), located in the central valley of Mexico. It housed perhaps 200,000 people in the middle of the first millennium C.E. Broad avenues, dozens of temples, two huge pyramids, endless stone carvings and many bright frescoes, small apartments for the ordinary, palatial homes for the wealthy—all of this must have seemed another world for a new visitor from a distant village. In shopping for obsidian blades, how was she to decide among the 350 workshops in the city? In seeking relatives, how could she find her way among many different compounds, each surrounded by a wall and housing a different lineage? And what would she make of a neighborhood composed entirely of Maya merchants from the distant coastal lowlands?

Cities, then, were central to most of the First Civilizations, though to varying degrees. They were political/administrative capitals; they functioned as centers for the production of culture, including art, architecture, literature, ritual, and ceremony; they served as marketplaces for both local and long-distance exchange; and they housed most manufacturing activity. Everywhere they generated a unique kind of society, compared to earlier agricultural villages or Paleolithic camps. Urban society was impersonal, for it was no longer possible to know everyone. Relationships of class and occupation emerged alongside those of kinship and village loyalty. Most notably, the degree of specialization and inequality far surpassed that of all preceding human communities.

The Erosion of Equality

Among the most novel features of early urban life, at least to our imaginary village visitor, was the amazing specialization of work outside of agriculture—scholars, officials, merchants, priests, and artisans of all kinds. In ancient Mesopotamia, even scribes were subdivided into many categories: junior and senior scribes, temple scribes and royal scribes, scribes for particular administrative or official functions. None of these people, of course, grew their own food; they were supported by the highly productive agriculture of farmers.

Hierarchies of Class

Alongside the occupational specialization of the First Civilizations lay their vast inequalities—in wealth, status, and power. As ingenuity and technology created more productive economies, the greater wealth now available was everywhere piled up rather than spread out. Early signs of this erosion of equality were evident in the more settled and complex gathering and hunting societies and in agricultural chiefdoms, but the advent of urban-based civilizations multiplied and magnified these inequalities many times over, as the more egalitarian values of earlier cultures were everywhere displaced. This transition represents one of the major turning points in the social history of humankind.

As the First Civilizations took shape, inequality and hierarchy soon came to be regarded as normal and natural. Upper classes everywhere enjoyed great wealth in land or salaries, were able to avoid physical labor, had the finest of everything, and occupied the top positions in political, military, and religious life. Frequently, they were distinguished by the clothing they wore, the houses they lived in, and the manner of their burial. Early Chinese monarchs bestowed special robes, banners, chariots, weapons, and ornaments on their regional officials, and all of these items were graded according to the officials' precise location in the hierarchy. In Mesopotamia, the punishments prescribed in the famous Code of Hammurabi (hahm-moo-RAH-bee) depended on social status. A free-born commoner who struck a person of equal rank had to pay a small fine, but if he struck "a man who is his superior, he [would] receive 60 strokes with an oxtail whip in public." Clearly, class had consequences.

In all of the First Civilizations, free commoners represented the vast majority of the population and included artisans of all kinds, lower-level officials, soldiers and police, servants, and, most numerous of all, farmers. It was their surplus production—appropriated through a variety of taxes, rents, required labor, and tribute payments—that supported the upper classes. At least some of these people were aware of, and resented, these forced extractions and their position in the social hierarchy. Most Chinese peasants, for example, owned little land of their own and worked on plots granted to them by royal or aristocratic landowners. An ancient poem compared the exploiting landlords to rats and expressed the farmers' vision of a better life:

> Large rats! Large rats!
> Do not eat our spring grain!
> Three years have we had to do with you.
> And you have not been willing to think of our toil.

■ **Change**
In what ways was social inequality expressed in early civilizations?

War and Slavery
This Mesopotamian victory monument, dating to about 2200 B.C.E., shows the Akkadian ruler Naram-Sin crushing his enemies. Prisoners taken in such wars were a major source of slaves in the ancient world. (Musée du Louvre, Paris, France/Bridgeman Images)

We will leave you,
And go to those happy borders.
Happy borders, happy borders!
Who will there make us always to groan?[8]

At the bottom of social hierarchies everywhere were slaves. Evidence for slavery dates to well before the emergence of civilization and was clearly present in some gathering and hunting societies and early agricultural communities. But the practice of "people owning people" flourished on a larger scale in the urban- and state-based societies of civilizations. Female slaves, captured in the many wars among rival Mesopotamian cities, were put to work in large-scale semi-industrial weaving enterprises, while males helped to maintain irrigation canals and construct ziggurats. Others worked as domestic servants in the households of their owners. In all of the First Civilizations, slaves—derived from prisoners of war, criminals, and debtors—were available for sale; for work in the fields, mines, homes, and shops of their owners; or on occasion for sacrifice. From the days of the earliest civilizations until the nineteenth century, slavery was everywhere an enduring feature of these more complex societies.

Its practice in ancient times, however, varied considerably from place to place. Egypt and the Indus Valley civilizations initially had far fewer slaves than did Mesopotamia, which was highly militarized. Later, the Greeks of Athens and the Romans employed slaves far more extensively than did the Chinese or Indians (see Chapter 5). Furthermore, most ancient slavery differed from the type of slavery practiced in the Americas during recent centuries: in the early civilizations, slaves were not a primary agricultural labor force; many children of slaves could become free people; and slavery was not associated primarily with "blackness" or with Africa.

Hierarchies of Gender

No division of human society has held greater significance for the lives of individuals than those of sex and gender. Sex describes the obvious biological differences between males and females. More important to historians, however, has been gender, which refers to the many and varied ways that cultures have assigned meaning to those sexual differences. To be gendered as masculine or feminine defines the roles and behavior considered appropriate for men and women in every human community. At least since the emergence of the First Civilizations, and in some cases even earlier, gender systems have been patriarchal, meaning that women have been subordinate to men in the family and in society generally. The inequalities of gender, like those of class, decisively shaped the character of the First Civilizations and those that followed.

The patriarchal ideal regarded men as superior to women and sons preferable to daughters. Men had legal and property rights unknown to most women. Public life in general was associated with masculinity, which defined men as rulers, warriors, scholars, and heads of households. Women's roles—both productive and reproductive—took place in the home, mostly within a heterosexual family, where women were defined largely by their relationship to a man: as a daughter, wife, mother, or widow. Frequently men could marry more than one woman and claim the right to regulate the social and sexual lives of the wives, daughters, and sisters in their families. Widely seen as weak but feared as potentially disruptive, women required both the protection and control of men.

But the reality of the lives of men and women did not always correspond to these ideals. Most men, of course, were far from prominent and exercised little power, except perhaps over the women and children of their own families. Gender often interacted with class to produce a more restricted but privileged life for upper-class women, who were largely limited to the home and the management of servants or slaves. By contrast, the vast majority of women always had to be out in public, working in the fields, tending livestock, buying and selling in the streets, or serving in the homes of their social superiors. A few women also operated in roles defined as masculine, acting as rulers, priests, and scholars, while others pushed against the limits and restrictions assigned to women. But most women no doubt accepted their assigned roles, unable to imagine anything approaching gender equality, even as most men genuinely believed that they were protecting and providing for their women.

The big question for historians lies in trying to explain the origins of this kind of pervasive patriarchy. Clearly it was neither natural nor of long standing. For millennia beyond measure, gathering and hunting societies had developed gender systems without the sharp restrictions and vast inequalities that characterized civilizations. Early farming societies, those using a hoe or digging stick for cultivation, continued the relative gender equality that had characterized Paleolithic peoples. What was it, then, about civilization that seemed to generate a more explicit and restrictive patriarchy? One approach to answering this question highlights the role of a new and more intensive form of agriculture, involving the use of animal-drawn plows and the keeping and milking of large herds of animals. Unlike earlier farming practices that relied on a hoe or digging stick, plow-based agriculture meant heavier work, which men were better able to perform. Taking place at a distance from the village, this new form of agriculture was perhaps less compatible with women's primary responsibility for child rearing and food preparation. Furthermore, the growing population of civilizations meant that women were more often pregnant and thus more deeply involved in child care than before. Hence, in plow-based

■ **Change**
In what ways have historians tried to explain the origins of patriarchy?

communities, men took over most of the farming work, and the status of women declined correspondingly, even though their other productive activities—weaving and food preparation, for example—continued. "As women were increasingly relegated to secondary tasks," writes archeologist Margaret Ehrenberg, "they had fewer personal resources with which to assert their status."[9] In much of Africa, all of the agricultural areas of the Americas, and parts of Southeast Asia, hoe-based farming persisted and with it, arguably, less restrictive lives for women.

Women have long been identified not only with the home but also with nature, for they are central to the primordial natural process of reproduction. But civilization seemed to highlight culture, or the human mastery of nature, through agriculture, monumental art and architecture, and creation of large-scale cities and states. Did this mean, as some scholars have suggested, that women were now associated with an inferior dimension of human life (nature), while men assumed responsibility for the higher order of culture?[10]

A further aspect of civilization that surely contributed to patriarchy was warfare. While earlier forms of human society certainly experienced violent conflict, large-scale military clashes with professionally led armies were a novel feature of almost all of the First Civilizations, and female prisoners of war often were the first slaves. With military service largely restricted to men, its growing prominence in the affairs of civilizations enhanced the values, power, and prestige of a male warrior class and cemented the association of masculinity with organized violence and with the protection of society, especially its women.

Private property and commerce, central elements of the First Civilizations, may also have helped to shape early patriarchies. Without sharp restrictions on women's sexual activity, how could a father be certain that family property would be inherited by his offspring? In addition, the buying and selling associated with commerce were soon applied to male rights over women, as female slaves, concubines, and wives were exchanged among men.

Patriarchy in Practice

Whatever the precise origins of patriarchy, women's subordination permeated the First Civilizations, marking a gradual change from the more equal relationships of men and women within agricultural villages or Paleolithic bands. By the second millennium B.C.E. in Mesopotamia, various written laws codified and sought to enforce a patriarchal family life that offered women a measure of paternalistic protection while insisting on their submission to the unquestioned authority of men. Central to these laws was the regulation of female sexuality. A wife caught sleeping with another man might be drowned at her husband's discretion, whereas he was permitted to enjoy sexual relations with his female servants, though not with another man's wife. Divorce was far easier for the husband than for the wife. Rape was a serious offense, but the injured party was primarily the father or the husband of the victim, rather than the violated woman herself. While wealthy women might own and operate their own businesses or act on behalf of their powerful husbands, they too saw themselves as dependent. "Let all be well with [my husband]," prayed one such wife, "that I may prosper under his protection."[11]

Furthermore, women in Mesopotamian civilization were sometimes divided into two sharply distinguished categories. Under an Assyrian law code that was in effect between the fifteenth and eleventh centuries B.C.E., respectable women, those under the protection and sexual control of one man, were required to be veiled when outside the home, whereas nonrespectable women, such as slaves and prostitutes, were forbidden to wear veils and were subject to severe punishment if they presumed to cover their heads.

■ **Comparison**
How did Mesopotamian and Egyptian patriarchy differ from each other?

Finally, in some places, the powerful goddesses of earlier times were gradually relegated to the home and hearth. They were replaced in the public arena by dominant male deities, who now were credited with the power of creation and fertility and viewed as the patrons of wisdom and learning. This "demotion of the goddess," argued historian Gerda Lerner, found expression in the Hebrew Scriptures, in which a single male deity, Yahweh (YAH-way), alone undertakes the act of creation without any participation of a female counterpart. Yet this demotion did not occur always or everywhere; in Mesopotamia, for example, the prominent goddess Inanna, or Istar, long held her own against male gods and was regarded as a goddess of love and sexuality as well as a war deity. In a hymn to Inanna dating to around 2250 B.C.E., the poet and priestess Enheduanna declared: "It is her game to speed conflict and battle, untiring, strapping on her sandals."

Thus expressions of patriarchy varied among the First Civilizations. Egypt, while clearly patriarchal, afforded its women greater opportunities than did most other First Civilizations. In Egypt, women were recognized as legal equals to men, able to own property and slaves, to administer and sell land, to make their own wills, to sign their own marriage contracts, and to initiate divorce. Moreover, married women in Egypt were not veiled as they were at times in Mesopotamia. Royal women occasionally exercised significant political power, acting as regents for their young sons or, more rarely, as queens in their own right. Clearly, though, this was seen as abnormal, for Egypt's most famous queen, Hatshepsut (r. 1472–1457 B.C.E.), was sometimes portrayed in statues as a man, dressed in male clothing and sporting the traditional false beard of the pharaoh.

The Rise of the State

What, we might reasonably ask, held ancient civilizations together despite the many tensions and complexities of urban living and the vast inequalities of civilized societies? Why did they not fly apart amid the resentments born of class and gender hierarchies? The answer, in large part, lay in yet another distinctive feature of the First Civilizations—states. Organized around particular cities or larger territories, early states were headed almost everywhere by kings, who employed a variety of ranked officials, exercised a measure of control over society, and defended against external enemies. To modern people, the state is such a familiar reality that we find it difficult to imagine life without it. Nonetheless, it is a quite recent invention in human history, with the state replacing, or at least supplementing, kinship as the basic organizing principle of society and exercising far greater power than earlier chiefdoms. But the power of central states in the First Civilizations was limited and certainly not "totalitarian" in the modern sense of that term. The temple and the private economy rivaled and checked the power of rulers, and most authority was local rather than directed from the capital.

Coercion and Consent

Yet early states in Mesopotamia, Egypt, China, Mesoamerica, and elsewhere were influential, drawing their power from various sources, all of which assisted in providing cohesion for the First Civilizations. One basis of authority lay in the recognition that the complexity of life in cities or densely populated territories required some authority to coordinate and regulate the community. Someone had to organize the irrigation systems of river valley civilizations. Someone had to direct efforts to defend the city or territory against aggressive outsiders. Someone had to adjudicate conflicts among the many different peoples, unrelated to one another, who rubbed elbows in the streets of early cities. The state, in short, solved certain widely shared problems and therefore had a measure of voluntary support among the population. For many people, it was surely useful.

■ **Change**
What were the sources of state authority in the First Civilizations?

The state, however, was more useful for some people than for others, for it also served to protect the privileges of the upper classes, to require farmers to give up a portion of their product to support city-dwellers, and to demand work on large public projects such as pyramids and fortifications. If necessary, state authorities had the ability, and the willingness, to use force to compel obedience. An Egyptian document described what happens to a peasant unable to pay his tax in grain:

> Now the scribe lands on the shore. He surveys the harvest. Attendants are behind him with staffs, Nubians with clubs. One says [to the peasant], "Give grain." There is none. He is beaten savagely. He is bound, thrown into a well, submerged head down. His wife is bound in his presence. His children are in fetters. His neighbors abandon them and flee.[12]

Such was the power of the state, as rulers accumulated the resources to pay for officials, soldiers, police, and attendants. This capacity for violence and coercion marked off the states of the First Civilizations from earlier chiefdoms, whose leaders had only persuasion, prestige, and gifts to back up their authority. But as states increasingly monopolized the legitimate right to use violence, rates of death from interpersonal violence declined as compared to earlier nonstate communities.[13]

Force, however, was not always necessary, for the First Civilizations soon generated ideas suggesting that state authority as well as class and gender inequalities were normal, natural, and ordained by the gods. Rulers in many places were thought to be morally responsible for the care of their subjects, especially in times of crisis or catastrophe. Kingship everywhere was associated with the sacred. Ancient Chinese kings were known as the Son of Heaven, and only they or their authorized priests could perform the rituals and sacrifices necessary to keep the cosmos in balance, thus preventing war, pestilence, and natural disaster. Mesopotamian rulers were thought to be the stewards of their city's patron gods. Their symbols of kingship—crown, throne, scepter, mace—were said to be of divine origin, sent to earth when the gods established monarchy. Egyptians, most of all, invested their pharaohs with divine qualities. Rulers claimed to embody all the major gods of Egypt, and their supernatural power ensured the regular flooding of the Nile and the defeat of the country's enemies.

A Mesopotamian Ziggurat
This massive ziggurat/temple to the Mesopotamian moon god Nanna was built around 2100 B.C.E. in the city of Ur. The solitary figure standing atop the staircase illustrates the size of this huge structure. (© Richard Ashworth/Robert Harding World Imagery/Corbis)

But if religion served most often to justify unequal power and privilege, it might also on occasion be used to restrain, or even undermine, the established order. Hammurabi claimed that his law code was inspired by Marduk, the chief god of Babylon, and was intended to "bring about the rule of righteousness in the land, to destroy the wicked and the evil-doers; so that the strong should not harm the weak."[14] Another Mesopotamian monarch, Urukagina from the city of Lagash, claimed authority from the city's patron god for reforms aimed at ending the corruption and tyranny of a previous ruler. In China during the Western Zhou dynasty (1046–771 B.C.E.), emperors ruled by the Mandate of Heaven, but their bad behavior could result in the removal of that mandate and their overthrow.

Writing and Accounting

A further support for state authority lay in the remarkable invention of writing. It was a powerful and transforming innovation, regarded almost everywhere as a gift from the gods, while people without writing often saw it as something magical or supernatural. Distinctive forms of writing emerged in most of the First Civilizations (see Snapshot, page 78), sustaining them and their successors in many ways. Literacy defined elite status and conveyed enormous prestige to those who possessed it. For Egyptians, a scribe earned a kind of immortality through his writing, for it persisted long after his death. Because it can be learned, writing also provided a means for some commoners to join the charmed circle of the literate. Writing as propaganda, celebrating the great deeds of the kings, was prominent, especially

SNAPSHOT   Writing in Ancient Civilizations

Most of the early writing systems were logophonetic, using symbols to designate both whole words and particular sounds or syllables. Chinese characters, which indicated only words, were an exception. None of the early writing systems employed alphabets.

Location	Type	Initial Use	Example	Comment
Sumer	Cuneiform: wedge-shaped symbols on clay tablets representing objects, abstract ideas, sounds, and syllables	Records of economic transactions, such as temple payments and taxes	bird	Regarded as the world's first written language; other languages such as Babylonian and Assyrian were written with Sumerian script
Egypt	Hieroglyphs ("sacred carvings"): a series of signs that denote words and consonants (but not vowels or syllables)	Business and administrative purposes; later used for religious inscriptions, stories, poetry, hymns, and mathematics	rain, dew, storm	For everyday use, less formal systems of cursive writing (known as hieratic and demotic) were developed
Andes	Quipu: a complex system of knotted cords in which the color, length, type, and location of knots conveyed mostly numerical meaning	Various accounting functions; perhaps also used to express words	numerical data (possibly in codes), words, and ideas	Widely used in the Inca Empire; recent discoveries place quipus in Caral some 5,000 years ago
Indus River Valley	Some 400 pictographic symbols representing sounds and words, probably expressing a Dravidian language currently spoken in southern India	Found on thousands of clay seals and pottery; probably used to mark merchandise	6 fish	As yet undeciphered
China	Oracle bone script: pictographs (stylized drawings) with no phonetic meaning	Inscribed on turtle shells or animal bones; used for divination (predicting the future) in the royal court of Shang dynasty rulers	horse	Direct ancestor of contemporary Chinese characters
Olmec	Signs that represent sounds (syllables) and words; numbering system using bars and dots	Used to record the names and deeds of rulers and shamans, as well as battles and astronomical data	jaguar	Structurally similar to later Mayan script; Olmec calendars were highly accurate and the basis for later Mesoamerican calendars

among the Egyptians and later among the Maya. A hymn to the pharaoh, dating to about 1850 B.C.E., extravagantly praised the Egyptian ruler:

> He has come unto us . . . and has given peace to the two Riverbanks
> and has made Egypt to live; he hath banished its suffering;
> he has caused the throat of the subjects to breathe
> and has trodden down foreign countries;
> he has delivered them that were robbed; he has come unto us, that we may
>   [nurture up?] our children and bury our aged ones.[15]

In Mesopotamia and elsewhere, writing served an accounting function, recording who had paid their taxes, who owed what to the temple, and how much workers had earned. Thus it immensely strengthened bureaucracy. Complex calendars indicated precisely when certain rituals should be performed. Writing also gave weight and specificity to orders, regulations, and laws. Hammurabi's famous law code, while correcting certain abuses, made crystal clear that fundamental distinctions divided men and women and separated slaves, commoners, and people of higher rank.

Once it had been developed, writing, like religion, proved hard to control and operated as a wild card in human affairs. It gave rise to literature and philosophy, to astronomy and mathematics, and, in some places, to history, often recording what had long been oral traditions. On occasion, the written word proved threatening, rather than supportive, to rulers. China's so-called First Emperor, Qin Shihuangdi (r. 221–210 B.C.E.), allegedly buried alive some 460 scholars and burned their books when they challenged his brutal efforts to unify China's many warring states, or so his later critics claimed (see Chapter 3). Thus writing became a major arena for social and political conflict, and rulers have always sought to control it.

The Grandeur of Kings

Yet another source of state authority derived from the lavish lifestyle of elites, the impressive rituals they arranged, and the imposing structures they created. Everywhere, kings, high officials, and their families lived in luxurious palaces or homes, dressed in splendid clothing, bedecked themselves with the loveliest jewelry, and were attended by endless servants. Their deaths triggered elaborate burials, of which the pyramids of the Egyptian pharaohs were perhaps the most ostentatious. Monumental palaces, temples, ziggurats, pyramids, and statues conveyed the imposing power of the state and its elite rulers. The Olmec civilization of Mesoamerica (1200– 400 B.C.E.) erected enormous human heads,

Olmec Head
This colossal statue, some six feet high and five feet wide, is one of seventeen such carvings, dating to the first millennium B.C., that were discovered in the territory of the ancient Olmec civilization. Thought to represent individual rulers, each of the statues has a distinct and realistically portrayed face. (© Danny Lehman/Corbis)

SUMMING UP SO FAR

In what ways might the advent of "civilization" have marked a revolutionary change in the human condition? And in what ways did it carry on earlier patterns from the past?

more than ten feet tall and weighing at least twenty tons, carved from blocks of basalt and probably representing particular rulers. Somewhat later, the Maya Temple of the Great Jaguar, towering 154 feet tall, was the most impressive among many temples, pyramids, and palaces that graced the city of Tikal. All of this must have seemed overwhelming to common people in the cities and villages of the First Civilizations.

Comparing Mesopotamia and Egypt

A productive agricultural technology, city living, distinct class and gender inequalities, the emerging power of states—all of these were common features of First Civilizations across the world and also of those that followed. Still, these civilizations were not everywhere the same, for differences in political organization, religious beliefs and practices, the role of women, and much more gave rise to distinctive traditions. Nor were they static. Like all human communities, they changed over the centuries. Finally, these civilizations did not exist in complete isolation, for they participated in networks of interactions with near and sometimes more distant neighbors. In looking more closely at two of these First Civilizations—Mesopotamia and Egypt—we can catch a glimpse of the differences, changes, and connections that characterized early civilizations.

Environment and Culture

■ Comparison

In what ways did Mesopotamian and Egyptian civilizations differ from each other?

The civilizations of both Mesopotamia and Egypt grew up in river valleys and depended on their rivers to sustain a productive agriculture in otherwise-arid lands. Those rivers, however, were radically different. At the heart of Egyptian life was the Nile, "that green gash of teeming life," which rose predictably every year to bring the soil and water that nurtured a rich Egyptian agriculture. The Tigris and Euphrates rivers, which gave life to Mesopotamian civilization, also rose annually, but "unpredictably and fitfully, breaking man's dikes and submerging his crops"[16] (see Map 2.2). Furthermore, an open environment without serious obstacles to travel made Mesopotamia far more vulnerable to invasion than the much more protected space of Egypt, which was surrounded by deserts, mountains, seas, and cataracts. For long periods of its history, Egypt enjoyed a kind of "free security" from external attack that Mesopotamians clearly lacked.

But does the physical environment shape the human cultures that develop within it? Most historians are reluctant to endorse any kind of determinism, especially one suggesting that "geography is destiny," but in the case of Mesopotamia and Egypt, it is hard to deny some relationship between the physical setting and culture.

Mesopotamia's location within a precarious, unpredictable, and often-violent environment arguably contributed to an outlook suggesting that humankind was caught in an inherently disorderly world, subject to the whims of capricious and

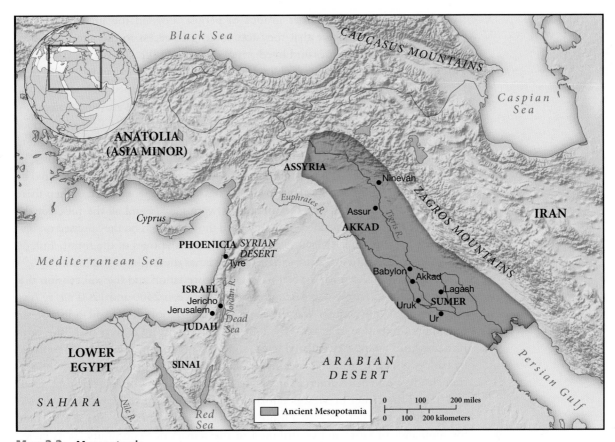

Map 2.2 Mesopotamia

After about 1,000 years of independent and competitive existence, the city-states of Sumer were incorporated into a number of larger imperial states based in Akkad, Babylon, and then Assyria.

quarreling gods, and faced death without much hope of a blessed life beyond. A Mesopotamian poet complained: "I have prayed to the gods and sacrificed, but who can understand the gods in heaven? Who knows what they plan for us? Who has ever been able to understand a god's conduct?"[17] One character in the famous *Epic of Gilgamesh* declared: "When the gods created man, they allotted to him death, but life they retained in their own keeping."

By contrast, elite literate culture in Egypt, developing in a more stable, predictable, and beneficent environment, produced a rather more cheerful and hopeful outlook on the world. The rebirth of the sun every day and of the river every year seemed to assure Egyptians that life would prevail over death. The amazing pyramids, constructed during Egypt's Old Kingdom (2663–2195 B.C.E.), reflected the firm belief that at least the pharaohs and other high-ranking people could successfully make the journey to eternal life in the Land of the West. Incantations for the dead describe an afterlife of abundance and tranquillity that Gilgamesh could only have envied. Over time, larger groups of people, beyond the pharaoh and his entourage, came to believe that they too could gain access to the afterlife if they followed proper procedures and lived a morally upright life. Thus Egyptian civilization not only affirmed the possibility of eternal life but also expanded access to it.

If the different environments of Mesopotamia and Egypt shaped their societies and cultures, those civilizations, with their mounting populations and growing demand for resources, likewise had an impact on the environment.[18] The *Epic of Gilgamesh* inscribed in mythology the deforestation of Mesopotamia. When the ruler Gilgamesh sought to make for himself "a name that endures" by building walls, ramparts, and temples, he required much timber. But to acquire it, he had first to kill Humbaba, appointed by the gods to guard the forests. The epic describes what happened next: "Then there followed confusion. . . . Now the mountains were moved and all the hills, for the guardian of the forest was killed. They attacked the cedars. . . . So they pressed on into the forest . . . and while Gilgamesh felled the first of the trees of the forest, Enkidu [the friend of Gilgamesh] cleared their roots as far as the banks of Euphrates."[19]

In Sumer (southern Mesopotamia), such deforestation and the soil erosion that followed from it sharply decreased crop yields between 2400 and 1700 B.C.E. Also contributing to this disaster was the increasing salinization of the soil, a long-term outcome of intensive irrigation. By 2000 B.C.E., there were reports that "the earth turned white" as salt accumulated in the soil. As a result, wheat was largely replaced by barley, which is far more tolerant of salty conditions. This ecological deterioration clearly weakened Sumerian city-states, facilitated their conquest by foreigners, and shifted the center of Mesopotamian civilization permanently to the north.

Egypt, by contrast, created a more sustainable agricultural system, which lasted for thousands of years and contributed to the remarkable continuity of its civilization. Whereas Sumerian irrigation involved a complex and artificial network of canals and dikes that led to the salinization of the soil, its Egyptian counterpart was much less intrusive, simply regulating the natural flow of the Nile. Such a system avoided the problem of salty soils, allowing Egyptian agriculture to emphasize wheat production, but it depended on the general regularity and relative gentleness of the Nile's annual flooding. On occasion, that pattern was interrupted, with serious consequences for Egyptian society. An extended period of low floods between 2250 and 1950 B.C.E. led to sharply reduced agricultural output, large-scale starvation, the loss of livestock, and, consequently, social upheaval and political disruption. Nonetheless, Egypt's ability to work *with* its more favorable natural environment enabled a degree of stability and continuity that proved impossible in Sumer, where human action intruded more heavily into a less benevolent natural setting.

Cities and States

Politically as well as culturally and environmentally, Mesopotamian and Egyptian civilizations differed sharply. For its first thousand years (3200–2350 B.C.E.), Mesopotamian civilization, located in the southern Tigris-Euphrates region known as

Sumer, was organized in a dozen or more separate and independent city-states. Each city-state was ruled by a king, who claimed to represent the city's patron deity and who controlled the affairs of the walled city and surrounding rural area. Quite remarkably, some 80 percent of the population of Sumer lived in one or another of these city-states, making Mesopotamia the most thoroughly urbanized society of ancient times. The chief reason for this massive urbanization, however, lay in the great flaw of this system, for frequent warfare among these Sumerian city-states caused people living in rural areas to flee to the walled cities for protection. With no overarching authority, rivalry over land and water often led to violent conflict.

These conflicts, together with environmental devastation, eventually left Sumerian cities vulnerable to outside forces, and after about 2350 B.C.E., stronger peoples from northern Mesopotamia conquered Sumer's warring cities, bringing an end to the Sumerian phase of Mesopotamian civilization. First the Akkadians (2350–2000 B.C.E.), and later the Babylonians (1900–1500 B.C.E.) and the Assyrians (900–612 B.C.E.), created larger territorial states or bureaucratic empires that encompassed all or most of Mesopotamia. Periods of political unity now descended upon this First Civilization, but it was unity imposed from outside.

Egyptian civilization, by contrast, began its history around 3100 B.C.E., with the merger of several earlier states or chiefdoms into a unified territory that stretched some 1,000 miles along the Nile. For an amazing 3,000 years, the Egypt of the pharaohs maintained its unity and independence, though with occasional interruptions. A combination of wind patterns that made it easy to sail south along the Nile and a current flowing north facilitated communication, exchange, unity, and stability within the Nile Valley. Here was a record of political longevity and continuity that the Mesopotamians and many other ancient peoples could not replicate. An Egyptian territorial state and cultural identity persist still in northeastern Africa.

Cities in Egypt were less important than in Mesopotamia, although political capitals, market centers, and major burial sites gave Egypt an urban presence as well. Most people lived in agricultural villages along the river rather than in urban centers, perhaps because Egypt's greater security made it less necessary for people to gather in fortified towns. The focus of the Egyptian state resided in the pharaoh, believed to be a god in human form. He alone ensured the daily rising of the sun and the annual flooding of the Nile. All of the country's many officials served at his pleasure, and access to the afterlife lay in proximity to him and burial in or near his towering pyramids.

This image of the pharaoh and his role as an enduring symbol of Egyptian civilization persisted over the course of three millennia, but the realities of Egyptian political life did not always match the ideal, as the Zooming In feature on Paneb so vividly illustrates (see page 84). By 2400 B.C.E., the power of the pharaoh had diminished, as local officials and nobles, who had been awarded their own land and were able to pass their positions on to their sons, assumed greater authority. When changes in the weather resulted in the Nile's repeated failure to flood properly around 2200 B.C.E., the authority of the pharaoh was severely discredited, and Egypt dissolved for several centuries into a series of local principalities.

Paneb, an Egyptian Troublemaker

The life of Paneb (ca. thirteenth century B.C.E.) illuminates an underside of Egyptian life rather different from the images of order and harmony portrayed in much of ancient Egyptian art and literature.[20] Paneb was born into a family and a village of tomb workers—people who quarried, sculpted, and painted the final resting places of the pharaohs and other elite figures at a time when royal pyramids were no longer being constructed. Granted generous allowances of grain, beer, fish, vegetables, firewood, and clothing, tomb workers represented a prestigious occupation in ancient Egypt.

Paneb was apparently orphaned as a youngster and raised by another tomb-working family, that of the childless Neferhotep, a foreman of the tomb workers' crew who brought his adopted son into the profession. But Paneb quarreled violently with Neferhotep, on one occasion smashing the door to his house and threatening to kill him.

As an adult, Paneb married and sired a large family of eight or nine children. He also indulged in numerous

Paneb worshipping a coiled cobra representing the goddess Meretseger, patron deity of the burial grounds in Thebes, where Paneb worked.

affairs with married women and was involved in at least one rape. One of his lovers was the wife of a man with whom Paneb had grown up in Neferhotep's home; the couple subsequently divorced, a frequent occurrence in ancient Egypt. In another case, Paneb seduced both a married woman and her daughter and shared the sexual favors of the daughter with his son Aapehty. It is not difficult to imagine the tensions that such behavior created in a small, close-knit village.

When Paneb's adoptive father, Neferhotep, died—he was perhaps murdered—Paneb succeeded him as workplace foreman, thus incurring the lifelong hostility of Neferhotep's brother, Amennakht, who felt he had better claim to the job. What turned the tide in Paneb's favor was his "gift" of five servants, made to the vizier, the pharaoh's highest official, who was responsible for such appointments. To add insult to Amennakht's injury, those servants had belonged to Neferhotep himself.

Even when centralized rule was restored around 2000 B.C.E., the pharaohs never regained their old power and prestige. Kings were now warned that they too would have to account for their actions at the Day of Judgment. Nobles no longer sought to be buried near the pharaoh's pyramid but instead created their own more modest tombs in their own areas. Osiris, the god of the dead, became increasingly prominent, and all worthy men, not only those who had been close to the pharaoh in life, could aspire to immortality in his realm.

Interaction and Exchange

Although Mesopotamia and Egypt represented separate and distinct civilizations, they interacted frequently with each other and with both near and more distant

While such bribes were common practice in obtaining promotions, it was Paneb's use of his position as foreman of the tomb workers' crew that got him into ever-deeper trouble. He actively harassed his rival Amennakht, preventing him and his family from using the small chapel in which workers celebrated the festivals of their gods. He quarreled with the foreman of another work crew, saying, "I'll attack you on the mountain and I'll kill you." Such angry outbursts led to frequent fighting and gained Paneb a reputation for brutality.

Paneb also exploited his position as foreman to his own advantage. He used—or stole—expensive tools given to the work crew for his own purposes. He ordered members of his work crew to do personal work for him—making a bed that he then sold to a high official, feeding his oxen, weaving baskets for his personal use, and preparing and decorating his own tomb, using materials pilfered from the royal tombs he was charged with constructing. On one occasion he stole the covering of a royal chariot, and another time he entered a royal tomb, drank the wine intended for the pharaoh's afterlife, and in an act of enormous disrespect—even blasphemy—actually sat on the sarcophagus containing the embalmed body of the ruler.

Although Paneb was rebuked from time to time by high officials, his bad behavior continued. "He could not stop his clamor," according to an official document. At some point, Paneb's son publicly denounced his father's sexual escapades. But the final straw that broke his career came from Amennakht, Paneb's longtime rival. He apparently had had enough and drew up a long list of particulars detailing Paneb's crimes. That document, from which our knowledge of Paneb largely derives, has survived. It concluded in this fashion:

> He is thus not worthy of this position. For truly, he seems well, [but] he is like a crazy person. And he kills people to prevent them from carrying out a mission of the Pharaoh. See, I wish to convey knowledge of his condition to the vizier.

The outcome of this complaint is unclear, for Paneb subsequently disappears from the historical record, and a new foreman was appointed in his place. It was not, however, Amennakht.

Questions: Since most of the evidence against Paneb comes from his archrival, how much weight should historians grant to that account? How might the story appear if written from Paneb's viewpoint? What perspectives on the Egypt of his time does Paneb's career disclose? How do those perspectives differ from more conventional and perhaps idealized understandings?

---

neighbors. Even in these ancient times, the First Civilizations were embedded in larger networks of commerce, culture, and power. None of them stood alone.

The early beginnings of Egyptian civilization illustrate the point. Its agriculture drew upon wheat and barley, which likely reached Egypt from Mesopotamia, as well as gourds, watermelon, domesticated donkeys, and cattle, which came from the Sudan to the south. The practice of "divine kingship" probably derived from the central or eastern Sudan, where small-scale agricultural communities had long viewed their rulers as sacred and buried them with various servants and officials. From this complex of influences, the Egyptians created something distinct and unique, but that civilization had roots in both Africa and Southwest Asia.

Furthermore, once they were established, both Mesopotamia and Egypt carried on long-distance trade, mostly in luxury goods destined for the elite. Sumerian

■ **Connection**
In what ways were Mesopotamian and Egyptian civilizations shaped by their interactions with near and distant neighbors?

merchants had established seaborne contact with the Indus Valley civilization as early as 2300 B.C.E., while Indus Valley traders and their interpreters had taken up residence in Mesopotamia. Other trade routes connected it to Anatolia (present-day Turkey), Egypt, Iran, and Afghanistan. During Akkadian rule over Mesopotamia, a Sumerian poet described its capital of Agade:

> In those days the dwellings of Agade were filled with gold,
> its bright-shining houses were filled with silver,
> into its granaries were brought copper, tin, slabs of
> lapis lazuli [a blue gemstone], its silos bulged at the sides . . .
> its quay where the boats docked were all bustle.[21]

All of this and more came from far away.

Egyptian trade likewise extended far afield. Beyond its involvement with the Mediterranean and the Middle East, Egyptian trading journeys extended deep into Africa, including Nubia, south of Egypt in the Nile Valley, and Punt, along the East African coast of Ethiopia and Somalia. One Egyptian official described his return from an expedition to Nubia: "I came down with three hundred donkeys laden with incense, ebony, . . . panther skins, elephant tusks, throw sticks, and all sorts of good products."[22] What most intrigued the very young pharaoh who sent him, however, was a dancing dwarf who accompanied the expedition back to Egypt.

Along with trade goods went cultural influence from the civilizations of Mesopotamia and Egypt. Among the smaller societies of the region to feel this influence were the Hebrews. Their sacred writings, recorded in the Old Testament, showed the influence of Mesopotamia in the "eye for an eye" principle of their legal system and in the story of a flood that destroyed the world. The Phoenicians, who were commercially active in the Mediterranean basin from their homeland in present-day Lebanon, also were influenced by Mesopotamian civilization. They venerated

Egypt and Nubia

By the fourteenth century B.C.E., Nubia was a part of an Egyptian empire. This wall painting shows Nubian princes bringing gifts or tribute, including rings and bags of gold, to Huy, the Egyptian viceroy of Nubia. The mural comes from Huy's tomb. (© The Trustees of the British Museum/Art Resource, NY)

Asarte, a local form of the Mesopotamian fertility goddess Istar. They also adapted the Sumerian cuneiform method of writing to a much easier alphabetic system, which later became the basis for Greek and Latin writing. Various Indo-European peoples, dispersing probably from north-central Anatolia, also incorporated Sumerian deities into their own religions as well as bronze metallurgy and the wheel into their economies. When their widespread migrations carried them across much of Eurasia, they took these Sumerian cultural artifacts with them.

Egyptian cultural influence likewise spread in several directions. Nubia, located to the south of Egypt in the Nile Valley, not only traded with its more powerful neighbor but also was subject to periodic military intervention and political control from Egypt. Skilled Nubian archers were actively recruited for service as mercenaries in Egyptian armies. They often married Egyptian women and were buried in Egyptian style. All of this led to the diffusion of Egyptian culture in Nubia, expressed in building Egyptian-style pyramids, worshipping Egyptian gods and goddesses, and making use of Egyptian hieroglyphic writing. Despite this cultural borrowing, Nubia remained a distinct civilization, developing its own alphabetic script, retaining many of its own gods, developing a major ironworking industry by 500 B.C.E., and asserting its political independence whenever possible. The Nubian kingdom of Kush, in fact, invaded Egypt in 760 B.C.E. and ruled it for about 100 years. (See Zooming In: Piye, Kushite Conqueror of Egypt, Chapter 6, page 236.)

In the Mediterranean basin, clear Egyptian influence is visible in the art of Minoan civilization, which emerged on the island of Crete about 2500 B.C.E. More controversial has been the claim by historian Martin Bernal in a much-publicized book, *Black Athena* (1987), that ancient Greek culture—its art, religion, philosophy, and language—drew heavily upon Egyptian as well as Mesopotamian precedents. His book lit up a passionate debate among scholars. To some of his critics, Bernal seemed to undermine the originality of Greek civilization by suggesting that it had Afro-Asian origins. His supporters accused the critics of Eurocentrism. Whatever its outcome, the controversy surrounding Bernal's book served to focus attention on Egypt's relationship to black Africa and to the world of the Mediterranean basin.

Influence was not a one-way street, however, as Egypt and Mesopotamia likewise felt the impact of neighboring peoples. Pastoral peoples, speaking Indo-European languages and living in what is now southern Russia, had domesticated the horse by perhaps 4000 B.C.E. and later learned to tie that powerful animal to wheeled carts and chariots. This new technology provided a fearsome military potential that enabled various chariot-driving peoples, such as the Hittites, to threaten ancient civilizations. Based in Anatolia, the Hittites sacked the city of Babylon in 1595 B.C.E. Several centuries later, conflict between the Hittites and Egypt over control of Syria resulted in the world's first written peace treaty. But chariot technology was portable, and soon both the Egyptians and the Mesopotamians incorporated it into their own military forces. In fact, this powerful military innovation, together with the knowledge of bronze metallurgy, spread quickly and widely, reaching China by 1200 B.C.E. There it enabled the creation of a strong Chinese state ruled by the Shang dynasty.

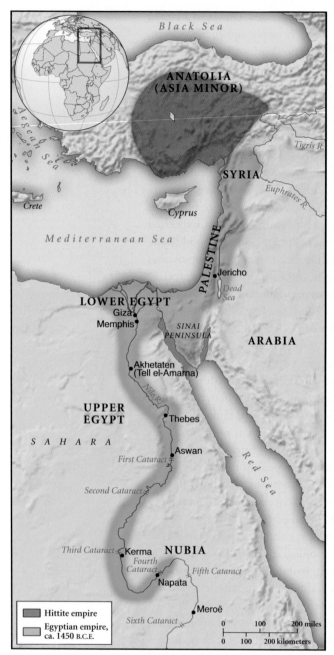

Map 2.3   An Egyptian Empire

During the New Kingdom period after 1550 B.C.E., Egypt became for several centuries an empire, extending its political control southward into Nubia and northward into Palestine and Syria.

All of these developments provide evidence of at least indirect connections across parts of the Afro-Eurasian landmass in ancient times. Even then, no civilization was wholly isolated from larger patterns of interaction.

In Egypt, the centuries following 1650 B.C.E. witnessed the migration of foreigners from surrounding regions and conflict with neighboring peoples, shaking the sense of security that this Nile Valley civilization had long enjoyed. It also stimulated the normally complacent Egyptians to adopt a number of technologies pioneered earlier in Asia, including the horse-drawn chariot; new kinds of armor, bows, daggers, and swords; improved methods of spinning and weaving; new musical instruments; and olive and pomegranate trees. Absorbing these foreign innovations, Egyptians went on to create their own empire, both in Nubia and in the eastern Mediterranean regions of Syria and Palestine. By 1500 B.C.E., the previously self-contained Egypt became for several centuries an imperial state bridging Africa and Asia, ruling over substantial numbers of non-Egyptian peoples (see Map 2.3). It also became part of an international political system that included the Babylonian and later Assyrian empires of Mesopotamia as well as many other peoples of the region. Egyptian and Babylonian rulers engaged in regular diplomatic correspondence, referred to one another as "brother," exchanged gifts, and married their daughters into one another's families. Or at least they tried to. While Babylonian rulers were willing to send their daughters to Egypt, the Egyptians were exceedingly reluctant to return the favor, claiming that "from ancient times the daughter of the king of Egypt has not been given to anyone." To this rebuff, the disappointed Babylonian monarch replied: "You are a king and you can do as pleases you. . . . Send me [any] beautiful woman as if she were your daughter. Who is to say this woman is not the daughter of the king?"[23]

"Civilization": What's in a Word?

In examining the cultures of ancient Mesopotamia and Egypt, we are worlds away from life in agricultural villages or Paleolithic camps. Much the same holds for those of the Indus Valley, Central Asia, China, Mesoamerica, and the Andes. Strangely enough, historians have been somewhat uncertain as to how to refer to these new forms of human community. Following common practice, we have called them "civilizations," but scholars have reservations about the term for two reasons. The first is its implication of superiority. In popular usage, "civilization" suggests refined behavior, a "higher" form of society, something unreservedly positive. The opposite of "civilized"—"barbarian," "savage," or "uncivilized"—is normally understood as an insult implying inferiority. That, of course, is precisely how the inhabitants of many civilizations have viewed outsiders, particularly those neighboring peoples living without the alleged benefit of cities and states.

Modern assessments of the First Civilizations reveal a profound ambiguity about these new, larger, and more complex societies. On the one hand, these civilizations have given us inspiring art, profound reflections on the meaning of life, more productive technologies, increased control over nature, and the art of writing—all of which have been cause for celebration. On the other hand, as anthropologist Marvin Harris noted, "human beings learned for the first time how to bow, grovel, kneel, and kowtow."[24] Massive inequalities, state oppression, slavery, large-scale warfare, the subordination of women, and epidemic disease also accompanied the rise of civilization, generating discontent, rebellion, and sometimes the urge to escape. This ambiguity about the character of civilizations has led some historians to avoid the word, referring to early Egypt, Mesopotamia, and other regions instead as complex societies, urban-based societies, state-organized societies, or some other more neutral term.

A second reservation about using the term "civilization" derives from its implication of solidity—the idea that civilizations represent distinct and widely shared identities with clear boundaries that mark them off from other such units. It is unlikely, however, that many people living in Mesopotamia, Norte Chico, or ancient China felt themselves part of a shared culture. Local identities defined by occupation, clan affiliation, village, city, or region were surely more important for most people than those of some larger civilization. At best, members of an educated upper class who shared a common literary tradition may have felt themselves part of some more inclusive civilization, but that left out most of the population. Moreover, unlike modern nations, none of the earlier civilizations had definite borders. Any identification with that civilization surely faded as distance from its core region increased. Finally, the line between civilizations and other kinds of societies is not always clear. Just when does a village or town become a city? At what point does a chiefdom become a state? Scholars continue to argue about these distinctions.

Given these reservations, should historians discard the notion of civilization? Maybe so, but this book continues to use it both because it is so deeply embedded in our way of thinking about the world and because no alternative concept has achieved widespread acceptance for making distinctions among different kinds of human communities. But it is important to recall that historians use "civilization" as a purely descriptive term, referring to a particular and distinctive type of human society—one with cities and states—without implying any judgment or assessment, any sense of superiority or inferiority. Furthermore "civilization" serves to define broad cultural patterns in particular geographic regions—Mesopotamia, the Peruvian coast, or China, for example—even though many people living in those regions may have been more aware of differences and conflicts than of those commonalities.

Second Thoughts

What's the Significance?

Norte Chico / Caral, 61; 64

Indus Valley civilization, 65

Central Asian / Oxus
   civilization, 67

Olmec civilization, 67; 79

Uruk, 69

Epic of Gilgamesh, 69; 82

Mohenjo Daro / Harappa, 69; 70

Code of Hammurabi, 71

patriarchy, 73–75

rise of the state, 75–79

Egypt, 80–88

Sumer, 83–87

Paneb, 84–85

Nubia, 87

Big Picture Questions

1. How does historians' use of the term "civilization" differ from popular usage? How do you use it?
2. "Civilizations were held together largely by force." Do you agree with this assessment, or were there other mechanisms of integration as well?
3. How did the various First Civilizations differ from one another?
4. **Looking Back:** To what extent did civilizations represent "progress" in comparison with earlier Paleolithic and Neolithic societies? And in what ways did they constitute a setback for humankind?

Next Steps: For Further Study

Cyril Aldred, *The Egyptians* (1998). A brief account from a widely recognized expert.

Jonathan M. Kenoyer, *Ancient Cities of the Indus Valley Civilization* (1998). A thorough and beautifully illustrated study by a leading archeologist of the area.

Samuel Noah Kramer, *History Begins at Sumer* (1981). A classic account of Sumerian civilization, filled with wonderful stories and anecdotes.

David B. O'Connor, *Ancient Nubia: Egypt's Rival in Africa* (1994). An overview of this ancient African civilization, with lovely illustrations based on a museum exhibit.

Christopher A. Pool, *Olmec Archeology and Early Mesoamerica* (2007). A scholarly and up-to-date account of the earliest civilization in Mesoamerica.

Robert Thorp, *China in the Early Bronze Age: Shang Civilization* (2006). An accessible and scholarly account of early Chinese civilization informed by recent archeological discoveries.

The British Museum, "Ancient Egypt," http://www.ancientegypt.co.uk/menu.html. An interactive exploration of Egyptian civilization.

"The Indus Civilization," http://www.harappa.com/har/har0.html. Hundreds of vivid pictures and several brief essays on the Indus Valley civilization.

WORKING WITH EVIDENCE

Indus Valley Civilization

In most accounts of the First Civilizations, Egypt and Mesopotamia hold center stage. And yet the civilization of the Indus River valley was much larger, and its archeological treasures have been equally impressive, though clearly distinctive. This civilization flourished around 2000 B.C.E., about a thousand years later than its better-known counterparts in the Middle East and Northeast Africa. By 1700 B.C.E., Indus Valley civilization was in decline, as the center of Indian or South Asian civilization shifted gradually eastward to the plains of the Ganges River. In the process, all distinct memory of the earlier Indus Valley civilization vanished, to be rediscovered only in the early twentieth century as archeologists uncovered its remarkable remains. Here is yet another contrast with Egypt and Mesopotamia, where conscious memory of earlier achievements persisted long after those civilizations had passed into history.

Among the most distinctive elements of Indus Valley civilization were its cities, of which Mohenjo Daro and Harappa were the largest and are the most thoroughly investigated. Laid out systematically on a grid pattern and clearly planned, they were surrounded by substantial walls made from mud bricks of a standardized size and interrupted by imposing gateways. Inside the walls, public buildings, market areas, large and small houses, and craft workshops stood in each of the cities' various neighborhoods. Many houses had indoor latrines, while wide main streets and narrow side lanes had drains to carry away polluted water and sewage. (See page 70 for an image of a ritual bathing pool in Mohenjo Daro.)

The images that follow are drawn from archeological investigations of the Indus Valley civilization and offer us a glimpse of its achievements and unique features. Since its written language was limited in extent and has not yet been deciphered, scholars have been highly dependent on its physical remains for understanding this First Civilization.

In many ancient and more recent societies, seals have been used for imprinting an image on a document or a product. Such seals have been among the most numerous artifacts found in the Indus Valley cities. They often carried the image of an animal—a bull, an elephant, a crocodile, a buffalo, or even a mythic creature such as a unicorn—as well as a title or inscription in a still-undeciphered script. Thus the seals were accessible to an illiterate worker loading goods on a boat as well as to literate merchants or officials. Particular seals may well have represented a specific clan, a high official, a particular business, or a prominent individual. Unicorn seals have been the most numerous finds and were often used to make impressions on clay tags attached to bundled goods, suggesting that their owners were involved in trade or commerce. Because bull seals, such as the one shown in Source 2.1, were rarer, their owners may have been high-ranking officials or members of a particularly powerful clan. The bull, speculates archeologist Jonathan Kenoyer, "may symbolize the leader of the herd, whose strength and virility protects the herd and ensures the procreation of the species, or it may stand for a sacrificial animal."[25] Indus Valley seals, as well as pottery, have been found in Mesopotamia, indicating an established trade between these two First Civilizations.

- How might a prominent landowner, a leading official, a clan head, or a merchant make use of such a seal?

- What meaning might you attach to the use of animals as totems or symbols of a particular group or individual?

- Notice the five characters of the Indus Valley script at the top of the seal. Do a little research on the script with an eye to understanding why it has proved so difficult to decipher.

De Agostini Picture Library/A. Dagli Orti/Bridgeman Images

Source 2.1 A Seal from the Indus Valley

The most intriguing features of Indus Valley civilization involve what is missing, at least in comparison with ancient Egypt and Mesopotamia. Archeologists have found no grand temples or palaces; no elite burial places filled with great wealth; no images of warfare, conquest, or the seizing of captives; no monuments to celebrate powerful rulers. These absences have left scholars guessing about the social and political organization of this civilization. Kenoyer has suggested that the great cities were likely controlled not by a single ruler, but by "a small group of elites, comprised of merchants, landowners, and ritual specialists."[26]

Source 2.2, a statue seven inches tall and found in Mohenjo Daro, likely depicts one of these elite men.

Jean-Louis Nou/akg-images

Source 2.2 Man from Mohenjo Daro

■ What specific features of the statue can you point out?

■ What possible indication of elite status can you identify?

■ What overall impression does the statue convey?

Limited archeological evidence suggests that some urban women played important social and religious roles in the Indus Valley civilization. Figurines of women or goddesses are more common than those of men. Women, apparently, were buried near their mothers and grandmothers, while men were not interred with their male relatives. The great variety of clothing, hairstyles, and decorations displayed on female figurines indicates considerable class, ethnic, and perhaps individual variation.

Among the most delightful discoveries in the Indus Valley cities is the evocative statue shown in Source 2.3. It is about four inches tall and dates to

National Museum of India, New Delhi, India/Bridgeman Images

Source 2.3 Dancing Girl

around 2500 B.C.E. This young female nude is known generally as the "dancing girl." Cast in bronze using a sophisticated "lost wax" method, this statue provides evidence for a well-developed copper/bronze industry. The figure herself was portrayed in a dancer's pose, her hair gathered in a bun and her left arm covered with bangles and holding a small bowl. Both her arms and legs seem disproportionately long. She has been described variously as a queen, a high-status woman, a sacred temple dancer, and a tribal girl. Although no one really knows her precise identity, she has evoked wide admiration and appreciation. Mortimer Wheeler, a famous British archeologist, described her as "a girl perfectly, for the moment, perfectly confident of herself and the world." American archeologist Gregory Possehl, also active in the archeology of the Indus Valley civilization, commented, "We may not be certain that she was a dancer, but she was good at what she did and she knew it."[27]

■ What features of this statue may have provoked such observations?

■ How do you react to this statue? What qualities does the figure evoke?

■ What does Source 2.3 suggest about views of women, images of female beauty, and attitudes about sexuality and the body?

DOING HISTORY

Indus Valley Civilization

1. **Using art as evidence:** What can we learn about Indus Valley civilization from these visual sources? How does our level of understanding of this civilization differ from that of Egypt and Mesopotamia, where plentiful written records are available?

2. **Considering accessibility:** Do you find the art of civilizations, such as that of the Indus Valley, more accessible to modern people than artistic products of earlier eras? Is it possible to speak of artistic "progress" or "development," or should we be content with simply noticing differences?

3. **Comparing representations of people:** Notice the various ways that human figures were portrayed in the images shown in Chapters 1 and 2, both those in the chapter narrative and in the Working with Evidence section. How might you define those differences? Can you identify changes from the Paleolithic to the Neolithic eras and then to the age of First Civilizations? How are gender differences represented in these images?

4. **Seeking further evidence:** What additional kinds of archeological discoveries would be helpful in furthering our understanding of Indus Valley civilization?

PART TWO
SECOND-WAVE CIVILIZATIONS IN WORLD HISTORY
500 B.C.E.–500 C.E.

Contents

AFTER THE FIRST CIVILIZATIONS: WHAT CHANGED AND WHAT DIDN'T?

Studying world history has much in common with using the zoom lens of a camera. Sometimes, we pull the lens back to get a picture of the broadest possible panorama. At other times, we zoom in a bit for a middle-range shot, or even farther for a close-up of some particular feature of the historical landscape. Students of world history soon become comfortable with moving back and forth among these several perspectives.

As we bid farewell to the First Civilizations, we will take the opportunity to pull back the lens and look broadly, and briefly, at the entire age of agricultural civilizations, a period from about 3500 B.C.E., when the earliest of the First Civilizations arose, to about 1750 C.E., when the first Industrial Revolution launched a new and distinctively modern phase of world history. During these more than 5,000 years, the most prominent large-scale trend was the globalization of civilization as this new form of human community increasingly spread across the planet, encompassing more people and larger territories.

The first wave of that process, addressed in Chapter 2, was already global in scope, with expressions in Asia, Africa, and the Americas. Those First Civilizations generated the most impressive and powerful human societies created thus far, but they proved fragile and vulnerable as well. The always-quarreling city-states of ancient Mesopotamia had long ago been absorbed into the larger empires of Babylon and Assyria. By the middle of the second millennium B.C.E., the Indus Valley, Central Asian, and Norte Chico civilizations had collapsed or faded away. Egypt too fell victim to a series of foreign invaders during the first millennium B.C.E., including the forces of Nubia, Assyria, Alexander the Great, and the Roman Empire. The end of Olmec civilization around 400 B.C.E. has long puzzled historians, for it seems that the Olmecs themselves razed and then abandoned their major cities even as their civilizational style spread to neighboring peoples. About the same time, China's Zhou dynasty kingdom fragmented into a series of competing states.

Even though these First Civilizations broke down, there was no going back. Civilization as a form of human community proved durable and resilient as well as periodically fragile. Thus, in the thousand years between 500 B.C.E. and 500 C.E., new or enlarged urban-centered and state-based societies emerged to replace the First Civilizations in the Mediterranean basin, the Middle East, India,

China, Mesoamerica, and the Andes. Furthermore, smaller expressions of civilization began to take shape elsewhere—in Ethiopia and West Africa, in Japan and Indonesia, in Vietnam and Cambodia. In short, the development of civilization was becoming a global process.

Many of these second-wave civilizations likewise perished, as the collapse of the Roman Empire, Han dynasty China, and the Maya cities reminds us. They were followed by yet a third wave of civilizations, from roughly 500 to 1500 C.E. (see Part Three). Some of them represented the persistence or renewal of older patterns, as in the case of China, for example, while elsewhere—such as in Western Europe, Russia, Japan, and West Africa—newer civilizations emerged, all of which borrowed heavily from their more-established neighbors. The largest of these, Islamic civilization, incorporated a number of older centers of civilization, Egypt and Mesopotamia, for example, under the umbrella of a new religion. Thus the globalization of civilization continued apace. So too did the interaction of civilizations with one another and with the gathering and hunting peoples, agricultural village societies, and pastoral communities who were their neighbors.

Continuities in Civilization

As this account of the human journey moves into the second and third waves of civilization, the question arises as to how they differed from the first ones. From a panoramic perspective, the answer is "not much." States and empires rose, expanded, and collapsed with a tiresome regularity. It is arguable, however, that little fundamental change occurred amid these constant fluctuations. Monarchs continued to rule most of the new civilizations; women remained subordinate to men in all of them; a sharp divide between the elite and everyone else persisted almost everywhere, as did the practice of slavery.

Furthermore, no technological or economic breakthrough occurred to create new kinds of human societies as the Agricultural Revolution had done earlier or as the Industrial Revolution would do much later. Landowning elites had little incentive to innovate, for they benefited enormously from simply expropriating the surplus that peasant farmers produced. Nor would peasants have any reason to invest much effort in creating new forms of production when they knew full well that any gains they might generate would be seized by their social superiors. Merchants, who often were risk takers, might have spawned innovations, but they usually were dominated by powerful states and were viewed with suspicion and condescension by more prestigious social groups.

Many fluctuations, repetitive cycles, and minor changes characterize this long era of agricultural civilization, but no fundamental or revolutionary transformation of social or economic life took place. The major turning points in human history had occurred earlier with the emergence of agriculture and the birth of the First Civilizations and would occur later with the breakthrough of industrialization.

Changes in Civilization

While this panoramic perspective allows us to see the broadest outlines of the human journey, it also obscures much of great importance that took place during the second and third waves of the age of agrarian civilization. If we zoom in a bit more closely, significant changes emerge, even if they did not result in a thorough transformation of human life. Population, for example, grew more rapidly than ever before during this period, as the Snapshot illustrates. Even though the overall trend was up, important fluctuations interrupted the pattern, especially during the first millennium C.E., when little overall growth took place. Moreover, the rate of growth, though rapid in comparison with Paleolithic times, was quite slow if we measure it against the explosive expansion of recent centuries, when human numbers quadrupled in the twentieth century alone. This modest and interrupted pattern of population growth during the age of agrarian civilization reflected the absence of any fundamental economic breakthrough, which could have supported much larger numbers.

Another change lies in the growing size of the states or empires that structured civilizations. The Roman, Persian, Indian, and Chinese empires of second-wave civilizations, as well as the Arab, Mongol, and Inca empires of the third wave, all dwarfed the city-states of Mesopotamia and the Egypt of the pharaohs. Each of these empires brought together in a single political system a vast diversity

SNAPSHOT   World Population during the Age of Agricultural Civilization[1]

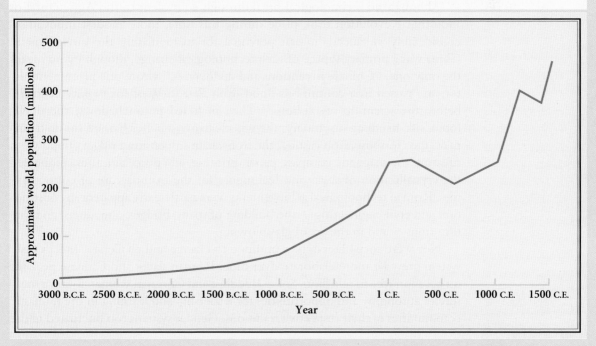

of peoples. Even so, just to keep things in perspective, as late as the seventeenth century C.E., only one-third of the world's landmass was under the control of any state-based system, although these societies now encompassed a considerable majority of the world's people.

The rise and fall of these empires likewise represented very consequential changes to the people who experienced them. In the course of its growth, the Roman Empire utterly destroyed the city of Carthage in North Africa, with the conquerors allegedly sowing the ground with salt so that nothing would ever grow there again. Similar bloodshed and destruction accompanied the creation of other much-celebrated states. Their collapse also had a dramatic impact on the lives of their people. Scholars have estimated that the large population of Maya civilization shrank by some 85 percent in less than a century as that society dissolved around 840 C.E. It is difficult to imagine the sense of trauma and bewilderment associated with a collapse of this magnitude.

Second- and third-wave civilizations also generated important innovations in many spheres. Those in the cultural realm have been perhaps the most widespread and enduring. Distinctive "wisdom traditions"—the great philosophical/religious systems of Confucianism and Daoism in China; Hinduism and Buddhism in India; Greek rationalism in the Mediterranean; and Judaism, Zoroastrianism, Christianity, and Islam in the Middle East—have provided the moral and spiritual framework within which most of the world's peoples have sought to order their lives and define their relationship to the mysteries of life and death. All of these philosophical and religious systems are the product of second- and third-wave civilizations.

Although no technological breakthrough equivalent to the Agricultural or Industrial Revolution took place during this time, more modest innovations considerably enhanced human potential for manipulating the environment. China was a primary source of such technological change, though by no means the only one. "Chinese inventions and discoveries," wrote one prominent historian, "passed in a continuous flood from East to West for twenty centuries before the scientific revolution."[2] They included piston bellows, the drawloom, silk-handling machinery, the wheelbarrow, a better harness for draft animals, the crossbow, iron casting, the iron-chain suspension bridge, gunpowder, firearms, the magnetic compass, paper, printing, and porcelain. India pioneered the crystallization of sugar and techniques for the manufacture of cotton textiles. Roman technological achievements were particularly apparent in construction and civil engineering—the building of roads, bridges, aqueducts, and fortifications—and in the art of glassblowing.

Nor were social hierarchies immune to change and challenge. India's caste system grew far more elaborate over time. Roman slaves and Chinese peasants on occasion rose in rebellion. Some Buddhist and Christian women found a measure of autonomy and opportunities for leadership and learning in the monastic communities of their respective traditions. Gender systems too fluctuated in the intensity with which women were subordinated to men. Generally women were less restricted in the initial phase of a civilization's development and during times of disruption, while patriarchy limited women more sharply as a civilization matured and stabilized.

A further process of change following the end of the First Civilizations lay in the emergence of far more elaborate, widespread, and dense networks of communication and exchange that connected many of the world's peoples to one another. Many of the technologies mentioned here diffused widely across large areas, as did the religious and cultural traditions of second- and third-wave civilizations. Long-distance trade routes represented another form of transregional interaction. Caravan trade across northern Eurasia, seaborne commerce within the Indian Ocean basin, the exchange of goods across the Sahara, river-based commerce in the eastern woodlands of North America, various trading networks radiating from Mesoamerica—all of these carried goods, and sometimes disease, technology, culture, and religion as well. In the early centuries of the Common Era, for example, Southeast Asia attracted distant merchants and some settlers from both China and India, bringing Confucianism, Hinduism, and Buddhism to various parts of that vast region. Disease also increasingly linked distant human communities. According to the famous Greek historian Thucydides, a mysterious plague "from parts of Ethiopia above Egypt" descended on Athens in 430 B.C.E., decimating the city.[3]

In all of these ways, the world became quite different from what it had been in the age of the First Civilizations, even though fundamental economic and social patterns had not substantially changed.

The first three chapters of Part Two focus in a thematic fashion on the Eurasian / North African civilizations of the second-wave era (500 B.C.E.–500 C.E.), which hosted the vast majority of the world's population, some 80 percent or more. Chapter 3 introduces them by examining and comparing their political frameworks and especially the empires (great or terrible, depending on your point of view) that took shape in most of them. Far more enduring than their empires were the cultural or religious traditions that second-wave civilizations generated. These are examined, also comparatively, in Chapter 4. The social life of these civilizations, expressed in class, caste, slavery, and gender relationships, also varied considerably, as Chapter 5 spells out. In Chapter 6, the historical spotlight turns to inner Africa, the Americas, and Pacific Oceania during the second-wave era, asking whether their histories paralleled Eurasian patterns or explored alternative possibilities.

In recalling this second-wave phase of the human journey, we will have occasion to compare the experiences of its various peoples, to note their remarkable achievements, to lament the tragedies that befell them and the suffering to which they gave rise, and to ponder their continuing power to fascinate us still.

MAPPING PART TWO

Ancestral Pueblo
Chapter 6

Mound Builders
Chapter 6

Maya / Teotihuacán
Chapter 6

Chavín / Moche
Chapter 6

Wari / Tiwanaku
Chapter 6

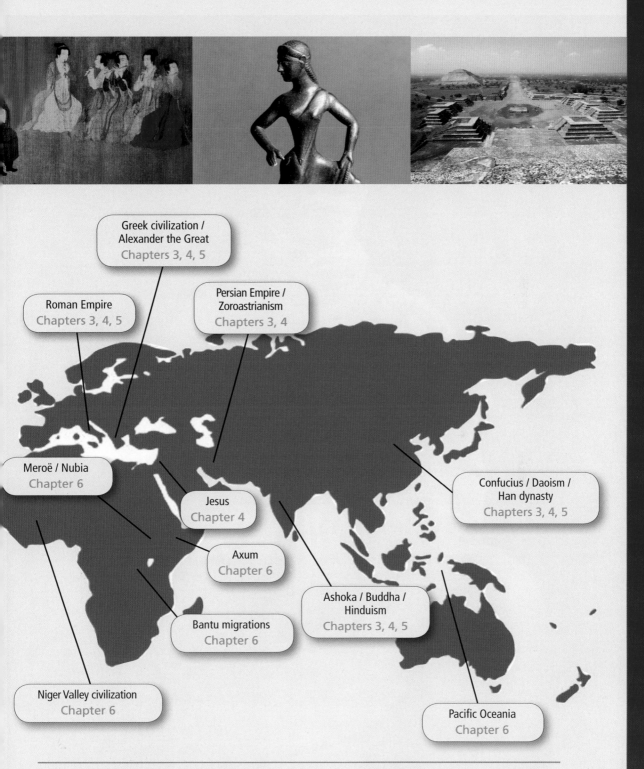

Greek civilization /
Alexander the Great
Chapters 3, 4, 5

Persian Empire /
Zoroastrianism
Chapters 3, 4

Roman Empire
Chapters 3, 4, 5

Meroë / Nubia
Chapter 6

Jesus
Chapter 4

Confucius / Daoism /
Han dynasty
Chapters 3, 4, 5

Axum
Chapter 6

Ashoka / Buddha /
Hinduism
Chapters 3, 4, 5

Bantu migrations
Chapter 6

Niger Valley civilization
Chapter 6

Pacific Oceania
Chapter 6

CHAPTER 3

State and Empire in Eurasia/North Africa

500 B.C.E.–500 C.E.

Are We Rome? It was the title of a thoughtful book, published in 2007, asking what had become a familiar question in the early twenty-first century: "Is the United States the new Roman Empire?"[1] With the collapse of the Soviet Union by 1991 and the subsequent U.S. invasions of Afghanistan and Iraq, some commentators began to make the comparison. The United States' enormous multicultural society, its technological achievements, its economically draining and overstretched armed forces, its sense of itself as unique and endowed with a global mission, its concern about foreigners penetrating its borders, its apparent determination to maintain military superiority—all of this invited comparison with the Roman Empire. Supporters of a dominant role for the United States argued that Americans must face up to their responsibilities as "the undisputed master of the world" as the Romans did in their time. Critics warned that the Roman Empire became overextended abroad and corrupt and dictatorial at home and then collapsed, suggesting that a similar fate may await the U.S. empire. Either way, the point of reference was an empire that had passed into history some 1,500 years earlier, a continuing reminder of the significance of the distant past to our contemporary world. In fact, for at least several centuries, that empire has been a source of metaphors and "lessons" about personal morality, corruption, political life, military expansion, and much more.

Even in a world largely critical of empires, they still excite the imagination of historians and readers of history alike. The earliest ones show up in the era of the First Civilizations when Akkadian, Babylonian, and Assyrian empires encompassed the city-states of Mesopotamia and established an enduring imperial tradition in the Middle East.

Terra-Cotta Archer Part of the immense funerary complex constructed for the Chinese ruler Qin Shihuangdi, this kneeling archer represents the military power that reunified a divided China under the Qin dynasty in 221 B.C.E.

Egypt became an imperial state when it temporarily ruled Nubia and the lands of the eastern Mediterranean. Following in their wake were many more empires, whose rise and fall have been central features of world history for the past 4,000 years.

But what exactly is an empire? At one level, empires are simply states, political systems that exercise coercive power. The term, however, is normally reserved for larger and more aggressive states, those that conquer, rule, and extract resources from other states and peoples. Thus empires have generally encompassed a considerable variety of peoples and cultures within a single political system, and they have often been associated with political or cultural oppression. Frequently, empires have given political expression to a civilization or culture, as in the Chinese and Persian empires. But civilizations have also flourished without a single all-encompassing state or empire, as in the competing city-states of Mesopotamia, Greece, and Mesoamerica or the many rival states of post-Roman Europe. In such cases, civilizations were expressed in elements of a common culture rather than in a unified political system.

The Eurasian empires of the second-wave era—those of Persia, Greece under Alexander the Great, Rome, China during the Qin (chihn) and Han dynasties, and India during the Mauryan (MORE-yuhn) and Gupta dynasties—shared a set of common problems. Would they seek to impose the culture of the imperial heartland on their varied subjects? Would they rule conquered people directly or through established local authorities? How could they extract the wealth of empire in the form of taxes, tribute, and labor while maintaining order in conquered territories? And, no matter how impressive they were at their peak, they all sooner or later collapsed, providing a useful reminder to their descendants of the fleeting nature of all human projects.

Why have these and other empires been of such lasting fascination to both ancient and modern people? Perhaps in part because they were so big, creating a looming presence in their respective regions. Their armies and their tax collectors were hard to avoid. Maybe also because they were so bloody. The violence of conquest easily grabs our attention, and certainly all of these empires were founded and sustained at a great cost in human life. The collapse of these once-powerful states is likewise intriguing, for the fall of the mighty seems somehow satisfying, perhaps even a delayed form of justice. The study of empires also sets off by contrast those times and places in which civilizations have prospered without an enduring imperial state.

But empires have also commanded attention simply because they were important. While the political values of recent times have almost universally condemned empire building, very large numbers of people—probably the majority of humankind before the twentieth century—have lived out their lives in empires, where they were often governed by rulers culturally different from themselves. These imperial states brought together people of quite different traditions and religions and so stimulated the exchange of ideas, cultures, and values. Despite their violence, exploitation, and oppression, empires also imposed substantial periods of

A MAP OF TIME

750–336 B.C.E.	Era of Greek city-states
553–330 B.C.E.	Persian Achaemenid Empire
509 B.C.E.	Founding of the Roman Republic
500–221 B.C.E.	Chinese age of warring states
490 and 480 B.C.E.	Major battles between Persians and Greeks
479–429 B.C.E.	Golden Age of Athens
431–404 B.C.E.	Peloponnesian War
336–323 B.C.E.	Reign of Alexander the Great
326–184 B.C.E.	India's Mauryan dynasty empire
221–206 B.C.E.	China's Qin dynasty empire
206 B.C.E.–220 C.E.	China's Han dynasty empire
200 B.C.E.–200 C.E.	High point of Roman Empire
1st century B.C.E.	Transition from republic to empire in Rome
184 C.E.	Yellow Turban Rebellion in China
220 C.E.	Collapse of Chinese Han dynasty
320–550 C.E.	India's Gupta dynasty empire
5th century C.E.	Collapse of western Roman Empire

peace and security, which fostered economic and artistic development, commercial exchange, and cultural mixing. In many places, empire also played an important role in defining masculinity, as conquest generated a warrior culture that gave particular prominence to the men who created and ruled those imperial states.

SEEKING THE MAIN POINT

How might you assess—both positively and negatively—the role of empires in the history of the second-wave era?

Empires and Civilizations in Collision: The Persians and the Greeks

The millennium between 500 B.C.E. and 500 C.E. in North Africa and Eurasia witnessed the flowering of second-wave civilizations in the Mediterranean world, the Middle East, India, and China. For the most part, these distant civilizations did not directly encounter one another, as each established its own political system, cultural values, and ways of organizing society. A great exception to that rule lay in the Mediterranean world and in the Middle East, where the emerging Persian Empire and Greek civilization, physically adjacent to each other, experienced a centuries-long interaction and clash. It was one of the most consequential cultural encounters of the ancient world. (For another example of contact among second-wave empires, see the Zooming In feature on the Kushan Empire, page 128.)

The Persian Empire

In 500 B.C.E., the largest and most impressive of the world's empires was that of the Persians, an Indo-European people whose homeland lay on the Iranian plateau just north of the Persian Gulf. Living on the margins of the earlier Mesopotamian civilization, the Persians under the Achaemenid (ah-KEE-muh-nid) dynasty (553–330 B.C.E.) constructed an imperial system that drew on previous examples, such as the Babylonian and Assyrian empires, but far surpassed them all in size and splendor. Under the leadership of the famous monarchs Cyrus (r. 557–530 B.C.E.) and Darius (r. 522–486 B.C.E.), Persian conquests quickly reached from Egypt to India, encompassing in a single state some 35 to 50 million people, an immensely diverse realm containing dozens of peoples, states, languages, and cultural traditions (see Map 3.1).

■ **Comparison**

How did Persian and Greek civilizations differ in their political organization and values?

The Persian Empire centered on an elaborate cult of kingship in which the monarch, secluded in royal magnificence, could be approached only through an elaborate ritual. When the king died, sacred fires all across the land were extinguished, Persians were expected to shave their hair in mourning, and the manes of horses were cut short. Ruling by the will of the great Persian god Ahura Mazda (uh-HOORE-uh MAHZ-duh), kings were absolute monarchs, more than willing to crush rebellious regions or officials. Interrupted on one occasion while he was with his wife, Darius ordered the offender, a high-ranking nobleman, killed, along with his entire clan. In the eyes of many, Persian monarchs fully deserved their effusive title—"Great king, King of kings, King of countries containing all kinds of men, King in this great earth far and wide." Darius himself best expressed the authority of the Persian ruler when he observed, "What was said to them by me, night and day, it was done."[2]

But more than conquest and royal decree sustained the empire. An effective administrative system placed Persian governors, called *satraps* (SAY-traps), in each of the empire's twenty-three provinces, while lower-level officials were drawn from local authorities. A system of imperial spies, known as the "eyes and ears of the King," represented a further imperial presence in the far reaches of the empire. A general policy of respect for the empire's many non-Persian cultural traditions also cemented the state's authority. Cyrus won the gratitude of the Jews when in 539 B.C.E. he allowed those exiled in Babylon to return to their homeland and rebuild their temple in Jerusalem (see Chapter 4, pages 166–67). In Egypt and Babylon, Persian kings took care to uphold local religious cults in an effort to gain the support of their followers and officials. The Greek historian Herodotus commented that "there is no nation which so readily adopts foreign customs. They have taken the dress of the Medes and in war they wear the Egyptian breastplate.

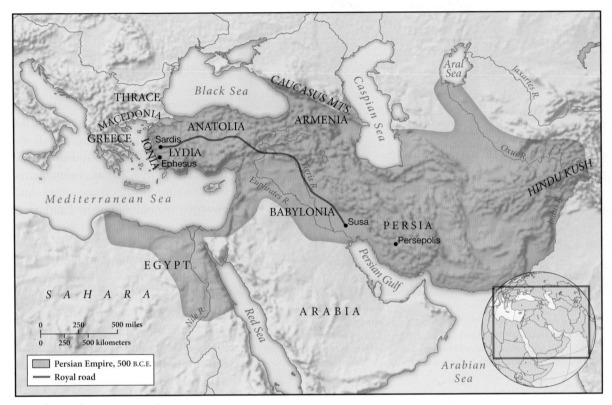

Map 3.1   The Persian Empire

At its height, the Persian Empire was the largest in the world. It dominated the lands of the First Civilizations in the Middle East and was commercially connected to neighboring regions.

As soon as they hear of any luxury, they instantly make it their own."[3] (See more on Herodotus's perceptions of Persia in Working with Evidence, Source 3.1, page 137.) For the next 1,000 years or more, Persian imperial bureaucracy and court life, replete with administrators, tax collectors, record keepers, and translators, provided a model for all subsequent regimes in the region, including, later, those of the Islamic world.

The infrastructure of empire included a system of standardized coinage, predictable taxes levied on each province, and a newly dug canal linking the Nile with the Red Sea, which greatly expanded commerce and enriched Egypt. A "royal road," some 1,700 miles in length, facilitated communication and commerce across this vast empire. Caravans of merchants could traverse this highway in three months, but agents of the imperial courier service, using a fresh supply of horses every twenty-five to thirty miles, could carry a message from one end of the road to another in a week or two. Herodotus was impressed. "Neither snow, nor rain, nor heat, nor darkness of night," he wrote, "prevents them from accomplishing the task proposed to them with utmost speed." And an elaborate underground irrigation

Persepolis
The largest palace in Persepolis, the Persian Empire's ancient capital, was the Audience Hall. The emperor officially greeted visiting dignitaries at this palace, which was constructed around 500 B.C.E. This relief, which shows a lion attacking a bull and Persian guards at attention, adorns a staircase leading to the Audience Hall. (Giraudon/Bridgeman Images)

system sustained a rich agricultural economy in the semi-arid conditions of the Iranian plateau and spread from there throughout the Middle East and beyond.

Elaborate imperial centers, particularly Susa and Persepolis, reflected the immense wealth and power of the Persian Empire. Palaces, audience halls, quarters for the harem, monuments, and carvings made these cities into powerful symbols of imperial authority. Materials and workers alike were drawn from all corners of the empire and beyond. Inscribed in the foundation of Persepolis was Darius's commentary on what he had set in motion: "And Ahura Mazda was of such a mind, together with all the other gods, that this fortress [should] be built. And [so] I built it. And I built it secure and beautiful and adequate, just as I was intending to."[4]

The Greeks

It would be hard to imagine a sharper contrast than that between the huge and centralized Persian Empire, governed by an absolute and almost unapproachable monarch, and the small competing city-states of classical Greece, which allowed varying degrees of popular participation in political life. Like the Persians, the Greeks were an Indo-European people whose early history drew on the legacy of the First Civilizations. The classical Greece of historical fame emerged around 750 B.C.E. as a new civilization and flourished for about 400 years before it was incorporated into a succession of foreign empires. During that relatively short period, the civilization of Athens and Sparta, of Plato and Aristotle, of Zeus and Apollo took shape and collided with its giant neighbor to the east.

Calling themselves Hellenes, the Greeks created a civilization that was distinctive in many ways, particularly in comparison with that of the Persians. The total population of Greece and the Aegean basin was just 2 million to 3 million, a fraction of that of the Persian Empire. Furthermore, Greek civilization took shape on a small peninsula, deeply divided by steep mountains and valleys. Its geography certainly contributed to the political shape of that civilization, which found expression not in a Persian-style empire, but in hundreds of city-states or small settlements (see Map 3.2). Most were quite modest in size, with between 500 and 5,000 male

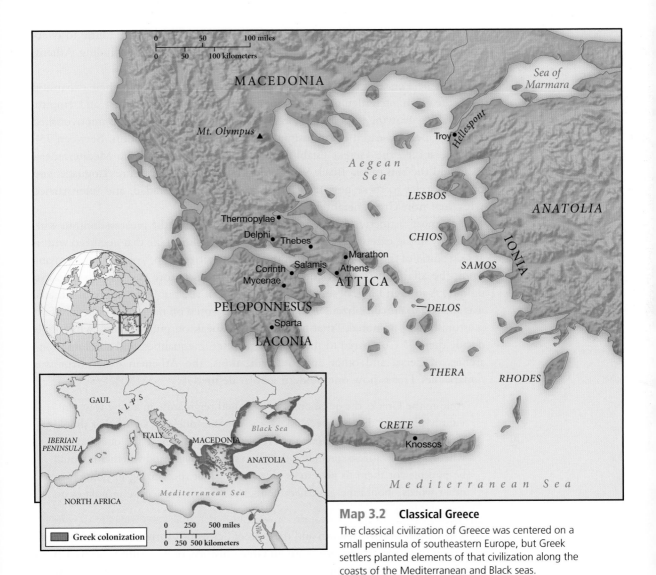

Map 3.2   Classical Greece

The classical civilization of Greece was centered on a small peninsula of southeastern Europe, but Greek settlers planted elements of that civilization along the coasts of the Mediterranean and Black seas.

citizens. But Greek civilization, like its counterparts elsewhere, also left a decisive environmental mark on the lands it encompassed. Smelting metals such as silver, lead, copper, bronze, and iron required enormous supplies of wood, leading to deforestation and soil erosion. Plato declared that the area around Athens had become "a mere relic of the original country. . . . All the rich soil has melted away, leaving a country of skin and bone."[5]

Each of these city-states was fiercely independent and in frequent conflict with its neighbors, yet they had much in common, speaking the same language and worshipping the same gods. Every four years they temporarily suspended their continual conflicts to participate together in the Olympic Games, which had begun

■ **Change**

How did semidemocratic governments emerge in some of the Greek city-states?

in 776 B.C.E. But this emerging sense of Greek cultural identity did little to overcome the endemic political rivalries of the larger city-states, including Athens, Sparta, Thebes, and Corinth, among many others.

Like the Persians, the Greeks were an expansive people, but their expansion took the form of settlement in distant places rather than conquest and empire. Pushed by a growing population, Greek traders in search of iron and impoverished Greek farmers in search of land stimulated a remarkable emigration. Between 750 and 500 B.C.E., the Greeks established settlements all around the Mediterranean basin and the rim of the Black Sea. Settlers brought Greek culture, language, and building styles to these new lands, even as they fought, traded, and intermarried with their non-Greek neighbors.

The most distinctive feature of Greek civilization, and the greatest contrast with Persia, lay in the extent of popular participation in political life that occurred within at least some of the city-states. It was the idea of "citizenship," of free people managing the affairs of state, of equality for all citizens before the law, that was so unique. A foreign king, observing the operation of the public assembly in Athens, was amazed that male citizens as a whole actually voted on matters of policy: "I find it astonishing," he noted, "that here wise men speak on public affairs, while fools decide them."[6] Compared to the rigid hierarchies, inequalities, and absolute monarchies of Persia and other ancient civilizations, the Athenian experiment was remarkable. This is how one modern scholar defined it:

> Among the Greeks the question of who should reign arose in a new way. Previously the most that had been asked was whether one man or another should govern and whether one alone or several together. But now the question was whether all the citizens, including the poor, might govern and whether it would be possible for them to govern as citizens, without specializing in politics. In other words, should the governed themselves actively participate in politics on a regular basis?[7]

The extent of participation and the role of "citizens" varied considerably, both over time and from city to city. Early in Greek history, only wealthy and well-born men had the rights of full citizenship, such as speaking and voting in the assembly, holding public office, and fighting in the army. Gradually, men of the lower classes, mostly small-scale farmers, also obtained these rights. At least in part, this broadening of political rights was associated with the growing number of men able to afford the armor and weapons that would allow them to serve as hoplites, or infantrymen, in the armies of the city-states. In many places, strong but benevolent rulers known as tyrants emerged for a time, usually with the support of the poorer classes, to challenge the prerogatives of the wealthy. Sparta—famous for its extreme forms of military discipline and its large population of helots, conquered people who lived in slave-like conditions—vested most political authority in its Council of Elders. The council was composed of twenty-eight men over the age of sixty, derived from the wealthier and more influential segment of society, who served for life and provided political leadership for Sparta.

It was in Athens that the Greek experiment in political participation achieved its most distinctive expression. Early steps in this direction were the product of intense class conflict, leading almost to civil war. A reforming leader named Solon emerged in 594 B.C.E. to push Athenian politics in a more democratic direction, breaking the hold of a small group of aristocratic families. Debt slavery was abolished, access to public office was opened to a wider group of men, and all citizens were allowed to take part in the Assembly. Later reformers such as Cleisthenes (KLEYE-sthuh-nees) and Pericles extended the rights of citizens even further. By 450 B.C.E., all holders of public office were chosen by lot and were paid, so that even the poorest could serve. The Assembly, where all citizens could participate, became the center of political life.

Athenian democracy, however, was different from modern democracy. It was direct, rather than representative, democracy, and it was distinctly limited. Women, slaves, and foreigners, together far more than half of the population, were wholly excluded from political participation. Nonetheless, political life in Athens was a world away from that of the Persian Empire and even from that of many other Greek cities.

Collision: The Greco-Persian Wars

In recent centuries, many writers and scholars have claimed classical Greece as the foundation of Western or European civilization. But the ancient Greeks themselves looked primarily to the East—to Egypt and the Persian Empire. In Egypt, Greek scholars found impressive mathematical and astronomical traditions on which they built. And Persia represented both an immense threat and later, under Alexander the Great, an opportunity for Greek empire building.

If ever there was an unequal conflict between civilizations, surely it was the collision of the Greeks and the Persians. The confrontation between the small and divided Greek cities and Persia, the world's largest empire, grew out of their respective patterns of expansion. A number of Greek settlements on the Anatolian seacoast, known to the Greeks as Ionia, came under Persian control as that empire extended its domination to the west. In 499 B.C.E., some of these Ionian Greek cities revolted against Persian domination and found support from Athens on the Greek mainland. Outraged by this assault from the remote and upstart Greeks, the Persians, twice in ten years (490 and 480 B.C.E.), launched major military expeditions to punish the Greeks in general and Athens in particular. Against all odds and all expectations, the Greeks held them off, defeating the Persians on both land and sea.

Though no doubt embarrassing, their defeat on the far western fringes of the empire had little effect on the Persians. However, it had a profound impact on the Greeks and especially on Athens, whose forces had led the way to victory. Beating the Persians in battle was a source of enormous pride for Greece. Years later, elderly Athenian men asked one another how old they had been when the Greeks triumphed in the momentous Battle of Marathon in 490 B.C.E. In their view, this

■ **Connection**
What were the consequences for both sides of the encounter between the Persians and the Greeks?

victory was the product of Greek freedoms because those freedoms had motivated men to fight with extraordinary courage for what they valued so highly. It led to a Western worldview in which Persia represented Asia and despotism, whereas Greece signified Europe and freedom. Thus was born the notion of an East/West divide, which has shaped European and North American thinking about the world into the twenty-first century.

The Greek victory also radicalized Athenian democracy, for it had been men of the poorer classes who had rowed their ships to victory and who were now in a position to insist on full citizenship. The fifty years or so after the Greco-Persian Wars were not only the high point of Athenian democracy but also the Golden Age of Greek culture. During this period, the Parthenon, that marvelous temple to the Greek goddess Athena, was built; Greek theater was born from the work of Aeschylus, Sophocles, and Euripides; and Socrates was beginning his career as a philosopher and an irritant in Athens.

But Athens's Golden Age was also an era of incipient empire. In the Greco-Persian Wars, Athens had led a coalition of more than thirty Greek city-states on the basis of its naval power, but Athenian leadership in the struggle against Persian aggression had spawned an imperialism of its own. After the war, Athenian efforts to solidify Athens's dominant position among the allies led to intense resentment and finally to a bitter civil war (431–404 B.C.E.), with Sparta taking the lead in defending the traditional independence of Greek city-states. In this bloody conflict, known as the Peloponnesian War, Athens was defeated, while the Greeks exhausted themselves and magnified their distrust of one another. Thus the way was open to their eventual takeover by the growing forces of Macedonia, a frontier kingdom on the northern fringes of the Greek world. The glory days of the Greek experiment were over, but the spread of Greek culture was just beginning.

Collision: Alexander and the Hellenistic Era

The Macedonian takeover of Greece, led by its king, Philip II, finally accomplished by 338 B.C.E. what the Greeks themselves had been unable to achieve—the political unification of Greece, but at the cost of much of the prized independence of its various city-states. It also set in motion a second round in the collision of Greece and Persia as Philip's son, Alexander, prepared to lead a massive Greek expedition against the Persian Empire. Such a project appealed to those who sought vengeance for the earlier Persian assault on Greece, but it also served to unify the fractious Greeks in a war against their common enemy.

■ **Connection**
What changes did Alexander's conquests bring in their wake?

The story of this ten-year expedition (333–323 B.C.E.), accomplished while Alexander was still in his twenties, has become the stuff of legend (see Map 3.3). Surely it was among the greatest military feats of the ancient world in that it created a Greek empire from Egypt and Anatolia in the west to Afghanistan and India in the east. In the process, the great Persian Empire was thoroughly defeated; its capital, Persepolis (per-SEP-uh-lis), was looted and burned; and Alexander was hailed as

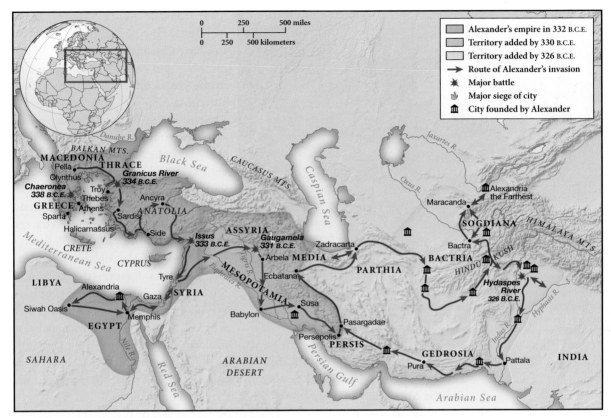

Map 3.3   Alexander's Empire and Successor States

Alexander's conquests, though enormous, did not long remain within a single empire, for his generals divided them into three successor states shortly after his death. This was the Hellenistic world within which Greek culture spread.

the "king of Asia." In Egypt, Alexander, then just twenty-four years old, was celebrated as a liberator from Persian domination, was anointed as pharaoh, and was declared by Egyptian priests to be the "son of the gods." Arrian, a later Greek historian, described Alexander in this way:

> His passion was for glory only, and in that he was insatiable. . . . Noble indeed was his power of inspiring his men, of filling them with confidence, and in the moment of danger, of sweeping away their fear by the spectacle of his own fearlessness.[8]

Alexander died in 323 B.C.E., without returning to Greece, and his empire was soon divided into three kingdoms, ruled by leading Macedonian generals.

From the viewpoint of world history, the chief significance of Alexander's amazing conquests lay in the widespread dissemination of Greek culture during what historians call the Hellenistic era (323–30 B.C.E.). Elements of that culture, generated

Alexander the Great
This mosaic of Alexander on horseback comes from the Roman city of Pompeii. It depicts the Battle of Issus (333 B.C.E.), in which Greek forces, although considerably outnumbered, defeated the Persian army, led personally by Emperor Darius III. (Museo Archeologico Nazionale, Naples, Italy/De Agostini Picture Library/G. Nimatallah/Bridgeman Images)

in a small and remote Mediterranean peninsula, now penetrated the lands of the First Civilizations—Egypt, Mesopotamia, and India—resulting in one of the great cultural encounters of the ancient world.

The major avenue for the spread of Greek culture lay in the many cities that Alexander and later Hellenistic rulers established throughout the empire. Complete with Greek monuments, sculptures, theaters, markets, councils, and assemblies, these cities attracted many thousands of Greek settlers serving as state officials, soldiers, or traders. Alexandria in Egypt—the largest of these cities, with half a million people— was an enormous cosmopolitan center where Egyptians, Greeks, Jews, Babylonians, Syrians, Persians, and many others rubbed elbows. A harbor with space for 1,200 ships facilitated long-distance commerce. Greek learning flourished thanks to a library of some 700,000 volumes and the Museum, which sponsored scholars and writers of all kinds.

From cities such as these, Greek culture spread. From the Mediterranean to India, Greek became the language of power and elite culture. The Indian monarch Ashoka published some of his decrees in Greek, while an independent Greek state was established in Bactria in what is now northern Afghanistan. The attraction of many young Jews to Greek culture prompted the Pharisees to develop their own school system, as this highly conservative Jewish sect feared for the very survival of Judaism. (See Zooming In: The Kushan Empire, page 128, for Greek influence on this Central Asian kingdom.)

Cities such as Alexandria were very different from the original city-states of Greece, both in their cultural diversity and in the absence of the independence so valued by Athens and Sparta. Now they were part of large conquest states ruled by Greeks: the Ptolemaic (TOL-uh-MAY-ik) empire in Egypt and the Seleucid empire in Persia. These were imperial states, which, in their determination to preserve order, raise taxes, and maintain the authority of the monarch, resembled the much older empires of Mesopotamia, Egypt, Assyria, and Persia. Macedonians and Greeks, representing perhaps 10 percent of the population in these Hellenistic kingdoms, were clearly the elite and sought to keep themselves separate from non-Greeks. In Egypt, different legal systems for Greeks and native Egyptians maintained this separation. An Egyptian agricultural worker complained that because he was an Egyptian, his supervisors despised him and refused to pay him.[9] Periodic rebellions expressed resentment at Greek arrogance, condescension, and exploitation. But the separation between the Greeks and native populations was by no means complete, and a fair amount of cultural interaction and blending occurred. Alexander himself had taken several Persian princesses as his wives and actively encouraged intermarriage between his troops and Asian women. In both Egypt and Mesopotamia, Greek rulers patronized the building of temples to local gods and actively supported their priests. A growing number of native peoples were able to become Greek citizens by obtaining a Greek education, speaking the language, dressing appropriately, and assuming Greek names. In India, Greeks were assimilated into the hierarchy of the caste system as members of the Kshatriya (warrior) caste, while in Bactria a substantial number of Greeks converted to Buddhism, including one of their kings, Menander. A school of Buddhist art that emerged in the early centuries of the Common Era depicted the Buddha in human form for the first time, but in Greek-like garb with a face resembling the god Apollo. (See Working with Evidence, Source 4.2, page 186.) Clearly, not all was conflict between the Greeks and the peoples of the East.

In the long run, much of this Greek cultural influence faded as the Hellenistic kingdoms that had promoted it weakened and vanished by the first century B.C.E. While it lasted, however, it represented a remarkable cultural encounter, born of the collision of two empires and two second-wave civilizations. In the western part of that Hellenistic world, Greek rule was replaced by that of the Romans, whose empire, like Alexander's, also served as a vehicle for the continued spread of Greek culture and ideas.

Comparing Empires: Roman and Chinese

While the adjacent civilizations of the Greeks and the Persians collided, two other empires were taking shape—the Roman Empire on the far western side of Eurasia and China's imperial state on the far eastern end. They flourished at roughly the same time (200 B.C.E.–200 C.E.); they occupied a similar area (about 1.5 million square miles); and they encompassed populations of a similar size (50 to 60 million). They were the giant empires of their time, shaping the lives of close to half of the world's population. Unlike the Greeks and the Persians, the Romans and the Chinese were only dimly aware of each other and had almost no direct contact. Historians, however, have seen them as fascinating variations on an imperial theme and have long explored their similarities and differences.

Rome: From City-State to Empire

The rise of empires is among the perennial questions that historians tackle. Like the Persian Empire, that of the Romans took shape initially on the margins of the civilized world and was an unlikely rags-to-riches story. Rome began as a small and impoverished city-state on the western side of central Italy in the eighth century

B.C.E. According to legend, the city was so weak that Romans were reduced to kidnapping neighboring women to maintain its population. In a transformation of epic proportions, Rome subsequently became the center of an enormous imperial state that encompassed the Mediterranean basin and included parts of continental Europe, Britain, North Africa, and the Middle East.

Originally ruled by a king, around 509 B.C.E. Roman aristocrats threw off the monarchy and established a republic in which the men of a wealthy class, known as patricians, dominated. Executive authority was exercised by two consuls, who were advised by a patrician assembly, the Senate. Deepening conflict with the poorer classes, called plebeians (plih-BEE-uhns), led to important changes in Roman political life. A written code of law offered plebeians some protection from abuse; a system of public assemblies provided an opportunity for lower classes to shape public policy; and a new office of tribune, who represented plebeians, allowed them to block unfavorable legislation. Romans took great pride in this political system, believing that they enjoyed greater freedom than did many of their more autocratic neighbors. The values of the republic—rule of law, the rights of citizens, the absence of pretension, upright moral behavior, keeping one's word—were later idealized as "the way of the ancestors."

With this political system and these values, the Romans launched their empire-building enterprise, a prolonged process that took more than 500 years (see Map 3.4). It began in the 490s B.C.E. with Roman control over its Latin neighbors in central Italy and over the next several hundred years encompassed most of the Italian peninsula. Between 264 and 146 B.C.E., victory in the Punic Wars with Carthage, a powerful empire with its capital in North Africa, extended Roman control over the western Mediterranean, including Spain, and made Rome a naval power. Subsequent expansion in the eastern Mediterranean brought the ancient civilizations of Greece, Egypt, and Mesopotamia under Roman domination. Rome also expanded into territories in Southern and Western Europe, including present-day France and Britain. By early in the second century C.E., the Roman Empire had reached its maximum extent. Like classical Greece, that empire has been associated with Europe. But in its own time, elites in North Africa and Southwest Asia likewise claimed Roman identity, and the empire's richest provinces were in the east.

■ **Change**

How did Rome grow from a single city to the center of a huge empire?

No overall design or blueprint drove the building of empire, nor were there any precedents to guide the Romans. What they created was something wholly new—an empire that encompassed the entire Mediterranean basin and beyond. It was a piecemeal process, which the Romans invariably saw as defensive. Each addition of territory created new vulnerabilities, which could be assuaged only by more conquests. For some, the growth of empire represented opportunity. Poor soldiers hoped for land, loot, or salaries that might lift their families out of poverty. The well-to-do or well-connected gained great estates, earned promotions, and sometimes achieved public acclaim and high political office. The wealth of long-established societies in the eastern Mediterranean (Greece and Egypt, for example) beckoned, as did the resources and food supplies of the less developed regions, such

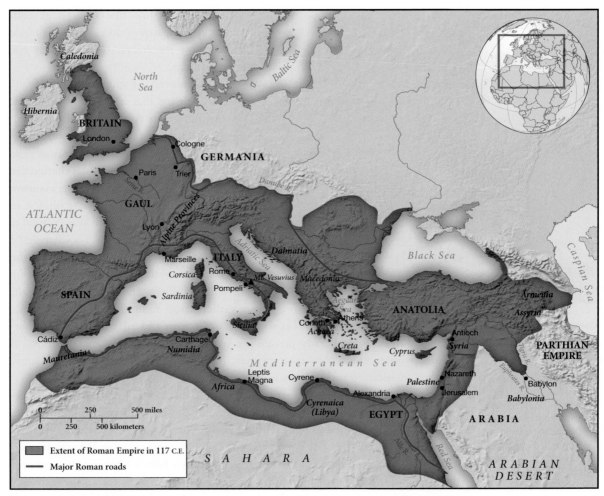

Map 3.4   The Roman Empire

At its height in the second century C.E., the Roman Empire incorporated the entire Mediterranean basin, including the lands of the Carthaginian Empire, the less developed region of Western Europe, the heartland of Greek civilization, and the ancient civilizations of Egypt and Mesopotamia.

as Western Europe. There was no shortage of motivation for the creation of the Roman Empire.

Although Rome's central location in the Mediterranean basin provided a convenient launching pad for empire, it was the army, "well-trained, well-fed, and well-rewarded," that built the empire.[10] Drawing on the growing population of Italy, that army was often brutal in war. Carthage, for example, was utterly destroyed; the city was razed to the ground, and its inhabitants were either killed or sold into slavery. Nonetheless, Roman authorities could be generous to former enemies. Some were granted Roman citizenship; others were treated as allies and allowed to maintain their local rulers. As the empire grew, so too did political

Queen Boudica
This statue in London commemorates the resistance of the Celtic people of eastern Britain against Roman rule during a revolt in 60–61 C.E., led by Queen Boudica. A later Roman historian lamented that "all this ruin was brought upon the Romans by a woman, a fact which in itself caused them the greatest shame." (Daniel Boulet, photographer)

forces in Rome that favored its continued expansion and were willing to commit the necessary manpower and resources.

Centuries of empire building and the warfare that made it possible had an impact on Roman society and values. That vast process, for example, shaped Roman understandings of gender and the appropriate roles of men and women. Rome was becoming a warrior society in which the masculinity of upper-class male citizens was defined in part by a man's role as a soldier and a property owner. In private life, this translated into absolute control over his wife, children, and slaves, including the theoretical right to kill them without interference from the state. This ability of a free man and a Roman citizen to act decisively in both public and private life lay at the heart of ideal male identity. A Roman woman could participate proudly in this warrior culture by bearing brave sons and inculcating these values in her offspring.

Strangely enough, by the early centuries of the Common Era the wealth of empire, the authority of the imperial state, and the breakdown of older Roman social patterns combined to offer women in the elite classes a less restricted life than they had known in the early centuries of the republic. Upper-class Roman women had never been as secluded in the home as were their Greek counterparts, and now the legal authority of their husbands was curtailed by the intrusion of the state into what had been private life. The head of household, or *pater familias*, lost his earlier power of life and death over his family. Furthermore, such women could now marry without transferring legal control to their husbands and were increasingly able to manage their own finances and take part in the growing commercial economy of the empire. According to one scholar, Roman women of the wealthier classes gained "almost complete liberty in matters of property and marriage."[11] At the other end of the social spectrum, Roman conquests brought many thousands of women as well as men into the empire as slaves, who were often brutally treated and subject to the whims of their masters (see Chapter 5, pages 203–8).

The relentless expansion of empire raised yet another profound question for Rome: could republican government and values survive the acquisition of a huge empire? The wealth of empire enriched a few, enabling them to acquire large estates and many slaves, while pushing growing numbers of free farmers into the cities and poverty. Imperial riches also empowered a small group of military leaders—

Marius, Sulla, Pompey, Julius Caesar—who recruited their troops directly from the ranks of the poor and whose fierce rivalries brought civil war to Rome during the first century B.C.E. Traditionalists lamented the apparent decline of republican values—simplicity, service, free farmers as the backbone of the army, the authority of the Senate—amid the self-seeking ambition of the newly rich and powerful. When the dust settled from the civil war, Rome was clearly changing, for authority was now vested primarily in an emperor, the first of whom was Octavian, later granted the title of Augustus (r. 27 B.C.E.–14 C.E.), which implied a divine status for the ruler. The republic was history; Rome had become an empire and its ruler an emperor.

But it was an empire with an uneasy conscience, for many felt that in acquiring an empire, Rome had betrayed and abandoned its republican origins. Augustus was careful to maintain the forms of the republic—the Senate, consuls, public assemblies—and referred to himself as "first man" rather than "king" or "emperor," even as he accumulated enormous personal power. And in a bow to republican values, he spoke of the empire's conquests as reflecting the "power of the Roman people" rather than of the Roman state. Despite this rhetoric, he was emperor in practice, if not in name, for he was able to exercise sole authority, backed up by his command of a professional army. Later emperors were less reluctant to flaunt their imperial prerogatives.

During the first two centuries C.E., this empire in disguise provided security, grandeur, and relative prosperity for the Mediterranean world. In 155 C.E., Aelius Aristides, one of the empire's Greek subjects from the west coast of Anatolia and himself a Roman citizen, expressed this perspective as he praised the empire to the sky in front of the emperor Antonius:

> Everywhere you have made citizens all those who are the more accomplished, noble and powerful people, even if they retain their native affinities. . . . No envy walks in your empire. . . . There has arisen a single harmonious government which has embraced all men. . . . And the whole inhabited world, as it were attending a national festival, has laid aside . . . the carrying of weapons. . . . Now it is possible for both Greek and barbarian to travel easily wherever he wishes.[12]

This was the *pax Romana*, the Roman peace, the era of imperial Rome's greatest extent and greatest authority.

China: From Warring States to Empire

About the same time, on the other side of Eurasia, another huge imperial state was in the making—China. Here, however, the task was understood differently. It was not a matter of creating something new, as in the case of the Roman Empire, but of restoring something old. As one of the First Civilizations, a Chinese state had emerged as early as 2200 B.C.E. and under the Xia, Shang, and Zhou dynasties had grown progressively larger. By 500 B.C.E., however, this Chinese state was in shambles. Any earlier unity vanished in an "age of warring states," featuring the endless rivalries of seven competing kingdoms.

■ **Comparison**

Why was the Chinese empire able to take shape so quickly, while that of the Romans took centuries?

To many Chinese, this was a wholly unnatural and unacceptable condition, and rulers in various states vied to reunify China. One of them, known to history as Qin Shihuangdi (chihn shee-HUANG-dee) (i.e., Shihuangdi from the state of Qin), succeeded brilliantly. The state of Qin had already developed an effective bureaucracy, subordinated its aristocracy, equipped its army with iron weapons, and enjoyed rapidly rising agricultural output and a growing population. It also had adopted a political philosophy called Legalism, which advocated clear rules and harsh punishments as a means of enforcing the authority of the state. With these resources, Shihuangdi (r. 221–210 B.C.E.) launched a military campaign to reunify China and in just ten years soundly defeated the other warring states. Believing that he had created a universal and eternal empire, he grandly named himself Shihuangdi, which means the "first emperor." Unlike Augustus, he showed little ambivalence about empire. Subsequent conquests extended China's boundaries far to the south into the northern part of Vietnam, to the northeast into Korea, and to the northwest, where the Chinese pushed back the nomadic pastoral people of the steppes. (See Zooming In: Trung Trac, page 124, for an example of resistance to Chinese expansion.) Although the boundaries fluctuated over time, Shihuangdi laid the foundations for a unified Chinese state, which has endured, with periodic interruptions, to the present (see Map 3.5).

Building on earlier precedents, the Chinese process of empire formation was far more compressed than the centuries-long Roman effort, but it was no less dependent on military force and no less brutal. Scholars who opposed Shihuangdi's policies were executed and their books burned. Aristocrats who might oppose his centralizing policies were moved physically to the capital. Hundreds of thousands of laborers were recruited to construct the Great Wall of China, designed to keep out northern "barbarians," and to erect a monumental mausoleum as the emperor's final resting place. More positively, Shihuangdi imposed a uniform system of weights, measures, and currency and standardized the length of axles for carts and the written form of the Chinese language.

As in Rome, the creation of the Chinese empire had domestic repercussions, but they were brief and superficial compared to Rome's transition from republic to empire. The speed and brutality of Shihuangdi's policies ensured that his own Qin dynasty did not last long, and it collapsed unmourned in 206 B.C.E. The Han dynasty that followed (206 B.C.E.–220 C.E.) retained the centralized features of Shihuangdi's creation, although it moderated the harshness of his policies, adopting a milder and moralistic Confucianism in place of Legalism as the governing philosophy of the state. It was Han dynasty rulers who consolidated China's imperial state and established the political patterns that lasted into the twentieth century.

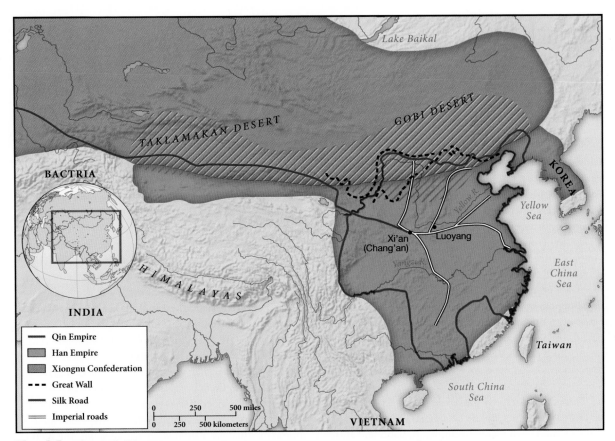

Map 3.5   Classical China

The brief Qin dynasty brought unity to the heartland of Chinese civilization, and the much longer Han dynasty extended its territorial reach south toward Vietnam, east to Korea, and west into Central Asia. To the north lay the military confederacy of the nomadic Xiongnu.

Consolidating the Roman and Chinese Empires

Once established, these two huge imperial systems shared a number of common features. Both, for example, defined themselves in universal terms. The Roman writer Polybius spoke of bringing "almost the entire world" under the control of Rome, while the Chinese state was said to encompass "all under heaven." Both of them invested heavily in public works—roads, bridges, aqueducts, canals, protective walls—all designed to integrate their respective domains militarily and commercially.

Furthermore, Roman and Chinese authorities both invoked supernatural sanctions to support their rule. By the first century C.E., Romans began to regard their deceased emperors as gods and established a religious cult to bolster the authority of living rulers. It was the refusal of early Christians to take part in this cult that provoked their periodic persecution by Roman authorities.

■ **Explanation**

Why were the Roman and Chinese empires able to enjoy long periods of relative stability and prosperity?

Trung Trac: Resisting the Chinese Empire

Empires have long faced resistance from people they conquer and never more fiercely than in Vietnam, which was incorporated into an expanding Chinese empire for over a thousand years (111 B.C.E.–939 C.E.). Among the earliest examples of Vietnamese resistance to this occupation was that led around 40 C.E. by Trung Trac and her younger sister Trung Nhi,

Trung Trac and Trung Nhi.

daughters in an aristocratic, military family. Trung Trac married a prominent local lord, Thi Sach, who was a vocal opponent of offensive Chinese policies—high taxes, even on the right to fish in local rivers; required payoffs to Chinese officials; and the imposition of Chinese culture on the Vietnamese. In response to this opposition, the Chinese governor of the region ordered Thi Sach's execution.

This personal tragedy provoked Trung Trac to take up arms against the Chinese occupiers, and she quickly gained a substantial following among peasants and aristocrats alike. Famously addressing some 30,000 soldiers, while dressed in full military regalia rather than the expected mourning clothes, she declared to the assembled crowd:

Foremost I will avenge my country.
Second I will restore the Hung lineage.
Third I will avenge the death of my husband.
Lastly I vow that these goals will be accomplished.

Within months, her forces had captured sixty-five towns, and, for two years, they held the Chinese at bay, while Trung Trac and Trung Nhi ruled a briefly independent state as co-queens. Chinese sources referred to Trung Trac as a "ferocious warrior." During their rule,

the sisters eliminated the hated tribute taxes imposed by the Chinese and sought to restore the authority of Vietnamese aristocrats. A large military force, said to number some 80,000, counted among its leaders thirty-six female "generals," including the Trung sisters' mother.

Soon, however, Chinese forces overwhelmed the rebellion, and Trung Trac's support faded. Later Vietnamese records explained the failure of the revolt as a consequence of its female leadership. In traditional Vietnamese accounts, the Trung sisters committed suicide, jumping into a nearby river, as did a number of their followers.

Although the revolt failed, it lived on in stories and legends to inspire later Vietnamese resistance to invaders—Chinese, French, Japanese, and American alike. Men were reminded that women had led this rebellion. "What a pity," wrote a thirteenth-century Vietnamese historian, "that for a thousand years after this, the men of our land bowed their heads, folded their arms, and served the northerners [Chinese]."[13] To this day, temples, streets, and neighborhoods bear the name of the Trung sisters, and a yearly celebration in their honor coincides with International Women's Day. Usually depicted riding on war elephants and wielding swords, these two women also represent the more fluid gender roles then available to some Vietnamese women in comparison to the stricter patriarchy prevalent in China.

Question: How might you imagine the reactions to the Trung sisters' revolt from Chinese officials; Vietnamese aristocrats; Vietnamese peasants, both male and female; and later generations of Vietnamese men and women?

photo: CPA Media

In China, a much older tradition had long linked events on Earth with the invisible realm called "Heaven." In this conception, Heaven was neither a place nor a supreme being, but rather an impersonal moral force that regulated the universe. Emperors were called the Son of Heaven and were said to govern by the Mandate of Heaven so long as they ruled morally and with benevolence. Peasant rebellions, "barbarian" invasions, or disastrous floods were viewed as signs that the emperor had ruled badly and had thus lost the Mandate of Heaven. Among the chief duties of the emperor was the performance of various rituals thought to maintain the appropriate relationship between Heaven and Earth. What moral government meant in practice was spelled out in the writings of Confucius and his followers, which became the official ideology of the empire (see Chapter 4).

Both of these second-wave civilizations also absorbed a foreign religious tradition—Christianity in the Roman world and Buddhism in China—although the process unfolded somewhat differently. In the case of Rome, Christianity was born as a small sect in a remote corner of the empire. Aided by the *pax Romana* and Roman roads, the new faith spread slowly for several centuries, particularly among the poor and lower classes. Women were prominent in the leadership of the early Church, as were a number of more well-to-do individuals from urban families. After suffering intermittent persecution, Christianity in the fourth century C.E. obtained state support from emperors who hoped to shore up a tottering empire with a common religion, and thereafter the religion spread quite rapidly.

In the case of China, by contrast, Buddhism came from India, far beyond the Chinese world. It was introduced to China by Central Asian traders and received little support from Han dynasty rulers. In fact, the religion spread only modestly among Chinese until after the Han dynasty collapsed (220 C.E.), when it appealed to people who felt bewildered by the loss of a predictable and stable society. Not until the Sui (sway) dynasty emperor Wendi (r. 581–604 C.E.) reunified China did the new religion gain state support, and then only temporarily. Buddhism thus became one of several alternative cultural traditions in a complex Chinese mix, while Christianity, though divided internally, ultimately became the dominant religious tradition throughout Europe (see Chapters 8 and 10).

The Roman and Chinese empires also had a different relationship to the societies they governed. Rome's beginnings as a small city-state meant that Romans, and even Italians, were always a distinct minority within the empire. The Chinese empire, by contrast, grew out of a much larger cultural heartland, already ethnically Chinese. Furthermore, as the Chinese state expanded, especially to the south, it actively assimilated the non-Chinese, or "barbarian," people. In short, they became Chinese, culturally, linguistically, and through intermarriage in physical appearance as well. Many Chinese in modern times are in fact descended from people who at one point or another were not Chinese at all.

The Roman Empire offered a different kind of assimilation to its subject peoples. Gradually and somewhat reluctantly, the empire granted Roman citizenship to various individuals, families, or whole communities for their service to the empire or in recognition of their adoption of Roman culture. In 212 C.E., Roman citizenship was bestowed on almost all free people of the empire. Citizenship offered clear advantages—the right to hold public office, to serve in the Roman military units known as legions, to wear a toga, and more—but it conveyed a legal status, rather than cultural assimilation, and certainly did not erase other identities, such as being Greek, Egyptian, or a citizen of a particular city.

Various elements of Roman culture—its public buildings, its religious rituals, its Latin language, its style of city life—were attractive, especially in Western Europe, where urban civilization was something new. In the eastern half of the empire, however, things Greek retained tremendous prestige. Many elite Romans in fact regarded Greek culture—its literature, philosophy, and art—as superior to their own and proudly sent their sons to Athens for a Greek education. To some extent, the two blended into a mixed Greco-Roman tradition, which the empire served to disseminate throughout the realm. Other non-Roman cultural traditions—such as the cult of the Persian god Mithra or the compassionate Egyptian goddess Isis, and, most extensively, the Jewish-derived religion of Christianity—also spread throughout the empire. Nothing similar occurred in Han dynasty China, except for Buddhism, which established a modest presence, largely among foreigners. Chinese culture experienced little competition from older, venerated, or foreign traditions. It was widely recognized across much of East Asia—in Japan, Korea, and Vietnam, for example—as the model to which others should conform.

Language served these two empires in important but contrasting ways. Latin, an alphabetic language depicting sounds, gave rise to various distinct languages—Spanish, Portuguese, French, Italian, Romanian—whereas Chinese did not. Chinese characters, which represented words or ideas more than sounds, were not easily transferable to other languages. Written Chinese, however, could be understood by all literate people, no matter which spoken dialect of the language they used. Thus Chinese, more than Latin, served as an instrument of elite assimilation. For all of these reasons, the various peoples of the Roman Empire were able to maintain their separate cultural identities far more than was the case in China.

Politically, both empires established effective centralized control over vast regions and huge populations, but the Chinese, far more than the Romans, developed an elaborate bureaucracy to hold the empire together. The Han emperor Wudi (r. 141–87 B.C.E.) established an imperial academy for training officials for an emerging bureaucracy with a curriculum based on the writings of Confucius. This was the beginning of a civil service system, complete with examinations and selection by merit, which did much to integrate the Chinese empire and lasted into the early twentieth century. Roman administration was a somewhat ramshackle affair, relying more on regional aristocratic elites and the army to provide cohesion. Unlike the Chinese, however, the Romans developed an elaborate body of law, applicable equally to all people of the realm, dealing with matters of justice, property, commerce, and family life. Chinese and Roman political development thus generated different answers to the question of what made for good government. For those who inherited the Roman tradition, it was good laws, whereas for those in the Chinese tradition, it was good men.

Finally, both Roman and Chinese civilizations had marked effects on the environment in various ways. The Roman poet Horace complained of the noise and smoke of the city and objected to the urban sprawl that extended into the adjacent fertile lands. Roman mining operations, the smelting of metals, its large-scale agriculture, and its growing population—all of this led to extensive deforestation and consequent soil erosion. The shortage of wood in the heartland of the empire led to the relocation of some ceramic workshops to Gaul, where timber was more plentiful. Lead pollution, derived from the smelting of lead ores in open furnaces and from lead water pipes and cooking pots, shows up in the bones of Roman burials and in bones found as far away as Greenland, where studies of the icecap indicate that lead in the atmosphere increased during Roman times. Here is perhaps the earliest example of international atmospheric pollution.

Large-scale Chinese ironworking during the Han dynasty likewise contributed to substantial urban air pollution, while a rapidly growing and dense population practicing intensive agriculture stripped the North China plain of its ancient forest cover, causing sufficient soil erosion to turn the Hwang-ho River its characteristic yellow-brown color. What had been known simply as "the River" now became the Yellow River, which frequently flooded with devastating results and over many centuries dramatically changed course. In addition, as China expanded north and west into the steppe lands of the pastoral peoples, military/agricultural colonies of Chinese farmers turned pasturelands into farmlands, plowing up long-established sod. When the Chinese state subsequently grew weaker or actually collapsed, such farms were abandoned, wind erosion took hold, and deserts emerged.[14]

The Collapse of Empires

Empires rise, and then, with some apparent regularity, they fall, and in doing so, they provide historians with one of their most intriguing questions: what causes the collapse of these once-mighty structures? In China, the Han dynasty empire came to an end in 220 C.E.; the traditional date for the final disintegration of the Roman Empire is 476 C.E., although a process of decline had been under way for several centuries. In the Roman case, however, only the western half of the empire collapsed, while the eastern part, subsequently known as the Byzantine Empire, maintained the tradition of imperial Rome for another thousand years.

Despite these differences, a number of common factors have been associated with the end of these imperial states. At one level, they both simply got too big, too overextended, and too expensive to be sustained by the available resources, and no fundamental technological breakthrough was available to enlarge these resources. Furthermore, the growth of large landowning families with huge estates and political

The Kushan Empire

Often lost among the giant second-wave empires of Persia, Macedonia/Greece, Rome, China, and India is the story of a smaller empire—that of the Kushan people—whose Central Asian state interacted directly or indirectly with all the others. At its height during the first two centuries of the Common Era, the Kushan Empire, according to one recent account, "created stable conditions at the heart of Central Asia, allowing for the great flowering of trans-Eurasian mercantile and cultural exchange that occurred along the Silk Roads."[15]

The Kushans, originally a pastoral nomadic people from an area around Dunhuang at the far western edge of China, had migrated in the early centuries B.C.E. to the region that now makes up northwestern India, Pakistan, Afghanistan, and Tajikistan, where they established a sizable and prosperous empire linked to the Silk Road trading network. It was a remarkably cosmopolitan place, illustrating the mixing and blending of many cultural

A pendant from the Kushan Empire.

traditions. Since parts of this empire had earlier been ruled by Alexander the Great and his Greek successors (see pages 114–17), classical Mediterranean culture was a prominent element of Kushan life. The Kushans used the Greek alphabet to write their official language, which was derived from India. Roman bronze and glassware items have been found in Kushan merchant warehouses, and scholars suspect that Roman gold coins, used to pay for Eastern imports, were melted down and recast as Kushan coins. From the other end of Eurasia, Kushans imported Chinese lacquer goods, and on at least one occasion, Kushan military forces clashed with those of an expanding Han dynasty China. The greatest of the Kushan rulers, Kanishka (r. ca. 127–153 C.E.), styled himself "Great King, King of Kings, Son of God," a title that had both Persian and Chinese precedents.

photo: Victoria & Albert Museum/V&A Images/Art Resource, NY

clout enabled them to avoid paying taxes, turned free peasants into impoverished tenant farmers, and diminished the authority of the central government. In China, such conditions led to a major peasant revolt, known as the Yellow Turban Rebellion, in 184 C.E. (see Chapter 5, pages 197–98).

Rivalry among elite factions created instability in both empires and eroded imperial authority. In China, persistent tension between castrated court officials (eunuchs) loyal to the emperor and Confucian-educated scholar-bureaucrats weakened the state. In the Roman Empire between 235 and 284 C.E., some twenty-six individuals claimed the title of Roman emperor, only one of whom died of natural causes. In addition, epidemic disease ravaged both societies, though more extensively in the Roman world. The population of the Roman Empire declined by 25 percent in the two centuries following 250 C.E., a demographic disaster that meant diminished production, less revenue for the state, and fewer men available for the defense of the empire's long frontiers.

Religiously, the Kushan Empire was a diverse and apparently tolerant place. Hindu devotional cults as well as Buddhism flourished, and evidence of Persian Zoroastrian religious practice is found on many Kushan coins, which depict the ruler conducting a sacrifice over a fire altar. It was in the Kushan realm that the earliest human representations of the Buddha were sculpted, and often with distinctly Greek features. (See Working with Evidence, Source 4.2, page 186.) Despite these outside influences, Kushan artists recalled their nomadic past as they depicted their rulers in typical steppe nomadic style: on horseback, wearing loose trousers, heavy boots, and knee-length robes.

A Kushan pendant dating to the fourth century C.E., shown opposite, illustrates the cultural blending so characteristic of Kushan life. It features Hariti, originally a fearsome Hindu goddess who abducted and killed children, feeding their flesh to her own offspring. But in an encounter with the Buddha, Hariti repented and was transformed into a compassionate protector of children. Here she is depicted holding in her right hand a lotus blossom, a prominent Buddhist symbol; her left hand holds another lotus flower supporting a flask or cornucopia overflowing with pomegranates (symbolizing food and abundance). According to local mythology, the Buddha had offered Hariti pomegranates (often said to resemble human flesh) as a substitute for the children she was devouring.

While the content of this pendant is thoroughly Indian and Buddhist, its representation of Hariti was probably modeled after the Greek goddess Tyche (TEE-chee), also portrayed holding a cornucopia. Furthermore, her short tunic worn with a belt was likewise of Greek or Hellenistic origin. And the border of pearls and stylized flowers that surround the image derives from Persia.

During the time of the Kushan Empire, Central Asia, so often regarded as a backwater in recent centuries, was a place where the political, cultural, and economic influences of all the Eurasian civilizations overlapped and intermingled. For those several centuries, the Kushan Empire was at the center of an interacting world.

Questions: How does the Kushan Empire challenge impressions that second-wave civilizations of Eurasia existed in isolation from one another? Why do you think the Kushan artist who created this pendant chose to weave together so many distinct cultural strands?

Historians have often linked the collapse of empires with environmental factors as well, more often with reference to Rome than to Han dynasty China. Considerable fluctuations in the climate after about 250 C.E. led to drought in the third century, cold and wet conditions in the fourth, and increased rainfall and cooler temperatures in the fifth, all of which generated substantial soil erosion and declining agricultural productivity. The North African breadbasket of the empire suffered from serious salinization and increasingly desert-like conditions. The extent to which such factors contributed to the collapse of the Roman Empire remains a point of dispute among scholars.

To these mounting internal problems was added a growing threat from nomadic or semi-agricultural peoples occupying the frontier regions of both empires. The Chinese had long developed various ways of dealing with the Xiongnu and other nomadic people to the north—building the Great Wall to keep them out, offering them trading opportunities at border markets, buying them off with lavish gifts,

■ **Change**
What internal and external factors contributed to the collapse of the Roman and Chinese empires?

Meeting of Attila and Pope Leo I
Among the "barbarian" invaders of the Roman Empire, none were more feared than the Huns, led by the infamous Attila. In a celebrated meeting in 452 C.E., Pope Leo I persuaded Attila to spare the city of Rome and to withdraw from Italy. This seventeenth-century Spanish painting records one view of that remarkable meeting. (Mural in church, El Hospital de Los Venerables, Seville, Spain/© Islandstock/Alamy)

contracting marriage alliances with nomadic leaders, and conducting periodic military campaigns against them. But as the Han dynasty weakened in the second and third centuries C.E., such peoples more easily breached the frontier defenses and set up a succession of "barbarian states" in north China. Culturally, however, many of these foreign rulers gradually became Chinese, encouraging intermarriage, adopting Chinese dress, and setting up their courts in Chinese fashion.

A weakening Roman Empire likewise faced serious problems from Germanic-speaking peoples living on its northern frontier. Growing numbers of these people began to enter the empire in the fourth century C.E.—some as mercenaries in Roman armies and others as refugees fleeing the invasions of the ferocious Huns, who were penetrating Europe from Central Asia. Once inside the declining empire, various Germanic groups established their own kingdoms, at first controlling Roman emperors and then displacing them altogether by 476 C.E. Unlike the nomadic groups in China, who largely assimilated Chinese culture, Germanic kingdoms in Europe developed their own ethnic identities—Visigoths, Franks, Anglo-Saxons, and others—even as they drew on Roman law and adopted Roman Christianity. Far more than in China, the fall of the western Roman Empire produced a new culture, blending Latin and Germanic elements, which provided the foundation for the hybrid civilization that would arise in Western Europe.

The collapse of empire meant more than the disappearance of centralized government and endemic conflict. In post-Han China and post-Roman Europe, it also meant the decline of urban life, a contracting population, less area under cultivation, diminishing international trade, and vast insecurity for ordinary people. It must have seemed that civilization itself was unraveling.

The most significant difference between the collapse of empire in China and that in the western Roman Empire lay in what happened next. In China, after about 350 years of disunion, disorder, frequent warfare, and political chaos, a Chinese imperial state, similar to that of the Han dynasty, was reassembled under the Sui (589–618 C.E.), Tang (618–907), and Song (960–1279) dynasties. Once again, a single emperor ruled; a bureaucracy selected by examinations governed; and the ideas of Confucius informed the political system. Such a Chinese empire persisted into the early twentieth century, establishing one of the most continuous political traditions of any civilization in world history.

The story line of European history following the end of the western Roman Empire was very different indeed. No large-scale, centralized, imperial authority encompassing all of Western Europe has ever been successfully reestablished there for any length of time. The memory of Roman imperial unity certainly persisted, and many subsequently tried unsuccessfully to re-create it. But most of Western Europe dissolved into highly decentralized political systems involving nobles, knights and vassals, kings with little authority, various city-states in Italy, and small territories ruled by princes, bishops, or the pope. From this point on, Europe would be a civilization without an encompassing imperial state.

From a Chinese point of view, Western Europe's post-Roman history must seem an enormous failure. Why were Europeans unable to reconstruct something of the unity of their classical empire, while the Chinese clearly did? Surely the greater cultural homogeneity of Chinese civilization made that task easier than it was amid the vast ethnic and linguistic diversity of Europe. The absence in the Roman legacy of a strong bureaucratic tradition also contributed to European difficulties, whereas in China the bureaucracy provided some stability even as dynasties came and went. The Chinese also had in Confucianism a largely secular ideology that placed great value on political matters in the here and now. The Roman Catholic Church in Europe, however, was frequently at odds with state authorities, and its "otherworldliness" did little to support the creation of large-scale empires. Finally, Chinese agriculture was much more productive than that of Europe, and for a long time its metallurgy was more advanced.[16] These conditions gave Chinese state builders more resources to work with than were available to their European counterparts.

SUMMING UP SO FAR

In comparing the Roman and Chinese empires, which do you find more striking—their similarities or their differences?

Intermittent Empire: The Case of India

Among the second-wave civilizations of Eurasia, empire loomed large in Persian, Mediterranean, and Chinese history, but it played a rather less prominent role in Indian history. In the Indus River valley flourished the largest of the First Civilizations, embodied in exquisitely planned cities such as Harappa but with little evidence of any central political authority (see Chapter 2). The demise of this early civilization by 1500 B.C.E. was followed over the next thousand years by the creation of a new civilization based farther east, along the Ganges River on India's northern plain. That process has occasioned considerable debate, which has focused on the role of the Aryans, a pastoral Indo-European people long thought to have invaded and destroyed the Indus Valley civilization and then created the new one along the Ganges. More recent research questions this interpretation. Did the Aryans invade suddenly, or did they migrate slowly into the Indus River valley? Were they already there as a part of the Indus Valley population? Was the new civilization largely the work of Aryans, or did it evolve gradually from Indus Valley culture? Scholars have yet to reach agreement on any of these questions.[17]

■ **Comparison**

Why were centralized empires so much less prominent in India than in China?

However it occurred, by 600 B.C.E. what would become the second-wave civilization of South Asia had begun to take shape across northern India. Politically, that civilization emerged as a fragmented collection of towns and cities, some small republics governed by public assemblies, and a number of regional states ruled by kings. An astonishing range of ethnic, cultural, and linguistic diversity also characterized this civilization, as an endless variety of peoples migrated into India from Central Asia across the mountain passes in the northwest. These features of Indian civilization—political fragmentation and vast cultural diversity—have informed much of South Asian history throughout many centuries, offering a sharp contrast to the pattern of development in China. What gave Indian civilization a recognizable identity and character was neither an imperial tradition nor ethno-linguistic commonality, but rather a distinctive religious tradition, known later to outsiders as Hinduism, and a unique social organization, the caste system. These features of Indian life are explored further in Chapters 4 and 5.

Nonetheless, empires and emperors were not entirely unknown in India's long history. Northwestern India had been briefly ruled by the Persian Empire and then conquered by Alexander the Great. These Persian and Greek influences helped stimulate the first and largest of India's short experiments with a large-scale political system, the Mauryan Empire (326–184 B.C.E.), which encompassed all but the southern tip of the subcontinent (see Map 3.6).

The Mauryan Empire was an impressive political structure, equivalent to the Persian, Chinese, and Roman empires, though not nearly as long-lasting. With a population of perhaps 50 million, the Mauryan Empire boasted a large military force, reported to include 600,000 infantry soldiers, 30,000 cavalry, 8,000 chariots, and 9,000 elephants. A civilian bureaucracy featured various ministries and a large contingent of spies to provide the rulers with local information. A famous treatise called the *Arthashastra* (*The Science of Worldly Wealth*) articulated a pragmatic, even amoral, political philosophy for Mauryan rulers. It was, according to one scholar, a book that showed "how the political world does work and not very often stating how it ought to work, a book that frequently discloses to a king what calculating and sometimes brutal measures he must carry out to preserve the state and the common good."[18] The state also operated many industries—spinning, weaving, mining, shipbuilding, and armaments. This complex apparatus was financed by taxes on trade, on herds of animals, and especially on land, from which the monarch claimed a quarter or more of the crop.

Mauryan India is perhaps best known for one of its emperors, Ashoka (r. 268–232 B.C.E.), who left a record of his activities and his thinking in a series of edicts carved on rocks and pillars throughout the kingdom. Ashoka's conversion to Buddhism and his moralistic approach to governance gave his reign a different tone than that of China's Shihuangdi or Greece's Alexander the Great, who, according to legend, wept because he had no more worlds to conquer. Ashoka's legacy to modern India has been that of an enlightened ruler, who sought to govern in accord with the religious values and moral teachings of Hinduism and Buddhism.

Despite their good intentions, these policies did not long preserve the empire, which broke apart soon after Ashoka's death. About 600 years later, a second brief imperial experiment, known as the Gupta Empire (320–550 C.E.), took shape. Faxian, a Chinese Buddhist traveler in India at the time, noted a generally peaceful, tolerant, and prosperous land, commenting that the ruler "governs without decapitation or corporal punishment." Free hospitals, he reported, were available to "the destitute, crippled and diseased," but he also noticed "untouchables" carrying bells to warn upper-caste people of their polluting presence.[19] Culturally, the Gupta era witnessed a flourishing of art, literature, temple building, science, mathematics, and medicine, much of it patronized by rulers. Indian trade with China also thrived, and elements of Buddhist and Hindu culture took root in Southeast Asia (see Chapter 7). Indian commerce reached as far as the Roman world. A Germanic leader named Alaric laid siege to Rome in 410 C.E., while demanding 3,000 pounds of Indian pepper to spare the city.

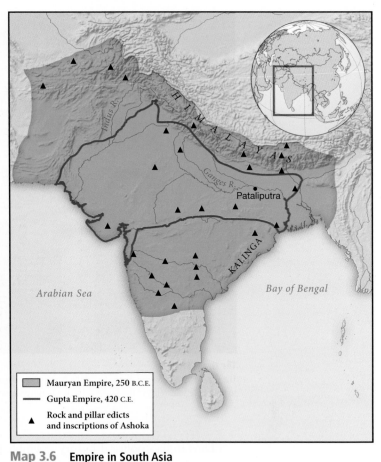

Map 3.6 Empire in South Asia

Large-scale empires in the Indian subcontinent were less frequent and less enduring than those in China. Two of the largest efforts were those of the Mauryan and Gupta dynasties.

The Great Stupa
The Great Stupa of Sanchi, the oldest stone building in India, was commissioned by Ashoka in the third century B.C.E. to house precious relics of the Buddha. (© Luca Tettoni/Bridgeman Images)

Thus India's political history resembled that of Western Europe after the collapse of the Roman Empire far more than that of China or Persia. Neither imperial nor regional states commanded the kind of loyalty or exercised the degree of influence that they did in other second-wave civilizations. India's unparalleled cultural diversity surely was one reason, as was the frequency of invasions from Central Asia, which repeatedly smashed emerging states that might have provided the nucleus for an all-India empire. Finally, India's social structure, embodied in a caste system linked to occupational groups, made for intensely local loyalties at the expense of wider identities (see Chapter 5).

Nonetheless, a frequently vibrant economy fostered a lively internal commerce and made India the focal point of an extensive network of trade in the Indian Ocean basin. In particular, its cotton textile industry long supplied cloth throughout the Afro-Eurasian world. Strong guilds of merchants and artisans provided political leadership in major towns and cities, and their wealth supported lavish temples, public buildings, and religious festivals. Great creativity in religious matters generated Hindu and Buddhist traditions that later penetrated much of Asia. Indian mathematics and science, especially astronomy, were also impressive; Indian scientists plotted the movements of stars and planets and recognized quite early that the earth was round. Clearly, the absence of consistent imperial unity did not prevent the evolution of a lasting civilization.

REFLECTIONS

Enduring Legacies of Second-Wave Empires

The second-wave empires discussed in this chapter have long ago passed into history, but their descendants have kept them alive in memory, for they have proved useful, even in the twentieth and early twenty-first centuries. Those empires have provided legitimacy for contemporary states, inspiration for new imperial ventures, and abundant warnings and cautions for those seeking to criticize more recent empires. For example, in bringing communism to China in the twentieth century, the Chinese leader Mao Zedong compared himself to Shihuangdi, the unifier of China and the brutal founder of its Qin dynasty. Reflecting on his campaign against intellectuals in general and Confucianism in particular, Mao declared to a Communist Party conference: "Emperor Qin Shihuang was not that outstanding. He only buried alive 460 Confucian scholars. We buried 460 thousand Confucian scholars. . . . To the charge of being like Emperor Qin, of being a dictator, we plead guilty."[20]

In contrast, modern-day Indians, who have sought to present their country as a model of cultural tolerance and nonviolence, have been quick to link themselves to Ashoka and his policies of inclusiveness. When the country became independent from British colonial rule in 1947, India soon placed an image of Ashoka's Pillar on the new nation's currency.

In the West, it has been the Roman Empire that has provided a template for thinking about political life. Many in Great Britain celebrated their own global empire as a modern version of the Roman Empire. If the British had been "civilized" by Roman rule, then surely Africans and Asians would benefit from falling under the control of the "superior" British. Likewise, to the Italian fascist dictator Benito Mussolini, his country's territorial expansion during the 1930s and World War II represented the creation of a new Roman Empire. Most recently, the United States' dominant role in the world has prompted the question, are the Americans the new Romans?

Historians frequently cringe as politicians and students use (and perhaps misuse) historical analogies to make their case for particular points of view in the present. But we have little else to go on except history in making our way through the complexities of contemporary life, and historians themselves seldom agree on the "lessons" of the past. Lively debate about the continuing relevance of these ancient empires shows that although the past may be gone, it surely is not dead.

Second Thoughts

What's the Significance?

Persian Empire, 108

Athenian democracy, 112

Greco-Persian Wars, 113

Alexander the Great, 114

Hellenistic era, 115

Augustus, 121

pax Romana, 121

Qin Shihuangdi, 122

Han dynasty, 122

Trung Trac, 124

Kushan Empire, 128

Mauryan Empire, 132

Ashoka, 133

Big Picture Questions

1. What common features can you identify in the empires described in this chapter? In what ways did they differ from one another? What accounts for those differences?
2. Are you more impressed with the "greatness" of empires or with their destructive and oppressive features? Why?
3. Do you think that these second-wave empires hold "lessons" for the present, or are contemporary circumstances sufficiently unique as to render the distant past irrelevant?
4. **Looking Back:** How do these empires of the second-wave civilizations differ from the political systems of the First Civilizations?

Next Steps: For Further Study

Jane Burbank and Frederick Cooper, *Empires in World History* (2010). A fascinating account by two major scholars of the imperial theme across the world. Chapter 2 compares the Roman and Chinese empires.

Arthur Cotterell, *The First Emperor of China* (1988). A biography of Shihuangdi.

Christopher Kelley, *The Roman Empire: A Very Short Introduction* (2006). A brief, up-to-date, and accessible account of the Roman achievement.

Cullen Murphy, *Are We Rome? The Fall of an Empire and the Fate of America* (2007). A reflection on the usefulness and the dangers of comparing the Roman Empire to the present-day United States.

Sarah Pomeroy et al., *Ancient Greece* (1999). A highly readable survey of Greek history by a team of distinguished scholars.

Romila Thapar, *Ashoka and the Decline of the Mauryas* (1961). A classic study of India's early empire builder.

Illustrated History of the Roman Empire, http://www.roman-empire.net. An interactive Web site with maps, pictures, and much information about the Roman Empire.

The Story of Han Dynasty, episode 1, http://www.youtube.com/watch?v=9U45tvzxP74. The first episode of a Chinese TV series dramatizing the founding of the Han dynasty, with English subtitles.

Perceptions of Outsiders
in the Ancient World

The peoples of ancient Eurasia did not live in splendid isolation from one another. Nor did they inhabit the kind of deeply interconnected and globalized world that the past century has created. But through war, commerce, the migration of peoples, the spread of religions, and sheer geographic proximity, some of those peoples became sharply aware of one another.

Thus the Greeks went to war with Persia, and a few of them visited or lived in Egypt. Romans derived their much-beloved pepper from India and some silk from China, while facing those they regarded as "barbarians" in the European lands to the north of their imperial boundaries. For many centuries, the Chinese too had to deal with their own "barbarians" beyond the Great Wall, even as Chinese Buddhist pilgrims sought out the sources of their faith in India. These are but a few of the cross-cultural encounters that helped to shape histories of ancient peoples.

Such encounters with strangers have long been an important motor of change in human history, as foreign ideas, diseases, goods, technologies, and military challenges required adjustment in established ways of living. Here, however, we are more interested in the perceptions or understandings of outsiders that arose from these interactions, mental images of life beyond the familiar confines of one's own culture. How do we understand those who are "other" than ourselves? What distortions arise as we ponder those outside our circle? How can the "other" provide opportunities to question or critique one's own society? The documents that follow provide three examples of this process from the ancient world.

Source 3.1

A Greek Historian on Persia and Egypt

Born to a wealthy Greek family in Asia Minor, Herodotus (ca. 485–425 B.C.E.) came of age when the wars between the Greeks and Persians were still recent memories. He devoted much of his life to recording the history of that great conflict in a series of books known as *The Histories*. In doing so, he pretty much invented for the Western world the craft of history as a systematic and connected narrative based on research. As a man of means, he was able to travel widely in the Persian Empire, Egypt, Syria, Babylon, Sicily, and Italy, making notes of what he saw and collecting stories, myths, and oral recollections along the way. The selection that follows contains some of his personal impressions of Persia and Egypt.

- What cultural differences does Herodotus notice between Greek ways of living and those of Persia and Egypt?

- What posture does Herodotus take toward these differences? He does refer to Persians as "barbarians," but at the time that term may have meant simply "non-Greek," without the implication of "savage" or "uncivilized" that it later acquired. Does he express a critical view of the Persians and Egyptians or a more positive understanding?

- What parts of these accounts might be helpful to historians seeking to describe life in ancient Persia or Egypt? What might a historian learn about Greek culture itself from these descriptions?

HERODOTUS

The Histories

Mid-Fifth Century B.C.E.

On Persians

The customs that I know the Persians follow are these. They have no images of the gods and no temples or altars; they consider the use of them a sign of foolishness. This comes, I think, from their not believing the gods to have the same nature as human beings, as the Greeks imagine. The Persians' practice is to climb to the tops of the highest mountains to offer sacrifices to Zeus, the Greek name for the chief god of the universe. The Persians use this god's name to refer to the whole extent of the sky. They also sacrifice to the sun and moon, to the earth, to fire, to water, and to the winds. . . .

The Persians offer sacrifice to these gods in the following way: They do not construct an altar, light a fire, or pour a libation, and there is no flute music, no wearing of garlands, and no consecrated barley cake. The person who wishes to sacrifice brings the victim to a spot of ground that is pure from ritual pollution and there calls upon the name of the god for whom the sacrifice is meant. It is usual to have one's turban encircled with a wreath, most commonly of myrtle. The sacrificer is not allowed to pray for blessings on himself alone, but he prays for the welfare of the king and of the whole Persian people, among whom he is necessarily included. He cuts the [animal] victim in pieces, and having boiled the meat, he lays it out on the softest grass that he can find, clover in particular. When everything is ready, one of the mages [priests] comes forward and chants a hymn, which they say describes the origins of the gods. . . . After a short time, the sacrificer carries the meat of the victim away with him to use as he likes.

Of all the days in the year, the one they celebrate the most is their birthday. It is customary to serve much more food on that day than usual. The richer Persians have an ox, a horse, a camel, and an ass roasted whole for the meal; poorer people cook smaller kinds of cattle. They eat relatively few main courses but many extra courses, which they serve a few dishes at a time. For this reason, the Persians say that the Greeks leave a meal hungry because they have nothing worth mentioning served to them as an extra after the meats and that if the Greeks did have extra courses served, they would never stop eating. The Persians love wine and drink large amounts of it. . . .

When they meet another person in the street, you can tell if the people meeting are of equal status by the following indication: If they are, instead of speaking, they kiss each other on the lips. In the case where one is a little inferior to the other, the kiss is given on the cheek. Where the difference of rank is great, the inferior lies down on the ground in front of the superior. . . . The farther away other peoples live, the less the Persians respect them. The reason is that they regard themselves as very greatly superior in all respects to the rest of humanity, believing that other peoples' excellence is directly proportional to how close they live to Persia. . . .

No one so readily adopts foreign customs as the Persians. For this reason, they wear clothing like that of the Medes, considering it superior to their own. In war, they wear Egyptian armor to protect their chests. As soon as they hear of any luxury from any country, they instantly make it their own. In particular, they learned from the Greeks to have sex with adolescent boys. Each man has several wives and an even greater number of concubines.

In terms of manliness, manly courage on the battlefield is the greatest proof, with fathering many sons the second greatest. . . . They carefully educate their sons from the age of five to the age of twenty in only three subjects: riding horses, shooting arrows, and speaking the truth. Until boys are five, they are not allowed to come into the sight of their fathers, but instead spend their time with the women. They do this so that if the child dies young, the father will not be saddened at losing him.

I praise this custom and the following one too. The king does not put anyone to death for a single instance of wrong-doing, and no Persian inflicts an extreme penalty on a slave for a single instance of wrong-doing.

I can say all these things about the Persians with complete certainty, relying on my own personal knowledge.

On Egyptians

Concerning Egypt itself I am going to say a great deal because there is no country that possesses so many amazing things or has such a large number of buildings and monuments that defy description. Not only is the climate different from that of the rest of the world and the rivers unlike any other rivers, but the people also, in the majority of their ways and customs, exactly reverse what the rest of humanity usually does. The women there participate in the markets and in trade, while the men sit at home weaving on a loom. And while the rest of the world works the woof up the warp while weaving, the Egyptians work it down. The women also carry loads on their shoulders, while the men carry them on their heads. They eat their food out-of-doors in the streets, but they withdraw into their houses to go to the bathroom, explaining that what is shameful but necessary should be done in private, but that which has nothing shameful about it should be done openly. A woman cannot serve as a priest, either for a god or a goddess, but men are priests for both. Sons are not required to support their parents unless they choose to do so, but daughters must, whether they want to or not.

In other countries, the priests have long hair, but in Egypt their heads are shaved. In other lands, it is customary for close relatives while mourning their dead to cut their hair short. The Egyptians, who shave their hair the rest of the time, let their beards and the hair on their heads grow long when a relative dies. All other people live their lives separate from animals, but the Egyptians always have animals living with them. Others make barley and wheat their food; it is a disgrace to do so in Egypt, where the grain they live on is spelt, which some call *zea* [a distinct form of wheat, sometimes known as emmer]. They knead dough with their feet, but they mix clay, and even pick up dung, with their hands. They are the only people in the world, except for those who learned it from them, to use circumcision. . . . When they write or do math, they move their hand from right to left, instead of writing from left to right, like the Greeks. They insist that their method is "right-handed" and therefore dexterous, but that the Greeks' method is "left-handed" and awkward. They have two quite different kinds of writing, one of which is called sacred, the other "of the people."

They are excessively religious, far beyond any other peoples. . . . They drink out of bronze cups, which they clean every day. They wear linen clothes, which they are especially careful to have always freshly washed. They practice circumcision for the sake of cleanliness, considering it better to be clean than attractive.

Source: Herodotus, *The Histories*, 1:131–37, 140; 2:35–37, in Thomas R. Martin, ed., *Herodotus and Sima Qian: The First Great Historians of Greece and China* (Boston: Bedford/St. Martin's, 2010), 46–51.

Source 3.2
A Roman Historian on the Germans

Occupying much of Central Europe north of the Roman Empire, ancient Germanic-speaking peoples were never a single "nation" but rather a collection of tribes, clans, and chiefdoms. They were regarded by the Romans as barbarians, though admired and feared for their military skills. These Germanic peoples were famously described by Tacitus (56–117 C.E.), a Roman official and well-known historian. Tacitus himself had never visited the lands of the people he describes; rather, he relied on earlier written documents and interviews with merchants and soldiers who had traveled and lived in the region. Unlike Herodotus, he wrote about people who lived without the states and cities characteristic of civilizations.

■ What can we learn from Tacitus's account about the economy, politics, society, and culture of the Germanic peoples of the first century C.E.?

■ Which statements of Tacitus might you regard as reliable, and which are more suspect? Why?

■ Why did Tacitus regard Germanic peoples as distinctly inferior to Romans? How might he have responded to the idea that these people would play a major role in the collapse of the Roman Empire several centuries later?

■ Modern scholars have argued that Tacitus used the Germanic peoples to criticize aspects of his own Roman culture. What evidence might support this point of view?

■ What differences might you notice between Herodotus's description of neighboring civilizations and Tacitus's discussion of an agricultural village society?

TACITUS

Germania

First Century C.E.

The Germans themselves I should regard as aboriginal, and not mixed at all with other races through immigration or intercourse. . . . [W]ho would leave Asia, or Africa, or Italy for Germany, with its wild country, its inclement skies, its sullen manners and aspect, unless indeed it were his home? In their ancient songs, their only way of remembering or recording the past, they celebrate an earth-born god, Tuisco, and his son Mannus, as the origin of their race, as their founders. . . .

The tribes of Germany are free from all taint of intermarriages with foreign nations, and they appear as a distinct, unmixed race, like none but themselves. Hence, too, the same physical peculiarities throughout so vast a population. All have fierce blue eyes, red hair, huge frames, fit only for a sudden exertion. They are less able to bear laborious work. Heat and thirst they cannot in the least endure; to cold and hunger their climate and their soil inure them. . . .

They choose their kings by birth, their generals by merit. These kings have not unlimited or arbitrary power, and the generals do more by example than by authority. . . . But to reprimand, to imprison, even to flog, is permitted to the priests alone, and that not as a punishment, or at the general's bidding, but, as it were, by the mandate of the god whom they believe to inspire the warrior. . . . And what most stimulates their courage is that their squadrons or battalions, instead of being formed by chance or by a fortuitous gathering, are composed of families and clans. Close by them, too, are those dearest to them, so that they hear the shrieks of women, the cries of infants. . . .

Tradition says that armies already wavering and giving way have been rallied by women who, with earnest entreaties and bosoms laid bare, have vividly represented the horrors of captivity, which the Germans fear with such extreme dread on behalf of their women. . . . They even believe that the female sex has a certain sanctity and prescience, and they

do not despise their counsels, or make light of their answers. . . .

Mercury is the deity whom they chiefly worship, and on certain days they deem it right to sacrifice to him even with human victims. . . .

Augury and divination by lot no people practice more diligently. . . . In public questions the priest of the particular state, in private the father of the family, invokes the gods, and, with his eyes toward heaven, takes up each piece [of a small tree branch] three times, and finds in them a meaning according to the mark previously impressed on them. . . .

When they go into battle, it is a disgrace for the chief to be surpassed in valor, a disgrace for his followers not to equal the valor of the chief. And it is an infamy and a reproach for life to have survived the chief, and return from the field. To defend, to protect him, to ascribe one's own brave deeds to his renown, is the height of loyalty. The chief fights for victory; his vassals fight for their chief. . . . Feasts and entertainments, which though inelegant, are plentifully furnished, are their only pay. The means of this bounty come from war or rapine. Nor are they as easily persuaded to plough the earth and to wait for the year's produce as to challenge an enemy and earn the honor of wounds. Nay, they actually think it tame and stupid to acquire by the sweat of toil what they might win by their blood.

Whenever they are not fighting, they pass much of their time in hunting, and still more in idleness, giving themselves up to sleep and to feasting, the bravest and the most warlike doing nothing, and surrendering the management of the household of the home, and of the land, to the women, the old men, and all the weakest members of the family. . . . It is the custom of the states to bestow by voluntary and individual contribution on the chief a present of cattle or of grain, which, while accepted as a compliment, supplies their wants. They are particularly delighted by gifts from neighboring tribes . . . such as choice steeds, heavy armor, trappings, and neckchains. We have now taught them to accept money also.

It is well known that the nations of Germany have no cities, and that they do not even tolerate closely contiguous dwellings. They live scattered and apart, just as a spring, a meadow, or a wood has attracted them. Their villages they do not arrange in our fashion, . . . but every person surrounds his dwelling with an open space, either as a precaution against the disasters of fire, or because they do not know how to build. No use is made by them of stone or tile; they employ timber for all purposes, rude masses without ornament or attractiveness. . . .

They all wrap themselves in a cloak which is fastened with a clasp, or, if this is not forthcoming, with a thorn, leaving the rest of their persons bare. . . . They also wear the skins of wild beasts. . . .

Their marriage code, however, is strict, and indeed no part of their manners is more praiseworthy. Almost alone among barbarians they are content with one wife, except a very few among them. . . . Lest the woman should think herself to stand apart from aspirations after noble deeds and from the perils of war, she is reminded by the ceremony which inaugurates marriage that she is her husband's partner in toil and danger, destined to suffer and to dare with him alike both in peace and in war. . . .

Very rare for so numerous a population is adultery, the punishment of which is prompt, and in the husband's power. Having cut off the hair of the adulteress and stripped her naked, he expels her from the house in the presence of her kinfolk, and then flogs her through the whole village. The loss of chastity meets with no indulgence; neither beauty, youth, nor wealth will procure the culprit a husband.

No one in Germany laughs at vice, nor do they call it the fashion to corrupt and to be corrupted. . . . To limit the number of their children or to destroy any of their subsequent offspring is accounted infamous, and good habits are here more effectual than good laws elsewhere. . . .

It is the duty among them to adopt the feuds as well as the friendships of a father or a kinsman. These feuds are not implacable; even homicide is expiated by the payment of a certain number of cattle and of sheep, and the satisfaction is accepted by the entire family, greatly to the advantage of the state, since feuds are dangerous in proportion to a people's freedom. . . .

[S]laves are not employed after our manner with distinct domestic duties assigned to them, but each one has the management of a house and home of his own. The master requires from the slave a certain quantity of grain, of cattle, and of clothing, as he would from a tenant, and this is the limit of subjection. All other household functions are discharged by the wife and children. . . .

Of lending money on interest and increasing it by compound interest they know nothing—a more effectual safeguard than if it were prohibited.

Land proportioned to the number of inhabitants is occupied by the whole community in turn, and afterward divided among them according to rank. A wide expanse of plains makes the partition easy. They till fresh fields every year, and they have still more land than enough; . . . corn [wheat] is the only produce required from the earth.

Source: Alfred John Church and William Jackson Brodribb, *The Agricola and Germania of Tacitus* (London: Macmillan, 1877), 87ff.

Source 3.3
A Chinese Historian on the Xiongnu

During the time of the Han dynasty, the Chinese historian and high official Sima Qian (ca. 145–86 B.C.E.), like his Roman counterpart Tacitus, had occasion to observe and describe neighboring "barbarian" peoples and their history.

In Sima Qian's case, those people were the Xiongnu, pastoral nomads living to the north of China's Great Wall. China's fluctuating relationship with these peoples, involving war, trade, exchange of ambassadors, and periodic treaties, are described more fully in Chapter 8 (see pages 334–35). While the Chinese generally felt enormously superior to such "uncivilized" people, they were compelled on occasion to accommodate the military prowess of the Xiongnu. The following excerpts from Sima Qian's enormous history of ancient China illustrate his understanding of these people, who long represented a mirror through which the Chinese defined their image of themselves.

■ Based on this document and what you know about Chinese life, what aspects of Xiongnu culture would likely appear most different or distasteful to Sima Qian?

■ What purpose does the story about Maodun serve in this account?

■ What can you infer about the relationship between China and the Xiongnu from the letter of Emperor Wen? How do you imagine he and Sima Qian felt about that letter?

Sima Qian
Records of the Grand Historian
ca. 100 B.C.E.

The ancestor of the Xiongnu descended from the ruler of the Xia dynasty, whose name was Qun Wei. From before the time of Emperors [of the third millennium B.C.E.], there have been barbarians . . . living in northern uncivilized areas and wandering around herding animals. They herd mainly horses, cattle, and sheep, but also some unusual animals, such as camels, donkeys, mules, and wild horses. . . . They move around looking for water and pasture and have no walled settlements or permanent housing. They do not farm, but they do divide their land into separate holdings under different leaders. They have no writing, and all contracts are verbal. When their children can ride a sheep, they begin to use bows and arrows to shoot birds and rodents. When they are older, they shoot foxes and rabbits for food. In this way, all the young men are easily able to become archers and serve as cavalry. It is their custom when times are easy to graze their animals and hunt with the bow for their living, but when hard times come, they take up weapons to plunder and raid. This is their innate nature. Their long-range weapons are bows and arrows; they use swords and spears in close combat. When they have the advantage in battle, they advance, but if not, they retreat, since there is no shame in running away. They are only concerned with self-interest, knowing nothing of proper behavior or justice.

Everyone, including the chiefs, eats the meat of their domesticated animals and wears clothing of hides and coats of fur. The men who are in their prime eat the fattiest and best food, while the elderly eat what is left over, since the Xiongnu treasure the strong and healthy but place little value on the weak and old. When his father dies, a son marries his stepmother, and when brothers die, the surviving brothers marry their widows. They have personal names but no family names or additional names. . . .

[*Then Sima Qian relates a story about how Maodun became the Xiongnu ruler in 209 B.C.E.*]

Maodun had arrows made that whistled in flight and trained his men to shoot their bows as they were riding. He ordered, "He who does not shoot where my whistling arrow hits will be executed!" He then went out hunting birds and animals, and if any of his men failed to shoot at what he shot at with his whistling arrow, he immediately beheaded them. Next, he shot a whistling arrow at his own favorite horse. Some of his men hesitated, not daring to shoot the horse. Maodun beheaded them. A little later, he used a whistling arrow to shoot at his favorite wife. Again, some of his men, perhaps because they were afraid, did not dare to shoot. Once more, Maodun beheaded them. Later, he went hunting with his men and shot his father's best horse. All his men shot it, too. Then Maodun knew that he could rely on his troops. Accompanying Touman [Maodun's father] on a hunting trip, he shot a whistling arrow at his father. All his followers shot where the whistling arrow struck and killed the chief. Next, Maodun murdered his stepmother, his younger brother, and all the senior officers who refused to follow his commands. So Maodun made himself the chief [in 209 B.C.E.].

At the start of the year, their leaders hold a small gathering at the chief's location. By the fifth month, a large meeting takes place at Longcheng, during which they offer sacrifices to their ancestors Heaven and Earth, and the gods and spirits. In the fall, when the horses are fat, they hold another large meeting in the Dai forest. There they count up the number of persons and animals. According to their law, anyone who pulls out his sword one foot from its scabbard receives the death penalty, while those convicted of theft have their property confiscated. They punish minor crimes by whipping and major ones by execution. Nobody is held in confinement for more than ten days, and no more than a handful of men are in jail in the entire nation. At dawn the chief rises to worship the sun as it rises, and at night he does the same to the moon. . . . When a ruler dies, his favorite ministers and concubines must follow him in death,

and they often number in the hundreds or even thousands. . . .

Whenever they start some action, they track the stars and the moon. They launch attacks at the full moon and pull back their army when the moon wanes. Following a battle, they award a jug of wine to those who have cut off the heads of enemies, and they are allowed to keep the plunder that they have seized. They make slaves of any prisoners of war. Therefore, when they make war, each warrior works for his own profit. They are very skilled at using decoy soldiers to trick opponents to their destruction. As soon as they see the enemy, they go after their booty like a flock of birds hungry for prey, but when they are defeated they disperse and evaporate. . . . Anyone who brings back a fallen comrade's body from the battlefield is given all the dead man's property. . . .

[*In describing the fluctuating relationship between the Chinese and the Xiongnu, Sima Qian quotes a letter written from the Chinese emperor Wen in 162 B.C.E. to the Xiongnu.*]

"The emperor respectfully asks about the health of the chief of the Xiongnu. Your ambassadors . . . have brought us two horses. We accept them with respect.

In accordance with what the previous emperor decreed the chief of the Xiongnu was to command the region north of the Great Wall where men shoot arrows from their bows, while we were to rule the region south of the wall, where the people live in houses and wear hats and sashes. Under this arrangement, the multitudes of inhabitants of these areas would get their food and clothing by farming, weaving, or hunting, fathers and sons would live side by side, rulers and officials would both be safe, and no one would act violently or rebel. We have heard, however, that a number of evil and deluded men, whose greed for wealth has overcome them, have forsaken justice and broken our peace treaty, paying no heed to what will happen to the multitudes of inhabitants and destroying the harmony that has been in place between the rulers of our two lands.

This, however, is now past history. You said in your [earlier] letter to me that, since our two nations have been brought together again in peace and our two rulers are again in agreement, you want to rest your army and let your horses graze, so that there may be prosperity and happiness for generation upon generation, and so that we can begin again to exist peacefully and harmoniously. We enthusiastically agree with what you said. The sagely wise man, it is said, renews himself every day, reforming and starting over again so that the elderly can rest and the young can mature, with each one keeping his life secure and living out the span of time that Heaven bestows on him. As long as we and the chief of the Xiongnu join together to walk this path, obeying the will of Heaven and having mercy on the people, granting the benefits of peace to generations without end, then no one in the entire world will fail to benefit. Our two great nations, the Han and the Xiongnu, exist next to one another. Since the Xiongnu live in the north, where the country is cold and the severe frosts arrive early in the year, we have ordered our imperial officials to send annually to the chief of the Xiongnu a specified amount of grain, yeast, gold, silk cloth, thread, fiber stuffing for clothing, and other items.

The world currently is experiencing a secure peace, and our peoples are undisturbed. We and the chief of the Xiongnu must be like their parents. When we look back at the past, we recognize that the plans of our officials came to nothing as a result of minor things and insignificant causes. Nothing of this sort deserves to overturn the concord existing between brothers."

Source: Sima Qian, *The Records of the Historian*, chap. 110 in Thomas R. Martin, ed., *Herodotus and Sima Qian: The First Great Historians of Greece and China* (Boston: Bedford/St. Martin's, 2010), 129–33, 136–37.

DOING HISTORY

Perceptions of Outsiders in the Ancient World

1. **Making comparisons:** How might you compare the perceptions of outsiders in these three accounts? Did the authors notice the same features of these societies? Did they focus more on what was exotic or different rather than on what may have been familiar? Did they adopt a similar posture toward the peoples they were describing? Were they simply reporting what they observed or were they making judgments as well?

2. **Describing the "uncivilized":** Both Tacitus and Sima Qian wrote about peoples living beyond the boundaries of "civilization." To what extent did they describe these peoples in a similar fashion?

3. **Relating encounters and observations:** How might the actual relationships between the observers and the observed peoples affect the writers' perceptions of those peoples?

CHAPTER 4

Culture and Religion in Eurasia/North Africa

500 B.C.E.–500 C.E.

In September of 2009, Kong Dejun returned to China from her home in Great Britain. The occasion was a birthday celebration for her ancient ancestor Kong Fuzi, or Confucius, born 2,560 years earlier. Together with some 10,000 other people—descendants, scholars, government officials, and foreign representatives—Kong Dejun attended ceremonies at the Confucian Temple in Qufu, the hometown of China's famous sage. "I was touched to see my ancestor being revered by people from different countries and nations," she said.[1] What made this celebration remarkable was that it took place in a country still ruled by the Communist Party, which had long devoted enormous efforts to discrediting Confucius and his teachings. In the view of communist China's revolutionary leader, Mao Zedong, Confucianism was associated with class inequality, patriarchy, feudalism, superstition, and all things old and backward. But the country's ancient teacher and philosopher had apparently outlasted its revolutionary hero, for now the Communist Party claims Confucius as a national treasure and has established over 300 Confucian Institutes to study his writings. He appears in TV shows and movies, even as many anxious parents offer prayers at Confucian temples when their children are taking the national college entrance exams.

Buddhism and Daoism (DOW-i'zm) have also experienced something of a revival in China, as thousands of temples, destroyed during the heyday of communism, have been repaired and reopened. Christianity too has grown rapidly since the death of Mao in 1976. Here are reminders, in a Chinese context, of the continuing appeal of cultural traditions forged long ago. Those traditions are among the most enduring legacies that second-wave civilizations have bequeathed to the modern world.

China's Cultural Traditions   In this idealized painting, attributed to the Chinese artist Wang Shugu (1649–1730), the Chinese teacher Confucius presents a baby Buddha to the Daoist master Laozi. The image illustrates the assimilation of a major Indian religion into China as well as the generally peaceful coexistence of these three traditions.

In the several centuries surrounding 500 B.C.E., something quite remarkable happened all across Eurasia. More or less simultaneously, in China, India, the Middle East, and Greece, there emerged cultural traditions that have spread widely, have persisted in various forms into the twenty-first century, and have shaped the values and outlooks of most people who have inhabited the planet over the past 2,500 years. But we do well to remember that alongside these larger and more extensive cultural systems flourished a multitude of locally embedded and orally transmitted religious traditions. Within the major civilizations, these so-called "little traditions" interacted constantly with the "great traditions," and in societies that lay beyond the zone of civilization, such as those in Aboriginal Australia, they linked living human beings to the land, to the vegetable and animal worlds, to their ancestors, and to the gods or spirits that inhabited everything. (See, for example, the Aboriginal Dreamtime stories in Working with Evidence, Chapter 1, page 49, and the discussion of ancient African religious beliefs in Chapter 6, pages 254–55.) Here, however, the spotlight falls on those spiritual or religious traditions that emerged from the civilizations of the second-wave era.

In China, it was the time of Confucius and Laozi (low-ZUH), whose teachings gave rise to Confucianism and Daoism, respectively. In India, a series of religious writings known as the Upanishads gave expression to the classical philosophy of what we know as Hinduism, while a religious reformer, Siddhartha Gautama (sih-DHAR-tuh GOW-tau-mah), set in motion a separate religion known later as Buddhism. In the Middle East, a distinctively monotheistic religious tradition appeared. It was expressed in Zoroastrianism, derived from the teachings of the Persian prophet Zarathustra (zar-uh-THOO-struh), and in Judaism, articulated in Israel by a number of Jewish prophets such as Amos, Jeremiah, and Isaiah. Later, this Jewish religious outlook became the basis for both Christianity and Islam. Finally, in Greece, a rational and humanistic tradition found expression in the writings of Socrates, Plato, Aristotle, and many others.

These cultural traditions differed greatly. Chinese and Greek thinkers focused more on the affairs of this world and credited human rationality with the power to understand that reality. Indian, Persian, and Jewish intellectuals, by contrast, explored the unseen realm of the Divine and the relationship of God or the gods to human life. All these traditions sought an alternative to an earlier polytheism, in which the activities of various gods and spirits explained what happened in this world. These gods and spirits had generally been seen as similar to human beings, though much more powerful. Through ritual and sacrifice, men and women might placate the gods or persuade them to do human bidding. In contrast, the new cultural traditions of the second-wave era sought to define a single source of order and meaning in the universe, some moral or religious realm, sharply different from and higher than the sphere of human life. The task of humankind, according to these new ways of thinking, was personal moral or spiritual transformation—often expressed as the development of compassion—by aligning with that higher order.[2] These enormously rich and varied traditions have collectively posed the great questions of human life and society that have haunted and inspired much of humankind ever

A MAP OF TIME

800–400 B.C.E.	Upanishads composed
9th–6th centuries B.C.E.	Hebrew prophets (Amos, Hosea, Micah, Isaiah)
ca. 7th–6th centuries B.C.E.	Life of Zarathustra
600–300 B.C.E.	Emergence of Greek rationalism
6th–5th centuries B.C.E.	Life of Buddha, Confucius, Laozi
586–539 B.C.E.	Jewish exile in Babylon
558–330 B.C.E.	Achaemenid dynasty in Persia; state support for Zoroastrianism
500–221 B.C.E.	Age of warring states in China
469–399 B.C.E.	Life of Socrates
221–206 B.C.E.	Qin dynasty in China
Early 1st century C.E.	Life of Jesus
10–65 C.E.	Life of Paul
4th century C.E.	Christianity becomes state religion of Roman Empire, Armenia, Axum

since. They also defined and legitimated the hierarchies of class and gender that distinguished the various second-wave civilizations from one another.

Why did these traditions all emerge at roughly the same time? Here we encounter an enduring issue of historical analysis: What is the relationship between ideas and the circumstances in which they arise? Are ideas generated by particular political, social, and economic conditions? Or are they the product of creative human imagination independent of the material environment? Or do they derive from some combination of the two? In the case of these cultural traditions, many historians have noted the tumultuous social changes that accompanied their emergence. An iron-age technology, available since roughly 1000 B.C.E., made possible more productive economies and more deadly warfare. Growing cities, increased trade, the prominence of merchant classes, the emergence of new states and empires, new contacts among civilizations—all of these disruptions, occurring in already-literate societies, led thinkers to question older outlooks and to come up with new solutions to fundamental questions: What is the purpose of life? How should human society be ordered? What is the relationship between human life in this world and the moral or spiritual realms that lie beyond or within? But precisely why various societies developed their own distinctive answers to these questions remains elusive—a tribute, perhaps, to the unpredictable genius of human imagination.

SEEKING THE MAIN POINT

Fundamentally, religions are basically alike. Does the material of this chapter support or challenge this idea?

China and the Search for Order

As one of the First Civilizations, China had a tradition of state building that historians have traced back to around 2000 B.C.E. or earlier. When the Zhou dynasty took power in 1122 B.C.E., the notion of the Mandate of Heaven had already taken root, as had the idea that the normal and appropriate condition of China was one of political unity. By the eighth century B.C.E., the authority of the Zhou dynasty and its royal court had substantially weakened, and by 500 B.C.E. any unity that China had earlier enjoyed was long gone. What followed was a period (500–221 B.C.E.) of chaos, growing violence, and disharmony that became known as the age of warring states (see Chapter 3, pages 121–22).

During these dreadful centuries of disorder and turmoil, a number of Chinese thinkers began to consider how order might be restored, how the apparent tranquillity of an earlier time could be realized again. From their reflections emerged classical cultural traditions of Chinese civilization.

The Legalist Answer

One answer to the problem of disorder—though not the first to emerge—was a hardheaded and practical philosophy known as Legalism. To Legalist thinkers, the solution to China's problems lay in rules or laws, clearly spelled out and strictly enforced through a system of rewards and punishments. "If rewards are high," wrote Han Fei, one of the most prominent Legalist philosophers, "then what the ruler wants will be quickly effected; if punishments are heavy, what he does not want will be swiftly prevented."[3] Legalists generally entertained a rather pessimistic view of human nature. Most people, they believed, were stupid and shortsighted. Only the state and its rulers could act in their long-term interests. Doing so meant promoting farmers and soldiers, the only two groups in society who performed essential functions, while suppressing merchants, aristocrats, scholars, and other classes regarded as useless.

■ **Comparison**

What different answers to the problem of disorder arose in classical China?

Legalist thinking provided inspiration and methods for the harsh reunification of China under Shihuangdi and the Qin dynasty (221–206 B.C.E.), but the brutality of that short dynasty thoroughly discredited Legalism (see Chapter 3, page 122). Although its techniques and practices played a role in subsequent Chinese statecraft, few philosophers or rulers ever again openly advocated its ideas as the sole guide for Chinese political life. The Han and all subsequent dynasties drew instead on the teachings of China's greatest sage—Confucius.

The Confucian Answer

Born to an aristocratic family in the state of Lu in northern China, Confucius (551–479 B.C.E.) was both learned and ambitious. Believing that he had found the key to solving China's problem of disorder, he spent much of his adult life seeking a politi-

SNAPSHOT   Thinkers and Philosophies of the Second-Wave Era

Person	Date	Location	Religion/Philosophy	Key Ideas
Zoroaster	7th century B.C.E. (?)	Persia (present-day Iran)	Zoroastrianism	Single High God; cosmic conflict of good and evil
Hebrew prophets (such as Isaiah, Amos, Jeremiah)	9th–6th centuries B.C.E.	Eastern Mediterranean/ Palestine/Israel	Judaism	Transcendent High God; covenant with chosen people; social justice
Anonymous writers of Upanishads	800–400 B.C.E.	India	Brahmanism/Hinduism	Brahman (the single impersonal divine reality); karma; rebirth; goal of liberation (moksha)
Confucius	6th–5th centuries B.C.E.	China	Confucianism	Social harmony through moral example; secular outlook; importance of education; family as model of the state
Mahavira	6th century B.C.E.	India	Jainism	All creatures have souls; purification through non-violence; opposed to caste
Siddhartha Gautama	6th–5th centuries B.C.E.	India	Buddhism	Suffering caused by desire/ attachment; end of suffering through modest and moral living and meditation practice
Laozi, Zhuangzi	6th–3rd centuries B.C.E.	China	Daoism	Withdrawal from the world into contemplation of nature; simple living; end of striving
Socrates, Plato, Aristotle	5th–4th centuries B.C.E.	Greece	Greek rationalism	Style of persistent questioning; secular explanation of nature and human life
Jesus	Early 1st century C.E.	Palestine/Israel	Christianity	Supreme importance of love based on intimate relationship with God; at odds with established authorities
Saint Paul	1st century C.E.	Palestine/Israel/ eastern Roman Empire	Christianity	Christianity as a religion for all; salvation through faith in Jesus Christ

cal position from which he might put his ideas into action. But no such opportunity came his way. Perhaps it was just as well, for it was as a thinker and a teacher that Confucius left a profound imprint on Chinese history and culture and also on other East Asian societies, such as Korea's and Japan's. After his death, his students collected his teachings in a short book called the *Analects*, and later scholars elaborated and commented endlessly on his ideas, creating a body of thought known as Confucianism.

The Confucian answer to the problem of China's disorder was very different from that of the Legalists. Not laws and punishments, but the moral example of superiors was the Confucian key to a restored social harmony. For Confucius, human society consisted primarily of unequal relationships: the father was superior to the son; the husband to the wife; the older brother to the younger brother; and, of course, the ruler to the subject. If the superior party in each of these relationships behaved with sincerity, benevolence, and genuine concern for others, then the inferior party would be motivated to respond with deference and obedience. Harmony then would prevail. As Confucius put it, "The relation between superiors and inferiors is like that between the wind and the grass. The grass must bend when the wind blows across it." Thus, in both family life and in political life, the cultivation of *ren*—translated as human-heartedness, benevolence, goodness, nobility of heart—was the essential ingredient of a tranquil society.

But how were these humane virtues to be nurtured? Believing that people have a capacity for improvement, Confucius emphasized education as the key to moral betterment. He prescribed what we might call a broad liberal arts education emphasizing language, literature, history, philosophy, and ethics, all applied to the practical problems of government. Ritual and ceremonies were also important, for they conveyed the rules of appropriate behavior in the many and varying circumstances of life. For the "superior person," or "gentleman" in Confucian terms, this process of improvement involved serious personal reflection and a willingness to strive continuously to perfect his moral character.

■ Description

Why has Confucianism been defined as a "humanistic philosophy" rather than a supernatural religion?

Filial Piety

The long-enduring social order that Confucius advocated began at home with unquestioning obedience and the utmost respect for parents and other senior members of the family. This Qing dynasty woodcut illustrates the proper filial relationship between father and son in a variety of circumstances. (Chinese colored woodcut, Qing Dynasty [1644–1912]/Private Collection/Roland and Sabrina Michaud/akg-images)

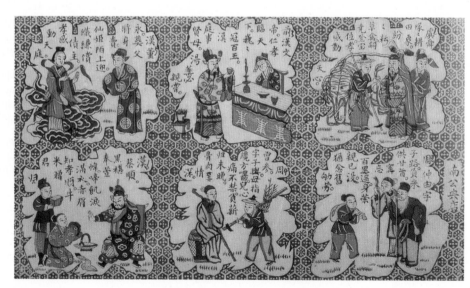

Such ideas left a deep mark on Chinese culture. The discrediting of Legalism during the Qin dynasty opened the door to the adoption of Confucianism as the official ideology of the Chinese state, to such an extent that Confucianism became almost synonymous with Chinese culture. As China's bureaucracy took shape during and after the Han dynasty, Confucianism became the central element of the educational system, which prepared students for the examinations required to gain official positions. In those examinations, candidates were required to apply the principles of Confucianism to specific situations that they might encounter in office. Thus generation after generation of China's male elite was steeped in the ideas and values of Confucianism.

Family life had long been central to Chinese popular culture, expressed in the practice of ancestor veneration, including visiting the graves of the deceased, presenting them with offerings, and erecting commemorative tablets and shrines in their honor. In Confucian thinking, the family became a model for political life, a kind of miniature state. Filial piety, the honoring of one's ancestors and parents, was both an end in itself and a training ground for the reverence due to the emperor and state officials.

Confucian views of the family were rigidly patriarchal and set the tone for defining the lives of women and men alike. Those views were linked to a hierarchical understanding of the cosmos in which an inferior and receptive earth was in balance with the superior and creative principle of Heaven. But these were gendered concepts, with Heaven associated with things male and earth with those female. Thus the subordinate and deferential position of women in relation to men was rooted in the structure of the cosmos itself. What this meant for women was spelled out by a somewhat later woman writer, Ban Zhao (bahn jow) (45–116 C.E.), in a famous work called *Lessons for Women*.

> Let a woman modestly yield to others. . . . Always let her seem to tremble and to fear. . . . Then she may be said to humble herself before others. . . . To guard carefully her chastity . . . , to choose her words with care . . . , to wash and scrub filth away . . . , with whole-hearted devotion to sew and to weave, to love not gossip and silly laughter, in cleanliness and order to prepare the wine and food for serving guests: [these] may be called the characteristics of womanly work.[4]

Ban Zhao called for greater attention to education for young girls, not because they were equal to boys, but so that a young woman might be better prepared to serve her husband. Education for boys, on the other hand, enabled them to more effectively control their wives.

Corresponding Confucian virtues for ideal men were contained in the paired concepts of *wen* and *wu*, both limited largely to males. The superior principle of wen referred to the refined qualities of rationality, scholarship, and literary and artistic abilities, while wu focused attention on physical and martial achievements. Thus men alone, and superior men at that, were eligible for the civil service exams that led to political office and high prestige, while military men and merchants occupied a distinctly lower position in a male social hierarchy.[5]

Beyond defining gender expectations, Confucianism also placed great importance on history, for the ideal good society lay in the past. Confucian ideas were reformist, perhaps even revolutionary, but they were consistently presented as an effort to restore a past golden age. Those ideas also injected a certain democratic element into Chinese elite culture, for the great sage had emphasized that "superior men" and potential government officials were those of outstanding moral character and intellectual achievement, not simply those of aristocratic background. Usually only young men from wealthy families could afford the education necessary for passing examinations, but on occasion villagers could find the resources to sponsor one of their bright sons, potentially propelling him into the stratosphere of the Chinese elite while bringing honor and benefit to the village itself.

Confucian values clearly justified the many inequalities of Chinese society, but they also established certain expectations for the superior parties in China's social hierarchy. Thus emperors should keep taxes low, administer justice, and provide for the material needs of the people. Those who failed to govern by the moral norms of Confucian values forfeited the Mandate of Heaven and invited upheaval and their replacement by another dynasty. Likewise, husbands should deal kindly with their wives and children, lest they invite conflict and disharmony in the family.

Finally, Confucianism marked Chinese elite culture by its secular, or nonreligious, character. Confucius did not deny the reality of gods and spirits. In fact, he advised people to participate in family and state rituals "as if the spirits were present," and he believed that the universe had a moral character with which human beings should align themselves. But the thrust of Confucian teaching was distinctly this-worldly and practical, concerned with human relationships, effective government, and social harmony. Asked on one occasion about his view of death and the spirits, Confucius replied that because we do not fully understand this life, we cannot possibly know anything about the life beyond. Members of the Chinese elite generally acknowledged that magic, the gods, and spirits were perhaps necessary for the lower orders of society, but educated people, they argued, would find them of little help in striving for moral improvement and in establishing a harmonious society.

The Daoist Answer

No civilization has ever painted its cultural outlook in a single color. As Confucian thinking became generally known in China, a quite different school of thought also took shape. Known as Daoism, it was associated with the legendary figure Laozi, who, according to tradition, was a sixth-century B.C.E. archivist. He is said to have penned a short poetic volume, the *Daodejing* (DOW-DAY-JIHNG) (*The Way and Its Power*), before vanishing in the wilderness to the west of China on his water buffalo. Daoist ideas were later expressed in a more explicit fashion by the philosopher Zhuangzi (369–286 B.C.E.).

In many ways, Daoist thinking ran counter to that of Confucius, who had emphasized the importance of education and earnest striving for moral improvement and good government. The Daoists ridiculed such efforts as artificial and useless, claiming that they generally made things worse. In the face of China's disorder and chaos, Daoists urged withdrawal into the world of nature and encouraged behavior that was spontaneous, individualistic, and natural. Whereas Confucius focused on the world of human relationships, the Daoists turned the spotlight on the immense realm of nature and its mysterious unfolding patterns. "Confucius roams within society," the Chinese have often said. "Laozi wanders beyond."

The central concept of Daoist thinking is *dao*, an elusive notion that refers to the way of nature, the underlying and unchanging principle that governs all natural phenomena. The dao "moves around and around, but does not on this account suffer," wrote Laozi in the *Daodejing*. "All life comes from it. It wraps everything with its love as in a garment, and yet it claims no honor, for it does not demand to be lord. I do not know its name and so I call it the Dao, the Way, and I rejoice in its power."[6]

Amid the world of civilization, so highly valued by Confucius, the Daoists yearned for an earlier time, "an age of perfect virtue" that had been disrupted by Confucian striving for something better. Then, according to one Daoist master, "there were no paths and ramps on the mountains and no boats upon the bridges. . . . There were vast numbers of animals and grasses, and trees reached their natural growth. Wild animals could be taken for walks on leashes, and one could climb up to the nests of magpies and other birds." Such a vision of human harmony with nature contrasted sharply with the Confucian outlook, which urged "the development of a world of culture from a nature experienced as hostile." To Confucians, humankind "disposes over the world of [wild] things, tames wild animals, and brings cowed vermin under his control."[7] Thus individual Daoists often fled to the mountains, where they might experience the dao in union with nature. Li Po, a much-acclaimed Chinese poet of the eighth century, expressed a Daoist sensibility in this short poem:

The birds have vanished into the sky,
And now the last cloud drains away.

■ **Comparison**
How did the Daoist outlook differ from that of Confucianism?

Chinese Landscape Paintings
Focused largely on mountains and water, Chinese landscape paintings were much influenced by the Daoist search for harmony with nature. Thus human figures and buildings were usually eclipsed by towering peaks, waterfalls, clouds, and trees. This thirteenth-century ink-on-silk painting illustrates that sensibility. The poem at the top reads: "Night rains cleansed the capital's suburban farms, / Morning sun brightens the emperor's city; / People work happily in a good year, / Dancing and singing they cross a path in the field." (*Singing and Dancing*, Southern Song Period [960–1279], [ink and watercolor on silk], Ma Yuan [1190–1235]/Palace Museum, Beijing, China/Bridgeman Images)

We sit together, the mountain and me,
until only the mountain remains.[8]

Applied to human life, Daoism invited people to withdraw from the world of political and social activism, to disengage from the public life so important to Confucius, and to align themselves with the way of nature. It meant simplicity in living, small self-sufficient communities, limited government, and the abandonment of education and active efforts at self-improvement. "Give up learning," declares the *Daodejing*, "and put an end to your troubles." The flavor of the Daoist approach to life is evident in this passage from the *Daodejing*, describing a small and simple society:

Though there were individuals with the abilities of ten or a hundred men,
there should be no employment of them . . . ;
Though they had boats and carriages, they should have no occasion to ride in them;
though they had buff coats and sharp weapons, they should have no occasion to
use them.
I would make the people return to the use of knotted cords (instead of written
characters).
They should think their (coarse) food sweet; their (plain) clothes beautiful;
their (poor) dwellings places of rest;
and their common (simple) ways sources of enjoyment.
There should be a neighbouring state within sight . . . ,
but I would make the people . . . not have any intercourse with it.[9]

Like Confucianism, the Daoist perspective viewed family life as central to Chinese society, though the element of male/female hierarchy was downplayed in favor of complementarity and balance between the sexes.

Despite its various differences with the ideas of Confucianism, the Daoist perspective was widely regarded by elite Chinese as complementing rather than contradicting Confucian values (see the chapter-opening image on page 146). Such an outlook was facilitated by the ancient Chinese concept of *yin* and *yang*, which expressed a belief in the unity of opposites (see figure).

The Yin Yang Symbol

Thus a scholar-official might pursue the Confucian project of "government by goodness" during the day, but upon returning home in the evening or following his retirement, he might well behave in a more Daoist fashion—pursuing the simple life, reading Daoist philosophy, practicing Daoist meditation and breathing exercises, or enjoying landscape paintings in which tiny human figures are dwarfed by the vast peaks and valleys of the natural world (see image on page 155). Daoism also shaped the culture of ordinary people as it entered popular religion. This kind of Daoism sought to tap the power of the dao for practical uses and came to include magic, fortune-telling, and the search for immortality. It also on occasion provided an ideology for peasant uprisings, such as the Yellow Turban Rebellion (184–204 C.E.), which imagined a utopian society without the oppression of governments and landlords (see Chapter 5, pages 197–98). In its many and varied forms, Daoism, like Confucianism, became an enduring element of the Chinese cultural tradition.

Cultural Traditions of Classical India

The cultural development of Indian civilization was far different from that of China. Whereas Confucianism paid little attention to the gods, spirits, and speculation about religious matters, Indian elite culture embraced the Divine and all things spiritual with enthusiasm and generated elaborate philosophical visions about the nature of ultimate reality. But the Indian religious tradition—later called Hinduism—differed from other world religions as well. Unlike Buddhism, Christianity, or Islam, Hinduism had no historical founder; rather, it grew up over many centuries along with Indian civilization. Although it later spread into Southeast Asia, Hinduism was not a missionary religion seeking converts, but was, like Judaism, associated with a particular people and territory.

In fact, "Hinduism" was never a single tradition at all, and the term itself derived from outsiders—Greeks, Muslims, and later the British—who sought to reduce the infinite variety of Indian cultural patterns into a recognizable system. From the inside, however, Hinduism dissolved into a vast diversity of gods, spirits, beliefs, practices, rituals, and philosophies. This endlessly variegated Hinduism served to incorporate into Indian civilization the many diverse peoples who migrated into or invaded the South Asian peninsula over many centuries and several millennia. Its ability to accommodate this diversity gave India's cultural development a distinctive quality.

South Asian Religion: From Ritual Sacrifice to Philosophical Speculation

Despite the fragmentation and variety of Indian cultural and religious patterns, an evolving set of widely recognized sacred texts provided some commonality. The earliest of these texts, known as the Vedas (VAY-duhs), were collections of poems, hymns, prayers, and rituals. Compiled by priests called Brahmins, the Vedas were for centuries transmitted orally and were reduced to writing in Sanskrit around 600 B.C.E. In the Vedas, historians have caught fleeting glimpses of Indian civilization in its formative centuries (1500–600 B.C.E.). Those sacred writings tell of small competing chiefdoms or kingdoms, of sacred sounds and fires, of numerous gods, rising and falling in importance over the centuries. They also suggest a clearly patriarchal society, but one that afforded upper-class women somewhat greater opportunities than they later enjoyed. Vedic women participated in religious sacrifices, sometimes engaged in scholarship and religious debate, were allowed to wear the sacred thread that symbolized ritual purity in the higher castes, and could on occasion marry a man of their own choosing. The Vedas described as well the elaborate ritual sacrifices that Brahmin priests required. Performing these sacrifices and rituals with great precision enabled the Brahmins to acquire enormous power and wealth, sometimes exceeding even that of kings and warriors. But Brahmins also generated growing criticism, as ritual became mechanical and formal and as Brahmins required heavy fees to perform them.

■ Change
In what ways did the religious traditions of South Asia change over the centuries?

From this dissatisfaction arose another body of sacred texts, the Upanishads (oo-PAHN-ee-shahds). Composed by largely anonymous thinkers between 800 and 400 B.C.E., these were mystical and highly philosophical works that sought to probe the inner meaning of the sacrifices prescribed in the Vedas. In the Upanishads, external ritual gave way to introspective thinking, which expressed in many and varied formulations the central concepts of philosophical Hinduism that have persisted into modern times. Chief among them was the idea of Brahman, the World Soul, the final and ultimate reality. Beyond the multiplicity of material objects and individual persons and beyond even the various gods themselves lay this primal unitary energy or divine reality infusing all things, similar in some ways to the Chinese notion of the dao. This alone was real; the immense diversity of existence that human beings perceived with their senses was but an illusion.

The fundamental assertion of philosophical Hinduism was that the individual human soul, or *atman*, was in fact a part of Brahman. Beyond the quest for pleasure, wealth, power, and social position, all of which were perfectly normal and quite legitimate, lay the effort to achieve the final goal of humankind—union with Brahman, an end to our illusory perception of a separate existence. This was *moksha* (MOHK-shuh), or liberation, compared sometimes to a bubble in a glass of water breaking through the surface and becoming one with the surrounding atmosphere.

Achieving this exalted state was held to involve many lifetimes, and the notion of *samsara*, or rebirth/reincarnation, became a central feature of Hindu thinking. Human souls migrated from body to body over many lifetimes, depending on one's actions. This was the law of *karma*. Pure actions, appropriate to one's station in life, resulted in rebirth in a higher social position or caste. Thus the caste system of distinct and ranked groups, each with its own duties, became a register of spiritual progress. Birth in a higher caste was evidence of "good karma," based on actions in a previous life, and offered a better chance to achieve moksha, which brought with it an end to the painful cycle of rebirth.

If Hinduism underpinned caste, it also legitimated and expressed India's gender system. As South Asian civilization crystallized during the second-wave era, its patriarchal features tightened. Women were increasingly seen as "unclean below the navel," forbidden to learn the Vedas, and excluded from public religious rituals. The Laws of Manu, probably composed in the early centuries of the Common Era, described a divinely ordained social order and articulated a gender system whose ideals endured for a millennium or more. It taught that all embryos were basically male and that only weak semen generated female babies. It advocated child marriage for girls to men far older than themselves. "A virtuous wife," the Laws proclaimed, "should constantly serve her husband like a god" and should never remarry after his death. In a famous prescription similar to that of Chinese and other patriarchal societies, the Laws declared: "In childhood a female must be subject to her father; in youth to her husband; when her lord is dead to her sons; a woman must never be independent."[10]

Hindu Ascetics
Hinduism called for men in the final stage of life to leave ordinary ways of living and withdraw into the forests to seek spiritual liberation, or moksha. Here, in an illustration from an early thirteenth-century Indian manuscript, a holy man explores a text with three disciples in a secluded rural setting. (Musée des Arts Asiatiques—Guimet, Paris, France/© RMN–Grand Palais/Art Resource, NY)

And yet some aspects of Hinduism served to empower women. Sexual pleasure was considered a legitimate goal for both men and women, and its many and varied techniques were detailed in the *Kamasutra*. Many Hindu deities were female, some life-giving and faithful, others, like Kali, fiercely destructive. Women were particularly prominent in the growing devotional cults dedicated to particular deities, where neither gender nor caste was an obstacle to spiritual fulfillment.

A further feature of Hindu religious thought lay in its provision of different paths to the ultimate goal of liberation, or moksha. Various ways to this final release, appropriate to people of different temperaments, were spelled out in Hindu teachings. Some might achieve moksha through knowledge or study; others by means of detached action in the world, doing one's work without regard to consequences; still others through passionate devotion to some deity or through extended meditation practice. Such ideas—carried by Brahmin priests and wandering ascetics or holy men, who had withdrawn from ordinary life to pursue their spiritual development—became widely known throughout India.

The Buddhist Challenge

About the same time as philosophical Hinduism was emerging, another movement took shape that soon became a distinct and separate religious tradition—Buddhism. Unlike Hinduism, this new faith had a historical founder, Siddhartha Gautama (ca. 566–ca. 486 B.C.E.), a prince from a small north Indian state. According to Buddhist tradition, the prince had enjoyed a sheltered and delightful youth but was shocked to his core upon encountering old age, sickness, and death. Leaving family and fortune behind, he then set out on a six-year spiritual quest, finally achieving insight, or "enlightenment," at the age of thirty-five. For the rest of his life, he taught what he had learned and gathered a small but growing community whose members came to see him as the Buddha, the Enlightened One, a human being who had awakened.

■ **Comparison**

In what ways did Buddhism reflect Hindu traditions, and in what ways did it challenge them?

"I teach but one thing," the Buddha said, "suffering and the end of suffering." To the Buddha, suffering or sorrow—experiencing life as imperfect, impermanent, and unsatisfactory—was the central and universal feature of human life. Widely known to Buddhists as *dukkha*, this kind of suffering derived from desire or craving for individual fulfillment, from attachment to that which inevitably changes, particularly to the notion of a core self or ego that is uniquely and solidly "me." The cure for this "dis-ease" lay in living a modest and moral life combined with meditation practice. Those who followed the Buddhist path most fully could expect to achieve enlightenment, or *nirvana*, a virtually indescribable state in which individual identity would be "extinguished" along with all greed, hatred, and delusion. With the pain of unnecessary suffering finally ended, the enlightened person would experience an overwhelming serenity, even in the midst of difficulty, as well as an immense loving-kindness, or compassion, for all beings. It was a simple message, elaborated endlessly and in various forms by those who followed the Buddha.

Much of the Buddha's teaching reflected the Hindu traditions from which it sprang. The idea that ordinary life is an illusion, the concepts of karma and rebirth, the goal of overcoming the incessant demands of the ego, the practice of meditation, the hope for final release from the cycle of rebirth—all of these Hindu elements found their way into Buddhist teaching. In this respect, Buddhism was a simplified and more accessible version of Hinduism.

Other elements of Buddhist teaching, however, sharply challenged prevailing Hindu thinking. Rejecting the religious authority of the Brahmins, the Buddha ridiculed their rituals and sacrifices as irrelevant to the hard work of dealing with one's suffering. Nor was he much interested in abstract speculation about the creation of the world or the existence of God, for such questions, he declared, "are not useful in the quest for holiness; they do not lead to peace and to the direct knowledge of *nirvana*." Individuals had to take responsibility for their own spiritual development with no help from human authorities or supernatural beings. It was a path of intense self-effort, based on personal experience. The Buddha also challenged the inequalities of a Hindu-based

Classic Indian Buddha

This sixth-century C.E. image of the Buddha from eastern India shows a classical representation of the great teacher. The Buddha's right hand with palm facing the viewer indicates reassurance, or "have no fear." The partially webbed fingers are among the *lakshanas*, or signs of a Buddha image, that denote the Buddha's unique status. So too is the knot on the top of his head, symbolizing enlightenment. The elongated earlobes remind the viewer that earlier in his life the Buddha wore heavy and luxurious earrings, while his partially closed and downcast eyes and his bare feet indicate detachment from the world. (Standing Buddha, India [probably Bihar]. Gupta period. Late 6th–early 7th century. Bronze. H. 18½ x 6⅛ in. [47.0 × 15.6 cm.]. Hands: Diam. 5⅝ in. [14.3 cm.]. Purchase, Florance Waterbury Bequest, 1969 [69.222]. Photo: Bruce White. The Metropolitan Museum of Art, New York, NY, USA/Image copyright © Metropolitan Museum of Art/Image source: Art Resource, NY)

caste system, arguing that neither caste position nor gender was a barrier to enlightenment. The possibility of "awakening" was available to all.

But when it came to establishing a formal organization of the Buddha's most devoted followers, the prevailing patriarchy of Indian society made itself felt. Buddhist texts recount that the Buddha's foster mother, Prajapati Gotami, sought to enter the newly created order of monks but was repeatedly refused admission by the Buddha himself. Only after the intervention of the Buddha's attendant, Ananda, did he relent and allow women to join a separate order of nuns. Even then, these nuns were subjected to a series of rules that clearly subordinated them to men. Male monks, for example, could officially admonish the nuns, but the reverse was forbidden. Such policies reflected a particular strain of Buddhist thinking that viewed women as a distracting obstacle to male enlightenment.

Nonetheless, thousands of women flocked to join the Buddhist order of nuns, where they found a degree of freedom and independence unavailable elsewhere in Indian society. Buddhist nuns delighted in the relative freedom of their order, where they largely ran their own affairs, were forbidden to do household chores, and devoted themselves wholly to the search for "awakening," which many apparently achieved. A nun named Mutta declared: "I am free from the three crooked things: mortar, pestle, and my crooked husband. I am free from birth and death and all that dragged me back."[11]

Gradually, Buddhist teachings found an audience in India. Buddhism's egalitarian message appealed especially to lower-caste groups and to women. The availability of its teaching in the local language of Pali, rather than the classical Sanskrit, made it accessible. Establishing monasteries and stupas (commemorative monuments containing relics of the Buddha) on the site of neighborhood shrines to earth spirits or near a sacred tree linked the new religion to local traditions. The most dedicated followers joined monasteries, devoting their lives to religious practice and spreading the message among nearby people. (See Zooming In: Nalanda, page 162.) State support during the reign of Ashoka (r. 268–232 B.C.E.) (see Chapter 3, page 133) likewise helped the new religion gain a foothold in India as a distinct tradition separate from Hinduism.

As Buddhism spread, both within and beyond India, differences in understanding soon emerged, particularly as to how nirvana could be achieved or, in a common Buddhist metaphor, how to cross the river to the far shore of enlightenment. The Buddha had taught a rather austere doctrine of intense self-effort, undertaken most actively by monks and nuns who withdrew from society to devote themselves fully to the quest. This early version of the new religion, known as Theravada (Teaching of the Elders), portrayed the Buddha as an immensely wise teacher and model, but certainly not divine. It was more psychological than religious, a set of practices rather than a set of beliefs. The gods, though never completely denied, played little role in assisting believers in their search for enlightenment. In short, individuals were on their own in crossing the river. Each person had to row his or her own boat. Clearly, this was not for everyone.

■ **Comparison**

What is the difference between the Theravada and Mahayana expressions of Buddhism?

Nalanda, India's Buddhist University

Nalanda, a village in the Bihar region of northeastern India, has a storied past in the world of Buddhism, for tradition has it that the Buddha himself visited on several occasions and the Mauryan dynasty emperor Ashoka built a temple there. But the village came to a wider prominence much later during the fifth century C.E. when a huge monastic complex, dedicated to Buddhist learning, began to take shape. Many have viewed it as the world's first university. With eight separate compounds, ten temples, many meditation halls and class-rooms, and numerous sculptures, Nalanda was a stunning architectural achievement.

One of the many temples in the Nalanda complex.

Patronized by the emperors of India's Gupta dynasty and later rulers, Nalanda was supported by the dedicated revenue from 100 or more villages in the region and operated under state supervision. Students, numbering in the many thousands, lived in dormitories and were taught by hundreds of instructors. Scholars and students alike came to Nalanda from all over the Buddhist world and beyond—China, Korea, Japan, Tibet, Indonesia, Persia, and Central Asia. Many spent a few years in Indonesia or elsewhere to improve their Sanskrit before moving on to the highly prestigious Nalanda center. There they had access to a huge library occupying three buildings, one of them a nine-story structure, housing endless books and manuscripts.

If the student body was international, the curriculum was likewise inclusive. While focused on distinctly Buddhist writings, students also studied Hindu sacred texts, Sanskrit grammar, logic, astronomy, medicine, and philosophy. Numerous Buddhist images were joined by those representing Hindu deities. Nalanda was a cosmopolitan place of lively discussion and controversy among rival schools of thought.

Visitors from the more remote regions of the Buddhist world were stunned at what they witnessed at

photo: Votive stupa of the principal temple of Site III/Giraudon/Bridgeman Images

By the early centuries of the Common Era, a modified form of Buddhism called Mahayana (mah-huh-YAH-nah) (Great Vehicle) had taken root in parts of India, proclaiming that help was available for the strenuous voyage. Buddhist thinkers developed the idea of *bodhisattvas* (BOH-dih-SAT-vuhs), spiritually developed people who postponed their own entry into nirvana to assist those who were still suffering. The Buddha himself became something of a god, and both earlier and future Buddhas were available to offer help. Elaborate descriptions of these supernatural beings, together with various levels of Heavens and Hells, transformed Buddhism into a popular religion of salvation. Furthermore, religious merit, leading to salvation, might now be earned by acts of piety and devotion, such as contributing to the support of a monastery, and that merit might be transferred to others. This was the Great Vehicle, allowing far more people to make the voyage across the river. (See Working with Evidence, page 183, for the evolution of Buddhism reflected in images.)

Nalanda. In the seventh century C.E., the Chinese Buddhist monk Xuanzang recorded some of his impressions:

> Ten thousand monks always lived there, both hosts and guests. They studied Mahayana [Buddhist] teachings and the doctrines of the eighteen schools, as well as worldly books such as the [Hindu] Vedas. They also learned about works on logic, grammar, medicine, and divination. . . . Lectures were given at more than a hundred places in the monastery every day, and the students studied diligently without wasting a single moment. As all the monks who lived there were men of virtue, the atmosphere in the monastery was naturally solemn and dignified. For more than seven hundred years since its establishment, none of the monks had committed any offence.[12]

Xuanzang's comments about the "solemn and dignified" atmosphere of Nalanda may have been a little exaggerated, for reports of dice and board games, tumbling, shooting marbles, sword play, and even performances by dancing girls cast a somewhat different picture. Students apparently will be students.

Turkish Muslim invasions of India around 1200 badly damaged Nalanda; many monks were killed, others fled to Tibet or Nepal, and the library was burned. A Tibetan visitor in 1235 found a much-reduced Nalanda with only seventy students and one ninety-year-old teacher. The subsequent closure of Nalanda was part of a more general process by which Buddhism largely vanished within India. Even the name of Nalanda was apparently forgotten, as the area came to be called Bargaon. But the scholarship of Nalanda had enriched both Indian science and Buddhist learning and practice in Tibet, China, and elsewhere. In late 2013, the Dalai Lama paid tribute to the Nalanda tradition: "The name Nalanda was very familiar to me as the source of the tradition we follow in Tibet. First we memorize the root text, then study it word by word and then debate it with our fellow students to penetrate the depths of its meaning."[13]

The spectacular ruins of Nalanda began to be excavated in the nineteenth century when India was a British colony. And in 2014, a new, revived, and modern Nalanda University, now a secular institution, welcomed students for the first time, some 1,500 years after the opening of the original Nalanda complex.

Questions: What is most striking to you about Nalanda? How might the experiences of its students compare to your university experience? In what ways did Nalanda's influence stretch beyond India's borders and persist even after its collapse?

Hinduism as a Religion of Duty and Devotion

Strangely enough, Buddhism as a distinct religious practice ultimately died out in the land of its birth as it was reincorporated into a broader Hindu tradition, but it spread widely and flourished, particularly in its Mahayana form, in other parts of Asia. Buddhism declined in India perhaps in part because the mounting wealth of monasteries and the economic interests of their leading figures separated them from ordinary people. Competition from Islam after 1000 C.E. also played a role. But the most important reason for the waning of Buddhism in India was the growth during the first millennium C.E. of a new kind of popular Hinduism, which the masses found more accessible than the elaborate sacrifices of the Brahmins or the philosophical speculations of intellectuals. Expressed in the widely known epic poems called the *Mahabharata* (mah-hah-BAH-rah-tah) and the *Ramayana*, this revived Hinduism indicated more clearly that action in the world and the detached performance of caste duties might also provide a path to liberation. It was perhaps a response to the challenge of Buddhism.

■ **Change**
What new emphases characterized Hinduism as it responded to the challenge of Buddhism?

In the much-beloved Hindu text known as the Bhagavad Gita (BUH-guh-vahd GEE-tuh), the troubled warrior-hero Arjuna is in anguish over the necessity of killing his kinsmen as a decisive battle approaches. But he is assured by his charioteer Lord Krishna, an incarnation of the god Vishnu, that performing his duty as a warrior, and doing so selflessly without regard to consequences, is an act of devotion that would lead to "release from the shackles of repeated rebirth." This was not an invitation to militarism, but rather an affirmation that ordinary people, not just Brahmins, could also find spiritual fulfillment by selflessly performing the ordinary duties of their lives: "The man who, casting off all desires, lives free from attachments, who is free from egoism, and from the feeling that this or that is mine, obtains tranquility." Withdrawal and asceticism were not the only ways to moksha.

Also becoming increasingly prominent was yet another religious path—the way of devotion to one or another of India's many gods and goddesses. Beginning in south India and moving northward, this *bhakti* (BAHK-tee) (worship) movement involved the intense adoration of and identification with a particular deity through songs, prayers, and rituals. By far the most popular deities were Vishnu, the protector and preserver of creation who was associated with mercy and goodness, and Shiva, a god representing the Divine in its destructive aspect, but many others also had their followers. This form of Hindu expression sometimes pushed against the rigid caste and gender hierarchies of Indian society by inviting all to an adoration of the Divine. After all, Krishna in the Bhagavad Gita had declared that "those who take shelter in Me, though they be of lower birth—women, vaishyas [merchants] and shudras [workers]—can attain the supreme destination."

The proliferation of gods and goddesses, and of their bhakti cults, occasioned very little friction or serious religious conflict. "Hinduism," writes a leading scholar, "is essentially tolerant, and would rather assimilate than rigidly exclude."[14] This capacity for assimilation extended to an already-declining Buddhism, which for many people had become yet another cult worshipping yet another god. The Buddha in fact was incorporated into the Hindu pantheon as the ninth incarnation of Vishnu. By 1000 C.E., Buddhism had largely disappeared as a separate religious tradition within India.

Thus a constantly evolving and enormously varied South Asian religious tradition had been substantially transformed. An early emphasis on ritual sacrifice gave way to that of philosophical speculation, devotional worship, and detached action in the world. In the process, that tradition had generated Buddhism, which became the first of the great universal religions of world history, and then had absorbed that new faith back into the fold of an emerging popular Hinduism.

SUMMING UP SO FAR

How did the evolution of cultural traditions in India and China differ during the era of second-wave civilizations?

Toward Monotheism: The Search for God in the Middle East

Paralleling the evolution of Chinese and Indian cultural traditions was the movement toward a distinctive monotheistic religious outlook in the Middle East, which found expression in Persian Zoroastrianism and in Judaism. Neither of these religions themselves spread very widely, but the monotheism that they nurtured became the basis for both Christianity and Islam, which have shaped so much of world history over the past 2,000 years. Amid the proliferation of gods and spirits that had long characterized religious life throughout the ancient world, monotheism—the idea of a single supreme deity, the sole source of all life and being—was a radical cultural innovation. That conception created the possibility of a universal religion, open to all of humankind, but it could also mean an exclusive and intolerant faith.

Zoroastrianism

During the glory years of the powerful Persian Empire, a new religion arose to challenge the polytheism of earlier times. Tradition dates its Persian prophet, Zarathustra (Zoroaster to the Greeks), to the sixth or seventh century B.C.E., although some scholars place him hundreds of years earlier. Whenever he actually lived, his ideas took hold in Persia and received a degree of state support during the Achaemenid dynasty (558–330 B.C.E.). Appalled by the endemic violence of recurring cattle raids, Zarathustra recast the traditional Persian polytheism into a vision of a single unique god, Ahura Mazda, who ruled the world and was the source of all truth, light, and goodness. This benevolent deity was engaged in a cosmic struggle with the forces of evil, embodied in an equivalent supernatural figure, Angra Mainyu. Ultimately this struggle would be decided in favor of Ahura Mazda, aided by the arrival of a final savior who would restore the world to its earlier purity and peace. At a day of judgment, those who had aligned with Ahura Mazda would be granted new resurrected bodies and rewarded with eternal life in Paradise. Those who had sided with evil and the "Lie" (which found expression as greed, wrath, and envy) were condemned to everlasting punishment. Zoroastrian (zohr-oh-ASS-tree-ahn) teaching thus placed great emphasis on the free will of humankind and the necessity for each individual to choose between good and evil.

The Zoroastrian faith achieved widespread support within the Persian heartland, although it also found adherents in other parts of the empire, such as Egypt, Mesopotamia, and Anatolia. But it never became an active missionary religion and did not spread widely beyond the region. Alexander the Great's invasion of the Persian Empire and the subsequent Greek-ruled Seleucid dynasty (330–155 B.C.E.) were disastrous for Zoroastrianism, as temples were plundered, priests slaughtered, and sacred writings burned. But the new faith managed to survive this onslaught

■ **Connection**
What aspects of Zoroastrianism and Judaism subsequently found a place in Christianity and Islam?

Zoroastrian Fire Altar
Representing the energy of the creator god Ahura Mazda, the fire altar became an important symbol of Zoroastrianism and was often depicted on Persian coins in association with images of Persian rulers. This particular coin dates from the third century C.E. (© AAAC/Topham/The Image Works)

and flourished again during the Parthian (247 B.C.E.–224 C.E.) and Sassanid (224–651 C.E.) dynasties. It was the arrival of Islam and an Arab empire that occasioned the final decline of Zoroastrianism in Persia, although a few believers fled to India, where they became known as Parsis ("Persians"). The Parsis have continued their faith into present times.

Like Buddhism, the Zoroastrian faith vanished from its place of origin, but unlike Buddhism, it did not spread beyond Persia in a recognizable form. Some elements of the Zoroastrian belief system, however, did become incorporated into other religious traditions. The presence of many Jews in the Persian Empire meant that they surely became aware of Zoroastrian ideas. Many of those ideas—including the conflict of God and an evil counterpart (Satan); the notion of a last judgment and resurrected bodies; and a belief in the final defeat of evil, the arrival of a savior (Messiah), and the remaking of the world at the end of time—found a place in an evolving Judaism. Some of these teachings, especially the concepts of Heaven and Hell, later became prominent in those enormously influential successors to Judaism—Christianity and Islam.[15] Thus the Persian tradition of Zoroastrianism continued to echo well beyond its disappearance in the land of its birth.

Judaism

While Zoroastrianism emerged in the greatest empire of its time, Judaism, the Middle East's other ancient monotheistic tradition, was born among one of the region's smaller and, at the time, less significant peoples—the Hebrews. Their traditions, recorded in the Hebrew scriptures, tell of an early migration from Mesopotamia to Canaan under the leadership of Abraham. Those same traditions report that a portion of these people later fled to Egypt, where they were first enslaved and then miraculously escaped to rejoin their kinfolk in Palestine. There, around 1000 B.C.E., they established a small state, which soon split into two parts—a northern kingdom called Israel and a southern state called Judah.

■ **Description**
What was distinctive about the Jewish religious tradition?

In a region politically dominated by the large empires of Assyria, Babylon, and Persia, these tiny Hebrew communities lived a precarious existence. Israel was conquered by Assyria in 722 B.C.E., and many of its inhabitants were deported to distant regions, where they assimilated into the local culture. In 586 B.C.E., the kingdom of Judah likewise came under Babylonian control, and its elite class was shipped off to exile. "By the rivers of Babylon," wrote one of their poets, "there we sat down, yea, we wept, when we remembered Zion [Jerusalem]." It was in Babylonian exile that these people, now calling themselves Jews, retained and renewed their cultural identity, and later a small number were able to return to their homeland. A large part of that identity lay in their unique religious ideas. It was in creating that religious tradition, rather than in building a powerful empire, that this small people cast a long shadow in world history.

Ancient Israel

From their unique historical memory of exodus from Egypt and exile in Babylon, the Hebrews evolved over many centuries a distinctive conception of God. Unlike the peoples of Mesopotamia, India, Greece, and elsewhere—all of whom populated the invisible realm with numerous gods and goddesses—Jews found in their God, whom they called Yahweh (YAH-way), a powerful and jealous deity, who demanded their exclusive loyalty. "Thou shalt have no other gods before me"—this was the first of the Ten Commandments. It was a difficult requirement, for as the Hebrews turned from a pastoral life to agriculture, many of them were attracted by the fertility gods of neighboring peoples. Their neighbors' goddesses were also attractive, offering a kind of spiritual support that the primarily masculine Yahweh could not. Foreign deities also entered Hebrew culture through royal treaty obligations with nearby states. Thus the emerging Hebrew conception of the Divine was not quite monotheism, for the repeated demands of the Hebrew prophets to turn away from other gods show that those deities remained real for many Jews. Over time, however, the priesthood that supported the one-god theory triumphed. The Jews came to understand their relationship to Yahweh as a contract or a covenant. In return for their sole devotion and obedience to God's laws, Yahweh would consider the Jews his chosen people, favoring them in battle, causing them to grow in numbers, and bringing them prosperity and blessing.

Unlike the bickering, arbitrary, polytheistic gods of Mesopotamia or ancient Greece, who were associated with the forces of nature and behaved in quite human fashion, Yahweh was increasingly seen as a lofty, transcendent deity of utter holiness and purity, set far above the world of nature, which he had created. But unlike the impersonal conceptions of ultimate reality found in Daoism and Hinduism, Yahweh was encountered as a divine person with whom people could actively communicate. He also acted within the historical process, bringing the Jews out of Egypt or using foreign empires to punish them for their disobedience.

Furthermore, for some, Yahweh was transformed from a god of war, who ordered his people to "utterly destroy" the original inhabitants of the Promised Land, to a god of social justice and compassion for the poor and the marginalized, especially in the passionate pronouncements of Jewish prophets such as Amos and Isaiah. The prophet Isaiah describes Yahweh as rejecting the empty rituals of his chosen but sinful people: "What to me is the multitude of your sacrifices, says the Lord. . . . Wash yourselves, make yourselves clean, . . . cease to do evil, learn to do good; seek justice; correct oppression; defend the fatherless; plead for the widow."[16]

Here was a distinctive conception of the Divine—singular, transcendent, personal, ruling over the natural order, engaged in history, and demanding social justice and moral righteousness above sacrifices and rituals. This set of ideas sustained a separate Jewish identity in both ancient and modern times, and it was this understanding of God that provided the foundation on which those later Abrahamic faiths of Christianity and Islam were built.

Jewish understanding of the natural world likewise informed all three religious traditions. The Jewish scriptures pronounced the world of nature as real and positively valued, not simply an illusion or a distraction from spiritual concerns, as in some versions of Hindu or Buddhist thinking. The first chapter of Genesis ends with God's review of his creation: "And God saw everything that he had made, and behold it was very good." Moreover, the material world disclosed or revealed something of the divine mystery. The writer of the Psalms affirmed that "the heavens declare the glory of God and the firmament shows his handiwork." Much later, the Quran echoed this understanding: "There are signs in the creation of the heavens and the earth, and in the alternation of night and day for people of understanding." Finally, Jewish tradition made human beings the stewards of creation. They were to "have dominion . . . over all the earth," even as Adam and Eve in the Garden of Eden were instructed "to till it and keep it." The Jewish teacher named Jesus affirmed this view of the world in the famous Lord's prayer: "Thy kingdom come, on earth as it is in heaven."

The Cultural Tradition of Classical Greece: The Search for a Rational Order

Unlike the Jews, the Persians, or the civilization of India, Greek thinkers of the second-wave era generated no lasting religious tradition of world historical importance. The religion of these city-states brought together the unpredictable, quarreling, and lustful gods of Mount Olympus, secret fertility cults, oracles predicting the future, and the ecstatic worship of Dionysus, the god of wine. The distinctive feature of the classical Greek cultural tradition was the willingness of many Greek intellectuals to abandon this mythological framework, to affirm that the world was a physical reality governed by natural laws, and to assert that human rationality could both understand these laws and work out a system of moral and ethical life as well. In separating science and philosophy from conventional religion, the Greeks developed a way of thinking that bore some similarity to the secularism of Confucian thought in China.

■ **Description**
What are the distinctive features of the Greek intellectual tradition?

Precisely why Greek thought evolved in this direction is hard to say. Perhaps the diversity and incoherence of Greek religious mythology presented its intellectuals with a challenge to bring some order to their understanding of the world. Greece's geographic position on the margins of the great civilizations of Mesopotamia, Egypt, and Persia certainly provided intellectual stimulation. Furthermore, the growing role of law in the political life of Athens possibly suggested that a similar regularity also underlay the natural order.

The Greek Way of Knowing

The foundations of this Greek rationalism emerged in the three centuries between 600 and 300 B.C.E., coinciding with the flourishing of Greek city-states, especially Athens, and with the growth of its artistic, literary, and theatrical traditions. The enduring significance of Greek thinking lay not so much in the answers it provided to life's great issues, for the Greeks seldom agreed with one another, but rather in its way of asking questions. Their emphasis on argument, logic, and the relentless questioning of received wisdom; their confidence in human reason; their enthusiasm for puzzling out the world without much reference to the gods—these were the defining characteristics of the major Greek thinkers.

The great exemplar of this approach to knowledge was Socrates (469–399 B.C.E.), an Athenian philosopher who walked about the city engaging others in conversation about the good life. He wrote nothing, and his preferred manner of teaching was not the lecture or exposition of his own ideas but rather a constant questioning of the assumptions and logic of his students' thinking. Concerned always to puncture the pretentious, he challenged conventional ideas about the importance of wealth and power in living well, urging instead the pursuit of wisdom and virtue. He was critical of Athenian democracy and on occasion had positive things to say about Sparta, the great enemy of his own city. Such behavior brought him into conflict with city authorities, who accused him of corrupting the youth of Athens and sentenced him to death. At his trial, he defended himself as the "gadfly" of Athens, stinging its citizens into awareness. To any and all, he declared, "I shall question, and examine and cross-examine him, and if I find that he does not possess virtue, but says he does, I shall rebuke him for scorning the things that are most important and caring more for what is of less worth."[17]

The earliest of the classical Greek thinkers, many of them living on the Ionian coast of Anatolia, applied this rational and questioning way of knowing to the world of nature. For example, Thales, drawing on Babylonian astronomy, predicted an eclipse of the sun and argued that the moon simply reflected the sun's light. He was also one of the first Greeks to ask about the fundamental nature of the universe and came up with the idea that water was the basic stuff from which all else derived, for it existed as solid, liquid, and gas. Others argued in favor of air or fire or some combination. Democritus suggested that atoms, tiny "uncuttable" particles, collided in various configurations to form visible matter. Pythagoras believed that beneath the chaos and complexity of the visible world lay a simple, unchanging mathematical order. What these thinkers had in common was a commitment to a rational and nonreligious explanation for the material world.

Such thinking also served to explain the functioning of the human body and its diseases. Hippocrates and his followers came to believe that the body was composed of four fluids, or "humors," which caused various ailments when out of proper balance. He also traced the origins of epilepsy, known to the Greeks as "the sacred disease," to simple heredity: "It appears to me to be nowise more divine nor more

The Death of Socrates
Condemned to death by an Athenian jury, Socrates declined to go into exile, voluntarily drank a cup of poison hemlock, and died in 399 B.C.E. in the presence of his friends. The dramatic scene was famously described by Plato and much later was immortalized on canvas by the French painter Jacques-Louis David in 1787. (*The Death of Socrates*, 1787. Oil on canvas, 51 x 77¼ in. [129.5 x 196.2 cm.]. Catharine Lorillard Wolfe Collection, Wolfe Fund, 1931 [31.45]./The Metropolitan Museum of Art, New York, NY, USA/Image copyright © The Metropolitan Museum of Art/Image source: Art Resource, NY)

sacred than other diseases, but has a natural cause . . . like other afflictions."[18] A similar approach informed Greek thinking about the ways of humankind. Herodotus, who wrote about the Greco–Persian Wars, explained his project as an effort to discover "the reason why they fought one another." This assumption that human reasons lay behind the conflict, not simply the whims of the gods, was what made Herodotus a historian in the modern sense of that word. Ethics and government also figured importantly in Greek thinking. Plato (429–348 B.C.E.) famously sketched out in *The Republic* a design for a good society. It would be ruled by a class of highly educated "guardians" led by a "philosopher-king." Such people would be able to penetrate the many illusions of the material world and to grasp the "world of forms," in which ideas such as goodness, beauty, and justice lived a real and unchanging existence. Only such people, he argued, were fit to rule.

Aristotle (384–322 B.C.E.), a student of Plato and a teacher of Alexander the Great, represents the most complete expression of the Greek way of knowing, for he wrote or commented on practically everything. With an emphasis on empirical observation, he cataloged the constitutions of 158 Greek city-states, identified hundreds of species of animals, and wrote about logic, physics, astronomy, the weather, and much else besides. Famous for his reflections on ethics, he argued that "virtue" was a product of rational training and cultivated habit and could be learned. As to government, he urged a mixed system, combining the principles of monarchy, aristocracy, and democracy.

The Greek Legacy

The rationalism of the Greek tradition was clearly not the whole of Greek culture. The gods of Mount Olympus continued to be a reality for many people, and the ecstatic songs and dances that celebrated Dionysus, the god of wine, were anything but rational and reflective. The death of Socrates at the hands of an Athenian jury showed that philosophy could be a threat as well as an engaging pastime. Nonetheless, Greek rationalism, together with Greek art, literature, and theater, persisted long after the glory days of Athens were over. Alexander's empire and that of the Romans facilitated the spread of Greek culture within the Mediterranean basin and beyond, and not a few leading Roman figures sent their children to be educated in Athens at the Academy, which Plato had founded. An emerging Christian theology was expressed in terms of Greek philosophical concepts, especially those of Plato. Even after the western Roman Empire collapsed, classical Greek texts were preserved in the eastern half, known as the Byzantine Empire or Byzantium.

In the West, however, direct access to Greek texts was far more difficult in the chaotic conditions of post–Roman Europe, and for centuries Greek scholarship was neglected in favor of distinctly Christian writers. Much of that legacy was subsequently rediscovered after the twelfth century C.E. as European scholars gained access to classical Greek texts. From that point on, the Greek legacy has been viewed as a central element of an emerging "Western" civilization. It played a role in formulating an updated Christian theology, in fostering Europe's Scientific Revolution, and in providing a point of departure for much of European philosophy.

Long before this European rediscovery, the Greek legacy had also entered the Islamic world. Systematic translations of Greek works of science and philosophy into Arabic, together with Indian and Persian learning, stimulated Muslim thinkers and scientists, especially in the fields of medicine, astronomy, mathematics, geography, and chemistry. It was in fact largely from Arabic translations of Greek writers that Europeans became reacquainted with the legacy of classical Greece, especially during the twelfth and thirteenth centuries. Despite the many centuries that have passed since the flourishing of ancient Greek culture, that tradition has remained, especially in the West, an inspiration for those who celebrate the powers of the human mind to probe the mysteries of the universe and to explore the equally challenging domain of human life.

The Birth of Christianity . . . with Buddhist Comparisons

About 500 years after the time of Confucius, the Buddha, Zarathustra, and Socrates, a young Jewish peasant/carpenter in the remote province of Judaea in the Roman Empire began a brief three-year career of teaching and miracle working before he got in trouble with local authorities and was executed. In one of history's most unlikely stories, the life and teachings of that obscure man, barely noted in the historical records of the time, became the basis of the world's second great universal religion, after Buddhism. This man, Jesus of Nazareth, and the religion of Christianity that grew out of his brief career, had a dramatic impact on world history, similar to and often compared with that of India's Siddhartha Gautama, the Buddha.

The Lives of the Founders

■ Comparison

How would you compare the lives and teachings of Jesus and the Buddha? In what different ways did the two religions evolve after the deaths of their founders?

The family background of the two teachers could hardly have been more different. Gautama was born to royalty and luxury, whereas Jesus was a rural or small-town worker from a distinctly lower-class family. But both became spiritual seekers, mystics in their respective traditions, who claimed to have personally experienced another and unseen level of reality. Those powerful religious experiences provided the motivation for their life's work and the personal authenticity that attracted their growing band of followers.

Both were "wisdom teachers," challenging the conventional values of their time, urging the renunciation of wealth, and emphasizing the supreme importance of love or compassion as the basis for a moral life. The Buddha had instructed his followers in the practice of *metta*, or loving-kindness: "Just as a mother would protect her only child at the risk of her own life, even so, let [my followers] cultivate a boundless heart towards all beings."[19] In a similar vein during his famous Sermon on the Mount, Jesus told his followers: "You have heard that it was said 'Love your neighbor and hate your enemy,' but I tell you 'Love your enemies and pray for those who persecute you.' "[20] Both Jesus and the Buddha called for the personal transformation of their followers, through "letting go" of the grasping that causes suffering, in the Buddha's teaching, or "losing one's life in order to save it," in the language of Jesus.[21]

Despite these similarities, there were also some differences in their teachings and their life stories. Jesus inherited from his Jewish tradition an intense devotion to a single personal deity with whom he was on intimate terms, referring to him as Abba ("papa" or "daddy"). According to the New Testament, the miracles he performed reflected the power of God available to him as a result of that relationship. The Buddha's original message, by contrast, largely ignored the supernatural, involved no miracles, and taught a path of intense self-effort aimed at ethical living and mindfulness as a means of ending suffering. Furthermore, Jesus' teachings had a sharper social and political edge than did those of the Buddha. Jesus spoke more clearly on behalf of the poor and the oppressed, directly criticized the hypocrisies of the powerful, and deliberately associated with lepers, adulterous women, and tax collectors, all of whom were regarded as "impure." These actions reflected his lower-class background, the Jewish tradition of social criticism, and the reality of Roman imperial rule over his people, none of which corresponded to the Buddha's experience. Finally, Jesus' public life was very brief, probably less than three years, compared to more than forty years for the Buddha. His teachings had so antagonized both Jewish and Roman authorities that he was crucified as a political rebel. The Buddha's message was apparently less threatening to the politically powerful, and he died a natural death at age eighty.

The Spread of New Religions

Neither Jesus nor the Buddha had any intention of founding a new religion; rather, they sought to revitalize the traditions from which they had come. Nonetheless, Christianity and Buddhism soon emerged as separate religions, distinct from Judaism and Hinduism, proclaiming their messages to a much wider and more inclusive audience. In the process, both teachers were transformed by their followers into gods. According to many scholars, Jesus never claimed divine status, seeing himself as a teacher or a prophet, whose close relationship to God could be replicated by anyone. The Buddha likewise viewed himself as an enlightened but fully human person, an example of what was possible for all who followed the path. But in Mahayana Buddhism, the Buddha became a supernatural being who could be worshipped and prayed to and was spiritually available to his followers. Jesus also soon became divine in the eyes of his early followers, such as Saint Paul and Saint John. According to one of the first creeds of the Church, he was "the Son of God, Very God of Very God," while his death and resurrection made possible the forgiveness of sins and the eternal salvation of those who believed.

The transformation of Christianity from a small Jewish sect to a world religion began with Saint Paul (10–65 C.E.), an early convert whose missionary journeys in the eastern Roman Empire led to the founding of small Christian communities that included non-Jews. The Good News of Jesus, Paul argued, was for everyone, and Gentile (non-Jewish) converts need not follow Jewish laws or rituals such as circumcision. In one of his many letters to these new communities, later collected as part of the New Testament, Paul wrote, "There is neither Jew nor Greek . . . neither slave nor free . . . neither male nor female, for you are all one in Christ Jesus."[22]

Despite Paul's egalitarian pronouncement, early Christianity, like Buddhism, offered a mix of opportunities and restrictions for women. Jesus himself had interacted easily with a wide range of women, and they had figured prominently among his followers. Some scholars have argued that Mary Magdalene was a part of his inner circle.[23] And women played leadership roles in the "house churches" of the first century C.E. Nonetheless, some New Testament writings counseled women to "be subject to your husbands" and declared that "it is shameful for a woman to

■ **Change**
In what ways was Christianity transformed in the five centuries following the death of Jesus?

speak in church." Men were identified with the role of Christ himself, for "the husband is head of the wife as Christ is head of the Church."[24] It was not long before male spokesmen for the faith had fully assimilated older and highly negative views of women. As daughters of Eve, they were responsible for the introduction of sin and evil into the world and were the source of temptation for men. On the other hand, Jesus' mother, Mary, soon became the focus of a devotional cult; women were among the martyrs of the early Church; and growing numbers of Christian women, like their Buddhist counterparts, found a more independent space in the monasteries, even as the official hierarchy of the Church became wholly male.

Nonetheless, the inclusive message of early Christianity was one of the attractions of the new faith as it spread very gradually within the Roman Empire during the several centuries after Jesus' death (see Map 4.1). The earliest converts were usually lower-stratum people—artisans, traders, and a considerable number of women—mostly from towns and cities, while a scattering of wealthier, more prominent, and better-educated people subsequently joined the ranks of Christians. The spread of the faith was often accompanied by reports of miracles, healings, and the casting out of demons—all of which were impressive to people thoroughly accustomed to seeing the supernatural behind the events of ordinary life. Christian communities also attracted converts by the way their members cared for one another. In the middle of the third century C.E., the Church in Rome supported 154 priests (of whom 52 were exorcists) and some 1,500 widows, orphans, and destitute people.[25] By 300 C.E., perhaps 10 percent of the Roman Empire's population (some 5 million people) identified themselves as Christians.

Although Christians in the West often think of their faith as a European-centered religion, during the first six centuries of the Christian era, most followers of Jesus lived in the non-European regions of the Roman Empire—North Africa, Egypt, Anatolia, Syria—or outside the empire altogether in Arabia, Persia, Ethiopia, India, and China. Saint Paul's missionary journeys had established various Christian communities in the Roman province of Asia—what is now Turkey—and also in Syria, where the earliest recorded Christian church building was located. The Syrian Church also developed a unique liturgy with strong Jewish influences and a distinctive musical tradition of chants and hymns. The language of that liturgy was neither Greek nor Latin, but Syriac, a Semitic tongue closely related to Aramaic, which Jesus spoke.

From Syria, the faith spread eastward into Persia, where it attracted a substantial number of converts, many of them well educated in the sciences and medicine, by the third century C.E. Those converts also encountered periodic persecution from the Zoroastrian rulers of Persia and were sometimes suspected of political loyalty to the Roman Empire, Persia's longtime enemy and rival. To the north of Syria on the slopes of the Caucasus Mountains, the Kingdom of Armenia became the first place where rulers adopted Christianity as a state religion. In time, Christianity

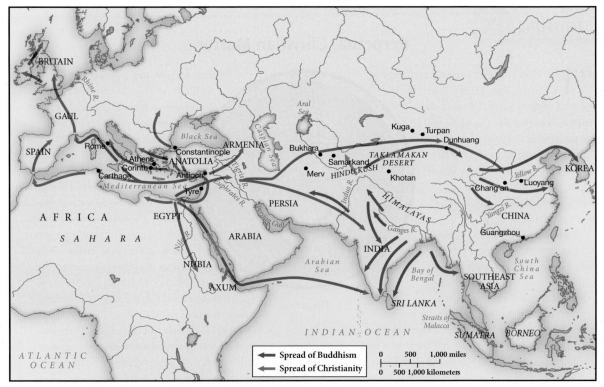

Map 4.1   The Spread of Early Christianity and Buddhism

In the five centuries after the birth of Jesus, Christianity found converts from Spain to northeast Africa, the Middle East, Central Asia, and India. In the Roman Empire, Axum, and Armenia, the new religion enjoyed state support as well. Subsequently, Christianity took root solidly in Europe and after 1000 C.E. in Russia as well. Meanwhile, Buddhism was spreading from its South Asian homeland to various parts of Asia, even as it was weakening in India itself.

became—and remains to this day—a central element of Armenian national identity. A distinctive feature of Armenian Christianity involved the ritual killing of animals at the end of the worship service, probably a continuation of earlier pre-Christian practices.

Syria and Persia represented the core region of the Church of the East, distinct both theologically and organizationally from the Latin Church focused on Rome and an emerging Eastern Orthodox Church based in Constantinople. Its missionaries took Christianity even farther to the east. By the fourth century, and perhaps much earlier, a well-organized Church had taken root in southern India, which later gained tax privileges and special rights from local rulers. In the early seventh century, a Persian monk named Alopen initiated a small but remarkable Christian experiment in China, described more fully in Chapter 10. A modest Christian presence in Central Asia was also an outgrowth of this Church of the East.

Perpetua, Christian Martyr

"The blood of the martyrs," declared the Christian writer Tertullian, "is the seed of the church." Few of those martyrs, whose stories so inspired the persecuted converts of the early Christian centuries, could match that of Perpetua, a young woman whose prison diary provides a highly personal account of her arrest and trial.[26]

Born in 181 C.E. in the North African city of Carthage, Perpetua hailed from an upper-class Roman family and was quite well educated, literate in Latin and probably Greek, and acquainted with Roman philosophical writings. By the time she entered the historical record at age twenty-two, she had given birth to a son, had lost her husband to either death or abandonment, and had recently begun to study Christianity, becoming part of a small but growing group of educated people who were turning toward the new faith. Coinciding with her conversion was a wave of persecutions ordered by the Roman emperor Septimus Severus, also of North

Perpetua.

African descent and a devotee of the Egyptian cult of Isis and Osiris. Severus sought to forbid new conversions rather than punish long-established Christians. In line with this policy, in 203 C.E., the hard-line governor of the region ordered the arrest of Perpetua along with four others—two slaves, one of them a woman named Felicitas who was eight months pregnant, and two free men. Before she was taken to the prison, however, Perpetua decisively confirmed her commitment to Christianity by accepting baptism.

Once in the "dark hole" of the prison, Perpetua was terrified. It was crowded and stiflingly hot, and she was consumed with anxiety for her child. Several fellow Christians managed to bribe the prison guards to permit Perpetua to nurse her baby son. Reunited with her child, she found that "my prison had suddenly

photo: Detail from vault mosaic, Archbishop's Palace, Ravenna, Italy/Scala/ Art Resource, NY

In other directions as well, Christianity spread from its Palestinian place of origin. By the time Muhammad was born in 570, a number of Arabs had become Christians. One of them, in fact, was among the first to affirm Muhammad as an authentic prophet. A particularly vibrant center of Christianity developed in Egypt, where tradition holds that Jesus' family fled to escape persecution by King Herod. Egyptian priests soon translated the Bible into the Egyptian language known as Coptic, and Egyptian Christians pioneered various forms of monasticism. By 400 C.E., hundreds of monasteries, cells, and caves dotted the desert, inhabited by reclusive monks dedicated to their spiritual practices. Increasingly, the language, theology, and practice of Egyptian Christianity diverged from that of Rome and Constantinople, giving expression to Egyptian resistance against Roman or Byzantine oppression. To the west of Egypt, a Church of North Africa furnished a number of the intellectuals of the early Church, including Saint Augustine, as well as many

become a palace, so that I wanted to be there rather than anywhere else."

A few days later, Perpetua's deeply distressed non-Christian father arrived for a visit, hoping to persuade his only daughter to recant her faith and save her life and the family's honor. It was a heartbreaking encounter. "Daughter," he said, "have pity on my grey head. . . . Do not abandon me to be the reproach of men. Think of your brothers, think of your mother and your aunt, think of your child, who will not be able to live once you are gone. Give up your pride! You will destroy all of us! None of us will ever be able to speak freely again if anything happens to you." Firm in her faith, Perpetua refused his entreaties, and she reported that "he left me in great sorrow."

On the day of her trial, with her distraught father in attendance, the governor Hilarianus also begged Perpetua to consider her family and renounce her faith by offering a sacrifice to the emperor. Again she refused and together with her four companions was "condemned to the beasts," a humiliating form of execution normally reserved for the lower classes. Although she was now permanently separated from her child, she wrote, "We returned to the prison in high spirits." During her last days in the prison, Perpetua and the others were treated "more humanely" and were allowed to visit with family and friends, as the head of the jail was himself a Christian.

But then, on the birthday of the emperor, this small band of Christians was marched to the amphitheater, "joyfully as though they were going to heaven," according to an eyewitness account. After the prisoners strenuously and successfully resisted dressing in the robes of pagan priests, the three men were sent into the arena to contend with a boar, a bear, and a leopard. Then it was the turn of the women, Perpetua and the slave Felicitas, who had given birth only two days earlier. When a mad cow failed to kill them, a soldier was sent to finish the work. As he approached Perpetua, he apparently hesitated, but as an eyewitness account put it, "she took the trembling hand of the young gladiator and guided it to her throat." Appended to her diary was this comment from an unknown observer: "It was as though so great a woman, feared as she was by the unclean spirit, could not be dispatched unless she herself were willing."

Questions: How might you understand the actions and attitudes of Perpetua? Is her experience accessible to people living in a largely secular modern society?

Christian martyrs to Roman persecution. (See Zooming In: Perpetua, above.) Here and elsewhere, the coming of Christianity provoked not only hostility from Roman political authorities but also tensions within families. The North African Carthaginian writer Tertullian (160–220 C.E.), known as the "father of Latin Christianity," described the kind of difficulties that might arise between a Christian wife and her "pagan" husband:

> She is engaged in a fast; her husband has arranged a banquet. It is her Christian duty to visit the streets and the homes of the poor; her husband insists on family business. She celebrates the Easter Vigil throughout the night; her husband expects her in his bed. . . . She who has taken a cup at Eucharist will be required to take of a cup with her husband in the tavern. She who has foresworn idolatry must inhale the smoke arising from the incense on the altars of the idols in her husband's home.[27]

Further south in Africa, Christianity became during the fourth century the state religion of Axum, an emerging kingdom in what is now Eritrea and Ethiopia (see Chapter 6). This occurred at about the same time as both Armenia and the Roman Empire officially endorsed Christianity. In Axum, a distinctively African expression of Christianity took root with open-air services, the use of drums and stringed instruments in worship, and colorful umbrellas covering priests and musicians from the elements. Linked theologically and organizationally to Coptic Christianity in Egypt, the Ethiopian Church used Ge'ez, a local Semitic language and script, for its liturgy and literature.

In the Roman world, the strangest and most offensive feature of the new faith was its exclusive monotheism and its antagonism to all other supernatural powers, particularly the cult of the emperors. Christians' denial of these other gods caused them to be tagged as "atheists" and was one reason behind the empire's intermittent persecution of Christians during the first three centuries of the Common Era. All of that ended with Emperor Constantine's conversion in the early fourth century C.E. and with growing levels of state support for the new religion in the decades that followed.

Roman rulers sought to use an increasingly popular Christianity as glue to hold together a very diverse population in a weakening imperial state. Constantine and his successors thus provided Christians with newfound security and opportunities. The emperor Theodosius (r. 379–395 C.E.) enforced a ban on all polytheistic ritual sacrifices and ordered the temples that practiced them closed. Christians, by contrast, received patronage for their buildings, official approval for their doctrines, suppression of their rivals, prestige from imperial recognition, and, during the late fourth century, the proclamation of Christianity as the official state religion. All of this set in motion a process by which the Roman Empire, and later all of Europe, became overwhelmingly Christian. At the time, however, Christianity was expanding at least as rapidly to the east and south as it was to the west. In 500, few observers could have predicted that the future of Christianity would lie primarily in Europe rather than in Asia and Africa.

The spread of Buddhism in India was quite different from that of Christianity in the Roman Empire. Even though Ashoka's support gave Buddhism a considerable boost, it was never promoted to the exclusion of other faiths. Ashoka sought harmony among India's diverse population through religious tolerance rather than uniformity. The kind of monotheistic intolerance that Christianity exhibited in the Roman world was quite foreign to Indian patterns of religious practice. Although Buddhism subsequently died out in India as it was absorbed into a reviving Hinduism, no renewal of Roman polytheism occurred, and Christianity became an enduring element of European civilization. Nonetheless, Christianity did adopt some elements of religious practice from the Roman world, including, perhaps, the cult of saints and the dating of the birth of Jesus to the winter solstice. In both cases, however, these new religions spread widely beyond their places of origin. Buddhism provided a network of cultural connections across much of Asia, while Christianity during its early centuries established an Afro-Eurasian presence.

Institutions, Controversies, and Divisions

As Christianity spread within the Roman Empire and beyond, it developed a hierarchical organization, with patriarchs, bishops, and priests—all men—replacing the house churches of the early years, in which women played a more prominent part. At least in some places, however, women continued to exercise leadership and even priestly roles, prompting Pope Gelasius in 494 to speak out sharply against those who encouraged women "to officiate at the sacred altars, and to take part in all matters imputed to the offices of the male sex, to which they do not belong."[28] In general, though, the exclusion of women from the priesthood established a male-dominated clergy and a patriarchal church, which has lasted into the twenty-first century.

The emerging Christian movement was, however, anything but unified. Its immense geographic reach, accompanied by inevitable differences in language, culture, and political regime, ensured that a single focus for Christian belief and practice was difficult to achieve. Doctrinal differences also tore at the unity of Christianity and embroiled church authorities in frequent controversy about the nature of Jesus (was he human, divine, or both?), his relationship to God (equal or inferior?), and the always-perplexing concept of the Trinity (God as Father, Son, and Holy Spirit). There was debate as well about what writings belonged in the official New Testament, as dozens of letters, gospels, poems, and songs circulated among the early Christian communities. A series of church councils—at Nicaea (325 C.E.), Chalcedon (451 C.E.), and Constantinople (553 C.E.), for example—sought to define an orthodox, or correct, position on these and other issues, declaring those who disagreed as *anathema* and expelling them from the Church. Thus Egyptian Christians, for example, held to the unorthodox position called Monophysite. This view, that Jesus had a single divine nature simply occupying a human body, expressed resistance to domination from Rome or Constantinople, which held that Jesus was both fully human and fully divine. Likewise, the Church of the East adopted Nestorianism, another unorthodox view that emphasized the human side of Jesus' nature and distinguished its theology from the Latin and Eastern Orthodox Churches.

Beyond these theological debates, political and cultural differences generated division even among the orthodox. The bishop of Rome gradually emerged as the dominant leader, or pope, of the Church in the western half of the empire, but his authority was sharply contested in the East. This division contributed to the later split between the Latin, or Roman Catholic, and the Greek, or Eastern Orthodox, branches of Christendom, a division that continues to the present (see Chapter 10). Thus the Christian world of 500 C.E. was not only geographically extensive but also politically and theologically very diverse and highly fragmented.

Buddhists too clashed over various interpretations of the Buddha's teachings, and a series of councils failed to prevent the division between Theravada, Mahayana, and other approaches. A considerable proliferation of different sects, practices, teachings, and meditation techniques subsequently emerged within the Buddhist world, but these divisions generally lacked the "clear-cut distinction between 'right' and 'wrong' ideas" that characterized conflicts within the Christian world.[29] Although Buddhist states and warrior classes (such as the famous samurai of Japan) sometimes engaged in warfare, religious differences among Buddhists seldom provided the basis for the bitterness and violence that often accompanied religious conflict within Christendom. Nor did Buddhists develop the kind of overall religious hierarchy that characterized Christianity, although communities of monks and nuns, organized in monasteries, created elaborate rules to govern their internal affairs.

SUMMING UP SO FAR

How might you understand the appeal of Buddhism and Christianity as opposed to the more rationalist approaches of Greek and Confucian philosophy?

REFLECTIONS

Religion and Historians

To put it mildly, religion has always been a sensitive subject, and no less so for historians than for anyone else. Throughout human history, the vast majority of people have simply assumed the existence of an unseen realm, that of the gods, the spirits, the sacred, or the Divine. They further accepted the capacity of human beings, guided often by tradition, ritual, or religious authority, to align themselves with that other world. But more recently, as an outgrowth of the Scientific Revolution and the European Enlightenment, some have challenged those assumptions, arguing that the only realities worth considering are those that can be accessed with the techniques of science and our five senses. This situation has generated various tensions or misunderstandings between historians and religious practitioners because modern secular historians, whatever their personal beliefs, can rely only on evidence available in this world.

One of these tensions involves the question of change. Most religions present themselves as timeless revelations from the beyond, partaking of eternity or at least reflecting ancient practice. In the eyes of historians, however, the religious aspect of human life changes as much as any other. The Hindu tradition changed from a religion of ritual and sacrifice to one of devotion and worship. Buddhism became more conventionally religious, with an emphasis on the supernatural, as it evolved from Theravada to Mahayana forms. A male-dominated hierarchical Christian Church, with its pope, bishops, priests, and state support, was very different from the small house churches that suffered persecution by imperial authorities in the early Christian centuries. The implication—that religions are largely a human phenomenon—has been troublesome to some believers.

Historians, on the other hand, have sometimes been uncomfortable in the face of claims by believers that they have actually experienced a divine reality, and therein lies a second problem. How could such experiences be verified, when even the biographical details for Buddha and Jesus are difficult to prove by the standards of historians? Certainly, modern historians are in no position to validate or refute the spiritual claims of these teachers, but we need to take them seriously. Although we will never know precisely what happened to the Buddha as he sat in meditation in northern India or what transpired when Jesus spent forty days in the wilderness, clearly those experiences changed the two men and motivated their subsequent actions. Later, Muhammad likewise claimed to have received revelations from God in the caves outside Mecca. Millions of the followers of these religious leaders have also acted on the basis of what they perceived to be an encounter with the Divine or the unseen. This interior dimension of human experience, though difficult to grasp with any precision and impossible to verify, has been a significant mover and shaper of the historical process.

Yet a third problem arises from debates within particular religious traditions about which group most accurately represents the "real" or authentic version of the faith. Historians usually refuse to take sides in such disputes. They simply notice with interest that most human cultural traditions generate conflicting views, some of which become the basis for serious conflict in societies.

Reconciling personal religious convictions with the perspectives of modern historical scholarship is no easy task. At the very least, all of us can appreciate the immense human effort that has gone into the making of religious traditions, and we can acknowledge the enormous significance of these traditions in the unfolding of the human story. They have shaped the meanings that billions of people over thousands of years have attached to the world they inhabit. These religious traditions have justified the vast social inequalities and oppressive states of human civilizations, but they have also enabled human beings to endure the multiple sufferings that attend human life, and on occasion they have stimulated reform and rebellion. And the religions born in second-wave civilizations have guided much of humankind in our endless efforts to penetrate the mysteries of the world beyond and of the world within.

Second Thoughts

What's the Significance?

Big Picture Questions

1. Is a secular outlook on the world an essentially modern phenomenon, or does it have precedents in the second-wave era?

2. "Religion is a double-edged sword, both supporting and undermining political authority and social elites." How would you support both sides of this statement?

3. How would you define the appeal of the religious/cultural traditions discussed in this chapter? To what groups were they attractive, and why?

4. Imagine that you were a Roman Christian traveler in the Eurasian world of 500 C.E. writing home about your encounter with other religious traditions. What similarities and differences might you notice? What might you appreciate in those traditions? And what might you find appalling?

5. **Looking Back:** What relationships can you see between the political dimensions of second-wave civilizations described in Chapter 3 and their cultural or religious aspects discussed in this chapter?

Next Steps: For Further Study

Karen Armstrong, *The Great Transformation* (2006). A comparative and historical study of the major religions by a well-known scholar.

Robert N. Bellah, *Religion in Human Evolution: From the Paleolithic to the Axial Age* (2011). An impressive but controversial account of the origins of religion in general and those of second-wave civilizations in particular.

Peter Brown, *The Rise of Western Christendom* (2003). A history of the first 1,000 years of Christianity, cast in a global framework.

Huston Smith, *An Illustrated World's Religions* (1994). A sympathetic account of major world religions, beautifully illustrated, by a prominent scholar of comparative religion.

Arthur Waley, *Three Ways of Thought in Ancient China* (1983). A classic work, first published more than half a century ago, about the major philosophies of old China.

Jonathan S. Walters, *Finding Buddhists in Global History* (1998). A brief account that situates Buddhism in a world history framework.

BBC, "Religions," http://www.bbc.co.uk/religion/religions/. A succinct introduction to the history, beliefs, and practices of many of the world's religious traditions.

Bridging World History, "Early Belief Systems," http://www.learner.org/courses/worldhistory/unit_main_5 .html. A thoughtful Web site that explores the origins of the religious impulse and many of the traditions covered in this chapter.

WORKING WITH EVIDENCE

Representations of the Buddha

Buddhism derived from a single individual, Siddhartha Gautama, born in northern India, probably in the sixth century B.C.E. The son of royalty, the young Siddhartha enjoyed a splendid but sheltered upbringing encased in luxury, and his father spared no effort to protect the child from anything painful or difficult. At the age of sixteen, he was married to a beautiful cousin, Yasodhara, who bore him a son thirteen years later. Buddhist tradition tells us that while riding beyond the palace grounds, this curious and lively young man encountered human suffering in the form of an old man, a sick person, and a corpse. Shattered by these revelations of aging, illness, and death, Siddhartha determined to find the cause of such sufferings and a remedy for them. And so, at the age of twenty-nine and on the very day his son was born, the young prince left his luxurious life as well as his wife and child, shed his royal jewels, cut off his hair, and set off on a quest for enlightenment. This act of severing his ties to the attachments of ordinary life is known in Buddhist teaching as the Great Renunciation.

What followed were six years of spiritual experimentation that finally led Siddhartha to an ancient fig tree in northern India, now known as the Bodhi (enlightenment) tree. There, Buddhist sources tell us, he began a forty-nine-day period of intensive meditation that ended with an almost indescribable experience of spiritual realization. Now he was the Buddha, the man who had awakened. For the next forty years, he taught what he had learned, setting in motion the cultural tradition of Buddhism. Over many centuries, the religion evolved as it grew in numbers and intersected with various cultures throughout Asia, including those of China, Japan, Tibet, Korea, and Vietnam.

For almost five centuries after his death, which likely took place in the early fifth century B.C.E., artists represented the Buddha as an empty throne, a horse with no rider, a tree, a wheel, or in some other symbolic way, while largely shunning any depiction of him in human form. Among the most widespread of these early symbolic representations of the Buddha were images of his footprints. Found throughout Buddhist Asia, such footprints indicated the Buddha's spiritual presence and served as a focus for devotion or contemplation. They also reminded his followers that since he had passed into nirvana, he could not be physically present. One Buddhist text declared that those who looked on those footprints "shall be freed from the bonds of error, and conducted upon the Way of Enlightenment."[30]

Permission courtesy of John Eskenazi, photo courtesy of AC Cooper

Source 4.1 Footprints of the Buddha

Source 4.1 shows a footprint image from northwestern India dating probably from the second century C.E. and containing a number of Buddhist symbols. In the center of each footprint is a *dharmachakra*, a wheel-like structure that had long symbolized the Buddha's teaching. Here, it surrounds a lotus flower, representing the Buddha's purity. Near the heel is a three-pronged emblem known as a *triratna*. It symbolizes the three things in which Buddhists can take refuge: the Buddha himself, his teaching, and the *sangha* (the Buddhist community). This particular footprint image also includes in the bottom corners two *yakshis*, Indian female earth spirits suggesting fertility. The position of their hands conveys a respectful greeting.

■ Why might artists have been reluctant to portray the human figure of the Buddha?

■ Why might the wheel serve as an effective symbol of the Buddha's message?

■ What does the inclusion of the yakshis add to the message of this image?

■ What overall religious message might this footprint convey to those who gazed on it?

By the first century C.E., the impulse to depict the Buddha in human form had surfaced, with some of the earliest examples coming from the region of South Asia known as Gandhara in what is now northern Pakistan and eastern Afghanistan (see Map 3.3, page 115). That area had been a part of the empire of Alexander the Great and his Hellenistic successors from about 322 B.C.E. to 50 B.C.E. and had developed commercial ties to the Roman Empire as well. These early images of the Buddha reflect this Greco-Roman influence, depicting him with a face similar to that of the Greek god Apollo, dressed in a Roman-style toga, and with curly hair characteristic of the Mediterranean region.

Source 4.2, from India of the second or third century C.E., depicts in Gandhara style a famous scene from the life of the Buddha—his temptation by the demon Mara and Mara's seductive daughters while meditating under the Bodhi tree.

■ How are Mara and his daughters, shown on the right, portrayed in this relief?

■ What attitude characterizes the Buddha, shown on the left and surrounded by attendants?

■ Why might Greco-Roman cultural influence have stimulated physical representations of the Buddha?

■ What larger meaning might the Buddha's followers take from this story?

By the time of India's Gupta dynasty (320–550 C.E.), the Greco-Roman influence of the Gandhara style was fading, replaced by more completely Indian images of the Buddha, which became the "classic" model, shown on page 160. Yet, as the message of the Buddha gained a mass following and spread across much of Asia, some of its early features—rigorous and time-consuming meditation practice, a focus on monks and nuns withdrawn from ordinary life, the absence of accessible supernatural figures able to provide help and comfort—proved difficult for many converts. And so the religion adapted. A new form of the faith, Mahayana Buddhism, offered greater accessibility, a spiritual path available to a much wider range of people beyond the monks and ascetics, who were the core group in early Buddhism.

In most expressions of Mahayana Buddhism, enlightenment (or becoming a Buddha) was available to everyone; it was possible within the context of ordinary life, rather than a monastery; and it might occur within a single lifetime rather than over the course of many lives. While Buddhism had

Siddhartha at the Bodhi Tree, 100–200 A.D. (stone), Indian School/Cleveland Museum of Art, Cleveland, OH, USA/Bridgeman Images

Source 4.2 A Gandhara Buddha

originally put a premium on spiritual wisdom, leading to liberation from rebirth and the achievement of nirvana, Mahayana expressions of the faith emphasized compassion—the ability to feel the sorrows of other people as if they were one's own. This compassionate religious ideal found expression in the notion of bodhisattvas, fully enlightened beings who postponed their own final liberation in order to assist a suffering humanity. They were spiritual beings, intermediaries between mortal humans and the Buddhas, whose countless images in sculpture or painting became objects of worship and sources of comfort and assistance to many Buddhists.

Across the world of Asian Mahayana Buddhism, the most widely popular of the many bodhisattva figures was that of Avalokitesvara, known in China as Guanyin and in Japan as Kannon. This Bodhisattva of Compassion, often portrayed as a woman or with distinctly feminine characteristics, was known as "the one who hears the cries of the world." Calling on him or her for assistance, devotees could be rescued from all kinds of danger and distress. Women, for example, might petition for a healthy child. Moral transformation too was possible. According to the *Lotus Sutra*, a major Mahayana text, "Those who act under the impulse of hatred will, after adoring the Bodhisattva Avalokitesvara, be freed from hatred."

Among the most striking of the many representations of this bodhisattva are those that portray him or her with numerous heads, with which to hear the many cries of a suffering humanity, or with multiple arms to aid them. Source 4.3 provides an illustration of such a figure, a gilded wooden statue from Korea dating to the tenth or eleventh century C.E.

■ What elements of Buddhist imagery can you identify in this statue?

■ To whom might such an image appeal? And why?

■ Some scholars have identified similarities between the Bodhisattva of Compassion and the Virgin Mary in the Christian tradition. What common elements and what differences can you identify?

Beyond providing numerous bodhisattvas, Mahayana Buddhism also populated the spiritual universe with various Buddhas in addition to the historical Buddha. One of these is the Maitreya Buddha, or the Buddha of the future, predicted to appear when the teachings of the historical Buddha have been lost or forgotten. In China, this Buddha of the future was sometimes portrayed as the "laughing Buddha," a fat, smiling, contented figure, said to be modeled on a tenth-century monk named Budai, who wandered the country merrily spreading happiness and good cheer, while evoking contentment and abundance. Source 4.4 illustrates this Chinese Maitreya Buddha together with some of his disciples in a carving, dating to the tenth through fourteenth centuries, in China's Feilai Feng caves.

Source 4.3 A Bodhisattva of Compassion: Avalokitesvara with a Thousand Arms

- How does this Buddha image differ, both physically and in its religious implications, from the other Buddhas already discussed in this feature?

- Why might this image be appealing to some Buddhists, and why might others take exception to it?

- In what ways does this figure represent an adaptation of Buddhist imagery to Chinese culture? Consider what you know about Confucian and Daoist postures to the world.

© Nazima Kowall/Corbis

Source 4.4 The Chinese Maitreya Buddha

DOING HISTORY

Representations of the Buddha

1. **Tracing change:** What transformations in Buddhist belief and practice are disclosed in these images?

2. **Identifying cultural adaptation:** What evidence do these images provide about the blending of Buddhism into a variety of cultural settings?

3. **Understanding the growth of Buddhism:** What do these images suggest about the appeal of Buddhism to growing numbers of people across Asia?

4. **Considering cultural boundaries:** To what extent are these images meaningful to people outside the Buddhist tradition? In what ways do they speak to universal human needs or desires? What is specifically Buddhist or Asian about them?

CHAPTER 5

Society and Inequality in Eurasia/North Africa

500 B.C.E.–500 C.E.

"Caste has no impact on life today," declared Chezi K. Ganesan in 2010.[1] Certainly, Mr. Ganesan's low-caste background as a Nadar, ranking just above the "untouchables," has had little impact on the career of this prosperous high-tech businessman, who shuttles between California's Silicon Valley and the city of Chennai in southern India. Yet his grandfather could not enter Hindu temples, and until the mid-nineteenth century, the women of his caste, as a sign of their low status, were forbidden to cover their breasts in the presence of Brahmin men. But if caste has proven no barrier to Mr. Ganesan, it remains significant for many others in contemporary India. Personal ads for those seeking a marriage partner in many online services often indicate an individual's caste as well as other personal data. Affirmative action programs benefiting low-caste Indians have provoked great controversy and resentment among some upper-caste groups. The brutal murder of an entire Dalit, or "untouchable," family in 2006 sparked much soul-searching in the Indian media. So while caste has changed in modern India, it has also persisted. Both the changes and the persistence have a long history.

The most recent 250 years of world history have called into question social patterns long assumed to be natural and permanent. The French, Russian, and Chinese revolutions challenged and destroyed ancient monarchies and class hierarchies; the abolitionist movement of the nineteenth century attacked slavery, largely unquestioned for millennia; the women's movement has confronted long and deeply held patriarchal assumptions about the proper

---

Mother and Child Mothers and their children have been at the core of social life everywhere and a prominent theme of many artistic traditions. This lovely statue comes from the Sunga dynasty, which flourished in northeastern India from about 185 to 73 B.C.E., after the collapse of the Mauryan Empire.

relationship between the sexes; and Mahatma Gandhi, during India's struggle for independence in the twentieth century, sought to raise the status of "untouchables," referring to them as Harijan, or "children of God." Nevertheless, caste, class, patriarchy, and even slavery have certainly not vanished from human society, even now. During the era of second-wave civilizations in Eurasia, these patterns of inequality found expressions and generated social tensions that endured well beyond that era.

As Chapter 3 pointed out, millions of individual men and women inhabiting the civilizations of Eurasia and North Africa lived within a political framework of states or empires. They also occupied a world of ideas, religions, and values that derived both from local folkways and from the teaching of the great religious or cultural traditions of these civilizations, as described in Chapter 4. In this chapter, we explore the social arrangements of these civilizations—relationships between rich and poor, powerful and powerless, slaves and free people, and men and women. Those relationships shaped the daily lives and the life chances of everyone and provided the foundation for political authority as well as challenges to it.

Like the First Civilizations, those of the second-wave era were sharply divided along class lines, and they too were patriarchal, with women clearly subordinated to men in most domains of life. In constructing their societies, however, these second-wave civilizations differed substantially from one another. Chinese, Indian, and Mediterranean civilizations provide numerous illustrations of the many and varied ways in which these peoples organized their social lives. The assumptions, tensions, and conflicts accompanying these social patterns provided much of the distinctive character and texture that distinguished these diverse civilizations from one another.

SEEKING THE MAIN POINT

To what extent were the massive inequalities of second-wave civilizations generally accepted, and in what ways were they resisted or challenged?

Society and the State in China

Chinese society was unique in the ancient world in the extent to which it was shaped by the actions of the state. Nowhere was this more apparent than in the political power and immense social prestige of Chinese state officials, all of them male. For more than 2,000 years, these officials, bureaucrats acting in the name of the emperor both in the capital and in the provinces, represented the cultural and social elite of Chinese civilization. This class had its origins in the efforts of early Chinese rulers to find administrators loyal to the central state rather than to their own families or regions. Philosophers such as Confucius had long advocated selecting such officials on the basis of merit and personal morality rather than birth or wealth. As the Han dynasty established its authority in China around 200 B.C.E., its rulers required each province to send men of promise to the capital, where they were examined and chosen for official positions on the basis of their performance.

A MAP OF TIME

470–400 B.C.E.	Life of Aspasia in Athens
124 B.C.E.	Imperial academy for training Chinese officials established
1st century B.C.E.	Poetry of Buddhist nuns set to writing
73 B.C.E.	Spartacus slave rebellion in Italy
1–200 C.E.	Laws of Manu prescribing proper social behavior in India
Early 1st century C.E.	Reforming emperor Wang Mang in power in China
45–116 C.E.	Life of Ban Zhao in China
79 C.E.	Eruption of Mount Vesuvius destroys Pompeii
184 C.E.	Yellow Turban Rebellion in China
After 221 C.E.	Loosening of restrictions on elite Chinese women as Han dynasty collapsed
After 500 C.E.	Slavery replaced by serfdom in Roman world
690–705 C.E.	Empress Wu reigned in China

An Elite of Officials

Over time, this system of selecting administrators evolved into the world's first professional civil service. In 124 B.C.E., Emperor Wu Di established an imperial academy where potential officials were trained as scholars and immersed in texts dealing with history, literature, art, and mathematics, with an emphasis on Confucian teachings. By the end of the Han dynasty, it enrolled some 30,000 students, who were by then subjected to a series of written examinations to select officials of various grades. Private schools in the provinces funneled still more aspiring candidates into this examination system, which persisted until the early twentieth century. In theory open to all men, this system in practice favored those whose families were wealthy enough to provide the years of education required to pass even the lower-level exams. Proximity to the capital and family connections to the imperial court also helped in gaining a position in this highest of Chinese elites. Nonetheless, village communities or a local landowner might sponsor the education of a bright young man from a commoner family, enabling him to enter the charmed circle of officialdom. One rags-to-riches story told of a pig farmer who became an adviser to the emperor himself. Thus the examination system provided a modest measure of social mobility in an otherwise quite hierarchical society.

■ **Description**
How would you characterize the social hierarchy of China during the second-wave era?

In later dynasties, that system grew even more elaborate and became an endur-ing and distinguishing feature of Chinese civilization. During the Tang dynasty, the famous poet and official Po Chu-I (772–846 C.E.) wrote a poem titled "After Pass-ing the Examination," which shows something of the fame and fortune that awaited an accomplished student as well as the continuing loyalty to family and home that ideally marked those who succeeded:

> For ten years I never left my books,
> I went up . . . and won unmerited praise.
> My high place I do not much prize;
> The joy of my parents will first make me proud.
> Fellow students, six or seven men,
> See me off as I leave the City gate.
> My covered coach is ready to drive away;
> Flutes and strings blend their parting tune.
> Hopes achieved dull the pains of parting;
> Fumes of wine shorten the long road. . . .
> Shod with wings is the horse of him who rides
> On a Spring day the road that leads to home.[2]

Those who made it into the bureaucracy entered a realm of high privilege and great prestige. Senior officials moved about in carriages and were bedecked with robes, ribbons, seals, and headdresses appropriate to their rank. Even lower officials who served in the provinces rather than the capital were distinguished by their polished speech, their cultural sophistication, and their urban manners as well as their political authority. Proud of their learning, they were the bearers, and often the makers, of Chinese culture. "Officials are the leaders of the populace," stated an imperial edict of 144 B.C.E., "and it is right and proper that the carriages they ride in and the robes that they wear should correspond to the degrees of their dignity."[3] Some of these men, particularly in times of political turmoil, experienced tension between their official duties and their personal inclination toward a more with-drawn life of reflective scholarship. (See Zooming In: Ge Hong, page 196.)

The Landlord Class

Most officials came from wealthy families, and in China wealth meant land. When the Qin dynasty unified China by 210 B.C.E., most land was held by small-scale peas-ant farmers. But by the first century B.C.E., the pressures of population growth, taxa-tion, and indebtedness had generated a class of large landowners as impoverished peasants found it necessary to sell their lands to more prosperous neighbors. This accumulation of land in sizable estates was a persistent theme in Chinese history and one that was frequently, though not very successfully, opposed by state authorities. Landlords of such large estates were often able to avoid paying taxes, thus decreas-ing state revenues and increasing the tax burden for the remaining peasants. In some cases, they could also mount their own military forces that might challenge the authority of the emperor.

One of the most dramatic state efforts to counteract the growing power of large landowners is associated with Wang Mang, a high court official of the Han dynasty who usurped the emperor's throne in 8 C.E. and immediately launched a series of startling reforms. A firm believer in Confucian good government, Wang Mang saw his reforms as re-creating a golden age of long ago in which small-scale peasant farmers represented the backbone of Chinese society. Accordingly, he ordered the great private estates to be nationalized and divided up among the landless. Government loans to peasant families, limits on the amount of land a family might own, and an end to private slavery were all part of his reform program, but these measures proved impossible to enforce. Opposition from wealthy landowners, nomadic invasions, poor harvests, floods, and famines led to the collapse of Wang Mang's reforms and his assassination in 23 C.E.

Large landowning families, therefore, remained a central feature of Chinese society, although the fate of individual families rose and fell as the wheel of fortune raised them to great prominence or plunged them into poverty and disgrace. As a class, they benefited both from the wealth that their estates generated and from the power and prestige that accompanied their education and their membership in the official elite. The term "scholar-gentry" reflected their twin sources of privilege. With homes in both urban and rural areas, members of the scholar-gentry class lived luxuriously. Multi-storied houses, the finest of silk clothing, gleaming carriages, private orchestras, high-stakes gambling—all of this was part of the life of China's scholar-gentry class.

Peasants

Throughout the long course of China's civilization, the vast majority of its population consisted of peasants, living in small households representing two or three generations. Some owned enough land to support their families and perhaps even sell something on the local market. Many others could barely survive. Nature, the state, and landlords combined to make the life of most peasants extremely vulnerable. Famines, floods, droughts, hail, and pests could wreak havoc without warning. State authorities required the payment of taxes, demanded about a month's labor every year on various public projects, and conscripted young men for military service. During the Han dynasty, growing numbers of impoverished and desperate peasants had to sell

Chinese Peasants
For many centuries, the normal activities of Chinese peasant farmers included plowing, planting, and threshing grain, as shown in this painting from China's Song dynasty (960–1279 C.E.). (Mogao Caves, Dunhuang, Gansu Province, China/ Bridgeman Images)

Ge Hong, a Chinese Scholar in Troubled Times

Had Ge Hong lived at a different time, he might have pursued the life of a Confucian scholar and civil servant, for he was born to a well-established aristocratic family in southern China. But when he entered the world in 283 C.E., the times were clearly out of joint. The Han dynasty, which had given China four centuries of relative peace and prosperity, had fragmented into a number of competing states. Nomadic peoples invaded and ruled the northern parts of the country. Coups and rebellions were frequent. Many northern Chinese fled south to escape the chaos. The life of Ge Hong illustrates how these larger historical circumstances shaped the life of a single individual.[4]

Ge Hong's family directly experienced the disorder when the family library was destroyed during the repeated wars of the time. Furthermore, the family patriarch, Ge Hong's father, died when the young boy was only thirteen years old, an event that brought hardship and a degree of impoverishment to the family. Ge Hong reported later in his autobiography that he had to "walk long distances to borrow books" and that he cut and

A solitary scholar in China, such as Ge Hong sought to become.

sold firewood to buy paper and brushes. Nonetheless, like other young men of his class, he received a solid education, reading the classic texts of Confucianism along with history and philosophy.

At about the age of fourteen or fifteen, Ge Hong began to study with the aged Daoist master Zheng Yin. He had to sweep the floor and perform other menial chores for the master while gaining access to rare and precious texts of the esoteric and alchemical arts aimed at creating the "gold elixir" that could promote longevity and transcendence. Withdrawal into an interior life, reflected in both Daoist and Buddhist thought, had a growing appeal to the elite classes of China in response to the political disturbances and disorder of public life. It was the beginning of a life-long quest for Ge Hong.

And yet the Confucian emphasis on office holding, public service, and moral behavior in society persisted,

photo: *Scholar Walking with a Staff in a Landscape*, Qing Dynasty [ink and color on silk], Chinese School/Saint Louis Art Museum, Saint Louis, Missouri, USA/Bridgeman Images

out to large landlords and work as tenants or sharecroppers on their estates, where rents could run as high as one-half to two-thirds of the crop. Other peasants fled, taking to a life of begging or joining gangs of bandits in remote areas.

An eighth-century C.E. Chinese poem by Li Shen reflects poignantly on the enduring hardships of peasant life:

■ **Change**
What class conflicts disrupted Chinese society?

> The cob of corn in springtime sown
> In autumn yields a hundredfold.
> No fields are seen that fallow lie:
> And yet of hunger peasants die.

sending Ge Hong into a series of military positions. Here too was a reflection of the disordered times of his life, for in more settled circumstances, young elite men would have disdained military service, favoring a career in the civil bureaucracy. Thus in 303, at the age of twenty, he organized and led a small group of soldiers to crush a local rebellion, later reporting that he alone among military leaders prevented his troops from looting the valuables of the enemy. For his service, he received the title of "wave conquering general" and 100 bolts of cloth. "I was the only one," he wrote, "to distribute it among my officers, soldiers, and needy friends." At several other points in his life as well, Ge Hong accepted official appointments, some of them honorary and others more substantive.

But his heart lay elsewhere, as he yearned for a more solitary and interior life. "Honor, high posts, power, and profit are like sojourning guests," he wrote in his memoir. "They are not worth all the regret and blame, worry and anxiety they cause." Thus he spent long periods of his life in relative seclusion, refusing a variety of official positions. "Unless I abandon worldly affairs," he asked, "how can I practice the tranquil Way?" To Ge Hong, withdrawal was primarily for the purpose of seeking immortality, "to live as long as heaven and earth," a quest given added urgency no doubt by the chaotic world of his own time. In his writings, he explored various techniques for enhancing *qi*, the vital energy that sustains all life, including breathing exercises, calisthenics, sexual practices, diet, and herbs. But it was the search for alchemically generated elixirs, especially those containing liquid gold and cinnabar (derived from mercury), that proved most compelling to Ge Hong. Much to his regret, he lacked the resources to obtain and process these rare ingredients.

However, Ge Hong did not totally abandon the Confucian tradition and its search for social order, for he argued in his writings that the moral virtues advocated by China's ancient sage were a necessary prerequisite for attaining immortality. And he found a place in his philosophy also for the rewards and punishments of Legalist thinking. Thus he sought to reconcile the three major strands of Chinese thought—Confucianism, Daoism, and Legalism—even as he acknowledged that his practices were "always ill-suited to the times."

Ge Hong spent the last years of his life on the sacred mountain of Luofu in the far south of China, continuing his immortality research until he died in 343 at the age of sixty. When his body was lifted into its coffin, contemporaries reported that it was "exceedingly light as if one were lifting empty clothing."[5] They concluded from this that Ge Hong had in fact achieved transcendence, joining the immortals in everlasting life, as he had so fervently hoped.

Question: In what ways did the larger conditions of China shape the life of Ge Hong?

As at noontide they hoe their crops,
Sweat on the grain to earth down drops.
How many tears, how many a groan,
Each morsel on thy dish did mould![6]

Such conditions provoked periodic peasant rebellions, which have punctuated Chinese history for over 2,000 years. Toward the end of the second century C.E., wandering bands of peasants began to join together as floods along the Yellow River and resulting epidemics compounded the misery of landlessness and poverty. What emerged was a massive peasant uprising known as the Yellow Turban Rebellion

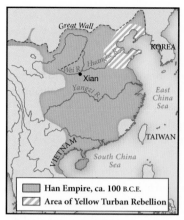

Yellow Turban Rebellion

because of the yellow scarves the peasants wore around their heads. That movement, which swelled to about 360,000 armed followers by 184 C.E., found leaders, organization, and a unifying ideology in a popular form of Daoism. Featuring supernatural healings, collective trances, and public confessions of sin, the Yellow Turban movement looked forward to the "Great Peace"—a golden age of equality, social harmony, and common ownership of property. Although the rebellion was suppressed by the military forces of the Han dynasty, the Yellow Turban and other peasant upheavals devastated the economy, weakened the state, and contributed to the overthrow of the dynasty a few decades later. Repeatedly in Chinese history, such peasant movements, often expressed in religious terms, registered the sharp class antagonisms of Chinese society and led to the collapse of more than one ruling dynasty.

Merchants

Peasants were oppressed in China and certainly exploited, but they were also honored and celebrated in the official ideology of the state. In the eyes of the scholar-gentry, peasants were the solid productive backbone of the country, and their hard work and endurance in the face of difficulties were worthy of praise. Merchants, however, did not enjoy such a favorable reputation in the eyes of China's cultural elite. They were widely viewed as unproductive, making a shameful profit from selling the work of others. Stereotyped as greedy, luxury loving, and materialistic, merchants stood in contrast to the presumed frugality, altruism, and cultured tastes of the scholar-gentry. They were also seen as a social threat, as their ill-gained wealth impoverished others, deprived the state of needed revenues, and fostered resentments.

Such views lay behind periodic efforts by state authorities to rein in merchant activity and to keep them under control. Early in the Han dynasty, merchants were forbidden to wear silk clothing, ride horses, or carry arms. Nor were they permitted to sit for civil service examinations or hold public office. State monopolies on profitable industries such as salt, iron, and alcohol limited merchant opportunities. Later dynasties sometimes forced merchants to loan large sums of money to the state. Despite this active discrimination, merchants frequently became quite wealthy. Some tried to achieve a more respectable elite status by purchasing landed estates or educating their sons for the civil service examinations. Many had backdoor relationships with state officials and landlords who found them useful and were not averse to profiting from business connections with merchants, despite their unsavory reputation.

Class and Caste in India

India's social organization shared certain broad features with that of China. In both civilizations, birth determined social status for most people; little social mobility was available for the vast majority; sharp distinctions and great inequalities characterized social life; and religious or cultural traditions defined these inequalities as natural, eternal, and ordained by the gods. Despite these similarities, the organization, flavor, and texture of ancient Indian society were distinctive compared to almost all other civilizations. These unique aspects of Indian society have long been embodied in what we now call the caste system, a term that comes from the Portuguese word *casta*, which means "race" or "purity of blood." That social organization emerged over thousands of years and in some respects has endured into modern times.

Caste as Varna

The origins of the caste system are at best hazy. An earlier idea—that caste evolved from a racially defined encounter between light-skinned Aryan invaders and the darker-hued native peoples—has been challenged in recent years, but no clear alternative theory has emerged. Perhaps the best we can say at this point is that the distinctive social system of India grew out of the interactions among South Asia's immensely varied cultures together with the development of economic and social differences among these peoples as the inequalities of "civilization" spread throughout the Ganges River valley and beyond. Notions of race, however, seem less central to the growth of the caste system than those of economic specialization and of culture.

■ **Description**
What set of ideas underlies India's caste-based society?

Caste in India
This 1947 photograph from *Life* magazine illustrates the "purity and pollution" thinking that has long been central to the ideology of caste. It shows a high-caste landowner carefully dropping wages wrapped in a leaf into the outstretched hands of his low-caste workers. By avoiding direct physical contact with them, he escapes the ritual pollution that would otherwise ensue. (Margaret Bourke-White/The LIFE Picture Collection/Getty Images)

Whatever the precise origins of the caste system, by around 500 B.C.E., the idea that society was forever divided into four ranked classes, or *varnas*, was deeply embedded in Indian thinking. Everyone was born into and remained within one of these classes for life. At the top of this hierarchical system were the Brahmins, priests whose rituals and sacrifices alone could ensure the proper functioning of the world. They were followed by the Kshatriya class, warriors and rulers charged with protecting and governing society. Next was the Vaisya class, originally commoners who cultivated the land. These three classes came to be regarded as pure Aryans and were called the "twice-born," for they experienced not only a physical birth but also formal initiation into their respective varnas and status as people of prestigious Aryan descent. Far below these twice-born in the hierarchy of varna groups were the Sudras, native peoples incorporated into the margins of Aryan society in very subordinate positions. Regarded as servants of their social betters, they were not allowed to hear or repeat the Vedas or to take part in Aryan rituals. So little were they valued that a Brahmin who killed a Sudra was penalized as if he had killed a cat or a dog.

According to varna theory, these four classes were formed from the body of the god Purusha and were therefore eternal and changeless. Although these divisions are widely recognized in India even today, historians have noted considerable social flux in ancient Indian history. Members of the Brahmin and Kshatriya groups, for example, were frequently in conflict over which ranked highest in the varna hierarchy, and only slowly did the Brahmins emerge clearly in the top position. Although theoretically purely Aryan, both groups absorbed various tribal peoples as Indian civilization expanded. Tribal medicine men or sorcerers found a place as Brahmins, while warrior groups entered the Kshatriya varna. The Vaisya varna, originally defined as cultivators, evolved into a business class with a prominent place for merchants, while the Sudra varna became the domain of peasant farmers. Finally a whole new category, ranking lower even than the Sudras, emerged in the so-called untouchables, men and women who did the work considered most unclean and polluting, such as cremating corpses, dealing with the skins of dead animals, and serving as executioners. (See Snapshot, opposite.)

Caste as Jati

As the varna system took shape in India, another set of social distinctions also arose, based largely on occupations. In India as elsewhere, urban-based civilization gave rise to specialized occupations, many organized in guilds that regulated their own affairs in a particular region. Over time, these occupationally based groups, known as *jatis*, blended with the varna system to create India's unique caste-based society.

The many thousands of jatis became the primary cell of India's social life beyond the family or household, but each of them was associated with one of the great classes (varnas). Thus Brahmins were divided into many separate jatis, or subcastes,

■ **Comparison**
What is the difference between varna and jati as expressions of caste?

SNAPSHOT   Social Life and Duty in Classical India

Much personal behavior in classical India, at least ideally, was regulated according to caste. Each caste was associated with a particular color, with a part of the body of the god Purusha, and with a set of duties.

Caste (Varna)	Color/Symbolism	Part of Purusha	Duties
Brahmin	white/spirituality	head	priests, teachers
Kshatriya	red/courage	shoulders	warriors, rulers
Vaisya	yellow/wealth	thighs	farmers, merchants, artisans
Sudra	black/ignorance	feet	labor
Untouchables (outside of the varna system; thus no color and not associated with Purusha)	—	—	polluted labor

Beyond caste, behavior was ideally defined in terms of four stages of life, at least for the first three varna groups. Each new stage was marked by a *samskara*, a ritual initiating the person into this new phase of life.

Stage of Life	Duties
Student	Boys live with a teacher (guru); learn Sanskrit, rituals, Vedas; practice obedience, respect, celibacy, nonviolence.
Householder	Marriage and family; men practice caste-based career/occupation; women serve as wives and mothers, perform household rituals and sacrifices, actively support children and elders.
Retirement	Both husband and wife withdraw to the forests following birth of grandchildren; diminished household duties; greater focus on spiritual practice; sex permitted once a month.
Wandering ascetic	Only for men (women return to household); total rejection of ordinary existence; life as wandering hermit without shelter or possessions; caste becomes irrelevant; focus on achieving moksha and avoiding future rebirth.

as were each of the other varnas as well as the untouchables. In a particular region or village, each jati was ranked in a hierarchy known to all, from the highest of the Brahmins to the lowest of the untouchables. Marriage and eating together were permitted only within an individual's own jati. Each jati was associated with a particular set of duties, rules, and obligations, which defined its members' unique and separate place in the larger society. Brahmins, for example, were forbidden to eat meat, while Kshatriyas were permitted to do so. Upper-caste women covered their breasts, while some lower-caste women were forbidden this privilege as a sign of their subordination. "It is better to do one's own duty badly than another's well"— this frequently quoted saying summed up the underlying idea of Indian society. With its many separate, distinct, and hierarchically ranked social groups, Indian society was quite different from that of China or the Greco-Roman world. It was also unique in the set of ideas that explained and justified that social system. Foremost among them was the notion of ritual purity and pollution applied to caste groups. Brahmins or other high-caste people who came in contact with members of lower castes, especially those who cleaned latrines, handled corpses, or butchered and skinned dead animals, were in great danger of being polluted, or made ritually unclean. Thus untouchables were forbidden to use the same wells or to enter the temples designated for higher-caste people. Sometimes they were required to wear a wooden clapper to warn others of their approach. A great body of Indian religious writing defined various forms of impurity and the ritual means of purification.

A further support for this idea of inherent inequality and permanent difference derived from emerging Hindu notions of *karma*, *dharma*, and rebirth. Being born into a particular caste was generally regarded as reflecting the good or bad deeds (karma) of a previous life. Thus an individual's prior actions were responsible for his or her current status. Any hope for rebirth in a higher caste rested on the faithful and selfless performance of one's present caste duties (dharma) in this life. Doing so contributed to spiritual progress by subduing the relentless demands of the ego. Such teachings, like that of permanent impurity, provided powerful sanctions for the inequalities of Indian society. So too did the threat of social ostracism, because each jati had the authority to expel members who violated its rules. No greater catastrophe could befall a person than this, for it meant the end of any recognized social life and the loss of all social support.

As caste restrictions tightened, it became increasingly difficult—virtually impossible—for individuals to raise their social status during their lifetimes. However, another kind of upward mobility enabled entire jatis, over several generations, to raise their standing in the local hierarchy of caste groups. By acquiring land or wealth, by adopting the behaviors of higher-caste groups, by finding some previously overlooked "ancestor" of a higher caste, a particular jati might slowly be redefined in a higher category. India's caste system was in practice rather more fluid and changing than the theory of caste might suggest.

India's social system thus differed from that of China in several ways. It gave priority to religious status and ritual purity (the Brahmins), whereas China elevated political officials to the highest of elite positions. The caste system divided Indian society into vast numbers of distinct social groups; China had fewer, but broader, categories of society—scholar-gentry, landlords, peasants, merchants. Finally, India's caste society defined these social groups far more rigidly than in China and provided even less opportunity for social mobility.

The Functions of Caste

This caste-based social structure shaped India's emerging civilization in various ways. Because caste (jati) was a very local phenomenon, rooted in particular regions or villages, it focused the loyalties of most people on a quite restricted territory and weakened the appeal or authority of larger all-Indian states. This localization is one reason that India, unlike China, seldom experienced an empire that encompassed the entire subcontinent (see Chapter 3, pages 131–35). Caste, together with the shared culture of a diverse Hinduism, provided a substitute for the state as an integrative mechanism for Indian civilization. It offered a distinct and socially recognized place for almost everyone. In looking after widows, orphans, and the destitute, jatis provided a modest measure of social security and support. Even the lowest-ranking jatis had the right to certain payments from the social superiors whom they served.

Furthermore, caste represented a means of accommodating the many migrating or invading peoples who entered the subcontinent. The cellular, or honeycomb, structure of caste society allowed various peoples, cultures, and traditions to find a place within a larger Indian civilization while retaining something of their unique identity. The process of assimilation was quite different in China, where it meant becoming Chinese ethnically, linguistically, and culturally. Finally, India's caste system facilitated the exploitation of the poor by the wealthy and powerful. The multitude of separate groups into which it divided the impoverished and oppressed majority of the population made class consciousness and organized resistance across caste lines much more difficult to achieve.

SUMMING UP SO FAR

How did India's caste system differ from China's class system?

Slavery: The Case of the Roman Empire

Beyond the inequalities of class and caste lay those of slavery, a social institution with deep roots in human history, extending into the Paleolithic era of gathering and hunting peoples. Some have suggested that the early domestication of animals provided a model for enslaving people. Certainly, slave owners have everywhere compared their slaves to tamed animals. Aristotle, for example, observed that the ox is "the poor man's slave." War, patriarchy, and the notion of private property, all of which accompanied the First Civilizations, also contributed to the growth of slavery. Large-scale warfare generated numerous prisoners, and everywhere in the ancient world capture in war meant the possibility of enslavement. Early records suggest that women captives were the first slaves, usually raped and then enslaved as concubines, whereas male captives were killed. Patriarchal societies, in which men sharply controlled and perhaps even "owned" women, may have suggested the possibility of using other people, men as well as women, as slaves. The class inequalities of early civilizations, which were based on great differences in privately owned property, also made it possible to imagine people owning other people.

Slavery and Civilization

Whatever its precise origins, slavery generally meant ownership by a master, the possibility of being sold, working without pay, and the status of an "outsider" at the bottom of the social hierarchy. For most, it was a kind of "social death,"[7] for slaves usually lacked any rights or independent personal identity recognized by the larger society. By the time Hammurabi's law code casually referred to Mesopotamian slavery (around 1750 B.C.E.), it was already a long-established tradition in the region and in all the First Civilizations. Likewise, virtually all subsequent civilizations—in the Americas, Africa, and Eurasia—practiced some form of slavery.

■ **Comparison**

How did the inequalities of slavery differ from those of caste?

Slave systems throughout history have varied considerably. In some times and places, such as ancient Greece and Rome, a fair number of slaves might be emancipated in their own lifetimes, through the generosity or religious convictions of their owners, or to avoid caring for them in old age, or by allowing slaves to purchase their freedom with their own funds. In some societies, the children of slaves inherited the status of their parents, while in others, such as the Aztec Empire, they were considered free people. Slaves likewise varied considerably in the labor they were required to do, with some working for the state in high positions, others performing domestic duties in their owner's household, and still others toiling in fields or mines in large work gangs.

The second-wave civilizations of Eurasia differed considerably in the prominence and extent of slavery in their societies. In China, it was a minor element, amounting to perhaps 1 percent of the population. Convicted criminals and their families, confiscated by the government and sometimes sold to wealthy private individuals, were among the earliest slaves in Han dynasty China. In desperate circumstances, impoverished or indebted peasants might sell their children into slavery. In southern China, teenage boys of poor families could be purchased by the wealthy, for whom they served as status symbols. Chinese slavery, however, was never very widespread and did not become a major source of labor for agriculture or manufacturing.

In India as well, people could fall into slavery as criminals, debtors, or prisoners of war and served their masters largely in domestic settings, but religious writings and secular law offered, at least in theory, some protection for slaves. Owners were required to provide adequately for their slaves and were forbidden to abandon them in old age. According to one ancient text, "A man may go short himself or stint his wife and children, but never his slave who does his dirty work for him."[8] Slaves in India could inherit and own property and earn money in their spare time. A master who raped a slave woman was required to set her free and pay compensation. The law encouraged owners to free their slaves and allowed slaves to buy their freedom. All of this suggests that Indian slavery was more restrained than that of other ancient civilizations. Nor did Indian civilization depend economically on slavery, for most work was performed by lower-caste, though free, men and women.

The Making of Roman Slavery

In sharp contrast to other second-wave civilizations, slavery played an immense role in the Mediterranean, or Western, world. Although slavery was practiced in Chinese, Indian, and Persian civilizations, in the Greco-Roman world society was based on slavery. By a conservative estimate, classical Athens alone was home to perhaps 60,000 slaves, or about one-third of the total population. In Athens, ironically, the growth of democracy and citizenship was defined and accompanied by the simultaneous growth of slavery on a mass scale. The greatest of the Greek philosophers, Aristotle, developed the notion that some people were "slaves by nature" and should be enslaved for their own good and for that of the larger society.

"The ancient Greek attitude toward slavery was simple," writes one modern scholar. "It was a terrible thing to become a slave, but a good thing to own a slave."[9] Even poor households usually had at least one or two female slaves, providing domestic work and sexual services for their owners. Although substantial numbers of Greek slaves were granted freedom by their owners, they usually did not become citizens or gain political rights. Nor could they own land or marry citizens, and particularly in Athens they had to pay a special tax. Their status remained "halfway between slavery and freedom."[10]

Practiced on an even larger scale, slavery was a defining element of Roman society. By the time of Christ, the Italian heartland of the Roman Empire had some 2 to 3 million slaves, representing 33 to 40 percent of the population.[11] Not until the modern slave societies of the Caribbean, Brazil, and the southern United States was slavery practiced again on such an enormous scale. Wealthy Romans could own many hundreds or even thousands of slaves. One woman in the fifth century C.E. freed 8,000 slaves when she withdrew into a life of Christian monastic practice. Even people of modest means frequently owned two or three slaves. In doing so, they confirmed their own position as free people, demonstrated their social status, and expressed their ability to exercise power. Slaves and former slaves also might be slave owners. One freedman during the reign of Augustus owned 4,116 slaves at the time of his death. (See Working with Evidence, page 220, for more on Roman society viewed through the lens of Pompeii.)

■ Comparison

How did Greco-Roman slavery differ from that of other classical civilizations?

Roman Slavery

This Roman mosaic from the third century C.E. shows the slave Myro serving a drink to his master, Fructus. (Bardo Museum, Tunis, Tunisia/Gianni Dagli Orti/The Art Archive at Art Resource, NY)

The vast majority of Roman slaves had been prisoners captured in the many wars that accompanied the creation of the empire. In 146 B.C.E., following the destruction of the North African city of Carthage, some 55,000 people were enslaved en masse. From all over the Mediterranean basin, men and women were funneled into the major slave-owning regions of Italy and Sicily. Pirates also furnished slaves, kidnapping tens of thousands and selling them to Roman slave traders on the island of Delos. Roman merchants purchased still other slaves through networks of long-distance commerce extending to the Black Sea, the East African coast, and northwestern Europe. The supply of slaves also occurred through natural reproduction, as the children of slave mothers were regarded as slaves themselves. Such "home-born" slaves had a certain prestige and were thought to be less troublesome than those who had known freedom earlier in their lives. Finally, abandoned or exposed children could legally become the slave of anyone who rescued them.

Unlike American slavery of later times, Roman practice was not identified with a particular racial or ethnic group. Egyptians, Syrians, Jews, Greeks, Gauls, North Africans, and many other people found themselves alike enslaved. From within the empire and its adjacent regions, an enormous diversity of people were bought and sold at Roman slave markets.

Like slave owners everywhere, Romans regarded their slaves as "barbarians"—lazy, unreliable, immoral, prone to thieving—and came to think of certain peoples, such as Asiatic Greeks, Syrians, and Jews, as slaves by nature. Nor was there any serious criticism of slavery in principle, although on occasion owners were urged to treat their slaves in a more benevolent way. Even the triumph of Christianity within the Roman Empire did little to undermine slavery, for Christian teaching held that slaves should be "submissive to [their] masters with all fear, not only to the good and gentle, but also to the harsh."[12] In fact, the New Testament used the metaphor of slavery to describe the relationship of believers to God, styling them as "slaves of Christ," while Saint Augustine (354–430 C.E.) described slavery as God's punishment for sin. Thus slavery was deeply embedded in the religious thinking and social outlook of elite Romans.

Similarly, slavery was entrenched throughout the Roman economy. No occupation was off-limits to slaves except military service, and no distinction existed between jobs for slaves and those for free people. Frequently they labored side by side. In rural areas, slaves provided much of the labor force on the huge estates, or *latifundia*, which produced grain, olive oil, and wine, mostly for export, much like the later plantations in the Americas. There they often worked chained together. In the cities, slaves worked in their owners' households, but also as skilled artisans, teachers, doctors, business agents, entertainers, and actors. In the empire's many mines and quarries, slaves and criminals labored under brutal conditions. Slaves in the service of the emperor provided manpower for the state bureaucracy, maintained temples and shrines, and kept Rome's water supply system functioning.

Trained in special schools, they also served as gladiators in the violent spectacles of Roman public life. Female slaves usually served as domestic servants but were also put to work in brothels, served as actresses and entertainers, and could be used sexually by their male owners. Thus slaves were represented among the highest and most prestigious occupations and in the lowest and most degraded.

Slave owners in the Roman Empire were supposed to provide the necessities of life to their slaves. When this occurred, slaves may have had a more secure life than was available to impoverished free people, who had to fend for themselves, but the price of this security was absolute subjection to the will of the master. Beatings, sexual abuse, and sale to another owner were constant possibilities. Lacking all rights in the law, slaves could not legally marry, although many contracted unofficial unions. Slaves often accumulated money or possessions, but such property legally belonged to their masters and could be seized at any time. If a slave murdered his master, Roman law demanded the lives of all of the victim's slaves. When one Roman official was killed by a slave in 61 C.E., every one of his 400 slaves was condemned to death. For an individual slave, the quality of life depended almost entirely on the character of the master. Brutal owners made life a living hell. Benevolent owners made life tolerable and might even grant favored slaves their freedom or permit them to buy that freedom. As in Greece, manumission of slaves was a widespread practice, and in the Roman Empire, unlike in Greece, freedom was accompanied by citizenship.

Roman slaves, like their counterparts in other societies, responded to enslavement in many ways. Most, no doubt, did what was necessary to survive, but there are recorded cases of Roman prisoners of war who chose to commit mass suicide rather than face the horrors of slavery. Others, once enslaved, resorted to the "weapons of the weak"—small-scale theft, sabotage, pretending illness, working poorly, and placing curses on their masters. Fleeing to the anonymous crowds of the city or to remote rural areas prompted owners to post notices in public places, asking for information about their runaways. Catching runaway slaves became an organized private business. Occasional murders of slave owners made masters conscious of the dangers they faced. "Every slave we own is an enemy we harbor" ran one Roman saying.[13]

On several notable occasions, the slaves themselves rose in rebellion. The most famous uprising occurred in 73 B.C.E. when a slave gladiator named Spartacus led seventy other slaves from a school for gladiators in a desperate bid for freedom that mushroomed into a huge uprising. (See Zooming In: The Spartacus Slave Revolt, page 208, for a more detailed account.) Nothing on the scale of Spartacus's rebellion occurred again in the Western world of slavery until the Haitian Revolution of the 1790s. But Haitian rebels sought the creation of a new society free of slavery altogether. None of the Roman slave rebellions, including that of Spartacus, had any such overall plan or goal. The rebels simply wanted to escape

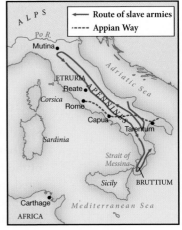

The Rebellion of Spartacus

The Spartacus Slave Revolt

Despite the prominence of slavery in ancient civilizations, large-scale slave revolts were rare. One of the most impressive began in the Roman Empire during the summer of 73 B.C.E. when around seventy slaves escaped from a gladiator school at Capua, about 125 miles south of Rome. Grabbing knives and skewers from the kitchen on their way out, this small band of men, who had been trained to fight to the death for the enter-

The death of Spartacus, 71 B.C.E.

tainment of spectators, established a stronghold on nearby Mount Vesuvius and chose as their leader Spartacus, described by the historian Sallust as "a man of immense bodily strength and spirit."[14] The defeat of Roman forces sent to seize them encouraged other slaves and some free men to join the rebellion. Their numbers eventually swelled to as many as 120,000 men, women, and children at the height of the uprising, reflecting the large number of slaves employed on the great estates of southern Italy.

Roman authorities became increasingly concerned when Spartacus and his followers began to manufacture

their own weapons and to organize into a more coherent military force, which defeated in turn several hurriedly assembled Roman armies and plundered the rich farming region of Campania. The fortunes of the rebels peaked in 72 B.C.E. when they briefly threatened Rome itself. Both sides treated their opponents brutally. The Greek historian Appian reported that Spartacus ordered the sacrifice of 300 Roman prisoners in honor of the slain rebel leader Crixus, while another historian claimed that Spartacus staged gladiatorial games using 400 captives. When the revolt was finally suppressed, captured rebel slaves received similarly brutal treatment from the Roman authorities.

Fearful for the safety of the capital, the Roman authorities acted decisively. They appointed Marcus Licinius Crassus, a rich and ambitious Roman aristocrat

Roman slavery. Although rebellions created a perpetual fear in the minds of slave owners, slavery itself was hardly affected.

Comparing Patriarchies

Social inequality was embedded not only in the structures of class, caste, and slavery, but also in the gender systems of second-wave civilizations, as the patriarchies of the First Civilizations (see Chapter 2, pages 72–75) were replicated and elaborated in those that followed. Until quite recently, women's subordination in all civilizations has been so widespread and pervasive that historians have been slow to recognize that gender systems had a history, changing over time. New agricultural technologies, the rise or decline of powerful states, the incorporation of world religions, interaction with culturally different peoples—all of these developments and

and military commander, to lead eight Roman legions, totaling perhaps 40,000 troops, against Spartacus and his rebels. Crassus cornered the slave army in the far south of Italy, and Spartacus soon realized that his followers faced a fight to the death.

- According to the historian Appian, he advertised their precarious situation to his troops by crucifying a Roman soldier "as a visual reminder to his own men of what would happen to them if they did not win."[15] Rather than be captured, Spartacus and the slaves with him chose to make a last stand.

The Greek historian Plutarch reports that Spartacus killed his horse in front of his troops to show that he had no intention of fleeing, and led his forces in a final desperate engagement with Crassus's army. Even the most hostile of later historians recounted that Spartacus died bravely during the battle, even if some claimed that his body was never found. For those that survived, a terrible vengeance followed as some 6,000 captured rebel slaves were nailed to crosses along the Appian Way, between Capua, where the rebellion began, and Rome. These crucified prisoners, spaced some thirty-five to forty yards apart for over a hundred miles, provided a clear warning to all others who contemplated rebellion.

Spartacus's revolt had little lasting effect on the society in which he lived. No further large-scale revolts took place in the Roman Empire, and Rome continued its economic system based on slave labor. Moreover, the rebellion occasioned little historical comment until the eighteenth century. However, over the past two and a half centuries, a number of groups have embraced Spartacus, casting him as an inspirational leader of the downtrodden who resisted injustice and subjugation. Marxists, socialists, and nationalists have all found something to admire in Spartacus and his rebellion. In the United States, Spartacus entered the popular imagination due in no small part to the success of the 1960 epic film *Spartacus*, starring Kirk Douglas as the rebel leader fighting against the odds to free the oppressed. While there is no historical evidence that Spartacus ever intended to abolish slavery or fundamentally reform Roman society, in modern times his heroic, if ultimately failed, quest for freedom has been recovered from the past, becoming for many an inspirational symbol of just resistance to oppression. In such ways, the past continues to resonate in the present.

Questions: What can Spartacus's revolt tell us about the nature of the slave system in the Roman Empire? How might you account

more generated significant change in understandings of what was appropriate masculine and feminine behavior. Most often, patriarchies were lighter and less restrictive for women in the early years of a civilization's development and during times of upheaval, when established patterns of male dominance were disrupted.

Furthermore, women were often active agents in the histories of their societies, even while largely accepting their overall subordination. As the central figures in family life, they served as repositories and transmitters of their peoples' culture. Some were able to occupy unorthodox and occasionally prominent positions outside the home as scholars, religious functionaries, managers of property and participants in commerce, and even as rulers or military leaders. In Britain, Egypt, and Vietnam, for example, women led efforts to resist their countries' incorporation into the Roman or Chinese empires. (See Zooming In: Trung Trac, page 124, and the statue of Boudica, page 120.) Both Buddhist and Christian nuns carved out small domains of relative freedom from male control. But these changes or challenges to male dominance occurred within a patriarchal framework, and nowhere did they evolve out of or beyond that framework. Thus a kind of "patriarchal equilibrium" ensured the long-term persistence of women's subordination despite fluctuations and notwithstanding various efforts to redefine gender roles or push against gendered expectations.[16]

Nor was patriarchy everywhere the same. Restrictions on women were far sharper in urban-based civilizations than in those pastoral or agricultural societies that lay beyond the reach of cities and empires. The degree and expression of patriarchy also varied from one civilization to another, as the discussion of Mesopotamia and Egypt in Chapter 2 illustrated. And within particular civilizations, elite women both enjoyed privileges and suffered the restrictions of seclusion in the home to a much greater extent than their lower-class counterparts whose economic circumstances required them to operate in the larger social arena. China provides a fascinating example of how patriarchy changed over time, while the contrasting patriarchies of Athens and Sparta illustrate clear variations even within the much smaller world of Greek civilization.

A Changing Patriarchy: The Case of China

As Chinese civilization took shape during the Han dynasty, elite thinking about gender issues became more explicitly patriarchal, more clearly defined, and linked to an emerging Confucian ideology. Long-established patterns of thinking in terms of pairs of opposites were now described in gendered and unequal terms. The superior principle of *yang* was viewed as masculine and related to Heaven, rulers, strength, rationality, and light, whereas *yin*, the lower feminine principle, was associated with the earth, subjects, weakness, emotion, and darkness. Thus female inferiority was seen as permanent and embedded in the workings of the universe.

■ **Change**

In what ways did the expression of Chinese patriarchy change over time, and why did it change?

What this view meant more practically was spelled out repeatedly over the centuries in various Confucian texts. Two notions in particular summarized the ideal position of women, at least in the eyes of elite male writers. The adage "Men go out, women stay in" emphasized the public and political roles of men in contrast to the domestic and private domain of women. A second idea, known as the "three obediences," emphasized a woman's subordination first to her father, then to her husband, and finally to her son. "Why is it," asked one text, "that according to the rites the man takes his wife, whereas the woman leaves her house [to join her husband's family]? It is because the *yin* is lowly, and should not have the initiative; it proceeds to the *yang* in order to be completed."[17]

The Chinese woman writer and court official Ban Zhao (45–116 C.E.) observed that the ancients had practiced three customs when a baby girl was born. She was placed below the bed to show that she was "lowly and weak," required always to "humble herself before others." Then she was given a piece of broken pottery to play with, signifying that "her primary duty [was] to be industrious." Finally, her

Chinese Women Musicians
This tenth-century rendering by the painter Gu Hongzhong shows these upper-class women serving as musicians for a high official of a Tang dynasty emperor. It was titled *The Night Revels of Han Xizai*. The painter was apparently sent by the emperor to spy on the suspicious behavior of the minister, who in various tellings was suspected of either rebellion or undignified activity. (Beijing Palace Museum, Imperial Palace [Forbidden City], Beijing, China/Werner Forman/Art Resource, NY)

birth was announced to the ancestors with an offering to indicate that she was responsible for "the continuation of [ancestor] worship in the home."[18]

Yet such notions of passivity, inferiority, and subordination were not the whole story of women's lives in ancient China. A few women, particularly the wives, concubines, or widows of emperors, were able on occasion to exercise considerable political authority. Several others led peasant rebellions. In doing so, they provoked much antifemale hostility on the part of male officials, who understood governance as a masculine task and often blamed the collapse of a dynasty or natural disasters on the "unnatural" and "disruptive" influence of women in political affairs. Others, however, praised women of virtue as wise counselors to their fathers, husbands, and rulers and depicted them positively as active agents.

Within her husband's family, a young woman was clearly subordinate as a wife and daughter-in-law, but as a mother of sons, she was accorded considerable honor for her role in producing the next generation of male heirs to carry on her husband's lineage. When her sons married, she was able to exercise the significant authority of a mother-in-law. Furthermore, a woman, at least in the upper classes, often brought with her a considerable dowry, which was regarded as her own property and gave her some leverage within her marriage. Women's roles in the production of textiles, often used to pay taxes or to sell commercially, made a woman's

Chinese Women at Work
For a long time, the spinning and weaving of cloth were part of women's domestic work in China. In this detail from a Ming dynasty vase, women are shown weaving silk. (Detail from a ceramic vase, Chinese School, Ming Dynasty [1368–1644]/Goleston Palace, Tehran, Iran/Giraudon/Bridgeman Images)

labor quite valuable to the family economy. And a man's wife was sharply distinguished from his concubines, for she was legally mother to all her husband's children. Furthermore, peasant women could hardly follow the Confucian ideal of seclusion in the home, as their labor was required in the fields. Thus women's lives were more complex and varied than the prescriptions of Confucian orthodoxy might suggest.

Much changed in China following the collapse of the Han dynasty in the third century C.E. Centralized government vanished amid much political fragmentation and conflict. Confucianism, the main ideology of Han China, was discredited, while Daoism and Buddhism attracted a growing following. Pastoral and nomadic peoples invaded northern China and ruled a number of the small states that had replaced the Han government. These new conditions resulted in some loosening of the strict patriarchy of Han dynasty China over the next five or six centuries.

The cultural influence of nomadic peoples, whose women were far less restricted than those of China, was noticed, and criticized, by more Confucian-minded male observers. One of them lamented the sad deterioration of gender roles under the influence of nomadic peoples:

> In the north of the Yellow river it is usually the wife who runs the household. She will not dispense with good clothing or expensive jewelry. The husband has to settle for old horses and sickly servants. The traditional niceties between husband and wife are seldom observed, and from time to time he even has to put up with her insults.[19]

Others criticized the adoption of nomadic styles of dress, makeup, and music. By the time of the Tang dynasty (618–907), writers and artists depicted elite women as capable of handling legal and business affairs on their own and on occasion riding horses and playing polo, bareheaded and wearing men's clothing. Tang legal codes even recognized a married daughter's right to inherit property from her family of birth. Such images of women were quite different from those of Han dynasty China.

A further sign of a weakening patriarchy and the cause of great distress to advocates of Confucian orthodoxy lay in the unusual reign of Empress Wu (r. 690–705 C.E.), a former high-ranking concubine in the imperial court, who came to power amid much palace intrigue and was the only woman ever to rule China with the title of emperor. With the support of China's growing Buddhist establishment, Empress Wu governed despotically, but she also consolidated China's civil service examination system for the selection of public officials and actively patronized scholarship and the arts. Some of her actions seem deliberately designed to elevate the position of women. She commissioned the biographies of famous women, decreed that the mourning period for mothers be made equal to that for fathers, and ordered the creation of a Chinese character for "human being" that suggested the process of birth flowing from one woman without a prominent male role. Her reign was brief and unrepeated.

The growing popularity of Daoism provided new images of the feminine and new roles for women. Daoist texts referred to the *dao* as "mother" and urged the traditionally feminine virtues of yielding and passive acceptance rather than the male-oriented striving of Confucianism. Daoist sects often featured women as priests, nuns, or reclusive meditators, able to receive cosmic truth and to use it for the benefit of others. A variety of female deities from Daoist or Buddhist traditions found a place in Chinese village religion, while growing numbers of women found an alternative to family life in Buddhist monasteries. None of this meant an end to patriarchy, but it does suggest some change in the tone and expression of that patriarchy. However, during the Song dynasty that followed, a more restrictive patriarchy reemerged. (See Chapter 8.)

Contrasting Patriarchies: Athens and Sparta

The patriarchies of second-wave civilizations not only fluctuated over time but also varied considerably from place to place. Nowhere is this variation more apparent than in the contrasting cases of Athens and Sparta, two of the leading city-states of Greek civilization (see Map 3.2, page 111). Even within this small area, the opportunities available to women and the restrictions imposed on them differed substantially. Although Athens has been celebrated as a major expression of democracy and rationalism, its posture toward women was far more restrictive than that of the highly militaristic and much less democratic Sparta.

In the several centuries between about 700 and 400 B.C.E., as the free male citizens of Athens moved toward unprecedented participation in political life, the city's women experienced growing limitations. They had no role whatsoever in the Assembly, the councils, or the juries of Athens, which were increasingly the focus of life for free men. In legal matters, women had to be represented by a guardian, and court proceedings did not even refer to them by name, but only as someone's wife or mother.

■ Comparison
How did the patriarchies of Athens and Sparta differ from each other?

Greek thinkers, especially Aristotle, provided a set of ideas that justified women's exclusion from public life and their general subordination to men. According to Aristotle, "A woman is, as it were, an infertile male. She is female in fact on account of a kind of inadequacy." That inadequacy lay in her inability to generate

A Woman of Athens
This grave stele from about 400 B.C.E. marked the final resting place of Hegeso, a wealthy Athenian woman, shown in the women's quarter of a Greek home examining her jewelry, perhaps for the last time, while attended by her slave. The domestic setting of this grave marker contrasts with that common for men, which usually showed them as warriors in a public space. (National Archeological Museum, Athens, Greece/Marie Mauzy/Art Resource, NY)

sperm, which contained the "form" or the "soul" of a new human being. Her role in the reproductive process was passive, providing a receptacle for the vital male contribution. Compared often to children or domesticated animals, women were associated with instinct and passion and lacked the rationality to take part in public life. "It is the best for all tame animals to be ruled by human beings," wrote Aristotle. "In the same way, the relationship between the male and the female is by nature such that the male is higher, the female lower, that the male rules and the female is ruled."[20]

As in China, elite Athenian women were expected to remain inside the home, except perhaps for religious festivals or funerals. Even within the home, women's space was quite separate from that of men. Although poorer women, courtesans, and prostitutes had to leave their homes to earn money, collect water, or shop, ideal behavior for upper-class women meant assigning these tasks to slaves or to men and involved a radical segregation of male and female space. "What causes women a bad reputation," declared Andromache, a female character in the Greek playwright Euripides' *The Trojan Women*, "is not remaining inside."

Within the domestic realm, Athenian women were generally married in their midteens to men ten to fifteen years older than themselves. Their main function was the management of domestic affairs and the production of sons who would become active citizens. These sons were expected to acquire a literate education, while their sisters were normally limited to learning spinning, weaving, and other household tasks. The Greek writer Menander exclaimed: "Teaching a woman to read and write? What a terrible thing to do! Like feeding a vile snake on more poison." Nor did women have much economic power. Although they could own personal property obtained through dowry, gifts, or inheritance, land was usually passed through male heirs. By law, women were forbidden to buy or sell land and could negotiate contracts only if the sum involved was valued at less than a bushel of barley.

There were exceptions, although rare, to the restricted lives of upper-class Athenian women, the most notable of which was Aspasia (ca. 470–400 B.C.E.). She was born in the Greek city of Miletus, on the western coast of Anatolia, to a wealthy family that believed in educating its daughters. As a young woman, Aspasia found her way to Athens, where her foreign birth gave her somewhat more freedom than was normally available to the women of that city. She soon attracted the attention of Pericles, Athens's leading political figure. The two lived together as husband and wife until Pericles' death in 429 B.C.E., although they were not officially married. Treated as an equal partner by Pericles, Aspasia proved to be a learned and witty conversationalist who moved freely in the cultured circles of Athens. Her foreign birth and her apparent influence on Pericles provoked critics to suggest that she was a *hetaera*, a professional, educated, high-class entertainer and sexual companion, similar to a Japanese geisha. Although little is known about Aspasia, a number of major Athenian writers commented about her, both positively and negatively. She was, by all accounts, a rare and remarkable woman in a city that offered little opportunity for individuality or achievement to its female population.

The evolution of Sparta differed in many ways from that of Athens. Early on, Sparta solved the problem of feeding a growing population not by creating overseas colonies as did many Greek city-states, but by conquering its immediate neighbors and reducing them to a status of permanent servitude, not far removed from slavery. Called helots, these dependents far outnumbered the free citizens of Sparta and represented a permanent threat of rebellion. Solving this problem shaped Spartan society decisively. Sparta's answer was a militaristic regime, constantly ready for war to keep the helots in their place. To maintain such a system, all boys were removed from their families at the age of seven to be trained by the state in military camps, where they learned the ways of war. There they remained until the age of thirty. The ideal Spartan male was a warrior, skilled in battle, able to endure hardship, and willing to die for his city. Mothers are said to have told their sons departing for battle to "come back with your shield . . . or on it." Although economic equality for men was the ideal, it was never completely realized in practice. And unlike Athens, political power was exercised primarily by a small group of wealthy men.

This militaristic and far-from-democratic system had implications for women that, strangely enough, offered them greater freedoms and fewer restrictions. As in many warrior societies, their central task was reproduction—bearing warrior sons for Sparta. To strengthen their bodies for childbearing, girls were encouraged to take part in sporting events— running, wrestling, throwing the discus and javelin,

A Girl of Sparta
This figurine portrays a young female Spartan athlete or runner. Compare her clothing with that worn by Hegeso in the photo opposite. (The British Museum, London, UK/Bridgeman Images)

even driving chariots. At times, women and men alike competed in the nude before mixed audiences. Their education, like that of boys, was prescribed by the state, which also insisted that newly married women cut their hair short, unlike adult Greek women elsewhere. Thus Spartan women were not secluded or segregated, as were their Athenian counterparts.

Furthermore, Spartan young women, unlike those of Athens, usually married men of their own age, about eighteen years old, thus putting the new couple on a more equal basis. Marriage often began with a trial period to make sure the new couple could produce children, with divorce and remarriage readily available if they could not. Because men were so often away at war or preparing for it, women exercised much more authority in the household than was the case in Athens.

It is little wonder that the freedom of Spartan women appalled other Greeks, who believed that it undermined good order and state authority. Aristotle complained that the more egalitarian inheritance practices of Spartans led to their women controlling some 40 percent of landed estates. In Sparta, he declared, women "live in every sort of intemperance and luxury" and "the [male] rulers are ruled by women." Plutarch, a Greek writer during the heyday of the Roman Empire, observed critically that "the men of Sparta always obeyed their wives." The clothing worn by Spartan women to give them greater freedom of movement seemed immodest to other Greeks.

Nonetheless, in another way, Sparta may have been more restrictive than Athens and other Greek city-states, particularly in its apparent prohibition of homosexuality. At least, this was the assertion of the Athenian writer Xenophon (427–355 B.C.E.), who stated that Sparta's legendary founder Lycurgus "caused lovers to abstain from sexual intercourse with boys."[21] Elsewhere, however, homoerotic relationships were culturally approved and fairly common for both men and women, although this did not prevent their participants from entering heterosexual marriages as well. The ideal homosexual relationship—between an older man and a young adolescent boy—was viewed as limited in time, for it was supposed to end when the boy's beard began to grow. Unlike contemporary Western societies where sexuality is largely seen as an identity, ancient Greek society viewed sexual choice more casually and as a matter of taste.

Sparta clearly was a patriarchy, with women serving as breeding machines for its military system and lacking any formal role in public life, but it was a lighter patriarchy than that of Athens. The joint efforts of men and women seemed necessary to maintain a huge class of helots in permanent subjugation. Death in childbirth was considered the equivalent of death in battle, for both contributed to the defense of Sparta, and both were honored alike. In Athens, on the other hand, growing freedom and democracy were associated with the strengthening of the male-dominated, property-owning household, and within that household, the cornerstone of Athenian society, men were expected to exercise authority. Doing so required increasingly severe limitations and restrictions on the lives of women.

Together, the cases of Athens and Sparta illustrate how the historical record appears in a different light when viewed through the lens of gender. Athens, so celebrated for its democracy and philosophical rationalism, offered little to its women, whereas Sparta, often condemned for its militarism and virtual enslavement of the helots, provided a somewhat wider scope for the free women of the city.

REFLECTIONS

What Changes? What Persists?

So what is more impressive in human history—the innovations and changes or the enduring patterns and lasting features? At the level of personal history, most people have no doubt noticed the brevity and transience of life, marked as it is by childhood, coming of age, marriage, the birth of children, illness, decline, and death. Every culture has developed rituals to honor these changes. And yet we also recognize some enduring sense of self across the span of a life, some continuity, at least in memory, between the child and the elder.

Beyond our individual histories, however, our perception of change or continuity in the wider arenas of life surely depends on when we are living. During the long Paleolithic and Neolithic eras, few people were aware of major changes in the larger patterns of life. Of course, change happened: nomadic peoples settled down in villages; agriculture developed; cities arose; states and empires took shape; class structures evolved; patriarchy emerged more sharply defined. But few of these changes occurred quickly enough to be noticeable in a single lifetime. It is among the great contributions of world history to call attention to transformations of which we might otherwise be unaware. In the modern era, and certainly in our own time, the pace of change has dramatically accelerated. We have come to value, celebrate, expect, and promote change in ways that many of our distant—and not so distant—ancestors would find unimaginable.

What might we say about the balance of change and persistence in the era of second-wave civilizations? Clearly, there was much that was new, even if those innovations had roots in earlier times. The Greek conquest of the Persian Empire under the leadership of Alexander the Great was both novel and unexpected. The Roman Empire encompassed the entire Mediterranean basin in a single political system for the first time. Buddhism and Christianity emerged as new, distinct, and universal religious traditions, although both bore the marks of their origin in Hindu and Jewish religious thinking, respectively. The collapse of dynasties, empires, and civilizations long thought to be solidly entrenched—the Chinese and Roman, for example—must surely have seemed to people of the time to be something fearfully new.

But much that was created in the second-wave era—particularly its social and cultural patterns—has demonstrated an impressive continuity throughout many centuries, even if it also changed in particular ways over time. China's scholar-gentry class retained its prominence throughout the ups and downs of changing dynasties into the twentieth century. India's caste-based social structure still endures as a way of thinking and behaving for hundreds of millions of men and women on the South Asian peninsula. Although slavery gave way to serfdom in post-Roman Europe, it was widely practiced in the Islamic world and massively extended in Europe's American colonies after 1500. In various expressions, slavery remained an important and largely unquestioned feature of all civilizations until the nineteenth century, and in a few places it still exists. Patriarchy, with its assumptions of male superiority and dominance, has surely been the most fundamental, long-lasting, and taken-for-granted feature of all civilizations. Not until recent centuries have those assumptions effectively been challenged, and even so, patriarchy has continued to shape the lives and the thinking of the vast majority of humankind. And many hundreds of millions of people in the twenty-first century still honor or practice religious and cultural traditions begun during the second-wave era.

Persistence and change alike have long provided the inextricable warp and woof of both individual experience and historical study. Each of us no doubt ponders the tension between them in our own lives. Untangling their elusive relationship has figured prominently in the task of historians and has contributed much to the enduring fascination of historical study.

Second Thoughts

What's the Significance?

Wang Mang, 195

China's scholar-gentry class, 195

Ge Hong, 196–97

Yellow Turban Rebellion, 197–98

caste as *varna* and *jati*, 199–202

"ritual purity" in Indian social practice, 202

Greek and Roman slavery, 203–8

Spartacus, 208

patriarchy, 208–17

the "three obediences," 210–11

Empress Wu, 212

Aspasia and Pericles, 214

helots, 215–17

Big Picture Questions

1. What might an observant Chinese traveler from the Han dynasty era find surprising or offensive in India or the Greco-Roman world? What similarities might he or she notice?

2. Why do you think slavery was so much more prominent in Greco-Roman civilization than in India or China?

3. What philosophical, religious, or cultural ideas served to legitimate the class and gender inequalities of second-wave civilizations?

4. What changes in the patterns of social life in second-wave civilizations can you identify? What accounts for these changes?

5. **Looking Back:** Cultural and social patterns of civilizations seem to endure longer than the political framework of states and empires. What evidence from Chapters 3, 4, and 5 might support this statement? How might you account for this phenomenon? Is there evidence that could support a contrary position?

Next Steps: For Further Study

Jeannine Auboyer, *Daily Life in Ancient India* (2002). A social history of ancient India, with a focus on caste, ritual, religion, and art.

Sue Blundell, *Women in Ancient Greece* (1999). A well-written academic study, with occasional humorous stories and anecdotes.

Keith Bradley, *Slavery and Society at Rome* (1994). A scholarly but very readable account of slavery in the Roman Empire.

Michael Lowe, *Everyday Life in Early Imperial China* (1968). A vivid description of social life during the Han dynasty.

Merry Weisner-Hanks, *Gender in History* (2001). A thoughtful overview by a leading scholar in both women's history and world history.

"The Indian Caste System: An Introduction," http://www.youtube.com/watch?v=Oh_xvKLhZHg. A brief BBC documentary on the beginnings of caste in India.

"Women in World History," http://chnm.gmu.edu/wwh/index.html. Documents, reviews, and lesson plans for learning and teaching about women's history in a global context.

Pompeii as a Window on the Roman World

You could hear the shrieks of women, the wailing of infants, and the shouting of men; some were calling their parents, others their children or their wives, trying to recognize them by their voices. People bewailed their own fate or that of their relatives, and there were some who prayed for death in their terror of dying. Many besought the aid of the gods, but still more imagined there were no gods left, and that the universe was plunged into eternal darkness for evermore.[22]

Written by a prominent Roman known as Pliny the Younger, this eye-witness account details reactions to the volcanic eruption of Mount Vesuvius, located on the southwestern side of the Italian peninsula, on August 24, 79 C.E. That eruption buried the nearby city of Pompeii, located about 150 miles south of Rome, but it also preserved the city, frozen in time, until archeologists began to uncover it in the mid-eighteenth century (see Map 3.4, page 119). Now substantially excavated, Pompeii is an archeological and historical treasure, offering a unique window into the life of a Roman city during the first century C.E.

As this city of perhaps 20,000 people emerged from layers of ash, it stood revealed as a small but prosperous center of commerce and agriculture, serving as a point of entry for goods coming to southern Italy by sea. Pompeii also hosted numerous vineyards, production facilities for wine and olive oil, and a fisheries industry. In addition, the city was a tourist destination for well-to-do Romans. The houses of the wealthy were elegant structures, often built around a central courtyard, and were decorated with lovely murals displaying still-life images, landscapes, and scenes from Greek and Roman mythology. An inscription found on the threshold of one house expressed the entrepreneurial spirit of the town: "Gain is pure joy."[23]

Laid out in a grid pattern with straight streets, the city's numerous public facilities included a central bathing/swimming pool, some twenty-five street fountains, various public bathhouses, and a large food market as well as many bars and small restaurants. More than thirty brothels, often featuring explicit erotic art, offered sexual services at relatively inexpensive prices. One inscription, apparently aimed at local tourists, declared: "If anyone is looking for some tender love in this town, keep in mind that here all the girls are very

Source 5.1 Terentius Neo and His Wife

Source 5.2 A Pompeii Banquet

friendly." Graffiti too abounded, much of it clearly sexual. Here are three of the milder examples: "Atimetus got me pregnant"; "Sarra, you are not being very nice, leaving me all alone like this"; and "If anyone does not believe in Venus, they should gaze at my girlfriend."[24]

The preserved art of Pompeii, especially the wall paintings, provides a glimpse into the social life of that city. Most of that art, of course, catered to and reflected the life of the more prosperous classes. Source 5.1 shows a portrait of Terentius Neo, a prominent businessman and magistrate (an elected public official), and his unnamed wife. He is wearing a toga and holding a papyrus scroll, while she wears a tunic and is holding to her lips a stylus, used for writing on the wax-covered wooden tablet that she carries. Her hair is styled in a fashion popular in the mid-first century.

■ What significance do you attribute to the absence in the painting's title of a name for the woman?

■ What do you think the artist is trying to convey by highlighting the literacy of this couple?

■ What overall impression of these two people and their relationship to each other does this painting suggest?

Terentius Neo and his wife were no doubt served by slaves in their home, as slave owning was common in the Roman world, particularly among the upper classes. In the streets and homes of urban areas, slaves and free people mingled quite openly. Roman slavery was not distinguished by race, and the outward signs of urban slavery were few, especially for those practicing professions. Such a couple no doubt gave and attended banquets similar to the one depicted in Source 5.2, where well-to-do guests reclined on padded couches while slaves served them food and drink. Dancers, acrobats, and singers often provided entertainment at such events, which provided an occasion for elites to impress others with their lavish display of wealth and generosity.

■ What signs of social status are evident in this painting?

■ How are slaves, shown here in the foreground, portrayed? See also the mosaic of a slave and master on page 205.

The lives of the less exalted appear infrequently in the art of Pompeii, but the images in Source 5.3 provide some entrée into their world. These are frescoes painted on the wall of a *caupona*, an inn or tavern catering to the lower classes. The first image shows Myrtale, a prostitute, kissing a man, while the caption above reads: "I don't want to, with Myrtale." In the second image, a

Source 5.3 Scenes in a Pompeii Tavern

Museo Archeologico Nazionale, Naples, Italy/Photos: Fotografica Foglia/Scala/Art Resource, NY

female barmaid serves two customers with a large jug and a cup, while they compete for her attention. In the third image, two men playing dice are arguing.

- Why do you think a tavern owner might have such paintings in his place of business?

- What might we learn about tavern life from these images?

- What roles did women play in the tavern?

- What differences do you notice between these paintings and those depicting the lives of the upper classes?

The excavated ruins of Pompeii have much to tell us about the religious as well as the social life of the Roman world in the first century C.E., before Christianity had spread widely. Based on ritual observance rather than doctrine or theology, Roman religious practice sought to obtain the favor of the gods as a way of promoting success, prosperity, and good fortune. A core expression of the diverse and eclectic world of Roman religion was the imperial cult. In Pompeii, a number of temples were dedicated to one or another of the deified emperors, employing together a large cadre of priests and priestesses. Linked to the imperial cult were temples devoted to the traditional Greco-Roman gods such as Apollo, Venus, and Jupiter.

Probably more important to ordinary people were their *lararia* (household shrines), often a niche in the wall that housed paintings or sculptures of *lares* (guardian spirits or deities believed to provide protection within the home). Families offered gifts of fruit, cakes, and wine to these spirits, and the lararia were the focal point for various sacrifices and rituals associated with birth, marriage, and death. Source 5.4 shows one of these shrines, uncovered in the home of a well-to-do freedman (former slave) named Vetti. Protecting the family from external danger were two lares, standing on either side of the lararium and holding their drinking horns. In the center was the *genius*, the spirit of the male head of household. Dressed in a toga and offering a sacrifice, this spirit embodied the character of the man, especially his procreative powers, and so guaranteed many children for the household. The snake at the bottom represented still other benevolent guardian spirits of the family in a fashion very different from Christian symbolism of the snake.

- Why might such a shrine and the spirits it accommodated be more meaningful for many people than the state-approved cults?

- What significance might you find in the temple-like shape of the lararium?

In addition to the official cults and the veneration of household gods, by the first century C.E. a number of newer traditions, often called "mystery

Werner Forman Archive/Bridgeman Images

Source 5.4 A Domestic Shrine

religions," were spreading widely in the Roman Empire. Deriving from the eastern realm of the empire and beyond (Greece, Egypt, and Persia, for example), these mystery religions illustrate the kinds of cultural exchange that took place within the empire. They offered an alternative to the official cults, for they were more personal, emotional, and intimate, usually featuring a ritual initiation into sacred mysteries, codes of moral behavior, and the promise of an afterlife. Among the most popular of these mystery cults in Pompeii was that of Isis, an Egyptian goddess who restored her husband/brother, Osiris, to life and was worshipped as a compassionate protector of the downtrodden.

Another mystery cult, this one of Greek origin, was associated with Dionysus, a god of wine, ecstasy, and poetic inspiration, who was especially popular with women. Often associated with drunkenness, trance states, wild dancing, and unrestrained sexuality, the cult of Dionysus encouraged at least

Werner Forman Archive/Bridgeman Images

Source 5.5 Mystery Religions: The Cult of Dionysus

the temporary abandonment of conventional inhibitions and social restrictions as initiates sought union with Dionysus. A series of wall paintings on a Pompeii building known as the Villa of Mysteries depicts the process of initiation into the cult of Dionysus, perhaps in preparation for marriage.

Source 5.5 shows a particularly dramatic phase of that initiation in which a woman is ritually whipped, while a naked devotee dances ecstatically with a pair of cymbals above her head and a companion holds a rod of phallic symbolism sacred to Dionysus. In any such process of religious initiation, the initiate undergoes a series of trials or purifications in which he or she "dies" symbolically, achieves mystical union with the god, and is "reborn" into the new community of the cult.

- What aspects of the initiation process are visible in this image?

- How might you understand the role of whipping in the initiation process? How would you interpret the relationship of the initiate and the woman on whose lap she is resting her head?

- In what way is sexual union, symbolized by the rod, significant in the initiation?

- Why do you think Roman authorities took action against these mystery religions, even as they did against Christianity?

- What did the mystery cults of Isis or Dionysus provide that neither the state cults nor household gods might offer?

DOING HISTORY

Pompeii as a Window on the Roman World

1. **Characterizing Pompeii:** What does the art of Pompeii, as reflected in these sources, tell us about the social and religious life of this small Roman city in the first century C.E.?

2. **Noticing class differences:** What class or social distinctions are apparent in these visual sources?

3. **Identifying gender roles:** What do these sources suggest about the varied lives and social roles of women and men in Pompeii?

CHAPTER 6

Commonalities and Variations

Africa, the Americas, and Pacific Oceania
500 B.C.E.–1200 C.E.

In early 2010, Bolivian president Evo Morales was inaugurated for his second term in office, the only person from the country's Native American population ever elected to that post since independence from Spain in 1825. The day before the official ceremony in the capital of La Paz, Morales traveled to Tiwanaku (tee-wah-NAH-coo), the center of an impressive empire that had flourished in the Andean highlands between 400 and 1000 C.E., long before either the Incas or the Spanish ruled the area. There he sought to link himself and his administration to this ancient culture, a symbol of Bolivian nationalism and indigenous pride. On his arrival, Morales was ritually cleansed with holy water and herbs and dressed in a llama wool robe. After offerings were made to Pachamama, an Andean earth goddess, and to Tata Inti, the Inca sun god, Morales was invested with symbols of both kingship and spiritual leadership, thus joining political and religious sources of authority. Proclaiming a new multinational state, Morales declared: "Gone forever is the colonial state, which allowed the looting of our natural resources, and gone also is the discriminatory [against native peoples] colonial state."[1] This recent ceremony provides a reminder that memories of American second-wave civilizations remained alive and were available for mobilizing political support and legitimating political authority in the very different circumstances of the early twenty-first century.

For many people, the second-wave era evokes most vividly the civilizations of Eurasia—the Greeks and the Romans, the Persians and the Chinese, and the Indians of South Asia—yet those were not the only civilizations of that era. During this period, the

---

The Maya Temple of the Great Jaguar in Tikal   Located in the Maya city of Tikal in present-day Guatemala, this temple was constructed in the eighth century C.E. and excavated by archeologists in the late nineteenth century. It served as the tomb of the Tikal ruler Jasaw Chan K'awiil I (682–734). Some 144 feet tall, it was topped by a three-room temple complex and a huge roofcomb showing the ruler on his throne. Carved on a wooden beam inside the temple is an image of the ruler protected by a huge jaguar, along with illustrations of his military victories.

Mesoamerican Maya and the Andean Tiwanaku thrived, as did several civilizations in sub-Saharan Africa, including Meroë (MER-oh-ee), Axum (AHK-soom), and the Niger River valley. Furthermore, those peoples who did not organize themselves around cities or states likewise had histories of note and alternative ways of constructing their societies, although they are often neglected in favor of civiliza-

tions. This chapter explores the histories of the varied peoples of Africa, the Americas, and Pacific Oceania during this phase of world history. On occasion, those histories will extend some centuries beyond the chronological boundaries of the second-wave era in Eurasia because patterns of historical development around the world did not always coincide precisely.

Continental Comparisons

At the broadest level, human cultures evolved in quite similar fashion around the world. All, of course, were part of that grand process of human migration that initially peopled the planet. Beginning in Africa, that vast movement of humankind subsequently encompassed Eurasia, Australia, the Americas, and Pacific Oceania. Almost everywhere, gathering, hunting, and fishing long remained the sole basis for sustaining life and society. Then, on the three supercontinents—Eurasia, Africa, and the Americas—the momentous turn of the Agricultural Revolution took place independently and in several distinct areas of each landmass (see Chapter 1). That revolutionary transformation of human life subsequently generated, in particularly rich agricultural environments of all three regions, those more complex societies that we know as civilizations, featuring cities, states, monumental architecture, and great social inequality (see Chapter 2). In these ways, the historical trajectory of the human journey has a certain unity and similarity across quite distinct continental regions. These commonalities provide the foundation for a genuinely global history of humankind. At the beginning of the Common Era, that trajectory had generated a total world population of about 250 million people, substantially less than the current population of the United States alone. By modern standards, it was still a sparsely populated planet.

■ **Comparison**
What similarities and differences are noticeable among the three major continents of the world?

The world's human population was then distributed very unevenly across the three giant continents, as the Snapshot on page 232 indicates. Eurasia was then home to more than 85 percent of the world's people, Africa about 10 percent, the Americas around 5 percent, and Oceania less than 1 percent. That unevenness in population distribution, a pattern that has persisted to the present, is part of the reason why world historians focus more attention on Eurasia than on these other regions. Here lies one of the major differences among the continents.

There were others as well. The absence of most animals capable of domestication meant that few pastoral societies developed in the Americas, and only in pockets of the Andes Mountains based on the herding of llamas and alpacas. No animals

A MAP OF TIME

1400–800 B.C.E.	Lapita culture in Oceania
900–200 B.C.E.	Chavín religious movement in Peruvian Andes
730 B.C.E.	Nubian conquest of Egypt
300 B.C.E.–100 C.E.	Kingdom of Meroë in upper Nile Valley
300 B.C.E.–900 C.E.	Niger Valley civilization in West Africa
200 B.C.E.–400 C.E.	Hopewell "mound-building" culture in U.S. eastern woodlands
1st–8th centuries C.E.	Flourishing of Axum (East Africa) and Moche (coastal Peru) civilizations; spread of Bantu-speaking people in eastern and southern Africa
250–900 C.E.	Classical Maya civilization
300–600	Flourishing of Teotihuacán
4th century	Introduction of Christianity to Axum
400–1000	Tiwanaku and Wari in the Andes
860–1130	Chaco culture in U.S. Southwest
900–1250	Cahokia
After 1000	Flourishing of Tonga trading network
1100–1600	Saudeleur dynasty on island of Pohnpei
1200	Initial settlement of New Zealand

were available in the Americas to pull plows or carts or to be ridden into combat. Africa too lacked wild sheep, goats, chickens, horses, and camels, but its proximity to Eurasia meant that these animals, once domesticated, became widely available to African peoples. Metallurgy in the Americas was likewise far less developed than in Eurasia and Africa, where iron tools and weapons played such an important role in economic and military life. In the Americas, writing was limited to the Mesoamerican region and was most highly developed among the Maya, whereas in Africa it was confined to the northern and northeastern parts of the continent. In Eurasia, by contrast, writing emerged elaborately in many regions. Furthermore, civilizations in Africa and the Americas were fewer in number and generally smaller than those of Eurasia, and larger numbers of people in those two continents lived outside the confines of any civilization in communities that did not feature cities and states.

A final continental comparison distinguishes the history of Africa from that of the Americas. Geography placed Africa adjacent to Eurasia, while it separated the Americas from both Africa and Eurasia. This has meant that parts of Africa frequently

SNAPSHOT   Continental Population in the Second-Wave Era and Beyond

(Note: Population figures for such early times are merely estimates and are often controversial among scholars. Percentages do not always total 100 percent due to rounding.[2])

	Eurasia	Africa	North America	Central/South America	Australia/ Oceania	Total World
Area (in square miles and as percentage of world total)						
	21,049,000 (41%)	11,608,000 (22%)	9,365,000 (18%)	6,880,000 (13%)	2,968,000 (6%)	51,870,000
Population (in millions and as percentage of world total)						
400 B.C.E.	127 (83%)	17 (11%)	1 (0.7%)	7 (5%)	1 (0.7%)	153
10 C.E.	213 (85%)	26 (10%)	2 (0.8%)	10 (4%)	1 (0.4%)	252
200 C.E.	215 (84%)	30 (12%)	2 (0.8%)	9 (4%)	1 (0.4%)	257
600 C.E.	167 (80%)	24 (12%)	2 (1%)	14 (7%)	1 (0.5%)	208
1000 C.E.	195 (77%)	39 (15%)	2 (0.8%)	16 (6%)	1 (0.4%)	253
1500	329 (69%)	113 (24%)	4.5 (0.9%)	53 (11%)	3 (0.6%)	477
1750	646 (83%)	104 (13%)	3 (0.4%)	15 (1.9%)	3 (0.4%)	771
2013	5,041 (70.4%)	1,110 (15.5%)	355 (5%)	617 (8.6%)	38 (0.5%)	7,162

interacted with Eurasian civilizations. In fact, Mediterranean North Africa was long part of a larger zone of Afro-Eurasian interaction. Ancient Egyptian civilization was certainly in contact with Crete, Syria, and Mesopotamia and provided inspiration for the Greeks. The entire North African coastal region was incorporated into the Roman Empire and used to produce wheat and olives on large estates with slave labor. Christianity spread widely across North Africa, giving rise to some of the early Church's most famous martyrs and theologians. The Christian faith found an even more permanent foothold in the lands now known as Ethiopia.

Arabia, located between Africa and Asia, was another point of contact with a wider world for African peoples. The arrival of the domesticated camel, probably from Arabia, generated a pastoral way of life among some of the Berber peoples of the western Sahara during the first three centuries C.E. A little later, camels also made possible trans-Saharan commerce, which linked interior West Africa to the world of Mediterranean civilization. Over many centuries, the East African coast was a port of call for Egyptian, Roman, and Arab merchants, and that region subsequently became an integral part of Indian Ocean trading networks. The transoceanic voyages of Austronesian-speaking sailors from Southeast Asia brought various food crops of that region, bananas for example, to Madagascar and from there to the East African mainland. The Americas and Oceania, by contrast, developed almost wholly apart from this Afro-Eurasian network until that separation was breeched by the voyages of Columbus from 1492.

To illustrate the historical developments of the second-wave era beyond Eurasia / North Africa, this chapter examines first the civilizations that emerged in sub-Saharan Africa and the Americas. Then our historical spotlight turns to several regions on both continents as well as the islands of the Pacific that remained outside the zone of civilization, reminding us that the histories of many peoples took shape without the cities, states, and empires that were so prominent within that zone.

Civilizations of Africa

When historians refer to Africa in premodern times, they are speaking generally of a geographic concept, a continental landmass, and not a cultural identity. Certainly few, if any, people living on the continent at that time thought of themselves as Africans. Like Eurasia or the Americas, Africa hosted numerous separate societies, cultures, and civilizations with vast differences among them as well as some interaction between them.

Many of these differences grew out of the continent's environmental variations. Small regions of Mediterranean climate in the northern and southern extremes, large deserts (the Sahara and the Kalahari), even larger regions of savanna grasslands, tropical rain forest in the continent's center, highlands and mountains in eastern Africa—all of these features, combined with the continent's enormous size, ensured endless variation among Africa's many peoples. Africa did, however, have one distinctive environmental feature: bisected by the equator, it was the most tropical of the world's three supercontinents. While some regions, such as highland Ethiopia, sustained very productive agriculture, elsewhere a variety of factors generated lower crop yields and diminished soil fertility. These included heavy but sometimes-erratic rainfall frequently followed by long dry seasons and the leaching of nutrients from often very ancient soils. Climatic conditions also spawned numerous disease-carrying insects and parasites, which have long created serious health problems in many parts of the continent. It was within these environmental constraints that African peoples made their histories. In several distinct regions of the continent—the upper Nile Valley, northern Ethiopia/Eritrea, and the Niger River valley—small civilizations flourished during the second-wave era, while others followed later. A further African civilization falling partly within this time period grew up along the East African coast in conjunction with Indian Ocean commerce. Known as Swahili civilization, it is treated in greater detail in Chapter 7.

Meroë: Continuing a Nile Valley Civilization

In the Nile Valley south of Egypt lay the lands of Nubian civilization, almost as old as Egypt itself. Over many centuries, Nubians both traded and fought with Egypt, and on one occasion the Nubian Kingdom of Kush conquered Egypt and ruled it for a century. (See Zooming In: Piye, page 236.) While borrowing heavily from Egypt, Nubia remained a distinct and separate civilization. As Egypt fell increasingly under foreign control, Nubian civilization came to center on the southern city of Meroë (MER-oh-ee), where it flourished between 300 B.C.E. and 100 C.E. (see Map 6.1).

■ **Connection**

How did the history of Meroë and Axum reflect interaction with neighboring civilizations?

Politically, the Kingdom of Meroë was governed by an all-powerful and sacred monarch, a position held on at least ten occasions by women, governing alone or as co-rulers with a male monarch. Unlike the female pharaoh Hatshepsut in Egypt, who was portrayed in male clothing, Meroë queens appeared in sculptures as women and with a prominence and power equivalent to their male counterparts. In accordance with ancient traditions, such rulers were buried along with a number of human sacrificial victims. The city of Meroë and other urban centers housed a wide variety of economic specialties—merchants, weavers, potters, and masons, as well as servants, laborers, and slaves. The smelting of iron and the manufacture of iron tools and weapons were especially prominent industries. The rural areas surrounding Meroë were populated by peoples who practiced some combination of herding and farming and paid periodic tribute to the ruler. Rainfall-based agriculture was possible in Meroë, and consequently farmers were less dependent on irrigation. This meant that the rural population did not need to concentrate so heavily near the Nile as was the case in Egypt.

The wealth and military power of Meroë derived in part from extensive long-distance trading connections, to the north via the Nile and to the east and west by means of camel caravans. Its iron weapons and cotton cloth, as well as its access to gold, ivory, tortoiseshells, and ostrich feathers, gave Meroë a reputation for great riches in the world of northeastern Africa and the Mediterranean. The discovery in Meroë of a statue of the Roman emperor Augustus, probably seized during a raid on Roman Egypt,

A Bracelet from Meroë

This gold bracelet, dating to about 100 B.C.E., illustrates the skill of Meroë's craftsmen as well as the kingdom's reputation as one of the wealthiest states of the ancient world. The bracelet's depiction of a seated Hathor, a popular Egyptian goddess, shows the influence of Egyptian culture in Nubia. (Bracelet with an image of Hathor, from Pyramid B, Gebel Barkal, Nubia, Meroitic Period, 250–100 B.C. [gold and enamel], Nubian/Museum of Fine Arts, Boston, Massachusetts, USA/Harvard University–Boston Museum of Fine Arts Expedition/Bridgeman Images)

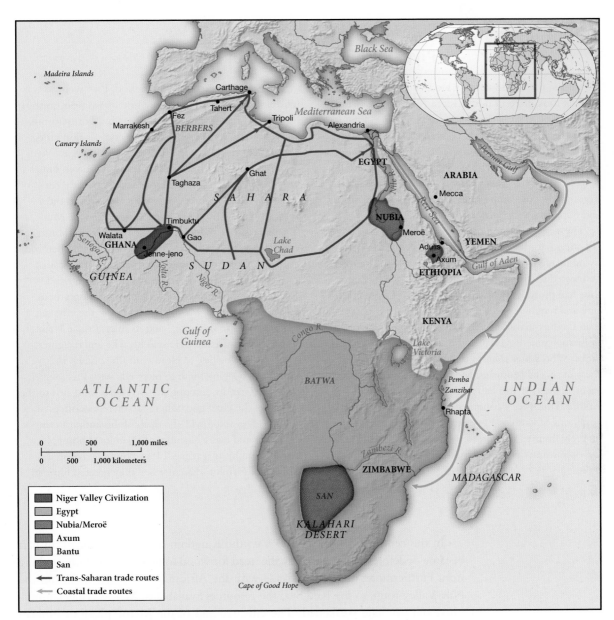

Map 6.1   Africa in the Second-Wave Era

During the second-wave era, older African civilizations such as Egypt and Nubia persisted and changed, while new civilizations emerged in Axum and the Niger River valley. South of the equator, the process of Bantu expansion created many new societies and identities.

testifies to contact with the Mediterranean world. Culturally, Meroë seemed to move away from the heavy Egyptian influence of earlier times. A local lion god, Apedemek, grew more prominent than Egyptian deities such as Isis and Osiris, while the use of Egyptian-style writing declined as a new and still-undeciphered Meroitic script took its place.

Piye, Kushite Conqueror of Egypt

During the eighth century B.C.E., a remarkable reversal took place in northeastern Africa. The ancient Kingdom of Kush in the southern Nile Valley, long under the control of Egypt, conquered its former ruler and governed it for a century. The primary agent of that turnabout was Piye, a Kushite ruler (r. 752–721 B.C.E.), who recorded his great victory in a magnificent inscription that provides some hints about his own personality and outlook on the world.[3]

The very beginning of the inscription discloses Piye's self-image, for he declares himself a "divine emanation, living image of Atum," the Egyptian creator-god closely connected to kingship. Like most of the Kushite elite, Piye had thoroughly assimilated much of Egyptian culture and religion, becoming perhaps "more Egyptian than the Egyptians."[4] Even the inscription was written in hieroglyphic Egyptian and in the style of earlier pharaohs. Who better then to revive an Egypt that, over the past several centuries, had become hopelessly fragmented and that also had neglected the worship of Amun? Thus Piye's conquest reflected the territorial ambitions of Kush's "Egyptianized" rulers, a sense of divinely inspired mission to set things right in Egypt, and the opportunity presented by the sorry state of Egyptian politics.

If we are to believe the inscription, Piye went to war reluctantly and only in response to requests from various Egyptian "princes, counts, and generals." Furthermore, he was careful to pay respect to the gods all along the way. After celebrating the new year in 730 B.C.E., Piye departed from his capital of Napata and made an initial stop in Thebes, a southern Egyptian city already controlled by Kushite forces. There he took part in the annual Opet Festival, honoring Amun, his wife Mut (Egypt's mother goddess), and their offspring Khonsu, associated with the moon. Moving north, Piye then laid siege to Hermopolis, located in middle Egypt. From a high tower, archers poured arrows into the city and "slingers" hurled stones, "slaying people among them daily," according to the inscription. Soon the city had become "foul to the nose," and its ruler, Prince Namlot, prepared for surrender. He sent his wife and daughter, lying on their bellies, to plead with the women in Piye's entourage, begging them to intercede with Piye, which they did. Grandly entering the city, Piye went first to the temple of the chief god, where he offered sacrifices of "bulls, calves and fowl." To establish his authority, he then "entered every chamber of [Namlot's] house, his treasury and his magazines." Piye pointedly ignored the women of Namlot's harem when they greeted him "in

In the centuries following 100 C.E., the Kingdom of Meroë declined, in part because of deforestation caused by the need for wood to make charcoal for smelting iron. Furthermore, as Egyptian trade with the African interior switched from the Nile Valley route to the Red Sea, the resources available to Meroë's rulers diminished and the state weakened. The effective end of the Meroë phase of Nubian civilization came with the kingdom's conquest in the 340s C.E. by the neighboring and rising state of Axum. In the centuries that followed, three separate Nubian states emerged, and Coptic (Egyptian) Christianity penetrated the region. For almost a thousand years, Nubia was a Christian civilization, using Greek as a liturgical language and constructing churches in Coptic or Byzantine fashion. After 1300 or so, political division, Arab immigration, and the penetration of Islam eroded this Christian civilization, and Nubia became part of the growing world of Islam (see Chapter 10).

the manner of women." Yet in the stable, he was moved by the suffering of the horses. He seized Namlot's possessions for his treasury and assigned his enemy's grain to the temple of Amun.

And so it went as Piye moved northward. Many cities capitulated without resistance, offering their treasure to the Kushites. Presenting himself as a just and generous conqueror, Piye declared that "not a single one has been slain therein, except the enemies who blasphemed against the god, who were dispatched as rebels." However, it was a different story when he arrived outside the major north Egyptian city of Memphis, then ruled by the Libyan chieftain Tefnakht. There "a multitude of people were slain" before Tefnakht was induced to surrender. He sent an envoy to Piye to deliver an abject and humiliating speech: "Be thou appeased! I have not beheld thy face for shame; I cannot stand before thy flame, I tremble at thy might." The city was ritually cleansed; proper respect was paid to the gods, who confirmed Piye's kingship; and tribute was collected. Soon all resistance collapsed, and Piye, once ruler of a small Kushite kingdom, found himself master of all Egypt.

And then, surprisingly, he departed, leaving his underlings in charge and his sister as the high priestess and wife of Amun in Thebes. His ships "were laden with silver, gold, copper, clothing, and everything of the Northland, every product of Syria, and all sweet woods of God's Land [Egypt]. His majesty sailed up-stream, with glad heart." Never again did Piye set foot in Egypt, preferring to live out his days in his native country, where he was buried in an Egyptian-style pyramid. But he had laid the foundation for a century of Kushite rule in Egypt, reunifying that ancient country, reinvigorating the cult of Amun, and giving expression to the vitality of an important African civilization.

The stele of Piye, showing Piye to the right of the seated god Amun, receiving the surrender of his Egyptian enemies, while below defeated rulers prostrate themselves before him.

Questions: How did Piye understand himself and his actions in Egypt? How might ancient Egyptians or modern historians view his conquests?

photo: James Henry Breasted, *The Piankhi Stela, Ancient Records of Egypt* (Chicago, 1906), Part IV, 816ff/Visual Connection Archive

Axum: The Making of a Christian Kingdom

If Meroë represented the continuation of an old African/Nubian civilization, Axum marked the emergence of a new one. (For various accounts about or from Axum, see Working with Evidence: Axum and the World, page 265.) Axum lay in the Horn of Africa, in what is now Eritrea and northern Ethiopia (see Map 6.1). Its economic foundation was a highly productive agriculture that used a plow-based farming system, unlike most of the rest of Africa, which relied on the hoe or digging stick. Axum's agriculture generated substantial amounts of wheat, barley, millet, and teff, a highly nutritious grain unique to that region. By 50 C.E. or so, a substantial state had emerged, stimulated by its participation in the rapidly increasing Red Sea and Indian Ocean commerce, which was itself a product of growing Roman demand for Indian pearls, textiles, and especially pepper. At Adulis, then the largest

The Columns of Axum
Dating to the time when Axum first encountered Christianity (300–500 C.E.), this column, measuring some seventy-nine feet tall, probably served as a funeral monument for the kingdom's ancient rulers. (McPhoto/ZAD/age fotostock)

port on the East African coast, a wide range of merchants sought the products of the African interior — animal hides, rhinoceros horn, ivory, obsidian, tortoiseshells, and slaves. Taxes on this trade provided a major source of revenue for the Axumite state and the complex society that grew up within it. Thus the decline of Meroë and the rise of Axum were both connected to changing patterns of long-distance commerce.

The interior capital city, also known as Axum, was a center of monumental building and royal patronage for the arts. The most famous structures were huge stone obelisks, which most likely marked royal graves. Some of them were more than 100 feet tall and at the time were the largest structures in the world hewn from a single piece of rock. The language used at court, in the towns, and for commerce was Ge'ez, written in a script derived from South Arabia. The Axumite state exercised a measure of control over the mostly Agaw-speaking people of the country through a loose administrative structure focusing on the collection of tribute payments. To the Romans, Axum was the third major empire within the world they knew, following their own and the Persian Empire.

Through its connections to Red Sea trade and the Roman world, particularly Egypt, Axum was introduced to Christianity in the fourth century C.E. Its monarch at the time, King Ezana, adopted the new religion about the same time as Constantine did in the Roman Empire. Early in his reign, the kingdom's coins featured images of gods derived from southern Arabia, while by the end, they were inscribed with the Christian cross. Supported by royal authority, Christianity took root in Axum, linking that kingdom religiously to Egypt, where a distinctive Christian Church known as Coptic was already well established. (See Chapter 4, page 176, and Chapter 10, page 414.) Although Egypt subsequently became largely Islamic, reducing its Christian community to a small minority, Christianity maintained a dominant position in the mountainous terrain of highland Ethiopia and in the early twenty-first century still represents the faith of perhaps 60 percent of the country's population.

During the fourth through the sixth centuries C.E., Axum mounted a campaign of imperial expansion that took its forces into the Kingdom of Meroë and across the Red Sea into Yemen in South Arabia. By 571, the traditional date for the birth of Muhammad, an Axumite army, including a number of African war elephants, had reached the gates of Mecca, but it was a fairly short-lived imperial venture. The next several centuries were ones of decline for the Axumite state, owing partly to environmental changes, such as soil exhaustion, erosion, and deforestation, brought about by intensive farming. Equally important was the rise of Islam, which altered trade routes and diminished the revenue available to the Axumite state. Its last coins were struck in the early seventh century. When the state revived several centuries later, it was centered farther south on the Ethiopian plateau. In this new location, there emerged the Christian Church and the state that present-day Ethiopia has inherited, but the link to ancient Axum was long remembered and revered.

With their long-distance trading connections, urban centers, centralized states, complex societies, monumental architecture, written languages, and imperial ambitions, both Meroë and Axum paralleled on a smaller scale the major features of the second-wave civilizations of Eurasia. Furthermore, both were in direct contact with the world of Mediterranean civilizations. Across the continent in West Africa, a rather different civilization took shape.

Along the Niger River: Cities without States

The middle stretches of the Niger River in West Africa witnessed the emergence of a remarkable urbanization (see Map 6.1, page 235). A prolonged dry period during the five centuries after 500 B.C.E. brought growing numbers of people from the southern Sahara into the fertile floodplain of the middle Niger in search of more reliable access to water. Accompanying them were their domesticated cattle, sheep, and goats; their agricultural skills; and their ironworking technology. Over many centuries (roughly 300 B.C.E.–900 C.E.), the peoples of this region created a distinctive city-based civilization. The most fully studied of the urban clusters that grew up along the middle Niger was the city of Jenne-jeno (jihn-AY jihn-OH), which at its high point probably housed more than 40,000 people.

Among the most distinctive features of the Niger Valley civilization was the apparent absence of a corresponding state structure. Unlike the cities of Egypt, China, the Roman Empire, or Axum, these middle Niger urban centers were not encompassed within some larger imperial system. Nor were they like the city-states of ancient Mesopotamia, in which each city had its own centralized political structure, embodied in a monarch and his accompanying bureaucracy. According to a leading historian of the region, they were "cities without citadels," complex urban centers that apparently operated without the coercive authority of a state, for archeologists have found in their remains few signs of despotic power, widespread warfare, or deep social inequalities.[5] In this respect, these urban centers resemble the early cities of Norte Chico or the Indus Valley civilization, where likewise little archeological evidence of centralized state structures has been found (see Chapter 2).

In place of such hierarchical organization, Jenne-jeno and other cities of the region emerged as clusters of economically specialized settlements surrounding a larger central town. The earliest and most prestigious of these specialized occupations was iron smithing. Working with fire and earth (ore) to produce this highly useful metal, the smiths of the Niger Valley were both feared and revered. Archeologist

■ **Description**
How does the experience of the Niger Valley challenge conventional notions of "civilization"?

Terra-Cotta Statue from Jenne-jeno
The artistic tradition of Niger Valley civilization includes a number of terra-cotta couples, reflecting perhaps the emphasis on the separate but complementary roles of men and women in much of African thought. This statue and others like it date to sometime after the twelfth century and may express the resistance of an indigenous tradition to the growing penetration of Islam. (Entwistle Gallery, London, UK/ Werner Forman/Art Resource, NY)

Roderick McIntosh, a leading figure in the excavation of Jenne-jeno, argued that "their knowledge of the transforming arts—earth to metal, insubstantial fire to the mass of iron—was the key to a secret, occult realm of immense power and immense danger."[6]

Other specializations followed. Villages of cotton weavers, potters, leather workers, and griots (praise-singers who preserved and recited the oral traditions of their societies) grew up around the central towns. Gradually these urban artisan communities became occupational castes, whose members passed their jobs and skills to their children and could marry only within their own group. In the surrounding rural areas, as in all urban-based civilizations, farmers tilled the soil and raised their animals, but specialization also occurred in food production as various ethnic groups focused on fishing, rice cultivation, or some other agricultural pursuit. At least for a time, these middle Niger cities represented an African alternative to an oppressive state, which in many parts of the world accompanied an increasingly complex urban economy and society. A series of distinct and specialized economic groups shared authority and voluntarily used the services of one another, while maintaining their own identities through physical separation.

Accompanying this unique urbanization, and no doubt stimulating it, was a growing network of indigenous West African commerce. The middle Niger floodplain supported a rich agriculture and contained clay for pottery, but it lacked stone, iron ore, salt, and fuel. This scarcity of resources was the basis for a long-distance commerce that operated by boat along the Niger River and overland by donkey to the north and south. Iron ore from more than 50 miles away, copper from mines 200 miles distant, gold from even more distant sources, stones and salt from the Sahara—all of these items have been found in Jenne-jeno, exchanged no doubt for grain, fish, smoked meats, iron implements, and other staples. Jenne-jeno itself was an important transshipment point in this commerce, in which goods were transferred from boat to donkey or vice versa. By the 500s C.E., there is evidence of an even wider commerce, and at least indirect contact, from Mauritania in the west to present-day Mali and Burkina Faso in the east.

In the second millennium C.E., new historical patterns developed in West Africa (see Chapter 7). A number of large-scale states or empires emerged in the region—Ghana, Mali, and Songhay, among the most well-known. At least partially responsible for this development was the flourishing of a camel-borne trans-Saharan commerce, previously but a trickle across the great desert. As West Africa became more firmly connected to North Africa and the Mediterranean, Islam penetrated the region, marking a gradual but major cultural transformation. All of this awaited West Africa in later centuries, submerging, but not completely eliminating, the decentralized city life of the Niger Valley.

Civilizations of Mesoamerica

Westward across the Atlantic Ocean lay an altogether separate world, later known as the Americas. Although geography encouraged some interaction between African and Eurasian peoples, the Atlantic and Pacific oceans ensured that the cultures and societies of the Western Hemisphere operated in a world apart from their Afro-Eurasian counterparts. Nor were the cultures of the Americas stimulated by the kind of fruitful interaction among their own peoples that played such an important role in the Eastern Hemisphere. Nothing similar to the contact between Egypt and Mesopotamia, or Persia and the Greeks, or the extensive communication along the Silk Road trading network, enriched the two major centers of civilization in the Americas—Mesoamerica and the Andes—which had little if any direct contact with each other.

Another geographic feature that distinguished these centers of civilization from those in the Afro-Eurasian world was their rugged mountainous terrain. Sharp changes in the landscape ascending from sea level to summit gave rise to an enormous range of microclimates as well as great ecological and biological diversity. Arid coastal environments, steamy lowland rain forests, cold and windy highland plateaus cut by numerous mountains and valleys—all of this was often encompassed in a relatively small area. Such conditions contributed to substantial linguistic and ethnic diversity and to the development of many distinct and competing cities, chiefdoms, and states. It also meant that states, and sometimes individual families, sought "vertical integration," an effort to control a variety of ecological zones where a number of different crops and animals could flourish.

Finally, the remarkable achievements of early American civilizations and cultures occurred without the many large domesticated animals or ironworking technologies that were so important throughout the Eastern Hemisphere. In the Andes, an important exception to this generalization involved the domestication of the llama and alpaca, which offered food, fiber, and transport for the civilizations of that region and in a few places provided for a time the basis for largely pastoral communities.

Accounts of pre-Columbian American societies often focus primarily on the Aztec and Inca empires (see Chapter 12), yet these impressive creations, flourishing in the fifteenth and early sixteenth centuries, were but the latest in a long line of civilizations that preceded them in Mesoamerica and the Andes, respectively. These two regions housed the vast majority of the population of the Americas. Here the historical spotlight focuses on the long period following the First Civilizations of the Olmecs and Norte Chico but preceding the Aztecs and Incas, roughly 500 B.C.E. to 1300 C.E.

The region housing Mesoamerican civilizations stretched from central Mexico to northern Central America. Despite its environmental and ethnic diversity, Mesoamerica was also a distinct region, bound together by elements of a common culture. Its many peoples shared an intensive agricultural technology devoted to raising maize, beans, chili peppers, and squash. They prepared maize in a distinctive and highly nutritious fashion and based their economies on market exchange. They practiced religions featuring a similar pantheon of male and female deities, understood time as a cosmic cycle of creation and destruction, practiced human sacrifice, and constructed monumental ceremonial centers. Furthermore, they employed a common ritual calendar of 260 days and hieroglyphic writing, and they interacted frequently among themselves. During the first millennium B.C.E., for example, the various small states and chiefdoms of the region, particularly the Olmec, exchanged a number of luxury goods used to display social status and for ritual purposes—jade, serpentine, obsidian tools, ceramic pottery, shell ornaments, stingray spines, and turtle shells. As a result, aspects of Olmec culture, such as artistic styles, temple pyramids, the calendar system, and rituals involving human sacrifice, spread widely throughout Mesoamerica and influenced many of the civilizations that followed.

The Maya: Writing and Warfare

Among Mesoamerican civilizations, none has attracted more attention than that of the Maya. Scholars have traced the beginnings of the Maya people to ceremonial centers constructed as early as 2000 B.C.E. in present-day Guatemala and the Yucatán region of Mexico (see Map 6.2). During the first millennium B.C.E., a number of substantial urban centers with concentrated populations and monumental architecture had emerged in the region. In northern Guatemala, for example, the archeological site of El Mirador was home to tens of thousands of people, a pyramid/temple said by some to be the largest in the world, and a stone-carved frieze depicting the Maya creation story known as the Popul Vuh.

But it was during a later phase of Maya civilization, between 250 and 900 C.E., that their most well-known

Map 6.2   Civilizations of Mesoamerica

During the second-wave era, Maya civilization and the large city of Teotihuacán represented the most prominent features of Mesoamerican civilization.

cultural achievements emerged. Intellectuals, probably priests, developed a mathematical system that included the concept of zero and place notation and was capable of complex calculations. They combined this mathematical ability with careful observation of the night skies to plot the cycles of planets, to predict eclipses of the sun and the moon, to construct elaborate calendars, and to calculate accurately the length of the solar year. The distinctive art of the Maya elite was likewise impressive to later observers.

Accompanying these intellectual and artistic achievements was the creation of the most elaborate writing system in the Americas, which used both pictographs and phonetic or syllabic elements. Carved on stone and written on bark paper or deerskin books, Mayan writing recorded historical events, masses of astronomical data, and religious or mythological texts. Temples, pyramids, palaces, and public plazas abounded, graced with painted murals and endless stone carving. It is not surprising that early scholars viewed Maya civilization somewhat romantically as a peaceful society led by gentle stargazing priest-kings devoted to temple building and intellectual pursuits.

■ **Comparison**

With what Eurasian civilizations might the Maya be compared?

The economic foundations for these cultural achievements were embedded in an "almost totally engineered landscape."[7] The Maya drained swamps, terraced hillsides, flattened ridgetops, and constructed an elaborate water-management system. Much of this underpinned a flourishing agriculture, which supported a very rapidly growing and dense population by 750 C.E. This agriculture sustained substantial elite classes of nobles, priests, merchants, architects, and sculptors, as well as specialized artisans producing pottery, tools, and cotton textiles. And it was sufficiently productive to free a large labor force for work on the many public structures that continue to amaze contemporary visitors.

The earlier romantic view of Maya civilization changed as scholars realized that its many achievements took place within a highly fragmented political system of city-states, local lords, and regional kingdoms with no central authority, with frequent warfare, and with the extensive capture and sacrifice of prisoners. The larger political units of Maya civilization were densely populated urban and ceremonial centers, ruled by powerful kings and on a few occasions queens. They were divine rulers or "state shamans" able to mediate between humankind and the supernatural. One of these cities, Tikal (tee-KAHL), contained perhaps 50,000 people, with another 50,000 or so in the surrounding countryside, by 750 C.E. (See the chapter-opening photo, page 228, of a temple from Tikal.) Some of these city-states had imperial ambition, but none succeeded in creating a unified Maya empire. Various centers of Maya civilization rose and fell; fluctuating alliances among them alternated with periods of sporadic warfare; ruling families intermarried; the elite classes sought luxury goods from far away—jade, gold, shells, feathers from exotic birds, cacao—to bolster their authority and status. In its political dimensions, Maya civilization more closely resembled the competing city-states of ancient Mesopotamia or classical Greece than the imperial structures of Rome, Persia, or China.

But large parts of that imposing civilization collapsed with a completeness and finality rare in world history. Clearly, this was not a single or uniform phenomenon, as flourishing centers of Maya civilization persisted in the northern Yucatán, and many Maya survived to fight the Spanish in the sixteenth century. But in the southern regions where the collapse was most complete, its outcomes were devastating. In less than a century following the onset of a long-term drought in 840, the population of the low-lying southern heartland of the Maya dropped by 85 percent or more as famine, epidemic, and fratricidal warfare reaped a horrific toll. It was a catastrophe from which there was no recovery. Elements of Maya culture survived in scattered settlements, but the great cities were deserted, and large-scale construction and artistic work ceased. The last date inscribed in stone corresponds to 909 C.E. As a complex civilization, the Maya had passed into history.

Explaining this remarkable demise has long kept scholars guessing, with recent accounts focusing on ecological and political factors. Rapid population growth after 600 C.E. pushed total Maya numbers to perhaps 5 million or more and soon outstripped available resources, resulting in deforestation and the erosion of hillsides. Under such conditions, climate change in the form of prolonged droughts in the 800s may well have placed unbearable pressures on Maya society. Political disunity and endemic rivalries, long a prominent feature of Maya civilization, prevented a coordinated and effective response to the emerging catastrophe. Warfare in fact became more frequent as competition for increasingly scarce land for cultivation became sharper. Rulers dependent on ritual splendor for their legitimacy competed to mount ever more elaborate temples, palaces, and pageants, requiring more labor and taxes from their subjects and tribute from their enemies. Whatever the precise explanation, the Maya collapse, like that of the Romans and others, illustrates the fragility of civilizations, whether they are embodied in large empires or organized in a more decentralized fashion.

Teotihuacán: The Americas' Greatest City

At roughly the same time as the Maya flourished in the southern regions of Mesoamerica, the giant city of Teotihuacán (tay-uh-tee-wah-KAHN) was also thriving further north in the Valley of Mexico. Begun around 150 B.C.E. and apparently built to a plan rather than evolving haphazardly, the city came to occupy about eight square miles and by 550 C.E. had a population variously estimated between 100,000 and 200,000. It was by far the largest urban complex in the Americas at the time and one of the six largest in the world. Beyond this, much about Teotihuacán is unknown, such as its original name, the language of its people, the kind of government that ordered its life, and the precise function of its many deities.

■ **Connection**
In what ways did Teotihuacán shape the history of Mesoamerica?

Physically, the city was enormously impressive, replete with broad avenues, spacious plazas, huge marketplaces, temples, palaces, apartment complexes, slums, waterways, reservoirs, drainage systems, and colorful murals. Along the main north/south boulevard, now known as the Street of the Dead, were the grand homes of

Teotihuacán
Taken from the summit of the Pyramid of the Moon, this photograph looks down the famous Avenue of the Dead to the Pyramid of the Sun in the upper left. (Alison Wright/Science Source)

the elite, the headquarters of state authorities, many temples, and two giant pyramids. One of them, the Pyramid of the Sun, had been constructed over an ancient tunnel leading to a cave and may well have been regarded as the site of creation itself, the birthplace of the sun and the moon. At the Temple of the Feathered Serpent, archeologists have found the remains of some 200 people, their hands and arms tied behind them; they were the apparently unwilling sacrificial victims meant to accompany the high-ranking persons buried there into the afterlife.

Off the main avenues in a grid-like pattern of streets lay thousands of residential apartment compounds, home to the city's commoners, each with its own kitchen area, sleeping quarters, courtyards, and shrines. In these compounds, perhaps in groups of related families or lineages, lived many of the farmers who tilled the lands outside the city. Thousands of Maya specialists—masons, leather workers, potters, construction laborers, merchants, civil servants—also made their homes in these apartments. So too did skilled makers of obsidian blades, who plied their trade in hundreds of separate workshops, generating products that were in great demand throughout Mesoamerica. At least two small sections of the city were reserved exclusively for foreigners.

Buildings, both public and private, were decorated with mural paintings, sculptures, and carvings. Many of these works of art display abstract geometric and stylized images. Others depict gods and goddesses, arrayed in various forms—feathered serpents, starfish, jaguars, flowers, and warriors. One set of murals shows happy people cavorting in a paradise of irrigated fields, playing games, singing, and chasing butterflies, which were thought to represent the souls of the dead. Another, however, portrays dancing warriors carrying elaborate curved knives, to which were attached bleeding human hearts.

The art of Teotihuacán, unlike that of the Maya, has revealed few images of self-glorifying rulers or individuals. Nor did the city have a tradition of written public inscriptions as the Maya did, although a number of glyphs or characters indicate at least a limited form of writing. One scholar has suggested that "the rulers of Teotihuacán might have intentionally avoided the personality cult of the dynastic art and writing" so characteristic of the Maya.[8] Perhaps those rulers constituted an oligarchy or council of high-ranking elites rather than a single monarch.

However it was governed, Teotihuacán cast a huge shadow over Mesoamerica, particularly from 300 to 600 C.E. A core region of perhaps 10,000 square miles was administered directly from the city itself, while tribute was no doubt exacted from other areas within its broader sphere of influence. At a greater distance, the power of Teotihuacán's armies gave it a presence in the Maya heartland more than 600 miles to the east. At least one Maya city, Kaminaljuyú in the southern highlands, was completely taken over by the Teotihuacán military and organized as a colony. In Tikal, a major lowland Maya city, in the year 378 C.E., agents of Teotihuacán apparently engineered a coup that placed a collaborator on the throne and turned the city for a time into an ally or a satellite. Elsewhere—in the Zapotec capital of Monte Albán, for example—murals show unarmed persons from Teotihuacán engaged in what seem to be more equal diplomatic relationships.

At least some of this political and military activity was no doubt designed to obtain, either by trade or by tribute, valued commodities from afar—food products, cacao beans, tropical bird feathers, honey, salt, medicinal herbs. The presence in Teotihuacán of foreigners, perhaps merchants, from the Gulf Coast and Maya lowlands, as well as much pottery from those regions, provides further evidence of long-distance trade. Moreover, the sheer size and prestige of Teotihuacán surely persuaded many, all across Mesoamerica, to imitate the architectural and artistic styles of the city. Thus, according to a leading scholar, "Teotihuacán meant something of surpassing importance far beyond its core area."[9] Almost a thousand years after its still-mysterious collapse around 650 C.E., the great metropolis was dubbed Teotihuacán, the "city of the gods," by the peoples of the Aztec Empire.

Civilizations of the Andes

Yet another and quite separate center of civilization in the Americas lay in the dramatic landscape of the Andes. Bleak deserts along the coast supported human habitation only because they were cut by dozens of rivers flowing down from the mountains, offering the possibility of irrigation and cultivation. The offshore waters of the Pacific Ocean also provided an enormously rich marine environment with an endless supply of seabirds and fish. The Andes themselves, a towering mountain chain with many highland valleys, afforded numerous distinct ecological niches, depending on altitude. Andean societies generally sought access to the resources of these various environments through colonization, conquest, or trade—seafood from the coastal regions; maize and cotton from lower-altitude valleys; potatoes, quinoa, and pastureland for their llamas in the high plains; tropical fruits and coca leaves from the moist eastern slope of the Andes and the arid western slope as well (see Map 6.3).

The most well-known of the civilizations to take shape in this environment was that of the Incas, which encompassed practically the entire region, some 2,500 miles in length, in the fifteenth century. Yet the Incas represented only the most recent and the largest in a long history of civilizations in the area.

The coastal region of central Peru had in fact generated one of the world's First Civilizations, known as Norte Chico, dating back to around 3000 B.C.E. (see Chapter 2). During the two millennia between roughly 1000 B.C.E. and 1000 C.E., a number of Andean civilizations rose and passed away. Because none of them had developed writing, historians are largely dependent on archeology for an understanding of these civilizations.

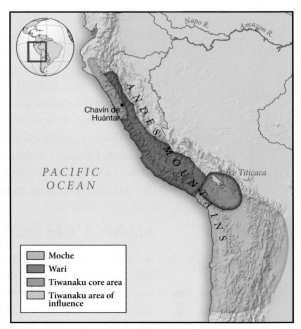

Map 6.3 Civilizations of the Andes

No single civilization dominated the Andes region during the second-wave era. Rather, a number of religious movements, states, and empires rose and fell before the entire region was encompassed by the Inca Empire in the fifteenth century.

Chavín: A Pan-Andean Religious Movement

In both the coastal and highland regions of Peru, archeologists have uncovered numerous local ceremonial centers or temple complexes, dating to between 2000 and 1000 B.C.E. Then around 900 B.C.E., one of them, situated in the Andean highlands at a village called Chavín (cha-BEEN) de Huántar, became the focus of a religious movement that soon swept through both coastal and highland Peru, aided by its strategic location on trade routes to both the coastal region to the west and the Amazon rain forest to the east.

By perhaps 750 B.C.E., this small center had become a town of 2,000 to 3,000 people, with clear distinctions between an elite class, who lived in stone houses, and ordinary people, with adobe dwellings. An elaborate temple complex included numerous galleries, hidden passageways, staircases, ventilation shafts, drainage canals, and distinctive carvings. Chavín artwork suggests influences from both the desert coastal region and the rain forests. Major deities were represented as jaguars, crocodiles, and snakes, all of them native to the Amazon basin. Shamans or priests likely made use of the San Pedro cactus, native to the Andes Mountains, employing its

■ **Connection**
What kind of influence did Chavín exert in the Andes region?

hallucinogenic properties to penetrate the supernatural world. Some of the fantastic artwork of this civilization—its jaguar-human images, for example—may well reflect the visions of these religious leaders.

Over the next several centuries, this blended religious movement proved attractive across much of Peru and beyond, as Chavín-style temple architecture, sculpture, pottery, religious images, and painted textiles were widely imitated within the region. Chavín itself became a pilgrimage site and perhaps a training center for initiates. Although some evidence suggests violence and warfare, no Chavín "empire" emerged. Instead, a widespread religious cult, erected on the back of a trading network, provided for the first time and for several centuries a measure of economic and cultural integration to much of the Peruvian Andes.

Moche: A Civilization of the Coast

By 200 B.C.E., the pan-Andes Chavín cult had faded, replaced by a number of regional civilizations. Among them, Moche (MOH-chee) civilization clearly stands out. Dominating a 250-mile stretch of Peru's northern coast and incorporating thirteen river valleys, the Moche people flourished between about 100 and 800 C.E. Their economy was rooted in a complex irrigation system, requiring constant maintenance, which funneled runoff from the Andes into fields of maize, beans, and squash and acres of cotton, all fertilized by rich bird droppings called guano. Moche fishermen also harvested millions of anchovies from the bountiful Pacific.

■ **Description**
What features of Moche life characterize it as a civilization?

Politically, Moche was governed by warrior-priests, some of whom lived atop huge pyramids, the largest of which was constructed from 143 million sun-dried bricks. There shaman-rulers, often under the influence of hallucinogenic drugs, conducted ancient rituals that mediated between the world of humankind and that of the gods. They also presided over the ritual sacrifice of human victims, drawn from their many prisoners of war, which became central to the politico-religious life of the Moche. Images on Moche pottery show a ruler attired in a magnificent feather headdress and seated on a pyramid, while a parade of naked prisoners marches past him. Other scenes of decapitation and dismemberment indicate the fate that awaited those destined for sacrifice. For these rulers, the Moche world was apparently one of war, ceremony, and diplomacy.

The immense wealth of this warrior-priest elite and the exquisite artistry of Moche craftsmen are reflected in the elaborate burials accorded the rulers. (See Zooming In: The Lord of Sipan and the Lady of Cao, page 250.) In the absence of written texts, these artistic products are the most accessible aspect of Moche life, and much of what scholars know about the Moche world derives from the superb skill of its craftspeople, such as metalworkers, potters, weavers, and painters. Face masks, figures of animals, small earrings, and other jewelry items, many plated in gold, display amazing technical abilities and a striking artistic sensibility. Decorating Moche ceramic pottery are naturalistic portraits of noble lords and rulers and images from the life of common people, including the blind and the sick. Battle scenes show warriors confronting their enemies with raised clubs. Erotic encounters between men and women and gods making love to humans likewise represent common themes, as do grotesque images of the many Moche gods and goddesses. Much of this, of course, reflects the culture of the Moche elite. We know much less about the daily life of the farmers, fishermen, weavers, traders, construction workers, and servants whose labor made that elite culture possible.

These cultural achievements, however, rested on fragile environmental foundations, for the region was subject to drought, earthquakes, and occasional torrential rains associated with El Niño episodes (dramatic changes in weather patterns caused by periodic warming of Pacific Ocean currents). During the sixth century C.E., some combination of these forces caused extended ecological disruption, which seriously undermined Moche civilization. In these circumstances, the Moche were vulnerable to aggressive neighbors and possibly to internal social tensions as well. By the end of the eighth century C.E., that civilization had passed into history.

Wari and Tiwanaku: Empires of the Interior

Far more than the Moche and other coastal civilizations, the interior empires of Wari (wah-ree) and Tiwanaku provided a measure of political integration and cultural commonality for the entire Andean region. Growing out of ancient settlements, these two states flourished between 400 and 1000 C.E., Wari in the northern highlands and Tiwanaku to the south. Both were centered in large urban capitals, marked by monumental architecture and stratified populations numbering in the tens of thousands. Both governments collected surplus food in warehouses as an insurance against times of drought and famine.

But neither state controlled a continuous band of territory. Adapting to their vertical environment, both empires established colonies at lower elevations on the eastern and western slopes of the Andes as well as throughout the highlands, seeking access to resources such as seafood, maize, chili peppers, cocoa, hallucinogenic plants, obsidian, and feathers from tropical birds. Caravans of llamas linked distant centers, allowing the exchange and redistribution of goods, while the religious prestige and ceremonial power of the capital city provided further integration. Cultural influences from the center, such as styles of pottery and textiles, spread well beyond the regions of direct political control. Similar religious symbols and images prevailed in both places, including the ancient Andean Staff God, a deity portrayed with a staff in each hand. Versions of this image have been found in Norte Chico, Chavín, and Moche sites as well, suggesting a long-term continuity in the religious culture of the Andean region.

But Wari and Tiwanaku were hardly carbon copies of each other. Wari's agriculture employed an elaborate system of hillside terracing and irrigation, using snowmelt from the Andes. A seventeenth-century Jesuit missionary thought the hillsides of the Wari region "were covered with flights of stairs." Tiwanaku's highly productive farming economy, by contrast, utilized a "raised field" system in which artificially

■ **Description**

What was the significance of Wari and Tiwanaku in the history of Andean civilization?

The Lord of Sipan and the Lady of Cao

In the mid- to late third century C.E., a prominent man of Moche society died in what is now Peru. We do not know his name, for a written language was not a part of Moche life. But since archeologists uncovered his final resting place in 1987, scholars have learned a great deal about him and about his culture. He was five feet four inches in height, relatively tall for his time and place, and was somewhere around forty years of age. The condition of his teeth and bones suggests that he ate a well-balanced diet and probably performed little physical labor during his life. The cause of his death is unclear, but scholars think that he may well have died of an epidemic disease during a severe famine.

The Moche ruler in the center of the grave, dating to about 250 C.E., was about forty years old when he died and, at five feet four inches, was quite tall for the time.

Much more obvious is his high social status, for which he has been dubbed the Lord of Sipan, named for the town in Peru where the archeological site is located. Laid to rest in the official and ceremonial finery he likely donned in life, the Lord of Sipan was bedecked in gold. He wore a huge gold crescent headdress, a gold face mask, two necklaces with gold and silver beads in the shape of oversized peanuts, and gold earspools exquisitely inlaid with turquoise; he had a gold warrior's shield on his back and a golden scepter in his hand. Hundreds of pots contained food and drink, while 451 ceremonial objects also accompanied the burial. Guarding the entrance to his tomb was the skeleton of a man with his feet cut off, presumably to prevent him from leaving his post. Buried with the Lord of Sipan were six other individuals: a young child (perhaps his own?); two robust men (perhaps ritually sacrificed warriors?); and three young women (perhaps his wives?). A dog, claimed by local traditions to guide the dead into the afterworld, and two llamas also attended the lord in death. In its archeological significance and its material splendor, this burial site has been compared to that of Tutankhamen, the young pharaoh of Egypt. (See the photo of his burial site above.)

Clearly, the Lord of Sipan was a very high-ranking member of Moche's highly stratified society. Such lords received food from their subjects, some of which they passed on to lesser lords, and they had access to the rare and prestigious objects created for them by Moche's

photo: © Karl Heinz Raach/laif/Redux

elevated planting surfaces in swampy areas were separated by small irrigation canals. Tiwanaku, furthermore, has become famous for its elaborately fitted stone walls and buildings, while Wari's tombs and temples were built of fieldstone set in mud mortar and covered with smooth plaster. Cities in the Wari region seemed built to a common plan and linked to the capital by a network of highways, which suggests a political system more tightly controlled from the center than in Tiwanaku.[10]

Despite these differences and a 300-mile common border, little overt conflict or warfare occurred between Wari and Tiwanaku. In areas where the two peoples lived near one another, they apparently did not mingle much. They each spoke their own language, wore different clothing, furnished their homes with distinctive goods, and looked to their respective capital cities for inspiration.

immensely skillful artisans. Various objects in the tomb correspond closely to images on Moche pottery and temples of prisoners being slaughtered and a warrior-priest collecting and drinking their blood. Perhaps the Lord of Sipan was one such warrior-priest.

At the time the Lord of Sipan came to light, it was widely assumed that the ruling elite of Moche society was all male. Then in 2005, another remarkable burial site was uncovered, containing the intact body of a young woman who had died in childbirth around 450 C.E. while still in her twenties. Now known as the Lady of Cao, she had been carefully wrapped in hundreds of yards of cotton strips, wore long braided hair, and bore numerous tattoos of snakes, crabs, and spiders on her arms and legs. Accompanying her was a huge collection of elaborate grave goods indicating great wealth: fifteen elaborate necklaces, gold sewing needles, weaving tools, beautiful jewelry, and a vessel depicting a nursing mother. But beyond these feminine objects were more surprising signs of real power. Her nose rings featured designs of men wielding war clubs and heads being pecked by condors. Two copper and wood staffs, symbols of authority, were entombed with her, as well as many weapons, including

Object found in the tomb of the Lady of Cao.

two massive war clubs and twenty-three spear throwers. "The war clubs are clear symbols not only of combat but of power," declared one member of the archeological team.[11]

So was the Lady of Cao a local ruler in her own right or simply a woman from an elite family? The case for her political and religious role has been strengthened by the subsequent discovery of eight more burials of prominent Moche women. One of them contained a tall silver goblet, very similar to those depicted in Moche artistic scenes of ritual sacrifice and the consumption of blood. Some scholars suggest that Moche society was highly decentralized, with men in positions of authority in some communities and women in others. Thus the Lord of Sipan and the Lady of Cao, though living several hundred years apart, may have played equivalent roles in Moche society.

Questions: What do we learn about Moche society from these two figures? If you could interview these individuals, what would you want to ask them? What might be inferred from these burials about Moche understandings of the afterlife?

photo: © EFE/Zuma Press

In the several centuries following 1000 C.E., both civilizations collapsed, their impressive cities permanently abandoned. What followed was a series of smaller kingdoms, one of which evolved into the Inca Empire that gave to Andean civilization a final and spectacular expression before all of the Americas was swallowed up in European empires from across the sea. The Incas themselves clearly drew on the legacy of Wari and Tiwanaku, adopting aspects of their imperial models and systems of statecraft, building on the Wari highway system, and utilizing similar styles of dress and artistic expression. Such was the prestige of Tiwanaku centuries after its collapse that the Incas claimed it as their place of origin.

SUMMING UP SO FAR

What features common to all civilizations can you identify in the civilizations of Africa and the Americas? What distinguishing features give each of them a distinctive identity?

Alternatives to Civilization

World historians are frequently occupied, sometimes almost preoccupied, with civilizations, and understandably so, since those urban and state-based communities were clearly the most powerful, expansive, and innovative societies, later embracing almost the entire population of the planet. And yet it is useful to remind ourselves that other ways of organizing human communities evolved alongside civilizations, and they too made history. Two such regions were Africa south of the equator and North America. They shared environments that featured plenty of land and relatively few people compared to the greater population densities and pressure on the land that characterized many civilizations. And a third was Pacific Oceania, where small numbers of people navigated a sea covering about one-third of the world's surface, settled the mostly tiny specks of land that rose above the surface of that ocean, and created there a remarkable range of human communities.

Bantu Africa: Cultural Encounters and Social Variation

In the vast region of Africa south of the equator, the most significant development during the second-wave era involved the accelerating movement of Bantu-speaking peoples, cultures, and technologies into the enormous subcontinent. That process had begun many centuries earlier, probably around 3000 B.C.E., from a homeland region in what are now southeastern Nigeria and the Cameroons. Over the long run, some 400 distinct but closely related languages emerged, known collectively as Bantu. By the first century C.E., agricultural peoples speaking Bantu languages and now bearing an ironworking technology had largely occupied the forest regions of equatorial Africa, and at least a few of them had probably reached the East African coast. In the several centuries that followed, they established themselves quite rapidly in most of eastern and southern Africa (see Map 6.1, page 235), introducing immense economic and cultural changes to a huge region of the continent.

Bantu expansion was not a conquest or invasion such as that of Alexander the Great; nor was it a massive and self-conscious migration like that of Europeans to the Americas in more recent times. Rather, it was a slow movement of peoples, perhaps a few extended families at a time. And sometimes Bantu expansion was less a movement of people than the diffusion of new patterns of living involving language, root crops, grains, sheep and cattle, pottery styles, and ironworking technology. In this way, already-established communities could "become Bantu" without the wholesale migration of outsiders. Taken as a whole, these processes brought to Africa south of the equator a measure of cultural and linguistic commonality, marking it as a distinct region of the continent.

That movement of individuals and cultural patterns also generated numerous situations that required decisions about how to respond to new peoples, ideas, and technologies. Among those encounters, none was more significant than that between the agricultural Bantu and the gathering and hunting peoples who earlier occupied this region of Africa. Their interaction was part of a long-term global phenomenon in which farmers largely replaced foragers as the dominant people on the planet (see Chapter 1).

In these encounters, Bantu-speaking farmers had various advantages. One was numerical, as agriculture generated a more productive economy, enabling larger numbers to live in a smaller area than was possible with a gathering and hunting way of life. A second advantage was a greater immunity to animal-borne disease, acquired by prolonged exposure to both parasitic and infectious illnesses common to farming and herding societies. Foraging peoples lacked that immunity, and many quickly succumbed when they encountered the agricultural newcomers. A third advantage was iron, so useful for tools and weapons, which accompanied Bantu expansion in its interactions with peoples still operating with stone-age technology. Thus gathering and hunting peoples were displaced, absorbed, or largely eliminated in most parts of Africa south of the equator—but not everywhere.

In the rain forest region of Central Africa, the foraging Batwa (Pygmy) people, at least some of them, became "forest specialists" who produced honey, wild game, elephant products, animal skins, and medicinal barks and plants, all of which entered regional trading networks in exchange for the agricultural products of their Bantu neighbors. Some also adopted Bantu languages, thus becoming Bantu linguistically, while maintaining a gathering and hunting lifestyle and a separate identity.

Bantu-speaking peoples themselves also changed as they encountered different environments and peoples. In the drier climate of East Africa, the yam-based agriculture of the West African Bantu homeland was unable to support their growing numbers, so Bantu farmers increasingly adopted grains as well as domesticated sheep and cattle from the already-established people of the region. They also enriched their agriculture by acquiring a variety of food crops from Southeast Asia—coconuts, sugarcane, and especially bananas—which were brought to East Africa by Indonesian Malay sailors and immigrants early in the first millennium C.E. This agricultural package and its associated ironworking technology then spread throughout the vast area of eastern and southern Africa, probably reaching present-day South Africa by 400 C.E. Some newly "Bantuized" areas incorporated musical traditions, linguistic patterns, and kinship systems derived from the earlier inhabitants. From these interactions a common set of cultural and social practices diffused widely across Bantu Africa. One prominent historian described these practices:

> [They encompassed] in religion, the centrality of ancestor observances; in philosophy, the problem of evil understood as the consequence of individual malice or of the failure to honor one's ancestors; in music, an emphasis on polyrhythmic performance with drums as the key instrument; in dance, a new form of expression in which a variety of prescribed body movements took preference over footwork; and in agriculture, the pre-eminence of women as the workers and innovators.[12]

All of this became part of the common culture of Bantu-speaking Africa.

As Bantu-derived patterns of living became established in Africa south of the equator during the thousand or so years between 500 and 1500 C.E., a wide variety

■ **Connection**

In what ways did the process of Bantu expansion stimulate cross-cultural interaction?

of quite distinct societies and cultures took shape. Some societies—in present-day Kenya, for example—organized themselves without any formal political specialists at all. Instead, they made decisions, resolved conflicts, and maintained order by using kinship structures or lineage principles supplemented by age grades, which joined men of a particular generation together across various lineages. Elsewhere, lineage heads who acquired a measure of personal wealth, or who proved skillful at mediating between the local spirits and the people, might evolve into chiefs with a modest political authority. In several areas, such as the region around Lake Victoria or present-day Zimbabwe, larger and more substantial kingdoms evolved. Along the East African coast after 1000 C.E., dozens of rival city-states linked the African interior with the commerce of the Indian Ocean basin (see Chapter 7, pages 291–93).

A Female Luba Ancestral Statue
Representations of powerful women, often ancestral figures, were frequent in the wood carvings of the Bantu-speaking Luba people of Central Africa. Many of them showed women touching their breasts, a gesture signifying devotion, respect, and the holding of secret knowledge. (Scala/Art Resource, NY)

Many societies in the Bantu-speaking world developed gender systems that were markedly less patriarchal than those of established urban-based civilizations. Male ironworkers in the Congo River basin, for example, sought to appropriate the power and prestige of female reproductive capacity by decorating their furnaces with clay breasts and speaking of their bellows as impregnating the furnaces. Among the Luba people of Central Africa, male rulers operated in alliance with powerful women, particularly spirit mediums, who were thought to contain the spirit of the king. Only a woman's body was considered sufficiently strong to acquire this potent and dangerous presence. Luba art represented female ancestors as "keepers of secret royal knowledge." And across a wide area of south-central Africa, a system of "gender parallelism" associated female roles with village life (child care, farming, food preparation, making pots, baskets, and mats), while masculine identity revolved around hunting and forest life (fishing, trapping, collecting building materials and medicinal plants). It was a complementary or "separate but equal" definition of gender roles.[13]

In terms of religion, Bantu practice in general placed less emphasis on a High or Creator God, who was viewed as remote and largely uninvolved in ordinary life, and focused instead on ancestral or nature spirits. The power of dead ancestors might be accessed through rituals of sacrifice, especially of cattle. Supernatural power deriving from ancient heroes, ancestors, or nature spirits also resided in charms, which could be activated by proper rituals and used to control the rains, defend the village, achieve success in hunting, or identify witches. Belief in witches was widespread, reflecting the idea that evil or misfortune was the work of malicious people. Diviners, skilled in penetrating the unseen world, used dreams, visions, charms, or trances to identify the source of misfortune and to prescribe remedies. Was a particular illness the product of broken taboos, a dishonored ancestor, an unhappy nature spirit, or a witch? Was a remedy to be found in a cleansing ceremony, a sacrifice to an ancestor, the activation of a charm, or the elimination of a witch?[14]

Unlike the major monotheistic religions, with their "once and for all" revelations from God through the Christian Bible or the Muslim Quran, Bantu religious practice was predicated on the notion of "continuous revelation"—the possibility of constantly receiving new messages from the world beyond through dreams, visions, or trance states. Moreover, unlike Buddhism, Christianity, or Islam, Bantu religions were geographically confined, intended to explain, predict, and control local affairs, with no missionary impulse or inclination toward universality.

North America: Ancestral Pueblo and Mound Builders

If the Americas played host to civilizations, cities, and empires in Mesoamerica and the Andes, they also housed various alternative forms of human community during the second-wave era and beyond. Arctic and subarctic cultures, the bison hunters of the Great Plains, the complex and settled communities of the Pacific coast of North America, nomadic bands living in the arid regions of southern South America—all of these represent the persistence of gathering and hunting ways of living.

Even more widespread—in the eastern woodlands of the United States, Central America, the Amazon basin, the Caribbean islands—were societies sustained by village-based agriculture. Owing to environmental or technological limitations, it was a less intensive and productive agriculture than in Mesoamerica or the Andes and supported usually much smaller populations (see Map 6.4 and Map 12.5, page 523). These peoples too made their own histories, changing in response to their unique environments, their interactions with outsiders, and their own visions of the world. The Anasazi of the southwestern United States, now called the Ancestral Pueblo, and the mound-building cultures of the eastern woodlands provide two illustrations from North America.

The southwestern region of North America, an arid land cut by mountain ranges and large basins, first acquired maize from its place of origin in Mesoamerica during the second millennium B.C.E., but it took roughly 2,000 years for that crop, later supplemented by beans and squash, to become the basis of a settled agricultural way of living. In a desert region, farming was risky, and maize had to be gradually adapted to the local environment. Not until around 600 to 800 C.E. did permanent village life take hold widely. People then lived in pit houses with floors sunk several feet below ground level. Some settlements had only a few such homes, whereas others contained twenty-five or more. By 900 C.E., many of these villages also included kivas, much larger pit structures used for ceremonial purposes, which symbolized the widespread belief that humankind emerged into this world from another world below. Individual settlements were linked to one another in local trading networks and sometimes in wider webs of exchange that brought them buffalo hides, copper, turquoise, seashells, macaw feathers, and coiled baskets from quite distant locations.

■ **Comparison**

In what ways were the histories of the Ancestral Pueblo and the Mound Builders similar to each other, and how did they differ?

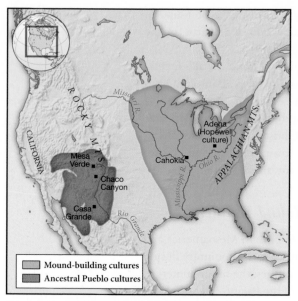

Map 6.4   North America in the Second-Wave Era

A sparsely populated North America hosted a number of semi-sedentary agricultural societies as well as various gathering and hunting peoples rather than the "civilizations" characteristic of Mesoamerica and the Andes.

These processes of change—growing dependence on agriculture, increasing population, more intensive patterns of exchange—gave rise to larger settlements and adjacent aboveground structures known as pueblos. The most spectacular of these took shape in Chaco canyon in what is now northwestern New Mexico. There, between 860 and 1130 C.E., five major pueblos emerged. This Chaco Phenomenon encompassed 25,000 square miles and linked some seventy outlying settlements to the main centers. The population was not large, perhaps as few as 5,000 people, although experts continue to debate the issue. The largest of these towns, or "great houses," Pueblo Bonito, stood five stories high and contained more than 600 rooms and many kivas. Hundreds of miles of roads, up to forty feet wide, radiated out from Chaco, likewise prompting much debate among scholars. Without wheeled carts or large domesticated animals, such an elaborate road system seems unnecessary for ordinary trade or travel. Did the roads represent, as some scholars speculate, a "sacred landscape which gave order to the world," joining its outlying communities to a "Middle Place," an entrance perhaps to the underworld?[15]

Among the Chaco elite were highly skilled astronomers who constructed an observatory of three large rock slabs situated so as to throw a beam of light across a spiral rock carving behind it at the summer solstice. By the eleventh century, Chaco also had become a dominant center for the production of turquoise ornaments, which became a major item of regional commerce, extending as far south as Mesoamerica. Not all was sweetness and light, however. Warfare, internal conflict, and occasional cannibalism (a matter of much controversy among scholars) apparently increased in frequency as an extended period of drought in the half century following 1130 brought this flourishing culture to a rather abrupt end. By 1200, the great houses had been abandoned and their inhabitants scattered in small communities that later became the Pueblo peoples of more recent times.

Unlike the Chaco region in the southwest, the eastern woodlands of North America and especially the Mississippi River valley hosted an independent Agricultural Revolution. By 2000 B.C.E., many of its peoples had domesticated local plant species, including sumpweed, goosefoot, some gourds and squashes, and a form of artichoke. Sunflowers, originally domesticated in Mesoamerica, also found a place in diets of eastern woodland peoples. These few plants, however, were not sufficient to support a fully settled agricultural village life; rather, they supplemented diets derived from gathering and hunting without fundamentally changing that ancient way of life. Such peoples created societies distinguished by arrays of large earthen mounds, found all over the United States east of the Mississippi, prompting archeologists to dub them the Mound Builders. The earliest of these mounds date to around 2000 B.C.E., but the most elaborate and widespread took shape between 200 B.C.E. and 400 C.E., commonly called the Hopewell culture, after an archeological site in Ohio.

Several features of the Hopewell culture have intrigued archeologists. Particularly significant are the striking burial mounds and geometric earthworks, sometimes covering areas equivalent to several city blocks, and the wide variety of artifacts found within them—smoking pipes, human figurines, mica mirrors, flint blades, fabrics, and jewelry of all kinds. The mounds themselves were no doubt the focus of elaborate burial rituals, but some of them were aligned with the moon with such precision as to mark lunar eclipses. Developed most elaborately in the Ohio River valley, Hopewell-style earthworks, artifacts, and ceremonial pottery have also been found throughout the eastern woodlands region of North America. Hopewell centers in Ohio contained mica from the Appalachian Mountains, volcanic glass from Yellowstone, conch shells and a few sharks' teeth from the Gulf of Mexico, and copper from the Great Lakes. All of this suggests a large "Hopewell Interaction Sphere," linking this entire region in a loose network of exchange, as well as a measure of cultural borrowing of religious ideas and practices.[16]

The next and most spectacular phase in the history of these mound-building peoples took shape as corn-based agriculture, derived ultimately but indirectly from Mexico, gained ground in the Mississippi valley after 800 C.E., allowing larger populations and more complex societies to emerge. The dominant center was Cahokia, near present-day St. Louis, Missouri, which flourished from about 900 to 1250 C.E. Its central mound, a terraced pyramid of four levels, measured 1,000 feet long by 700 feet wide, rose more than 100 feet above the ground, and occupied fifteen acres. It was the largest structure north of Mexico, the focal point of a community numbering 10,000 or more people, and the center of a widespread trading network (see an artist's reconstruction of Cahokia on page 45).

Evidence from burials and from later Spanish observers suggests that Cahokia and other centers of this Mississippi culture were stratified societies with a clear elite and with rulers able to mobilize the labor required to build such enormous structures. One high-status male was buried on a platform of 20,000 shell beads, accompanied by 800 arrowheads, sheets of copper and mica, and a number of sacrificed men and women nearby.[17] Well after Cahokia had declined and was abandoned, sixteenth-century Spanish and French explorers encountered another such chiefdom among the Natchez people, located in southwestern Mississippi. Paramount chiefs, known as Great Suns, dressed in knee-length fur coats and lived luxuriously in deerskin-covered homes. An elite class of "principal men" or "honored peoples" clearly occupied a different status from commoners, sometimes referred to as "stinkards." These sharp class distinctions were blunted by the requirement that upper-class people, including the Great Suns, had to marry "stinkards."

The military capacity of these Mississippi chiefdoms greatly impressed European observers, as this Spanish account indicates:

> The next day the cacique [paramount chief] arrived with 200 canoes filled with men, having weapons, . . . the warriors standing erect from bow to stern, holding bows and arrows. . . . [F]rom under the canopy where the chief man was, the course was directed and orders issued to the rest. . . . [W]hat with the awnings, the plumes, the shields, the pennons, and the number of people in the fleet, it appeared like a famous armada of galleys.[18]

Here then, in the eastern woodlands of North America, were peoples who independently generated a modest Agricultural Revolution, assimilated corn and beans from distant sources, developed increasingly complex chiefdoms, and created monumental structures, new technologies, and artistic traditions. Beyond the separate societies that emerged within this large area, scholars have noticed some similarities in artifacts, symbols, ceremonies, mythologies, and artistic styles, many of which seem related to marking the status of elites. A horned serpent, sometimes depicted with wings, and various animal-god representations were widely shared symbols, though the meaning of these symbols no doubt changed as they entered new cultural environments. Dubbed the Southeast Ceremonial Complex, the loose networks of connection that generated these similarities grew outward from Cahokia for several centuries after 1200 or so, continuing earlier patterns of interaction associated with the Hopewell cultural region. While no linguistic, cultural, or political unity emerged from these relationships, they testify to a measure of exchange, borrowing, and cultural adaptation across an enormous region of North America.

Pacific Oceania: Peoples of the Sea

The peoples of Pacific Oceania, like those of Bantu Africa and North America, created enduring human communities without the large cities, states, and empires so prominent in civilizations. But the ecological setting for these historical journeys was distinctive, for they took place on the islands of the immense Pacific: a few larger territories, such as New Guinea and New Zealand, as well as thousands of much smaller islands, many of them specks in the sea, barely visible from space (see Map 6.5). New Guinea had been settled for perhaps 50,000 years, initially at a time when it was connected to Australia by a land bridge. But the rest of Oceania was the last part of the world to receive human settlers, who began arriving from Island Southeast Asia only about 3,500 years ago (see Chapter 1, pages 19–20). By 1200 C.E., they had achieved a presence on every habitable piece of land throughout this enormous region. It was, as one historian summarized the process, "the greatest maritime expansion known to history."[19]

The settlers' arrival, however, produced an enormous and sometimes devastating environmental impact as humans entered and disrupted bountiful but fragile ecosystems, especially as their populations grew. Referring to some of the early settlers

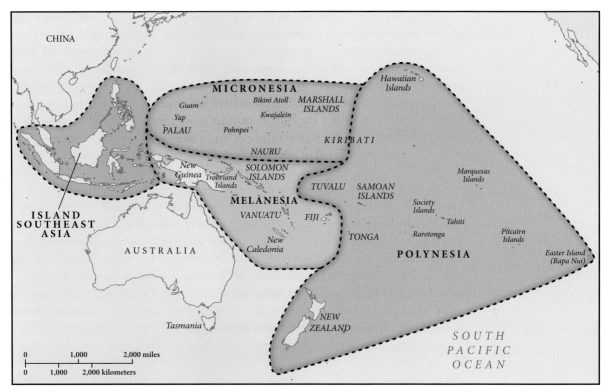

Map 6.5 Pacific Oceania

Covering about one-third of the world's surface, the Pacific Ocean encompasses thousands of islands, which were home to many distinct societies but also constituted a cultural region that shared numerous commonalities and connections.

in Melanesia during the first millennium B.C.E., Pacific historian Ian Campbell wrote: "They hunted, gathered, and fished profligately, and burnt large tracts of previously undisturbed forests."[20] In New Zealand, initially settled much later, around 1200 C.E., human hunting largely eliminated the huge flightless *moa* bird within a century. Archeologists have discovered the remains of some 90,000 moa at a single butchery. A similar impact occurred in Hawaii and elsewhere as smaller birds fell victim to the rats, pigs, and dogs introduced by the settlers. Resource depletion, deforestation, and soil erosion followed, no doubt contributing to the abandonment of at least several dozen islands, as their inhabitants found themselves forced to flee or perish. Rapa Nui (Easter Island) in easternmost Polynesia had come almost to the point of ecological collapse by the time Europeans arrived in the eighteenth century, as much of its tree cover had vanished and many bird species had likewise disappeared. Human activity had surely contributed to this outcome with overhunting, overfishing, and the cutting down of forests. But Polynesian rats, whether introduced accidentally or intentionally by the original settlers to the island, were at least equally responsible, as their numbers exploded and they devoured the seeds of the palm trees.[21]

Another change occasioned by growing populations lay in increased social complexity on some of the most densely populated islands. One example comes from the Micronesian island of Pohnpei, where an urban complex, constructed from stone and coral, served as the ceremonial, administrative, and burial center of a powerful Saudeleur dynasty that governed the island for several centuries. Probably emerging in the tenth century, this impressive urban center, later dubbed by Europeans the "Venice of the Pacific," contained numerous seawalls and canals, over ninety small artificial islands, marketplaces, and a large tomb and funerary complex. However, local legends tell of increasingly despotic rulers whose oppressive policies triggered a revolt by lower-ranking chiefs.

The Polynesian Tonga Islands witnessed yet another example of growing social complexity. By the fourteenth century, powerful rulers, known as Tu'i Tonga, stood at the head of a royal court including many wives and concubines, various relatives, ceremonial attendants, prisoners of war, and specialized craftsmen such as carvers, navigators, and fishermen. The court collected and redistributed food and various gifts to lesser chiefs, who then did the same for their followers. The widespread military and commercial influence of Tonga in the central Pacific has led some scholars to regard it as an incipient empire, while others view it as a tributary network or a system of economic interdependence.

Given the vast distances separating these island societies, considerable diversity among them is hardly surprising. And yet they also participated in the making of a single cultural region with numerous commonalities and connections. Many of their cultural and dietary similarities derive from their common origin in Island Southeast Asia and ultimately from southern China as well as from a common Pacific environment. Variations developed from the adaptation of this shared heritage to the distinctive environment of particular islands—large or small, tropical or semitropical, sea-level coastal terrain or mountainous interior, uninhabited or containing established societies as in New Guinea. The relative isolation of these societies, as well as periodic contact with near and more distant neighboring islands, also shaped their histories.

Linguistically, the peoples of Oceania, despite their small numbers, have spoken hundreds of different languages, over 100 on the small island chain of Melanesian Vanuatu alone. But almost all of them are members of the Austronesian family of languages, whose speakers also include those of Malaysia, Indonesia, and Madagascar. New Guinea, however, is a different story, with well over 1,000 languages, most of which are part of the Papuan language family, derived from its much earlier settlement. Similarly, Pacific islanders everywhere practiced the art of body decoration called *tatau* (which became "tattoo" in English), but particularly in Polynesia each archipelago developed distinctive designs, reflecting its unique identity.

This pattern of diversity and unity found other expression as well, both among the three major regions of Melanesia, Micronesia, and Polynesia and within them. In economic life, for example, these people of the sea drew heavily on the ocean as a major source of food, while its shells were used as currency and tools. But they were also farmers, raising pigs, dogs, and fowl, while everywhere cultivating taro, a starchy root vegetable. Other crops—yams, sweet potatoes, breadfruit, coconut palms—were cultivated variously as availability and conditions allowed.

In political and social life, Oceanic societies were generally organized as chiefdoms, but with considerable variation. On small islands, chiefs and priests could hardly be distinguished from anyone else, while village councils, operating by consensus, made decisions. In parts of Melanesia, so-called "big men," or locally influential individuals, exercised authority through ceremony, feasts, and gift giving. Elsewhere, societies were more stratified and authority more centralized. In New Zealand, the Maori people distinguished among chiefly families, commoners, and slaves derived from prisoners of war. Frequent warfare among its chiefdoms prevented greater political unity. In Hawaii and Tonga, by contrast, elaborate social hierarchies emerged with powerful rulers who had hundreds or even thousands of warriors at their disposal.

Women everywhere in ancient Oceania were considered dangerous and polluting, especially during menstruation and childbirth, and were isolated at those times. However, gender roles differed substantially from place to place. In Melanesia, women were more actively involved in food production, but in Polynesia their labor was directed more toward the making of mats and cloth. Throughout Polynesia, women were accorded high status, and women of chiefly families could exercise considerable power through their male relatives. Melanesian women, by contrast, were more sharply subordinated to men than their counterparts in other regions of Oceania.

Religious life in Oceania was pragmatic, designed to protect against harm and to manipulate the spirits or gods in one's favor. It found expression in two pervasive concepts: *mana* and *tapu*. Mana was a spiritual energy or power, associated especially with chiefs and demonstrated by remarkable actions or great success. To maintain the purity of mana, ritual restriction or prohibitions known as tapu (which came into English as "taboo") served to make someone or something sacred or elevated far above the ordinary. Throughout Polynesia, only a particular official could handle the chief's food or his possessions. A Maori chief in New Zealand could not allow even his shadow to fall on food, for doing so made it forbidden to all others. Hawaiians prostrated themselves on the ground before their major chiefs. Since

The Moai of Rapa Nui
The most iconic artistic representations of Polynesian culture are these huge stone figures called *moai*. Carved from volcanic rock on the island of Rapa Nui sometime between 1200 and 1600, they are thought to depict sacred ancestors or clan chiefs. Around 1,000 of them were quarried and carved, and hundreds were somehow transported up to eight miles to stand on stone platforms near the coast. The largest reached some thirty-three feet tall and weighed over eighty tons. (Ken Welsh/Bridgeman Images)

violating a tapu could result in death, religion provided supernatural sanctions for political authorities and social elites, as it has in so many other societies. While much of this was common across all of Pacific Oceania, the gods, ghosts, ancestors, and spirits differed considerably, as did the role of priests or shamans as well as the associated rituals and artistic expression of religious life.

Despite the distances between these island societies, they were not wholly isolated from one another. Networks of exchange and communication—both regional and at a greater distance—allowed for some interaction among the various peoples of Oceania. Between roughly 1400 and 800 B.C.E., the spread of a distinctive pottery style known as Lapita throughout Melanesia and as far as Tonga and Samoa suggests a widespread pattern of exchange involving both commercial and ceremonial elements. During this time, obsidian from the island of New Britain off the northeastern coast of New Guinea had a distribution that extended over 4,000 miles from Borneo in Island Southeast Asia to Fiji in eastern Melanesia.

In western Micronesia, another system of exchange arose in the Caroline Island chain, with a particular focus on the island of Yap. It involved trade in commodities such as sea turtles, coconuts, and breadfruit; permission to fish near neighboring islands; and promises of refuge and shelter in times of famine. But it was also a set of tributary relationships in which the high-ranking island of Yap periodically received payments such as woven cloth, various coconut products, mats, and shells from islands of lesser rank up to 1,200 miles farther east. In return, the subordinates received gifts from Yap that exceeded the value of their tribute: wood for canoes, flint stone, food, and powdered turmeric, used as a skin paste and in coming-of-age rituals. Cast in terms of a parent–child relationship between Yap and the other islands, the whole system was supported by fears of powerful Yapese sorcery capable of generating great storms, should the required tribute not be forthcoming. Such trading circuits often contained an elaborate ceremonial element in which the exchange of noneconomic items—bracelets, necklaces, feathers, or shells—served to display status, to cement bonds of mutual assistance across great distances, and to confirm relationships of dominance and submission. Small island societies were invariably vulnerable and limited in resources; such networks of exchange provided insurance for their survival.

Polynesian networks of exchange also flourished in the centuries after 1000 C.E., with Tonga at the center of a system linked by trade with Samoa and Fiji. Finely woven Samoan mats were highly valued for displaying prestige, and large logs from Fiji were prized for the huge canoes that could be carved from them for Tonga's impressive warships. From the far eastern edge of Polynesia, sailors had apparently reached the coast of South America, from which they returned with sweet potatoes and bottle gourds. Taking hold in Rapa Nui, those domesticates from the Americas then entered Polynesian voyaging networks and found their way to Hawaii, New Zealand, and elsewhere, becoming a major food source.

Linked to Asia by their distant origins and to the Americas by the slender thread of the sweet potato, the peoples of Pacific Oceania lived largely, but not entirely, in a world apart from the rest of humankind.

Deciding What's Important: Balance in World History

Among the perennial problems that teachers and writers of world history confront is sorting through the vast record of times past and choosing what to include and what to leave out. A related issue involves the extent to which particular peoples or civilizations will be treated. Should the Persians get as much space as the Greeks? Does Africa merit equal treatment with Eurasia? Where do the Americas fit in the larger human story? What, in short, are the criteria for deciding what is important in recalling the history of the human venture?

One standard might be duration. Should ways of living that have endured for longer periods of time receive greater attention than those of lesser length? If historians followed only this criterion, then the Paleolithic era of gathering, hunting, and fishing societies should occupy 90 percent or more of any world history text. On the other hand, perhaps change is more important than continuity. If so, then something new merits more space than something old. Thus we pay attention to both agriculture and civilizations because they represent significant turning points in human experience. Population provides yet another principle for determining inclusion. That, of course, is the reason that Eurasia / North Africa, with over 80 percent of the world's population, is addressed in three chapters of this section, whereas inner Africa, the Americas, and Pacific Oceania together receive just one chapter. There is also the related issue of range of influence. Buddhism, Christianity, and Islam spread more widely and shaped the lives of more people than did the religions of the Maya or the Bantu-speaking peoples of Africa. Do they therefore deserve more extended treatment? Still another factor involves the availability of evidence. In this respect, Eurasia generated far more written records than either Africa or the Americas did, and therefore its history has been investigated far more thoroughly.

A final possible criterion involves the location of the historian and his or her audience. Those who have recently developed world history as a field of study have vigorously sought to counteract a Eurocentric telling of the human story. Still, is there anything inherently wrong with an account of world history that is centered on one's own people? When I taught history in an Ethiopian high school in the mid–1960s, I was guided by an Afrocentric curriculum, which focused first on Ethiopian history, then on Africa as a whole, and finally on the larger world. Might a world historian from the Middle East, for example, legitimately strike a somewhat different balance in the treatment of various civilizations than someone writing for a largely Western audience or for Chinese readers?

Any account of the world's past will mix and match these criteria in various and contested ways. Among historians, there exists neither a consensus about this question nor any formula to ensure a "proper" balance. You may want to consider whether the balance struck in this chapter, this section, and the book as a whole is appropriate or somehow out of line.

Second Thoughts

What's the Significance?

Meroë, 234–36

Piye, 236–37

Axum, 237–39

Niger Valley civilization, 239–41

Maya civilization, 242–44

Teotihuacán, 244–46

Chavín, 247–48

Moche, 248–49

Wari and Tiwanaku, 249–51

Bantu expansion, 252–55

Chaco Phenomenon, 256

Mound Builders / Cahokia, 256–58

Pohnpei, 260

Tonga, 260

mana and *tapu*, 261

Yap, 262

Big Picture Questions

1. "The particular cultures and societies of Africa, the Americas, and Pacific Oceania discussed in this chapter developed largely in isolation." What evidence would support this statement, and what might challenge it?

2. How do you understand areas of the world, such as Bantu Africa, North America, and Pacific Oceania, that did not generate "civilizations"? Do you see them as "backward," as moving slowly toward civilization, or as simply different?

3. How did Africa's proximity to Eurasia shape its history? And how did America's separation from the Eastern Hemisphere affect its development?

4. **Looking Back:** "The histories of Africa and the Americas during the second-wave era largely resemble those of Eurasia." Do you agree with this statement? Explain why or why not.

Next Steps: For Further Study

Christopher Ehret, *The Civilizations of Africa* (2002). An overview of African history before 1800 by a prominent scholar.

Brian M. Fagan, *Ancient North America* (2005). A prominent archeologist's account of North American history.

Steven R. Fischer, *A History of the Pacific Islands* (2013). A recent account of the history of Pacific Oceania from ancient times to the present.

Eric Gilbert and Jonathan T. Reynolds, *Africa in World History* (2004). An accessible account of African history set in a global context.

Guy Gugliotta, "The Maya: Glory and Ruin," *National Geographic* (August 2007). A beautifully illustrated account of the rise and fall of Maya civilization.

Charles C. Mann, *1491: New Revelations of the Americas before Columbus* (2005). A journalist's thoughtful account, delightfully written, of the controversies surrounding the history of the Americas before 1492.

Ancient Africa's Black Kingdoms, http://www.homestead.com/wysinger/ancientafrica.html. A Web site exploring the history of Nubia.

Maya Adventure, http://www.smm.org/sln/ma. A collection of text and pictures about the Maya, past and present.

Maya Videos, http://www.history.com/topics/maya/videos/the-mayans. A series of brief video depictions of Maya history and culture from the History channel.

WORKING WITH EVIDENCE

Axum and the World

In the world of ancient African history, Axum has occupied a unique position in several ways (see Map 6.1, page 235, and pages 237–39). It is one of the few places in Africa, outside of Egypt, for which considerable documentary evidence exists. Some of the written sources—royal inscriptions and coins, for example—derive from within Axum itself, while others come from Greco-Roman and Christian visitors. Furthermore, after the rise of Islam, Axum—and its Ethiopian successor state—was the major surviving outpost of a Christian tradition that had earlier spread widely across northern and northeastern Africa. Finally, Axum has demonstrated an impressive cultural and religious continuity. Even after the decline of the Axumite Empire by the eighth century C.E., the city of Axum remained a major pilgrimage site for Christians, while Ethiopian kings into the twentieth century were crowned there.[22] The documents that follow offer a series of windows on this African kingdom.

Source 6.1

A Guidebook to the World of Indian Ocean Commerce

The earliest documentary reference to Axum was composed during the first century C.E. in an anonymous text known as *The Periplus of the Erythraean Sea*. Likely written by a sea captain from Roman-controlled Egypt, the *Periplus* offers a guide to the places and conditions that merchants might encounter as they traversed the Red Sea and the East African coast while on their way to India.

■ According to this text, why is the Axumite port of Adulis significant?

■ What evidence does the *Periplus* provide about Axum's cultural and economic ties to the larger world?

■ Based on the list of imports and exports, how would you describe Axum's role in the international commerce of the first century C.E.?

■ How might Axum's participation in long-distance trade have stimulated and sustained its growth as an empire?

The Periplus of the Erythraean Sea
First Century C.E.

Below Ptolemais of the Hunts [near modern Port Sudan on the Red Sea] . . . there is Adulis, a port established by law. . . . Before the harbor lies the so-called Mountain Island, about two hundred stadia sea-ward [1 stadium = ⅛ mile] from the very head of the bay, with the shores of the mainland close to it on both sides. Ships bound for this port now anchor here because of attacks from the land. . . . Opposite Mountain Island, on the mainland twenty stadia from shore, lies Adulis, a fair-sized village, from which there is a three-days' journey to Coloe, an inland town and the first market for ivory. From that place to the city of the people called Axumites there is a five days' journey more; to that place all the ivory is brought from the country beyond the Nile . . . and thence to Adulis. Practically the whole number of elephants and rhinoceros that are killed live in the places inland, although at rare intervals they are hunted on the seacoast even near Adulis. Before the harbor of that market-town, out at sea on the right hand, there lie a great many little sandy islands called Alalaei, yielding tortoise-shell, which is brought to market there by the Fish-Eaters.

And about eight hundred stadia beyond there is another very deep bay, with a great mound of sand piled up at the right of the entrance; at the bottom of which the opsian [obsidian] stone is found, and this is the only place where it is produced. These places . . . are governed by Zoscales [an Axumite ruler], who is miserly in his ways and always striving for more, but otherwise upright, and acquainted with Greek literature.

There are imported into these places undressed cloth made in Egypt for the Berbers; robes from Arsinoe [an Egyptian port]; cloaks of poor quality dyed in colors; double-fringed linen mantles; many articles of flint glass, and others of murrhine [used for making Roman vases] made in Diospolis [Thebes in Egypt]; and brass, which is used for ornament and in cut pieces instead of coin; sheets of soft copper, used for cooking utensils and cut up for bracelets and anklets for the women; iron, which is made into spears used against the elephants and other wild beasts, and in their wars. Besides these, small axes are imported, and adzes and swords; copper drinking-cups, round and large; a little coin [Roman money] for those coming to the market [probably foreign merchants living in Adulis]; wine of Laodicea and Italy, not much; olive oil, not much; for the king, gold and silver plate made after the fashion of the country, and for clothing, military cloaks, and thin coats of skin, of no great value. Likewise from the district of Ariaca [in western India] across this sea, there are imported Indian iron, and steel, and Indian cotton cloth; . . . and girdles, and coats of skin and mallow-colored cloth, and a few muslins, and colored lac [a resinous secretion of an insect, used in the form of shellac]. There are exported from these places ivory, and tortoise-shell and rhinoceros-horn. The most from Egypt is brought to this market from the month of January.

Source: Wilfred H. Schoff, trans. and ed., *The Periplus of the Erythraean Sea* (New York: Longman, Green, 1912), secs. 4–6.

Source 6.2
The Making of an Axumite Empire

At its high point in the mid-fourth century C.E., Axum ruled an empire stretching from Meroë in the upper Nile Valley, across much of what is now Eritrea and Ethiopia, and incorporating parts of southern Arabia on the opposite side of the Red Sea. Source 6.2 comes from an Axumite inscription written in Greek on a stone throne adorned with figures of the Greek gods Hercules and Mercury. Commissioned by an unknown Axumite monarch, the inscription dates probably from the second or third century C.E. It was copied and then published in the sixth century by Cosmas, a Greek merchant born in Alexandria, Egypt, who had become a monk. This text describes some of the conquests that generated the Axumite Empire.

- What internal evidence from the document itself dates it prior to Axum's acceptance of Christianity?

- How would you describe the point of view from which the document was written?

- What techniques of imperial control does the document reveal?

- How might you account for the obvious Greek influence that is apparent in the inscription?

- How would you describe the religious or ideological underpinnings of this empire? Why might the Axumite ruler who commissioned this inscription single out Ares, Zeus, and Poseidon for special attention?

Inscription on a Stone Throne
Second or Third Century C.E.

Having after this with a strong hand compelled the nations bordering on my kingdom to live in peace, I made war upon the following nations, and by force of arms reduced them to subjection. I warred first with the nation of Gaze [Axum, probably in an internal struggle for power], then with Agame and Sigye, and having conquered them, I exacted the half of all that they possessed. . . . [*There follows a long list of other peoples that this ruler conquered.*]

I proceeded next against the Tangaltae, who adjoin the borders of Egypt; and having reduced them I made a footpath giving access by land into Egypt from that part of my dominions. Next I reduced Annine and Metine — tribes inhabiting precipitous mountains. My arms were next directed against the Sesea nation. These had retired to a high mountain difficult of access; but I blockaded the mountain on every side, and compelled them to come down and surrender. I then selected for myself the best of their young men and their women, with their sons and daughters and all besides that

they possessed. The tribes of Rhausi I next brought to submission: a barbarous race spread over wide waterless plains in the interior of the frankincense country. [Advancing thence toward the sea,] I encountered the Solate, whom I subdued, and left with instructions to guard the coast.

All these nations, protected though they were by mountains all but impregnable, I conquered, after engagements in which I was myself present. Upon their submission I restored their territories to them, subject to the payment of tribute. Many other tribes besides these submitted of their own accord, and became likewise tributary. And I sent a fleet and land forces against the Arabitae and Cinaedocolpitae who dwelt on the other side of the Red Sea [southern Arabia], and having reduced the sovereigns of both, I imposed on them a land tribute and charged them to make traveling safe both by sea and by land. . . .

I first and alone of the kings of my race made these conquests. For this success I now offer my thanks to my mighty god, Ares [the Greek god of warfare and slaughter], who begat me, and by whose aid I reduced all the nations bordering on my own country. . . . Of these expeditions, some were conducted by myself in person, and ended in victory, and the others I entrusted to my officers. Having thus brought all the world under my authority to peace, I came down to Adulis and offered sacrifice to Zeus [chief god of the Greek pantheon], and to

Ares, and to Poseidon [Greek god of the sea], whom I entreated to befriend all who go down to the sea in ships. Here also I reunited all my forces, and setting down this Chair [throne] in this place, I consecrated it to Ares in the twenty-seventh year of my reign.

Source: J. W. McCrindle, trans. and ed., *The Christian Topography of Cosmas, an Egyptian Monk* (London: Hakluyt Society, 1897), 59–66.

Source 6.3

The Coming of Christianity to Axum

The introduction of Christianity in the mid-fourth century C.E. represented a major change in the cultural history of Axum. It meant that Axum would be more closely aligned to Christian Egypt and Byzantium than to South Arabia, from which many of its earlier cultural traditions had derived. Source 6.3 relates the story of the coming of Christianity to Axum. It was written by Rufinus (345–410 C.E.), a Christian monk and writer who was born in Italy but spent much of his life in Jerusalem, where he heard this story from those who had taken part in it. Note that Greco-Roman writers of this time used "India" to refer vaguely to East Africa and southern Arabia as well as the South Asian peninsula.

- According to this document, by what means was Christianity introduced to Axum? What do you think was the relative importance of Frumentius and Aedesius, as opposed to Roman merchants living in Axum?

- Why do you think the Axumite royal family was so receptive to this foreign religion? How might the story differ if told from the ruling family's perspective?

- How does the fact that this document was written by outsiders shape the emphasis of the story?

RUFINUS

On the Evangelization of Abyssinia

Late Fourth Century C.E.

A certain philosopher Metrodorus is said to have penetrated the more remote parts of India in order to study their world and investigate its regions. Meropius, a philosopher from Tyre, was motivated by his example and decided to go to India for similar reasons. Two little boys went with

him. He had been educating them in the liberal arts because they were his relatives. The younger boy was named Aedesius, the older Frumentius.

During the journey the things Meropius studied and learned nourished his mind. Then, while headed home, the philosopher's ship had to land because the travelers needed water or some other necessities. Where they landed the barbarians had a custom of cutting the throats of all Romans they found among them whenever neighboring nations announced that their treaties with the Romans were broken. The barbarians attacked the philosopher's ship. They killed him and all with him likewise. But the little boys they found studying and doing their reading under a tree. The barbarians spared the boys out of pity and led them to their king [the ruler of Axum].

The king made Aedesius his cup bearer. But he trusted Frumentius to be his accountant and scribe because he understood that the boy had a sharp mind and wisdom. From then on the king honored and loved them both. When the king died, he left as his successor his wife, who had a little son. He granted the boys, now young men, free opportunity to do whatever they wanted. And the queen, as if she trusted no one in the kingdom more, humbly asked them to share in taking care of the kingdom with her until her son was a young man. She especially wanted Frumentius to help because he had enough wisdom to direct a kingdom, while Aedesius displayed only a pure faith and sober mind.

While this was happening as well as during the time Frumentius directed the government of the kingdom, he carefully began to inquire—for God moved his mind and spirit—whether there were any Christians among the Roman merchants. And he gave the greatest power to these Christians and advised them to make meeting places in every part of the country so that they could congregate in them for prayer in the Roman manner. Moreover, he himself did the same to a much greater degree, and so encouraged others, motivated them with favor and benefits, offered whatever might be useful, supplied land for buildings and other necessi-

ties, and acted in every way to grow the Christian seed in the kingdom.

When the royal child for whom Aedesius and Frumentius were taking care of the kingdom became a young man, their task was fulfilled and they faithfully handed over everything to him. Then they returned again to our world [the Roman Empire], even though the queen and her son delayed their journey and asked them to remain.

While Aedesius hurried to Tyre to visit his parents and relatives, Frumentius went to Alexandria, saying that it was not right to hide the work of the Lord. As such, he presented everything as it had happened to the Bishop [Athanasius] and advised him to provide some worthy man whom he might send as a bishop to the churches built in the barbarian land and their already large number of Christians.

Then in truth Athanasius . . . after he readily and attentively considered Frumentius' words and deeds, said in a council of the priests, "What other man will we find who can achieve such things and in whom the spirit of God is as in you, Frumentius?" Athanasius made Frumentius a priest and ordered him to return with the grace of God to the place from which he had come. And when he had gone out as a bishop to India, they say that so much virtuous grace was given to him by God that miracles were worked through him and a countless number of barbarians was converted to the faith. From then on, Christian peoples and churches were created in the regions of India, and a clerical hierarchy was instituted. We know these things happened not by the report of common people, but because Aedesius himself, the former companion of Frumentius and later made a priest of Tyre, related them.

Source: *The Church History of Rufinus of Aquileia,* book 10, sections 9 and 10. Translation from Latin by Edward M. Gutting, Missouri State University.

Source 6.4
Axum and the Gold Trade

The foundations of the Axumite state lay not only in its military conquests and its adoption of a new religion but also in its economic ties to the larger world. Among these ties was its reputation as a major source of gold for the

Roman Empire. Source 6.4 describes the distinctive fashion in which Axumite traders obtained the gold from the African peoples living on the margins of the Axumite state. The author, Cosmas (see Source 6.2, page 266), was involved in this trade.

■ How would you define the pattern of exchange described in this document? Was it state-directed trade, private enterprise, or both? To what problems of cross-cultural interaction was it a response?

■ Who, if anyone, had the upper hand in this trade? Was it conducted between politically equal parties?

■ What purposes did this trade serve for the people who mined and "sold" the gold?

■ Beyond the peaceful trade for gold described here, what other purposes did this region serve for Axum?

Cosmas
The Christian Topography
Sixth Century C.E.

The country known as that of Sasu is itself near the ocean . . . in which there are many gold mines. The King of the Axumites accordingly, every other year, through the governor of Agau, sends thither special agents to bargain for the gold, and these are accompanied by many other traders—upwards, say, of five hundred—bound on the same errand as themselves. They take along with them to the mining district oxen, lumps of salt, and iron, and when they reach its neighborhood, they make a halt at a certain spot and form an encampment, which they fence round with a great hedge of thorns. Within this they live, and having slaughtered the oxen, cut them in pieces, and lay the pieces on the top of the thorns, along with the lumps of salt and the iron. Then come the natives bringing gold in nuggets like peas, and lay one or two or more of these upon what pleases them—the pieces of flesh or the salt or the iron, and then they retire to some distance off. Then the owner of the meat approaches, and if he is satisfied he takes the gold away, and upon seeing this, its owner comes and takes the flesh or the salt or

the iron. If, however, he is not satisfied, he leaves the gold, when the native, seeing that he has not taken it, comes and either puts down more gold, or takes up what he had laid down, and goes away. Such is the mode in which business is transacted with the people of that country, because their language is different and interpreters are hardly to be found.

The time they stay in that country is five days more or less, according as the natives, more or less readily coming forward, buy up all their wares. On the journey homeward they all agree to travel well-armed, since some of the tribes through whose country they must pass might threaten to attack them from a desire to rob them of their gold. The space of six months is taken up with this trading expedition, including both the going and the returning. In going they march very slowly, chiefly because of the cattle, but in returning they quicken their pace lest on the way they should be overtaken by winter and its rains. For the sources of the river Nile lie somewhere in these parts, and in winter, on account of the heavy rains, the numerous rivers which they generate obstruct the path of the traveler. The people there have their winter at the time we have our summer . . . and during the three months the rain falls in torrents, and makes a multitude of rivers all of which flow into the Nile.

The facts which I have just recorded fell partly under my own observation and partly were told me by traders who had been to those parts. . . .

For most of the slaves which are now found in the hands of merchants who resort to these parts are taken from the tribes of which we speak. As for the Semenai, where . . . there are snows and ice, it is to that country the King of the Axumites expatriates anyone whom he has sentenced to be banished.

Source: J. W. McCrindle, trans. and ed., *The Christian Topography of Cosmas, an Egyptian Monk* (London: Hakluyt Society, 1897), 52–54, 67.

DOING HISTORY

Axum and the World

1. **Assessing sources:** How does each of these documents reflect the distinctive perspective of its author? What different perspectives can you notice between those documents written from within Axum and those written by outsiders? How did the particular social role that each author represents (missionary, monarch, merchant) affect his view of Axum?

2. **Considering external influences:** Based on these documents, how would you describe Axum's various relationships with the world beyond its borders? How did its geographic location shape those relationships? (See Map 6.1, page 235.) In what ways did those external connections influence Axum's historical development? From another perspective, how did Axum actively assimilate foreign influences or deliberately take advantage of opportunities that came from outside?

3. **Explaining the rise and significance of Axum:** How might you account for the flourishing of Axum? What was the religious and military significance of Axum within the region?

4. **Comparing civilizations:** In what ways might Axum be viewed as a smaller-scale version of the second-wave civilizations of Eurasia? In what ways did it differ from them?

5. **Seeking further evidence:** What else would you like to know about Axum? If you could uncover one additional document, what would you want it to reveal?

PART THREE

AN AGE OF ACCELERATING CONNECTIONS

500–1500

Contents

photos: left, World History Archive/age fotostock; center, From the Psalter of Charles the Bold, 15th century/Victoria & Albert Museum, London, UK/Bridgeman Images; right, From *History of the Mongols*, India (Lahore), Moghul, Court of Akbar the Great, ca. 1590/Library, Golestan Palace, Teheran, Iran/Werner Forman/Art Resource, NY

THE BIG PICTURE

DEFINING A MILLENNIUM

History seldom turns sharp corners, and historians often have difficulty deciding just when one phase of the human story ends and another begins. Between roughly 200 and 850 C.E., many of the second-wave states and civilizations (Han dynasty China, the western Roman Empire, Gupta India, Meroë, Axum, Maya, Teotihuacán, Moche) experienced severe disruption, decline, or collapse. For many historians, this has marked the end of an era and the start of a new period of world history. Furthermore, almost everyone agrees that the transatlantic voyages of Columbus beginning in 1492 represent yet another new departure in world history. This coupling of the Eastern and Western hemispheres set in motion historical processes that transformed most of the world and signaled the beginning of the modern era.

But how are we to understand the thousand years (roughly 500 to 1500) between the end of the second-wave era and the beginning of modern world history? Frankly, historians have had some difficulty defining a distinct identity for this millennium, a problem reflected in the vague terms used to describe it: a postclassical era, a medieval or "middle" period between the ancient and modern, or, as in this book, an age of third-wave civilizations. At best, these terms indicate where this period falls in the larger time frame of world history, but none of them are very descriptive.

Third-Wave Civilizations: Something New, Something Old, Something Blended

A large part of the problem lies in the rather different trajectories of various regions of the world during this millennium. It is not easy to identify clearly defined features that encompass all major civilizations or human communities during this period and to distinguish them from what went before. We can, however, point to several distinct patterns during this third-wave era.

In some areas, for example, wholly new but smaller civilizations arose where none had existed before. Along the East African coast, Swahili civilization emerged in a string of thirty or more city-states, very much engaged in the commercial life of the Indian Ocean basin. The kingdoms of Ghana, Mali, Songhay, and others, stimulated and sustained by long-distance trade across the Sahara, represented a new West African civilization. In the area now encompassed by

Ukraine and western Russia, another new civilization, known as Kievan Rus, likewise took shape with a good deal of cultural borrowing from Mediterranean civilization. East and Southeast Asia also witnessed new centers of civilization. Those in Japan, Korea, and Vietnam were strongly influenced by China, while Srivijaya on the Indonesian island of Sumatra, and later the Angkor kingdom centered in present-day Cambodia, drew on the Hindu and Buddhist traditions of India.

All of these represent a continuation of a well-established pattern in world history—the globalization of civilization. Each of the new third-wave civilizations was, of course, culturally unique, but like their predecessors of the first and second waves, they too featured states, cities, specialized economic roles, sharp class and gender inequalities, and other elements of "civilized" life. As newcomers to the growing number of civilizations, all of them borrowed heavily from larger or more established centers.

The largest, most expansive, and most widely influential of the new third-wave civilizations was surely that of Islam. It began in Arabia in the seventh century C.E., projecting the Arab peoples into a prominent role as builders of an enormous empire while offering a new, vigorous, and attractive religion. Viewed as a new civilization defined by its religion, the world of Islam came to encompass many other centers of civilization—Egypt, Mesopotamia, Persia, India, the interior of West Africa and the coast of East Africa, Spain, southeastern Europe, and more. Here was a uniquely cosmopolitan or "umbrella" civilization that "came closer than any had ever come to uniting all mankind under its ideals."[1]

Yet another, and quite different, historical pattern during the third-wave millennium involved those older civilizations that persisted or were reconstructed. The Byzantine Empire, embracing the eastern half of the old Roman Empire, continued the patterns of Mediterranean Christian civilization and persisted until 1453, when it was overrun by the Ottoman Turks. In China, following almost four centuries of fragmentation, the Sui, Tang, and Song dynasties (589–1279) restored China's imperial unity and reasserted its Confucian tradition. Indian civilization retained its ancient patterns of caste and Hinduism amid vast cultural diversity, even as parts of India fell under the control of Muslim rulers.

Variations on this theme of continuing or renewing older traditions took shape in the Western Hemisphere, where two centers of civilization—in Mesoamerica and in the Andes—had been long established. In Mesoamerica, the collapse of classical Maya civilization and of the great city-state of Teotihuacán by about 900 C.E. opened the way for other peoples to give new shape to this ancient civilization. The most well-known of these efforts was associated with the Mexica or Aztec people, who created a powerful and impressive state in the fifteenth century. About the same time, on the western rim of South America, a Quechua-speaking people, now known as the Incas, incorporated various centers of Andean civilization into a huge bureaucratic empire. Both the Aztecs and the Incas gave a new political expression to much older patterns of civilized life.

Yet another pattern took shape in Western Europe following the collapse of the Roman Empire. There, would-be kings and church leaders alike sought to maintain links with the older Greco-Roman-Christian traditions of classical Mediterranean civilization. In the absence of empire, however, new and far more decentralized societies emerged, led now by Germanic peoples and centered in Northern and Western Europe, considerably removed from the older centers of Rome and Athens. It was a hybrid civilization, combining old and new, Greco-Roman and Germanic elements, in a distinctive blending. For five centuries or more, this region was a relative backwater, compared to the more vibrant, prosperous, and powerful civilizations of Byzantium, the Islamic world, and China. During the centuries after 1000 C.E., however, Western European civilization emerged as a rapidly growing and expansive set of competitive states, willing, like other new civilizations, to borrow extensively from their more developed neighbors.

The Ties That Bind: Transregional Interaction in the Third-Wave Era

These quite-different patterns of development within particular civilizations have made it difficult to devise a single, all-encompassing definition of the third-wave era. In one way, however, a common theme emerges, for during this time, the world's various regions, cultures, and peoples interacted with one another far more extensively. More than before, change in human societies was the product of contact with strangers, or at least with their ideas, armies, goods, or diseases. In a variety of places—Island Southeast Asia, coastal East Africa, Central Asian cities, parts of Western Europe, the Islamic Middle East, and the Inca Empire—local cosmopolitan regions emerged in which trade, migration, or empire had brought peoples of different cultures together in a restricted space. These "mini-globalizations," both larger and more common than before, became a distinctive feature of third-wave civilizations.

None of these civilizations were wholly isolated or separate from their neighbors, although the range and intensity of cross-cultural interaction certainly varied over time. In limited ways, this had been true for earlier civilizations as well. But the scale and pace of such interaction accelerated considerably between 500 and 1500. Much of Part Three highlights these intersections and spells out their many and varied consequences.

One pattern of interaction lay in long-distance trade, which grew considerably during the third-wave millennium—along the Silk Roads of Eurasia, within the Indian Ocean basin, across the Sahara, and along the Mississippi and other rivers. Everywhere it acted as an agent of change for all its participants. In places where such commerce was practiced extensively, it required that more people devote their energies to producing for a distant market rather than for the consumption of their own communities. Those who controlled this kind of trade often became extremely wealthy, exciting envy or outrage among those less fortunate. Many societies learned about new products via these trade routes. Europe's knowledge of pepper and other spices, for example, derived from Roman seaborne trade with India beginning in the first century C.E. Such exchange among distant lands also had political consequences, as many new states or empires were constructed on the basis of resources derived from long-distance commerce. Furthermore, religious ideas, technologies, and diseases also made their ways along these paths of commerce, disrupting older ways of living and offering new opportunities as well.

Yet another mechanism of cross-cultural interaction lay in large empires. Not only did they incorporate many distinct cultures within a single political system, but their size and stability also provided the security that encouraged travelers and traders to journey long distances from their homelands. Empires, of course, were nothing new in world history, but many of those associated with third-wave civilizations were distinctive. In the first place, they were larger. The Arab Empire, which accompanied the initial spread of Islam, stretched from Spain to India. Even more extensive was the Mongol Empire of the thirteenth and fourteenth centuries. In the Western Hemisphere, the Inca Empire encompassed dozens of distinct peoples in a huge state that ran some 2,500 miles along the spine of the Andes Mountains.

Furthermore, the largest of these empires were the creation of nomadic or pastoral peoples. Earlier empires in the Mediterranean basin, China, India, and Persia had been the work of settled farming societies. But now, in the thousand years between 500 and 1500, peoples with a recent history of a nomadic or herding way of life entered the stage of world history as empire builders— Arabs, Berbers, Turks, Mongols, Aztecs—ruling over agricultural peoples and established civilizations.

Together, large-scale empires and long-distance trade facilitated the spread of ideas, technologies, food crops, and germs far beyond their points of origin. Buddhism spread from India to much of Asia; Christianity encompassed Europe and took root in distant Russia, even as it contracted in the Middle East and North Africa. Hinduism attracted followers in Southeast Asia; and more than any other religion, Islam became an Afro-Eurasian phenomenon with an enormous reach. Beyond the connections born of commerce and conquest, those of culture and religion generated lasting ties among many peoples of the Eastern Hemisphere.

Technologies, too, were diffused widely. Until the sixth century C.E., China maintained a monopoly on the manufacture of raw silk. Then this technology spread beyond East Asia, allowing the development of a silk industry in the eastern Mediterranean and later in Italy. India too contributed much to the larger world—many food crops, crystallized sugar, a system of numerals and the concept of zero, and techniques for making cotton textiles. In the Americas, corn gradually diffused from Mesoamerica, where it was initially domesticated, to North America, where it stimulated population growth and the development of more complex societies. Disease also linked distant communities. The plague, or Black Death, decimated many parts of Eurasia and North Africa as it made its deadly way from east to west in the fourteenth century.

A focus on these accelerating connections across cultural boundaries puts the historical spotlight on merchants, travelers, missionaries, migrants, soldiers, and administrators—people who traveled abroad rather than those who stayed at home. This cross-cultural emphasis in world history raises provocative questions about what happens when cultures interact or when strangers meet. How did external stimuli operate to produce change within particular societies? How did individuals or societies decide what to accept and what to reject when confronted with new ideas or practices? In what ways did they alter foreign customs or traditions to better meet their own needs and correspond to their own values?

Much of the readily visible "action" in third-wave civilizations, as in all earlier civilizations, featured male actors. The vast majority of rulers, traders, soldiers, religious officials, and long-distance travelers were men, as were most heads of households and families. The building of states and empires, so prominent in the third-wave era, meant war and conquest, fostering distinctly masculine warrior values and reinforcing the dominant position of men. Much of what follows in Part Three is, frankly, men's history.

But it is useful to remember that behind all of this lay a vast realm of women's activity, long invisible to historians or simply assumed. Women sustained the family life that was the foundation of all human community; they were the repositories of language, religious ritual, group knowledge, and local history; their labor generated many of the products that entered long-distance trade routes as well as those that fed and clothed their communities. The changing roles and relationships of men and women and their understandings of gender also figure in the chapters that follow.

MAPPING PART THREE

Complex gathering and hunting cultures
Chapter 12

Iroquois Confederacy
Chapters 7, 12

Ancestral Pueblo
Chapter 7

Eastern woodlands
Chapters 7, 12

Aztec Empire
Chapters 7, 12

Amazon River trade
Chapter 12

Maya cities
Chapter 7

Inca Empire
Chapters 7, 12

Byzantine /
Ottoman Empire
Chapter 10

Kievan Russia
Chapter 10

Mongol homeland
Chapter 11

Silk Roads
Chapter 7

Korean civilization
Chapter 8

Western civilization /
Renaissance
Chapters 10, 12

Crusades
Chapter 10

Delhi sultanate
Chapters 9, 12

Japanese civilization
Chapter 8

Muhammad / Islam
Chapters 9, 10

Song / Tang dynasties
Chapter 8

Vietnamese civilization
Chapter 8

Trans-Saharan trade
Chapters 7, 9

Swahili civilization
Chapter 7

Songhay Empire
Chapter 12

Great Zimbabwe
Chapter 7

Mali
Chapter 9

Igbo
Chapter 12

Srivijaya
Chapter 7

photos: opposite left, © Jose Fuste Raga/Corbis; center, Library of Congress, ID #pd 01046; right: Antonello Lanzellotto/TIPS Images/age fotostock; above left, Erich Lessing/Art Resource, NY; center, By Rashid al-Din, Djamil el Tawarak, 15th century Persian illumination/Bibliothèque Nationale de France, Paris, France/akg-images; right, fStop/Superstock

CHAPTER 7

Commerce and Culture

500–1500

"In the spring of 2004, I was looking for an appropriate college graduation present for my son Ateesh and decided on an Apple iPod music player. . . . I placed my order online. . . . I was astonished by what followed. I received a confirmation e-mail within minutes . . . [and learned that] the product was being shipped not from California but from Shanghai, China. . . . Ateesh's personalized iPod landed on our New Haven [Connecticut] doorstep barely 40 hours after I had clicked 'Buy.'"[1] To Nayan Chanda, a fifty-eight-year-old journalist, born and educated in India and at the time working at Yale University, this was an astonishing transaction. Probably it was less surprising to his son. But both of them, no doubt, understood this kind of commercial exchange as something quite recent in human history.

And in the speed of the transaction, it surely was. But from the perspective of world history, exchange among distant peoples is not altogether new, and the roots of economic globalization lie deep in the past. In fact, just three years after purchasing his son's iPod, Nayan Chanda wrote a well-received book titled *Bound Together*, describing how traders, preachers, adventurers, and warriors had long created links among peoples living in widely separated cultures and civilizations. Those early transregional interactions and their capacity for transforming human societies, for better and for worse, played an increasingly significant role in this era of third-wave civilizations, a millennium of accelerating connections.

The exchange of goods among communities occupying different ecological zones has long been a prominent feature of human history. Coastlands and highlands, steppes and farmlands,

Travels on the Silk Road This Chinese ceramic figurine from the Tang dynasty (618–907 C.E.) shows a group of musicians riding on a camel along the famous Silk Road commercial network that long linked the civilizations of western and eastern Eurasia. The bearded figures represent Central Asian merchants, while the others depict Chinese.

281

islands and mainlands, valleys and mountains, deserts and forests—each generates different products. Furthermore, some societies have been able to monopolize, at least temporarily, the production of particular products—such as silk in China, certain spices in Southeast Asia, and incense in southern Arabia—that others have found valuable. This uneven distribution of goods and resources, whether natural or resulting from human activity, has long motivated exchange, not only within particular civilizations or regions but among them as well. In the world of 500 to 1500, long-distance trade became more important than ever before in linking and shaping distant societies and peoples. For the most part, it was indirect, a chain of separate transactions in which goods traveled farther than individual merchants. Nonetheless, a network of exchange and communication extending all across the Afro-Eurasian world, and separately in parts of the Americas as well, slowly came into being.

Why was trade important? How did it generate change within the societies that it connected? Economically speaking, commerce often altered consumption and shaped daily life. West Africans, for example, imported scarce salt, necessary for human diets and useful for seasoning and preserving food, from distant mines in the Sahara in exchange for the gold of their region. Over several millennia, incense such as frankincense and myrrh, grown in southern Arabia and the adjacent region of northern Somalia, found eager consumers in ancient Egypt and Babylon, India and China, Greece and Rome. Used for medicinal purposes, religious ceremonies, and as an antidote to the odors of unsanitary cities, incense also bore the "aroma of eros." "I have perfumed my bed with myrrh, aloes, and cinnamon," declared a harlot featured in the Old Testament book of Proverbs. "Come, let us take our fill of love till morning."[2] Trade also affected the working lives of many people, encouraging them to specialize in producing particular products for sale in distant markets rather than for use in their own communities.

Trade, in short, diminished the economic self-sufficiency of local societies, even as it altered the structure of those societies as well. Merchants often became a distinct social group, viewed with suspicion by others because of their impulse to accumulate wealth without actually producing anything themselves. In some societies, trade became a means of social mobility, as Chinese merchants, for example, were able to purchase landed estates and establish themselves within the gentry class. Long-distance trade also enabled elite groups in society to distinguish themselves from commoners by acquiring prestigious goods from a distance—silk, tortoise-shell, jade, rhinoceros horn, or particular feathers. The association with faraway or powerful societies, signaled by the possession of their luxury goods, often conveyed status in communities more remote from major civilizations.

Trade also had the capacity to transform political life. The wealth available from controlling and taxing trade motivated the creation of states in various parts of the world and sustained those states once they had been constructed. Furthermore, commerce posed a set of problems to governments everywhere. Should trade be left in private hands, as in the Aztec Empire, or should it be controlled by the state,

A MAP OF TIME

430 B.C.E.	Trade-borne disease enters Greece from Egypt
200 B.C.E.–200 C.E.	Initial flourishing of Silk Road commerce
By 1st century B.C.E.	Spread of Buddhism to Central Asian cities and northern China
Early centuries C.E.	Knowledge of monsoons enables expansion of Indian Ocean commerce
300–400 C.E.	Beginning of trans-Saharan trade
350	All-water route opened between India and China
6th century	Chinese monopoly on silk production broken
7th century	Rise of Islam
670–1025	Srivijaya kingdom
800–1300	Khmer kingdom of Angkor
1000–1500	Swahili civilization along East African coast
13th and 14th centuries	Mongol Empire revitalizes Silk Road commerce
1250–1350	Kingdom of Zimbabwe in southeastern Africa
1275–1292	Marco Polo in China
1346–1350	Black Death enters Europe via transcontinental trade routes
1354	Ibn Battuta visits West Africa
15th century	Aztec and Inca empires facilitate commercial exchange in the Americas

as in the Inca Empire? How should state authorities deal with men of commerce, who were both economically useful and potentially disruptive?

Moreover, the saddlebags of camel caravans or the cargo holds of merchant vessels carried more than goods. Trade became a vehicle for the spread of religious ideas, technological innovations, disease-bearing germs, and plants and animals to regions far from their places of origin. In just this fashion, Buddhism made its way from India to Central and East Asia, and Islam crossed the Sahara into West Africa. So did the pathogens that devastated much of Eurasia during the Black Death. These immense cultural and biological transformations were among the most significant outcomes of the increasingly dense network of long-distance commerce during the era of third-wave civilizations.

SEEKING THE MAIN POINT

In what ways did long-distance commerce act as a motor of change in premodern world history?

Silk Roads: Exchange across Eurasia

The Eurasian landmass has long been home to the majority of humankind as well as to the world's most productive agriculture, largest civilizations, and greatest concentration of pastoral peoples. Beyond its many separate societies and cultures, Eurasia also gave rise to one of the world's most extensive and sustained networks of exchange among its diverse peoples. Known as the Silk Roads, a reference to their most famous product, these land-based trade routes linked pastoral and agricultural peoples as well as the large civilizations on the continent's outer rim (see Map 7.1). None of its numerous participants knew the full extent of this network's reach, for it was largely a "relay trade" in which goods were passed down the line, changing hands many times before reaching their final destination. Nonetheless, the Silk Roads provide a certain unity and coherence to Eurasian history alongside the distinct stories of its separate civilizations and peoples.

The Growth of the Silk Roads

The beginnings of the Silk Roads lay in both geography and history. As a geographic unit, Eurasia is often divided into inner and outer zones that represent quite different environments. Outer Eurasia consists of relatively warm, well-watered areas, suitable for agriculture, which provided the setting for the great civilizations of China, India, the Middle East, and the Mediterranean. Inner Eurasia — the lands of eastern Russia and Central Asia — lies farther north and has a harsher and drier climate, much of it not conducive to agriculture. Herding their animals from horseback, the pastoral people of this region had for centuries traded with and raided their agricultural neighbors to the south. Products of the forest and of semi-arid northern grasslands known as the steppes — such as hides, furs, livestock, wool, and amber — were exchanged for the agricultural products and manufactured goods of adjacent civilizations. The movement of pastoral peoples for thousands of years also served to diffuse Indo-European languages, bronze metallurgy, horse-based technologies, and more all across Eurasia.

■ **Change**

What lay behind the emergence of Silk Road commerce, and what kept it going for so many centuries?

The construction of the second-wave civilizations and their imperial states during the last five centuries B.C.E. added another element to these earlier Eurasian connections. From the south, the Persian Empire invaded the territory of pastoral peoples in present-day Turkmenistan and Uzbekistan. From the west, Alexander the Great's empire stretched well into Central Asia. From the east, China's Han dynasty extended its authority westward, seeking to control the nomadic Xiongnu and to gain access to the powerful "heavenly horses" that were so important to Chinese military forces. By the early centuries of the Common Era, indirect trading connections, often brokered by pastoral peoples, linked these Eurasian civilizations in a network of transcontinental exchange.

Silk Road trading networks prospered most when large and powerful states provided security for merchants and travelers. Such conditions prevailed during the

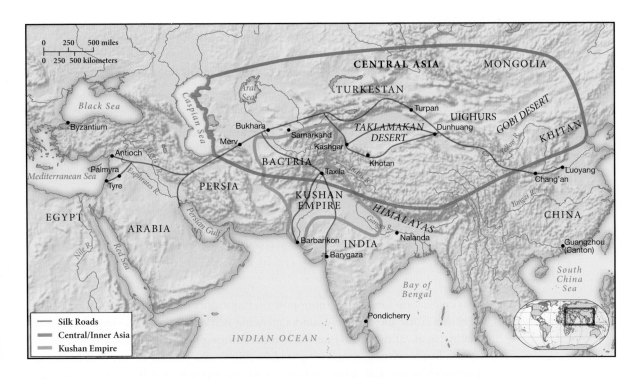

Map 7.1
The Silk Roads

For 2,000 years, goods, ideas, technologies, and diseases made their way across Eurasia on the several routes of the Silk Roads.

second-wave era when the Roman and Chinese empires anchored long-distance commerce at the western and eastern ends of Eurasia. Silk Road trade flourished again during the seventh and eighth centuries C.E. as the Byzantine Empire, the Muslim Abbasid (ah-BAH-sihd) dynasty, and Tang dynasty China created an almost continuous belt of strong states across Eurasia. In the thirteenth and fourteenth centuries, the Mongol Empire briefly encompassed almost the entire route of the Silk Roads in a single state, giving a renewed vitality to long-distance trade. Over many centuries, various technological innovations, such as yokes, saddles, and stirrups, made the use of camels, horses, and oxen more effective means of transportation across the vast distances of the Silk Roads.

Goods in Transit

During prosperous times especially, a vast array of goods (detailed in the Snapshot on page 286) made its way across the Silk Roads, often carried in large camel caravans that traversed the harsh and dangerous steppes, deserts, and oases of Central Asia. In high demand and hard to find, most of these goods were luxury products, destined for an elite and wealthy market, rather than staple goods, for only readily moved commodities of great value could compensate for the high costs of transportation across such long and forbidding distances.

Of all these luxury goods, it was silk that came to symbolize this Eurasian network of exchange. From the time of silk's origin in China, by 3000 B.C.E. or earlier,

SNAPSHOT   Economic Exchange along the Silk Roads

Region	Products Contributed to Silk Road Commerce
China	silk, bamboo, mirrors, gunpowder, paper, rhubarb, ginger, lacquerware, chrysanthemums
Forest lands of Siberia and grasslands of Central Asia	furs, walrus tusks, amber, livestock, horses, falcons, hides, copper vessels, tents, saddles, slaves
India	cotton textiles, herbal medicine, precious stones, spices, pepper, pearls, ebony
Middle East	dates, nuts, dried fruit, dyes, lapis lazuli, swords
Mediterranean basin	gold coins, glassware, glazes, grapevines, jewelry, artworks, perfume, wool and linen textiles, olive oil

that civilization long held a monopoly on its production. After 300 B.C.E. or so, that precious fabric increasingly found a growing market all across the linked commercial network of the Afro-Eurasian world. Although the silk trade itself was largely in the hands of men, women figured hugely in the process in terms of both supply and demand. For many centuries, Chinese women, mostly in rural areas, were responsible for every step of the ingenious and laborious enterprise of silk production. They tended the mulberry trees on whose leaves silkworms fed; they unwound the cocoons in very hot water to extract the long silk fibers; they turned these fibers into thread and wove them into textiles. Thus Chinese homes became the primary site of textile production with rural women as its main labor force. By the time of the Tang dynasty (618–907 C.E.), women were making a large contribution to the household economy, to technological innovation in the silk industry, and to the state, which depended heavily on peasant taxes, often paid in cloth. Despite these contributions, many rural families persisted in poverty, as the thirteenth-century writer Wen-hsiang indicated:

> The silkworms have finished their third sleep and are famished. The family is poor, without cash to buy the mulberry leaves to feed them. What can they do? Hungry silkworms do not produce silk. . . . The daughter is twenty but does not have wedding clothes. Those the government sends to collect taxes are like tigers. If they have no clothes to dress their daughter, they can put the [wedding] off. If they have no silk to turn over to the government, they will go bankrupt.[3]

■ **Significance**
What made silk such a highly desired commodity across Eurasia?

Elite Chinese women, and their men as well, also furnished part of the demand for these luxurious fabrics, which marked their high status. So too did Chinese officials, who required huge quantities of silk to exchange for much-needed horses and to buy off "barbarian" invaders from the north. Beyond China, women in many cultures ardently sought Chinese silk for its comfort and its value as a fashion statement. The demand for silk, as well as for cotton textiles from India, was so great in the Roman Empire that various Roman writers were appalled at the drain of resources that it represented. They also were outraged at the moral impact of wearing revealing silk garments. "I can see clothes of silk," lamented Seneca the Younger in the first century C.E., "if materials that do not hide the body, nor even one's decency, can be called clothes. . . . Wretched flocks of maids labour so that the adulteress may be visible through her thin dress, so that her husband has no more acquaintance than any outsider or foreigner with his wife's body."[4]

By the sixth century C.E., the knowledge and technology for producing raw silk had spread beyond China. An old Chinese story attributes it to a Chinese princess who smuggled out silkworms in her turban when she was married off to a Central Asian ruler. In a European version of the tale, Christian monks living in China did the deed by hiding some silkworms in a bamboo cane, an act of industrial espionage that allowed an independent silk-producing and silk-weaving industry to take hold in the Byzantine Empire. However it happened, Koreans, Japanese, Indians, and Persians likewise learned how to produce this precious fabric.

As the supply of silk increased, its many varieties circulated even more extensively across Afro-Eurasian trade routes. In Central Asia, silk was used as currency and as a means of accumulating wealth. In both China and the Byzantine Empire, silk became a symbol of high status, and governments passed laws that restricted silk clothing to members of the elite. Furthermore, silk became associated with the sacred in the expanding world religions of Buddhism and Christianity. Chinese Buddhist pilgrims who made their way to India seeking religious texts and relics took with them large quantities of silk as gifts to the monasteries they visited. Buddhist monks in China received purple silk robes from Tang dynasty emperors as a sign of high honor. In the world of Christendom, silk wall hangings, altar covers, and vestments became highly prestigious signs of devotion and piety. Because no independent silk industry developed in Western Europe until the twelfth century C.E., a considerable market developed for silks imported from the Islamic world. Ironically, the splendor of Christian churches depended in part on Islamic trading networks and on silks manufactured in the Muslim world. Some of those silks were even inscribed with passages in Arabic from the Quran, unbeknownst to their European buyers.[5] By the twelfth century, the West African king of Ghana was wearing silk, and that fabric circulated in Egypt, Ethiopia, and along the East African coast as well.

Compared to contemporary global commerce, the volume of trade on the Silk Roads was modest, and its focus on luxury goods limited its direct impact on most people. Nonetheless, it had important economic and social consequences. Peasants in the Yangzi River delta of southern China sometimes gave up the cultivation of food crops, choosing to focus instead on producing silk, paper, porcelain, lacquerware, or iron tools, many of which were destined for the markets of the Silk Roads. In this way, the impact of long-distance trade trickled down to affect the lives of ordinary farmers. Furthermore, favorably placed individuals could benefit immensely

■ **Connection**
What were the major economic, social, and cultural consequences of Silk Road commerce?

from long-distance trade. The twelfth-century Persian merchant Ramisht made a personal fortune from his long-distance trading business and with his profits purchased an enormously expensive silk covering for the Kaaba, the central shrine of Islam in Mecca.

Cultures in Transit

More important even than the economic impact of the Silk Roads was their role as a conduit of culture. Buddhism in particular, a cultural product of Indian civilization, spread widely throughout Central and East Asia, owing much to the activities of merchants along the Silk Roads. From its beginnings in India during the sixth century B.C.E., Buddhism had appealed to merchants, who preferred its universal message to that of a Brahmin-dominated Hinduism that privileged the higher castes. Indian traders and Buddhist monks, sometimes supported by rulers such as Ashoka, brought the new religion to the trans-Eurasian trade routes. To the west, Persian Zoroastrianism largely blocked the spread of Buddhism, but in the oasis cities of Central Asia, such as Merv, Samarkand, Khotan, and Dunhuang, Buddhism quickly took hold. By the first century B.C.E., many of the inhabitants of these towns had converted to Buddhism, and foreign merchant communities soon introduced it to northern China as well.

■ Change
What accounted for the spread of Buddhism along the Silk Roads?

Particularly important in this process were the Sogdians, a Central Asian people, whose merchants established an enduring network of exchange with China. Two such Sogdians, living in China during the second century C.E., were instrumental in translating Sanskrit Buddhist texts into Chinese. Sogdians dominated Silk Road trade for much of the first millennium C.E., and their language became a medium of communication all along that commercial network. In their Central Asian homeland, however, Sogdians practiced Zoroastrianism, Manichaeism, and local traditions as well as Buddhism.

Conversion to Buddhism in the oasis cities was a voluntary process, without the pressure of conquest or foreign rule. Dependent on long-distance trade, the inhabitants and rulers of those sophisticated and prosperous cities found in Buddhism a link to the larger, wealthy, and prestigious civilization of India. Well-to-do Buddhist merchants could earn religious merit by building monasteries and supporting monks. The monasteries in turn provided convenient and culturally familiar places of rest and resupply for merchants making the long and arduous trek across Central Asia. Many of these cities became cosmopolitan centers of learning and commerce. Scholars have found thousands of Buddhist texts in the city of Dunhuang, where several branches of the Silk Roads joined to enter western China, together with hundreds of cave temples, lavishly decorated with murals and statues.

Outside of the oasis communities, Buddhism progressed only slowly among pastoral peoples of Central Asia. The absence of a written language was an obstacle to the penetration of a highly literate religion, and their nomadic ways made the founding of monasteries, so important to Buddhism, quite difficult. But as pastoralists became involved in long-distance trade or came to rule settled agricultural

Dunhuang
Located in western China at a critical junction of the Silk Road trading network, Dunhuang was also a center of Buddhist learning, painting, and sculpture as that religion made its way from India to China and beyond. In some 492 caves, carved out of the rock between about 400 and 1400 C.E., a remarkable gallery of Buddhist art has been preserved, of which this painting is but one example. (Steve Vidler/© Prisma Bildagentur AG/Alamy)

peoples, Buddhism seemed more attractive. The nomadic Jie people, who controlled much of northern China after the collapse of the Han dynasty, are a case in point. Their ruler in the early fourth century C.E., Shi Le, became acquainted with a Central Asian Buddhist monk called Fotudeng, who had traveled widely on the Silk Roads. The monk's reputation as a miracle worker, a rainmaker, and a fortune-teller and his skills as a military strategist cemented a personal relationship with Shi Le and led to the conversions of thousands and the construction of hundreds of Buddhist temples. In China itself, Buddhism remained for many centuries a religion of foreign merchants or foreign rulers. Only slowly did it become popular among the Chinese themselves, a process examined more closely in Chapter 8.

As Buddhism spread across the Silk Roads from India to Central Asia, China, and beyond, it also changed. The original faith had shunned the material world, but Buddhist monasteries in the rich oasis towns of the Silk Roads found themselves very much involved in secular affairs. Some of them became quite wealthy, receiving gifts from well-to-do merchants, artisans, and local rulers. The begging bowls of the monks became a symbol rather than a daily activity. Sculptures and murals in the monasteries depicted musicians and acrobats, women applying makeup, and even drinking parties.

Doctrines changed as well. It was the more devotional Mahayana form of Buddhism (see Chapter 4)—featuring the Buddha as a deity, numerous bodhisattvas, an emphasis on compassion, and the possibility of earning merit—that flourished on the Silk Roads, rather than the more austere psychological teachings of the original Buddha. Moreover, Buddhism picked up elements of other cultures while in transit on the Silk Roads. In the Sogdian city of Samarkand, the use of Zoroastrian fire rituals apparently became a part of Buddhist practice. And in the area northwest of India that had been influenced by the invasions of Alexander the Great, statues of the Buddha reveal distinctly Greek influences. The Greco-Roman mythological figure of Heracles, the son of Zeus and a figure associated with great strength, courage, masculinity, and sexual prowess, was used to represent Vajrapani, one of the divine protectors of the Buddha. In a similar way, the gods of many peoples along the Silk Roads were incorporated into Buddhist practice as bodhisattvas.

Disease in Transit

Beyond goods and cultures, diseases too traveled the trade routes of Eurasia, and with devastating consequences. Each of the major population centers of the Afro-Eurasian world had developed characteristic disease patterns, mechanisms for dealing with them, and in some cases immunity to them. But when contact among previously isolated human communities occurred, people were exposed to unfamiliar diseases for which they had little immunity or few effective methods of coping. The epidemics that followed often brought suffering and death on an enormous scale to rich and poor alike. An early example involved the Greek city-state of Athens, which in 430–429 B.C.E. was suddenly afflicted by a new and still-unidentified infectious disease that had entered Greece via seaborne trade from Egypt, killing perhaps 25 percent of its army and permanently weakening the city-state.

■ Connection

What was the impact of disease along the Silk Roads?

Even more widespread diseases affected the Roman Empire and Han dynasty China as the Silk Roads promoted contact all across Eurasia. Smallpox and measles devastated the populations of both empires, contributing to their political collapse. Paradoxically, these disasters may well have strengthened the appeal of Christianity in Europe and Buddhism in China, for both of them offered compassion in the face of immense suffering.

Again in the period between 534 and 750 C.E., intermittent outbreaks of bubonic plague ravaged the coastal areas of the Mediterranean Sea as the black rats that carried the disease arrived via the seaborne trade with India, where they originally lived. What followed was catastrophic. Constantinople, the capital city of the Byzantine Empire, lost thousands of people per day during a forty-day period in 534 C.E., according to a contemporary historian. Disease played an important role in preventing Byzantium from reintegrating Italy into its version of a renewed Roman Empire encompassing the Mediterranean basin. The repeated recurrence of the disease over the next several centuries also weakened the ability of Christendom to resist Muslim armies from Arabia in the seventh century C.E.

The most well-known dissemination of disease was associated with the Mongol Empire, which briefly unified much of the Eurasian landmass during the thirteenth and fourteenth centuries C.E. (see Chapter 11). That era of intensified interaction facilitated the spread of the Black Death—identified variously with the bubonic plague, anthrax, or a package of epidemic diseases—from China to Europe. Its consequences were enormous. Between 1346 and 1348, up to half of the population of Europe perished from the plague. "A dead man," wrote the Italian writer Boccaccio, "was then of no more account than a dead goat."[6] Despite the terrible human toll, some among the living benefited. Tenant farmers and urban workers, now in short supply, could demand higher wages or better terms. Some landowning nobles, on the other hand, were badly hurt as the price of their grains dropped and the demands of their dependents grew.

A similar death toll afflicted China and parts of the Islamic world. The Central Asian steppes, home to many nomadic peoples, including the Mongols, also suffered terribly, undermining Mongol rule and permanently altering the balance between pastoral and agricultural peoples to the advantage of settled farmers. In these and many other ways, disease carried by long-distance trade shaped the lives of millions and altered their historical development. (See Chapter 11 for more on the Black Death.)

In the long run of world history, the exchange of diseases gave Europeans a certain advantage when they confronted the peoples of the Western Hemisphere after 1500. Exposure over time had provided them with some degree of immunity to Eurasian diseases. In the Americas, however, the absence of domesticated animals, the less intense interaction among major centers of population, and isolation from the Eastern Hemisphere ensured that native peoples had little defense against the diseases of Europe and Africa. Thus, when their societies were suddenly confronted by Europeans and Africans from across the Atlantic, they perished in appalling numbers. Such was the long-term outcome of the very different histories of the two hemispheres.

Sea Roads: Exchange across the Indian Ocean

If the Silk Roads linked Eurasian societies by land, sea-based trade routes likewise connected distant peoples all across the Eastern Hemisphere. For example, since the days of the Phoenicians, Greeks, and Romans, the Mediterranean Sea had been an avenue of maritime commerce throughout the region, a pattern that continued during the third-wave era. The Italian city of Venice emerged by 1000 C.E. as a major center of that commercial network, with its ships and merchants active in the Mediterranean and Black seas as well as on the Atlantic coast. Much of its wealth derived from control of expensive and profitable imported goods from Asia, many of which came up the Red Sea through the Egyptian port of Alexandria. There Venetian merchants picked up those goods and resold them throughout the Mediterranean basin. This type of transregional exchange linked the maritime commerce of the Mediterranean Sea to the much larger and more extensive network of seaborne trade in the Indian Ocean basin.

Until the creation of a genuinely global oceanic system of trade after 1500, the Indian Ocean represented the world's largest sea-based system of communication

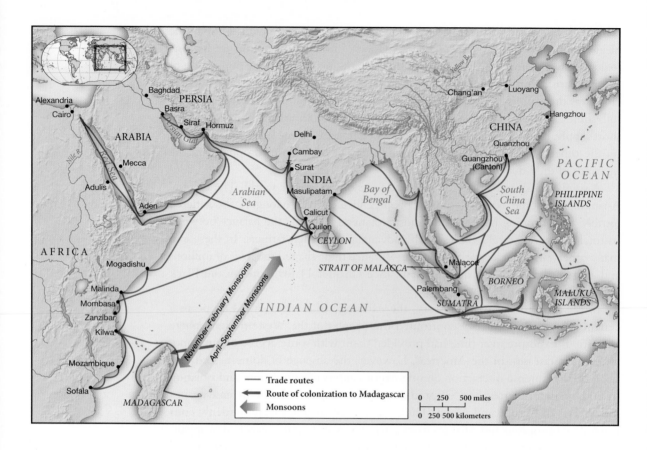

Map 7.2
The Sea Roads

Paralleling the Silk Road trading network, a sea-based commerce in the Indian Ocean basin connected the many peoples between China and East Africa.

and exchange, stretching from southern China to eastern Africa (see Map 7.2). Like the Silk Roads, these transoceanic trade routes—the Sea Roads—also grew out of the vast environmental and cultural diversities of the region. The desire for various goods not available at home—such as porcelain from China, spices from the islands of Southeast Asia, cotton goods and pepper from India, ivory and gold from the East African coast, incense from southern Arabia—provided incentives for Indian Ocean commerce. Transportation costs were lower on the Sea Roads than on the Silk Roads because ships could accommodate larger and heavier cargoes than camels. This meant that the Sea Roads could eventually carry more bulk goods and products destined for a mass market—textiles, pepper, timber, rice, sugar, wheat— whereas the Silk Roads were limited largely to luxury goods for the few.

What made Indian Ocean commerce possible were the monsoons, alternating wind currents that blew predictably northeast during the summer months and southwest during the winter (see Map 7.2). An understanding of monsoons and a gradually accumulating technology of shipbuilding and oceanic navigation drew on the ingenuity of many peoples—Chinese, Malays, Indians, Arabs, Swahilis, and others. Collectively they made "an interlocked human world joined by the common highway of the Indian Ocean."[7]

But this world of Indian Ocean commerce did not occur between entire regions and certainly not between "countries," even though historians sometimes write about India, Indonesia, Southeast Asia, or East Africa as a matter of shorthand or convenience. It operated rather across an "archipelago of towns" whose merchants often had more in common with one another than with the people of their own hinterlands.[8] These urban centers, strung out around the entire Indian Ocean basin, provided the nodes of this widespread commercial network.

Weaving the Web of an Indian Ocean World

The world of Indian Ocean commerce was long in the making, dating back to the time of the First Civilizations. Seaborne trade via the Persian Gulf between ancient Mesopotamia and the Indus Valley civilization is reflected in archeological finds in both places. Perhaps the still-undeciphered Indian writing system was stimulated by Sumerian cuneiform. The ancient Egyptians, and later the Phoenicians, likewise traded down the Red Sea, exchanging their manufactured goods for gold, ivory, frankincense, and slaves from the coasts of Ethiopia, Somalia, and southern Arabia. These ventures mostly hugged the coast and took place over short distances. Malay sailors, however, were an exception to this rule. Speaking Austronesian languages, they jumped off from the islands of present-day Indonesia during the first millennium B.C.E. and made their way in double-outrigger canoes across thousands of miles of open ocean to the East African island of Madagascar. There they introduced their language and their crops—bananas, coconuts, and taro—which soon spread to the mainland, where they greatly enriched the diets of African peoples. Also finding its way to the continent was a Malayo-Polynesian xylophone, which is still played in parts of Africa today. A casualty of this migration, coupled with the later arrival of Bantu-speaking Africans, was the extinction of the "elephant bird," a huge flightless bird weighing up to 600 pounds and found only in Madagascar.

The tempo of Indian Ocean commerce picked up in the era of second-wave civilizations during the early centuries of the Common Era, as mariners learned how to ride the monsoons. Various technological innovations also facilitated Indian Ocean trade—improvements in sails, new kinds of ships called junks with stern-post rudders and keels for greater stability, new means of calculating latitude such as the astrolabe, and evolving versions of the magnetic needle or compass. Around the time of Christ, the Greek geographer Strabo reported that "great fleets [from the Roman Empire] are sent as far as India, whence the most valuable cargoes are brought back to Egypt and thence exported again to other places."[9] Merchants from the Roman world, mostly Greeks, Syrians, and Jews, established settlements in southern India and along the East African coast. The introduction of Christianity into both Axum and Kerala (in southern India) testifies to the long-term cultural impact of that trade. In the eastern Indian Ocean and the South China Sea, Chinese and Southeast Asian merchants likewise generated a growing commerce, and by 100 C.E. Chinese traders had reached India.

SNAPSHOT   Economic Exchange in the Indian Ocean Basin

Region	Products Contributed to Indian Ocean Commerce
Mediterranean basin	ceramics, glassware, wine, gold, olive oil
East Africa	ivory, gold, iron goods, slaves, tortoiseshells, quartz, leopard skins
Arabia	frankincense, myrrh, perfumes
India	grain, ivory, precious stones, cotton textiles, spices, timber, tortoiseshells
Southeast Asia	tin, sandalwood, cloves, nutmeg, mace
China	silks, porcelain, tea

The fulcrum of this growing commercial network lay in India itself. Its ports bulged with goods from both west and east, as illustrated in the Snapshot above. Its merchants were in touch with Southeast Asia by the first century C.E., and settled communities of Indian traders appeared throughout the Indian Ocean basin and as far away as Alexandria in Egypt. Indian cultural practices, such as Hinduism and Buddhism, as well as South Asian political ideas began to take root in Southeast Asia.

■ **Change**

What lay behind the flourishing of Indian Ocean commerce in the post-classical millennium?

In the era of third-wave civilizations between 500 and 1500, two major processes changed the landscape of the Afro-Eurasian world and wove the web of Indian Ocean exchange even more densely than before. One was the economic and political revival of China, some four centuries after the collapse of the Han dynasty (see Chapter 8). Especially during the Tang and Song dynasties (618–1279), China reestablished an effective and unified state, which actively encouraged maritime trade. Furthermore, the impressive growth of the Chinese economy sent Chinese products pouring into the circuits of Indian Ocean commerce, while providing a vast and attractive market for Indian and Southeast Asian goods. Chinese technological innovations, such as larger ships and the magnetic compass, likewise added to the momentum of commercial growth.

A second transformation in the world of Indian Ocean commerce involved the sudden rise of Islam in the seventh century C.E. and its subsequent spread across much of the Afro-Eurasian world (see Chapter 9). Unlike Confucian culture, which was quite suspicious of merchants, Islam was friendly to commercial life; the Prophet Muhammad himself had been a trader. The creation of an Arab Empire, stretching from the Atlantic Ocean through the Mediterranean basin and all the way to India, brought together in a single political system an immense range of economies and cultural traditions and provided a vast arena for the energies of Muslim traders.

Those energies greatly intensified commercial activity in the Indian Ocean basin. Middle Eastern gold and silver flowed into southern India to purchase pepper, pearls, textiles, and gemstones. Muslim merchants and sailors, as well as Jews and Christians living within the Islamic world, established communities of traders from East Africa to the south China coast. Efforts to reclaim wasteland in Mesopotamia to produce sugar and dates for export stimulated a slave trade from East Africa, which landed thousands of Africans in southern Iraq to work on plantations and in salt mines under horrendous conditions. A massive fifteen-year revolt (868–883) among these slaves badly disrupted the Islamic Abbasid Empire before that rebellion was brutally crushed.

Beyond these specific outcomes, the expansion of Islam gave rise to an international maritime culture by 1000, shared by individuals living in the widely separated port cities around the Indian Ocean. The immense prestige, power, and prosperity of the Islamic world stimulated widespread conversion, which in turn facilitated commercial transactions. Even those who did not convert to Islam, such as Buddhist rulers in Burma, nonetheless regarded it as commercially useful to assume Muslim names. Thus was created "a maritime Silk Road . . . a commercial and informational network of unparalleled proportions."[10] After 1000, the culture of this network was increasingly Islamic.

Sea Roads as a Catalyst for Change: Southeast Asia

Oceanic commerce transformed all of its participants in one way or another, but nowhere more so than in Southeast Asia and East Africa, at opposite ends of the Indian Ocean network. In both regions, trade stimulated political change as ambitious or aspiring rulers used the wealth derived from commerce to construct larger and more centrally governed states or cities. Both areas likewise experienced cultural change as local people were attracted to foreign religious ideas from Confucian, Hindu, Buddhist, or Islamic sources. As on the Silk Roads, trade was a conduit for culture.

Located between the major civilizations of China and India, Southeast Asia was situated by geography to play an important role in the evolving world of Indian Ocean commerce. During the third-wave era, a series of cities and states or kingdoms emerged on both the islands and mainland of Southeast Asia, representing new civilizations in this vast region (see Map 7.3). That process paralleled a similar development of new civilizations in East and West Africa, Japan, Russia, and Western Europe in what was an Afro-Eurasian phenomenon. In Southeast Asia, many of those new societies were stimulated and decisively shaped by their interaction with the sea-based trade of the Indian Ocean.[11]

The case of Srivijaya (SREE-vih-juh-yuh) illustrates the connection between commerce and state building. When Malay sailors, long active in the waters around Southeast Asia, opened an all-sea route between India and China through the Straits of Malacca around 350 C.E., the many small ports along the Malay Peninsula and the coast of Sumatra began to compete intensely to attract the growing number of traders and travelers making their way through the straits. From this competition emerged the Malay kingdom of Srivijaya, which dominated this critical choke

■ Connection
In what ways did Indian influence register in Southeast Asia?

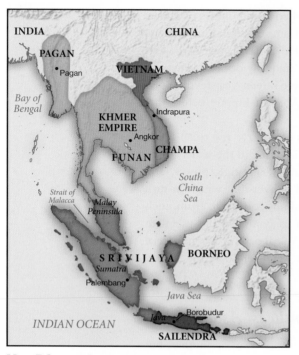

Map 7.3   Southeast Asia, ca. 1200 C.E.

Both mainland and island Southeast Asia were centrally
involved in the commerce of the Indian Ocean basin, and
both were transformed by that experience.

point of Indian Ocean trade from 670 to 1025. A number of factors—Srivijaya's plentiful supply of gold; its access to the source of highly sought-after spices, such as cloves, nutmeg, and mace; and the taxes levied on passing ships—provided resources to attract supporters, to fund an embryonic bureaucracy, and to create the military and naval forces that brought some security to the area.

The inland states on the mainland of Southeast Asia, whose economies were based more on domestically produced rice than on international trade, nonetheless participated in the commerce of the region. The state of Funan, which flourished during the first six centuries of the Common Era in what is now southern Vietnam and eastern Cambodia, hosted merchants from both India and China. Archeologists have found Roman coins as well as trade goods from Persia, Central Asia, and Arabia in the ruins of its ancient cities. The Khmer kingdom of Angkor (flourished 800–1300) exported exotic forest products, receiving in return Chinese and Indian handicrafts, while welcoming a considerable community of Chinese merchants. Traders from Champa in what is now central and southern Vietnam operated in China, Java, and elsewhere, practicing piracy when trade dried up. Champa's effort to control the trade between China and Southeast Asia provoked warfare with its commercial rivals.

Beyond the exchange of goods, commercial connections served to spread elements of Indian culture across much of Southeast Asia, even as Vietnam was incorporated into the Chinese sphere of influence. (See Chapter 8 for more on Chinese influence in Vietnam.) Indian alphabets such as Sanskrit and Pallava were used to write a number of Southeast Asian languages. Indian artistic forms provided models for Southeast Asian sculpture and architecture, while the Indian epic *Ramayana* became widely popular across the region.

Politically, Southeast Asian rulers and elites found attractive the Indian belief that leaders were god-kings, perhaps reincarnations of a Buddha or the Hindu deity Shiva, while the idea of karma conveyed legitimacy to the rich and powerful based on their moral behavior in earlier lives. Srivijayan monarchs, for example, employed Indians as advisers, clerks, or officials and assigned Sanskrit titles to their subordinates. The capital city of Palembang was a cosmopolitan place, where even the parrots were said to speak four languages. While these rulers drew on indigenous beliefs that chiefs possessed magical powers and were responsible for the prosperity of their people, they also made use of imported Indian political ideas and Buddhist religious concepts, which provided a "higher level of magic" for rulers as well as the prestige of association with Indian civilization.[12] They also sponsored the crea-

tion of images of the Buddha and various bodhisattvas whose faces resembled those of deceased kings and were inscribed with traditional curses against anyone who would destroy them. Srivijaya grew into a major center of Buddhist observance and teaching, attracting thousands of monks and students from throughout the Buddhist world. The seventh-century Chinese monk Yi Jing was so impressed that he advised Buddhist monks headed for India to study first in Srivijaya for several years.

Elsewhere as well, elements of Indian culture took hold in Southeast Asia. The Sailendra kingdom in central Java, an agriculturally rich region closely allied with Srivijaya, mounted a massive building program between the eighth and tenth centuries featuring Hindu temples and Buddhist monuments. The most famous, known as Borobudur, is an enormous mountain-shaped structure of ten levels, with a three-mile walkway and elaborate carvings illustrating the spiritual journey from ignorance and illusion to full enlightenment. The largest Buddhist monument anywhere in the world, it is nonetheless a distinctly Javanese creation, whose carved figures have Javanese features and whose scenes are clearly set in Java, not India. Its shape resonated with an ancient Southeast Asian veneration of mountains as sacred places and the abode of ancestral spirits. Borobudur represents the process of Buddhism becoming culturally grounded in a new place.

Hinduism too, though not an explicitly missionary religion, found a place in Southeast Asia. It was well rooted in the Champa kingdom, for example, where Shiva was worshipped, cows were honored, and phallic imagery was prominent. But it was in the prosperous and powerful Angkor kingdom of the twelfth century C.E. that Hinduism found its most stunning architectural expression in the temple complex known as Angkor Wat. The largest religious structure in the premodern

Borobudur
This huge Buddhist monument, constructed probably in the ninth century C.E., was subsequently abandoned and covered with layers of volcanic ash and vegetation as Java came under Islamic influence. It was rediscovered by British colonial authorities in the early nineteenth century and has undergone several restorations over the past two centuries. Although Indonesia is a largely Muslim country, its small Buddhist minority still celebrates the Buddha's birthday at Borobudur. (© Luca Tettoni/ Robert Harding World Imagery/ Alamy)

Angkor Wat
Constructed in the early twelfth century, the Angkor Wat complex was designed as a state temple, dedicated to the Hindu god Vishnu and lavishly decorated with carved bas-reliefs depicting scenes from Hindu mythology. By the late thirteenth century, it was in use by Buddhists, as it is to this day. This photo shows a small section of the temple and three Buddhist monks in their saffron robes. (© Jose Fuste Raga/Corbis)

world, it sought to express a Hindu understanding of the cosmos, centered on a mythical Mount Meru, the home of the gods in Hindu tradition. Later, it was used by Buddhists as well, with little sense of contradiction. To the west of Angkor, the state of Pagan likewise devoted enormous resources to shrines, temples, and libraries inspired by both Hindu and Buddhist faiths.

This extensive Indian influence in Southeast Asia has led some scholars to speak of the "Indianization" of the region, similar perhaps to the earlier spread of Greek culture within the empires of Alexander the Great and Rome. In the case of Southeast Asia, however, no imperial control accompanied Indian cultural influence. It was a matter of voluntary borrowing by independent societies that found Indian traditions and practices useful and were free to adapt those ideas to their own needs and cultures. Traditional religious practices mixed with the imported faiths or existed alongside them with little conflict. And much that was distinctively Southeast Asian persisted despite influences from afar. In family life, for example, most Southeast Asian societies traced an individual's ancestry from both the mother's and father's line in contrast to India and China, where patrilineal descent was practiced. Furthermore, women had fewer restrictions and a greater role in public life than in the more patriarchal civilizations of both East and South Asia. They were generally able to own property together with their husbands and to initiate divorce. A Chinese visitor to Angkor observed, "It is the women who are concerned with commerce." Women in Angkor also served as gladiators, warriors, and members of the palace staff, and as poets, artists, and religious teachers. Almost 1,800 realistically carved images of women decorate the temple complex of Angkor Wat. In neighboring Pagan, a thirteenth-century queen, Pwa Saw, exercised extensive political and religious influence for some forty years amid internal intrigue and external threats, while donating some of her lands and property to a Buddhist temple. Somewhat later, but also via Indian Ocean commerce, Islam too began to penetrate Southeast Asia as the world of seaborne trade brought yet another cultural tradition to the region.

Sea Roads as a Catalyst for Change: East Africa

On the other side of the Indian Ocean, the transformative processes of long-distance trade were likewise at work, giving rise to an East African civilization known as Swahili. Emerging in the eighth century C.E., this civilization took shape as a set of commercial city-states stretching all along the East African coast, from present-day Somalia to Mozambique.

The earlier ancestors of the Swahili lived in small farming and fishing communities, spoke Bantu languages, and traded with the Arabian, Greek, and Roman merchants who occasionally visited the coast during the second-wave era. But what stimulated the growth of Swahili cities was the far more extensive commercial life of the western Indian Ocean following the rise of Islam. As in Southeast Asia, local people and aspiring rulers found opportunity for wealth and power in the growing demand for East African products associated with an expanding Indian Ocean commerce. Gold, ivory, quartz, leopard skins, and sometimes slaves acquired from interior societies, as well as iron and processed timber manufactured along the coast, found a ready market in Arabia, Persia, India, and beyond. At least one East African giraffe found its way to Bengal in northeastern India, and from there was sent on to China. In response to such commercial opportunities, an African merchant class developed, villages turned into sizable towns, and clan chiefs became kings. A new civilization was in the making.

Between 1000 and 1500, that civilization flourished along the coast, and it was a very different kind of society from the farming and pastoral cultures of the East African interior. It was thoroughly urban, centered in cities of 15,000 to 18,000 people, such as Lamu, Mombasa, Kilwa, Sofala, and many others. Like the city-states of ancient Greece, each Swahili city was politically independent, was generally governed by its own king, and was in sharp competition with other cities. No imperial system or larger territorial states unified the world of Swahili civilization. Nor did any of these city-states control a critical choke point of trade, as Srivijaya did for the Straits of Malacca. Swahili cities were commercial centers that accumulated goods from the interior and exchanged them for the products of distant civilizations, such as Chinese porcelain and silk, Persian rugs, and Indian cottons. While the transoceanic journeys occurred largely in Arab vessels, Swahili craft navigated the coastal waterways, concentrating goods for shipment abroad. This long-distance trade generated class-stratified urban societies with sharp distinctions between a mercantile elite and commoners.

■ **Connection**
What was the role of Swahili civilization in the world of Indian Ocean commerce?

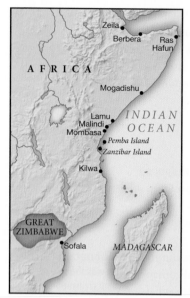

The Swahili Coast of East Africa

Culturally as well as economically, Swahili civilization participated in the larger Indian Ocean world. Arab, Indian, and Persian merchants were welcome visitors, and some settled permanently. Many ruling families of Swahili cities claimed Arab or Persian origins as a way of bolstering their prestige, even while they dined from Chinese porcelain and dressed in Indian cottons. The Swahili language, widely spoken in East Africa today, was grammatically an African tongue within the larger Bantu family of languages, but it was written in Arabic script and contained a number of Arabic loan words. A small bronze lion found in the Swahili city of Shanga and dating to about 1100 illustrates the distinctly cosmopolitan character of Swahili culture. It depicted a clearly African lion, but it was created in a distinctly Indian artistic style and was made from melted-down Chinese copper coins.[13]

Furthermore, Swahili civilization rapidly became Islamic. Introduced by Arab traders, Islam was voluntarily and widely adopted within the Swahili world. Like Buddhism in Southeast Asia, Islam linked Swahili cities to the larger Indian Ocean world, and these East African cities were soon dotted with substantial mosques. When Ibn Battuta (IH-buhn ba-TOO-tuh), a widely traveled Arab scholar, merchant, and public official, visited the Swahili coast in the early fourteenth century, he found altogether Muslim societies in which religious leaders often spoke Arabic, and all were eager to welcome a learned Islamic visitor. But these were African Muslims, not colonies of transplanted Arabs. A prominent historian of Ibn Battuta's travels commented on Swahili society: "The rulers, scholars, officials, and big merchants as well as the port workers, farmers, craftsmen, and slaves, were dark-skinned people speaking African tongues in everyday life."[14]

Islam sharply divided the Swahili cities from their African neighbors to the west, for neither the new religion nor Swahili culture penetrated much beyond the coast until the nineteenth century. Economically, however, the coastal cities acted as intermediaries between the interior producers of valued goods and the Arab merchants who carried them to distant markets. Particularly in the southern reaches of the Swahili world, this relationship extended the impact of Indian Ocean trade well into the African interior. Hundreds of miles inland, between the Zambezi and Limpopo rivers, lay rich sources of gold, much in demand on the Swahili coast. The emergence of a powerful state, known as Great Zimbabwe, seems clearly connected to the growing trade in gold to the coast as well as to the wealth embodied in its large herds of cattle. At its peak between 1250 and 1350, Great Zimbabwe had the resources and the labor power to construct huge stone enclosures entirely without mortar, with walls sixteen feet thick and thirty-two feet tall. "[It] must have been an astonishing sight," writes a recent historian, "for the subordinate chiefs and kings who would have come there to seek favors at court."[15] Here in the interior of southeastern Africa lay yet another example of the reach and transforming power of Indian Ocean commerce.

SUMMING UP SO FAR

To what extent did the Silk Roads and the Sea Roads operate in a similar fashion? How did they differ?

Sand Roads: Exchange across the Sahara

In addition to the Silk Roads and the Sea Roads, another important pattern of long-distance trade—this one across the vast reaches of the Sahara—linked North Africa and the Mediterranean world with the land and peoples of interior West Africa. Like the others, these Sand Road commercial networks had a transforming impact, stimulating and enriching West African civilization and connecting it to larger patterns of world history during the third-wave era.

Commercial Beginnings in West Africa

Trans-African trade, like the commerce of the Silk Roads and the Sea Roads, was rooted in environmental variation. The North African coastal regions, long part of Roman or later Arab empires, generated cloth, glassware, weapons, books, and other manufactured goods. The great Sahara held deposits of copper and especially salt, while its oases produced sweet and nutritious dates. While the sparse populations of the desert were largely pastoral and nomadic, farther south lived agricultural peoples who grew a variety of crops, produced their own textiles and metal products, and mined a considerable amount of gold. These agricultural regions of sub-Saharan Africa are normally divided into two ecological zones: the savanna grasslands immediately south of the Sahara, which produced grain crops such as millet and sorghum, and the forest areas farther south, where root and tree crops such as yams and kola nuts predominated. These quite varied environments provided the economic incentive for the exchange of goods.

The earliest long-distance trade within this huge region was not across the Sahara at all, but largely among the agricultural peoples themselves in the area later known to Arabs as the Sudan, or "the land of black people." During the first millennium B.C.E., the peoples of Sudanic West Africa began to exchange metal goods, cotton textiles, gold, and various food products across considerable distances using boats along the Niger River and donkeys overland. On the basis of this trade, a number of independent urban clusters emerged by the early centuries of the Common Era. The most well known was Jenne-jeno, which was located at a crucial point on the Niger River where goods were transshipped from boat to donkey or vice versa. This was the Niger Valley civilization, described in Chapter 6.

Gold, Salt, and Slaves: Trade and Empire in West Africa

A major turning point in African commercial life occurred with the introduction of the camel to North Africa and the Sahara in the early centuries of the Common Era. (See Zooming In: The Arabian Camel, page 302.) This remarkable animal, which could go for ten days without water, finally made possible the long trek across the Sahara. It was camel-owning dwellers of desert oases who initiated regular trans-Saharan commerce by 300 to 400 C.E. Several centuries later, North African Arabs, now bearing the new religion of Islam, also organized caravans across the desert.

The Arabian Camel

Part of a camel caravan.

Animals have their own histories, and they have long played a large role in human history as well. Consider the single-humped Arabian camel, for thousands of years an important means of transport and a beast of burden on the Silk and Sand Roads. Even today, the Arabian camel is a common sight across northern Africa and the Middle East. But it took millennia for this breed of camel to spread beyond its native Arabian Peninsula, where it had been domesticated by 3000 B.C.E. Camels were initially valued by Arab tribesmen for their milk; however, over time their endurance and ability to carry heavy loads resulted in their adoption as pack animals along the caravan routes between the frankincense- and myrrh-producing regions of southern Arabia and cities on the northern edges of the peninsula.

This trade slowly introduced Arabian camels to the rest of the Middle East, where they were well established by 500 B.C.E. But it was the invention of a new saddle, which allowed each animal to carry a heavier load, that transformed the camel into the most versatile and efficient form of transport in the region by 100 B.C.E. Ultimately the camel displaced the ox and cart, which for millennia had been a mainstay for moving goods. The advantages of the camel were significant. Camels ate desert plants that thrived on lands unsuitable to agriculture, while oxen required fodder grown on arable land. Moreover, camels carried loads on their backs rather than pulling carts made of wood, a scarce resource in the Middle East. In many parts of the region, the camel's triumph was complete. By 500 C.E., wheeled vehicles had disappeared entirely from most of the Middle East, and the camel maintained its dominance for fifteen

photo: From the "Maqamat" of Abu Mohammed al Qasim ibn Ali Hariri (1054–1122), 1237. © Scala/White Images/Art Resource, NY

■ **Connection**
What changes did trans-Saharan trade bring to West Africa?

What they sought, above all else, was gold, which was found in some abundance in the border areas straddling the grasslands and the forests of West Africa. From its source, it was transported by donkey to transshipment points on the southern edge of the Sahara and then transferred to camels for the long journey north across the desert. African ivory, kola nuts, and slaves were likewise in considerable demand in the desert, the Mediterranean basin, and beyond. In return, the peoples of the Sudan received horses, cloth, dates, various manufactured goods, and especially salt from the rich deposits in the Sahara.

Thus the Sahara was no longer simply a barrier to commerce and cross-cultural interaction; it quickly became a major international trade route that fostered new relationships among distant peoples. The caravans that made the desert crossing could be huge, with as many as 5,000 camels and hundreds of people. Traveling mostly at night to avoid the daytime heat, the journey might take up to seventy days, covering fifteen to twenty-five miles per day. For well over 1,000 years, such caravans traversed the desert, linking the interior of West Africa with lands and people far to the north.

hundred years. In the 1780s, a French traveler in Syria commented, "It is noteworthy that in all of Syria no wagon or cart is seen."[16] Only with the emergence of the automobile in the twentieth century did the camel decisively lose its advantage over wheeled vehicles. From the Middle East, Arabian camels and related hybrid species moved along the Silk Roads, becoming a major means of transport as far away as modern Afghanistan. Only the cold climatic conditions of Central Asia halted their spread. In the frigid Gobi Desert, it was the Arabian camel's cousin—the two-humped Bactrian camel— that traders relied upon to carry their loads.

The Arabian camel had perhaps an even more profound impact on long-distance trade across the Sahara. Before the arrival of the camel, the western Sahara proved an imposing barrier to trade. Just a trickle of goods flowed across the vast arid region, often through indirect exchange. The first camels most likely filtered into western Africa from the Middle East along the southern borders of the Sahara around 200 B.C.E., and they probably arrived after 100 C.E. in Roman North Africa, where they were used for a variety of purposes, including the plowing of fields. From the time of their arrival, camels stimulated trade and contact across the Sahara, but these exchanges really took off when the Arab conquerors of North Africa brought their expertise in camel caravan trading to the region in the sixth century C.E. At their height, caravans of up to 5,000 camels regularly crossed the Sahara on several established routes. It could take seventy days to traverse the desert, but profits from trade in gold, ivory, salt, and slaves made the journey worthwhile. These trade routes facilitated the emergence of empires in West Africa and the spread of Islam into the region. The Arabian camel remained the chief source of transport between sub-Saharan West Africa and the Mediterranean for over a thousand years, until European ships sailing along the Atlantic coast challenged their dominance in the fifteenth century.

Questions: Was the disappearance of the wheel an advance in terms of transport in the Middle East? What impact did the Arabian camel have on long-distance trade in Eurasia and Africa? How might reliance on the camel rather than the wheel affect human settlements?

As in Southeast Asia and East Africa, this long-distance trade across the Sahara provided both incentives and resources for the construction of new and larger political structures. It was the peoples of the western and central Sudan, living between the forests and the desert, who were in the best position to take advantage of these new opportunities. Between roughly 500 and 1600, they constructed a series of states, empires, and city-states that reached from the Atlantic coast to Lake Chad, including Ghana, Mali, Songhay, Kanem, and the city-states of the Hausa people (see Map 7.4). All of them were monarchies with elaborate court life and varying degrees of administrative complexity and military forces at their disposal. All drew on the wealth of trans-Saharan trade, taxing the merchants who conducted it. In the wider world, these states soon acquired a reputation for great riches. An Arab traveler in the tenth century C.E. described the ruler of Ghana as "the wealthiest king on the face of the earth because of his treasures and stocks of gold."[17] At its high point in the fourteenth century, Mali's rulers monopolized the import of strategic goods such as horses and metals; levied duties on salt, copper, and other merchandise; and reserved large nuggets of gold for themselves while

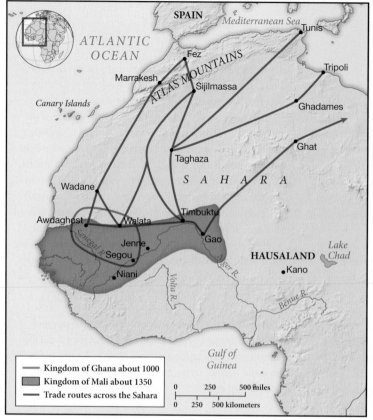

SPAIN

ATLANTIC OCEAN

Mediterranean Sea

Tunis

Fez

ATLAS MOUNTAINS

Marrakesh

Sijilmassa

Tripoli

Canary Islands

Ghadames

Ghat

Taghaza

S A H A R A

Wadane

Timbuktu

Awdaghost   Walata

Gao

Jenne

Lake Chad

Segou

HAUSALAND

Niani

Kano

Volta R.

Niger R.

Bénue R.

Senegal R.

Gulf of Guinea

    Kingdom of Ghana about 1000
    Kingdom of Mali about 1350
    Trade routes across the Sahara

0   250   500 miles
0   250   500 kilometers

Map 7.4   The Sand Roads

For a thousand years or more, the Sahara was an ocean of sand that linked the interior of West Africa with the world of North Africa and the Mediterranean but separated them as well.

permitting the free export of gold dust. (See Working with Evidence, Source 7.3, page 318, for an early sixteenth-century account of this West African civilization.)

This growing integration with the world of international commerce generated the social complexity and hierarchy characteristic of all civilizations. Royal families and elite classes, mercantile and artisan groups, military and religious officials, free peasants and slaves—all of these were represented in this emerging West African civilization. So too were gender hierarchies, although without the rigidity of more established Eurasian civilizations. Rulers, merchants, and public officials were almost always male, and by 1200 earlier matrilineal descent patterns had been largely replaced by those tracing descent through the male line. Male bards, the repositories for their communities' history, often viewed powerful women as dangerous, not to be trusted, and a seductive distraction for men. But ordinary women were central to agricultural production and weaving; royal women played important political roles in many places; and oral traditions and mythologies frequently portrayed a complementary rather than hierarchal relationship between the sexes. According to a recent scholar:

> Men [in West African civilization] derive their power and authority by releasing and accumulating *nyama* [a pervasive vital power] through acts of transforming one thing into another—making a living animal dead in hunting, making a lump of metal into a fine bracelet at the smithy. Women derive their power from similar acts of transformation—turning clay into pots or turning the bodily fluids of sex into a baby.[18]

Certainly, the famous Muslim traveler Ibn Battuta, visiting Mali in the fourteenth century, was surprised, and appalled, at the casual intimacy of unmarried men and women, despite their evident commitment to Islam.

As in all civilizations, slavery found a place in West Africa. Early on, most slaves had been women, working as domestic servants and concubines. As West African civilization crystallized, however, male slaves were put to work as state officials, porters, craftsmen, miners harvesting salt from desert deposits, and especially agricultural laborers producing for the royal granaries on large estates or plantations. Most came from non-Islamic and stateless societies farther south, which were raided during the dry season by cavalry-based forces of West African states, though some white slave women from the eastern Mediterranean also made an appearance in Mali. A song in honor of one eleventh-century ruler of Kanem boasted of his slave-raiding achievements:

> The best you took (and sent home) as the first fruits of battle.
> The children crying on their mothers you snatched away from their mothers. You took the slave wife from a slave, and set them in lands far removed from one another.[19]

Most of these slaves were used within this emerging West African civilization, but a trade in slaves also developed across the Sahara. Between 1100 and 1400, perhaps 5,500 slaves per year made the perilous trek across the desert, where most were put to work in the homes of the wealthy in Islamic North Africa.

These states of Sudanic Africa developed substantial urban and commercial centers—such as Koumbi-Saleh, Jenne, Timbuktu, Gao, Gobir, and Kano—where traders congregated and goods were exchanged. Some of these cities also became centers of manufacturing, creating finely wrought beads, iron tools, or cotton textiles, some of which entered the circuits of commerce. Visitors described them as cosmopolitan places where court officials, artisans, scholars, students, and local and foreign merchants all rubbed elbows. As in East Africa, Islam accompanied trade and became an important element in the urban culture of West Africa. The growth of long-distance trade had stimulated the development of a West African civilization, which was linked to the wider networks of exchange in the Eastern Hemisphere.

Manuscripts of Timbuktu
The West African city of Timbuktu, a terminus of the Sand Road commercial network, became an intellectual center of Islamic learning—both scientific and religious. Its libraries were stocked with books and manuscripts, often transported across the Sahara from the heartland of Islam. Many of these have been preserved and are now being studied once again. (Alex Dissanayake/Lonely Planet Images/Getty Images)

An American Network: Commerce and Connection in the Western Hemisphere

Before the voyages of Columbus, the world of the Americas developed quite separately from that of Afro-Eurasia. Intriguing hints of occasional contacts with Polynesia and other distant lands have been proposed, but the only clearly demonstrated connection was that occasioned by the brief Viking voyages to North America around the year 1000. (See Zooming In: Thorfinn Karlsefni, page 306.) Certainly, no sustained interaction between the peoples of the two hemispheres took place. But if the Silk, Sea, and Sand Roads linked the diverse peoples of the Eastern Hemisphere, did a similar network of interaction join and transform the various societies of the Western Hemisphere?

Thorfinn Karlsefni, Viking Voyager

While the peoples of the Eastern and Western hemispheres remained almost completely isolated from one another before Columbus, the Viking journeys to North America, part of a larger age of Viking expansion, represent an exception to that generalization. Between 800 and 1050, Scandinavian Vikings had raided, traded, and sometimes settled across much of Europe, generating a fearful reputation.

A Viking ship similar to that used by Thorfinn Karlsefni and other Viking explorers.

There he found winter accommodations with Eric the Red, a pioneer of Nordic settlement in Greenland. He also found a wife, Gudrid, the widow of one of Eric's sons. Two of Eric's sons, including Leif Ericsson, had previously made the journey to Vinland. And so, during that long winter, talk turned to another voyage, for that land was reputed to be rich in furs, timber, and other valuable resources. Thus Thorfinn came

They also colonized Iceland and Greenland, and from that base sought yet more land in North America. Yet their transatlantic voyages, although impressive feats of oceanic exploration, represented a historical dead end, for they bore no long-term consequences. Their significance lies in their role as a prelude to Columbus rather than in any immediate outcomes.

Among those voyagers was Thorfinn Karlsefni, who set off from southern Greenland in the spring of 1007 bound for what he called Vinland, and what we know as North America. A well-born, wealthy merchant and seaman of Norwegian Viking background, he had come the previous summer from his home in Iceland to the small Viking community in Greenland on a trading mission.

to lead 160 people, including his new wife and other women, on three ships heading to a virtually unknown land. The story of that voyage comes to us from two Icelandic sagas, based on oral traditions and committed to writing several hundred years after the events they describe.[20]

Arriving along the coast of what is now Newfoundland, Thorfinn and his people first looked for pastureland for the cattle that had accompanied them. With food in short supply, the first winter was very difficult and provoked a religious controversy. The Christians among the group "made prayers to God for food," but Thorhall, a

photo: © Yvette Cardozo/Alamy

■ **Comparison**

In what ways did networks of interaction in the Western Hemisphere differ from those in the Eastern Hemisphere?

Clearly, direct connections among the various civilizations and cultures of the Americas were less densely woven than in the Afro-Eurasian region. The llama and the potato, both domesticated in the Andes, never reached Mesoamerica; nor did the writing system of the Maya diffuse to Andean civilizations. The Aztecs and the Incas, contemporary civilizations in the fifteenth century, had little if any direct contact with each other. The limits of these interactions owed something to the absence of horses, donkeys, camels, wheeled vehicles, and large oceangoing vessels, all of which facilitated long-distance trade and travel in Afro-Eurasia.

Geographic or environmental differences added further obstacles. The narrow bottleneck of Panama, largely covered by dense rain forests, surely inhibited contact between South and North America. Furthermore, the north/south orientation

large, solitary, and "foul-mouthed" hunter, declared: "Has it not been that the Redbeard [Thor, the Norse god of thunder] has proved a better friend than your Christ?"

The following spring, the small Viking community had its first encounter with native peoples when dozens of canoes described in the sagas as "black, and ill favoured" appeared offshore. What followed was a kind of mutual inspection, as the natives "stayed a while in astonishment" and then rowed away. They returned the following year, this time to barter. The Vikings offered red cloth and milk porridge in exchange for furs and skins. But what began as a peaceful encounter ended badly when a bull from the Norsemen's herd erupted out of the forest, bellowing loudly. The surprised and frightened locals quickly departed, and when they returned three weeks later, violence erupted. Considerably outnumbered and attacked with catapults and a "great shower of missiles," Thorfinn and his company reacted with "great terror."

This encounter and the "fear of hostilities" that it provoked persuaded the Vikings "to depart and return to their own country." As they made their way north along the coast, they came upon a group of five natives sleeping near the sea. Perhaps in revenge, the Vikings simply killed them. In another incident before departing for home, they captured two boys, baptized them as Christians, and taught them the Viking language. After three difficult years in this remote land, Thorfinn and Gudrid returned home, with a son named Snorri, the first European born in the Western Hemisphere.

Although intermittent Viking voyages to North America probably occurred over the next several centuries, the Vikings established no permanent presence. Their numbers were small, and they lacked the support of a strong state, such as Columbus and the Spanish conquistadores later enjoyed. For some time, many doubted that those voyages had occurred at all. But in the 1960s, archeological work on the northern tip of the island of Newfoundland uncovered the remains of a Norse settlement dating to the time of Thorfinn's visit. Eight sod dwellings, evidence of ironworking and boat repair, and household items such as needles and spindles confirmed the existence of a Viking settlement, consisting of both men and women. The interaction of Thorfinn and the other Vikings with native peoples of North America raised, but did not answer, the question of how the epic encounter of these two continents would turn out. The later voyages of Columbus and other West Europeans provided that answer.

Question: How might these interactions have appeared if the descriptions of these encounters had been derived from the sagas of the native peoples of North America?

of the Americas—which required agricultural practices to move through, and adapt to, quite distinct climatic and vegetation zones—slowed the spread of agricultural products. By contrast, the east/west axis of Eurasia meant that agricultural innovations could diffuse more rapidly because they were entering roughly similar environments. Thus nothing equivalent to the long-distance trade of the Silk, Sea, or Sand Roads of the Eastern Hemisphere arose in the Americas, even though local and regional commerce flourished in many places. Nor did distinct cultural traditions spread widely to integrate distant peoples, as Buddhism, Christianity, and Islam did in the Afro-Eurasian world.

Nonetheless, scholars have discerned "a loosely interactive web stretching from the North American Great Lakes and upper Mississippi south to the Andes."[21]

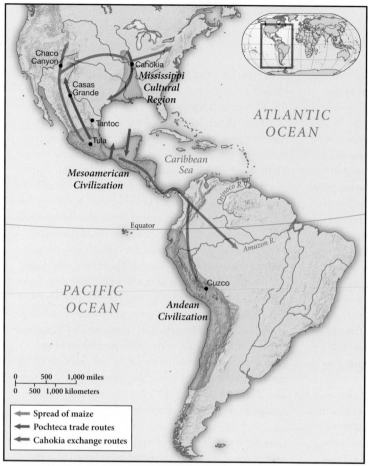

ATLANTIC
OCEAN

Caribbean
Sea

Equator

PACIFIC
OCEAN

Mesoamerican
Civilization

Andean
Civilization

0	500 1,000 miles
0	500 1,000 kilometers

Spread of maize
Pochteca trade routes
Cahokia exchange routes

Map 7.5   The American Web

Transcontinental interactions within the American web were more modest than those of the Afro-Eurasian hemisphere. The most intense areas of exchange and communication occurred within the Mississippi valley, Mesoamerican, and Andean regions.

(See Map 7.5.) Partly, it was a matter of slowly spreading cultural elements, such as the gradual diffusion of maize from its Mesoamerican place of origin to the southwestern United States and then on to eastern North America as well as to much of South America in the other direction. A game played with rubber balls on an outdoor court has left traces in the Caribbean, Mexico, and northern South America. Construction in the Tantoc region of northeastern Mexico resembled the earlier building styles of Cahokia, indicating the possibility of some interaction between the two regions. The spread of particular pottery styles and architectural conventions likewise suggests at least indirect contact over wide distances. This kind of diffusion likely extended from the Americas to the Pacific islands as well. Scholars believe that the sweet potato, indigenous to South America, passed into Pacific Oceania around 1000 to 1100 C.E., introduced by Polynesian voyagers who had landed on the west coast of that continent and then returned home with sweet potatoes, which spread widely within Oceania.[22]

Commerce too played an important role in the making of this "American web." A major North American chiefdom at Cahokia, near present-day St. Louis, flourished from about 900 to 1250 at the confluence of the Mississippi, Illinois, and Missouri rivers (see Chapter 6, pages 257–58). Cahokia lay at the center of a widespread trading network that brought it shells from the Atlantic coast, copper from the Lake Superior region, buffalo hides from the Great Plains, obsidian from the Rocky Mountains, and mica from the southern Appalachian Mountains. Sturdy dugout canoes plied the rivers of the eastern woodlands, loosely connecting their diverse societies. Early European explorers and travelers along the Amazon and Orinoco rivers of South America reported active networks of exchange that may well have operated for many centuries among densely populated settlements of agricultural peoples. Caribbean peoples using large oceangoing canoes had long conducted an inter-island trade, and the Chincha people of southern coastal Peru undertook a privately organized ocean-based exchange in copper, beads, and shells along the Pacific coasts of Peru and Ecuador in large seagoing rafts. Another regional commercial network, centered in Mesoamerica, extended north to what is now the southwestern United States and south to Ecuador and Colombia. Many items from Mesoamerica—copper bells, macaw feathers, tons of shells—have been found in the Chaco region of New Mexico. Residents of Chaco also drank liquid chocolate, using jars of Maya origin and cacao beans imported from Mesoamerica, where the practice began. Turquoise, mined and worked by the Ancestral Pueblo (see Chapter 6, pages 255–56), flowed in the other direction.

But the most active and dense networks of communication and exchange in the Americas lay within, rather than between, the regions that housed the two great civilizations of the Western Hemisphere—Mesoamerica and the Andes. During the flourishing of Mesoamerican civilization (200–900 C.E.), both the Maya cities in the Yucatán area of Mexico and Guatemala and the huge city-state of Teotihuacán in central Mexico maintained commercial relationships with one another and throughout the region. In addition to this land-based trade, the Maya conducted a seaborne commerce, using large dugout canoes holding forty to fifty people, along both the Atlantic and Pacific coasts.

Although most of this trade was in luxury goods rather than basic necessities, it was critical to upholding the position and privileges of royal and noble families. Items such as cotton clothing, precious jewels, and feathers from particular birds marked the status of elite groups and served to attract followers. Controlling access to such high-prestige goods was an important motive for war among Mesoamerican states. Among the Aztecs of the fifteenth century, professional merchants known as *pochteca* (pohch-TEH-cah) undertook large-scale trading expeditions both within and well beyond the borders of their empire, sometimes as agents for the state or for members of the nobility, but more often acting on their own as private businessmen.

Unlike in the Aztec Empire, in which private traders largely handled the distribution of goods, economic exchange in the Andean Inca Empire during the fifteenth century was a state-run operation, and no merchant group similar to the Aztec pochteca emerged there. Instead, great state storehouses bulged with immense quantities of food, clothing, military supplies, blankets, construction materials, and more, all carefully recorded on *quipus* (knotted cords used to record numerical data) by a highly trained class of accountants. From these state centers, goods were transported as needed by caravans of human porters and llamas across the numerous roads and bridges of the empire. Totaling some 20,000 miles, Inca roads traversed the coastal plain and the high Andes in a north/south direction, while lateral roads linked these diverse environments and extended into the eastern rain forests and

Inca Roads
Used for transporting goods by pack animal or sending messages by foot, the Inca road network included some 2,000 inns where travelers might find food and shelter. Messengers, operating in relay, could cover as many as 150 miles a day. Here contemporary hikers still make use of an old Inca trail road. (William H. Mullins/Science Source)

plains as well. Despite the general absence of private trade, local exchange took place at highland fairs and along the borders of the empire with groups outside the Inca state.

REFLECTIONS

Economic Globalization— Ancient and Modern

The densely connected world of the modern era, linked by ties of commerce and culture around the planet, certainly has roots in much earlier patterns. Particularly in the era of third-wave civilizations from 500 to 1500, the Silk, Sea, and Sand Roads of the Afro-Eurasian world and the looser networks of the American web linked distant peoples both economically and culturally, prompted the emergence of new states, and sustained elite privileges in many ancient civilizations. In those ways, they resembled the globalized world of modern times.

In other respects, though, the networks and webs of the premodern millennium differed sharply from those of more recent centuries. Most people still produced primarily for their own consumption rather than for the market, and a much smaller range of goods was exchanged in the marketplaces of the world. Far fewer people then were required to sell their own labor for wages, an almost universal practice in modern economies. Because of transportation costs and technological limitations, most trade was in luxury goods rather than in necessities. In addition, the circuits of commerce were rather more limited than the truly global patterns of exchange that emerged after 1500.

Furthermore, the world economy of the modern era increasingly had a single center—industrialized Western European countries—which came to dominate much of the world both economically and politically during the nineteenth century. Though never completely equal, the economic relationships of earlier times occurred among much more equivalent units. For example, no one region dominated the complex pattern of Indian Ocean exchange, although India and China generally offered manufactured goods, while Southeast Asia and East Africa mostly contributed agricultural products or raw materials. And with the exception of the brief Mongol control of the Silk Roads and the Inca domination of the Andes for a century, no single power exercised political control over the major networks of world commerce.

Economic relationships among third-wave civilizations, in short, were more balanced and multicentered than those of the modern era. Although massive inequalities occurred within particular regions or societies, interaction among the major civilizations operated on a rather more equal basis than in the globalized world of the past several centuries. With the rise of China, India, Turkey, and Brazil as major players in the world economy of the twenty-first century, are we perhaps witnessing a return to that earlier pattern?

Second Thoughts

What's the Significance?

Silk Roads, 284–91

Black Death, 290–91

Indian Ocean trading network, 291–300

Srivijaya, 295–97

Angkor Wat, 297–99

Swahili civilization, 299–300

Great Zimbabwe, 300

Sand Roads, 301–5

Arabian camel, 302–3

Ghana, Mali, Songhay, 303–4

trans-Saharan slave trade, 304–5

American web, 305–10

Thorfinn Karlsefni, 306–7

pochteca, 309

Big Picture Questions

1. What motivated and sustained the long-distance commerce of the Silk Roads, Sea Roads, and Sand Roads?

2. Why did the peoples of the Eastern Hemisphere develop long-distance trade more extensively than did those of the Western Hemisphere?

3. "Cultural change often derived from commercial exchange in the third-wave era." What evidence from this chapter supports this observation?

4. In what ways was Afro-Eurasia a single interacting zone, and in what respects was it a vast region of separate cultures and civilizations?

5. **Looking Back:** Compared to the cross-cultural interactions of earlier times, what was different about those of the third-wave era?

Next Steps: For Further Study

Jerry Bentley, *Old World Encounters* (1993). A wonderfully succinct and engaging history of cross-cultural interaction all across Afro-Eurasia before 1500.

William J. Bernstein, *A Splendid Exchange* (2008). A global account of "how trade shaped the world."

E. W. Bovill, *The Golden Trade of the Moors* (1970). A classic account of the trans-Saharan trade.

Nayan Chanda, *Bound Together* (2007). Places contemporary globalization in a rich world historical context.

K. N. Chaudhuri, *Trade and Civilization in the Indian Ocean* (1985). A well-regarded study that treats the Indian Ocean basin as a single region linked by both commerce and culture during the third-wave era.

Philip Curtin, *Cross-Cultural Trade in World History* (1984). Explores long-distance trade as a generator of social change on a global level.

Xinru Liu, *The Silk Road in World History* (2010). A brief, accessible, and up-to-date account by a leading scholar.

"The Last Salt Caravan," http://www.youtube.com/watch?v=yNwQeLFk74o. A ten-minute trailer for a documentary showing an early twenty-first-century camel caravan crossing the Sahara, reminiscent of much earlier caravans of the Sand Roads network.

Silk Road Seattle, http://depts.washington.edu/silkroad/. A wonderful Web site about the Silk Road with many artistic images and maps as well as extensive narrative description of that vast network of exchange.

WORKING WITH EVIDENCE

Travelers' Tales and Observations

During the third-wave millennium, as long-distance trade flourished and large transregional empires grew, opportunities increased for individuals to travel far beyond their homelands. Their accounts have provided historians with invaluable information about particular regions and cultures, as well as about interactions among disparate peoples. The authors of these accounts, perhaps inadvertently, also reveal much about themselves and about the perceptions and misperceptions generated by cross-cultural encounters. The selections that follow provide three examples of intrepid long-distance travelers and their impressions of the societies they encountered on their arduous journeys.

Source 7.1
A Chinese Buddhist in India

In 629, Xuanzang (SCHWEN-ZAHNG) (600–664 c.e.), a highly educated Buddhist monk from China, made a long and difficult journey to India through some of the world's most daunting deserts and mountain ranges, returning home in 645 c.e. after sixteen years abroad. His motives, like those of many other Buddhist travelers to India, were essentially religious. "I regretted that the teachings of [Buddhism] were not complete and the scriptures deficient in my own country," he wrote. "I have doubts and have puzzled in my mind, but I could find no one to solve them. That was why I decided to travel to the West."[23] In India, the homeland of Buddhism, he hoped to find the teachers and the sacred texts that would answer his questions, enrich Buddhist practice in China, and resolve the many disputes that had created serious divisions within the Buddhist community of his own country.

During a ten-year stay in India, Xuanzang visited many of the holy sites associated with the Buddha's life and studied with leading Buddhist teachers, particularly those at Nalanda University, a huge monastic complex dedicated to Buddhist scholarship (see Map 7.1, page 285, and the Zooming In feature on Nalanda in Chapter 4, page 162). He traveled widely within India and established a personal relationship with Harsha, the ruler of the state that then encompassed much of northern India. On his return journey to China, he carried hundreds of manuscripts, at least seven statues of the Buddha, and even some relics. Warmly greeted by the Chinese emperor, Xuanzang spent the last two decades of his life translating the texts he had collected into Chinese. He also wrote an account of his travels, known as the *Record of the Western Regions*, and shared his recollections with a fellow monk and translator named Huili, who subsequently wrote a biography of Xuanzang. The selections that follow derive from these two accounts and convey something of Xuanzang's impressions of Indian civilization in the seventh century C.E.

■ What surprised or impressed Xuanzang on his visit to India? What features of Indian life might seem most strange to a Chinese visitor?

■ How might these selections serve to illustrate or to contradict the descriptions of Indian civilization found in Chapters 3–5?

■ What can this document contribute to our understanding of Buddhist practice in India?

HUILI

A Biography of the Tripitaka Master

Seventh Century C.E.

[*Certainly the emotional highlight of Xuanzang's travels in India was his visit to the site of the Buddha's enlightenment under the famous Bodhi tree. The great traveler's biographer, Huili, recorded his Master's response.*]

Upon his arrival there, the Master worshipped the Bodhi tree and the image of the Buddha attaining enlightenment made by Maitreya Bodhisattva. After having looked at the image with deep sincerity, he prostrated himself before it and deplored sadly, saying with self-reproach, "I do not know where I was born in the course of transmigration at the time when the Buddha attained enlightenment. I could only come here at this time. . . . It makes me think that my karmic hindrances must have been very heavy!" While he was saying so, his eyes brimmed with sorrowful tears. As that was the time when the monks dismissed the summer retreat, several thousand people forgathered from far and near. Those who saw the Master were choked by sobs in sympathy with him.

Source: Li Rongxi, trans., *A Biography of the Tripitaka Master of the Great Ci'en Monastery of the Great Tang Dynasty* (Berkeley, CA: Numata Center for Buddhist Translation, 1995), 89–90.

XUANZANG

Record of the Western Region

Seventh Century C.E.

[*Selections from Xuanzang's more general description of Indian civilization follow here, drawn from his own account.*]

On Towns and Villages

The towns and villages have inner gates; the walls are wide and high; the streets and lanes are tortuous, and the roads winding. The thoroughfares are dirty and the stalls arranged on both sides of the road with appropriate signs. Butchers, fishers, dancers, executioners, and scavengers, and so on [untouchables], have their abodes without [outside] the city. In coming and going these persons are bound to keep on the left side of the road till they arrive at their homes. Their houses are surrounded by low walls and form the suburbs. The earth being soft and muddy, the walls of the towns are mostly built of brick or tiles. . . .

On Buddhist Studies

The different schools are constantly at variance, and their contending utterances rise like the angry waves of the sea. The different sects have their separate masters. . . . There are eighteen schools, each claiming pre-eminence. The partisans of the Great and Little Vehicle are content to dwell apart. There are some who give themselves up to quiet contemplation, and devote themselves, whether walking or standing still or sitting down, to the acquirement of wisdom and insight; others, on the contrary, differ from these in raising noisy contentions about their faith. According to their fraternity, they are governed by distinctive rules and regulations. . . .

The *Vinaya* discourses [rules governing monastic life] are equally Buddhist books. He who can entirely explain one class of these books is exempted from the control of the *karmadâna* [a high monastic official]. If he can explain two classes, he receives in addition the equipments of an upper seat (*room*); he who can explain three classes has allotted to him different servants to attend to and obey him; he who can explain four classes has "pure men" allotted to him as attendants; he who can explain five classes of books is then allowed an elephant carriage; he who can explain six classes of books is allowed a surrounding escort. When a man's renown has reached to a high distinction, then at different times he convokes an assembly for discussion. He judges of the superior or inferior talent of those who take part in it; he distinguishes their good or bad points; he praises the clever and reproves the faulty; if one of the assembly distinguishes himself by refined language, subtle investigation, deep pen-

etration, and severe logic, then he is mounted on an elephant covered with precious ornaments, and conducted by a numerous suite to the gates of the convent.

If, on the contrary, one of the members breaks down in his argument, or uses poor and inelegant phrases, or if he violates a rule in logic and adapts his words accordingly, they proceed to disfigure his face with red and white, and cover his body with dirt and dust, and then carry him off to some deserted spot or leave him in a ditch. Thus they distinguish between the meritorious and the worthless, between the wise and the foolish.

On Caste and Marriage

With respect to the division of families, there are four classifications. The first is called the Brâhman, men of pure conduct. They guard themselves in religion, live purely, and observe the most correct principles. The second is called Kshattriya, the royal caste. For ages they have been the governing class: they apply themselves to virtue and kindness. The third is called Vaiśyas, the merchant class: they engage in commercial exchange, and they follow profit at home and abroad. The fourth is called Sûdra, the agricultural class: they labor in plowing and tillage. In these four classes purity or impurity of caste assigns to every one his place. When they marry they rise or fall in position according to their new relationship. They do not allow promiscuous marriages between relations. A woman once married can never take another husband. Besides these there are other classes of many kinds that intermarry according to their several callings.

On Manners and Justice

With respect to the ordinary people, although they are naturally light-minded, yet they are upright and honorable. In money matters they are without craft, and in administering justice they are considerate. They dread the retribution of another state of existence, and make light of the things of the present world. They are not deceitful or treacherous in their conduct, and are faithful to their oaths and promises. In their rules of government there is remarkable rectitude, whilst in their behavior there is much gentleness and sweetness. With respect to criminals or rebels, these are few in number, and only occasionally troublesome. When the laws are broken or the power of the ruler violated, then the matter is clearly sifted and the offenders imprisoned. There is no infliction of corporal punishment; they are simply left to live or die, and are not counted among men. When the rules of propriety or justice are violated, or when a man fails in fidelity or filial piety, then they cut his nose or his ears off, or his hands and feet, or expel him from the country or drive him out into the desert wilds. For other faults, except these, a small payment of money will redeem the punishment. In the investigation of criminal cases there is no use of rod or staff to obtain proofs (*of guilt*).

Source: Samuel Beal, trans., *Su-Yu-Ki: Buddhist Records of the Western World* (London: K. Paul, Trench, Trubner, 1906), vol. 1, bk. 2, 73–74, 77, 79–84.

Source 7.2
A European Christian in China

Of all the travelers along the Silk Road network, the best known and most celebrated, at least in the West, was Marco Polo (1254–1324). Born and raised in the prosperous commercial city-state of Venice in northern Italy, Marco Polo was a member of a family prominent in the long-distance trade of the Mediterranean and Black sea regions. At the age of seventeen, Marco accompanied his father and an uncle on an immense journey across Eurasia that, by 1275, brought the Polos to China, recently conquered by the Mongols. It was, in fact, the relative peace that the Mongols had created in their huge transcontinental empire that facilitated the Polos' journey (see Map 11.1, page 466). For the next seventeen years, they lived in China, where they were employed in minor administrative positions by Khubilai Khan, the country's Mongol ruler. During these years, Marco Polo apparently traveled widely within China, where he gathered material for the book about his travels, which he dictated to a friend after returning home in 1295.

Marco Polo's journey and the book that described it, generally known as *The Travels of Marco Polo*, were important elements of the larger process by which an emerging West European civilization reached out to and became aware of the older civilizations of the East. Christopher Columbus carried a marked-up copy of the book on his transatlantic journeys, believing that he was seeking by sea the places Marco Polo had visited by land. Some modern scholars are skeptical about parts of Marco Polo's report, and a few even question whether he ever got to China at all, largely because he omitted any mention of certain prominent features of Chinese life, for example, foot binding, the Great Wall, and tea drinking. Most historians, however, accept the basic outlines of Marco Polo's account, even as they notice exaggerations as well as an inflated perception of his own role within China. The selection that follows conveys Marco Polo's description of the city of Hangzhou, which he referred to as Kinsay. At the time of Marco Polo's visit, it was among the largest cities in the world.

- How would you describe Marco Polo's impressions of the city? What did he notice? What surprised him?

- Why did Marco Polo describe the city as "the finest and the noblest in the world"?

- What marks his account of the city as that of a foreigner and a Christian?

- What evidence of China's engagement with a wider world does this account offer?

MARCO POLO

The Travels of Marco Polo
1299

The city is beyond dispute the finest and the noblest in the world. In this we shall speak according to the written statement which the Queen of this Realm sent to Bayan, the [Mongol] conqueror of the country for transmission to the Great Kaan, in order that he might be aware of the surpassing grandeur of the city and might be moved to save it from destruction or injury. I will tell you all the truth as it was set down in that document. For truth it was, as the said Messer Marco Polo at a later date was able to witness with his own eyes. . . .

First and foremost, then, the document stated the city of Kinsay to be so great that it hath an hundred miles of compass. And there are in it 12,000 bridges of stone. . . . [Most scholars consider these figures a considerable exaggeration.] And though the bridges be so high, the approaches are so well contrived that carts and horses do cross them.

The document aforesaid also went on to state that there were in this city twelve guilds of the different crafts, and that each guild had 12,000 houses in the occupation of its workmen. Each of these houses contains at least twelve men, whilst some contain twenty and some forty. . . . And yet all these craftsmen had full occupation, for many other cities of the kingdom are supplied from this city with what they require.

The document aforesaid also stated that the number and wealth of the merchants, and the amount of goods that passed through their hands, were so enormous that no man could form a just estimate thereof. And I should have told you with regard to those masters of the different crafts who are at the head of such houses as I have mentioned, that neither they nor their wives ever touch a piece of work with their own hands, but live as nicely and delicately as if they were kings and queens. The wives indeed are most dainty and angelical creatures! Moreover it was an ordinance laid down by the King that every man should follow his father's business and no other, no matter if he possessed 100,000 bezants [a Byzantine gold coin].

Inside the city there is a Lake . . . and all round it are erected beautiful palaces and mansions, of the richest and most exquisite structure that you can imagine, belonging to the nobles of the city. There are also on its shores many abbeys and churches of the Idolaters [Buddhists]. In the middle of the Lake are two Islands, on each of which stands a rich, beautiful, and spacious edifice, furnished in such style as to seem fit for the palace of an Emperor. And when any one of the citizens desired to hold a marriage feast, or to give any other entertainment, it used to be done at one of these palaces.

And everything would be found there ready to order, such as silver plate, trenchers, and dishes, napkins and table-cloths, and whatever else was needful. . . . Sometimes there would be at these palaces an hundred different parties; some holding a banquet, others celebrating a wedding . . . in so well-ordered a manner that one party was never in the way of another. . . .

Both men and women are fair and comely, and for the most part clothe themselves in silk, so vast is the supply of that material, both from the whole district of Kinsay, and from the imports by traders from other provinces. And you must know they eat every kind of flesh, even that of dogs and other unclean beasts, which nothing would induce a Christian to eat. . . .

You must know also that the city of Kinsay has some 3,000 baths, the water of which is supplied by springs. They are hot baths, and the people take great delight in them, frequenting them several times a month, for they are very cleanly in their persons. They are the finest and largest baths in the world. . . .

And the Ocean Sea comes within twenty-five miles of the city at a place called Ganfu, where there is a town and an excellent haven, with a vast amount of shipping which is engaged in the traffic to and from India and other foreign parts, export-ing and importing many kinds of wares, by which the city benefits. . . .

I repeat that everything appertaining to this city is on so vast a scale, and the Great Kaan's yearly revenues therefrom are so immense, that it is not easy even to put it in writing. . . .

In this part are the ten principal markets, though besides these there are a vast number of others in the different parts of the town. . . . [T]oward the [market] squares are built great houses of stone, in which the merchants from India and other foreign parts store their wares, to be handy for the markets. In each of the squares is held a market three days in the week, frequented by 40,000 or 50,000 persons, who bring thither for sale every possible necessary of life, so that there is always an ample supply of every kind of meat and game. . . .

Those markets make a daily display of every kind of vegetables and fruits. . . . [V]ery good raisins are brought from abroad, and wine likewise. . . . From the Ocean Sea also come daily supplies of fish in great quantity, brought twenty-five miles up the river. . . . All the ten market places are encompassed by lofty houses, and below these are shops where all sorts of crafts are carried on, and all sorts of wares are on sale, including spices and jewels and pearls. Some of these shops are entirely devoted to the sale of wine made from rice and spices, which is constantly made fresh, and is sold very cheap. Certain of the streets are occupied by the women of the town, who are in such a number that I dare not say what it is. They are found not only in the vicinity of the market places, where usually a quar-ter is assigned to them, but all over the city. They exhibit themselves splendidly attired and abundantly perfumed, in finely garnished houses, with trains of waiting-women. These women are extremely accomplished in all the arts of allurement, and read-ily adapt their conversation to all sorts of persons, insomuch that strangers who have once tasted their attractions seem to get bewitched, and are so taken with their blandishments and their fascinating ways that they never can get these out of their heads. . . .

Other streets are occupied by the Physicians, and by the Astrologers, who are also teachers of reading and writing; and an infinity of other pro-fessions have their places round about those squares. In each of the squares there are two great palaces facing one another, in which are established the officers appointed by the King to decide differ-ences arising between merchants, or other inhabi-tants of the quarter. . . .

The crowd of people that you meet here at all hours . . . is so vast that no one would believe it possible that victuals enough could be provided for their consumption, unless they should see how, on every market-day, all those squares are thronged and crammed with purchasers, and with the traders who have brought in stores of provisions by land or water; and everything they bring in is disposed of. . . .

The natives of the city are men of peaceful character, both from education and from the example of their kings, whose disposition was the same. They know nothing of handling arms, and keep none in their houses. You hear of no feuds or noisy quarrels or dissensions of any kind among them. Both in their commercial dealings and in their manufactures they are thoroughly honest and truthful, and there is such a degree of good will and neighborly attachment among both men and women that you would take the people who live in the same street to be all one family.

And this familiar intimacy is free from all jealousy or suspicion of the conduct of their women. These they treat with the greatest respect, and a man who should presume to make loose proposals to a married woman would be regarded as an infamous rascal. They also treat the foreigners who visit them for the sake of trade with great cordiality and entertain them in the most winning manner, affording them every help and advice on their business. But on the other hand they hate to see soldiers, and not least those of the Great Kaan's garrisons, regarding them as the cause of their having lost their native kings and lords.

Source: *The Book of Sir Marco Polo the Venetian Concerning the Kingdoms and Marvels of the East*, 3rd ed., translated and edited by Henry Yule, revised by Henri Cordier (London: John Murray, 1903), 2:185–206.

Source 7.3
A Moroccan Diplomat in West Africa

Known to the world by his European-derived nickname of Leo Africanus, this widely traveled Arabic-speaking Muslim of Berber background was actually born as al-Hassan Ibn Muhammad al Wazzan in Granada, Spain, during the late fifteenth century, just as Islam was being pushed out of that country. His family moved to Fez in Morocco, where he was educated in Islamic law. Later, he served the sultan of Morocco as a diplomat and commercial agent, traveling widely in North Africa, the Middle East, Italy, and West Africa. On one of these journeys, he was captured by pirates, winding up in Rome, where he came to the attention of Pope Leo X. There he was apparently converted to Christianity, at least for a time, though he later chose to live in Muslim North Africa and likely returned to his original Muslim faith. It was during his stay in Italy that he completed in 1526 the book for which he is most clearly remembered, *The History and Description of Africa*, based on observations and knowledge picked up during his travels. Later published in many languages, it became a major source of European knowledge of the African Islamic world, much as Marco Polo's writings introduced Europeans to China. In the following excerpts from that book, Leo Africanus describes several of the major kingdoms and cities of West African civilization.

■ Based on these accounts, how does Leo Africanus characterize West African civilization? What can you infer about his own attitude toward this civilization?

■ What connections between West Africa and a wider world are evident in these passages?

■ What can you learn about the role of slavery in West Africa at a time before the Atlantic slave trade had become big business?

■ Why do you think these passages say so little about the practice of Islam, focusing instead on political and economic matters? (Keep in mind that the book was first published in Italy and in Italian.) Despite this omission, what can you infer about variations in Islamic observance in West African civilization at this time?

LEO AFRICANUS

The History and Description of Africa
1526

The Kingdom of Mali

In this kingdom there is a large and ample village containing more than six thousand families, and named Mali, which is also the name of the whole kingdom. Here the king has his residence. The region itself yields great abundance of wheat, meat, and cotton. Here are many craftsmen and merchants in all places: and yet the king honorably entertains all strangers. The inhabitants are rich and have plenty of merchandise. Here is a great number of temples [mosques], clergymen, and teachers, who read their lectures in the mosques because they have no colleges at all. The people of the region excel all other Negroes in wit, civility, and industry, and were the first that embraced the law of Muhammad. . . .

The City of Timbuktu

All its houses are . . . cottages, built of mud and covered with thatch. However, there is a most stately mosque to be seen, whose walls are made of stone and lime, and a princely palace also constructed by the highly skilled craftsmen of Granada. Here there are many shops of artisans and merchants, especially of those who weave linen and cotton, and here Barbary [Muslim North African] merchants bring European cloth. The inhabitants, and especially resident aliens, are exceedingly rich, since the present king married both of his daughters to rich merchants. Here are many wells, containing sweet water. Whenever the Niger River overflows, they carry the water into town by means of sluices. This region yields great quantities of grain, cattle, milk, and butter, but salt is very scarce here, for it is brought here by land from Tegaza, which is five hundred miles away. When I was there, I saw one camel-load of salt sold for eighty ducats.

The rich king of Timbuktu has many plates and scepters of gold, some of which weigh 1,300 pounds, and he keeps a magnificent and well-furnished court. When he travels anywhere, he rides upon a camel, which is led by some of his noblemen. He does so likewise when going to war, and all his soldiers ride upon horses. Whoever wishes to speak to this king must first of all fall down before his feet and then taking up earth must sprinkle it on his own head and shoulders. . . . [The king] always has under arms 3,000 horsemen and a great number of foot soldiers who shoot poisoned arrows. They often skirmish with those who refuse to pay tribute and whomever they capture they sell to the merchants of Timbuktu. Here very few horses are bred. . . . Their best horses are brought out of North Africa. As soon as the king learns that any merchants have come to the town with horses, he commands that a certain number be brought before him. Choosing the best horse for himself, he pays a most liberal price for it. . . .

Here are great numbers of [Islamic] religious teachers, judges, scholars and other learned persons, who are bountifully maintained at the king's expense. Here too are brought various [Arabic] manuscripts or written books from Barbary, which are sold for more money than any other merchandise.

The coin of Timbuktu is gold, without any stamp or inscription, but in matters of small value they use certain shells from the kingdom of Persia. Four hundred of these are worth a ducat, and six pieces of Timbuktu's golden coin weigh two-thirds of an ounce.

The inhabitants are gentle and cheerful and spend a great part of the night in singing and dancing throughout the city streets. They keep large numbers of male and female slaves, and their town is greatly vulnerable to fire. At the time of my second visit, almost half the town burned down in the space of five hours.

The Town and Kingdom of Gao

Here are very rich merchants and to here journey continually large numbers of Negroes who purchase here cloth from Barbary and Europe. The town abounds in grain and meat but lacks wine, trees, and fruits. However, there are plenty of melons, lemons and rice. Here there are many wells, which also contain very sweet and wholesome water. Here also is a certain place where slaves are sold, especially upon those days when merchants assemble. A young slave of fifteen years of age is sold for six ducats, and children are also sold.

The king of this region has a certain private palace in which he keeps a large number of concubines and slaves, who are watched by eunuchs. To guard his person he maintains a sufficient troop of horsemen and foot soldiers. Between the first gate of the palace and the inner part, there is a walled enclosure wherein the king personally decides all of his subjects' controversies. Although the king is most diligent in this regard and conducts all business in these matters, he has in his company counsellors and such other officers as his secretaries, treasurers, stewards, and auditors.

It is a wonder to see the quality of merchandise that is daily brought here and how costly and sumptuous everything is. Horses purchased in Europe for ten ducats are sold here for forty and sometimes fifty ducats apiece. There is not European cloth so coarse as to sell for less than four ducats an ell [unit of measure]. If it is anywhere near fine quality, they will give fifteen ducats for an ell, and an ell of the scarlet of Venice or of Turkish cloth is here worth thirty ducats. A sword is here valued at three or four crowns, and likewise are spears, bridles, and similar commodities, and spices are all sold at a high rate. However, of all other items, salt is the most expensive.

The rest of this kingdom contains nothing but villages and hamlets inhabited by herdsmen and shepherds, who in winter cover their bodies with the skins of animals, but in summer they go naked, save for their private parts. . . . They are an ignorant and rude people, and you will scarcely find one learned person in the square of a hundred miles. They are continually burdened by heavy taxes; to the point that they scarcely have anything left on which to live.

The Kingdom of Borno

They embrace no religion at all, being neither Christian, Muhametans [Muslims], nor Jews, nor any other profession, but living after a brutish manner, having wives and children in common. . . . They have a most powerful prince. . . . He has in readiness as many as three thousand horsemen and a huge number of foot soldiers; for all his subjects are so serviceable and obedient to him, that whenever he commands them, they will arm themselves and will follow him wherever he leads them. They pay him no tribute except tithes on their grain; neither does the king have any revenues to support his state except the spoils he gets from his enemies by frequent invasions and assaults. He is in a state of perpetual hostility with a certain people who live beyond the desert of Seu, who in times past marching with a huge army of footsoldiers over the said desert, devastated a great part of the Kingdom of Borno. Whereupon the king sent for the merchants of Barbary and ordered them to bring him a great store of horses: for in this country they exchange horses for slaves, and sometimes give fifteen or twenty slaves for a horse. And by this means there were a great many horses bought although the merchants were forced to stay for their slaves until the king returned home as a conqueror with a great number of captives, and satisfied his creditors for his horses. Frequently it happens that the merchants must stay three months before the king returned from the wars. . . . Sometimes he does not bring home enough slaves to satisfy the merchants and sometimes they are forced to wait a whole year. . . . And yet the king seems marvelously rich, because his spurs, bridles, platters, dishes, pots, and other vessels are made of gold. The king is extremely covetous and would rather pay his debts in slaves rather than gold.

Source: Leo Africanus, *The History and Description of Africa*, edited by Robert Brown (London: The Hakluyt Society, 1896), 3:823–27, 832–34.

DOING HISTORY

Travelers' Tales and Observations

1. **Describing a foreign culture:** Each of these documents was written by an outsider to the people or society he is describing. What different postures toward these foreign cultures are evident in the sources? How did the travelers' various religions shape their perception of places they visited? How did they view the women of their host societies? Were these travelers more impressed by the similarities or by the differences between their home cultures and the ones they visited?

2. **Defining the self-perception of authors:** What can we learn from these documents about the men who wrote them? What motivated them to travel so far from home? How did they define themselves in relationship to the societies they observed?

3. **Assessing the credibility of sources:** What information in these sources would be most valuable for historians seeking to understand India, China, and West Africa in the third-wave era? What statements in these sources might be viewed with the most skepticism? You will want to consider the authors' purposes and their intended audiences in evaluating their writings.

4. **Considering outsiders' accounts:** What are the advantages and limitations for historians in drawing on the writings of foreign observers?

CHAPTER 8

China and the World

East Asian Connections
500–1300

"China will be the next superpower."[1] That was the frank assertion of an article in the British newspaper the *Guardian* in June 2006. Nor was it alone in that assessment. As the new millennium dawned, headlines with this message appeared with increasing frequency in public lectures, in newspaper and magazine articles, and in book titles all across the world. China's huge population, its booming economy, its massive trade surplus with the United States, its entry into world oil markets, its military potential, and its growing presence in global political affairs—all of this suggested that China was headed for a major role, perhaps even a dominant role, in the world of the twenty-first century. Few of these authors, however, paused to recall that China's prominence on the world stage was hardly something new or that its nineteenth- and twentieth-century position as a "backward," weak, or dependent country was distinctly at odds with its long history. Is China perhaps poised to resume in the twenty-first century a much older and more powerful role in world affairs?

I n the world of third-wave civilizations, even more than in earlier times, China cast a long shadow. Its massive and powerful civilization, widely imitated by adjacent peoples, gave rise to a China-centered set of relationships encompassing most of eastern Asia. China extended its borders deep into Central Asia, while its wealthy and cosmopolitan culture attracted visitors from all over Eurasia. None of its many neighbors—whether nomadic peoples to the north and west or smaller peripheral states such as Tibet, Korea, Japan, and Vietnam—could escape its gravitational pull. All of them

---

Chinese Astronomy   The impressive achievements of Chinese astronomy included the observation of sunspots, supernovae, and solar and lunar eclipses as well as the construction of elaborate star maps and astronomical devices such as those shown here. The print itself is of Japanese origin and depicts a figure wearing the dragon robes of a Chinese official. It illustrates the immense cultural influence of China on its smaller Japanese neighbor.

had to deal with China. Far beyond these near neighbors, China's booming economy and many technological innovations had ripple effects all across the Afro-Eurasia world.

Even as China so often influenced the world, it too was changed by its many interactions with non-Chinese peoples. Northern nomads—"barbarians" to the Chinese—frequently posed a military threat and on occasion even conquered and ruled parts of China. The country's growing involvement in international trade stimulated important social, cultural, and economic changes within China itself. Buddhism, a religion of Indian origin, took root in China, and, to a much lesser extent, so did Christianity and Islam. In short, China's engagement with the wider world became a very significant element in a global era of accelerating connections.

SEEKING THE MAIN POINT

Chinese history has often been viewed in the West as impressive perhaps, but largely static or changeless and self-contained or isolated. In what ways might the material in this chapter counteract such impressions?

Together Again: The Reemergence of a Unified China

The collapse of the Han dynasty around 220 C.E. ushered in more than three centuries of political fragmentation in China and signaled the rise of powerful and locally entrenched aristocratic families. It also meant the incursion of northern nomads, many of whom learned Chinese, dressed like Chinese, married into Chinese families, and governed northern regions of the country in a Chinese fashion. Such conditions of disunity, unnatural in the eyes of many thoughtful Chinese, discredited Confucianism and opened the door to a greater acceptance of Buddhism and Daoism among the elite. (See Zooming In: Ge Hong in Chapter 5, page 196.)

Those centuries also witnessed substantial Chinese migration southward toward the Yangzi River valley, a movement of people that gave southern China some 60 percent of the country's population by 1000. That movement of Chinese people, accompanied by their intensive agriculture, set in motion a vast environmental transformation, marked by the destruction of the old-growth forests that once covered much of the country and the retreat of the elephants that had inhabited those lands. Around 800 C.E., the Chinese official and writer Liu Zongyuan lamented what was happening:

A tumbled confusion of lumber as flames on the hillside crackle
Not even the last remaining shrubs are safeguarded from destruction
Where once mountain torrents leapt—nothing but rutted gullies.[2]

A "Golden Age" of Chinese Achievement

Unlike the fall of the western Roman Empire, where political fragmentation proved to be a permanent condition, China regained its unity under the Sui dynasty (589–618). Its emperors solidified that unity by a vast extension of the country's canal system, stretching some 1,200 miles in length and described by one scholar as

A MAP OF TIME

39 C.E.	Trung sisters' rebellion against China in Vietnam
4th–7th centuries	Early state building in Korea
300–800	Buddhism takes root in China
589–618	Sui dynasty and the reunification of China
604	Seventeen Article Constitution in Japan
618–907	Tang dynasty in China
688	Withdrawal of Chinese military forces from Korea
794–1192	Heian period in Japanese history
845	Suppression of Buddhism in China
868	First printed book in China
939	Vietnam establishes independence from China
960–1279	Song dynasty in China
ca. 1000	Invention of gunpowder in China; beginning of foot binding
1000	*The Tale of Genji* (Japan)
1279–1369	Mongol rule in China

"an engineering feat without parallel in the world of its time."[3] Those canals linked northern and southern China economically and contributed much to the prosperity that followed. But the ruthlessness of Sui emperors and a futile military campaign to conquer Korea exhausted the state's resources, alienated many people, and prompted the overthrow of the dynasty.

This dynastic collapse, however, witnessed no prolonged disintegration of the Chinese state. The two dynasties that followed—the Tang (618–907) and the Song (960–1279)—built on the Sui foundations of renewed unity (see Map 8.1). Together they established patterns of Chinese life that endured into the twentieth century, despite a fifty-year period of disunity between the two dynasties. Culturally, this era has long been regarded as a "golden age" of arts and literature, setting standards of excellence in poetry, landscape painting, and ceramics. (See Working with Evidence: The Leisure Life of China's Elites, page 356.) Particularly during the Song dynasty, an explosion of scholarship gave rise to Neo-Confucianism, an effort to revive Confucian thinking while incorporating into it some of the insights of Buddhism and Daoism.

Politically, the Tang and Song dynasties built a state structure that endured for a thousand years. Six major ministries—personnel, finance, rites, army, justice, and public works—were accompanied by the Censorate, an agency that exercised

■ **Change**
Why are the centuries of the Tang and Song dynasties in China sometimes referred to as a "golden age"?

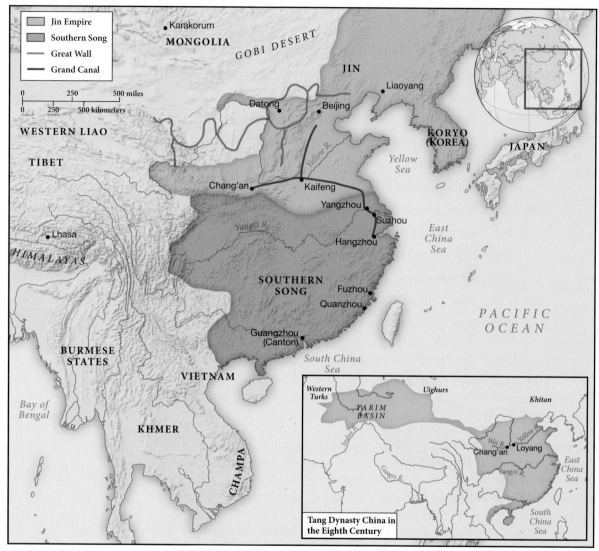

Map 8.1   Tang and Song Dynasty China

During the third-wave millennium, China interacted extensively with its neighbors. The Tang dynasty extended Chinese control deep into Central Asia, while the Song dynasty witnessed incursions by the nomadic Jurchen people, who created the Jin Empire, which ruled parts of northern China.

surveillance over the rest of the government, checking on the character and competence of public officials. To staff this bureaucracy, the examination system was revived and made more elaborate, facilitated by the ability to print books for the first time in world history. Efforts to prevent cheating on the exams included searching candidates entering the examination hall and placing numbers rather than names on their papers. Schools and colleges proliferated to prepare candidates for the rigorous exams, which became a central feature of upper-class life. A leading world historian has described Tang dynasty China as "the best ordered state in the world."[4]

Selecting officials on the basis of merit represented a challenge to established aristocratic families' hold on public office. Still, a substantial percentage of official positions went to the sons of the privileged, even if they had not passed the exams. Moreover, because education and the examination system grew far more rapidly than the number of official positions, many who passed lower-level exams could not be accommodated with a bureaucratic appointment. Often, however, they were able to combine landowning and success in the examination system to maintain an immense cultural prestige and prominence in their local areas. Despite the state's periodic efforts to redistribute land in favor of the peasantry, the great families of large landowners continued to encroach on peasant plots, a recurring pattern in rural China from ancient times to the present.

Underlying these cultural and political achievements was an "economic revolution" that made Song dynasty China "by far the richest, most skilled, and most populous country on earth."[5] The most obvious sign of China's prosperity was its rapid growth in population, which jumped from about 50 million or 60 million during the Tang dynasty to 120 million by 1200. Behind this doubling of the population were remarkable achievements in agricultural production, particularly the adoption of a fast-ripening and drought-resistant strain of rice from Vietnam.

Many people found their way to the cities, making China the most urbanized country in the world. Dozens of Chinese cities numbered over 100,000, while the Song dynasty capital of Hangzhou was home to more than a million people. A Chinese observer in 1235 provided a vivid description of that city.[6] Specialized markets abounded for meat, herbs, vegetables, books, rice, and much more, with troupes of actors performing for the crowds. Restaurants advertised their unique offerings — sweet bean soup, pickled dates, juicy lungs, meat pies, pigs' feet — and some offered vegetarian fare for religious banquets. Inns of various kinds appealed to different groups. Those that served only wine, a practice known as "hitting the cup," were regarded as "unfit for polite company." "Luxuriant inns," marked by red lanterns, featured prostitutes and "wine chambers equipped with beds." Specialized agencies managed elaborate dinner parties for the wealthy, complete with a Perfume and Medicine Office to "help sober up the guests." Schools for musicians offered thirteen different courses. Numerous clubs provided companionship for poets, fishermen, Buddhists, physical fitness enthusiasts, antiques collectors, horse lovers, and many other groups. No wonder the Italian visitor Marco Polo described Hangzhou later in the thirteenth century as "beyond dispute the finest and noblest [city] in the world."[7] (See Working with Evidence, Source 7.2, page 315, for a fuller description of Marco Polo's impressions of Hangzhou.)

Gunpowder

The Chinese Tang and Song dynasties (618–1279) witnessed a golden age of technological innovation in China. Both woodblock and movable type generated the world's first printed books, while Chinese innovations in navigational and shipbuilding technologies led the world. Among these many developments, the invention of gunpowder stands out because it spawned a permanent revolution in military affairs that had global dimensions. But gunpowder, a mixture of saltpeter, sulfur, and charcoal, was not originally developed for use in war. Instead, it was an accidental byproduct of the search by Daoist alchemists for an elixir of immortality. Indeed, the first reference to gunpowder appeared in a mid-ninth-century Daoist text that warns alchemists not to mix together its component parts because "smoke and flames result, so that [the alchemists'] hands and faces have been burnt, and even the whole house where they were working burned down."⁸ This association with alchemy may explain why the Chinese referred to gunpowder as *huo yao*, or "fire drug." The same properties that made gunpowder so dangerous in an alchemist's lab attracted the interest of those

A twelfth-century Chinese Buddhist carving showing an early handheld gun.

seeking to entertain and amaze audiences through fireworks and pyrotechnic displays, especially at the Chinese imperial court.

Military authorities also noticed its potential as a weapon, and its uses in war developed rapidly during the Song dynasty. At first, military engineers drew on the incendiary rather than the explosive possibilities of gunpowder. In 1044, an imperial official wrote a tract for the emperor on military technologies that included two recipes for gunpowder, both for weapons designed to set fire to their targets. Decades later, Song engineers borrowed techniques from fireworks makers to produce "Thunderclap Bombs" designed to scare and disorient opposing troops through noise and light. While these bombs were not yet powerful enough to kill large numbers of the enemy, a chronicler of a siege of the Song capital in 1127 described them as "hitting the lines of the enemy well and throwing them into great confusion."

Through the twelfth and early thirteenth centuries, both the Song dynasty, which controlled southern

photo: Cave number 149, Pei Shan complex, Temples at Ta-tsu, Szechuan, China/Ancient Art & Architecture Collection, Ltd.

Supplying these cities with food was made possible by an immense network of internal waterways—canals, rivers, and lakes—stretching perhaps 30,000 miles. They provided a cheap transportation system that bound the country together economically and created the "world's most populous trading area."⁹

Industrial production likewise soared. In both large-scale enterprises employing hundreds of workers and in smaller backyard furnaces, China's iron industry increased its output dramatically. By the eleventh century, it was providing the government with 32,000 suits of armor and 16 million iron arrowheads annually, in addition to supplying metal for coins, tools, construction, and bells in Buddhist

China, and the Jin, which controlled much of the north, continued to develop ever more powerful gunpowder weapons. Engineers experimented with gunpowder blends that included larger quantities of saltpeter, the nitrate-rich substance that gives gunpowder its explosiveness. When the Mongols invaded northern China in 1231, the defenders of the capital, Kaifeng, were able to deploy what they called the "Heaven-Shaking Thunder Crash Bomb" against Mongol forces. An eyewitness recorded that "the attacking soldiers were blown to bits, not even a trace being left behind."

The Mongols recognized the effectiveness of gunpowder and, following their conquest of China, encouraged engineers to continue to develop new weapons. During the thirteenth and fourteenth centuries, powerful bombs were produced with such names as "Match for Ten Thousand Enemies Bomb" and the "Bone-Burning and Bruising Fire Oil Magic Bomb." At the same time, Chinese technicians developed the first rockets, which were employed in battle from the middle of the thirteenth century. These experiments with more powerful forms of gunpowder culminated in the emergence of weapons designed to fire projectiles. The first of these evolved from earlier fire lances, bamboo or metal tubes filled with gunpowder that spewed flames and sparks. However, unlike the fire lance, which used the incendiary properties of gunpowder to attack the enemy, these new guns used its explosive power as a propellant to fire projectiles. Cannons were in common use in China by the 1350s. But the first evidence of a handheld gun comes from a carving, dating from the 1120s and located, strangely enough, in a Buddhist cave featuring Kuan-yin, "the one who answers every prayer." A prayer inscribed in that cave asks "that weapons of war be forever stilled."

Gunpowder and gunpowder-based weapons spread rapidly across Eurasia from the thirteenth century, changing the nature of warfare wherever they were adopted. While there is some debate as to exactly when gunpowder arrived in India, the Middle East, and Europe, it is clear that the Mongols' use of gunpowder weapons in their conquests spurred its spread and use. Its rapid adoption ensured that by the sixteenth century the "fire drug" developed by Daoist alchemists in search of immortality had sparked what scholars have labeled the gunpowder revolution in warfare, transforming military conflict across the globe. Gunpowder remained the dominant explosive used in war until the advent of nitroglycerin in the mid-nineteenth century.

It is more than a little ironic that a substance originally derived from a search for happiness and immortality would result in unimaginable human suffering and an untold number of deaths. Such are the unintended outcomes of human effort.

Question: What can the development of gunpowder-based weapons tell us about technological innovation in China?

monasteries. This industrial growth was fueled almost entirely by coal, which also came to provide most of the energy for heating homes and cooking. This no doubt generated considerable air pollution. Technological innovation in other fields also flourished. Inventions in printing, both woodblock and movable type, generated the world's first printed books, and by 1000 relatively cheap books on religious, agricultural, mathematical, and medical topics became widely available in China. Its navigational and shipbuilding technologies led the world. The Chinese invention of gunpowder created within a few centuries a revolution in military affairs that had global dimensions. (See Zooming In: Gunpowder, above.) But China's remarkable

Kaifeng
This detail comes from a huge watercolor scroll, titled *Upper River during Qing Ming Festival*, originally painted during the Song dynasty. It illustrates the urban sophistication of Kaifeng and other Chinese cities at that time and has been frequently imitated and copied since then. (View Stock RF/age fotostock)

industrial revolution stalled as the country was repeatedly invaded and devastated by nomadic peoples from the north, culminating in the Mongol conquests of the thirteenth century.

Most remarkably, perhaps, all of this occurred within the world's most highly commercialized society, in which producing for the market, rather than for local consumption, became a very widespread phenomenon. Cheap transportation allowed peasants to grow specialized crops for sale, while they purchased rice or other staples on the market. In addition, government demands for taxes paid in cash rather than in kind required peasants to sell something—their products or their labor—in order to meet their obligations. The growing use of paper money as well as financial instruments such as letters of credit and promissory notes further contributed to the commercialization of Chinese society. Two prominent scholars have described the outcome: "Output increased, population grew, skills multiplied, and a burst of inventiveness made Song China far wealthier than ever before—or than any of its contemporaries."[10] (See Snapshot, page 347.)

Women in the Song Dynasty

The "golden age" of Song dynasty China was perhaps less than "golden" for many of its women, for that era marked yet another turning point in the history of Chinese patriarchy. Under the influence of steppe nomads, whose women led less restricted lives, elite Chinese women of the Tang dynasty era, at least in the north, had participated in social life with greater freedom than in earlier times. Paintings and statues show aristocratic women riding horses, while the Queen Mother of the West, a Daoist deity, was widely worshipped by female Daoist priests and practitioners. (See Working with Evidence, Sources 8.2 and 8.4, pages 358 and 360.) By the Song dynasty, however, a reviving Confucianism and rapid economic growth seemed to tighten patriarchal restrictions on women and to restore some of the earlier Han dynasty notions of female submission and passivity.

Once again, Confucian writers highlighted the subordination of women to men and the need to keep males and females separate in every domain of life. The Song dynasty historian and scholar Sima Guang (1019–1086) summed up the prevailing view: "The boy leads the girl, the girl follows the boy; the duty of husbands to be resolute and wives to be docile begins with this."[11] For men, masculinity came to be defined less in terms of horseback riding, athleticism, and the warrior values of northern nomads and more in terms of the refined pursuits of calligraphy, scholarship, painting, and poetry. Corresponding views of feminine qualities emphasized women's weakness, reticence, and delicacy. Women were also frequently viewed as a distraction to men's pursuit of a contemplative and introspective life. The remarriage of widows, though legally permissible, was increasingly condemned, for "to walk through two courtyards is a source of shame for a woman."[12]

The most compelling expression of a tightening patriarchy lay in foot binding. Apparently beginning among dancers and courtesans in the tenth or eleventh century C.E., this practice involved the tight wrapping of young girls' feet, usually breaking the bones of the foot and causing intense pain. During and after the Song dynasty, foot binding found general acceptance among elite families and later became even more widespread in Chinese society. It was associated with new images of female beauty and eroticism that emphasized small size, frailty, and deference and served to keep women restricted to the "inner quarters," where Confucian tradition asserted that they belonged. Many mothers imposed this painful procedure on their daughters, perhaps to enhance their marriage prospects and to assist them in competing with concubines for the attention of their husbands.[13] For many women, it became a rite of passage, and their tiny feet and the beautiful slippers that encased them became a source of some pride, even a topic of poetry for some literate women. Foot binding also served to distinguish Chinese women from their "barbarian" counterparts and elite women from commoners and peasants.

Furthermore, a rapidly commercializing economy undermined the position of women in the textile industry. Urban workshops and state factories, run by men,

■ **Change**
In what ways did women's lives change during the Tang and Song dynasties?

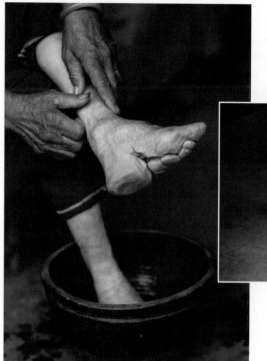

Foot Binding
While the practice of foot binding painfully deformed the feet of young girls and women, it was also associated aesthetically with feminine beauty, particularly in the delicate and elaborately decorated shoes that encased their bound feet. (foot: Jodi Cobb/National Geographic Creative; shoe: ClassicStock/Masterfile)

increasingly took over the skilled tasks of weaving textiles, especially silk, which had previously been the work of rural women in their homes. Although these women continued to tend silkworms and spin silk thread, they had lost the more lucrative income-generating work of weaving silk fabrics. But as their economic role in textile production declined, other opportunities beckoned in an increasingly prosperous Song China. In the cities, women operated restaurants, sold fish and vegetables, and worked as maids, cooks, and dressmakers. The growing prosperity of elite families funneled increasing numbers of women into roles as concubines, entertainers, courtesans, and prostitutes. Their ready availability surely reduced the ability of wives to negotiate as equals with their husbands, setting women against one another and creating endless household jealousies.

In other ways, the Song dynasty witnessed more positive trends in the lives of women. Their property rights expanded, allowing women to control their own dowries and to inherit property from their families. "Neither in earlier nor in later periods," writes one scholar, "did as much property pass through women's hands" as during the Song dynasty.[14] Furthermore, lower-ranking but ambitious officials strongly urged the education of women, so that they might more effectively raise their sons and increase the family's fortune. Song dynasty China, in short, offered a mixture of tightening restrictions and new opportunities to its women.

China and the Northern Nomads: A Chinese World Order in the Making

From early times to the nineteenth century, China's many interactions with a larger Eurasian world shaped both China's own development and that of world history more generally. The country's most enduring and intense interaction with foreigners lay to the north, involving the many nomadic pastoral or semi-agricultural peoples of the steppes. Living in areas unable to sustain Chinese-style farming, the northern nomads had long focused their economies around the raising of livestock (sheep, cattle, goats) and the mastery of horse riding. Organized locally in small, mobile, kinship-based groups, sometimes called tribes, these peoples also periodically created much larger and powerful states or confederations that could draw on the impressive horsemanship and military skills of virtually the entire male population of their societies. Such specialized pastoral societies needed grain and other agricultural products from China, and their leaders developed a taste for Chinese manufactured and luxury goods—wine and silk, for example—with which they could attract and reward followers. Thus the nomads were drawn like a magnet toward China, trading, raiding, and extorting to obtain the resources so vital to their way of life. For 2,000 years or more, pressure from the steppes and the intrusion of nomadic peoples were constant factors in China's historical development.

From the nomads' point of view, the threat often came from the Chinese, who periodically directed their own military forces deep into the steppes, built the Great Wall to keep the nomads out, and often proved unwilling to allow pastoral peoples easy access to trading opportunities within China. And yet the Chinese needed the nomads. Their lands were the source of horses, which were essential for the Chinese military. Other products of the steppes and the forests beyond, such as skins, furs, hides, and amber, were also of value in China. Furthermore, pastoral nomads controlled much of the Silk Road trading network, which funneled goods from the West into China. The continuing interaction between China and the northern nomads brought together peoples occupying different environments, practicing different economies, governing themselves with different institutions, and thinking about the world in quite different ways.

■ **Connection**

How did the Chinese and their nomadic neighbors to the north view each other?

The Tribute System in Theory

An enduring outcome of this cross-cultural encounter was a particular view the Chinese held of themselves and of their neighbors, fully articulated by the time of the Han dynasty (ca. 200 B.C.E.–200 C.E.) and lasting for more than two millennia. That understanding cast China as the "middle kingdom," the center of the world, infinitely superior to the "barbarian" peoples beyond its borders. With its long history, great cities, refined tastes, sophisticated intellectual and artistic achievements, bureaucratic state, literate elite, and prosperous economy, China represented "civilization." All of this, in Chinese thinking, was in sharp contrast to the rude cultures and primitive life of the northern nomads, who continually moved about "like beasts and birds," lived in tents, ate mostly meat and milk, and practically lived on their horses, while making war on everyone within reach. Educated Chinese saw their own society as self-sufficient, requiring little from the outside world, while barbarians, quite understandably, sought access to China's wealth and wisdom. Furthermore, China was willing to permit that access under controlled conditions, for its sense of superiority did not preclude the possibility that barbarians could become civilized Chinese. China was a "radiating civilization," graciously shedding its light most fully to nearby barbarians and with diminished intensity to those farther away.

■ **Connection**
What assumptions underlay the tribute system?

Such was the general understanding of literate Chinese about their own civilization in relation to northern nomads and other non-Chinese peoples. That worldview also took shape as a practical system for managing China's relationship with these people. Known as the tribute system, it was a set of practices that required non-Chinese authorities to acknowledge Chinese superiority and their own subordinate place in a Chinese-centered world order. Foreigners seeking access to China had to send a delegation to the Chinese court, where they would perform the kowtow, a series of ritual bowings and prostrations, and present their tribute—products of value from their countries—to the Chinese emperor. In return for these expressions of submission, he would grant permission for foreigners to trade in China's rich markets and would provide them with gifts or "bestowals," often worth far more than the tribute they had offered. This was the mechanism by which successive Chinese dynasties attempted to regulate their relationships with northern nomads; with neighboring states such as Korea, Vietnam, Tibet, and Japan; and, after 1500, with those European barbarians from across the sea.

Often, this system seemed to work. Over the centuries, countless foreign delegations proved willing to present their tribute, say the required words, and perform the rituals necessary for gaining access to the material goods of China. Aspiring non-Chinese rulers also gained prestige as they basked in the reflected glory of even this subordinate association with the great Chinese civilization. The official titles, seals of office, and ceremonial robes they received from China proved useful in their local struggles for power.

The Tribute System in Practice

But the tribute system also disguised some realities that contradicted its assumptions. On occasion, China was confronting not separate and small-scale barbarian societies, but large and powerful nomadic empires able to deal with China on at least equal terms. An early nomadic confederacy was that of the Xiongnu, established about the same time as the Han dynasty and eventually reaching from Manchuria to Central Asia (see Map 3.5, page 123). Devastating Xiongnu raids into northern China persuaded the Chinese emperor to negotiate an arrangement that recognized the nomadic state as a political equal, promised its leader a princess in marriage, and, most important, agreed to supply him annually with large quantities

The Tribute System
This Qing dynasty painting shows an idealized Chinese version of the tribute system. The Chinese emperor receives barbarian envoys, who perform rituals of subordination and present tribute in the form of a horse. (Musée des Arts Asiatiques–Guimet, Paris, France/© RMN–Grand Palais/Art Resource, NY)

of grain, wine, and silk. Although these goods were officially termed "gifts," granted in accord with the tribute system, they were in fact tribute in reverse or even protection money. In return for these goods, so critical for the functioning of the nomadic state, the Xiongnu agreed to refrain from military incursions into China. The basic realities of the situation were summed up in this warning to the Han dynasty in the first century B.C.E.:

> Just make sure that the silks and grain stuffs you bring the Xiongnu are the right measure and quality, that's all. What's the need for talking? If the goods you deliver are up to measure and good quality, all right. But if there is any deficiency or the quality is no good, then when the autumn harvest comes, we will take our horses and trample all over your crops.[15]

Something similar occurred during the Tang dynasty as a series of Turkic empires arose in Mongolia. Like the Xiongnu, they too extorted large "gifts" from the Chinese. One of these peoples, the Uighurs, actually rescued the Tang dynasty from a serious internal revolt in the 750s. In return, the Uighur leader gained one of the Chinese emperor's daughters as a wife and arranged a highly favorable exchange of poor-quality horses for high-quality silk, which brought half a million rolls of the precious fabric annually into the Uighur lands. Despite the rhetoric of the tribute system, the Chinese were not always able to dictate the terms of their relationship with the northern nomads.

Steppe nomads were generally not much interested in actually conquering and ruling China. It was easier and more profitable to extort goods from a functioning Chinese state. On occasion, however, that state broke down, and various nomadic groups moved in to "pick up the pieces," conquering and governing parts of China. Such a process took place following the fall of the Han dynasty and again after the collapse of the Tang dynasty, when the Khitan (kee-THAN) (907–1125) and then the Jin, or Jurchen (JER-chihn) (1115–1234), peoples established states that encompassed parts of northern China as well as major areas of the steppes to the north.

Both of them required the Chinese Song dynasty, located farther south, to deliver annually huge quantities of silk, silver, and tea, some of which found its way into the Silk Road trading network. The practice of "bestowing gifts on barbarians," long a part of the tribute system, allowed the proud Chinese to imagine that they were still in control of the situation even as they were paying heavily for protection from nomadic incursion. Those gifts, in turn, provided vital economic resources to nomadic states.

Cultural Influence across an Ecological Frontier

When nomadic peoples actually ruled parts of China, some of them adopted Chinese ways, employing Chinese advisers, governing according to Chinese practice, and, at least for the elite, immersing themselves in Chinese culture and learning. This process of "becoming Chinese" went furthest among the Jurchen, many of whom lived in northern China and learned to speak Chinese, wore Chinese clothing, married Chinese husbands and wives, and practiced Buddhism or Daoism. On the whole, however, Chinese culture had only a modest impact on the nomadic people of the northern steppes. Unlike the native peoples of southern China, who were gradually absorbed into Chinese culture, the pastoral societies north of the Great Wall generally retained their own cultural patterns. Few of them were incorporated, at least not for long, within a Chinese state, and most lived in areas where Chinese-style agriculture was simply impossible. Under these conditions, there were few incentives for adopting Chinese culture wholesale. But various modes of interaction — peaceful trade, military conflict, political negotiations, economic extortion, some cultural influence — continued across the ecological frontier that divided two quite distinct and separate ways of life. Each was necessary for the other.

■ **Connection**
In what ways did China and the nomads influence each other?

On the Chinese side, elements of steppe culture had some influence in those parts of northern China that were periodically conquered and ruled by nomadic peoples. The founders of the Sui and Tang dynasties were in fact of mixed nomad and Chinese ancestry and came from the borderland region where a blended Chinese/Turkic culture had evolved. High-ranking members of the imperial family personally led their troops in battle in the style of Turkic warriors. Furthermore, Tang dynasty China was awash with foreign visitors from all over Asia — delegations bearing tribute, merchants carrying exotic goods, bands of clerics or religious pilgrims bringing new religions such as Christianity, Islam, Buddhism, and Manichaeism. For a time in the Tang dynasty, almost anything associated with "Western barbarians" — Central Asians, Persians, Indians, Arabs — had great appeal among northern Chinese elites. Their music, dancing, clothing, foods, games, and artistic styles found favor among the upper classes. The more traditional southern Chinese, feeling themselves heir to the legacy of the Han dynasty, were sharply critical of their northern counterparts for allowing women too much freedom, for drinking yogurt rather than tea, and for listening to "Western" music, all of which they attributed to barbarian influence. Around 800 C.E., the poet Yuan Chen gave voice to a growing backlash against this too-easy acceptance of things "Western":

> Ever since the Western horsemen began raising smut and dust,
> Fur and fleece, rank and rancid, have filled Hsien and Lo [two Chinese cities].
> Women make themselves Western matrons by the study of Western makeup.
> Entertainers present Western tunes, in their devotion to Western music.[16]

Coping with China: Comparing Korea, Vietnam, and Japan

Also involved in tributary relationships with China were the newly emerging states and civilizations of Korea, Vietnam, and Japan. Unlike the northern nomads, these societies were thoroughly agricultural and sedentary. During the first millennium C.E., they were part of a larger process—the globalization of civilization—which produced new city- and state-based societies in various parts of the world. Proximity to their giant Chinese neighbor decisively shaped the histories of these new East Asian civilizations, for all of them borrowed major elements of Chinese culture. But unlike the native peoples of southern China, who largely became Chinese, the peoples of Korea, Vietnam, and Japan did not. They retained distinctive identities, which have lasted into modern times. While resisting Chinese political domination, they also appreciated Chinese culture and sought the source of Chinese wealth and power. In such ways, these smaller East Asian civilizations resembled the "developing" Afro-Asian societies of the twentieth century, which embraced "modernity" and elements of Western culture, while trying to maintain their political and cultural independence from the European and American centers of that modern way of life. Korea, Vietnam, and Japan, however, encountered China and responded to it in quite different ways.

Korea and China

Immediately adjacent to northeastern China, the Korean peninsula and its people have long lived in the shadow of their imposing neighbor (see Map 8.2). Temporary Chinese conquest of northern Korea during the Han dynasty and some colonization by Chinese settlers provided an initial channel for Chinese cultural influence, particularly in the form of Buddhism. Early Korean states, which emerged in the fourth through seventh centuries C.E., all referred to their rulers with the Chinese term *wang* (king). Bitter rivals with one another, these states strenuously resisted Chinese political control, except when they found it advantageous to join with China against a local enemy. In the seventh century, one of these states—the Silla (SHEE-lah) kingdom—allied with Tang dynasty China to bring some political

■ **Connection**

In what ways did China have an influence in Korea, Vietnam, and Japan? In what ways was that influence resisted?

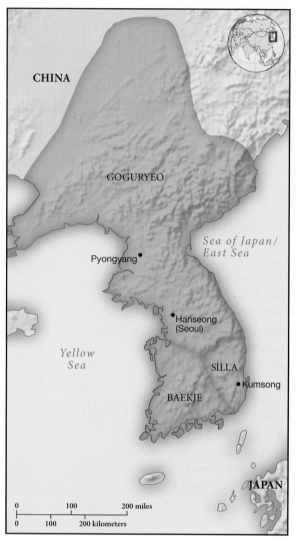

Map 8.2   Korean Kingdoms, ca. 500 C.E.

The three early kingdoms of Korea were brought together by the seventh century in a unified state, which was subsequently governed by a series of dynastic regimes.

unity to the peninsula for the first time. But Chinese efforts to set up puppet regimes and to assimilate Koreans to Chinese culture provoked sharp military resistance, persuading the Chinese to withdraw their military forces in 688 and to establish a tributary relationship with a largely independent Korea.

Under a succession of dynasties—the Silla (688–900), Koryo (918–1392), and Joseon (1392–1910)—Korea generally maintained its political independence while participating in China's tribute system. Its leaders actively embraced the connection with China and, especially during the Silla dynasty, sought to turn their small state into a miniature version of Tang China.

Tribute missions to China provided legitimacy for Korean rulers and knowledge of Chinese court life and administrative techniques, which they sought to replicate back home. A new capital city of Kumsong was modeled directly on the Chinese capital of Chang'an (chahng-ahn). Tribute missions also enabled both official and private trade, mostly in luxury goods such as ceremonial clothing, silks, fancy teas, Confucian and Buddhist texts, and artwork—all of which enriched the lives of a Korean aristocracy that was becoming increasingly Chinese in culture. Thousands of Korean students were sent to China, where they studied primarily Confucianism but also natural sciences and the arts. Buddhist monks visited centers of learning and pilgrimage in China and brought back popular forms of Chinese Buddhism, which quickly took root in Korea. Schools for the study of Confucianism, using texts in the Chinese language, were established in Korea. In these ways, Korea became a part of the expanding world of Chinese culture, and refugees from the peninsula's many wars carried Chinese culture to Japan as well.

These efforts to plant Confucian values and Chinese culture in Korea had what one scholar has called an "overwhelmingly negative" impact on Korean women, particularly after 1300.[17] Early Chinese observers noticed, and strongly disapproved of, "free choice" marriages in Korea as well as the practice of women singing and dancing together late at night. With the support of the Korean court, Chinese models of family life and female behavior, especially among the elite, gradually replaced the more flexible Korean patterns. Earlier, a Korean woman had generally given birth and raised her young children in her parents' home, where she was often joined by her husband. This was now strongly discouraged, for it was deeply offensive to those who espoused Confucian orthodoxy, which held that a married woman belonged to her husband's family. Some Korean customs—funeral rites in which a husband was buried in the sacred plot of his wife's family, the remarriage of widowed or divorced women, and female inheritance of property—eroded under the pressure of Confucian orthodoxy. So too did the practice of plural marriages for men. In 1413, a legal distinction between primary and secondary wives required men to identify one of their wives as primary. Because she and her children now had special privileges and status, sharp new tensions emerged within families. Korean restrictions on elite women, especially widows, came to exceed even those in China itself.

Still, Korea remained Korean. After 688, the country's political independence, though periodically threatened, was largely intact. Chinese cultural influence, except for Buddhism, had little impact beyond the aristocracy and certainly did not penetrate the lives of Korea's serf-like peasants. Nor did it register among Korea's many slaves, amounting to about one-third of the country's population by 1100. In fact, Korean Buddhist monasteries used slaves to cultivate their lands. A Chinese-style examination system to recruit government officials, though encouraged by some Korean rulers, never assumed the prominence that it gained in Tang and Song dynasty China. Korea's aristocratic class was able to maintain an even stronger monopoly on bureaucratic office than its Chinese counterpart did. And in the 1400s, Korea moved toward greater cultural independence by developing a phonetic alphabet, known as *hangul* (HAHN-gool), for writing the Korean language. Although resisted by conservative male elites, who were long accustomed to using the more prestigious Chinese characters to write Korean, this new form of writing gradually took hold, especially in private correspondence, in popular fiction, and among women. Clearly part of the Chinese world order, Korea nonetheless retained a distinctive culture as well as a separate political existence.

Vietnam and China

At the southern fringe of the Chinese cultural world, the people who eventually came to be called Vietnamese had a broadly similar historical encounter with China (see Map 8.3). As in Korea, the elite culture of Vietnam borrowed heavily from China—adopting Confucianism, Daoism, Buddhism, administrative techniques, the examination system, artistic and literary styles—even as its popular culture remained distinctive. And, like Korea, Vietnam achieved political independence, while participating fully in the tribute system as a vassal state.

But there were differences as well. The cultural heartland of Vietnam in the Red River valley was fully incorporated into the Chinese state for more than a thousand years (111 B.C.E.–939 C.E.), far longer than corresponding parts of Korea.

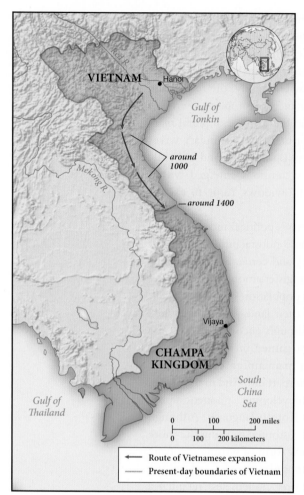

Map 8.3   Vietnam

As Vietnam threw off Chinese control, it also expanded to the south, while remaining wary of its larger Chinese neighbor to the north.

Regarded by the Chinese as "southern barbarians," the Vietnamese were ruled by Chinese officials who expected to fully assimilate this rich rice-growing region into China culturally as well as politically. To these officials, it was simply a further extension of the southward movement of Chinese civilization. Thus Chinese-style irrigated agriculture was introduced; Vietnamese elites were brought into the local bureaucracy and educated in Confucian-based schools; Chinese replaced the local language in official business; Chinese clothing and hairstyles became mandatory; and large numbers of Chinese, some fleeing internal conflicts at home, flooded into the relative security of what they referred to as "the pacified south," while often despising the local people. The heavy pressure of the Chinese presence generated not only a Vietnamese elite thoroughly schooled in Chinese culture but also periodic rebellions, on several occasions led by women. (See Zooming In: Trung Trac, Chapter 3, page 124.)

The weakening of the Tang dynasty in the early tenth century C.E. finally enabled a particularly large rebellion to establish Vietnam as a separate state, though one that carefully maintained its tributary role, sending repeated missions to do homage at the Chinese court. Nonetheless, successive Vietnamese dynasties found the Chinese approach to government useful, styling their rulers as emperors, claiming the Mandate of Heaven, and making use of Chinese court rituals, while expanding their state steadily southward. More so than in Korea, a Chinese-based examination system in Vietnam functioned to undermine an established aristocracy, to provide some measure of social mobility for commoners, and to create a merit-based scholar-gentry class to staff the bureaucracy. Furthermore, members of the Vietnamese elite class remained deeply committed to Chinese culture, viewing their own country less as a separate nation than as a southern extension of a universal civilization, the only one they knew.

Beyond the elite, however, there remained much that was uniquely Vietnamese, such as a distinctive language, a fondness for cockfighting, and the habit of chewing betel nuts. More importantly, Vietnam long retained a greater role for women in social and economic life, despite heavy Chinese influence. In the third century C.E., a woman leader of an anti-Chinese resistance movement declared: "I want to drive away the enemy to save our people. I will not resign myself to the usual lot of women who bow their heads and become concubines." Female nature deities and a "female Buddha" continued to be part of Vietnamese popular religion, even as Confucian-based ideas took root among the elite. In the centuries following independence from China, as Vietnam expanded to the south, northern officials tried in vain to impose more orthodox Confucian gender practices in place of local customs that allowed women to choose their own husbands and married men to live in the households of their wives. So persistent were these practices that a seventeenth-century Chinese visitor opined, with disgust, that Vietnamese preferred the birth of a girl to that of a boy. These features of Vietnamese life reflected larger patterns of Southeast Asian culture that distinguished it from China. And like Koreans, the Vietnamese developed a variation of Chinese writing called *chu nom* ("southern script"), which provided the basis for an independent national literature and a vehicle for the writing of most educated women.

Independence for Vietnam
In 938, Vietnamese forces under the leadership of General Ngo Quyen defeated the Chinese in the Battle of Bach Dang River, thus ending a thousand years of direct Chinese rule. This image is one of many that celebrate that victory. (Pictures from History/CPA Media)

Japan and China

Unlike Korea and Vietnam, the Japanese islands were physically separated from China by 100 miles or more of ocean and were never successfully invaded or conquered by their giant mainland neighbor (see Map 8.4). Thus Japan's very extensive borrowing from Chinese civilization was wholly voluntary, rather than occurring under conditions of direct military threat or outright occupation. The high point of that borrowing took place during the seventh to the ninth centuries C.E., as the first more or less unified Japanese state began to emerge from dozens of small clan-based aristocratic chiefdoms. That state found much that was useful in Tang dynasty China and set out, deliberately and systematically, to transform Japan into a centralized bureaucratic state on the Chinese model.

The initial leader of this effort was Shotoku Taishi (572–622), a prominent aristocrat from one of the major clans. He launched a series of large-scale missions to China, which took hundreds of Japanese monks, scholars, artists, and students to the mainland, and when they returned, they put into practice what they had learned. In 604 C.E. Shotoku issued the Seventeen Article Constitution, proclaiming the Japanese ruler as a Chinese-style emperor and encouraging both Buddhism and Confucianism. In good Confucian fashion, that document emphasized the

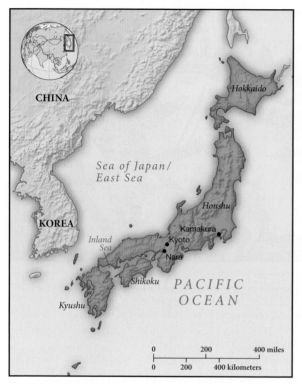

Map 8.4   Japan

Japan's distance from China enabled it to maintain its political independence and to draw selectively from Chinese culture.

moral quality of rulers as a foundation for social harmony. In the decades that followed, Japanese authorities adopted Chinese-style court rituals and a system of court rankings for officials as well as the Chinese calendar. Subsequently, they likewise established Chinese-based taxation systems, law codes, government ministries, and provincial administration, at least on paper. Two capital cities, first Nara and then Heian-kyo (Kyoto), arose, both modeled on the Chinese capital of Chang'an.

Chinese culture, no less than its political practices, also found favor in Japan. Various schools of Chinese Buddhism took root, first among the educated and literate classes and later more broadly in Japanese society, deeply affecting much of Japanese life. Art, architecture, education, medicine, views of the afterlife, attitudes toward suffering and the impermanence of life—all of this and more reflected the influence of Buddhist culture in Japan. The Chinese writing system—and with it an interest in historical writing, calligraphy, and poetry—likewise proved attractive among the elite.

The absence of any compelling threat from China made it possible for the Japanese to be selective in their borrowing. By the tenth century, deliberate efforts to absorb additional elements of Chinese culture diminished, and formal tribute missions to China stopped, although private traders and Buddhist monks continued to make the difficult journey to the mainland. Over many centuries, the Japanese combined what they had assimilated from China with elements of their own tradition into a distinctive Japanese civilization, which differed from Chinese culture in many ways.

In the political realm, for example, the Japanese never succeeded in creating an effective centralized and bureaucratic state to match that of China. Although the court and the emperor retained an important ceremonial and cultural role, their real political authority over the country gradually diminished in favor of competing aristocratic families, both at court and in the provinces. A Chinese-style university trained officials, but rather than serving as a mechanism for recruiting talented commoners into the political elite, it enrolled students who were largely the sons of court aristocrats.

As political power became increasingly decentralized, local authorities developed their own military forces, the famous *samurai* warrior class of Japanese society. Bearing their exquisite curved swords, the samurai developed a distinctive set of values featuring bravery, loyalty, endurance, honor, great skill in martial arts, and a preference for death over surrender. This was *bushido* (boo-shee-doh), the way of the warrior. Japan's celebration of the samurai and of military virtues contrasted sharply with China's emphasis on intellectual achievements and political office holding, which were accorded higher prestige than bearing arms. "The educated men of the land," wrote a Chinese minister in the eleventh century, "regard the carrying of arms as a disgrace."[18] The Japanese, clearly, did not agree.

Religiously as well, Japan remained distinctive. Although Buddhism in many forms took hold in the country, it never completely replaced the native beliefs and practices, which focused attention on numerous *kami*, sacred spirits associated with human ancestors and various natural phenomena. Much later referred to as Shinto, this tradition provided legitimacy to the imperial family, based on claims of descent from the sun goddess. Because veneration of the kami lacked an elaborate philosophy or ritual, it conflicted very little with Buddhism. In fact, numerous kami were assimilated into Japanese Buddhism as local expressions of Buddhist deities or principles.

Japanese literary and artistic culture likewise evolved in distinctive ways, despite much borrowing from China. As in Korea and Vietnam, there emerged a unique writing system that combined Chinese characters with a series of phonetic symbols. A highly stylized Japanese poetic form, known as tanka, developed early and has remained a favored means of expression ever since. (See Zooming In: Izumi Shikibu, page 344, for the life of Japan's best-known female tanka poet.) Particularly during the Heian period of Japanese history (794–1192), a highly refined aesthetic culture found expression at the imperial court, even as the court's real political authority melted away. Court aristocrats and their ladies lived in splendor, composed poems, arranged flowers, and conducted their love affairs. "What counted," wrote one scholar, "was the proper costume, the right ceremonial act, the successful turn of phrase in a poem, and the appropriate expression of refined taste."[19] Much of our knowledge of this courtly culture comes from the work of women writers, who composed their diaries and novels in the vernacular Japanese script, rather than in the

■ **Comparison**

In what different ways did Japanese and Korean women experience the pressures of Confucian orthodoxy?

The Samurai of Japan

This late nineteenth-century image shows a samurai warrior on horseback clad in armor and a horned helmet while carrying a sword as well as a bow and arrows. The prominence of martial values in Japanese culture was one of the ways in which Japan differed from its Chinese neighbor, despite much borrowing. (Library of Congress, ID #pd 01046)

Izumi Shikibu,
Japanese Poet and Lover

Nowhere in world history has poetry played a more central role than in the imperial court of Japan, located in the capital city of Heian-kyo (now Kyoto) between the ninth and twelfth centuries. There, amid the political posturing and the love affairs of aristocratic women and men, almost every event, public or private, called for a poem—the first sighting of spring blossoms or a new moon; births, deaths, and marriages; various official rituals; the morning after a romantic encounter. "It is poetry," wrote one famous Japanese author in the early tenth century, "which . . . awakens the world of invisible spirits . . . , softens the relationship between men and women, and consoles the hearts of fierce warriors."[20] Izumi Shikibu, Japan's most illustrious female poet, was a master of this art, particularly in the lyric five-line, thirty-one-syllable form known as tanka. In her exquisite poetry, we can catch a glimpse of her erotic intensity, expressed in many scandalous love affairs, as well as her engagement in more spiritual pursuits.

Born around 975 as the daughter of a mid-level official, Izumi grew up in the imperial court, where a literary

Izumi Shikibu.

education was essential for girls of her status, for at least in matters of poetry and the arts, women and men operated on an equal basis. At about the age of twenty, Izumi married a provincial governor, but she soon began an affair with Prince Tametaka, son of the emperor, shocking court society partly because of the sharp difference in their social positions. Tametaka's death in 1002, widely credited to his sexual excess with Izumi, only deepened the scandal and led to Izumi's divorce from her husband and estrangement from her family. Addressing her parents and sisters in a poem, she declared: "One of you / I was, but am no more."[21]

Less than a year later, she ignited another scandal by taking up with Tametaka's brother, Prince Atsumichi. The first year of this affair became the subject of Izumi's famous *Diary*. When the prince sent her a sprig of orange blossoms, she responded with a poem: "Rather than recall / in these flowers / the fragrance of the past, /

photo: Pictures from History/CPA Media

classical Chinese used by elite men. *The Tale of Genji*, a Japanese novel written by the woman author Murasaki Shikibu around 1000, provides an intimate picture of the intrigues and romances of court life.

At this level of society, Japan's women, unlike those in Korea, largely escaped the more oppressive features of Chinese Confucian culture, such as the prohibition of remarriage for widows, seclusion within the home, and foot binding. Perhaps this is because the most powerful Chinese influence on Japan occurred during the Tang dynasty, when Chinese elite women enjoyed considerable freedom. Japanese women continued to inherit property; Japanese married couples often lived apart or with the wife's family; and marriages were made and broken easily. None of this corresponded to Confucian values. When Japanese women did begin to lose status

I would like to hear this nightingale's voice, / to know if his song is as sweet." What followed was a year of nocturnal visits, frequent absences, rumors and gossip, doubts and longings, and the endless exchange of poems. Finally, Izumi took up residence in the prince's compound, much to the distress of his principal wife. Atsumichi's death in 1007 prompted an outpouring of poetry mourning the loss of her great love. "I long for the sound / of your voice. / The face / I see so clearly / doesn't say a word."[22]

Despite Izumi's behavior, she was subsequently appointed as a lady-in-waiting for the Empress Akiko, for her literary reputation added splendor to the court. But the scandal of her personal life continued to shadow her. A rival literary figure at the court, the renowned Lady Murasaki, author of *The Tale of Genji*, commented, "How interestingly Izumi Shikibu writes. Yet what a disgraceful person she is."[23] A subsequent marriage to a much older provincial governor took Izumi away from the court for the rest of her life. But her affairs continued. "I do not feel in the least disposed to sleep alone," she wrote.[24]

Her poetry gave frequent expression to erotic love and to the anguished yearning that accompanied it. "Lying alone, / my black hair tangled, / uncombed / I long for the one / who touched it first." To a monk who left his fan behind after a visit, she wrote, "I think / you may have briefly forgotten / this fan, / but everyone must know / how it came to be dropped."

Izumi's experiences of love within her social circle gave her an acute sense of the ephemerality of all things. "Come quickly — as soon as / these blossoms open, / they fall. / This world exists / as a sheen of dew on flowers." Her understanding of impermanence was reinforced by her Buddhist faith with its emphasis on the transience of human life. From time to time, she felt the desire to withdraw into a monastery, and she did take periodic retreats in mountain temples. Even there, however, Izumi experienced the pull of the world. "Although I try / to hold the single thought / of Buddha's teaching in my heart, / I cannot help but hear / the many crickets' voices calling as well."[25]

Perhaps Izumi's best-known poem was composed when she was still in her teens, though it has sometimes been viewed as a prayer on her deathbed. Written to a Buddhist cleric, it reveals her early and continuing desire for spiritual enlightenment, symbolized here as the light of the moon. "From utter darkness / I must embark upon an / even darker road / O distant moon, cast your light / from the rim of the mountains."[26]

Question: How do you understand Izumi's involvement in multiple love relationships and her religious sensibilities?

in the twelfth century and later, it had less to do with Confucian pressures than with the rise of a warrior culture. As the personal relationships of samurai warriors to their lords replaced marriage alliances as a political strategy, the influence of women in political life was reduced, but this was an internal Japanese phenomenon, not a reflection of Chinese influence.

Japan's ability to borrow extensively from China while developing its own distinctive civilization perhaps provided a model for its encounter with the West in the nineteenth century. Then, as before, Japan borrowed selectively from a foreign culture without losing either its political independence or its cultural uniqueness.

SUMMING UP SO FAR

In what different ways did Korea, Vietnam, Japan, and northern nomads experience and respond to Chinese influence?

China and the Eurasian World Economy

Beyond China's central role in East Asia was its economic interaction with the wider world of Eurasia generally. On the one hand, China's remarkable economic growth, taking place during the Tang and Song dynasties, could hardly be contained within China's borders and clearly had a major impact throughout Eurasia. On the other hand, China was recipient as well as donor in the economic interactions of the third-wave era, and its own economic achievements owed something to the stimulus of contact with the larger world.

Spillovers: China's Impact on Eurasia

One of the outcomes of China's economic revolution lay in the diffusion of its many technological innovations to peoples and places far from East Asia as the movements of traders, soldiers, slaves, and pilgrims conveyed Chinese achievements abroad. (See Snapshot, opposite, for a wider view of Chinese technological achievements.) Chinese techniques for producing salt by solar evaporation spread to the Islamic world and later to Christian Europe. Papermaking, known in China since the Han dynasty, spread to Korea and Vietnam by the fourth century C.E., to Japan and India by the seventh, to the Islamic world by the eighth, to Muslim Spain by 1150, to France and Germany in the 1300s, and to England in the 1490s. Printing, likewise a Chinese invention, rapidly reached Korea, where movable type became a highly developed technique, and Japan as well. Both technologies were heavily influenced by Buddhism, which accorded religious merit to the reproduction of sacred texts. The Islamic world, however, highly valued handwritten calligraphy and generally resisted printing as impious until the nineteenth century. The adoption of printing in Europe was likewise delayed because of the absence of paper until the twelfth century. Then movable type was reinvented by Johannes Gutenberg in the fifteenth century, although it is unclear whether he was aware of Chinese and Korean precedents. With implications for mass literacy, bureaucracy, scholarship, the spread of religion, and the exchange of information, papermaking and printing were Chinese innovations of revolutionary and global dimensions.

■ **Connection**

In what ways did China participate in the world of Eurasian commerce and exchange, and with what outcomes?

Chinese technologies were seldom simply transferred from one place to another. More often, a particular Chinese technique or product stimulated innovations in more distant lands in accordance with local needs.[27] For example, as the Chinese formula for gunpowder, invented around 1000, became available in Europe, together with some early and simple firearms, these innovations triggered the development of cannons in the early fourteenth century. Soon cannons appeared in the Islamic world and, by 1356, in China itself, which first used cast iron rather than bronze in their construction. But the highly competitive European state system drove the "gunpowder revolution" much further and more rapidly than in China's imperial state. Chinese textile, metallurgical, and naval technologies likewise stimulated

SNAPSHOT Chinese Technological Achievements

Before the technological explosion of the European Industrial Revolution during the eighteenth and nineteenth centuries, China had long been the major center of global technological innovation.[28] Many of those inventions spread to other civilizations, where they stimulated imitation or modification. Since Europe was located at the opposite end of the Eurasian continent from China, it often took considerable time for those innovations to give rise to something similar in the West. That lag is also a measure of the relative technological development of the two civilizations in premodern times.

Innovation	First Used in China (approximate)	Adoption/Recognition in the West: Time Lag in Years (approximate)
Iron plow	6th–4th century B.C.E.	2,000+
Cast iron	4th century B.C.E.	1,000–1,200
Efficient horse collar	3rd–1st century B.C.E.	1,000
Paper	2nd century B.C.E.	1,000
Wheelbarrow	1st century B.C.E.	900–1,000
Rudder for steering ships	1st century C.E.	1,100
Iron chain suspension bridge	1st century C.E.	1,000–1,300
Porcelain	3rd century C.E.	1,500
Magnetic compass for navigation	9th–11th century C.E.	400
Gunpowder	9th century C.E.	400
Chain drive for transmission of power	976 C.E.	800
Movable type printing	1045 C.E.	400

imitation and innovation all across Eurasia. An example is the magnetic compass, a Chinese invention eagerly embraced by mariners of many cultural backgrounds as they traversed the Indian Ocean.

In addition to its technological influence, China's prosperity during the Song dynasty greatly stimulated commercial life and market-based behavior all across the Afro-Eurasian trading world. China's products—silk, porcelain, lacquerware—found eager buyers from Japan to East Africa, and everywhere in between. The immense size and wealth of China's domestic economy also provided a ready market for hundreds of commodities from afar. For example, the lives of many thousands of people in the spice-producing islands of what is now Indonesia were transformed as they came to depend on Chinese consumers' demand for their products. "[O]ne hundred million [Chinese] people," wrote historian William McNeill, "increasingly caught up within a commercial network, buying and selling to supplement every day's livelihood, made a significant difference to the way other human beings made their livings throughout a large part of the civilized world."[29] Such was the ripple effect of China's economic revolution.

On the Receiving End: China as Economic Beneficiary

If Chinese economic growth and technological achievements significantly shaped the Eurasian world of the third-wave era, that pattern of interaction was surely not a one-way street, for China too was changed by its engagement with a wider world. During this period, for example, China had learned about the cultivation and processing of both cotton and sugar from India. From Vietnam, around 1000, China gained access to the new, fast-ripening, and drought-resistant strains of rice that made a highly productive rice-based agriculture possible in the drier and more rugged regions of southern China. This marked a major turning point in Chinese history as the frontier region south of the Yangzi River grew rapidly in population, overtaking the traditional centers of Chinese civilization in the north. In the process, the many non-Chinese peoples of the area were painfully overwhelmed by Chinese military forces and by the migration of at least a million Han Chinese farmers by 1400. Some of them were attracted by new economic opportunities, while others were forcibly relocated by the Chinese state, intent on thoroughly integrating the south into Chinese civilization.

Technologically as well, China's extraordinary burst of creativity owed something to the stimulus of cross-cultural contact. Awareness of Persian windmills, for example, spurred the development of a distinct but related device in China. Printing arose from China's growing involvement with the world of Buddhism, which put a spiritual premium on the reproduction of the Buddha's image and of short religious texts that were carried as charms. It was in Buddhist monasteries during the Tang dynasty that the long-established practice of printing with seals was elaborated by Chinese monks into woodblock printing. The first printed book, in 868 C.E., was a famous Buddhist text, the *Diamond Sutra*.

A further transforming impact of China's involvement with a wider world derived from its growing participation in Indian Ocean trade. By the Tang dynasty, thousands of ships annually visited the ports of southern China, and settled communities of foreign merchants—Arabs, Persians, Indians, Southeast Asians—turned some of these cities into cosmopolitan centers. Buddhist temples, Muslim mosques and cemeteries, and Hindu phallic sculptures graced the skyline of Quanzhou, a coastal city in southern China. Occasionally the tensions of cultural diversity erupted in violence, such as the massacre of tens of thousands of foreigners in Canton during the 870s when Chinese rebel forces sacked the city. Indian Ocean commerce also contributed much to the transformation of southern China from a subsistence economy to one more heavily based on producing for export.

In the process, merchants achieved a degree of social acceptance not known before, including their frequent appointment to high-ranking bureaucratic positions. Finally, much-beloved stories of the monkey god, widely popular even in contemporary China, derived from Indian sources transmitted by Indian Ocean commerce.

China and Buddhism

By far the most important gift that China received from India was neither cotton nor sugar, but a religion, Buddhism. The gradual assimilation of this South Asian religious tradition into Chinese culture illustrates the process of cultural encounter and adaptation and invites comparison with the spread of Christianity into Europe. Until the adoption of Marxism in the twentieth century, Buddhism was the only large-scale cultural borrowing in Chinese history. It also made China into a launching pad for Buddhism's dispersion to Korea and from there to Japan as well. Thus, as Buddhism faded in the land of its birth, it became solidly rooted in much of East Asia, providing an element of cultural commonality for a vast region (see Map 8.5).

Making Buddhism Chinese

Buddhism initially entered China via the Silk Road trading network during the first and second centuries C.E. The stability and prosperity of the Han dynasty, then at its height, ensured that the new "barbarian" religion held little appeal for native Chinese. Furthermore, the Indian culture from which Buddhism sprang was at odds with Chinese understandings of the world in many ways. Buddhism's commitment to a secluded and monastic life for monks and nuns seemed to dishonor Chinese family values, and its concern for individual salvation or enlightenment appeared selfish, contradicting the social orientation of Confucian thinking. Its abstract philosophy ran counter to the more concrete, "this-worldly" concerns of Chinese thinkers, and the Buddhist concept of infinite eons of time, endlessly repeating themselves, was quite a stretch for the Chinese, who normally thought in terms of finite family generations or dynastic cycles. No wonder that for the first several centuries C.E., Buddhism was largely the preserve of foreign merchants and monks living in China.

In the half millennium between roughly 300 and 800 C.E., however, Buddhism took solid root in China within both elite and popular culture, becoming a permanent, though fluctuating, presence in Chinese life. How did this remarkable transformation unfold? It began, arguably, with the collapse of the Han dynasty around 200 C.E. The chaotic, violent, and politically fragmented centuries that followed seriously discredited Confucianism and opened the door to alternative understandings of the world. Nomadic rulers, now governing much of northern China, found Buddhism useful in part because it was foreign. "We were born out of the marches," declared one of them, "and though we are unworthy, we have complied with our

■ **Change**
What facilitated the rooting of Buddhism within China?

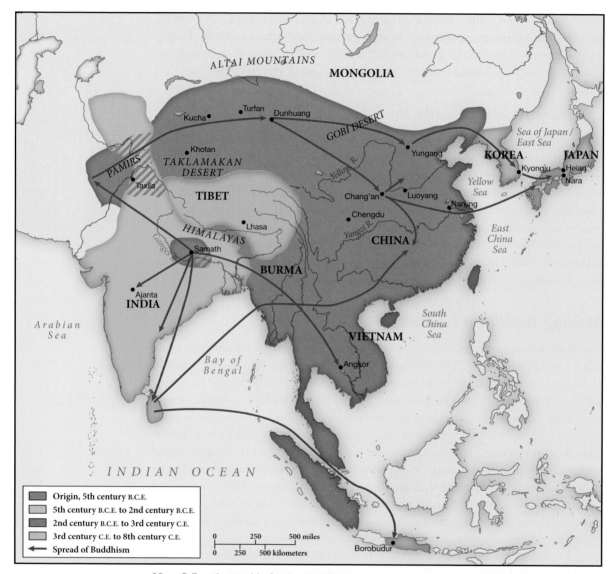

Map 8.5   The World of Asian Buddhism
Originating in India, Buddhism later spread widely throughout much of Asia to provide a measure of cultural or religious commonality across this vast region.

appointed destiny and govern the Chinese as their prince. . . . Buddha being a barbarian god is the very one we should worship."[30] Rulers and elite families provided patronage for Buddhist monasteries, temples, and works of art. In southern China, where many northern aristocrats had fled following the disastrous decline of the Han dynasty, Buddhism provided some comfort in the face of a collapsing society.

Its emphasis on ritual, morality, and contemplation represented an intellectually and aesthetically satisfying response to times that were so clearly out of joint.

Meanwhile, Buddhist monasteries increasingly provided an array of social services for ordinary people. In them, travelers found accommodation; those fleeing from China's many upheavals discovered a place of refuge; desperate people received charity; farmers borrowed seed for the next planting; the sick were treated; and children learned to read. And for many, Buddhism was associated with access to magical powers as reports of miracles abounded. Battles were won, rain descended on drought-ridden areas, diseases were cured, and guilt was relieved—all through the magical ministrations of charismatic monks.

Accompanying all of this was a serious effort by monks, scholars, and translators to present this Indian religion in terms that Chinese could more readily grasp. Thus the Buddhist term *dharma*, referring to the Buddha's teaching, was translated as *dao*, or "the way," a notion long familiar in both Daoist and Confucian thinking (see Chapter 4). The Buddhist notion of "morality" was translated with the Confucian term that referred to "filial submission and obedience." Some Indian concepts were modified in the process of translation. For example, the idea that "husband supports wife," which reflected a considerable respect for women and mothers in early Indian Buddhism, became in translation "husband controls wife."[31]

As Buddhism took hold in China, it was primarily in its broader Mahayana form—complete with numerous deities, the veneration of relics, many heavens and hells, and bodhisattvas to aid the believer—rather than its more psychological and individualistic Theravada form (see Chapter 4). One of the most popular expressions of Buddhism in China was the Pure Land School, in which faithfully repeating the name of an earlier Buddha, the Amitabha, was sufficient to ensure rebirth in a beautifully described heavenly realm, the Pure Land. In its emphasis on salvation by faith, without arduous study or intensive meditation, Pure Land Buddhism became a highly popular and authentically Chinese version of the Indian faith.

China's reunification under the Sui and early Tang dynasties witnessed growing state support for Buddhism. The Sui emperor Wendi (r. 581–604 C.E.) had monasteries constructed at the base of China's five sacred mountains, further identifying the imported religion with traditional Chinese culture. He even used Buddhism to justify his military campaigns. "With a hundred victories in a hundred battles," he declared, "we promote the practice of the ten Buddhist virtues."[32] By 600 C.E., some 4,000 monasteries had been established. With state support and growing popular acceptance, they became centers of great wealth. They were largely exempt from taxation and owned large estates; ran businesses such as oil presses, water mills, and pawn shops; collected gems, gold, and lavish works of art; and employed millions of slaves, serfs, and other unfree and dependent workers. But Buddhism, while solidly entrenched in Chinese life by the early Tang dynasty, never achieved the independence from state authorities that the Christian Church acquired in

Europe. The examinations for becoming a monk were supervised by the state, and education in the monasteries included the required study of the Confucian classics. In the mid-ninth century, the state showed quite dramatically just how much control it could exercise over the Buddhist establishment.

Losing State Support: The Crisis of Chinese Buddhism

The impressive growth of Chinese Buddhism was accompanied by a persistent undercurrent of resistance and criticism. Some saw the Buddhist establishment, at least potentially, as a "state within a state" and a challenge to imperial authority. More important was a deepening resentment of its enormous wealth. One fifth-century critic, referring to monks, put the issue squarely: "Why is it that their ideals are noble and far-reaching and their activities still are base and common? [They] become merchants and engage in barter, wrangling with the masses for profit."[33] Nor did the environmental impact of Buddhist monasteries escape the notice of state officials. In 707 C.E., one such official wrote: "Extensive construction of monasteries are undertaken and large mansions are built. Even though for such works trees are felled to the point of stripping the mountains, it does not suffice. . . . Though earth is moved to the point of obstructing roads, it does not suffice."[34] When state treasuries were short of funds, government officials cast a covetous eye on these wealthy and tax-exempt monasteries. Furthermore, Buddhism was clearly of foreign origin and offensive for that reason to some Confucian and Daoist thinkers. The celibacy of the monks and their withdrawal from society, the critics argued, undermined the Confucian-based family system of Chinese tradition.

■ **Change**

What were the major sources of opposition to Buddhism within China?

Such criticisms took on new meaning in the changed environment of China after about 800 C.E. Following centuries of considerable foreign influence in China, a growing resentment against foreign culture, particularly among the literate classes, increasingly took hold. The turning point may well have been the An Lushan rebellion (755–763), in which a general of foreign origin led a major revolt against the Tang dynasty. Whatever its origin, an increasingly xenophobic reaction set in among the upper classes, reflected in a desire to return to an imagined "purity" of earlier times. In this setting, the old criticisms of Buddhism became more sharply focused. In 819, Han Yu, a leading figure in the Confucian counterattack on Buddhism, wrote a scathing memorial to the emperor, criticizing his willingness to honor a relic of the Buddha's finger.

> Now the Buddha was of barbarian origin. His language differed from Chinese speech; his clothes were of a different cut; his mouth did not pronounce the prescribed words of the Former Kings. . . . He did not recognize the relationship between prince and subject, nor the sentiments of father and son. . . . I pray that Your Majesty will turn this bone over to the officials that it may be cast into water or fire.[35]

Several decades later, the Chinese state took direct action against the Buddhist establishment as well as against other foreign religions. A series of imperial decrees between 841 and 845 ordered some 260,000 monks and nuns to return to normal life as tax-paying citizens. Thousands of monasteries, temples, and shrines were either destroyed or turned to public use, while the state confiscated the lands, money, metals, and serfs belonging to monasteries. Buddhists were now forbidden to use gold, silver, copper, iron, and gems in constructing their images. These actions dealt a serious blow to Chinese Buddhism. Its scholars and monks were scattered, its creativity diminished, and its institutions came even more firmly under state control.

Despite this persecution, Buddhism did not vanish from China. At the level of elite culture, its philosophical ideas played a role in the reformulation of Confucian thinking that took place during the Song dynasty. At the village level, Buddhism became one element of Chinese popular religion, which also included the veneration of ancestors, the honoring of Confucius, and Daoist shrines and rituals. Temples frequently included statues of Confucius, Laozi, and the Buddha, with little sense of any incompatibility among them. "Every black-haired son of Han," the Chinese have long said, "wears a Confucian thinking cap, a Daoist robe, and Buddhist sandals." (See photo, page 146.) Unlike in Europe, where an immigrant religion triumphed over and excluded all other faiths, Buddhism in China became assimilated into Chinese culture alongside its other traditions.

REFLECTIONS

Why Do Things Change?

The rapidity of change in modern societies is among the most distinctive features of recent history, but change and transformation, though at various rates, have been constants in the human story since the very beginning. Explaining how and why human societies change is perhaps the central issue that historians confront, no matter which societies or periods of time they study. Those who specialize in the history of some particular culture or civilization often emphasize sources of change operating within those societies, although there is intense disagreement as to which are most significant. The ideas of great thinkers, the policies of leaders, struggles for power, the conflict of classes, the invention of new technologies, the growth or decline in population, variations in climate or weather—all of these and more have their advocates as the primary motor of historical transformation.

Of course, it is not necessary to choose among them. The history of China illustrates the range of internal factors that have driven change in that civilization. The political conflicts of the "era of warring states" provided the setting and the motivation for the emergence of Confucianism and Daoism, which in turn have certainly shaped the character and texture of Chinese civilization over many centuries. The personal qualities and brutal policies of Shihuangdi surely played a role in China's unification and in the brief duration of the Qin dynasty. The subsequent creation of a widespread network of canals and waterways as well as the country's technological achievements served to maintain that unity over very long periods of time. But the massive inequalities of Chinese society generated the peasant upheavals, which periodically shattered that unity and led to new ruling dynasties. Sometimes natural events, such as droughts and floods, triggered those rebellions.

World historians, more than those who study particular civilizations or nations, have been inclined to find the primary source of change in contact with strangers, in external connections and interactions, whether direct or indirect. The history of China and East Asia provides plenty of examples for this point of view as well. Conceptions of China as the "middle kingdom," infinitely superior to all surrounding societies, grew out of centuries of involvement with its neighbors. Some of those neighbors became Chinese as China's imperial reach grew, especially to the south. Even those that did not, such as Korea, Vietnam, and Japan, were decisively transformed by proximity to the "radiating civilization" of China. China's own cuisine, so distinctive in recent centuries, may well be a quite recent invention, drawing heavily on Indian and Southeast Asian cooking. Buddhism, of course, is an obvious borrowing from abroad, although its incorporation into Chinese civilization and its ups and downs within China owed much to internal cultural and political realities.

In the end, clear distinctions between internal and external sources of change in China's history—or that of any other society—are perhaps misleading. The boundary between "inside" and "outside" is itself a constantly changing line. Should the borderlands of northern China, where Chinese and Turkic peoples met and mingled, be regarded as internal or external to China itself? And, as the histories of Chinese Buddhism and of Japanese culture so clearly indicate, what comes from beyond is always transformed by what it encounters within.

Second Thoughts

What's the Significance?

Big Picture Questions

1. How can you explain the changing fortunes of Buddhism in China?
2. How did China influence the world of the third-wave era? How was China itself transformed by its encounters with a wider world?
3. How might China's posture in the world during the Tang and Song dynasty era compare to its emerging role in global affairs in the twenty-first century?
4. **Looking Back:** In what ways did Tang and Song dynasty China resemble the earlier Han dynasty period, and in what ways had China changed?

Next Steps: For Further Study

Samuel Adshead, *Tang China: The Rise of the East in World History* (2004). Explores the role of China within the larger world.

Patricia Buckley Ebrey, *The Inner Quarters* (1993). A balanced account of the gains and losses experienced by Chinese women during the changes of the Song dynasty.

Mark Elvin, *The Pattern of the Chinese Past* (1973). A classic account of the Chinese economic revolution.

James L. Huffman, *Japan in World History* (2010). The first three chapters of this recent work place Japan's early history in the framework of world history.

Paul S. Ropp, *China in World History* (2010). An up-to-date telling of China's historical development, cast in a global context.

Arthur F. Wright, *Buddhism in Chinese History* (1959). An older account filled with wonderful stories and anecdotes.

"Lost Treasurers of the Ancient World—Japan," http://www.youtube.com/watch?v=i9ObeuCWhiE. A Discovery Channel video presentation of Japanese history.

Upper River during the Qing Ming Festival, http://www.ibiblio.org/ulysses/gec/painting/qingming/full.htm. A scrolling reproduction of a huge Chinese painting, showing in detail the Song dynasty city of Kaifeng.

WORKING WITH EVIDENCE

The Leisure Life of China's Elites

From the earliest centuries of Chinese civilization, that country's artists have painted—on pottery, paper, wood, and silk; in tombs, on coffins, and on walls; in albums and on scrolls. Relying largely on ink rather than oils, their brushes depicted human figures, landscapes, religious themes, and images of ordinary life. While Chinese painting evolved over many centuries, in terms of both subject matter and technique, by most accounts it reached a high point of artistic brilliance during the Tang and Song dynasties.

Here, however, we are less interested in the aesthetic achievements of Chinese painting than in what those works can show us about the life of China's elite class—those men who had passed the highest-level examinations and held high office in the state bureaucracy and those women who lived within the circles of the imperial court. While they represented only a tiny fraction of China's huge population, such elite groups established the tone and set the standards of behavior for Chinese civilization. For such people, leisure was a positive value, a time for nurturing relationships and cultivating one's character in good Confucian or Daoist fashion. According to the Tang dynasty writer and scholar Duan Chengshi,

> Leisure is good.
> Dusty affairs don't entangle the mind.
> I sit facing the tree outside the window
> And watch its shadow change direction three times.[36]

Action and work, in the Chinese view of things, need to be balanced by self-reflection and leisure. In the images that follow, we can catch a glimpse of how the Chinese elite lived and interacted with one another, particularly in their leisure time.

Leading court officials and scholar-bureaucrats must have been greatly honored to be invited to an elegant banquet, hosted by the emperor himself, such as that shown in Source 8.1. Usually attributed to the emperor Huizong (1082–1135)—who was himself a noted painter, poet, calligrapher, and collector—the painting shows a refined dinner gathering of high officials drinking tea and wine with the emperor presiding at the left. This emperor's great attention to the arts rather than to affairs of state gained him a reputation as a negligent and dissolute ruler. His reign ended in disgrace as China suffered a humiliating defeat at the hands of northern nomadic Jin people, who took the emperor captive.

Source 8.1 A Banquet with the Emperor

- What features of this painting contribute to the impression of imperial elegance?

- What mood does this painting evoke?

- What social distinction among the figures in the painting can you discern?

- How is the emperor depicted in this painting in comparison to that on page 335? How would you explain the difference?

- How might you imagine the conversation around this table?

Elite women of the court likewise gathered to eat, drink, and talk, as illustrated in Source 8.2, an anonymous Tang dynasty painting on silk. Hosting the event is the empress, shown seated upright in the middle of the left side of the table, holding a fan and wearing a distinctive headdress. Her guests and paid professional musicians sit around the table.

- How does this gathering of elite women differ from that of the men in Source 8.1? How might their conversation differ from that of the men?

- To what extent are the emperor and empress in Sources 8.1 and 8.2 distinguished from their guests? How do you think the emperor and

National Palace Museum, Taipei, Taiwan/Werner Forman/Art Resource, NY

Source 8.2 At Table with the Empress

empress viewed their roles at these functions? Were they acting as private persons among friends or in an official capacity?

■ What differences in status among these women can you identify?

■ What view of these women does the artist seek to convey?

■ What does the posture of the women suggest about the event?

Confucian cultural ideals gave great prominence to literature, poetry, and scholarly pursuits as leisure activities appropriate for "gentlemen." Confucius himself had declared that "gentlemen make friends through literature, and through friendship increase their benevolence." For some, a more reclusive life devoted to study, painting, poetry, and conversation with friends represented an honorable alternative to government service. Thus literary gatherings of scholars and officials, often in garden settings, were common themes in Tang and Song dynasty paintings. Source 8.3, by the tenth-century painter Zhou Wenju, provides an illustration of such a gathering.

Source 8.3 A Literary Gathering

(Formerly attributed to) Scholars of the Liuli Hall, late 13th century, China. Song Dynasty (9601279). Handscroll: ink and color on silk. Image: 12⅜ × 50⁹⁄₁₆ in. (31.4 × 128.4 cm.). Overall with mounting: 15⅛ × 329½ in. (38.4 x 836.9 cm.). Gift of Mrs. Sheila Riddell, in memory of Sir Percival David, 1977 (1977.49). The Metropolitan Museum of Art, New York, NY, USA/Image copyright © The Metropolitan Museum of Art/Image Source: Art Resource, NY

- What marks these figures as cultivated men of literary or scholarly inclination?

- What meaning might you attribute to the outdoor garden setting of this image and that of Source 8.1?

- Notice the various gazes of the four figures. What do they suggest about the character of this gathering and the interpersonal relationships among its participants? Are they interacting or engaged in solitary pursuits?

- Do you think the artist was seeking to convey an idealized image of what a gathering of "gentlemen" ought to be or a realistic portrayal of an actual event? What elements of the painting support your answer?

Not all was poetry and contemplation of nature in the leisure-time activities of China's elite. Nor were men and women always so strictly segregated as the preceding sources may suggest. Source 8.4 illustrates another side of Chinese elite life. These images are part of a long tenth-century scroll painting

© Beijing Eastphoto Stockimages, Co., Ltd./Alamy

Source 8.4 An Elite Night Party

titled *The Night Revels of Han Xizai*. Apparently, the Tang dynasty emperor Li Yu became concerned that one of his ministers, Han Xizai, was overindulging in suspicious nightlong parties in his own home. He therefore commissioned the artist Gu Hongzhong to attend these parties secretly and to record the events in a painting, which he hoped would shame his wayward but talented official into more appropriate and dignified behavior. The entire scroll shows men and women together, sometimes in flirtatious situations, while open sleeping areas suggest sexual activity.

- What kinds of entertainment were featured at this gathering?

- What aspects of these parties shown in the scroll paintings might have caused the emperor some concern? Refer back to the female musicians shown on page 211, which derives from the same painting. In what respects might these kinds of gatherings run counter to Confucian values?

- How are women portrayed in these images? In what ways are they relating to the men in the paintings?

DOING HISTORY

The Leisure Life of China's Elites

1. **Describing elite society:** Based on these paintings, write a brief description of the social life of Chinese elites during the Tang and Song dynasties.

2. **Defining the self-image of an elite:** What do these sources suggest about how members of the elite ideally viewed themselves? In what ways do those self-portraits draw upon Confucian, Daoist, or Buddhist teachings?

3. **Noticing differences in the depiction of women:** In what different ways are women represented in these paintings? Keep in mind that all the artists were men. How might this affect the way women were depicted? How might female artists have portrayed them differently?

4. **Using images to illustrate change:** Reread the sections on Chinese women (pages 211–13 and 331–32). How might these images be used to illustrate the changes in women's lives that are described in those pages?

5. **Seeking additional sources:** What other kinds of visual sources might provide further insight into the lives of Chinese elites?

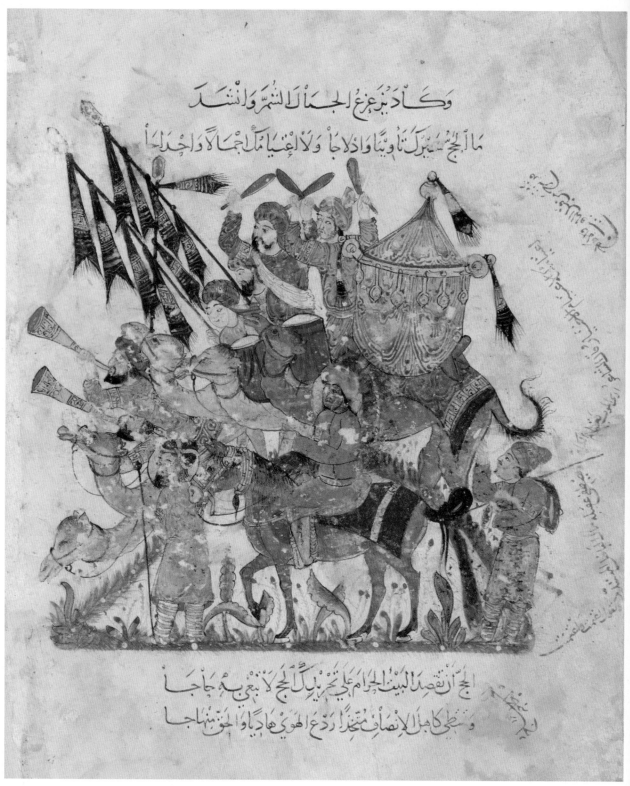

From the *"Maqamat"* of Abu Mohammed el Qasim ibn Ali Hariri (1054–1122), 1237/© BnF, Dist. RMN–Grand Palais/Art Resource, NY

CHAPTER 9

The Worlds of Islam

Afro-Eurasian Connections
600–1500

Hassan Kargbo, a citizen of the small West African country of Sierra Leone, is a "ChrisMus," which in local parlance is a person who identifies with both Christianity and Islam. "I see it as the same religion," he stated. Interviewed in early 2014, he acknowledged going to church every Sunday, wearing a Jesus bracelet, and praying at a mosque every day. Kelfala Conteh, the caretaker of an ancient mosque in Sierra Leone's capital of Freetown, reported, "Of course [Christians] come here. We have both Christians and Muslims praying side by side." Wurie Bah, another Muslim from Freetown, said, "We all believe in God. If my friends invite me to church, of course I will go." On one of the colorfully decorated minibuses that carry passengers around the city is the declaration that "God loves Allah."[1]

In the world of the early twenty-first century, where headlines often highlight violence among Muslims and violent conflict with Christians or Jews, it is perhaps useful to recall places such as Sierra Leone where religious tolerance is both practiced and celebrated. Nor is it alone. Indonesia, the most heavily populated Muslim country in the world, has inscribed freedom of religion in its constitution; has officially recognized Christian, Hindu, and Buddhist holidays as well as those of Islam; and has generally maintained peace among its various religious communities. Tunisia, the cradle of the Arab Spring, adopted a new constitution in early 2014 that represented a compromise between advocates of a secular state and those committed to a more Islamic regime. It commits the country to democracy, freedom of conscience, and gender equality.

The many faces of contemporary Islam echo the earlier history of this newest of humankind's major religions. During the first Muslim

The Hajj   The pilgrimage to Mecca, known as the hajj, has long been a central religious ritual in Islamic practice. It also embodies the cosmopolitan character of Islam as pilgrims from all over the vast Islamic realm assemble in the city where the faith was born. This painting shows a group of joyful pilgrims, led by a band, on their way to Mecca.

363

millennium (600–1600), the Islamic world found expression in various forms, some displaying a broad acceptance for diversity and others engaged in serious and at times violent conflict with those of a different religious outlook. Furthermore, both then and now, the world of Islam occupied a central position in the larger international arena, interacting with most of the other civilizations.

As in China, Muslim societies over much of the past century have been seeking to overcome several hundred years of humiliating European intrusion and to find their place in the modern world. In doing so, many Muslims have found inspiration and encouragement in the early history of their civilization and their faith. For a thousand years (roughly 600–1600), peoples claiming allegiance to Islam represented a highly successful, prosperous, and expansive civilization, encompassing parts of Africa, Europe, the Middle East, and Asia. While Chinese culture and Buddhism provided the cultural anchor for East Asia during the third-wave millennium and Christianity did the same for Europe, the realm of Islam touched on both of them and decisively shaped the history of the entire Afro-Eurasian world.

The significance of a burgeoning Islamic world during the third-wave era was enormous. It thrust the previously marginal and largely nomadic Arabs into a central role in world history, for it was among them and in their language that the newest of the world's major religions was born. The sudden emergence and rapid spread of that religion in the seventh century c.e. was accompanied by the creation of a huge empire that stretched from Spain to India. Both within that empire and beyond it, a new and innovative civilization took shape, drawing on Arab, Persian, Turkish, Greco-Roman, South Asian, and African cultures. It was clearly the largest and most influential of the new third-wave civilizations. Finally, the broad reach of Islam generated many of the great cultural encounters of this age of accelerating connections, as Islamic civilization challenged and provoked Christendom, penetrated and was transformed by African cultures, and also took root in India, Central Asia, and Southeast Asia. The spread of Islam continued in the modern era so that by 2013 some 1.6 billion people, or 23 percent of the world's population, identified as Muslims. It was second only to Christianity as the world's most widely practiced religion, and it extended far beyond the Arab lands where it had originated.

SEEKING THE MAIN POINT

In what ways did the civilization of Islam draw on other civilizations in the Afro-Eurasian world? And in what respects did it shape or transform those civilizations?

The Birth of a New Religion

Most of the major religious or cultural traditions of the second-wave era had emerged from the core of established civilizations—Confucianism and Daoism from China, Hinduism and Buddhism from India, Greek philosophy from the Mediterranean world, and Zoroastrianism from Persia. Christianity and Islam, by contrast, emerged more from the margins of Mediterranean and Middle Eastern civilizations. Christianity, of course, appeared among a small Middle Eastern people, the Jews, in a

A MAP OF TIME

570–632	Life of Muhammad
632–661	Era of Rightly Guided Caliphs
633–644	Muslim conquest of Persia
650s	Quran compiled
656–661; 680–692	Civil war; emergence of Sunni/Shia split
661–750	Umayyad caliphate
711–718	Conquest of Spain
750–900	High point of Abbasid caliphate
751	Battle of Talas River
756	Baghdad established as capital of Abbasid caliphate
800–1000	Emergence of Sufism
1099	Crusaders seize Jerusalem
1206	Delhi sultanate established in India
1258	Mongols sack Baghdad; formal end of Abbasid caliphate
1324	Mansa Musa's pilgrimage to Mecca
1453	Ottoman Empire conquers Constantinople; end of Byzantine Empire
1492	Christian reconquest of Spain complete; end of Muslim Spain
1526	Mughal Empire established in India

remote province of the Roman Empire, while Islam took hold in the cities and deserts of the Arabian Peninsula.

The Homeland of Islam

The central region of the Arabian Peninsula had long been inhabited by nomadic Arabs, known as Bedouins, who herded their sheep and camels in seasonal migrations. These peoples lived in fiercely independent clans and tribes, which often engaged in bitter blood feuds with one another. They recognized a variety of gods, ancestors, and nature spirits; valued personal bravery, group loyalty, and hospitality; and greatly treasured their highly expressive oral poetry. But there was more to Arabia than camel-herding nomads. In scattered oases, the highlands of Yemen, and interior mountain communities, sedentary village-based agriculture was practiced,

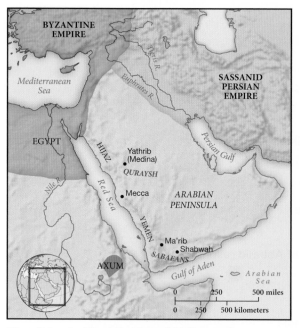

Map 9.1   Arabia at the Time of Muhammad

Located adjacent to the Byzantine and Persian empires, the eastern coast of Arabia was the site of a major trade route between the Indian Ocean and the Mediterranean Sea.

■ **Description**

In what ways did the early history of Islam reflect its Arabian origins?

and in the northern and southern regions of Arabia, small kingdoms had flourished in earlier times. Arabia also sat astride increasingly important trade routes that connected the Indian Ocean world with that of the Mediterranean Sea, a location that gave rise to cosmopolitan commercial cities, whose values and practices were often in conflict with those of traditional Arab tribes (see Map 9.1).

One of those cities, Mecca, came to occupy a distinctive role in Arabia. Though somewhat off the major long-distance trade routes, Mecca was the site of the Kaaba, the most prominent religious shrine in Arabia, which housed representations of some 360 deities and was the destination for many pilgrims. Mecca's dominant tribe, the Quraysh (koor-EYE'SH), had come to control access to the Kaaba and had grown wealthy by taxing the local trade that accompanied the annual pilgrimage season. By the sixth century, Mecca was home to people from various tribes and clans as well as an assortment of individual outlaws, exiles, refugees, and foreign merchants, but much of its growing wealth was concentrated in the hands of a few ruling Quraysh families.

Furthermore, Arabia was located on the periphery of two established and rival civilizations of that time—the Byzantine Empire, heir to the Roman world, and the Sassanid Empire, heir to the imperial traditions of Persia. This location, coupled with long-distance trade, ensured some familiarity with the larger world, particularly in the cities and settled farming regions of the peninsula. Many Jews and Christians as well as some Zoroastrians lived among the Arabs, and their monotheistic ideas became widely known. By the time of Muhammad, most of the settled Arabs had acknowledged the preeminent position of Allah, the supreme god of the Arab pantheon, although they usually found the lesser gods, including the three daughters of Allah, far more accessible. Moreover, they increasingly identified Allah with Yahweh, the Jewish High God, and regarded themselves too as "children of Abraham." A few Arabs were beginning to explore the possibility that Allah/Yahweh was the only God and that the many others, residing in the Kaaba and in shrines across the peninsula, were nothing more than "helpless and harmless idols."[2]

To an outside observer around 600, it might well have seemed that Arabs were moving toward Judaism religiously or that Christianity, the most rapidly growing religion in western Asia, would encompass Arabia as well. Any such expectations, however, were thoroughly confounded by the dramatic events of the seventh century.

The Messenger and the Message

The catalyst for those events and for the birth of this new religion was a single individual, Muhammad Ibn Abdullah (570–632 C.E.), who was born in Mecca to a Quraysh family. As a young boy, Muhammad lost his parents, came under the care of an uncle, and worked as a shepherd to pay his keep. Later he became a trader and traveled as far north as Syria. At the age of twenty-five, he married a wealthy widow, Khadija, herself a prosperous merchant, with whom he fathered six children. A highly reflective man deeply troubled by the religious corruption and social inequalities of Mecca, he often undertook periods of withdrawal and meditation in the arid mountains outside the city. There, like the Buddha and Jesus, Muhammad had a powerful, overwhelming religious experience that left him convinced, albeit reluctantly, that he was Allah's messenger to the Arabs, commissioned to bring to them a scripture in their own language. (See Working with Evidence: The Life of the Prophet, page 399, for images from the life of Muhammad.)

According to Muslim tradition, the revelations began in 610 and continued periodically over the next twenty-two years. Those revelations, recorded in the Quran, became the sacred scriptures of Islam, which to this day most Muslims regard as the very words of God and the core of their faith. Intended to be recited rather than simply read for information, the Quran, Muslims claim, when heard in its original Arabic, conveys nothing less than the very presence of the Divine. Its unmatched poetic beauty, miraculous to Muslims, convinced many that it was indeed a revelation from God. One of the earliest converts testified to its power: "When I heard the Quran, my heart was softened and I wept and Islam entered into me."[3]

■ **Description**
What did the Quran expect from those who followed its teachings?

In its Arabian setting, the Quran's message, delivered through Muhammad, was revolutionary. Religiously, it was radically monotheistic, presenting Allah as the only God, the all-powerful Creator, good, just, and ever merciful. Allah was the "Lord sustainer of the worlds, the Compassionate, the Caring, master of the day of reckoning" and known to human beings "on the farthest horizon and within their own selves."[4] Here was an exalted conception of Deity that drew heavily on traditions of Jewish and Christian monotheism. As "the Messenger of God," Muhammad presented himself in the line of earlier prophets—Abraham, Moses, Jesus, and many others. He was the last, "the seal of the prophets," bearing God's

Muslims, Jews, and Christians
The close relationship of three Middle Eastern monotheistic traditions is illustrated in this fifteenth-century Persian painting, which portrays Muhammad leading Moses, Abraham, and Jesus in prayer. The fire surrounding the Prophet's head represents his religious fervor. The painting reflects the Islamic belief that the revelations granted to Muhammad built on and completed those given earlier to Jews and Christians. (From *Miradj*, by Mir Haydar, Royal workshop of the Timurid Dynasty in Herat, Afghanistan, 1436. © BnF, Dist. RMN–Grand Palais/Art Resource, NY)

final revelation to humankind. It was not so much a call to a new faith as an invitation to return to the old and pure religion of Abraham from which Jews, Christians, and Arabs alike had deviated. Jews had wrongly conceived of themselves as a uniquely "chosen people"; Christians had made their prophet into a god; and Arabs had become wildly polytheistic. To all of this, the message of the Quran was a corrective.

Submission to Allah ("Muslim" means "one who submits") was the primary obligation of believers and the means of achieving a God-conscious life in this world and a place in Paradise after death. According to the Quran, however, submission was not merely an individual or a spiritual act, for it involved the creation of a whole new society. Over and again, the Quran denounced the prevailing social practices of an increasingly prosperous Mecca: the hoarding of wealth, the exploitation of the poor, the charging of high rates of interest on loans, corrupt business deals, the abuse of women, and the neglect of widows and orphans. Like the Jewish prophets of the Old Testament, the Quran demanded social justice and laid out a prescription for its implementation. It sought a return to the older values of Arab tribal life—solidarity, equality, concern for the poor—which had been undermined, particularly in Mecca, by growing wealth and commercialism.

The message of the Quran challenged not only the ancient polytheism of Arab religion and the social injustices of Mecca but also the entire tribal and clan structure of Arab society, which was so prone to war, feuding, and violence. The just and moral society of Islam was the *umma* (OOM-mah), the community of all believers, replacing tribal, ethnic, or racial identities. Such a society would be a "witness over the nations," for according to the Quran, "You are the best community evolved for mankind, enjoining what is right and forbidding what is wrong."[5] In this community, women too had an honored and spiritually equal place. "The believers, men and women, are protectors of one another," declared the Quran.[6] The umma, then, was to be a new and just community, bound by common belief rather than by territory, language, or tribe.

The core message of the Quran—the remembrance of God—was effectively summarized as a set of five requirements for believers, known as the Pillars of Islam. The first pillar expressed the heart of the Islamic message: "There is no god but God, and Muhammad is the messenger of God." The second pillar was ritual prayer, performed five times a day. Accompanying practices, including cleansing, bowing, kneeling, and prostration, expressed believers' submission to Allah and provided a frequent reminder, amid the busyness of daily life, that they were living in the presence of God. The third pillar, almsgiving, reflected the Quran's repeated demands for social justice by requiring believers to give generously to support the poor and needy of the community. The fourth pillar established a month of fasting during Ramadan, which meant abstaining from food, drink, and sexual relations from the first light of dawn to sundown. It provided an occasion for self-purification and a reminder of the needs of the hungry. The fifth pillar encouraged a pilgrimage to Mecca, known as the hajj (HAHJ), during which believers from all over the Islamic world assembled once a year and put on identical simple white clothing as they reenacted key events in Islamic history. For at least the few days of the hajj, the many worlds of Islam must surely have seemed a single realm.

A further requirement for believers, sometimes called the sixth pillar, was "struggle," or *jihad* in Arabic. Its more general meaning, which Muhammad referred to as the "greater jihad," was an interior personal effort of each believer against greed and selfishness, a spiritual striving toward living a God-conscious life. In its "lesser" form, the "jihad of the sword," the Quran authorized armed struggle against the forces of unbelief and evil as a means of establishing Muslim rule and of defending the umma from the threats of infidel aggressors. The understanding and use of the jihad concept have varied widely over the many centuries of Islamic history and remain a matter of much controversy among Muslims in the twenty-first century.

The Transformation of Arabia

As the revelations granted to Muhammad became known in Mecca, they attracted a small following of some close relatives, a few prominent Meccan leaders, and an assortment of lower-class dependents, freed slaves, and members of poorer clans. Those teachings also soon attracted the vociferous opposition of Mecca's elite families, particularly those of Muhammad's own tribe, the Quraysh. Muhammad's claim to be a "messenger of Allah," his unyielding monotheism, his call for social reform, his condemnation of Mecca's business practices, and his apparent disloyalty to his own tribe enraged the wealthy and ruling families of Mecca. So great had this opposition become that in 622 Muhammad and his small band of followers emigrated to the more welcoming town of Yathrib, soon to be called Medina, the city of the Prophet. This agricultural settlement of mixed Arab and Jewish population had invited Muhammad to serve as an arbitrator of their intractable conflicts. The emigration to Yathrib, known in Arabic as the *hijra* (HIJJ-ruh) ("the journey"), was a momentous turning point in the early history of Islam and thereafter marked the beginning of a new Islamic calendar.

The new community, or umma, that took shape in Medina was a kind of "supertribe," but very different from the traditional tribes of Arab society. Membership was a matter of belief rather than birth, allowing the community to expand rapidly. Furthermore, all authority, both political and religious, was concentrated in the hands of Muhammad, who proceeded to introduce radical changes. Usury was outlawed, tax-free marketplaces were established, and a mandatory payment to support the poor was imposed.

In Medina, Muhammad not only began to create a new society but also declared his movement's independence from its earlier affiliation with Judaism. In the early years, he had anticipated a warm response from Jews and Christians, based on a common monotheism and prophetic tradition, and had directed his followers to pray facing Jerusalem. But when some Jewish groups allied with his enemies, Muhammad acted harshly to suppress them, exiling some and enslaving or killing

■ **Change**
How was Arabia transformed by the rise of Islam?

others. This was not, however, a general suppression of Jews since others among them remained loyal to Muhammad's new state. But the Prophet now redirected his followers' prayer toward Mecca, essentially declaring Islam an Arab religion, though one with a universal message.

From its base in Medina, the Islamic community rapidly extended its reach throughout Arabia. Early military successes against Muhammad's Meccan opponents convinced other Arab tribes that the Muslims and their God were on the rise, and they sought to negotiate alliances with the new power. Growing numbers converted. The religious appeal of the new faith, its promise of material gain, the end of incessant warfare among feuding tribes, periodic military actions skillfully led by Muhammad, and the Prophet's willingness to enter into marriage alliances with leading tribes—all of this contributed to the consolidation of Islamic control throughout Arabia. In 630, Muhammad triumphantly and peacefully entered Mecca itself, purging the Kaaba of its idols and declaring it a shrine to the one God, Allah. By the time Muhammad died in 632, most of Arabia had come under the control of this new Islamic state, and many had embraced the new faith.

Thus the birth of Islam differed sharply from that of Christianity. Jesus' teaching about "giving to Caesar what is Caesar's and to God what is God's" reflected the minority and subordinate status of the Jews within the Roman Empire. Early Christians found themselves periodically persecuted by Roman authorities for more than three centuries, requiring them to work out some means of dealing with an often-hostile state. The answer lay in the development of a separate church hierarchy and the concept of two coexisting authorities, one religious and one political, an arrangement that persisted even after the state became Christian.

The young Islamic community, by contrast, constituted a state, and soon a huge empire, at the very beginning of its history. Muhammad was not only a religious figure but also, unlike Jesus or the Buddha, a political and military leader able to implement his vision of an ideal Islamic society. Nor did Islam give rise to a separate religious organization, although tension between religious and political goals frequently generated conflict. No professional clergy mediating between God and humankind emerged within Islam. Teachers, religious scholars, prayer leaders, and judges within an Islamic legal system did not have the religious role that priests held within Christianity. No distinction between religious law and civil law, so important in the Christian world, existed within the realm of Islam. One law, known as the *sharia* (shah-REE-ah), regulated every aspect of life. The sharia (literally, "a path to water," which is the source of life) evolved over the several centuries following the birth of this new religion and found expression in a number of separate schools of Islamic legal practice.

In little more than twenty years (610–632), a profound transformation had occurred in the Arabian Peninsula. What would subsequently become a new religion had been born, though it was one with roots in earlier Jewish, Christian, and Zoroastrian traditions. A new and vigorous state had emerged, bringing peace to the warring tribes of Arabia. Within that state, a distinctive society had begun to take shape, one that served ever after as a model for Islamic communities everywhere. In his farewell sermon, Muhammad described the outlines of this community:

> All mankind is from Adam and Eve, an Arab has no superiority over a non-Arab nor a non-Arab has any superiority over an Arab; also a white has no superiority over a black nor a black has any superiority over a white — except by piety and good action. Learn that every Muslim is a brother to every Muslim and that the Muslims constitute one brotherhood.[7]

The Making of an Arab Empire

It did not take long for the immense transformations occurring in Arabia to have an impact beyond the peninsula. In the centuries that followed, the energies born of those vast changes profoundly transformed much of the Afro-Eurasian world. The new Arab state became a huge empire, encompassing all or part of Egyptian, Roman/Byzantine, Persian, Mesopotamian, and Indian civilizations. The Islamic faith spread widely within and outside that empire. So too did the culture and language of Arabia, as many Arabs migrated far beyond their original homeland and many others found it advantageous to learn Arabic. From the mixing and blending of these many peoples emerged the new and distinctive third-wave civilization of Islam, bound by the ties of a common faith but divided by differences of culture, class, politics, gender, and religious understanding. These enormously consequential processes — the making of a new religion, a new empire, and a new civilization — were central to world history during the third-wave millennium.

War, Conquest, and Tolerance

Within a few years of Muhammad's death in 632, Arab armies engaged the Byzantine and Persian Sassanid empires, the great powers of the region. It was the beginning of a process that rapidly gave rise to an Arab empire that stretched from Spain to India, penetrating both Europe and China and governing most of the lands between them (see Map 9.2). In creating that empire, Arabs were continuing a long pattern of tribal raids into surrounding civilizations, but now these Arabs were newly organized in a state of their own with a central command able to mobilize the military potential of the entire population. The Byzantine and Persian empires had for a century or more suffered periodic epidemics of the plague that decimated their urban populations, while the more remote and scattered Arabs of the Arabian Desert were more protected from this pestilence. Furthermore, these great empires, weakened by decades of war with each other and by internal revolts, continued to view the Arabs as a mere nuisance rather than a serious threat. But by 644, the Sassanid Empire had been defeated by Arab forces, while Byzantium, the remaining eastern regions of the old Roman Empire, soon lost the southern half of its

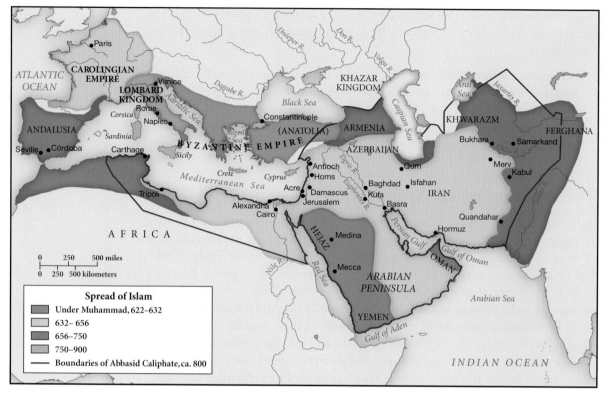

Map 9.2   **The Arab Empire and the Initial Expansion of Islam, 622–900 C.E.**

Far more so than with Buddhism or Christianity, the initial spread of Islam was both rapid and extensive. And unlike the other two world religions, Islam quickly gave rise to a huge empire, ruled by Muslim Arabs, which encompassed many of the older civilizations of the region.

territories. Beyond these victories, Muslim forces, operating on both land and sea, swept westward across North Africa, conquered Spain in the early 700s, and attacked southern France. To the east, Arab armies reached the Indus River and seized some of the major oases towns of Central Asia. In 751, they inflicted a crushing defeat on Chinese forces in the Battle of Talas River, which had lasting consequences for the cultural evolution of Asia, for it checked the further expansion of China to the west and made possible the conversion to Islam of Central Asia's Turkic-speaking people. Most of the violence of conquest involved imperial armies, though on occasion civilians too were caught up in the fighting and suffered terribly. In 634, for example, a battle between Byzantine and Arab forces in Palestine resulted in the death of some 4,000 villagers.

■ **Change**

Why were Arabs able to construct such a huge empire so quickly?

The motives driving the creation of the Arab Empire were broadly similar to those of other empires. The merchant leaders of the new Islamic community wanted to capture profitable trade routes and wealthy agricultural regions. Individual Arabs found in military expansion a route to wealth and social promotion. The need to harness the immense energies of the Arabian transformation was also important. The fragile unity of the umma threatened to come apart after Muhammad's death, and external expansion provided a common task for the community.

While many among the new conquerors viewed the mission of empire in terms of jihad, bringing righteous government to the peoples they conquered, this did not mean imposing a new religion. In fact, for the better part of a century after Muhammad's death, his followers usually referred to themselves as "believers," a term that appears in the Quran far more often than "Muslims" and one that included pious Jews and Christians as well as newly monotheistic Arabs. Such a posture eased the acceptance of the new political order, for many people recently incorporated in the emerging Arab Empire were already monotheists and familiar with the core ideas and practices of the Believers' Movement — prayer, fasting, pilgrimage, revelation, and prophets. Furthermore, the new rulers were remarkably tolerant of established Jewish and Christian faiths. The first governor of Arab-ruled Jerusalem was a Jew. Many old Christian churches continued to operate and new ones were constructed. A Nestorian Christian patriarch in Iraq wrote to one of his bishops around 647 C.E. observing that the new rulers "not only do not fight Christianity, they even commend our religion, show honor to the priests and monasteries and saints of the Lord, and make gifts to the monasteries and churches."[8] Formal agreements or treaties recognized Jews, Christians, and Zoroastrians as "people of the book," giving them the status of *dhimmis* (dihm-mees), protected but second-class subjects. Such people were permitted to freely practice their own religion, so long as they paid a special tax known as the *jizya*. Theoretically the tax was a substitute for military service, supposedly forbidden to non-Muslims. In practice, many dhimmis served in the highest offices within Muslim kingdoms and in their armies as well.

In other ways too, the Arab rulers of an expanding empire sought to limit the disruptive impact of conquest. To prevent indiscriminate destruction and exploitation of conquered peoples, occupying Arab armies were restricted to garrison towns, segregated from the native population. Local elites and bureaucratic structures were incorporated into the new Arab Empire. Nonetheless, the empire worked many changes on its subjects, the most enduring of which was the mass conversion of Middle Eastern peoples to what became by the eighth century the new and separate religion of Islam.

Conversion

For some people, no doubt, converting to Islam was or subsequently became a matter of profound spiritual or psychological transformation, but far more often, at least initially, it was "social conversion," motivated more by convenience than conviction.[9] It happened at various rates and in different ways, but in the four centuries or so after the death of Muhammad, millions of individuals and many whole societies within the Arab Empire found their cultural identity bound up with a belief in Allah and the message of his prophet. They had become Muslims. How had this immense cultural change occurred?

■ **Explanation**
What accounts for the widespread conversion to Islam?

In some ways, perhaps, the change was not so dramatic, as major elements of Islam—monotheism; ritual prayer and cleansing ceremonies; fasting; divine revelation; the ideas of Heaven, Hell, and final judgment—were quite familiar to Jews, Christians, and Zoroastrians. Furthermore, Islam was from the beginning associated with the sponsorship of a powerful state, quite unlike the experience of early Buddhism or Christianity. Conquest called into question the power of old gods, while the growing prestige of the Arab Empire attracted many to Allah. Although deliberately forced conversion was rare and forbidden, living in an Islamic-governed state provided a variety of incentives for claiming Muslim identity. Slaves and prisoners of war were among the early converts, particularly in Persia. Converts could also avoid the jizya, the tax imposed on non-Muslims. People aspiring to official positions found conversion to Islam an aid to social mobility. In Islam, merchants found a religion friendly to commerce. The Prophet himself had been a trader, acting as a commercial agent for his wife Khadija. As Islamic law developed over several centuries, it defined what merchants might expect from one another and so reduced the uncertainty of long-distance commerce. And in the expansive Arab Empire, merchants enjoyed a huge and secure arena for trade.

Conversion was not an automatic or easy process. Vigorous resistance delayed conversion for centuries among the Berbers of North Africa; a small group of zealous Spanish Christians in the ninth century provoked their own martyrdom by publicly insulting the Prophet; and some Persian Zoroastrians fled to avoid Muslim rule. More generally, though, a remarkable and lasting religious transformation occurred throughout the Arab Empire.

In Persia, for example, between 750 and 900, about 80 percent of the population made the transition to a Muslim religious identity. But they did so in a manner quite distinct from the people of Iraq, Syria, Egypt, and North Africa. In these regions, converts to Islam gradually abandoned their native languages, adopted Arabic, and came to see themselves as Arabs. In Iran or Persia, by contrast, Arab conquest did not involve cultural Arabization, despite some initial efforts to impose the Arabic language. By the tenth century, the vast majority of Persians had become Muslims, but the Persian language (called Farsi in Iran) flourished, enriched now by a number of Arabic loan words and written in an Arabic script. In 1010, that language received its classic literary expression when the Persian poet Ferdowsi completed his epic work, the *Shahnama* (*The Book of Kings*). A huge text of some 60,000 rhyming couplets, it recorded the mythical and pre-Islamic history of Iran and gave an enduring expression to a distinctly Persian cultural identity. Thus, in places where large-scale Arab migration had occurred, such as Egypt, North Africa, and Iraq, Arabic culture and language, as well as the religion of Islam, took hold. Such areas are today both Muslim and Arab, while the peoples of Iran, Turkey, Pakistan, Indonesia, and West Africa, for example, have "Islamized" without "Arabizing."

The preservation of Persian language and culture had enormous implications for the world of Islam. Many religious ideas of Persian Zoroastrianism—an evil satanic power, final judgment, Heaven and Hell, Paradise—found their way into

Islam, often indirectly via Jewish or Christian precedents. In Iran, Central Asia, India, and later in the Ottoman Empire, Islam was accompanied by pervasive Persian influences. Persian administrative and bureaucratic techniques; Persian court practices with their palaces, gardens, and splendid garments; Persian architecture, poetry, music, and painting—all of this decisively shaped the high culture of these eastern Islamic lands. One of the Abbasid caliphs, himself an Arab, observed: "The Persians ruled for a thousand years and did not need us Arabs even for a day. We have been ruling them for one or two centuries and cannot do without them for an hour."[10]

Divisions and Controversies

The ideal of a unified Muslim community, so important to Muhammad, proved difficult to realize as conquest and conversion vastly enlarged the Islamic umma. A central problem involved leadership and authority in the absence of Muhammad's towering presence. Who should hold the role of caliph (KAY-lihf), the successor to Muhammad as the political leader of the umma, the protector and defender of the faith? That issue crystallized a variety of emerging conflicts within the Islamic world—between early and later converts, among various Arab tribes and factions, between Arabs and non-Arabs, between privileged and wealthy rulers and their far less fortunate subjects. Many of these political and social conflicts found expression in religious terms as various understandings of the Quran and of Muhammad's life and teachings took shape within the growing Islamic community.

The first four caliphs, known among most Muslims as the Rightly Guided Caliphs (632–661), were close "companions of the Prophet," selected by the Muslim elders of Medina. Division surfaced almost immediately as a series of Arab tribal rebellions and new "prophets" persuaded the first caliph, Abu Bakr, to suppress them forcibly. The third and fourth caliphs, Uthman and Ali, were both assassinated, and by 656, less than twenty-five years after Muhammad's death, civil war pitted Muslim against Muslim.

■ **Comparison**
What is the difference between Sunni and Shia Islam?

Out of that conflict emerged one of the deepest and most enduring rifts within the Islamic world. On one side were the Sunni (SOON-nee) Muslims, who held that the caliphs were rightful political and military leaders, selected by the Islamic community. On the other side of this sharp divide was the Shia (SHEE-ah) (an Arabic word meaning "party" or "faction") branch of Islam. Its adherents felt strongly that leadership in the Islamic world should derive from the line of Ali and his son Husayn, blood relatives of Muhammad, both of whom died at the hands of their political or religious enemies. If the caliph was the idealized communal leader for Sunnis, *imams* (leaders) served this purpose for most of the Shia Muslims. They were widely thought to have some special charisma based on descent from the Prophet, giving them a religious authority that the caliphs lacked and allowing them to infallibly interpret divine revelation and law.

Thus what began as a purely political conflict acquired over time a deeper significance. For much of early Islamic history, Shia Muslims saw themselves as the

The Kaaba
Located in Mecca, this stone structure, covered with a black cloth and known as the Kaaba, was originally home to the numerous deities of pre-Islamic Arabia. Cleansed by Muhammad, it became the sacred shrine of Islam and the destination of countless pilgrims undertaking the hajj. Part of that ritual involves circling the Kaaba seven times, as shown here in a photograph from 2013. (Ibraheem Abu Mustafa/Reuters/Landov)

minority opposition within Islam. They felt that history had taken a wrong turn and that they were "the defenders of the oppressed, the critics and opponents of privilege and power," while the Sunnis were the advocates of the established order.[11] Various armed revolts by Shias over the centuries, most of which failed, led to a distinctive conception of martyrdom and to the expectation that their defeated leaders were merely in hiding and not really dead and that they would return in the fullness of time. Thus a messianic element entered Shia Islam. The Sunni/Shia schism became a lasting division in the Islamic world, reflected in conflicts among various Islamic states, and was exacerbated by further splits among the Shia. Those divisions echo still in the twenty-first century.

As the Arab Empire grew, its caliphs were transformed from modest Arab chiefs into absolute monarchs, "the shadow of God on earth," of the Byzantine or Persian variety, complete with elaborate court rituals, a complex bureaucracy, a standing army, and centralized systems of taxation and coinage. They were also subject to the dynastic rivalries and succession disputes common to other empires. The first dynasty, following the era of the Rightly Guided Caliphs, came from the Umayyad (oo-MEYE-ahd) family (r. 661–750). Under its leadership, the Arab Empire expanded greatly, caliphs became hereditary rulers, and the capital moved from Medina to the cosmopolitan Roman/Byzantine city of Damascus in Syria. Its ruling class was an

Arab military aristocracy, drawn from various tribes. But Umayyad rule provoked growing criticism and unrest. The Shia viewed the Umayyad caliphs as illegitimate usurpers, and non-Arab Muslims resented their second-class citizenship in the empire. Many Arabs protested the luxurious living and impiety of their rulers. The Umayyads, they charged, "made God's servants slaves, God's property something to be taken by turns among the rich, and God's religion a cause of corruption."[12]

Such grievances lay behind the overthrow of the Umayyads in 750 and their replacement by a new Arab dynasty, the Abbasids. With a splendid new capital in Baghdad, the Abbasid caliphs presided over a flourishing and prosperous Islamic civilization in which non-Arabs, especially Persians, now played a prominent role. But the political unity of the Abbasid Empire did not last long. Beginning in the mid-ninth century, many local governors or military commanders effectively asserted the autonomy of their regions, while still giving formal allegiance to the caliph in Baghdad. Long before Mongol conquest put an official end to the Abbasid Empire in 1258, the Islamic world had fractured politically into a series of "sultanates," many ruled by Persian or Turkish military dynasties.

A further tension within the world of Islam, though one that seldom produced violent conflict, lay in different answers to one central question: what does it mean to be a Muslim, to submit wholly to Allah? That question took on added urgency as the expanding Arab Empire incorporated various peoples and cultures that had been unknown during Muhammad's lifetime. One answer lay in the development of the sharia, the body of Islamic law developed primarily in the eighth and ninth centuries by religious scholars, Sunni and Shia alike, known as the *ulama*.

Based on the Quran, the life and teachings of Muhammad, deductive reasoning, and the consensus of scholars, the emerging sharia addressed in great detail practically every aspect of life. It was a blueprint for an authentic Islamic society, providing meticulous guidance for prayer and ritual cleansing; marriage, divorce, and inheritance; business and commercial relationships; the treatment of slaves; political life; personal hygiene; dietary requirements; and much more. Debates among the ulama led to the creation of four schools of law among Sunni Muslims and still others in the lands of Shia Islam. To the ulama and their followers, living as a Muslim meant following the sharia and thus participating in the creation of an Islamic society.

A second and quite different understanding of the faith emerged among those who saw the worldly success of Islamic civilization as a distraction and deviation from the purer

■ **Comparison**

In what ways were Sufi Muslims critical of mainstream Islam?

Sufis and Worldly Power

This early seventeenth-century painting from India illustrates the tension between Sufis and worldly authorities. Here the Muslim Mughal emperor Jahangir, seated on an hourglass throne, gives his attention to the white-bearded Sufi holy man rather than to the prominent men, including a European figure, shown in the bottom left. (bpk, Berlin/Museum für Islamische Kunst, Staatliche Museum, Berlin, Germany/Photo: Georg Niedermeiser/Art Resource, NY)

Mullah Nasruddin, the Wise Fool of Islam

In the Islamic world, a mullah was a man of some learning, often a local cleric or leader of a village mosque. Far and away the most famous and beloved of mullahs is Nasruddin, considered both a wise man and a fool, both a sage and a simpleton. Stories about him have circulated for centuries and were well known long before the earliest written references to him appeared in the thirteenth century. Many peoples have claimed him, some have sought to find a historical figure on which he is based, and in the Turkish city of Aksehir there is even a tomb and an annual Nasruddin festival, where people dress in costumes to reenact his jokes and stories.

In fact, Mullah Nasruddin has long been an imaginary folk character within the world of Islam and especially among Sufis, gently expressing a skeptical attitude toward the rational mind, sanctimonious posturing, human vanity, and the many faces of the ego. His tales usually take place in a village setting and highlight the limitations of the intellect; the role of humor and intuition in spiritual life; the

Mullah Nasruddin.

importance of generosity, tolerance, and humility; and the many mysteries of existence. The only way to get acquainted with Mullah Nasruddin is to reflect on some of his tales. Here are just a few of the thousands:[13]

- The Mullah was in Mecca for the pilgrimage and had fallen asleep with his feet pointing toward the Kaaba, the large black cube that is the central shrine of Islam. He was awakened and rebuked by some pious Muslims, who told him it was offensive to have his dirty feet pointing at the Kaaba, where God himself resided. The Mullah apologized profusely and then added, "Perhaps you could move my feet to some place where God is *not* present."

- Mullah Nasruddin was invited to a formal reception and upon entering took the seat of greatest honor. Approached by the chief of the guard, he was asked if he was a diplomat, a minister of the king, or perhaps the king himself in disguise. To each of these queries,

photo: Turkish miniature, ca. 1500/© akg-images/The Image Works

spirituality of Muhammad's time. Known as Sufis (SOO-fees), they represented Islam's mystical dimension, in that they sought a direct and personal experience of the Divine. Through renunciation of the material world, meditation on the words of the Quran, the chanting of the names of God, the use of music and dance, and the veneration of Muhammad and various "saints," Sufis pursued an interior life, seeking to tame the ego and achieve spiritual union with Allah. To describe that inexpressible experience, they often resorted to metaphors of drunkenness or the embrace of lovers. "Stain your prayer rug with wine," urged the famous Sufi poet Hafiz, referring to the intoxication of the believer with the Divine Presence. (See the Zooming In feature on Mullah Nasruddin, above, for an expression of popular or folk Sufism.)

he replied, "No, I am more than that." "Then who are you?" demanded the guard. His answer: "I am nobody."

- A villager rushed to tell the Mullah about visions of God he had been having. He asked if this meant he had become enlightened. The Mullah replied by asking him about his goats and servants. The man was enraged at this apparent dismissal of his visions. Then the Mullah explained, "If you are becoming more tender and kind toward your goats and servants, then you are on the way to enlightenment. If not, your visions are an illusion of your ego."

- Mullah Nasruddin was asked to present a lecture on "the nature of Allah" in the local mosque together with many highly learned scholars. When the scholars had finished their eloquent and wise expositions, the humble Mullah arose and hesitantly began his talk by declaring "Allah is an eggplant," while holding one of the vegetables aloft. An uproar followed at this blasphemy. When he was finally given a chance to explain himself, the Mullah declared, "Everyone before me has spoken of what they do not know or have never seen. But we can all see this eggplant. Can anyone deny that Allah is manifest in all things?" When no one was willing to dispute the point, the Mullah concluded, "Well, then Allah is an eggplant."

- One evening, after spending many hours in the local tavern, a thoroughly intoxicated Mullah was stumbling along the streets. A local police official approached him and asked, "Who are you? Where did you come from? Where are you going? Why are you out so late?" The Mullah replied, "If I had answers to all those questions, I'd be home already." [Note: To Sufis, taverns and drunkenness often symbolized spiritual insight or mystical "intoxication" with the Divine.]

- When some neighbors told Nasruddin that his donkey was lost, the Mullah exclaimed, "Thank goodness I was not on the donkey or I'd be lost as well." [Note: In Sufi circles, the donkey has long symbolized the unruly human ego.]

The Mullah's tales have been understood on several levels. Most obviously, they are jokes. But they also convey moral teachings about individual behavior as well as social commentary. And especially for Sufis, they have become a spiritual resource, gradually dissolving limited and culturally conditioned thinking, while opening the way to more fully realizing humanity's divine potential.

Questions: Pick several of these tales and explain in your own words the lessons they might convey for Muslims. In what ways might these tales be considered subversive of established authorities? Might they strike a chord with contemporary sensibilities of our own time?

This mystical tendency in Islamic practice, which became widely popular by the ninth and tenth centuries, was at times sharply critical of the more scholarly and legalistic practitioners of the sharia. To Sufis, establishment teachings about the law and correct behavior, while useful for daily living, did little to bring the believer into the presence of God. For some, even the Quran had its limits. Why spend time reading a love letter (the Quran), asked one Sufi master, when one might be in the very presence of the Beloved who wrote it?[14] Furthermore, Sufis felt that many of the ulama had been compromised by their association with worldly and corrupt governments. Sufis therefore often charted their own course to God, implicitly challenging the religious authority of the ulama. For these orthodox religious scholars, Sufi ideas and practice sometimes verged on heresy, as Sufis on occasion claimed unity with God, received new revelations, or incorporated novel religious practices from outside the Islamic world.

Despite their differences, adherents of the legalistic emphasis of the sharia and practitioners of Sufi spirituality coexisted, mostly peacefully, mixing and mingling, collaborating and disagreeing, in various combinations. For many centuries, roughly 1100 to 1800, Sufism was central to mainstream Islam, and many, perhaps most, Muslims affiliated with one or another Sufi organization, making use of its spiritual practices. A major Islamic thinker, al-Ghazali (1058–1111), himself both a legal scholar and a Sufi practitioner, in fact worked out an intellectual accommodation among these different strands of Islamic thought. Rational philosophy alone could never enable believers to know Allah, he argued. Nor were revelation and the law sufficient, for Muslims must know God in their hearts, through direct personal encounter with Allah. Nonetheless, differences in emphasis remained an element of tension and sometimes discord within the world of Islam.

Women and Men in Early Islam

What did the rise of Islam and the making of the Arab Empire mean for the daily lives of women and their relationship with men? Virtually every aspect of this question has been and remains highly controversial. The debates begin with the Quran itself. Did its teachings release women from earlier restrictions, or did they impose new limitations? At the level of spiritual life, the Quran was quite clear and explicit: men and women were equal. Numerous passages in the Quran use gender-inclusive language, referring to "believers, both men and women."

> Those who surrender themselves to Allah and accept the true faith; who are devout, sincere, patient, humble, charitable, and chaste; who fast and are ever mindful of Allah—on these, both men and women, Allah will bestow forgiveness and rich reward.[15]

■ **Change**
How did the rise of Islam change the lives of women?

But in social terms, and especially within marriage, the Quran, like the written texts of almost all civilizations, viewed women as inferior and subordinate: "Men have authority over women because Allah has made the one superior to the other, and because they spend their wealth to maintain them. Good women are obedient."[16] More specifically, the Quran provided a mix of rights, restrictions, and protections for women. Female infanticide, for example, widely practiced in many cultures as a means of gender selection, was now forbidden for Muslims. Women were given control over their own property, particularly their dowries, and were granted rights of inheritance, but at half the rate of their male counterparts. Marriage was considered a contract between consenting parties, thus making marriage by capture illegitimate. Divorce was possible for both parties, although it was far more readily available for men. The practice of taking multiple husbands, which operated in some pre-Islamic Arab tribes, was prohibited, while polygyny (the practice of having multiple wives) was permitted, though more clearly regulated than before. Men were limited to four wives and required to treat each of them equally. (The difficulty of doing so has been interpreted by some as virtually requiring monogamy.) Men were, however, permitted to have sexual relations with female slaves, but any children born of those unions were free, as was the mother once her owner died. Furthermore, men were strongly encouraged to marry orphans, widows, and slaves.

Such Quranic prescriptions were but one factor shaping the lives of women and men. At least as important were the long-established practices of the societies into which Islam spread and the growing sophistication, prosperity, and urbanization of Islamic civilization. As had been the case in Athens and China during their "golden ages," Muslim women, particularly in the upper classes, experienced growing restrictions as Islamic civilization flourished culturally and economically in the Abbasid era. In early Islamic times, a number of women played visible public roles, particularly Muhammad's youngest wife, Aisha. Women prayed in the mosques, although separately, standing beside the men. Nor were women generally veiled or secluded. As the Arab Empire grew in size and splendor, however, the position of women became more limited. The second caliph, Umar, asked women to offer prayers at home. Now veiling and the seclusion of women became standard practice among the upper and ruling classes, removing them from public life. Separate quarters within the homes of the wealthy were the domain of women, from which they could emerge only completely veiled. The caliph Mansur (r. 754–775) carried this separation of the sexes even further when he ordered a separate bridge for women to be built over the Euphrates River in the new capital of Baghdad. Such seclusion was less possible for lower-class women, who lacked the servants of the rich and had to leave the home for shopping or work.

Such practices derived far more from established traditions of Middle Eastern cultures than from the Quran itself, but they soon gained an Islamic rationale in the writings of Muslim thinkers. The famous philosopher and religious scholar al-Ghazali clearly saw a relationship between Muslim piety and the separation of the sexes:

> It is not permissible for a stranger to hear the sound of a pestle being pounded by a woman he does not know. If he knocks at the door, it is not proper for the woman to answer him softly and easily because men's hearts can be drawn to [women] for the most trifling [reason]. . . . However, if the woman has to answer the knock, she should stick her finger in her mouth so that her voice sounds like that of an old woman.[17]

Other signs of a tightening patriarchy—such as "honor killing" of women by their male relatives for violating sexual taboos and, in some places, clitoridectomy (female genital cutting)—likewise derived from local cultures, with no sanction in the Quran or Islamic law. Where they were practiced, such customs often came to be seen as Islamic, but they were certainly not limited to the Islamic world. In many cultures, concern with family honor linked to women's sexuality dictated harsh punishments for women who violated sexual taboos.

Negative views of women, presenting them variously as weak, deficient, and a sexually charged threat to men and social stability, emerged in the *hadiths* (hah-DEETHS), traditions about the sayings or actions of Muhammad, which became an important source of Islamic law. A changing interpretation of the Adam and Eve story illustrates the point. The Quran attaches equal blame to both Adam and Eve for yielding to the temptation of Satan, and both alike ask for and receive God's forgiveness. Nothing suggests that Eve tempted or seduced Adam into sin. In later centuries, however, several hadiths and other writings took up Judeo-Christian versions of the story that blamed Eve, and thus women in general, for Adam's sin and for the punishment that followed, including expulsion from the garden and pain in childbirth.[18]

Even as women faced growing restrictions in society generally, Islam, like Buddhism and Christianity, also offered new outlets for them in religious life. The Sufi practice of mystical union with Allah allowed a greater role for women than did mainstream Islam. Some Sufi orders had parallel groups for women, and a few welcomed women as equal members. Among the earliest of well-known Sufi practitioners was Rabia, an eighth-century woman from Basra in southern Iraq, who renounced numerous proposals of marriage and engaged, apparently successfully, in repeated religious debates with men. The greatest of the Sufi scholars, Ibn al-Arabi (1165–1240), sang the praises of divine beauty in an explicitly feminine form. The spiritual equality that the Quran accorded to male and female alike allowed women also to aspire to union with God. But for some male Sufi scholars, such as the twelfth-century mystical poet Attar, doing so meant that "she is a man and one cannot any more call her a woman."[19]

Beyond Sufi practice, within the world of Shia Islam, women teachers of the faith were called mullahs, the same as their male counterparts. Islamic education, either in the home or in Quranic schools, allowed some to become literate and a few to achieve higher levels of learning. Visits to the tombs of major Islamic figures as well as the ritual of the public bath likewise provided some opportunity for women to interact with other women beyond their own family circle.

Islam and Cultural Encounter: A Four-Way Comparison

In its earliest centuries, the rapid spread of Islam had been accompanied by the creation of an immense Arab Empire, very much in the tradition of earlier Mediterranean and Middle Eastern empires. By the tenth century, however, little political unity remained, and in 1258 even the powerless symbol of that earlier unity vanished as Mongol forces sacked Baghdad and killed the last Abbasid caliph. But even as the empire disintegrated, the civilization that was born within it grew and flourished. Perhaps the most significant sign of a flourishing Islamic civilization was the continued spread of the religion both within and beyond the boundaries of a vanishing Arab Empire (see Map 9.3), although that process differed considerably

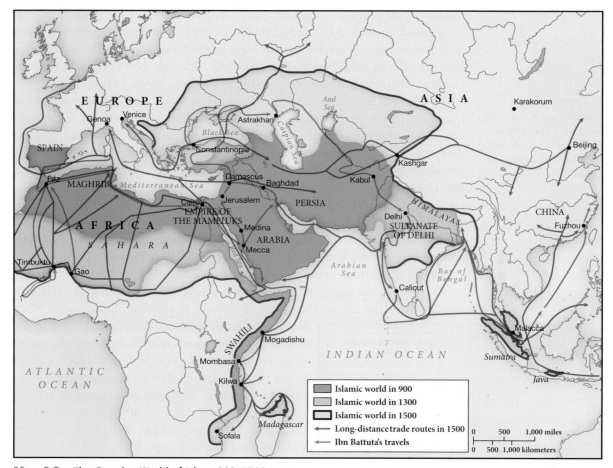

Map 9.3   The Growing World of Islam, 900–1500

Islam as a religion, a civilization, and an arena of commerce continued to grow even as the Arab Empire fragmented.

from place to place. The examples of India, Anatolia, West Africa, and Spain illustrate the various ways that Islam penetrated these societies as well as the rather different outcomes of these epic cultural encounters.

The Case of India

In South Asia, Islam found a permanent place in a long-established civilization as invasions by Turkic-speaking warrior groups from Central Asia, recently converted to Islam, brought the faith to northern India. Thus the Turks became the third major carrier of Islam, after the Arabs and Persians, as their conquests initiated an enduring encounter between Islam and a Hindu-based Indian civilization. Beginning around 1000, those conquests gave rise to a series of Turkic and Muslim regimes that governed much of India until the British takeover in the eighteenth and nineteenth centuries. The early centuries of this encounter were violent indeed, as the invaders smashed Hindu and Buddhist temples and carried off vast quantities of Indian treasure. With the establishment of the Sultanate of Delhi in 1206 (see Map 9.4), Turkic rule became more systematic, although the Turks' small numbers and internal conflicts allowed only a very modest penetration of Indian society.

■ **Comparison**

What similarities and differences can you identify in the spread of Islam to India, Anatolia, West Africa, and Spain?

In the centuries that followed, substantial Muslim communities emerged in India, particularly in regions less tightly integrated into the dominant Hindu culture. Disillusioned Buddhists as well as low-caste Hindus and untouchables found the more egalitarian Islam attractive. So did peoples just beginning to make the transition to settled agriculture. Others benefited from converting to Islam by avoiding the tax imposed on non-Muslims. Sufis were particularly important in facilitating conversion, for India had always valued "god-filled men" who were detached from worldly affairs. Sufi holy men, willing to accommodate local gods and religious festivals, helped to develop a "popular Islam" that was not always so sharply distinguished from the more devotional (*bhakti*) forms of Hinduism.

Unlike the earlier experience of Islam in the Middle East, North Africa, and Persia, where Islam rapidly became the dominant faith, in India it was never able to claim more than 20 to 25 percent of the total population. Furthermore, Muslim communities were especially concentrated in the Punjab and Sind regions of northwestern India and in Bengal to the east. The core regions of Hindu culture in the northern Indian plain were not seriously challenged by the new faith, despite centuries of Muslim rule. One reason perhaps lay in the sharpness of the cultural divide between Islam and Hinduism. Islam was the most radically monotheistic of the world's religions, forbidding any representation of Allah, while Hinduism was surely among the most prolifically polytheistic, generating endless statues and images of the Divine in many forms. The Muslim notion of the equality of all believers contrasted sharply with the hierarchical assumptions of the caste system. Believing in sexual modesty, Muslims were deeply offended by the open eroticism of some Hindu religious art.

Although such differences may have limited the appeal of Islam in India, they also may have prevented it from being absorbed into the tolerant and inclusive embrace of Hinduism, as so many other religious ideas, practices, and communities had been. The religious exclusivity of Islam, born of its firm monotheistic belief and the idea of a unique revelation, set a boundary that the great sponge of Hinduism could not completely absorb.

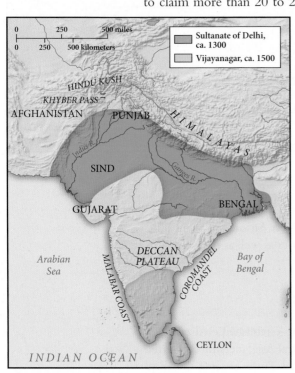

Map 9.4   The Sultanate of Delhi

Between 1206 and 1526 a number of Muslim dynasties ruled northern India as the Delhi sultanate, while an explicitly Hindu kingdom of Vijayanagar arose in the south after 1340. It drew on north Indian Muslim architectural features and made use of Muslim mercenaries for its military forces.

Certainly, not all was conflict across that boundary. Many prominent Hindus willingly served in the political and military structures of a Muslim–ruled India. Mystical seekers after the Divine blurred the distinction between Hindu and Muslim, suggesting that God was to be found "neither in temple nor in mosque." "Look within your heart," wrote the great fifteenth-century mystic poet Kabir, "for there you will find both [Allah] and Ram [a famous Hindu deity]."[20] During the early sixteenth century, a new and distinct religious tradition emerged in India, known as Sikhism (SIHK-iz'm), which blended elements of Islam, such as devotion to one universal God, with Hindu concepts, such as karma and rebirth. "There is no Hindu and no Muslim. All are children of God," declared Guru Nanak (1469–1539), the founder of Sikhism.

Nonetheless, Muslims usually lived quite separately, remaining a distinctive minority within an ancient Indian civilization, which they now largely governed but which they proved unable to completely transform.

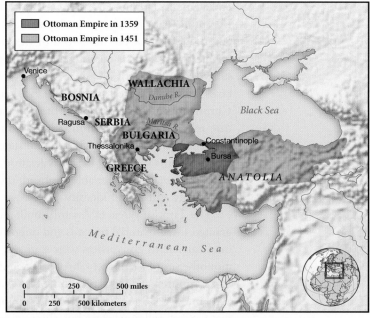

Map 9.5   The Ottoman Empire by the Mid-Fifteenth Century

As Turkic-speaking migrants bearing the religion of Islam penetrated Anatolia, the Ottoman Empire took shape, reaching into southeastern Europe and finally displacing the Christian Byzantine Empire. Subsequently, it came to control much of the Middle East and North Africa as well.

The Case of Anatolia

At the same time as India was being subjected to Turkic invasion, so too was Anatolia (now modern Turkey), where the largely Christian and Greek-speaking population was then governed by the Byzantine Empire (see Map 9.2 and Map 9.5). Here, as in India, the invaders initially wreaked havoc as Byzantine authority melted away in the eleventh century. Sufi practitioners likewise played a major role in the process of conversion. The outcome, however, was a far more profound cultural transformation than in India. By 1500, the population was 90 percent Muslim and largely Turkic-speaking, and Anatolia was the heartland of the powerful Turkish Ottoman Empire that had overrun Christian Byzantium. Why did the Turkic intrusion into Anatolia generate a much more thorough Islamization than in India?

One factor clearly lies in a very different demographic balance. The population of Anatolia—perhaps 8 million—was far smaller than India's roughly 48 million people, but far more Turkic-speaking peoples settled in Anatolia, giving them a much greater cultural weight than the smaller colonizing force in India. Furthermore, the disruption of Anatolian society was much more extensive. Massacres,

■ **Change**

In what ways was Anatolia changed by its incorporation into the Islamic world?

enslavement, famine, and flight led to a sharp drop in the native population. The Byzantine state had been fatally weakened. Church properties were confiscated, and monasteries were destroyed or deserted. Priests and bishops were sometimes unable to serve their congregations. Christians, though seldom forced to convert, suffered many discriminations. They had to wear special clothing and pay special taxes, and they were forbidden to ride saddled horses or carry swords. Not a few Christians came to believe that these disasters represented proof that Islam was the true religion. Thus Byzantine civilization in Anatolia, previously focused on the centralized institutions of church and state, was rendered leaderless and dispirited, whereas India's decentralized civilization, lacking a unified political or religious establishment, was better able to absorb the shock of external invasion while retaining its core values and identity.

The Turkish rulers of Anatolia built a new society that welcomed converts and granted them material rewards and opportunity for high office. Moreover, the cultural barriers to conversion were arguably less severe than in India. The common monotheism of Islam and Christianity, and Muslim respect for Jesus and the Christian scriptures, made conversion easier than crossing the great gulf between Islam and Hinduism. Such similarities lent support to the suggestion of some Sufi teachers that the two religions were but different versions of the same faith. Sufis also established schools, mills, orchards, hospices, and rest places for travelers and thus replaced the destroyed or decaying institutions of Christian Anatolia. All of this contributed to the thorough religious transformation of Anatolia and laid a foundation for the Ottoman Empire, which by 1500 had become the most impressive and powerful state within the Islamic world.

But the Islamization of Anatolia occurred within a distinctly Turkish context. A Turkish language, not Arabic, predominated. Some Sufi religious practices, such as ecstatic turning dances, actually derived from Central Asian Turkic shamanism. And Turkic tradition, common among pastoral peoples, offered a freer, more gender-equal life for women. This practice caught the attention of the Arab Moroccan visitor Ibn Battuta during his travels among the Turks in the fourteenth century. He commented, "A remarkable thing that I saw . . . was the respect shown to women by the Turks, for they hold a more dignified position than the men. . . . The windows of the tent are open and her face is visible, for the Turkish women do not veil themselves."[21] He was not pleased.

The Case of West Africa

Still another pattern of Islamic expansion prevailed in West Africa. Here Islam accompanied Muslim traders across the Sahara rather than being brought by invading Arab or Turkic armies. Its gradual acceptance in the emerging civilization of West African states in the centuries after 1000 was largely peaceful and voluntary, lacking the incentives associated elsewhere with foreign conquest. Introduced by Muslim merchants from an already-Islamized North Africa, the new faith was accepted primarily in the urban centers of the West African empires—Ghana, Mali,

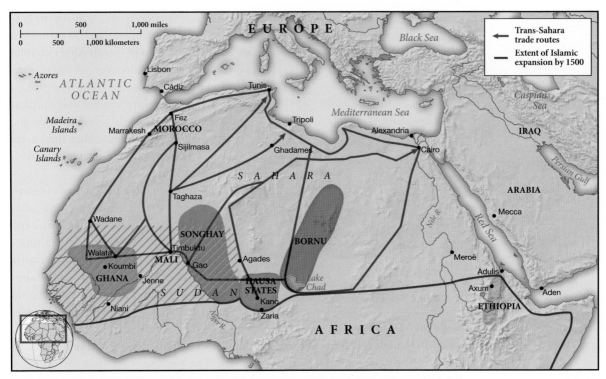

Map 9.6 West Africa and the World of Islam

Both trans-Saharan commerce and Islam linked the civilization of West Africa to the larger Muslim world.

Songhay, Kanem-Bornu, and others (see Map 9.6 and Zooming In: Mansa Musa, page 390). For African merchant communities, Islam provided an important link to Muslim trading partners, much as Buddhism had done in Southeast Asia. For the monarchs and their courts, it offered a source of literate officials to assist in state administration as well as religious legitimacy, particularly for those who gained the prestige conferred by a pilgrimage to Mecca. Islam was a world religion with a single Creator-God, able to comfort and protect people whose political and economic horizons had expanded well beyond the local realm where ancestral spirits and traditional deities might be effective. It had a religious appeal for societies that were now participating in a wider world.

By the sixteenth century, a number of West African cities had become major centers of Islamic religious and intellectual life, attracting scholars from throughout the Muslim world. Timbuktu boasted more than 150 lower-level Quranic schools and several major centers of higher education with thousands of students from all over West Africa and beyond. Libraries held tens of thousands of books and scholarly manuscripts (see the image on page 305). Monarchs subsidized the construction of mosques as West Africa became an integral part of a larger Islamic world. Arabic became an important language of religion, education, administration, and trade, but it did not become the dominant language of daily life. Nor did West

The Great Mosque at Jenne
This mosque in the city of Jenne, initially constructed in the thirteenth century, illustrates the assimilation of Islam into West African civilization. (Antonello Lanzellotto/TIPS Images/age fotostock)

Africa experience the massive migration of Arab peoples that had promoted the Arabization of North Africa and the Middle East. Moreover, in contrast to India and Anatolia, Sufi holy men played a far more modest role until at least the eighteenth century. Scholars, merchants, and rulers, rather than mystic preachers, initially established Islam in West Africa.

Islam remained the culture of urban elites and spread little into the rural areas of West Africa until the nineteenth century. No thorough religious transformation occurred in West Africa as it had in Anatolia. Although many rulers adopted Islam, they governed people who steadfastly practiced African religions and whose sensibilities they had to respect if social peace were to prevail. Thus they made few efforts to impose the new religion on their rural subjects or to govern in strict accordance with Islamic law. The fourteenth-century Arab visitor Ibn Battuta was appalled that practicing Muslims in Mali permitted their women to appear in public almost naked and to mingle freely with unrelated men. "The association of women with men is agreeable to us," he was told, "and a part of good conduct to which no suspicion attaches. They are not like the women of your country."[22] Ibn Battuta also noted with disapproval a "dance of the masks" on the occasion of an Islamic festival and the traditional practice of sprinkling dust on one's head as a sign of respect for the king. Sonni Ali, a fifteenth-century ruler of Songhay, observed Ramadan and built mosques, but he also consulted traditional diviners and performed customary sacrifices. In such ways, Islam became Africanized even as parts of West Africa became Islamized.

The Case of Spain

The chief site of Islamic encounter with Christian Europe occurred in Spain, called al-Andalus by Muslims, which was conquered by Arab and Berber forces in the early eighth century during the first wave of Islamic expansion. By the tenth century, Muslim Spain was a vibrant civilization, often portrayed as a place of harmony and tolerance between its Muslim rulers and its Christian and Jewish subjects.

Certainly, Spain's agricultural economy was the most prosperous in Europe during this time, and its capital of Córdoba was among the largest and most splendid cities in the world. Muslims, Christians, and Jews alike contributed to a brilliant high culture in which astronomy, medicine, the arts, architecture, and literature flourished. Furthermore, social relationships among upper-class members of different faiths were easy and frequent. By 1000, perhaps 75 percent of the population had converted to Islam. Many of the remaining Christians learned Arabic, veiled their women, stopped eating pork, appreciated Arabic music and poetry, and sometimes married Muslims. One Christian bishop complained that Spanish Christians knew the rules of Arabic grammar better than those of Latin. During the reign of Abd al-Rahman III (r. 912–961), freedom of worship was declared as well as the opportunity for all to rise in the bureaucracy of the state.

But this so-called golden age of Muslim Spain was both limited and brief. Even assimilated or Arabized Christians remained religious infidels and second-class citizens in the eyes of their Muslim counterparts, and by the late tenth century toleration began to erode. The Córdoba-based regime fragmented into numerous rival states. Warfare with the remaining Christian kingdoms in northern Spain picked up in the tenth and eleventh centuries, and more puritanical and rigid forms of Islam entered Spain from North Africa. Under the rule of al-Mansur (r. 981–1002), an official policy of tolerance turned to one of overt persecution against Christians, which now included the plundering of churches and the seizure of their wealth, although he employed many Christian mercenaries in his armies. Social life also changed. Devout Muslims avoided contact with Christians; Christian homes had to be built lower than those of Muslims; priests were forbidden to carry a cross or a Bible, lest they offend Muslim sensibilities; and Arabized Christians were permitted to live only in particular places. Thus, writes one scholar, "the era of harmonious interaction between Muslim and Christian in Spain came to an end, replaced by intolerance, prejudice, and mutual suspicion."[23]

That intolerance intensified as the Christian reconquest of Spain gained ground after 1200. The end came in 1492, when Ferdinand and Isabella, the Catholic monarchs of a unified Spain, took Granada, the last Muslim stronghold on the Iberian Peninsula. To Christopher Columbus, who witnessed the event before leaving on his first transatlantic voyage, it was a grand Christian triumph. "I saw the royal banners of your Highnesses planted by force of arms upon the towers of the Alhambra," he wrote. To Muslims, it was a catastrophe. Tradition has it that Abu Abdullah, the final ruler of Muslim Granada, wept as he left his beloved city for the last time. Observing his grief, Abu Abdullah's mother famously said to him: "Thou dost weep like a woman for what thou couldst not defend as a man."

After the conquest, many Muslims were forced to emigrate, replaced by Christian settlers. While those who remained under Christian rule were legally guaranteed freedom of worship, they were forbidden to make converts, to give the call to prayer, or to go on pilgrimage. And all Jews, some 200,000 of them, were expelled from the country. In the early seventeenth century, even Muslim converts to Christianity were likewise banished from Spain. And yet cultural interchange persisted for a time. The translation of Arab texts into Latin continued under Christian rule, while Christian churches and palaces were constructed on the sites of older mosques and incorporated Islamic artistic and architectural features.

Mansa Musa, West African Monarch and Muslim Pilgrim

In 1324, Mansa Musa, the ruler, or *mansa*, of the Kingdom of Mali, set out on an arduous journey from his West African homeland to the holy city of Mecca. His kingdom stretched from the Atlantic coast a thousand miles or more to the fabled inland city of Timbuktu and beyond, even as his pilgrimage to Mecca reflected the growing penetration of Islam in this emerging West African civilization. A pious Muslim, Mansa

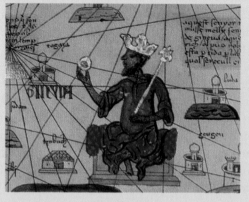

Mansa Musa.

Musa was fluent in Arabic, was an avid builder of mosques, and was inclined on occasion to free a few slaves.

In the fourteenth century, Mali was an expanding empire. According to Musa, one of his immediate predecessors had launched a substantial maritime expedition "to discover the furthest limits of the Atlantic Ocean."[24] The voyagers never returned, and no other record of this trip exists, but it is intriguing to consider that Africans and Europeans alike may have been exploring the Atlantic at roughly the same time. Mansa Musa, however, was more inclined to expand on land as he sought access to the goldfields to the south and the trans-Saharan

trade network to the north. Control of this lucrative commercial complex enriched Mansa Musa's empire, enabled a major building program of mosques and palaces, and turned the city of Timbuktu into a thriving center of trade, religion, and intellectual life. Merchants and scholars from across West and North Africa flocked to the city.

Mansa Musa's journey to Mecca fascinated observers at the time and continues to intrigue historians today. Such a pilgrimage has long been one of the duties—and privileges—of all Muslims. It also added the prestigious title of *hajji* to their names. For rulers in particular, it conveyed a spiritual power known as *baraka*, which helped legitimate their rule.

When Mansa Musa began his journey in 1324, he was accompanied by an enormous entourage, with thousands of fellow pilgrims, some 500 slaves, his wife and other women, hundreds of camels, and a huge quantity of gold. It was the gold that attracted the most attention, as he dis-

photo: Detail from the *Catalan Atlas*, 1375, by Abraham Cresques (1375–1387)/ Bibliothèque National de France, Paris, France/Bridgeman Images

Thus Spain, unlike most other regions incorporated into the Islamic world, experienced a religious reversal as Christian rule was reestablished and Islam painfully eradicated from the Iberian Peninsula. In world historical terms, perhaps the chief significance of Muslim Spain was its role in making the rich heritage of Islamic learning available to Christian Europe. As a cross-cultural encounter, it was largely a one-way street. European scholars wanted the secular knowledge—Greek as well as Arab—that had accumulated in the Islamic world, and they flocked to Spain to acquire it. That knowledge of philosophy, mathematics, medicine, optics, astronomy, botany, and more played a major role in the making of a new European civilization in the thirteenth century and beyond. Muslim Spain remained only as a memory.

SUMMING UP SO FAR

"Islam had a revolutionary impact on every society that it touched." What evidence might support this statement, and what might challenge it?

tributed it lavishly along his journey. Egyptian sources reported that the value of gold in their country was depressed for years after his visit. On his return trip, Mansa Musa apparently had exhausted his supply and had to borrow money from Egyptian merchants at high interest rates. Those merchants also made a killing on Musa's pilgrims, who, unsophisticated in big-city shopping, were made to pay far more than their purchases were worth. Europeans too now became aware of Mansa Musa, featuring him holding a large nugget of gold in a famous map from 1375 with a caption reading: "This Negro lord is called Musa Mali. . . . So abundant is the gold found in his country that he is the richest and most noble king in all the land."[25]

In Cairo, Mansa Musa displayed both his pride and his ignorance of Islamic law. Invited to see the sultan of Egypt, he was initially reluctant because of a protocol requirement to kiss the ground and the sultan's hand. He consented only when he was persuaded that he was really prostrating before God, not the sultan. And in conversation with learned clerics, Mansa Musa was surprised to learn that Muslim rulers were not allowed to take the beautiful unmarried women of their realm as concubines. "By God, I did not know that," he replied. "I hereby leave it and abandon it utterly."[26]

In Mecca, Mansa Musa completed the requirements of the hajj, dressing in the common garb of all pilgrims, repeatedly circling the Kaaba, performing ritual prayers, and visiting various sites associated with Muhammad's life, including a side trip to the Prophet's tomb in Medina. He also sought to recruit a number of sharifs, prestigious descendants of Muhammad's family, to add Islamic luster to his kingdom. After considerable difficulty and expense, he found four men who were willing to return with him to what Arabs understood to be the remote frontier of the Islamic world. Some reports suggested that they were simply freed slaves, hoping for better lives.

In the end, perhaps Mansa Musa's goals for the pilgrimage were achieved. On a personal level, one source reported that he was so moved by the pilgrimage that he actually considered abandoning his throne altogether and returning to Mecca, where he might live as "a dweller near the sanctuary [the Kaaba]."[27] His visit certainly elevated Mali's status in the Islamic world. Some 200 years after that visit, one account of his pilgrimage placed the sultan of Mali as one of four major rulers in the Islamic world, equal to those of Baghdad and Egypt. Mansa Musa would have been pleased.

Question: What significance did Mansa Musa likely attach to his pilgrimage? How might Egyptians, Arabians, and Europeans have viewed it?

The World of Islam as a New Civilization

As the religion spread and the Abbasid dynasty declined, the civilization of Islam, unlike that of China but similar to Western Christendom, operated without a dominant political center, bound more by a shared religious culture than by a shared state. Twice that civilization was threatened from outside. The most serious intrusion came during the thirteenth century from the Mongols, whose conquest of Central Asia and Persia proved devastating while incorporating many Muslims within the huge Mongol domains (see Chapter 11). Less serious but more well known, at least in the West, were the Christian Crusaders who established in the twelfth and thirteenth centuries several small and temporary outposts along the eastern Mediterranean (see Chapter 10).

Despite these external threats and its various internal conflicts, Islamic civilization flourished and often prospered, embracing at least parts of virtually every other civilization in the Afro-Eurasian hemisphere. It was in that sense "history's first truly global civilization," although the Americas, of course, were not involved.[28] What held this Islamic world together? What enabled many people to feel themselves part of a single civilization despite its political fragmentation, religious controversies, and cultural and regional diversity?

Networks of Faith

At the core of that vast civilization was a common commitment to Islam. No group was more important in the transmission of those beliefs and practices than the ulama. These learned scholars were not "priests" in the Christian sense, for in Islam, at least theoretically, no person could stand between the believer and Allah. Rather, they served as judges, interpreters, administrators, prayer leaders, and reciters of the Quran, but especially as preservers and teachers of the sharia. Supported mostly by their local communities, some also received the patronage of sultans, or rulers, and were therefore subject to criticism for corruption and undue submission to state authority. In their homes, mosques, shrines, and Quranic schools, the ulama passed on the core teachings of the faith. Beginning in the eleventh century, formal colleges called *madrassas* offered more advanced instruction in the Quran and the sayings of Muhammad; grammar and rhetoric; sometimes philosophy, theology, mathematics, and medicine; and, above all else, law. Teaching was informal, mostly oral, and involved much memorization of texts. It was also largely conservative, seeking to preserve an established body of Islamic learning.

■ **Description**

What makes it possible to speak of the Islamic world as a distinct and coherent civilization?

The ulama were an "international elite," and the system of education they created served to bind together an immense and diverse civilization. Common texts were shared widely across the world of Islam. Students and teachers alike traveled great distances in search of the most learned scholars. From Indonesia to West Africa, educated Muslims inhabited a "shared world of debate and reference."[29]

Paralleling the educational network of the ulama were the emerging religious orders of the Sufis. By the tenth century, particular Sufi *shaykhs* (shakes), or teachers, began to attract groups of disciples who were eager to learn their unique devotional practices and techniques of personal transformation. The disciples usually swore allegiance to their teacher and valued highly the chain of transmission by which those teachings and practices had come down from earlier masters. In the twelfth and thirteenth centuries, Sufis began to organize in a variety of larger associations, some limited to particular regions and others with chapters throughout the Islamic world. The Qadiriya order, for example, began in Baghdad but spread widely throughout the Arab world and into sub-Saharan Africa.

Sufi orders were especially significant in the frontier regions of Islam because they followed conquering armies or traders into Central and Southeast Asia, India, Anatolia, parts of Africa, and elsewhere. Their devotional teachings, modest ways of living, and reputation for supernatural powers gained a hearing for the new faith. Their emphasis on personal experience of the Divine, rather than on the law, allowed the Sufis to accommodate elements of local belief and practice and encouraged the growth of a popular or blended Islam. The veneration of deceased Sufi "saints," or "friends of God," particularly at their tombs, created sacred spaces that enabled Islam to take root in many places despite its foreign origins. But that flexibility also often earned Sufi practitioners the enmity of the ulama, who were sharply critical of any deviations from the sharia.

Like the madrassas and the sharia, Sufi religious ideas and institutions spanned the Islamic world and were yet another thread in the cosmopolitan web of Islamic civilization. Particular devotional teachings and practices spread widely, as did the writings of such famous Sufi poets as Hafiz and Rumi. Devotees made pilgrimages to the distant tombs of famous teachers, who, they often believed, might intercede with God on their behalf. Wandering Sufis, in search of the wisdom of renowned shaykhs, found fellow seekers and welcome shelter in the compounds of these religious orders.

In addition to the networks of the Sufis and the ulama, many thousands of people, from kings to peasants, made the grand pilgrimage to Mecca—the hajj— no doubt gaining some sense of the umma. There men and women together, hailing from all over the Islamic world, joined as one people to rehearse the central elements of their faith. The claims of local identities based on family, clan, tribe, ethnicity, or state never disappeared, but now overarching them all was the inclusive unity of the Muslim community.

Networks of Exchange

The world of Islamic civilization cohered not only as a network of faith but also as an immense arena of exchange in which goods, technologies, food products, and ideas circulated widely. Now large areas of the Afro-Eurasian world operated within a single political system, practiced Islam, and spoke Arabic. This huge region rapidly became a vast trading zone of hemispheric dimensions. In part, this was due to its central location in the Afro-Eurasian world and the breaking down of earlier political barriers between the Byzantine and Persian empires. Furthermore, commerce was valued positively within Islamic teaching, and laws regulating it figured prominently in the sharia, creating a predictable framework for exchange across many cultures. The pilgrimage to Mecca, as well as the urbanization that accompanied the growth of Islamic civilization, likewise fostered commerce. Baghdad, established in 756 as the capital of the Abbasid Empire, soon grew into a magnificent city of half a million people. The appetite of urban elites for luxury goods stimulated both craft production and the desire for foreign products.

Thus Muslim merchants, Arabs and Persians in particular, quickly became prominent and sometimes dominant players in all the major Afro-Eurasian trade routes of the third-wave era—in the Mediterranean Sea, along the revived Silk Roads, across the Sahara, and throughout the Indian Ocean basin (see Chapter 7).

■ **Connection**
In what ways was the world of Islam a "cosmopolitan civilization"?

By the eighth century, Arab and Persian traders had established a commercial colony in Canton in southern China, thus linking the Islamic heartland with Asia's other giant and flourishing economy. Various forms of banking, partnerships, business contracts, and instruments for granting credit facilitated these long-distance economic relationships and generated a prosperous, sophisticated, and highly commercialized economy that spanned the Old World.

The vast expanse of Islamic civilization also contributed to ecological change as agricultural products and practices spread from one region to another, a process already under way in the earlier Roman and Persian empires. Among the food crops that circulated within and beyond the Islamic world were different varieties of sugarcane, rice, apricots, artichokes, eggplants, lemons, oranges, almonds, figs, and bananas. Equally significant were water-management practices, so important to the arid or semi-arid environments of many parts of the Islamic world. Persian-style reservoirs and irrigation technologies spread as far as Tunisia and Morocco, the northern fringes of the Sahara, Spain, and Yemen. By connecting different environmental zones, particularly those where water availability was the major obstacle to agricultural growth, particular regions could draw upon a wide range of crops and practices. All of this contributed to an "Islamic Green Revolution" of increased food production as well as to population growth, urbanization, and industrial development across the Islamic world.

Technology too diffused widely within the realm of Islam. Muslim technicians made improvements on rockets, first developed in China, by developing one that carried a small warhead and another used to attack ships. Paper-making techniques entered the Abbasid Empire from China in the eighth century or earlier, with paper mills soon operating in Persia, Iraq, and Egypt. This revolutionary technology, which everywhere served to strengthen bureaucratic governments, passed from the Middle East into India and Europe over the following centuries. Everywhere it spurred the emergence of books and written culture at the expense of earlier orally based cultural expressions.

Ideas likewise circulated across the Islamic world. The religion itself drew heavily and quite openly on Jewish and Christian precedents. Persia also contributed much in the way of bureaucratic practice, court ritual, and poetry, with Persian becoming a major literary language in elite circles. Scientific, medical, and philosophical texts, especially from ancient Greece, the Hellenistic world, and India, were systematically translated into Arabic, providing an enormous boost to Islamic scholarship and science for several centu-

A Muslim Astronomical Observatory
Drawing initially on Greek, Indian, and Persian astronomy, the Islamic world after 1000 developed its own distinctive tradition of astronomical observation and prediction, reflected in this Turkish observatory constructed in 1557. Muslim astronomy subsequently exercised considerable influence in both China and Europe. (University Library, Istanbul, Turkey/Bridgeman Images)

SNAPSHOT   Key Achievements in Islamic Science and Scholarship

Person/Dates	Achievement
al-Khwarazim (790–840)	Mathematician; spread use of Arabic numerals in Islamic world; wrote first book on algebra
al-Razi (865–925)	Discovered sulfuric acid; wrote a vast encyclopedia of medicine drawing on Greek, Syrian, Indian, and Persian work and his own clinical observation
al-Biruni (973–1048)	Mathematician, astronomer, cartographer; calculated the radius of the earth with great accuracy; worked out numerous mathematical innovations; developed a technique for displaying a hemisphere on a plane
Ibn Sina (Avicenna) (980–1037)	Prolific writer in almost all fields of science and philosophy; especially known for *Canon of Medicine*, a fourteen-volume work that set standards for medical practice in Islamic and Christian worlds for centuries
Omar Khayyam (1048–1131)	Mathematician; critic of Euclid's geometry; measured the solar year with great accuracy; Sufi poet; author of *The Rubaiyat*
Ibn Rushd (Averroës) (1126–1198)	Translated and commented widely on Aristotle; rationalist philosopher; made major contributions in law, mathematics, and medicine
Nasir al-Din Tusi (1201–1274)	Founder of the famous Maragha observatory in Persia (data from Maragha probably influenced Copernicus); mapped the motion of stars and planets
Ibn Khaldun (1332–1406)	Greatest Arab historian; identified trends and structures in world history over long periods of time

ries. In 830, the Abbasid caliph al-Mamun, himself a poet and scholar with a passion for foreign learning, established the House of Wisdom in Baghdad as an academic center for this research and translation. Stimulated by Greek texts, a school of Islamic thinkers known as Mutazalites ("those who stand apart") argued that reason, rather than revelation, was the "surest way to truth."[30] In the long run, however, the philosophers' emphasis on logic, rationality, and the laws of nature was subject to increasing criticism by those who held that only the Quran, the sayings of the Prophet, or mystical experience represented a genuine path to God.

But the realm of Islam was much more than a museum of ancient achievements from the civilizations that it encompassed. Those traditions mixed and blended to generate a distinctive Islamic civilization with many new contributions to the world of learning. (See Snapshot, above.) Using Indian numerical notation, for example, Arab scholars developed algebra as a novel mathematical discipline. They also undertook much original work in astronomy and optics. They built on earlier Greek and Indian practice to create a remarkable tradition in medicine and pharmacology. Arab physicians such as al-Razi and Ibn Sina accurately diagnosed many diseases, such as hay fever, measles, smallpox, diphtheria, rabies, and diabetes. In addition, treatments such as using a mercury ointment for scabies, cataract and hernia operations, and filling teeth with gold emerged from Arab doctors. The first hospitals, traveling clinics, and examinations for physicians and pharmacologists were also developed within the Islamic world. In the eleventh and twelfth centuries, this enormous body of Arab medical scholarship entered Europe via Spain, and it remained at the core of European medical practice for many centuries.

REFLECTIONS

Past and Present: Choosing Our History

Prominent among the many uses of history is the perspective it provides on the present. Although historians sometimes worry that an excessive "present-mindedness" may distort our perception of the past, all of us look to history, almost instinctively, to comprehend the world we now inhabit. Given the obvious importance of the Islamic world in the international arena of the twenty-first century, how might some grasp of the early development of Islamic civilization assist us in understanding our present circumstances?

Certainly, that history reminds us of the central role that Islam played in the Afro-Eurasian world for a thousand years or more. From 600 to 1600 or later, it was a proud, cosmopolitan, often prosperous, and frequently powerful civilization that spanned Africa, Europe, the Middle East, and Asia. What followed were several centuries of European or Western imperialism that many Muslims found humiliating, even if some were attracted by elements of modern Western culture. In their recent efforts to overcome those centuries of subordination and exploitation, Muslims have found encouragement and inspiration in reflecting on the more distant and perhaps more glorious past. But they have not all chosen to emphasize the same past. Those labeled as "fundamentalists" have often viewed the early Islamic community associated with Medina, Mecca, and Muhammad as a model for Islamic renewal in the present. Others, often known as Islamic modernizers, have looked to the somewhat later achievements of Islamic science and scholarship as a foundation for a more open engagement with the West and the modern world.

The history of Islam also reveals to us a world of great diversity and debate. Sharp religious differences between Sunni and Shia understandings of the faith; differences in emphasis between advocates of the sharia and of Sufi spirituality; political conflicts among various groups and regions within the larger Islamic world; different postures toward women in Arab lands and in West Africa—all of this and more divided the umma and divide it still. Recalling that diversity is a useful reminder for any who would tag all Muslims with a single label.

A further dimension of that diversity lies in the many cultural encounters that the spread of Islam has spawned. Sometimes great conflict and violence have accompanied those encounters, as in the Crusades and in Turkic invasions of India and Anatolia. At other times and places, Muslims and non-Muslims have lived together in relative tranquillity and tolerance—in Spain, in West Africa, in India, and in the Ottoman Empire. Some commentaries on the current interaction of Islam and the West seem to assume an eternal hostility or an inevitable clash of civilizations. The record of the past, however, shows considerable variation in the interaction of Muslims and others. While the past certainly shapes and conditions what happens next, the future, as always, remains open. Within limits, we can choose the history on which we seek to build.

Second Thoughts

What's the Significance?

Quran, 367–69

umma, 368

Pillars of Islam, 368

hijra, 369

sharia, 370

jizya, 373

Umayyad caliphate, 376–77

Abbasid caliphate, 377

ulama, 377, 392

Sufism, 377–80

Mullah Nasruddin, 378–79

al-Ghazali, 380

Sikhism, 385

Ibn Battuta, 386–88

Timbuktu, 387

al-Andalus, 388–90

Mansa Musa, 390–91

madrassas, 392

House of Wisdom, 395

Ibn Sina, 395–96

Big Picture Questions

1. How might you account for the immense religious and political/military success of Islam in its early centuries?

2. In what ways might Islamic civilization be described as cosmopolitan, international, or global?

3. "Islam was simultaneously a single world of shared meaning and interaction and a series of separate, distinct, and conflicting communities." What evidence could you provide to support both sides of this argument?

4. What changes did Islamic expansion generate in those societies that encountered it, and how was Islam itself transformed by those encounters?

5. **Looking Back:** What distinguished the early centuries of Islamic history from a similar phase in the history of Christianity and Buddhism?

Next Steps: For Further Study

Reza Aslan, *No God but God* (2005). A well-written and popular history of Islam by an Iranian immigrant to the United States.

Fred M. Donner, *Muhammad and the Believers* (2010). An innovative account of the first century of Islam by a leading scholar of that era.

Richard Eaton, *Islamic History as Global History* (1990). A short account by a major scholar that examines Islam in a global framework.

John Esposito, ed., *The Oxford History of Islam* (1999). Up-to-date essays on various periods and themes in Islamic history. Beautifully illustrated.

Francis Robinson, ed., *Cambridge Illustrated History of the Islamic World* (1996). A series of essays by major scholars, with lovely pictures and maps.

Judith Tucker, *Gender and Islamic History* (1994). A brief overview of the changing lives of Islamic women.

The Man Who Walked across the World, http://topdocumentaryfilms.com/man-who-walked-across-world/. A documentary travelogue tracing the many journeys of Ibn Battuta.

"Religions: Islam," http://www.bbc.co.uk/religion/religions/islam/. A BBC Web site providing information about all aspects of Islamic life and culture.

WORKING WITH EVIDENCE

The Life of the Prophet

In addition to the teachings of the Quran, Muslims have long revered their Prophet as the most complete expression of God-conscious humanity and an example for all who would follow the path of Islam. In the several centuries after his death, Muslim scholars collected every detail of his life and sought to draw lessons about behavior based on his moral qualities and actions: his utter devotion to Allah; his bravery and decisiveness in battle; his honesty in business affairs; his flexibility, compassion, and willingness to forgive in dealing with enemies; his habit of consulting with companions before making a decision; his generosity and kindness to the poor and enslaved. Early biographies of Muhammad also made much of his sexual virility and attraction to women, which combined with his tenderness toward them to create a new model of Islamic masculinity.[31] The images that follow illustrate four major events in the life of Muhammad, long familiar to Muslims everywhere.

These images derive from the tradition of Persian or Turkish miniature painting—small, colorful, and exquisitely detailed works often used to illustrate books or manuscripts. One art historian described them as "little festivals of color in images separated from each other by pages of text."[32] Scenes from the life of the Prophet Muhammad appeared occasionally in this art form, which flourished especially from the thirteenth through the sixteenth centuries. They provide a window into the ways Muslims have understood their prophet and sought to learn from his example.

Representation of the Prophet Muhammad has long been controversial within Islamic societies. While not prohibited in the Quran, visual depictions of the Prophet have often been discouraged or even forbidden to prevent idolatry. Nonetheless, Muhammad was on occasion portrayed in Persian and Turkish miniature painting, sometimes in full face, but often with his face obscured. Such depictions, however, were limited to illustrations of particular events in books of history or poetry. They were never used to decorate mosques or the Quran. Nor were they employed as a teaching tool or for devotional purposes, as was frequently the case in Christian religious art.

According to all Muslims, the central and defining experience in Muhammad's life occurred in the year 610 C.E. in his initial encounter with an angel, usually identified as Gabriel, an event that marked the beginning of his revelations.[33] For some time before this dramatic event, Muhammad had been in the habit of withdrawing to a cave outside Mecca for prayer and meditation. On this occasion, however, a towering and overpowering presence of the angel appeared to him, filling the entire horizon, squeezing the very breath from his body, and commanding him to "recite" or to "read." After repeated protests that "I am not a reciter/reader," Muhammad found himself speaking what became the first revelation of the Quran.

When the vision passed, Muhammad fled in terror to his wife Khadija, fearing that he might be mad or possessed of some demonic spirit. Seeking to comfort him, Khadija took her husband to her learned cousin Waraqa, a Christian, who assured Muhammad that "he is the prophet of his people" and the recipient of revelation from the same God who had earlier granted similar messages to Abraham, Moses, and Jesus, among others. Further revelations followed over the next twenty-two years until Muhammad's death in 632, after which they were compiled into the Quran.

Source 9.1, an early fourteenth-century Persian miniature painting, depicts this encounter between Muhammad and Gabriel.

■ What impression of this encounter does the artist seek to convey by the posture of the two figures?

■ What religious meaning might Muslims derive from the idea that the revelation to Muhammad came through an angelic messenger rather than directly from Allah?

■ Traditional accounts of Muhammad's encounter with the angel stress the mysterious and overpowering "otherness" of the Divine Presence, which accounts for Muhammad's initial fear and terror. What is the religious significance of such a depiction of the Divine? To what extent does this image convey that impression?

■ Muslims have traditionally stressed that their prophet was illiterate, based in part on his response to the angel: "I am not a reader." Why might it be important to Muslims to believe that Muhammad was illiterate?

By far the most frequently portrayed event in the life of Muhammad was the *miraj*, the Prophet's Night Journey, said to have taken place in 619 or 620. The Quran refers briefly to God's taking the Prophet "from the sacred place of worship to the far distant place of worship." This passage became the basis for a story, much embellished over the centuries, of rich and deep meaning for Muslims. In this religious narrative, Muhammad was led one night by the angel Gabriel from Mecca to Jerusalem. For the journey he was given a *buraq*, a mythical winged creature with the body of a mule or donkey and the face of a woman. Upon arriving in Jerusalem, Muhammad led prayers for an assembly of earlier prophets including Abraham, Moses, and Jesus. (See page 367 for

Source 9.1 Muhammad and the Archangel Gabriel

Miniature from the "Jami' al-Tawarikh" of Rashid al-Din, ca. 1307/Edinburgh University Library, Scotland/With kind permission of the University of Edinburgh/Bridgeman Images

a fifteenth-century Persian painting illustrating this event.) Then, accompanied by many angels, Muhammad made his way through seven heavens almost into the presence of God, where, according to the Quran, "he did see some of the most profound of his Sustainer's symbols." There too Allah spoke to Muhammad about the importance of regular prayer, commanding fifty prayers a day, a figure later reduced to five on the advice of Moses.

From the beginning, Muslims have been divided on how to interpret this journey of the Prophet. For most, perhaps, it was taken quite literally as a miraculous event. Some, however, viewed it as a dream or a vision, while others understood it as the journey of Muhammad's soul but not his body.

Source 9.2 The Night Journey of Muhammad

The Prophet's youngest wife, Aisha, for example, reported that "his body did not leave its place." Source 9.2, dating from the early sixteenth century, is one of many representations of the Night Journey that emerged within Persian miniature painting.

- What significance might attach to the female head of the buraq?

- What are the accompanying angels offering to the Prophet during his journey?

- What meaning might the artist seek to convey by the image of the world below and slightly to the right of the buraq?

- What is the significance of Muhammad's encounter with earlier prophets such as Abraham, Moses, and Jesus?

- Review the discussion of the Sufi tradition of Islam on pages 377–80. How might Sufis have understood the Night Journey?

The circumstances of Muhammad's life required that he act as a political leader at the same time as he was seeking to convey a new religious message. By 622, intense hostility to that revolutionary message had forced him out of Mecca to a new base in Medina, where he became a lawgiver, creating a social and political framework for his small band of followers. Violent opposition from various quarters and the absence of any overall political authority in the Arabian Peninsula made it necessary for Muhammad to also become a military strategist to protect his fledgling community. In these ways, his task was very different from that of the Buddha or Jesus.

Among the leading adversaries of the embryonic community of "believers" in Medina were the forces of Muhammad's own Quraysh clan in Mecca. An important turning point in that struggle occurred in 624 at the Battle of Badr in western Arabia. Despite being outnumbered more than three to one (about 1,000 Meccans but only around 300 "believers" from Medina), Muhammad's forces emerged victorious. While the Meccans fought in traditional Arab style with much individual bravado and no unified command, Muhammad's men were carefully drilled, well organized, and effectively led. To Muslims, however, it was not human ingenuity but divine intervention that occasioned this unlikely triumph. The Quran reported that Allah had sent some 3,000 angels to assist Muhammad's forces and reminded the believers that "it was not you that slew the enemy, but it was God that slew them."

This battle established the new Muslim community as a force to be reckoned with in Arabia and was enormously encouraging to the "believers." It was also the occasion for a series of revelations to Muhammad about the treatment of prisoners. They should not be abused in any way, but released, offered for ransom, or allowed to earn enough money to purchase their freedom. According to a traditional saying (hadith) of the Prophet, Muhammad asked his followers to treat captives as members of their own families. "You must feed them as you feed yourselves and clothe them as you clothe yourselves."

Visual Source 9.3, a sixteenth-century Turkish miniature painting, shows the preparation for the battle at Badr. Muhammad, shown in green dress with his face obscured, is sending waves of horsemen into the struggle. While other followers watch from behind, two of his close associates appear at the bottom right, and an angel hovers over the scene.

From the *Siyar-i-Nabi* (Volume IV) of Murad III (1546–1595), 1595 / Musée du Louvre, Paris, France/© Christian Larrieu/Bridgeman Images

Source 9.3 The Battle at Badr

■ What elements of this image might suggest a natural or human understanding of the Muslim victory at Badr? And what might indicate divine intervention as an explanation?

■ Documentary sources report only two horses and seventy camels on the side of the "believers" at this battle and suggest a more ragtag group of fighters than the image portrays. Why do you think the artist presented a rather more impressive picture?

■ What religious meanings did Muhammad and Muslims in general extract from the battle at Badr?

In 630, just six years after the battle at Badr, Muhammad and some 10,000 soldiers triumphantly entered Mecca, almost completely without violence, and in a posture of reconciliation rather than revenge. In sharp contrast to traditional Arab practice, Muhammad issued a general amnesty for those who had opposed him. Then he turned his attention to the religious rationale of his entire movement. Riding his favorite camel, Muhammad circled the Kaaba seven times, shouting "Allahu Akbar" (God is greater), thus declaring the triumph of the Believer's Movement. Refusing to enter the Kaaba until it had been purified from its idolatry, Muhammad ordered its 360 idols and paintings removed. He then smashed each one, reciting a Quranic verse: "The truth has come and falsehood has vanished away." Muslim sources record that the Prophet invited his cousin and son-in-law Ali, the first male convert to the new faith, to stand on his shoulders to strike down the highest idols. Thus the Kaaba was cleansed and, in Muslim thinking, restored to its original purpose as a focal point for the worship of Allah alone.

Source 9.4, a fifteenth-century Persian image, portrays this dramatic event, showing Muhammad with Ali on his shoulders, both enveloped in holy fire, smashing the offensive idols while their followers look on.

■ What view of pre-Islamic Arab religion do the images of the idols suggest?

■ What fundamental religious teachings or spiritual truths does this painting seek to convey? How might you understand the Muslim concern with idolatry?

■ Some traditions suggest that Muhammad ordered pictures of Mary and Jesus within the Kaaba to be left intact. What purpose might this tradition serve?

Source 9.4 The Destruction of the Idols

Miniature from "Raudat as-Safa" ("Garden of Purity"), by Mir Havand (d. 1489), Iran: Shiraz, ca. 1590/bpk, Berlin/
Museum für Islamische Kunst, Staatliche Museen, Berlin, Germany/Photo: Wolfgang Selbach/Art Resource, NY

DOING HISTORY

The Life of the Prophet

1. **Noticing point of view:** Consider these four visual sources together with the other images within the chapter. What general impression of the Islamic world emerges? What point of view, if any, is reflected in this selection of visual sources? Do they convey a positive, negative, or neutral impression of Islamic civilization? Explain your answer with specific references to the various images.

2. **Considering Muhammad:** How might you describe the understanding of Muhammad that these images present? In what ways is Muhammad an exemplar for Muslims of a fully realized human being? Do such images have any usefulness for knowing "what really happened" as opposed to grasping Muslim views of their prophet?

3. **Reflecting on religious history:** What do these images reveal about Muslims' understandings of their relationship to earlier religious practices? What did they accept from the past, and what did they reject? How does that understanding compare with Buddhists' and Christians' views of their place in religious history?

4. **Comparing narrative textbook and visual sources:** What do these images add to the understanding of Islam you derived from the narrative text of this chapter?

From the Psalter of Charles the Bold, 15th century/Victoria & Albert Museum, London, UK/Bridgeman Images

CHAPTER 10

The Worlds of Christendom

Contraction, Expansion, and Division

500–1300

Yao Hong, a Chinese woman, was about twenty years of age around 1990, when, distraught at discovering that her husband was having an affair, she became a Christian. As a migrant from a rural village to the huge city of Shanghai, Yao Hong found support and a sense of family in a Christian community. Interviewed in 2010, she observed, "Whether they know you or not, they treat you as a brother or sister. If you have troubles, they help out with money or material assistance or spiritual aid." Nor did she find the Christian faith alien to her Chinese culture. To the contrary, she felt conversion to Christianity as a patriotic act, even a way of becoming more fully modern. "God is rising here in China," she declared. "If you look at the United States or England, their gospel is very advanced. Their churches are rich, because God blesses them. So I pray for China."[1]

Yao Hong is but one of many millions who have made Christianity a very rapidly growing faith in China over the past thirty years or so. Other Asian countries—South Korea, Taiwan, Singapore, the Philippines, Vietnam, and parts of India—also host substantial Christian communities. Even more impressively, the non-Muslim regions of Africa witnessed an explosive advance of Christianity during the twentieth century, while Latin America, long a primarily Catholic region, has experienced a spectacular growth of Pentecostal Protestant Christianity since the 1970s. In the early twenty-first century, over 60 percent of the world's Christians lived in Asia, Africa, or Latin America. Thus Europe and North America, long regarded as the centers of the Christian world, have been increasingly outnumbered in the census of global Christianity.

Charlemagne This fifteenth-century manuscript painting depicts Charlemagne, king of the Franks, who was crowned emperor by the pope in 800 C.E. His reign illustrates the close and sometimes-conflicted relationship of political and religious authorities in an emerging European civilization. It also represents the futile desire of many in Western Europe to revive the old Roman Empire, even as a substantially new civilization was taking shape in the aftermath of the Roman collapse several centuries earlier.

Interestingly enough, the sixth- and seventh-century world of Christendom revealed a broadly similar pattern. Christianity then enjoyed an Afro-Eurasian reach with flourishing communities in Anatolia, Arabia, Egypt, North Africa, Ethiopia, Nubia, Syria, Armenia, Persia, India, and China, as well as Europe (see Chapter 4, pages 172–80). But during the next thousand years, radical changes reshaped that Christian world. Its African and Asian outposts largely vanished, declined, or were marginalized as Christianity became primarily a European phenomenon for the next thousand years or more.

During this millennium, Christianity came to provide a measure of cultural commonality for the diverse peoples of western Eurasia, much as Chinese civilization and Buddhism did for those of East Asia and Islam did for the Middle East and beyond. By 1300, almost all of these societies—from Ireland and England in the west to Russia in the east—had embraced in some form the teachings of the Jewish artisan called Jesus. At the same time, that part of the Christian world became deeply divided. Its eastern half, known as the Byzantine Empire or Byzantium (bihz-ANN-tee-uhm), encompassed much of the eastern Mediterranean basin while continuing the traditions of the Greco-Roman world, though on a smaller scale, until its conquest by the Muslim Ottoman Empire in 1453. Centered on the magnificent city of Constantinople, Byzantium gradually evolved a particular form of Christianity known as Eastern Orthodoxy within a distinctive third-wave civilization.

In Western, or Latin, Christendom, encompassing what we now know as Western Europe, the setting was far different. There the Roman imperial order had largely vanished by 500 C.E., accompanied by the weakening of many features of Roman civilization. Roads fell into disrepair, cities decayed, and long-distance trade shriveled. What replaced the old Roman order was a highly localized society—fragmented, decentralized, and competitive—in sharp contrast to the unified state of Byzantium. Like Byzantium, the Latin West ultimately became thoroughly Christian, but it was a gradual process lasting centuries, and its Roman Catholic version of the faith, increasingly centered on the pope, had an independence from political authorities that the Eastern Orthodox Church did not. Moreover, the Western Church in particular and its society in general were far more rural than Byzantium and certainly had nothing to compare to the splendor of Constantinople. However, slowly at first and then with increasing speed after 1000, Western Europe emerged as an especially dynamic, expansive, and innovative third-wave civilization, combining elements of its Greco-Roman past with the culture of Germanic and Celtic peoples to produce a distinctive hybrid, or blended, civilization.

Thus the story of global Christendom in the era of third-wave civilizations is one of contractions and expansions. As a religion, Christianity contracted sharply in Asia and Africa even as it expanded in Western Europe and Russia. As a civilization, Christian Byzantium flourished for a time, then gradually con-

SEEKING THE MAIN POINT

In what different ways did the history of Christianity unfold in various parts of the Afro-Eurasian world during the third-wave era?

A MAP OF TIME

4th century	Christianity becomes state religion of Armenia, Axum, and Roman Empire
5th–6th centuries	Introduction of Christianity into Nubia
476	Collapse of western Roman Empire
527–565	Justinian rules Byzantine Empire
7th century	Introduction of Christianity into China; initial spread of Islam
726–843	Icon controversy in Byzantium
800	Charlemagne crowned as new "Roman emperor"
988	Conversion of Kievan Rus to Christianity
1054	Mutual excommunication of pope and patriarch
1095–1291	Crusaders in the Islamic world
12th–13th centuries	Translations of Greek and Arab works available in Europe
1346–1350	Black Death in Europe
1453	Turks capture Constantinople; end of Byzantine Empire
1492	Christian reconquest of Spain completed; Columbus's first voyage

tracted and finally disappeared. The trajectory of civilization in the West traced an opposite path, at first contracting as the Roman Empire collapsed and later expanding as a new and blended civilization took hold in Western Europe.

Christian Contraction in Asia and Africa

How had Christianity become by 1500 a largely European faith, with its earlier and promising Asian and African communities diminished, defeated, or dissolved? The answer, in large measure, was Islam. The wholly unforeseen birth of yet another monotheistic faith in the Middle East, its rapid spread across much of the Afro-Eurasian world, the simultaneous creation of a large and powerful Arab Empire, the emergence of a cosmopolitan and transcontinental Islamic civilization—these were the conditions, described more fully in Chapter 9, that led to the contraction of Christendom in Asia and Africa, leaving Europe as the principal center of the Christian faith.[2]

Asian Christianity

■ Comparison

What variations in the experience of African and Asian Christian communities can you identify?

It was in Arabia, the homeland of Islam, that the decimation of earlier Christian communities occurred most completely and most quickly, for within a century or so of Muhammad's death in 632, only a few Christian groups remained. During the eighth century, triumphant Muslims marked the replacement of the old religion by using pillars of a demolished Christian cathedral to construct the Grand Mosque of Sana'a in southern Arabia.

Elsewhere in the Middle East, other Jewish and Christian communities soon felt the impact of Islam. When expanding Muslim forces took control of Jerusalem in 638 and subsequently constructed the Muslim shrine known as the Dome of the Rock (687–691), that precise location had long been regarded as sacred. To Jews, it contained the stone on which Abraham prepared to offer his son Isaac as a sacrifice to God, and it was the site of the first two Jewish temples. To Christians, it was a place that Jesus had visited as a youngster to converse with learned teachers and later to drive out the money changers. Thus, when the Umayyad caliph (successor to the Prophet) Abd al-Malik ordered a new construction on that site, he was appropriating for Islam both Jewish and Christian legacies. But he was also demonstrating the victorious arrival of a new faith and announcing to Christians and Jews that "the Islamic state was here to stay."[3]

In Syria and Persia, with more concentrated populations of Christians, accommodating policies generally prevailed. Certainly, Arab conquest of these adjacent areas involved warfare, largely against the military forces of existing Byzantine and Persian authorities, but not to enforce conversion. In both areas, however, the majority of people turned to Islam voluntarily, attracted perhaps by its aura of success. A number of Christian leaders in Syria, Jerusalem, Armenia, and elsewhere negotiated agreements with Muslim authorities whereby remaining Christian communities were guaranteed the right to practice their religion, largely in private, in return for payment of a special tax.

Much depended on the attitudes of local Muslim rulers. On occasion, churches were destroyed, villages plundered, fields burned, and Christians forced to wear distinctive clothing. By contrast, a wave of church building took place in Syria under Muslim rule, and Christians were recruited into the

The Dome of the Rock, Jerusalem

To Muslims, the Dome of the Rock was constructed on the site from which Muhammad ascended into the presence of Allah during his Night Journey. It was the first large-scale building in the Islamic world and drew heavily on Roman, Byzantine, and Persian precedents. Its location in Jerusalem marked the arrival of a competing faith to Jews and Christians who had long considered the city sacred. (© Aaron Horowitz/Corbis)

administration, schools, translation services, and even the armed forces of the Arab Empire. In 649, only fifteen years after Damascus had been conquered by Arab forces, a Nestorian bishop wrote: "These Arabs fight not against our Christian religion; nay rather they defend our faith, they revere our priests and Saints, and they make gifts to our churches and monasteries."[4]

Thus the Nestorian Christian communities of Syria, Iraq, and Persia, sometimes called the Church of the East, survived the assault of Islam, but they did so as shrinking communities of second-class subjects, regulated minorities forbidden from propagating their message to Muslims. They also abandoned their religious paintings and sculptures, fearing to offend Muslims, who generally objected to any artistic representation of the Divine.

But further east, a small and highly creative Nestorian Church, initiated in

Nestorian Stele
The Nestorian Stele, erected in 781 c.e., is a large limestone block inscribed with a text detailing the early history of Christianity in China. (Nestorian Stele of the Tang Dynasty erected in 781, Xian, China/photo: Ancient Art & Architecture Collection Ltd./Kadokawa Shoten/Bridgeman Images)

635 by a Persian missionary monk, had taken root in China with the approval of the country's Tang dynasty rulers. Both its art and literature articulated the Christian message using Buddhist and Daoist concepts. The written texts themselves, known as the Jesus Sutras, refer to Christianity as the "Religion of Light from the West" or the "Luminous Religion." They describe God as the "Cool Wind," sin as "bad karma," and a good life as one of "no desire" and "no action." "People can live only by dwelling in the living breath of God," the Jesus Sutras declare. "All the Buddhas are moved by this wind, which blows everywhere in the world."[5] The contraction of this remarkable experiment owed little to Islam, but derived rather from the vagaries of Chinese politics. In the mid-ninth century, the Chinese state turned against all religions of foreign origin, Islam and Buddhism as well as Christianity (see Chapter 8, pages 352–53). Wholly dependent on the goodwill of Chinese authorities, this small outpost of Christianity withered.

Later the Mongol conquest of China in the thirteenth century offered a brief opportunity for Christianity's renewal, as the religiously tolerant Mongols welcomed Nestorian Christians as well as people of various other faiths. A number of prominent Mongols became Christians, including one of the wives of Chinggis Khan. Considering Jesus a powerful shaman, Mongols also appreciated that Christians, unlike Buddhists, could eat meat and, unlike Muslims, could drink alcohol, even including it in their worship. But Mongol rule was short, ending in 1368, and the small number of Chinese Christians ensured that the faith almost completely vanished with the advent of the vigorously Confucian Ming dynasty.

African Christianity

The churches of Africa, like those of the Middle East and Asia, also found themselves on the defensive and declining in the face of an expanding Islam. Across coastal North Africa, widespread conversion to Islam over several centuries reduced to virtual extinction Christian communities that had earlier provided many of the martyrs and intellectuals of the early Church.

In Egypt, however, Christianity had become the religion of the majority by the time of the Muslim conquest around 640, and for the next 500 years or so, large numbers continued to speak Coptic and practice their religion as *dhimmis*, legally inferior but protected people paying a special tax, under relatively tolerant Muslim rulers. Many found Arab government less oppressive than that of their former Byzantine overlords, who considered Egyptian Christians heretics. By the thirteenth century, things changed dramatically as Christian Crusaders from Europe and Mongol invaders from the east threatened Egypt. In these circumstances, the country's Muslim rulers came to suspect the political loyalty of their Christian subjects. The mid-fourteenth century witnessed violent anti-Christian pogroms, destruction of churches, and the forced removal of Christians from the best land. Many felt like "exiles in their own country." As a result, most rural Egyptians converted to Islam and moved toward the use of Arabic rather than Coptic, which largely died out. Although Egypt was becoming an Arab and Muslim country, a substantial Christian minority persisted among the literate in urban areas and in monasteries located in remote regions. In the early twenty-first century, Egyptian Christians still numbered about 10 percent of the population.

Even as Egyptian Christianity was contracting, a new center of African Christianity was taking shape during the fifth and sixth centuries in the several kingdoms of Nubia to the south of Egypt, where the faith had been introduced by Egyptian traders and missionaries. Parts of the Bible were translated into the Nubian language, while other writings appeared in Greek, Arabic, and the Ethiopian language of Ge'ez. A great cathedral in the Nubian city of Faras was decorated with magnificent murals, and the earlier practice of burying servants to provide for rulers in the afterlife stopped abruptly. At times, kings served as priests, and Christian bishops held state offices. By the mid-seventh century, both the ruling class and many commoners had become Christian. At the same time, Nubian armies twice defeated Arab incursions, and following these defeats an agreement with Muslim Egypt protected this outpost of Christianity for some 600 years. But pressures mounted in the thirteenth and fourteenth centuries as Egypt adopted a more hostile stance toward Christians, while Islamized tribes from the desert and Arab migrants pushed against Nubia. By 1500, Nubian Christianity, like its counterparts in coastal North Africa, had largely disappeared.

An important exception to these various contractions of Asian and African Christianity lay in Ethiopia. There the rulers of Axum had adopted Christianity in the fourth century, and it subsequently took root among the general population as well. (See Chapter 4, page 178, and Chapter 6, pages 237–39.) Over the centuries of Islamic expansion, Ethiopia became a Christian island in a Muslim sea, protected by its mountainous geography and its distance from major centers of Islamic power. Many Muslims also remembered gratefully that Christian Ethiopia had sheltered some of the beleaguered and persecuted followers of Muhammad in Islam's early years. Nonetheless, the spread of Islam largely cut Ethiopia off from other parts of Christendom and rendered its position in northeast Africa precarious.

The Church of St. George, Lalibela, Ethiopia
Excavated from solid rock in the twelfth century, the churches of Lalibela were distinctive Christian structures, invisible from a distance and apparent only when looking down on them from ground level. Local legend has it that their construction was aided by angels. This one in the shape of a cross is named for Saint George, the patron saint of Ethiopia. (© Gavin Hellier/Robert Harding World Imagery/Corbis)

In its isolated location, Ethiopian Christianity developed some of its most distinctive features. One of these was a fascination with Judaism and Jerusalem, reflected in a much-told story about the visit of an Ethiopian Queen of Sheba to King Solomon. The story includes an episode in which Solomon seduces the queen, producing a child who becomes the founding monarch of the Ethiopian state. Since Solomon figures in the line of descent to Jesus, it meant that Ethiopia's Christian rulers could legitimate their position by tracing their ancestry to Jesus himself. Furthermore, Ethiopian monks long maintained a presence in Jerusalem's Church of the Holy Sepulcher, said to mark the site where Jesus was crucified and buried. Then, in the twelfth century, the rulers of a new Ethiopian dynasty constructed a remarkable series of twelve linked underground churches, apparently attempting to create a New Jerusalem on Christian Ethiopian soil, as the original city lay under Muslim control. Those churches are in use to this day in modern Ethiopia, where over 60 percent of the country's population retains an affiliation with this ancient Christian church.

Byzantine Christendom: Building on the Roman Past

The contraction of the Christian faith and Christian societies in Asia and Africa left Europe and Anatolia, largely by default, as the centers of Christendom. The initial expansion of Islam and the Arab Empire had quickly stripped away what had been the Middle Eastern and North African provinces of the Roman Empire and had brought Spain under Muslim control. But after the Mediterranean frontier between the Islamic and Christian worlds stabilized somewhat in the early eighth century, the immediate threat of Muslim incursions into the heartland of Christendom lifted, although border conflicts persisted. It was within this space of relative security, unavailable to most African and Asian Christian communities, that the diverging histories of the Byzantine Empire and Western Europe took shape.

Unlike most empires, Byzantium has no clear starting point. Its own leaders, as well as its neighbors and enemies, viewed it as simply a continuation of the Roman Empire. Some historians date its beginning to 330 C.E., when the Roman emperor Constantine, who began to favor Christianity during his reign, established a new capital, Constantinople, on the site of an ancient Greek city called Byzantium. At the end of that century, the Roman Empire was formally divided into eastern and western halves, thus launching a division of Christendom that has lasted into the twenty-first century.

Although the western Roman Empire collapsed during the fifth century, the eastern half persisted for another thousand years. Housing the ancient civilizations of Egypt, Greece, Syria, and Anatolia, the eastern Roman Empire (Byzantium) was far wealthier, more urbanized, and more cosmopolitan than its western counterpart; it possessed a much more defensible capital in the heavily walled city of Constantinople; and it had a shorter frontier to guard. Byzantium also enjoyed access to the Black Sea and command of the eastern Mediterranean. With a stronger army, navy, and merchant marine as well as clever diplomacy, its leaders were able to deflect the Germanic and Hun invaders who had overwhelmed the western Roman Empire.

■ **Continuity and Change**

In what respects did Byzantium continue the patterns of the classical Roman Empire? In what ways did it diverge from those patterns?

Much that was late Roman—its roads, taxation system, military structures, centralized administration, imperial court, laws, Christian Church—persisted in the east for many centuries. Like Tang dynasty China seeking to restore the glory of the Han era, Byzantium consciously sought to preserve the legacy of classical Greco-Roman civilization. Constantinople was to be a "New Rome," and people referred to themselves as "Romans." Fearing contamination by "barbarian" customs, emperors forbade the residents of Constantinople from wearing boots, trousers, clothing made from animal skins, and long hairstyles, all of which were associated with Germanic peoples, and insisted instead on Roman-style robes and sandals. But much changed as well over the centuries, marking the Byzantine Empire as the home of a distinctive civilization.

The Byzantine State

Perhaps the most obvious change was one of scale, as the Byzantine Empire never approximated the size of its Roman predecessor (see Map 10.1). The western Roman Empire was permanently lost to Byzantium, despite Emperor Justinian's (r. 527–565) impressive but short-lived attempt to reconquer the Mediterranean basin. The rapid Arab/Islamic expansion in the seventh century resulted in the loss

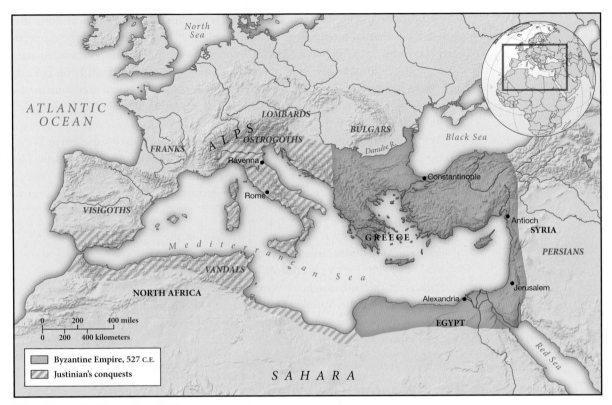

Map 10.1   The Byzantine Empire

The Byzantine Empire reached its greatest extent under Emperor Justinian in the mid-sixth century C.E. It subsequently lost considerable territory to various Christian European powers as well as to Muslim Arab and Turkic invaders.

of Syria/Palestine, Egypt, and North Africa. Nonetheless, until roughly 1200, a more compact Byzantine Empire remained a major force in the eastern Mediterranean, controlling Greece, much of the Balkans (southeastern Europe), and Anatolia. A reformed administrative system gave appointed generals civil authority in the empire's provinces and allowed them to raise armies from the landowning peasants of the region. From that territorial base, the empire's naval and merchant vessels were active in both the Mediterranean and Black seas.

In its heyday, the Byzantine state was an impressive creation. Political authority remained tightly centralized in Constantinople, where the emperor claimed to govern all creation as God's worldly representative, styling himself the "peer of the Apostles" and the "sole ruler of the world." The imperial court tried to imitate the awesome grandeur of what it thought was God's heavenly court, but in fact it resembled ancient Persian imperial splendor. Aristocrats trained in Greek rhetoric and literature occupied high positions in the administration, participating in court ceremonies that maintained their elite status. Parades of these silk-clad officials added splendor to the imperial court, which also included mechanical lions that roared, birds that sang, and an immense throne that quickly elevated the emperor high above his presumably awestruck visitors. Nonetheless, this centralized state touched only lightly on the lives of most people, as it focused primarily on collecting taxes, maintaining order, and suppressing revolts. "Personal freedom in the provinces was constrained more by neighbors and rival households," concluded one historian, "than by the imperial government."[6]

After 1085, Byzantine territory shrank, owing to incursions by aggressive Western European powers, by Catholic Crusaders, and by Turkic Muslim invaders. The end came in 1453 when the Turkic Ottoman Empire, then known as the "sword of Islam," finally took Constantinople. One eyewitness to the event wrote a moving lament to his fallen city:

> And the entire city was to be seen in the tents of the [Turkish] camp, the city deserted, lying lifeless, naked, soundless, without either form or beauty. O city, head of all cities, center of the four corners of the world, pride of the Romans, civilizer of the barbarians. . . . Where is your beauty, O paradise . . . ? Where are the bodies of the Apostle of my Lord . . . ? Where are the relics of the saints, those of the martyrs? Where are the remains of Constantine the Great and the other emperors? . . . Oh, what a loss![7]

The Byzantine Church and Christian Divergence

Intimately tied to the state was the Church, a relationship that became known as caesaropapism. Unlike in Western Europe, where the Roman Catholic Church maintained some degree of independence from political authorities, in Byzantium the emperor assumed something of the role of both "Caesar," as head of state, and the pope, as head of the Church. Thus he appointed the patriarch, or leader, of the Orthodox Church; sometimes made decisions about doctrine; called church councils into session; and generally treated the Church as a government department. "The [Empire] and the church have a great unity and community," declared a twelfth-century patriarch. "Indeed they cannot be separated."[8] A dense network of bishops and priests brought the message of the Church to every corner of the empire, while numerous monasteries accommodated holy men, whose piety, self-denial, and good works made them highly influential among both elite and ordinary people.

■ Comparison

How did Eastern Orthodox Christianity differ from Roman Catholicism?

Eastern Orthodox Christianity had a pervasive influence on every aspect of Byzantine life. It legitimated the supreme and absolute authority of the emperor, for he was a God-anointed ruler, a reflection of the glory of God on earth. It also provided a cultural identity for the empire's subjects. Even more than being "Roman," they were orthodox, or "right-thinking," Christians for whom the empire and the Church were equally essential to achieving eternal salvation. Constantinople was filled with churches and the relics of numerous saints. And the churches were filled with icons—religious paintings, some of them artistic masterpieces, of Jesus, Mary, and numerous saints—that many believed conveyed Divine Presence to the faithful. Complex theological issues about the Trinity and especially about the relationship of God and Jesus engaged the attention of ordinary people. One fourth-century bishop complained: "I wish to know the price of bread; one answers 'The Father is greater than the Son.' I inquire whether my bath is ready; one answers 'The Son has been made out of nothing.'"[9] Partisans of competing chariot-racing teams, known as the Greens and the Blues, vigorously debated theological issues as well as the merits of their favorite drivers.

In its early centuries and beyond, the Christian movement was rent by theological controversy and political division. Followers of Arius, an Egyptian priest, held that Jesus had been created by God the Father rather than living eternally with him. Nestorius, the fifth-century bishop of Constantinople, argued that Mary had given birth only to the human Jesus, who then became the "temple" of God. This view, defined as heretical in the Western Christian world, predominated in a separate Persian Church, which spread its views to India, China, and Arabia.

But the most lasting and deepest division within the Christian world occurred as Eastern Orthodoxy came to define itself against an emerging Latin Christianity centered on papal Rome. Both had derived, of course, from the growth of Christianity in the Roman Empire and therefore had much in common—the teachings of Jesus; the Bible; the sacraments; a church hierarchy of patriarchs, bishops, and priests; a missionary impulse; and intolerance toward other religions. Despite these shared features, any sense of a single widespread Christian community was increasingly replaced by an awareness of difference, competition, and outright hostility that even a common fear of Islam could not overcome. In part, this growing religious divergence reflected the political separation and rivalry between the Byzantine Empire and the emerging kingdoms of Western Europe. As the growth of Islam in the seventh century submerged earlier centers of Christianity in the Middle East and North Africa, Constantinople and Rome alone remained as alternative hubs of the Church. But they were now in different states that competed with each other for territory and for the right to claim the legacy of imperial Rome.

Beyond such political differences were those of language and culture. Although Latin remained the language of the Church and of elite communication in the West, it was abandoned in the Byzantine Empire in favor of Greek, which remained the basis for Byzantine education. More than in the West, Byzantine thinkers sought to formulate Christian doctrine in terms of Greek philosophical concepts.

Differences in theology and church practice likewise widened the gulf between Orthodoxy and Catholicism, despite agreement on fundamental doctrines. Disagreements about the nature of the Trinity, the source of the Holy Spirit, original sin, and the relative importance of faith and reason gave rise to much controversy. So too, for a time, did the Byzantine efforts to prohibit the use of icons, popular paintings of saints and biblical scenes, usually painted on small wooden panels. Other more modest differences also occasioned mutual misunderstanding and disdain.

St. Mark's Basilica
Consecrated in 1094, this ornate cathedral, although located in Venice, Italy, is a classic example of Byzantine architecture. Such churches represented perhaps the greatest achievement of Byzantine art and were certainly the most monumental expressions of Byzantine culture. (Erich Lessing/Art Resource, NY)

Priests in the West shaved and, after 1050 or so, were supposed to remain celibate, while those in Byzantium allowed their beards to grow long and were permitted to marry. Orthodox ritual called for using bread leavened with yeast in the Communion, but Catholics used unleavened bread. Far more significant was the question of authority. Eastern Orthodox leaders sharply rejected the growing claims of Roman popes to be the sole and final authority for all Christians everywhere.

This rift in the world of Christendom grew gradually from the seventh century on, punctuated by various efforts to bridge the mounting divide between the Western and Eastern branches of the Church. A sign of this continuing deterioration occurred in 1054 when representatives of both churches mutually excommunicated each other, declaring in effect that those in the opposing tradition were not true Christians. The Crusades, launched in 1095 by the Catholic pope against the forces of Islam, made things worse. Western Crusaders, passing through the Byzantine Empire on their way to the Middle East, engaged in frequent conflict with local people and thus deepened the distrust between them. From the Western viewpoint, Orthodox practices were "blasphemous, even heretical." One Western observer of the Second Crusade noted that the Greeks "were judged not to be Christians and the Franks [French] considered killing them a matter of no importance."[10] During the Fourth Crusade in 1204, Western forces seized and looted Constantinople and ruled Byzantium for the next half century. Their brutality only confirmed Byzantine views of their Roman Catholic despoilers as nothing more than barbarians. According to one Byzantine account, "They sacked the sacred places and trampled on divine things . . . they tore children from their mothers . . . and they defiled virgins in the holy chapels, fearing neither God's anger nor man's vengeance."[11] After this, the rupture in the world of Christendom proved irreparable.

Byzantium and the World

Beyond its tense relationship with Western Europe, the Byzantine Empire, located astride Europe and Asia, also interacted intensively with its other neighbors. On a political and military level, Byzantium continued the long-term Roman struggle with the Persian Empire. That persisting conflict weakened both of them and was one factor in the remarkable success of Arab armies as they marched out of Arabia in the seventh century. Although Persia quickly became part of the Islamic world, Byzantium held out, even as it lost considerable territory to the Arabs. A Byzantine military innovation known as "Greek fire"—a potent and flammable combination of oil, sulfur, and lime that was launched from bronze tubes—helped hold off the Arabs. It operated something like a flamethrower and subsequently passed into Arab and Chinese arsenals as well. Byzantium's ability to defend its core regions delayed for many centuries the Islamic advance into southeastern Europe, which finally occurred at the hands of the Turkish Ottoman Empire in the fifteenth and sixteenth centuries.

Economically, the Byzantine Empire was a central player in the long-distance trade of Eurasia, with commercial links to Western Europe, Russia, Central Asia, the Islamic world, and China. Its gold coin, the bezant, was a widely used currency in the Mediterranean basin for more than 500 years, and wearing such coins as pendants was a high-status symbol in the less developed kingdoms of Western Europe. The luxurious products of Byzantine craftspeople—jewelry, gemstones, silver and gold work, linen and woolen textiles, purple dyes—were much in demand. Its silk industry, based on Chinese technology, supplied much of the Mediterranean basin with this precious fabric.

■ **Connection**

In what ways was the Byzantine Empire linked to a wider world?

The cultural influence of Byzantium was likewise significant. Preserving much of ancient Greek learning, the Byzantine Empire transmitted this classical heritage to the Islamic world as well as to the Christian West. In both places, it had an immensely stimulating impact among scientists, philosophers, theologians, and other intellectuals. Some saw it as an aid to faith and to an understanding of the world, while others feared it as impious and distracting. (See "Reason and Faith," page 442.)

Byzantine religious culture also spread widely among Slavic-speaking peoples in the Balkans and Russia. As lands to the south and the east were overtaken by Islam, Byzantium looked to the north. By the early eleventh century, steady military pressure had brought many of the Balkan Slavic peoples and the Bulgars under Byzantine control. Christianity and literacy accompanied this Byzantine offensive. Already in the ninth century, two Byzantine missionaries, Cyril and Methodius, had developed an alphabet, based on Greek letters, with which Slavic languages could be written. This Cyrillic script made it possible to translate the Bible and other religious literature into these languages and greatly aided the process of conversion.

988 and the Conversion of Rus

The baptism of Prince Vladimir.

In 988, Prince Vladimir of Rus underwent his celebrated religious conversion, a decision that initiated the Christianization of what later became Russia and Ukraine. About 125 years later, a charming account of that event appeared in the *Russian Primary Chronicle*, a major source of information about early Russian history. In that account, the prince essentially went shopping for a religion, sending emissaries to investigate the faiths of Judaism, Islam, Roman Catholicism, and Eastern Orthodoxy. Based on these reports, Vladimir rejected Islam, for it prohibited eating pork and drinking alcohol, and "drinking is the joy of the Russes." Circumcision and the dispersal of the Jews from their homeland counted against Judaism, while the emissaries reported that they "beheld no glory" among the Catholics. It was a different story when they described Eastern Orthodox Christianity and the great church of Hagia Sophia in Constantinople. There, they declared, "we knew not whether we were in heaven or on earth." And so Vladimir was baptized; married a sister of the Byzantine emperor; threw an idol of Perun, the god of thunder, into the river; and ordered the inhabitants of Kiev to take part in a mass baptism. "There was joy in heaven and on earth," the *Chronicle* concludes, "to behold so many souls saved."[12]

Most historians are highly skeptical that any such systematic search for a new religion actually occurred. But the story reflects several historical realities of the time. Through trade and warfare, the emerging kingdom of Kievan Rus was becoming aware of its neighbors, especially the towering Byzantine Empire but also nearby Jewish, Catholic, and Muslim peoples. Nor is it hard to imagine that ruling elites sought ways to integrate the diverse peoples and cultures of their state. But the coming of Christianity to Rus was not nearly so abrupt as the *Chronicle* suggests. And the motives for this process were not quite so spiritual or religious as portrayed in this account.

In fact, the story began in 860, when the Byzantine Empire, subjected to fearsome raids by wild and ferocious warriors from Rus, sought to tame these "barbarians" by converting them to Christianity, a common practice

photo: Detail from the *Radziwill Chronicle*, Library of the Academy of Sciences of Russia, St. Petersburg, Russia/Photo by Fine Art Images/Heritage Images/Getty Images

The Conversion of Russia

The most significant expansion of Orthodox Christianity occurred among the Slavic peoples of what is now Ukraine and western Russia. In this culturally diverse region, which also included Finnic and Baltic peoples as well as Viking traders, a modest state known as Kievan Rus (KEE-yehv-ihn ROOS)—named after the most prominent city, Kiev—emerged in the ninth century. As in many of the new third-wave civilizations, the development of Rus was stimulated by trade, in this case along the Dnieper River, linking Scandinavia and Byzantium. Loosely led by various princes, especially the prince of Kiev, Rus was a society of slaves and freemen, privileged people and commoners, dominant men and subordinate women. This stratification marked it as a third-wave civilization in the making (see Map 10.3, page 429).

among threatened Christian rulers all across Europe. A Byzantine mission to the lands of Rus resulted in a church or two and a small number of individual converts, but no wholesale religious change. Then, in 911, a treaty between Rus and Byzantium was signed in Constantinople, where the delegates from Rus were shown "the beauties of the churches, the golden palace, and the riches contained therein." Furthermore, Byzantine clerics "instructed the Russes in their faith and expounded to them the true belief." By 957, some among the royal court in Rus had become interested in the new faith. A princess named Olga visited Constantinople and was baptized a Christian. But she was unable to persuade others in ruling circles to follow her example. Even her son spurned Christianity, fearing that his warrior followers would mock him if he converted. During this time, however, a brisk trade had developed between Rus and Byzantium; some warriors from Rus had served as mercenaries in Byzantine armies; and the notables of Rus had become aware of the cultural splendor and material riches of the Byzantine Empire.

And so it is perhaps not surprising that when Vladimir had consolidated his own power by 980, he moved decisively toward the Byzantine Empire and Orthodox Christianity. The occasion was a request in 987 for military assistance from a Byzantine emperor threatened by an internal rebellion. In the negotiations that followed, Vladimir agreed to supply 6,000 soldiers and to convert to Christianity. In return, he gained a new wife, Anna, the sister of the emperor, together with numerous priests and advisers. Perhaps most importantly, Vladimir gained recognition as an equal Christian ruler from the dominant civilization in the region. Here was a turning point in the century-long interaction of Rus and Byzantium and the beginning of an extended process, born of political need on both sides, by which Rus—and later Russia and Ukraine—became thoroughly Christian lands.

A thousand years after Vladimir's conversion, in 1988, the millennial anniversary of that event was celebrated in a Soviet Union still ruled by a Communist Party that had spared little effort to destroy the Russian Orthodox Church. As the Soviet Union disintegrated in the several years that followed, many closed churches, seminaries, and monasteries reopened, returning to the control of the faithful, who flooded into them. The Church has again become an important bulwark of the new Russian and Ukrainian states. And in the memory of many Russians, 988 still remains a major turning point in their country's history.

Questions: How did the *Russian Primary Chronicle* simplify the conversion story? What aspects of the conversion process are emphasized in the *Chronicle*?

Religion reflected the region's cultural diversity, with the gods and practices of many peoples much in evidence. Ancestral spirits, household deities, and various gods related to the forces of nature were in evidence, with Perun, the god of thunder, perhaps the most prominent. Small numbers of Christians, Muslims, and Jews were likewise part of the mix. Then, in the late tenth century, 988 to be precise, a decisive turning point occurred. The growing interaction of Rus with the larger world prompted Prince Vladimir of Kiev to affiliate with the Eastern Orthodox faith of the Byzantine Empire. He was searching for a religion that would unify the diverse peoples of his region, while linking Rus into wider networks of communication and exchange. (See Zooming In: 988 and the Conversion of Rus, above, for a closer look at this momentous decision.)

■ Connection
How did links to Byzantium transform the new civilization of Kievan Rus?

As elsewhere in Europe, the coming of Christianity to Rus was a top-down process in which ordinary people followed their rulers into the Church. It was also a slow process, and elements of traditional religious sensibility long lingered among those who defined themselves as Christian. Perun continued to speak to some, and "magicians" sometimes led people astray in the eyes of church authorities. But building churches on the site where idols to Perun and other gods once stood helped to anchor the new faith in its new land.

It was a fateful choice with long-term implications for Russian history, for it brought this fledgling civilization firmly into the world of Orthodox Christianity, separating it from both the realm of Islam and the Roman Catholic West. Like many new civilizations, Rus borrowed extensively from its older and more sophisticated neighbor. Among these borrowings were Byzantine architectural styles, the Cyrillic alphabet, the extensive use of icons, a monastic tradition stressing prayer and service, and political ideals of imperial control of the Church, all of which became part of a transformed Rus. Orthodoxy also provided a more unified identity for this emerging civilization and religious legitimacy for its rulers. Centuries later, when Byzantium had fallen to the Turks, a few Russian church leaders proclaimed the doctrine of a "third Rome." The original Rome had abandoned the true Orthodox faith for Roman Catholicism, and the second Rome, Constantinople, had succumbed to Muslim infidels. Moscow was now the third Rome, the final protector and defender of Orthodox Christianity. Though not widely proclaimed in Russia itself, such a notion reflected the "Russification" of Eastern Orthodoxy and its growing role as an element of Russian national identity. It was also a reminder of the enduring legacy of a thousand years of Byzantine history, long after the empire itself had vanished.

Western Christendom: Rebuilding in the Wake of Roman Collapse

The western half of the European Christian world followed a rather different path than that of the Byzantine Empire. For much of the third-wave millennium, it was distinctly on the margins of world history, partly because of its geographic location at the far western end of the Eurasian landmass. Thus it was at a distance from the growing routes of world trade—by sea in the Indian Ocean and by land across the Silk Roads to China and the Sand Roads to West Africa. Not until the Eastern and Western hemispheres were joined after 1500 did Western Europe occupy a geographically central position in the global network. Internally, Europe's geography made political unity difficult. It was a region in which population centers were divided by mountain ranges and dense forests as well as by five major peninsulas and two large islands (Britain and Ireland). However, its extensive coastlines and interior river systems facilitated exchange within Europe, while a moderate climate, plentiful rainfall, and fertile soils enabled a productive agriculture that could support a growing population.

Political Life in Western Europe

In the early centuries of this era, history must have seemed more significant than geography, for the Roman Empire, long a fixture of the western Mediterranean region, was gone. The traditional date marking the collapse of the empire is 476, when the German general Odoacer overthrew the last Roman emperor in the West. In itself not very important, this event has come to symbolize a major turning point in the West, for much that had characterized Roman civilization also weakened, declined, or disappeared in the several centuries before and after 476. Any semblance of large-scale centralized rule vanished. Disease and warfare reduced Western Europe's population by more than 25 percent. Land under cultivation contracted, while forests, marshland, and wasteland expanded. Urban life too diminished sharply, as Europe reverted to a largely rural existence. Rome at its height was a city of 1 million people, but by the tenth century it numbered perhaps 10,000. Public buildings crumbled from lack of care. Outside Italy, long-distance trade dried up as Roman roads deteriorated, and money exchange gave way to barter in many places. Literacy lost ground as well. Germanic peoples, whom the Romans had viewed as barbarians—Goths, Visigoths, Franks, Lombards, Angles, Saxons—now emerged as the dominant peoples of Western Europe. In the process, Europe's center of gravity moved away from the Mediterranean toward the north and west.

Yet much that was classical or Roman persisted, even as a new order emerged in Europe. On the political front, a series of regional kingdoms—led by Visigoths in Spain, Franks in France, Lombards in Italy, and Angles and Saxons in England— arose to replace Roman authority. But many of these Germanic peoples, originally organized in small kinship-based tribes with strong warrior values, had already been substantially Romanized. Contact with the Roman Empire in the first several centuries C.E. had generated more distinct ethnic identities among them, militarized their societies, and given greater prominence to Woden, their god of war. As Germanic peoples migrated into or invaded Roman lands, many were deeply influenced by Roman culture, especially if they served in the Roman army. On the funeral monument of one such person was a telling inscription: "I am a Frank by nationality, but a Roman soldier under arms."[13]

The prestige of things Roman remained high, even after the empire itself had collapsed. Now as leaders of their own kingdoms, the Germanic rulers actively embraced written Roman law, using fines and penalties to provide order and justice in their new states in place of feuds and vendettas. One Visigoth ruler named Athaulf (r. 410–415), who had married a Roman noblewoman, gave voice to the continuing attraction of Roman culture and its empire:

■ **Change**
What replaced the Roman order in Western Europe?

At first I wanted to erase the Roman name and convert all Roman territory into a Gothic empire. . . . But long experience has taught me that . . . without law a state is not a state. Therefore I have more prudently chosen the different glory of reviving the Roman name with Gothic vigour, and I hope to be acknowledged by posterity as the initiator of a Roman restoration.[14]

Several of the larger, though relatively short-lived, Germanic kingdoms also had aspirations to re-create something of the unity of the Roman Empire. Charlemagne (SHAHR-leh-mane) (r. 768–814), ruler of the Carolingian Empire, occupying what is now France, Belgium, the Netherlands, and parts of Germany and Italy, erected an embryonic imperial bureaucracy, standardized weights and measures, and began to act like an imperial ruler. On Christmas Day of the year 800, he was crowned as a new Roman emperor by the pope, although his realm splintered shortly after his death (see Map 10.2). Later Otto I of Saxony (r. 936–973) gathered much of Germany under his control, saw himself as renewing Roman rule, and was likewise invested with the title of emperor by the pope. Otto's realm, subsequently known as the Holy Roman Empire, was largely limited to Germany and soon proved little more than a collection of quarreling principalities. Though unsuccessful in reviving anything approaching Roman imperial authority, these efforts testify to the continuing appeal of the classical world, even as a new political system of rival kingdoms blended Roman and Germanic elements.

Map 10.2   Western Europe in the Ninth Century

Charlemagne's Carolingian Empire brought a temporary political unity to parts of Western Europe, but it was subsequently divided among his three sons, who waged war on one another.

Society and the Church

Within these new kingdoms, a highly fragmented and decentralized society widely known as feudalism emerged with great local variation. In thousands of independent, self-sufficient, and largely isolated landed estates or manors, power—political, economic, and social—was exercised by a warrior elite of landowning lords. In the constant competition of these centuries, lesser lords and knights swore allegiance to greater lords or kings and thus became their vassals, frequently receiving lands and plunder in return for military service.

Such reciprocal ties between superior and subordinate were also apparent at the bottom of the social hierarchy, as Roman-style slavery gradually gave way to serf-dom. Unlike slaves, serfs were not the personal property of their masters, could not be arbitrarily thrown off their land, and were allowed to live in families. However, they were bound to their masters' estates as peasant laborers and owed various pay-ments and services to the lord of the manor. One family on a manor near Paris in the ninth century owed four silver coins, wine, wood, three hens, and fifteen eggs per year. Women generally were required to weave cloth and make clothing for the lord, while men labored in the lord's fields. In return, the serf family received a small farm and such protection as the lord could provide. In a violent and insecure world adjusting to the absence of Roman authority, the only security available to many individuals or families lay in these communities, where the ties to kin, manor, and lord constituted the primary human loyalties. It was a world apart from the stability of life in imperial Rome or its continuation in Byzantium.

Also filling the vacuum left by the collapse of empire was the Church, later known as Roman Catholic, yet another link to the now-defunct Roman world. Its hierarchical organization of popes, bishops, priests, and monasteries was modeled on that of the Roman Empire and took over some of its political, administrative, educational, and welfare functions. Latin continued as the language of the Church even as it gave way to various vernacular languages in common speech. In fact, literacy in the classical languages of Greek and Latin remained the hallmark of edu-cated people in the West well into the twentieth century.

Like the Buddhist establishment in China, the Church subsequently became quite wealthy, with reformers often accusing it of forgetting its central spiritual mis-sion. It also provided a springboard for the conversion of Europe's many "pagan" peoples. Numerous missionaries, commissioned by the pope, monasteries, or already-converted rulers, fanned out across Europe, generally pursuing a "top-down" strat-egy. Frequently it worked, as local kings and warlords found status and legitimacy in association with a literate and "civilized" religion that still bore something of the grandeur that was Rome. With "the wealth and protection of the powerful," ordi-nary people followed their rulers into the fold of the Church.[15]

This process was similar to Buddhism's appeal for the nomadic rulers of north-ern and western China following the collapse of the Han dynasty. Christianity, like Buddhism, also bore the promise of superior supernatural powers, and its spread was frequently associated with reported miracles of healing, rainfall, fertility, and victory in battle.

But it was not an easy sell. Outright coercion was sometimes part of the process. More often, however, softer methods prevailed. The Church proved willing to accommodate a considerable range of earlier cultural practices, absorbing them into an emerging Christian tradition. For example, amulets and charms to ward off evil became medals with the image of Jesus or the Virgin Mary; traditionally sacred wells and springs became the sites of churches; and festivals honoring ancient gods became Christian holy days. December 25 was selected as the birthday of Jesus, for it was associated with the winter solstice, the coming of more light, and the birth or rebirth of various deities in pre-Christian European traditions. By 1100, most of Europe had embraced Christianity. Even so, for centuries priests and bishops had to warn their congregations against the worship of rivers, trees, and mountains, and for many people, ancient gods, monsters, trolls, and spirits still inhabited the land. The spreading Christian faith, like the new political framework of European civilization, was a blend of many elements. (For more on the rooting of Christianity in Western Europe, see Working with Evidence: The Making of Christian Europe, page 448.)

Church authorities and the nobles/warriors who exercised political influence reinforced each other. Rulers provided protection for the papacy and strong encouragement for the faith. In return, the Church offered religious legitimacy for the powerful and the prosperous. "It is the will of the Creator," declared the teaching of the Church, "that the higher shall always rule over the lower. Each individual and class should stay in its place [and] perform its tasks."[16] But Church and political authorities competed as well as cooperated, for they were rival centers of power in post-Roman Europe. Particularly controversial was the right to appoint bishops and the pope himself; this issue, known as the investiture conflict, was especially prominent in the eleventh and twelfth centuries. Was the right to make such appointments the responsibility of the Church alone, or did kings and emperors also have a role? In the compromise that ended the conflict, the Church won the right to appoint its own officials, while secular rulers retained an informal and symbolic role in the process.

Accelerating Change in the West

The pace of change in this emerging civilization picked up considerably in the several centuries after 1000. For many centuries before this, the world of European Christendom had been subject to repeated invasions. The incursion of Germanic peoples had accompanied the decline and fall of the western Roman Empire. In the fifth century C.E., the Central Asian Huns had penetrated as far as France and briefly, under the leadership of Attila, established a large state across much of Central and Eastern Europe. Muslim armies had conquered Christian North Africa and Spain and threatened the rest of Europe. In the ninth and tenth centuries, Magyar (Hungarian) invasions from the east and Viking incursions from the north likewise disrupted and threatened post-Roman Europe (see Map 10.3). But by the year 1000, these invasions had been checked; the invaders had been absorbed into settled society and in some cases had converted to Christianity. The greater security and stability that came with relative peace arguably opened the way to an accelerating tempo of change. The climate also seemed to cooperate. A generally warming trend after 750 reached its peak in the eleventh and twelfth centuries, enhancing agricultural production, especially in northern and highland regions.

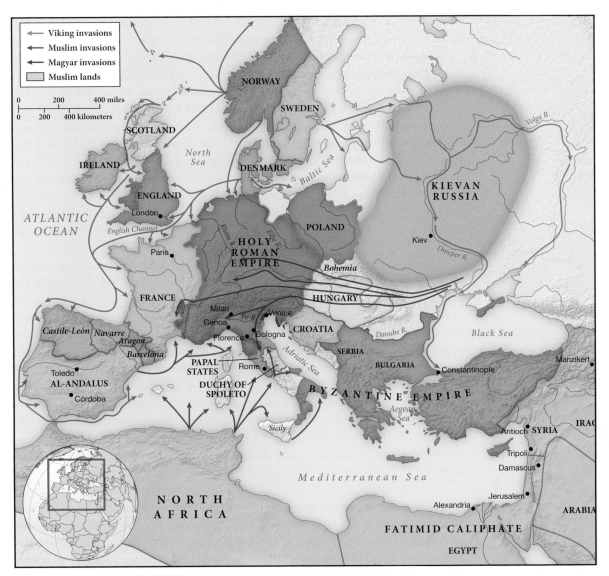

Map 10.3   Europe in the Middle Ages

By the eleventh century, the national monarchies that would organize European political life—France, Spain, England, Poland, and Germany—had begun to take shape. The earlier external attacks on Europe from Vikings, Magyars, and Muslims had largely ceased, although it was clear that European civilization was developing in the shadow of the Islamic world.

Whatever may have launched this new phase of European civilization, commonly called the High Middle Ages (1000–1300), the signs of expansion and growth were widely evident. The population of Europe grew from perhaps 35 million in 1000 to about 80 million in 1340. With more people, many new lands were opened for cultivation in a process paralleling China's expansion to the south at the same time. Great lords, bishops, and religious orders organized new villages on what had recently

■ **Change**

In what ways was European civilization changing after 1000?

been forest or wasteland. Marshes were drained in many regions, and land was reclaimed from the sea, especially along the North Sea coast.

Warmer weather during the summer months allowed farmers and pastoralists to herd their flocks into previously wild highland regions. Everywhere trees were felled at tremendous rates to clear agricultural land and to use as fuel or building material. By 1300, the forest cover of Europe had been reduced to about 20 percent of the land area. "I believe that the forest . . . covers the land to no purpose," declared a German abbot, "and hold this to be an unbearable harm."[17] These developments took a heavy toll on both the terrestrial and aquatic environments. Deforestation, overfishing, human waste, and the proliferation of new watermills and their associated ponds damaged freshwater ecosystems in many places. Lamenting the declining availability of fish, the French king Philip IV declared in 1289: "Today each and every river and waterside of our realm, large and small, yields nothing."[18]

The increased production associated with this agricultural expansion stimulated a considerable growth in long-distance trade, much of which had dried up in the aftermath of the Roman collapse. One center of commercial activity lay in Northern Europe from England to the Baltic coast and involved the exchange of wood, beeswax, furs, rye, wheat, salt, cloth, and wine. The other major trading network centered on northern Italian towns such as Florence, Genoa, and Venice. Their trading partners were the more established civilizations of Islam and Byzantium, and the primary objects of trade included silks, drugs, precious stones, and spices from Asia. At great trading fairs, particularly those in the Champagne area of France near Paris, merchants from Northern and Southern Europe met to exchange the products of their respective areas, such as northern woolens for Mediterranean spices. Thus the self-sufficient communities of earlier centuries increasingly forged commercial bonds among themselves and with more distant peoples.

The population of towns and cities likewise grew on the sites of older Roman towns, at trading crossroads and fortifications, and around cathedrals all over Europe. Some towns had only a few hundred people, but others became much larger. In the early 1300s, London had about 40,000 people, Paris had approximately 80,000, and Venice by the end of the fourteenth century could boast perhaps 150,000. To keep these figures in perspective, Constantinople housed some 400,000 people in 1000, Córdoba in Muslim Spain about 500,000, the Song dynasty capital of Hangzhou more than 1 million in the thirteenth century, and the Aztec capital of Tenochtitlán perhaps 200,000 by 1500. Nonetheless, urbanization was proceeding apace in Europe, though never hosting more than 10 percent of Europe's population. These towns gave rise to and attracted new groups of people, particularly merchants, bankers, artisans, and university-trained professionals such as lawyers, doctors, and scholars. Many of these groups, including university professors and students, organized themselves into guilds (associations of people pursuing the same line of work) to regulate their respective professions. Thus, from the rural social order of lord and peasant, a new more productive and complex division of labor took shape in European society.

A further sign of accelerating change in the West lay in the growth of territorial states with more effective institutions of government commanding the loyalty, or at least the obedience, of their subjects. Since the disintegration of the Roman Empire, Europeans' loyalties had focused on the family, the manor, or the religious community, but seldom on the state. Great lords may have been recognized as kings, but their authority was extremely limited and was exercised through a complex and decentralized network of feudal relationships with earls, counts, barons, and knights, who often felt little obligation to do the king's bidding. But in the eleventh through the thirteenth centuries, the nominal monarchs of Europe gradually and painfully began to consolidate their authority, and the outlines of French, English, Spanish, Scandinavian, and other states began to appear, each with its own distinct language and culture (see Map 10.3, page 429). Royal courts and fledgling bureaucracies were established, and groups of professional administrators appeared. Such territorial kingdoms were not universal, however. In Italy, city-states flourished as urban areas grew wealthy and powerful, whereas the Germans remained divided among a large number of small principalities within the Holy Roman Empire.

These changes, which together represented the making of a new civilization, had implications for the lives of countless women and men. (See Zooming In: Cecilia Penifader, page 432, for an account of a rural unmarried woman's life in England during this time.) Economic growth and urbanization initially offered European women substantial new opportunities. Women were active in a number of urban professions, such as weaving, brewing, milling grain, midwifery, small-scale retailing, laundering, spinning, and prostitution. In twelfth-century Paris, for example, a list of 100 occupations identified 86 as involving women workers, of which 6 were exclusively female. In England, women worked as silk weavers, hatmakers, tailors, brewers, and leather processors and were entitled to train female apprentices in some of these trades. In Frankfurt, about one-third of the crafts and trades were entirely female, another 40 percent were dominated by men, and the rest were open to both. Widows of great merchants sometimes continued their husbands' businesses, and one of them, Rose Burford, lent a large sum of money to the king of England to finance a war against Scotland in 1318.

Much as economic and technological change in China had eroded female silk production, by the fifteenth century artisan opportunities were declining for European women as well. Most women's guilds were gone, and women were restricted or banned from many others. Even brothels were run by men. In England, guild regulations now outlawed women's participation in manufacturing particular fabrics and forbade their being trained on new and larger weaving machines. Women might still spin thread, but the more lucrative and skilled task of weaving fell increasingly to men. Technological progress may have been one reason for this change. Water- and animal-powered grain mills replaced the hand-grinding previously undertaken by women, and larger looms making heavier cloth replaced the lighter looms that women had worked. Men increasingly took over these professions and trained their sons as apprentices, making it more difficult for women to remain active in these fields.

Cecilia Penifader, an English Peasant and Unmarried Woman

Born in 1297 in a small English village, Cecilia Penifader was an illiterate peasant woman, who seldom if ever traveled more than twenty miles beyond her birthplace. She was of no particular historical importance outside of her family and community. Nonetheless, her life, reconstructed from court records by historian Judith Bennett, provides a window into the conditions of ordinary rural people as a new European civilization was taking shape.[19]

From birth to death, Cecilia lived in Brigstock, a royal manor owned by the king of England or a member of the royal family. Free tenants such as Cecilia owed rents and various dues to the lord of the manor. Thus Cecilia occupied a social position above the serfs, unfree people who owed labor service to the lord, but infinitely below the clergy and nobility to whom the lower orders of society owed constant deference. But within the class of "those who work"—the peasantry—Cecilia was fortunate. She was born the seventh of eight children, six of whom survived to adulthood, an unusual occurrence at a time when roughly half of village children died. Her family had

A European peasant woman such as Cecilia Penifader.

substantially larger landholdings than most of their neighbors and no doubt lived in a somewhat larger house. Still, it was probably a single-room dwelling measuring about thirty by fifteen feet, with a dirt floor, and surely it was smoky, for chimneys were not a part of peasant homes.

Between 1315 and 1322, as Cecilia entered early adulthood, England and much of the rest of Europe experienced an immense famine, caused by several years of especially cold and wet weather that marked the end of centuries of favorable climatic conditions. During those years, Cecilia first entered the court records of Brigstock. In 1316, another peasant lodged a complaint against Cecilia and her father for ignoring his boundary stones and taking hay from his fields. Such petty quarrels and minor crimes proliferated as neighborliness broke down in the face of bad harvests and desperate circumstances. Furthermore, both of Cecilia's parents died during the famine years.

photo: *August*, from a series of labors of the month, ca. 1450. English stained glass roundel/Victoria & Albert Museum, London, UK/V&A Images/Art Resource, NY

The Church had long offered some women an alternative to home, marriage, family, and rural life. As in Buddhist lands, substantial numbers of women, particularly from aristocratic families, were attracted to the secluded monastic life of poverty, chastity, and obedience within a convent, in part for the relative freedom from male control that it offered. Here was one of the few places where women might exercise authority as abbesses of their orders and obtain a measure of education. The twelfth-century abbess Hildegard of Bingen, for example, won wide acclaim for her writings on theology, medicine, botany, and music.

But by 1300, much of the independence that such abbesses and their nuns had enjoyed was curtailed and male control tightened, even as veneration of the Virgin Mary swept across Western Christendom. Restrictions on women hearing confes-

Thus Cecilia was left a single woman in her early twenties, but the relative prosperity of her family allowed her to lead a rather independent life. In 1317, she acquired her first piece of land, probably with financial assistance from her father and her own earnings as a day laborer. In fact, Cecilia benefited from the famine because it forced desperate peasants to sell their land at reduced prices. As a result, Cecilia was able to accumulate additional land. By the time of her death in 1344, she was a fairly prosperous woman with a house and farmyard, seventy acres of pasture, and two acres of good farming land. She hired servants or day laborers to work her lands and depended considerably on her brothers, who lived nearby.

If class and family shaped Cecilia's life, so did gender. As a woman, she was unable to hold office in the manor; she was paid about one-third less than men when she worked as an unskilled day laborer; and she could not serve as an official ale-taster, responsible for the quality of the beverage, although women brewed the ale. Like all women, she suffered under a sexual double standard. Two of her brothers, one of whom was a priest, produced children out of wedlock, with no apparent damage to their reputations. But should Cecilia have done so, scandal would surely have ensued.

Unlike most women of her time, Cecilia never married. Did her intended perhaps die during the famine? Did she have a socially inappropriate lover? Did she have an intimate relationship with Robert Malin, a man to whom she left one-third of her estate? Or did she consider marriage a disadvantage? Married women and their property were legally under the control of their husbands, but as a free tenant and head of household, Cecilia bought and sold land on her own and participated as a full member in the deliberations of the local court, which regulated the legal affairs of the manor.

For a woman, the pros and cons of marriage depended very much on whom she married. As a medieval poem put it: "The good and bad happenstances that some women have had / Stands in the choice of a good husband or bad." So while Cecilia missed out on the social approval and support that marriage offered as well as the pleasures of intimacy and children, she also avoided the potential abuse and certain dependency that married life carried for women.

Cecilia's death in 1344 provoked sharp controversy within her family network over the familiar issues of inheritance, kinship, and land. She left her considerable property to the illegitimate son of her brother, to the daughter of her sister Agnes, and to the mysterious Robert Malin. Aggrieved parties, particularly her sister Christina and a nephew Martin, succeeded in having her will overturned.

Question: In what ways did class, family, gender, and natural catastrophe shape Cecilia's life?

sions, preaching, and chanting the Gospel were now more strictly enforced. The educational activities of monastic centers, where men and women could both participate, now gave way to the new universities, where only ordained men could study and teach. Furthermore, older ideas of women's intellectual inferiority, the impurity of menstruation, and their role as sexual temptresses were mobilized to explain why women could never be priests and must operate under male control.

Another religious opportunity for women, operating outside of monastic life and the institutional church, was that of the Beguines. These were groups of laywomen, often from poorer families in Northern Europe, who lived together, practiced celibacy, and devoted themselves to weaving and to working with the sick, the old, and the poor. Though widely respected for their piety and service, their independence from the church hierarchy prompted considerable opposition from both religious and secular authorities suspicious of women operating outside of male control, and the movement gradually faded away. More acceptable to male authorities was the role of anchoress, a woman who withdrew to a locked cell, usually attached to a church, where she devoted herself to prayer and fasting. Some anchoresses gained reputations for great holiness and were much sought after for spiritual guidance. The English mystic and anchoress Julian of Norwich (1342–1416), for example, acquired considerable public prominence and spiritual influence, even as she emphasized the feminine dimension of the Divine and portrayed Jesus as a mother, who "feeds us with Himself."[20]

Thus tightening male control of women took place in Europe as it did in Song dynasty China at about the same time. Accompanying this change was a new understanding of masculinity, at least in the growing towns and cities. No longer able to function as warriors protecting their women, men increasingly defined themselves as "providers"; a man's role was to brave the new marketplaces "to win wealth for himself and his children." In one popular tale, a woman praised her husband: "He was a good provider; he knew how to rake in the money and how to save it." By 1450, the English word "husband" had become a verb meaning "to keep" or "to save."[21]

Europe Outward Bound: The Crusading Tradition

Accompanying the growth of a new European civilization after 1000 were efforts to engage more actively with both near and more distant neighbors. This "medieval expansion" of Western Christendom took place as the Byzantine world was contracting under pressure from the West, from Arab invasion, and later from Turkish conquest (see Map 10.1, page 417). The western half of Christendom was on the rise, while the eastern part was in decline. It was a sharp reversal of their earlier trajectories.

■ Change

What was the impact of the Crusades in world history?

Expansion, of course, has been characteristic of virtually every civilization and has taken a variety of forms—territorial conquest, empire building, settlement of new lands, vigorous trading initiatives, and missionary activity. European civilization was no exception. As population mounted, settlers cleared new land, much of it on the eastern fringes of Europe. The Vikings of Scandinavia, having raided much of Europe, set off on a maritime transatlantic venture around 1000 that briefly established a colony in Newfoundland in North America, and more durably in Greenland and Iceland. (See Zooming In: Thorfinn Karlsefni, Chapter 7, page 306.) As Western economies grew, merchants, travelers, diplomats, and missionaries brought European society into more intensive contact with more distant peoples and with Eurasian commercial networks. By the thirteenth and fourteenth centuries, Europeans had direct, though limited, contact with India, China, and Mongolia. Europe clearly was outward bound.

Nothing more dramatically revealed European expansiveness and the religious passions that informed it than the Crusades, a series of "holy wars" that captured the imagination of Western Christendom for several centuries, beginning in 1095. In European thinking and practice, the Crusades were wars undertaken at God's command and authorized by the pope as the Vicar of Christ on earth. They required participants to swear a vow and in return offered an indulgence, which removed the penalties for any confessed sins, as well as various material benefits, such as immunity from lawsuits and a moratorium on the repayment of debts. Any number of political, economic, and social motives underlay the Crusades, but at their core they were religious wars. Within Europe, the amazing support for the Crusades reflected an understanding of them "as providing security against mortal enemies threatening the spiritual health of all Christendom and all Christians."[22] Crusading drew on both Christian piety and the warrior values of the elite, with little sense of contradiction between these impulses.

The most famous Crusades were those aimed at wresting Jerusalem and the holy places associated with the life of Jesus from Islamic control and returning them to Christendom (see Map 10.4). Beginning in 1095, wave after wave of Crusaders

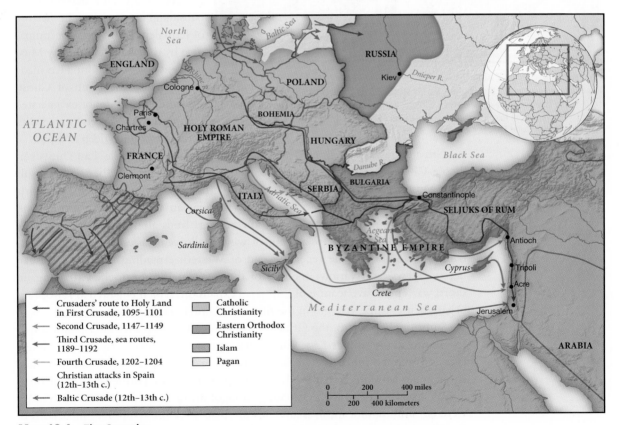

Map 10.4   The Crusades

Western Europe's crusading tradition reflected the expansive energy and religious impulses of an emerging civilization. It was directed against Muslims in the Middle East, Sicily, and Spain as well as the Eastern Orthodox Christians of the Byzantine Empire. The Crusades also involved attacks on Jewish communities, probably the first organized mass pogroms against Jews in Europe's history.

The Crusades
This fourteenth-century painting illustrates the Christian seizure of Jerusalem during the First Crusade in 1099. The crowned figure in the center is Godefroi de Bouillon, a French knight and nobleman who played a prominent role in the attack and was briefly known as the king of Jerusalem. (Bibliothèque Nationale de France, Paris, France/Bridgeman Images)

from all walks of life and many countries flocked to the eastern Mediterranean, where they temporarily carved out four small Christian states, the last of which was recaptured by Muslim forces in 1291. Led or supported by an assortment of kings, popes, bishops, monks, lords, nobles, and merchants, the Crusades demonstrated a growing European capacity for organization, finance, transportation, and recruitment, made all the more impressive by the absence of any centralized direction for the project. They also demonstrated considerable cruelty. The seizure of Jerusalem in 1099 was accompanied by the slaughter of many Muslims and Jews as the Crusaders made their way to the tomb of Christ, according to no doubt exaggerated reports, through streets littered with corpses and ankle deep in blood.

Crusading was not limited to targets in the Islamic Middle East, however. Those Christians who waged war for centuries to reclaim the Iberian Peninsula from Muslim hands were likewise declared "crusaders," with a similar set of spiritual and material benefits. So too were Scandinavian and German warriors who took part in wars to conquer, settle, and convert lands along the Baltic Sea. The Byzantine Empire and Russia, both of which followed Eastern Orthodox Christianity, were also on the receiving end of Western crusading, as were Christian heretics, Jews, and various enemies of the pope in Europe itself. Crusading, in short, was a pervasive feature of European expansion, which persisted as Europeans began their oceanic voyages in the fifteenth century and beyond.

Surprisingly perhaps, the Crusades had little lasting impact, either politically or religiously, in the Middle East. European power was not sufficiently strong or long-lasting to induce much conversion, and the small European footholds there had come under Muslim control by 1300. The penetration of Turkic-speaking peoples from Central Asia and the devastating Mongol invasions of the thirteenth century were far more significant in Islamic history than were the temporary incursions of European Christians. In fact, Muslims largely forgot about the Crusades until the late nineteenth and early twentieth centuries, when their memory was revived in the context of a growing struggle against European imperialism.

In Europe, however, crusading in general and interaction with the Islamic world in particular had very significant long-term consequences. Spain, Sicily, and the Baltic region were brought permanently into the world of Western Christendom, while a declining Byzantium was further weakened by the Crusader sacking of Constantinople in 1204 and left even more vulnerable to Muslim Turkish conquest. In Europe itself, popes strengthened their position, at least for a time, in their continuing struggles with secular authorities. Tens of thousands of Europeans came into personal contact with the Islamic world, from which they picked up a taste for the many luxury goods available there, stimulating a demand for Asian goods. They also learned techniques for producing sugar on large plantations using slave labor, a process that had incalculable consequences in later centuries as Europeans transferred the plantation system to the Americas. Muslim scholarship, together with the Greek learning that it incorporated, also flowed into Europe, largely through Spain and Sicily.

If the cross-cultural contacts born of crusading opened channels of trade, technology transfer, and intellectual exchange, they also hardened cultural barriers between peoples. The rift between Eastern Orthodoxy and Roman Catholicism deepened further and remains to this day a fundamental divide in the Christian world. Christian anti-Semitism was both expressed and exacerbated as Crusaders on their way to Jerusalem found time to massacre Jews, regarded as "Christ-killers," in a number of European cities, particularly in Germany. Such pogroms, however, were not sanctioned by the Church. A leading figure in the Second Crusade, Bernard of Clairvaux, declared, "It is good that you march against the Muslims, but anyone who touches a Jew to take his life, is as touching Jesus himself."[23] European empire building, especially in the Americas, continued the crusading notion that "God wills it." And more recently, over the past two centuries, as the world of the Christian West and that of Islam collided, both sides found many occasions for which images of the Crusades, however distorted, proved politically popular or ideologically useful.

> **SUMMING UP SO FAR**
>
> How did the historical development of the European West differ from that of Byzantium in the third-wave era?

The West in Comparative Perspective

At one level, the making of Western civilization was unremarkable. Civilizations had risen, fallen, renewed themselves, and evolved at many times and in many places. The European case has received extraordinary scrutiny, not so much because of its special significance at the time, but because of its later role as a globally dominant region. However we might explain Europe's subsequent rise to prominence on the world stage, its development in the several centuries after 1000 made only modest ripples beyond its own region. In some respects, Europe was surely distinctive, but it was not yet a major player in the global arena. Comparisons, particularly with China and the Islamic world, help to place these European developments in a world history context.

Catching Up

As the civilization of the West evolved, it was clearly less developed in comparison to Byzantium, China, India, and the Islamic world. Europe's cities were smaller, its political authorities weaker, its economy less commercialized, and its technology inferior. Muslim observers who encountered Europeans saw them as barbarians. An Arab geographer of the tenth century commented on Europeans: "Their bodies are large, their manners harsh, their understanding dull, and their tongues heavy. . . . Those of them who are farthest to the north are the most subject to stupidity, grossness and brutishness."[24] Muslim travelers over the next several centuries saw more to be praised in West African kingdoms, where Islam was practiced and gold was plentiful.

Furthermore, thoughtful Europeans who directly encountered other peoples often acknowledged their own comparative backwardness. "In our time," wrote a twelfth-century European scholar, "it is in Toledo [a Spanish city long under Muslim rule] that the teaching of the Arabs . . . is offered to the crowds. I hastened there to listen to the teaching of the wisest philosophers of this world."[25] The Italian traveler Marco Polo in the thirteenth century proclaimed Hangzhou in China "the finest and noblest [city] in the world." In the early sixteenth century, Spanish invaders of Mexico were stunned at the size and wealth of the Aztec capital, especially its huge market, claiming that they "had never seen such a thing before."[26]

■ Change

In what ways did borrowing from abroad shape European civilization after 1000?

Curious about the rest of the world, Europeans proved quite willing to engage with and borrow from the more advanced civilizations to the east. Growing European economies, especially in the northwest, reconnected with the Eurasian trading system, with which they had lost contact after the fall of Rome. Now European elites eagerly sought spices, silks, porcelain, and sugar from afar even as they assimilated various technological, intellectual, and cultural innovations, as the Snapshot opposite demonstrates. When the road to China opened in the thirteenth and fourteenth centuries, many Europeans, including the merchant-traveler Marco Polo, were more than willing to make the long and difficult journey, returning with amazing tales of splendor and abundance far beyond what was available in Europe. When Europeans took to the oceans in the fifteenth and sixteenth centuries, they were seeking out the sources of African and Asian wealth. Thus the accelerating growth of European civilization was accompanied by its reintegration into the larger Afro-Eurasian networks of exchange and communication.

In this willingness to borrow, Europe resembled several other third-wave civilizations of the time. Japan, for example, took much from China; West Africa drew heavily on Islamic civilization; and Russia actively imitated Byzantium. All of them were then developing civilizations, in a position analogous perhaps to the developing countries of the twentieth century.

Technological borrowing required adaptation to the unique conditions of Europe and was accompanied by considerable independent invention as well. Together these processes generated a significant tradition of technological innovation that

SNAPSHOT   European Borrowing

Like people in other emerging civilizations of the third-wave era, Europeans borrowed extensively from their near and more distant counterparts. They adapted these imports, both technological and cultural, to their own circumstances and generated distinctive innovations as well.

Borrowing	Source	Significance
Horse collar	China / Central Asia via Tunisia	Enabled heavy plowing and contributed to European agricultural development
Stirrup	India/Afghanistan	Revolutionized warfare by enhancing cavalry forces
Gunpowder	China	Enhanced the destructiveness of warfare
Paper	China	Enabled bureaucracy; fostered literacy; prerequisite for printing
Spinning wheel	India	Sped up production of yarn, usually by women at home
Wheelbarrow	China	Laborsaving device for farm and construction work
Aristotle	Byzantium / Islamic Spain	Recovery of classical Greek thought
Medical knowledge/treatments	Islamic world	Sedatives, antiseptics, surgical techniques, optics, and knowledge of contagious diseases enriched European medicine
Christian mysticism	Muslim Spain	Mutual influence of Sufi, Jewish, and Christian mysticism
Music/poetry	Muslim Spain	Contributed to tradition of troubadour poetry about chivalry and courtly love
Mathematics	India / Islamic world	Foundation for European algebra
Chess	India/Persia	A game of prestige associated with European nobility

allowed Europe by 1500 to catch up with, and in some areas perhaps to surpass, China and the Islamic world. That achievement bears comparison with the economic revolution of Tang and Song dynasty China, although Europe began at a lower level and depended more on borrowing than did its Chinese counterpart (see Chapter 8). But in the several centuries surrounding 1000, at both ends of Eurasia, major processes of technological innovation were under way.

In Europe, technological breakthroughs first became apparent in agriculture as Europeans adapted to the very different environmental conditions north of the Alps in the several centuries following 500 C.E. They developed a heavy wheeled plow that could handle the dense soils of Northern Europe far better than the light, or "scratch," plow used in Mediterranean agriculture. To pull the plow, Europeans began to rely increasingly on horses rather than oxen and to use iron horseshoes and a more efficient collar, which probably originated in China or Central Asia and could support much heavier loads. In addition, Europeans developed a

European Technology
Europeans' fascination with technology and their religious motivation for investigating the world are apparent in this thirteenth-century portrayal of God as a divine engineer, laying out the world with a huge compass. (From the *Bible Moralisée*, mid-13th century/Oesterreichische Nationalbibliothek, Vienna, Austria/Erich Lessing/Art Resource, NY)

new three-field system of crop rotation, which allowed considerably more land to be planted at any one time. These were the technological foundations for a more productive agriculture that could support the growing population of European civilization, especially in its urban centers, far more securely than before.

Beyond agriculture, Europeans began to tap non-animal sources of energy in a major way, particularly after 1000. A new type of windmill, very different from an earlier Persian version, was widely used in Europe by the twelfth and thirteenth centuries. The water-driven mill was even more important. The Romans had used such mills largely to grind grain, but their development was limited, since few streams flowed all year and many slaves were available to do the work. By the ninth century, however, watermills were rapidly becoming more evident in Europe. In the early fourteenth century, a concentration of sixty-eight mills dotted a one-mile stretch of the Seine River near Paris. In addition to grinding grain, these mills provided power for sieving flour, tanning hides, making beer, sawing wood, manufacturing iron, and making paper. Devices such as cranks, flywheels, camshafts, and complex gearing mechanisms, when combined with water or wind power, enabled Europeans of the High Middle Ages to revolutionize production in a number of industries and to break with the ancient tradition of depending almost wholly on animal or human muscle as sources of energy. So intense was the interest of European artisans and engineers in tapping mechanical sources of energy that a number of them experimented with perpetual-motion machines, an idea borrowed from Indian philosophers.

Technological borrowing was also evident in the arts of war. Gunpowder was invented in China, but Europeans were probably the first to use it in cannons, in the early fourteenth century, and by 1500 they had the most advanced arsenals in the world. In 1517, one Chinese official, on first encountering European ships and weapons, remarked with surprise, "The westerns are extremely dangerous because of their artillery. No weapon ever made since memorable antiquity is superior to their cannon."[27] Advances in shipbuilding and navigational techniques—including the magnetic compass and sternpost rudder from China and adaptations of the Mediterranean or Arab lateen sail, which enabled vessels to sail against the wind— provided the foundation for European mastery of the seas.

Europe's passion for technology was reflected in its culture and ideas as well as in its machines. About 1260, the English scholar and Franciscan friar Roger Bacon wrote of the possibilities he foresaw, and in doing so, he expressed the confident spirit of the age:

> Machines of navigation can be constructed, without rowers . . . which are borne under the guidance of one man at a greater speed than if they were full of men. Also a chariot can be constructed, that will move with incalculable speed without any draught animal. . . . Also flying machines may be constructed so that a man may sit in the midst of the machine turning a certain instrument by means of which wings artificially constructed would beat the air after the manner of a bird flying . . . and there are countless other things that can be constructed.[28]

Pluralism in Politics

Unlike the large centralized states of Byzantium, the Islamic world, and China, this third-wave European civilization never regained the earlier unity it had under Roman rule. Rather, political life gradually crystallized into a system of competing states (France, Spain, England, Sweden, Prussia, the Netherlands, and Poland, among others) that has persisted into the twenty-first century and that the European Union still confronts. Geographic barriers, ethnic and linguistic diversity, and the shifting balances of power among its many states prevented the emergence of a single European empire, despite periodic efforts to re-create something resembling the still-remembered unity of the Roman Empire.

This multicentered political system shaped the emerging civilization of the West in many ways. It gave rise to frequent wars, enhanced the role and status of military men, and drove the "gunpowder revolution." Thus European society and values were militarized far more than in China, which gave greater prominence to scholars and bureaucrats. Intense interstate rivalry, combined with a willingness to borrow, also stimulated European technological development. By 1500, Europeans had gone a long way toward catching up with their more advanced Asian counterparts in agriculture, industry, war, and sailing.

Thus endemic warfare did not halt European economic growth. Capital, labor, and goods found their way around political barriers, while the common assumptions of Christian culture and the use of Latin and later French by the literate elite fostered communication across political borders. Europe's multistate system thus provided enough competition to stimulate innovation, but it also preserved enough order and unity to allow the economy to grow.

The states within this emerging European civilization also differed from those to the east. Their rulers generally were weaker and had to contend with competing sources of power. Unlike the Orthodox Church in Byzantium, with its practice of caesaropapism, the Roman Catholic Church in the West maintained a degree of independence from state authority that served to check the power of kings and lords. European vassals had certain rights in return for loyalty to their lords and

■ **Comparison**

Why was Europe unable to achieve the kind of political unity that China experienced? What impact did this have on the subsequent history of Europe?

kings. By the thirteenth century, this meant that high-ranking nobles, acting through formal councils, had the right to advise their rulers and to approve new taxes.

This three-way struggle for power among kings, warrior aristocrats, and church leaders, all of them from the nobility, enabled urban-based merchants in Europe to achieve an unusual independence from political authority. Many cities, where wealthy merchants exercised local power, won the right to make and enforce their own laws and appoint their own officials. Some of them—Venice, Genoa, Pisa, and Milan, for example—became almost completely independent city-states. Elsewhere, kings granted charters that allowed cities to have their own courts, laws, and governments, while paying their own kind of taxes to the king instead of feudal dues. Powerful, independent cities were a distinctive feature of European life after 1100 or so. By contrast, Chinese cities, which were far larger than those of Europe, were simply part of the empire and enjoyed few special privileges. Although commerce was far more extensive in China than in the emerging European civilization, the powerful Chinese state favored the landowners over merchants, monopolized the salt and iron industries, and actively controlled and limited merchant activity far more than the new and weaker royal authorities of Europe were able to do.

The relative weakness of Europe's rulers allowed urban merchants more leeway and, according to some historians, opened the way to a more thorough development of capitalism in later centuries. It also led to the development of representative institutions or parliaments through which the views and interests of these contending forces could be expressed and accommodated. Intended to strengthen royal authority by consulting with major social groups, these embryonic parliaments did not represent the "people" or the "nation" but instead embodied the three great "estates of the realm"—the clergy (the first estate), the landowning nobility (the second estate), and urban merchants (the third estate).

Reason and Faith

A further feature of this emerging European civilization was a distinctive intellectual tension between the claims of human reason and those of faith. Christianity had developed in a world suffused with Greek rationalism. Some early Christian thinkers sought to maintain a clear separation between the new religion and the ideas of Plato and Aristotle. "What indeed has Athens to do with Jerusalem?" asked Tertullian (150–225 C.E.), an early church leader from North Africa. More common, however, was the notion that Greek philosophy could serve as a "handmaiden" to faith, more fully disclosing the truths of Christianity. In the reduced circumstances of Western Europe after the collapse of the Roman Empire, the Church had little direct access to the writings of the Greeks, although some Latin translations and commentaries provided a continuing link to the world of classical thought.

But intellectual life in Europe changed dramatically in the several centuries after 1000, amid a rising population, a quickening commercial life, emerging towns and cities, and the Church's growing independence from royal or noble authorities. Moreover, the West was developing a legal system that provided a measure of independence for a variety of institutions—towns and cities, guilds, professional associations, and especially universities. An outgrowth of earlier cathedral schools, these European universities—in Paris, Bologna, Oxford, Cambridge, Salamanca— became "zones of intellectual autonomy" in which scholars could pursue their studies with some freedom from the dictates of religious or political authorities, although that freedom was never complete and was frequently contested.[29]

This was the setting in which European Christian thinkers, a small group of literate churchmen, began to emphasize, quite self-consciously, the ability of human reason to penetrate divine mysteries and to grasp the operation of the natural order. An early indication of this new emphasis occurred in the late eleventh century when students in a monastic school in France asked their teacher, Anselm, to provide them a proof for the existence of God based solely on reason, without using the Bible or other sources of divine revelation.

The new interest in rational thought was applied first and foremost to theology, the "queen of the sciences" to European thinkers. Here was an effort to provide an intellectual foundation for faith, not to replace faith or to rebel against it. Logic, philosophy, and rationality would operate in service to Christ. Of course, some opposed this new emphasis on human reason. Bernard of Clairvaux, a twelfth-century French abbot, declared, "Faith believes. It does not dispute."[30] His contemporary and intellectual opponent, the French scholar William of Conches, lashed out: "You poor fools. God can make a cow out of a tree, but has he ever done so? Therefore show some reason why a thing is so or cease to hold that it is so."[31]

European intellectuals also applied their newly discovered confidence in human reason to law, medicine, and the world of nature, exploring optics, magnetism, astronomy, and alchemy. Slowly and never completely, the scientific study of nature, known as "natural philosophy," began to separate itself from theology. In European universities, natural philosophy was studied in the faculty of arts, which was separate from the faculty of theology, although many scholars contributed to both fields.

This mounting enthusiasm for rational inquiry stimulated European scholars to seek out original Greek texts, particularly those of Aristotle. They found them in the Greek-speaking world of Byzantium and in the Islamic world, where they had long ago been translated into Arabic. In the twelfth and thirteenth centuries, an explosion of translations from Greek and Arabic into Latin, many of them undertaken in Spain, gave European scholars direct access to the works of ancient Greeks and to the remarkable results of Arab scholarship in astronomy, optics, medicine, pharmacology, and more. Much of this Arab science was now translated into Latin and provided a boost to Europe's changing intellectual life, centered in the new universities. One of these translators, Adelard of Bath (1080–1142), remarked that

■ **Comparison**

In what different ways did classical Greek philosophy and science have an impact in the West, in Byzantium, and in the Islamic world?

European University Life in the Middle Ages
This fourteenth-century manuscript painting shows a classroom scene from the University of Bologna in Italy. Note the sleeping and disruptive students. Some things apparently never change. (From the *Liber ethicorum*, by Fra Henricus de Allemania, illuminated manuscript page by Laurentius de Voltolina, ca. 1360–1390/bpk, Berlin/Kupferstichkabinett, Staatliche Museen, Berlin, Germany/Photo: Joerg P. Anders/Art Resource, NY)

he had learned, "under the guidance of reason from Arabic teachers," not to trust established authority.[32]

It was the works of the prolific Aristotle, with his logical approach and "scientific temperament," that made the deepest impression. His writings became the basis for university education and largely dominated the thought of Western Europe in the five centuries after 1200. In the work of the thirteenth-century theologian Thomas Aquinas, Aristotle's ideas were thoroughly integrated into a logical and systematic presentation of Christian doctrine. In this growing emphasis on human rationality, which some considered to be at least partially separate from divine revelation, lay one of the foundations of the later Scientific Revolution and the secularization of European intellectual life.

Surprisingly, nothing comparable occurred in the Byzantine Empire, where knowledge of the Greek language was widespread and access to Greek texts was easy. Although Byzantine scholars kept the classical tradition alive, their primary interest lay in the humanities (literature, philosophy, history) and theology rather than in the natural sciences or medicine. Furthermore, both state and church had serious reservations about Greek learning. In 529, the emperor Justinian closed

Plato's Academy in Athens, claiming that it was an outpost of paganism. Its scholars dispersed into lands that soon became Islamic, carrying Greek learning into the Islamic world. Church authorities as well were suspicious of Greek thought, sometimes persecuting scholars who were too enamored with the ancients. Even those who did study the Greek writers did so in a conservative spirit, concerned with preserving and transmitting the classical heritage rather than with using it as a springboard for creating new knowledge. "The great men of the past," declared the fourteenth-century Byzantine scholar and statesman Theodore Metochites, "have said everything so perfectly that they have left nothing for us to say."[33]

In the Islamic world, Greek thought was embraced "with far more enthusiasm and creativity" than in Byzantium.[34] A massive translation project in the ninth and tenth centuries made Aristotle and many other Greek writers available in Arabic. That work contributed to a flowering of Arab scholarship, especially in the sciences and natural philosophy, between roughly 800 and 1200 (see Chapter 9), but it also stimulated a debate about faith and reason among Muslim thinkers, many of whom greatly admired Greek philosophical, scientific, and medical texts. As in the Christian world, the issue was whether secular Greek thought was an aid or a threat to the faith. Western European church authorities after the thirteenth century had come to regard natural philosophy as a wholly legitimate enterprise and had thoroughly incorporated Aristotle into university education, but learned opinion in the Islamic world swung the other way. Though never completely disappearing from Islamic scholarship, the ideas of Plato and Aristotle receded after the thirteenth century in favor of teachings that drew more directly from the Quran or from mystical experience. Nor was natural philosophy a central concern of Islamic higher education, as it was in the West. The integration of political and religious life in the Islamic world, as in Byzantium, contrasted with their separation in the West, where there was more space for the independent pursuit of scientific subjects.

REFLECTIONS

Remembering and Forgetting: Continuity and Surprise in the Worlds of Christendom

Many of the characteristic features of Christendom, which emerged during the era of third-wave civilizations, have had a long life, extending well into the modern era. The crusading element of European expansion was prominent among the motives of Spanish and Portuguese explorers. Europe's grudging freedom for merchant activity and its eagerness to borrow foreign technology arguably contributed to the growth of capitalism and industrialization in later centuries. The endemic military conflicts of European states, unable to recover the unity of the Roman Empire, found terrible expression in the world wars of the twentieth century. The controversy about reason and faith resonates still, at least in the United States, in debates about the authority of the Bible in secular and scientific matters. The rift between Eastern Orthodoxy and Roman Catholicism remains one of the major divides in the Christian world. Modern universities and the separation of religious and political authority likewise have their origins in the European Middle Ages. Such a perspective, linking the past with what came later, represents one of the great contributions that the study of history makes to human understanding. We are limited and shaped by our histories.

Yet that very strength of historical study can be misleading, particularly if it suggests a kind of inevitability, in which the past determines the future. Knowing the outcome of the stories we tell can be a serious disadvantage, for it may rob the people we study of the freedom and uncertainty that they surely experienced. In 500, few people would have predicted that Europe would become the primary center of Christianity, while the African and Asian expressions of that faith withered away. As late as 1000, the startling reversal of roles between the Eastern and Western wings of Christendom, which the next several centuries witnessed, was hardly on the horizon. At that time, the many small, rural, unsophisticated, and endlessly quarreling warrior-based societies of Western Europe would hardly have borne comparison with the powerful Byzantine Empire and its magnificent capital of Constantinople. Even in 1500, when Europe had begun to catch up with China and the Islamic world in various ways, there was little to predict its remarkable transformation over the next several centuries and the dramatic change in the global balance of power that this transformation produced.

Usually students of history are asked to remember. But forgetting can also be an aid to historical understanding. To recapture the unexpectedness of the historical process and to allow ourselves to be surprised, it may be useful on occasion to forget—or at least set aside—what we know about what happened next and to see the world as contemporaries viewed it.

Second Thoughts

What's the Significance?

Big Picture Questions

1. What accounts for the different historical trajectories of the Byzantine and West European expressions of Christendom?

2. How did Byzantium and Western Europe interact with each other and with the larger world of the third-wave era?

3. In what respects was the civilization of the Latin West distinctive and unique, and in what ways was it broadly comparable to other third-wave civilizations?

4. **Looking Back:** How does the evolution of the Christian world in the third-wave era compare with that of Tang and Song dynasty China and of the Islamic world?

Next Steps: For Further Study

Bonnie S. Anderson and Judith P. Zinsser, *A History of Their Own* (2000). An overview of European women's history by two prominent scholars.

Edward Grant, *Science and Religion from Aristotle to Copernicus* (2004). Demonstrates the impact of Greek philosophy and science in Europe, with comparisons to Byzantium and the Islamic world.

Barbara A. Hanawalt, *The Middle Ages: An Illustrated History* (1999). A brief and beautifully illustrated introduction to the Middle Ages in European history.

Rowena Loverance, *Byzantium* (2004). A lavishly illustrated history of the Byzantine Empire, drawing on the rich collection of artifacts in the British Museum.

Diarmaid MacCulloch, *Christianity: The First Three Thousand Years* (2010). A recent and much-praised overview of the history of Christendom.

Christopher Tyerman, *Fighting for Christendom: Holy Wars and the Crusades* (2005). A very well-written, up-to-date history of the Crusades designed for nonspecialists.

"Byzantine Empire," http://www.history.com/topics/ancient-history/byzantine-empire. A History channel Web site that features a number of short, thoughtful videos about Byzantium.

"Middle Ages," http://www.learner.org/interactives/middleages/. An interactive Web site with text and images relating to life in Europe after the collapse of the Roman Empire.

WORKING WITH EVIDENCE

The Making of Christian Europe

Like Buddhism and Islam, Christianity became a universal religion, taking root well beyond its place of origin. In its early centuries, this new faith, born in a Jewish context in Roman Palestine, spread throughout the Roman Empire, where it received state support during the fourth century C.E. In the centuries that followed the collapse of the western Roman Empire, Christianity also took hold among the peoples of Western Europe in what are now England, France, Germany, and Scandinavia. While we often think about this region as solidly Christian, Western Europe in the period between 500 and 1000 C.E. was very much on the frontier of the Christian world. During those centuries, a number of emerging monarchs of post-Roman Europe found the Christian faith and the Church useful in consolidating their new and fragile states by linking them to the legacy of the Roman Empire. But the making of Christian Europe was a prolonged and tentative process, filled with setbacks, resistance, and struggles among variant versions of the faith as well as growing acceptance and cultural compromise. The documents that follow illustrate that process.

Source 10.1
The Conversion of Clovis

Among the Germanic peoples of post-Roman Western Europe, none were of greater significance than the Franks, occupying the region of present-day France (see Map 10.1, page 417). By the early sixth century, a loosely unified Frankish kingdom had emerged under the leadership of Clovis (r. 485–511), whose Merovingian dynasty ruled the area until 751. Clovis's conversion to Christianity was described about a century later by a well-known bishop and writer, Gregory of Tours (538–594). It was an important step in the triumph of Christianity over Frankish "paganism." It also marked the victory of what would later become Roman Catholicism, based on the idea of the Trinity, over a rival form of the Christian faith, known as Arianism, which held that Jesus was a created divine being subordinate to God the Father.

■ According to Gregory, what led to the conversion of Clovis?

■ What issues are evident in the religious discussions of Clovis and his wife, Clotilda?

■ Notice how Gregory modeled his picture of Clovis on that of Constantine, the famous Roman emperor whose conversion to Christianity in the fourth century gave official legitimacy and state support to the faith (see Chapter 4). What message did Gregory seek to convey in making this implied comparison?

■ How might a modern secular historian use this document to help explain the spread of Christianity among the Franks?

GREGORY OF TOURS

History of the Franks

Late Sixth Century

[Clovis] had a first-born son by queen Clotilda, and as his wife wished to consecrate him in baptism, she tried unceasingly to persuade her husband, saying: "The gods you worship are nothing, and they will be unable to help themselves or any one else. For they are graven out of stone or wood or some metal. . . . They are endowed rather with the magic arts than with the power of the divine name. But he [God] ought rather to be worshipped who created by his word heaven and earth, the sea and all that in them is out of a state of nothingness . . . [and] by whose hand mankind was created. . . ."

But though the queen said this, the spirit of the king was by no means moved to belief, and he said: "It was at the command of our gods that all things were created and came forth, and it is plain that your God has no power and, what is more, he is proven not to belong to the family of the gods." Meantime the faithful queen made her son ready for baptism; she gave command to adorn the church with hangings and curtains, in order that he who could not be moved by persuasion might be urged to belief by this mystery. The boy, whom they named Ingomer, died after being baptized, still wearing the white garments in which he became regenerate. At this the king was violently angry, and reproached the queen harshly, saying: "If the boy had been dedicated in the name of my gods he would certainly have lived; but as it is, since he was baptized in the name of your God, he could not

live at all." To this the queen said: "I give thanks to the omnipotent God, creator of all, who has judged me not wholly unworthy, that he should deign to take to his kingdom one born from my womb. My soul is not stricken with grief for his sake, because I know that, summoned from this world as he was in his baptismal garments, he will be fed by the vision of God. . . ."

The queen did not cease to urge him to recognize the true God and cease worshipping idols. But he could not be influenced in any way to this belief, until at last a war arose with the Alamanni [a Germanic people], in which he was driven by necessity to confess what before he had of his free will denied. It came about that as the two armies were fighting fiercely, there was much slaughter, and Clovis's army began to be in danger of destruction. He saw it and raised his eyes to heaven, and with remorse in his heart he burst into tears and cried: "Jesus Christ, whom Clotilda asserts to be the son of the living God . . . , I beseech the glory of thy aid, with the vow that if thou wilt grant me victory over these enemies . . . , I will believe in thee and be baptized in thy name. For I have invoked my own gods but, as I find, they have withdrawn from aiding me; and therefore I believe that they possess no power, since they do not help those who obey them. . . ." And when he said thus, the Alamanni turned their backs, and began to disperse in flight. And when they saw that their king was killed, they submitted to the dominion of

Clovis, saying: "Let not the people perish further, we pray; we are yours now." And he stopped the fighting, and after encouraging his men, retired in peace and told the queen how he had had merit to win the victory by calling on the name of Christ. This happened in the fifteenth year of his reign. . . .

And so the king confessed all-powerful God in the Trinity, and was baptized in the name of the Father, Son and Holy Spirit, and was anointed with the holy ointment with the sign of the cross of Christ. And of his army more than 3,000 were baptized.

Source: Gregory Bishop of Tours, *History of the Franks*, translated by Ernest Brehaut (New York: Columbia University Press, 1916; copyright renewed 1944), bk. 2, selections from secs. 27, 29, 30, 31, 36–41.

Source 10.2
Advice on Dealing with "Pagans"

In their dealings with the "pagan," or non-Christian, peoples and kings of Western Europe, church authorities such as missionaries, bishops, and the pope himself sometimes advocated compromise with existing cultural traditions rather than overt hostility to them. Here Pope Gregory (r. 590–604) urges the bishop of England to adopt a strategy of accommodation with the prevailing religious practices of the Anglo-Saxon peoples of the island. Gregory's advice was included in a famous work about the early Christian history of England, composed by a Benedictine monk known as the Venerable Bede and completed about 731.

■ What can we learn about the religious practices of the Anglo-Saxons from Bede's account?

■ In what specific ways did the pope urge toleration? And why did he advocate accommodation or compromise with existing religious practices? Keep in mind that the political authorities in England at the time had not yet become thoroughly Christian.

■ What implication might Gregory's policies have for the beliefs and practices of English converts?

POPE GREGORY
Advice to the English Church
601

The temples of the idols in that nation [England] ought not to be destroyed; but let the idols that are in them be destroyed; let holy water be made and sprinkled in the said temples, let altars be erected, and relics placed. For if those temples are well built, it is requisite that they be converted from the worship of devils to the service of the true God; that the nation, seeing that their temples are not destroyed, may remove error from their hearts, and knowing and adoring the true God, may the more familiarly resort to the places to which they have been accustomed.

And because they have been used to slaughter many oxen in the sacrifices to devils, some solemnity must be exchanged for them on this account, as that on the day of the dedication, or the nativities of the holy martyrs, whose relics are there deposited, they may build themselves huts of the boughs of trees, about those churches which have been turned to that use from temples, and celebrate the solemnity with religious feasting, and no more offer beasts to the Devil, but kill cattle to the praise of God in their eating, and return thanks to the Giver of all things for their sustenance; to the end that, while some gratifications are outwardly permitted them, they may the more easily consent to the inward consolations of the grace of God. For there is no doubt that it is impossible to efface everything at once from their obdurate minds; because he who endeavors to ascend to the highest place, rises by degrees or steps, and not by leaps.

Thus the Lord made Himself known to the people of Israel in Egypt; and yet He allowed them the use of the sacrifices which they were wont to offer to the Devil, in his own worship; so as to command them in his sacrifice to kill beasts, to the end that, changing their hearts, they might lay aside one part of the sacrifice, while they retained another; that while they offered the same beasts which they were wont to offer, they should offer them to God, and not to idols; and thus they would no longer be the same sacrifices.

Source: The Venerable Bede, *The Ecclesiastical History of the English Nation*, edited by Ernest Rhys (London: J. M. Dent and Sons; New York: E. P. Dutton, 1910), 52–53.

Source 10.3
Charlemagne and the Saxons

The policies of peaceful conversion and accommodation described in Source 10.2 did not prevail everywhere, as Charlemagne's dealings with the Saxons reveals. During the late eighth and early ninth centuries C.E., Charlemagne (r. 768–814) was the powerful king of the Franks. He turned his Frankish kingdom into a Christian empire that briefly incorporated much of continental Europe, and he was crowned as a renewed Roman emperor by the pope. In the course of almost-constant wars of expansion, Charlemagne struggled for over thirty years (772–804) to subdue the Saxons, a "pagan" Germanic people who inhabited a region on the northeastern frontier of Charlemagne's growing empire (see Map 10.2, page 426). The document known as the *Capitulary on Saxony* outlines a series of laws, regulations, and punishments (known collectively as a capitulary) regarding religious practice of the Saxons. This source reveals both the coercive policies of Charlemagne and the vigorous resistance of the Saxons to their forcible incorporation into his Christian domain.

■ What does this document reveal about the kind of resistance that the Saxons mounted against their enforced conversion?

■ How did Charlemagne seek to counteract that resistance?

■ What does this document suggest about Charlemagne's views of his duties as ruler?

CHARLEMAGNE

Capitulary on Saxony

785

1. It was pleasing to all that the churches of Christ, which are now being built in Saxony and consecrated to God, should not have less, but greater and more illustrious honor, than the fanes [temples] of the idols had had. . . .

3. If any one shall have entered a church by violence and shall have carried off anything in it by force or theft, or shall have burned the church itself, let him be punished by death.

4. If any one, out of contempt for Christianity, shall have despised the holy Lenten fast and shall have eaten flesh, let him be punished by death. But, nevertheless, let it be taken into consideration by a priest, lest perchance any one from necessity has been led to eat flesh.

5. If any one shall have killed a bishop or priest or deacon, let him likewise be punished capitally.

6. If any one deceived by the devil shall have believed, after the manner of the pagans, that any man or woman is a witch and eats men, and on this account shall have burned the person, or shall have given the person's flesh to others to eat, or shall have eaten it himself, let him be punished by a capital sentence.

7. If any one, in accordance with pagan rites, shall have caused the body of a dead man to be burned and shall have reduced his bones to ashes, let him be punished capitally. . . .

9. If any one shall have sacrificed a man to the devil, and after the manner of the pagans shall have presented him as a victim to the demons, let him be punished by death.

10. If any one shall have formed a conspiracy with the pagans against the Christians, or shall have wished to join with them in opposition to the Christians, let him be punished by death; and whoever shall have consented to this same fraudulently against the king and the Christian people, let him be punished by death. . . .

17. Likewise, in accordance with the mandate of God, we command that all shall give a tithe of their property and labor to the churches and priests;

18. That on the Lord's day no meetings and public judicial assemblages shall be held, unless perchance in a case of great necessity or when war compels it, but all shall go to the church to hear the word of God, and shall be free for prayers or good works. Likewise, also, on the especial festivals they shall devote themselves to God and to the services of the church, and shall refrain from secular assemblies.

19. Likewise, . . . all infants shall be baptized within a year. . . .

21. If any one shall have made a vow at springs or trees or groves, or shall have made any offerings after the manner of the heathen and shall have partaken of a repast in honor of the demons, if he shall be a noble, [he must pay a fine of] 60 solidi [gold coins], if a freeman 30, if a litus [neither a slave nor a free person] 15.

Source: D. C. Munro, trans., *Translations and Reprints from the Original Sources of European History*, vol. 6, no. 5, *Selections from the Laws of Charles the Great* (Philadelphia: University of Pennsylvania Press, 1900), 2–4.

Sources 10.4 and 10.5
The Persistence of Tradition

Conversion to Christianity in Western Europe was neither easy nor simple. Peoples thought to have been solidly converted to the new faith continued to engage in earlier practices. Others blended older traditions with Christian rituals. The two documents that follow illustrate both patterns. Source 10.4 describes the encounter between Saint Boniface (672–754), a leading missionary to the Hessians, a Germanic people, during the eighth century. It was written by one of Boniface's devoted followers, Willibald, who subsequently composed a biography of the missionary. Source 10.5 comes from a tenth-century Anglo-Saxon manuscript known as the *Leechbook*, a medical text that describes cures for various problems caused by "elfkind and nightgoers."

- What practices of the Hessians conflicted with Boniface's understanding of Christianity? How did he confront the persistence of these practices?

- What do these documents reveal about the process of conversion to Christianity?

- How might Pope Gregory (Source 10.2), Charlemagne (Source 10.3), and Boniface (Source 10.4) have responded to the cures and preventions described in the *Leechbook*?

WILLIBALD
Life of Boniface
ca. 760

Now many of the Hessians who at that time had acknowledged the Catholic faith were confirmed by the grace of the Holy Spirit and received the laying-on of hands. But others, not yet strong in the spirit, refused to accept the pure teachings of the church in their entirety. Moreover, some continued secretly, others openly, to offer sacrifices to trees and springs, to inspect the entrails of victims; some practiced divination, legerdemain, and incantations; some turned their attention to auguries, auspices, and other sacrificial rites; while others, of a more reasonable character, forsook all the profane practices of the [heathens] and committed none of these crimes.

With the counsel and advice of the latter persons, Boniface in their presence attempted to cut down . . .

a certain oak of extraordinary size, called in the old tongue of the pagans the Oak of Jupiter. Taking his courage in his hands (for a great crowd of pagans stood by watching and bitterly cursing in their hearts the enemy of the gods), he cut the first notch. But when he had made a superficial cut, suddenly, the oak's vast bulk, shaken by a mighty blast of wind from above crashed to the ground shivering its topmost branches into fragments in its fall. As if by the express will of God (for the brethren present had done nothing to cause it) the oak burst asunder into four parts, each part having a trunk of equal length.

At the sight of this extraordinary spectacle the heathens who had been cursing ceased to revile and began, on the contrary, to believe and bless the Lord. Thereupon the holy bishop took counsel with the brethren, built an oratory [a place of prayer] from the timber of the oak and dedicated it to Saint Peter the Apostle. He then set out on a journey to Thuringia. . . . Arrived there, he addressed the elders and the chiefs of the people, calling on them to put aside their blind ignorance and to return to the Christian religion that they had formerly embraced.

Source: Willibald, "Life of Boniface," in *The Anglo-Saxon Missionaries in Germany*, translated by C. H. Talbot (London: Sheed and Ward, 1954), 45–46.

Leechbook
Tenth Century

Work a salve against elfkind and night-goers, . . . and the people with whom the Devil has intercourse. Take eowohumelan, worm-wood, bishopwort, lupin, ashthroat, henbane, harewort, haransprecel, heathberry plants, cropleek, garlic, hedgerife grains, githrife, fennel. Put these herbs into one cup, set under the altar, sing over them nine masses; boil in butter and in sheep's grease, add much holy salt, strain through a cloth; throw the herbs in running water. If any evil temptation, or an elf or nightgoers, happen to a man, smear his forehead with this salve, and put on his eyes, and where his body is sore, and cense him [with incense], and sign [the cross] often. His condition will soon be better.

. . . Against elf disease . . . Take bishopwort, fennel, lupin, the lower part of *ælfthone*, and lichen from the holy sign of Christ [cross], and incense; a handful of each. Bind all the herbs in a cloth, dip in hallowed font water thrice. Let three masses be sung over it, one "Omnibus sanctis [For all the saints]," a second "Contra tribulationem [Against tribulation]," a third "Pro infirmis [For the sick]." Put then coals in a coal pan, and lay the herbs on it.

Smoke the man with the herbs before . . . [9 A.M.] and at night; and sing a litany, the Creed [Nicene], and the Pater noster [Our Father]; and write on him Christ's mark on each limb. And take a little handful of the same kind of herbs, similarly sanctified, and boil in milk; drip holy water in it thrice. And let him sip it before his meal. It will soon be well with him.

Against the Devil and against madness, . . . a strong drink. Put in ale hassock, lupin roots, fennel, ontre, betony, hind heolothe, marche, rue, worm-wood, nepeta (catmint), helenium, *ælfthone*, wolfs comb. Sing twelve masses over the drink; and let him drink. It will soon be well with him.

A drink against the Devil's temptations: thefan-thorn, cropleek, lupin, ontre, bishopwort, fennel, hassock, betony. Sanctify these herbs; put into ale holy water. And let the drink be there in where the sick man is. And continually before he drinks sing thrice over the drink, . . . "God, in your name make me whole (save me)."

Source: Karen Louise Jolly, *Popular Religion in Late Saxon England: Elf Charms in Context* (Chapel Hill: University of North Carolina Press, 1996), 159–67.

DOING HISTORY

The Making of Christian Europe

1. **Describing cultural encounters:** Consider the spread of Christianity in Europe from the viewpoint of those seeking to introduce the new religion. What obstacles did they encounter? What strategies did they employ? What successes and failures did they experience?

2. **Describing cultural encounters . . . from another point of view:** Consider the same process from the viewpoint of new adherents to Christianity. What were the motives for or the advantages of conversion for both political elites and ordinary people? To what extent was it possible to combine prevailing practices and beliefs with the teachings of the new religion?

3. **Defining a concept:** The notion of "conversion" often suggests a quite rapid and complete transformation of religious commitments based on sincere inner conviction. In what ways do these documents support or challenge this understanding of religious change?

4. **Noticing point of view and assessing credibility:** From what point of view is each of the documents written? Which statements in each document might historians find unreliable, and which would they find most useful?

From *History of the Mongols,* India (Lahore), Moghul, Court of Akbar the Great, ca. 1590/Library, Golestan Palace, Teheran, Iran/Werner Forman/Art Resource, NY

CHAPTER 11

Pastoral Peoples on the Global Stage

The Mongol Moment
1200–1500

In late 2012, the Central Asian nation of Mongolia celebrated a "Day of Mongolian Pride," marking the birth of the country's epic hero Chinggis Khan 850 years earlier. Officials laid wreaths at a giant monument to the warrior leader; wrestlers and archers tested their skills in competition; dancers performed; over 100 scholars made presentations; traditional costumes abounded. In central London, no less, a large bronze statue of Mongolia's founder was unveiled for the occasion. For this small and somewhat remote country, seeking to navigate between its two giant neighbors, China and Russia, it was an occasion to express its own distinctive identity. And Chinggis Khan is central to that identity. With his bloody conquests played down, Chinggis Khan is celebrated as a unifier of the Mongolian peoples, the creator of an empire tolerant of various faiths, and a promoter of economic and cultural ties among distant peoples.

The 2012 celebrations marked a shift in Mongolian thinking about Chinggis Khan that has been under way since the 1990s. Under the country's earlier Soviet-backed communist government, the great Mongol leader had been regarded in very negative terms. After all, his forces had decimated Russia in the thirteenth century, and resentment lingered. But as communism faded in both Russia and Mongolia at the end of the twentieth century, the memory of Chinggis Khan made a remarkable comeback in the land of his birth. Vodka, cigarettes, a chocolate bar, two brands of beer, the country's best rock band, and the central square of the capital city all bore his name, while his picture appeared on Mongolia's stamps and money. Rural young people on horseback sang songs in his honor, and their counterparts in urban Internet cafés constructed Web sites to celebrate

Chinggis Khan at Prayer This sixteenth-century Indian painting shows Chinggis Khan at prayer in the midst of battle. He is perhaps praying to Tengri, the great sky god, on whom the Mongol conqueror based his power.

his achievements. The elaborate celebrations in 2012 for his 850th birthday represent just the latest expression of his continuing centrality to modern Mongolia.

All of this is a reminder of the enormous and surprising role that the Mongols played in the Eurasian world of the thirteenth and fourteenth centuries and of the continuing echoes of that long-vanished empire. More generally, the story of the Mongols serves as a useful corrective to the almost-exclusive focus that historians often devote to agricultural peoples and their civilizations, for the Mongols, and many other such peoples, were pastoralists who disdained farming while centering their economic lives around their herds of animals. Normally they did not construct elaborate cities, enduring empires, or monumental works of art, architecture, and written literature. Nonetheless, they left an indelible mark on the historical development of the entire Afro-Eurasian hemisphere, and particularly on the agricultural civilizations with which they so often interacted.

SEEKING THE MAIN POINT

What has been the role in world history of pastoral peoples in general and the Mongols in particular?

Looking Back and Looking Around: The Long History of Pastoral Peoples

The "revolution of domestication," beginning around 11,500 years ago, involved both plants and animals. People living in more favored environments were able to combine farming with animal husbandry and on this economic foundation generated powerful and impressive civilizations with substantial populations. But on the arid margins of agricultural lands, where productive farming was difficult or impossible, an alternative kind of food-producing economy emerged around 4000 B.C.E., focused on the raising of livestock. Peoples practicing such an economy learned to use the milk, blood, wool, hides, and meat of their animals, allowing them to occupy lands that could not support agricultural societies. Some of those animals also provided new baggage and transportation possibilities. Horses, camels, goats, sheep, cattle, yaks, and reindeer were the primary animals that separately, or in some combination, enabled the construction of pastoral or herding societies. Such societies took shape in the vast grasslands of inner Eurasia and sub-Saharan Africa, in the Arabian and Saharan deserts, in the subarctic regions of the Northern Hemisphere, and in the high plateau of Tibet. (See Snapshot, page 460.) Pastoralists had their greatest impact in the Afro-Eurasian world, because in most parts of the Americas the absence of large animals that could be domesticated precluded a herding economy. Only in the Andes did llamas and alpacas allow for some pastoralism.

The World of Pastoral Societies

Despite their many differences, pastoral societies shared several important features that distinguished them from settled agricultural communities and civilizations. Pastoral societies' generally less productive economies and their need for large graz-

A MAP OF TIME

ca. 4000 B.C.E.	Beginning of pastoral economies
ca. 1000 B.C.E.	Beginning of horseback riding
ca. 200 B.C.E.–200 C.E.	Xiongnu Empire
6th–10th centuries	Various Turkic empires
7th–10th centuries	Arab Empire
10th–14th centuries	Conversion of Turkic peoples to Islam
11th–12th centuries	Almoravid Empire
1162–1227	Life of Temujin (Chinggis Khan)
1209–1368	Mongol rule in China
1237–1480	Mongol rule in Russia
1241–1242	Mongol attacks on Eastern Europe
1258	Mongol seizure of Baghdad
1274, 1281	Failed Mongol attacks on Japan
1295	Mongol ruler of Persia converts to Islam
1348–1350	High point of Black Death in Europe

ing areas meant that they supported far smaller populations than did agricultural societies. People generally lived in small and widely scattered encampments or seasonal settlements made up of related kinfolk rather than in the villages, towns, and cities characteristic of agrarian civilizations. Beyond the family unit, pastoral peoples organized themselves in kinship-based groups or clans that claimed a common ancestry, usually through the male line. Related clans might on occasion come together as a tribe, which could also absorb unrelated people into the community. Although their values stressed equality and individual achievement, in some pastoral societies clans were ranked as noble or commoner, and considerable differences emerged between wealthy aristocrats owning large flocks of animals and poor herders. Many pastoral societies held slaves as well.

Furthermore, pastoral peoples generally offered women a higher status, fewer restrictions, and a greater role in public life than their counterparts in agricultural civilizations. Everywhere women were involved in productive labor as well as having domestic responsibility for food and children. The care of smaller animals such as sheep and goats usually fell to women, although only rarely did women own or control their own livestock. Among the Mongols, the remarriage of widows carried none of the negative connotations that it did among the Chinese, and women could initiate divorce. Mongol women frequently served as political advisers and

■ Comparison

In what ways did pastoral societies differ from their agricultural counterparts?

SNAPSHOT   Varieties of Pastoral Societies

Region and Peoples	Primary Animals	Features
Inner Eurasian steppes (Xiongnu, Yuezhi, Turks, Uighurs, Mongols, Huns, Kipchaks)[1]	Horses; also sheep, goats, cattle, Bactrian (two-humped) camel	Domestication of horse by 4000 B.C.E.; horseback riding by 1000 B.C.E.; site of largest pastoral empires
Southwestern and Central Asia (Seljuks, Ghaznavids, Mongol il-khans, Uzbeks, Ottomans)	Sheep and goats; used horses, camels, and donkeys for transport	Close economic relationship with neighboring towns; pastoralists provided meat, wool, milk products, and hides in exchange for grain and manufactured goods
Arabian and Saharan deserts (Bedouin Arabs, Berbers, Tuareg)	Dromedary (one-humped) camel; sometimes sheep	Camel caravans made possible long-distance trade; camel-mounted warriors central to early Arab/Islamic expansion
Grasslands of sub-Saharan Africa (Fulbe, Nuer, Turkana, Masai)	Cattle; also sheep and goats	Cattle were a chief form of wealth and central to ritual life; little interaction with wider world until nineteenth century
Subarctic Scandinavia, Russia (Sami, Nenets)	Reindeer	Reindeer domesticated only since 1500 C.E.; many also fished
Tibetan plateau (Tibetans)	Yaks; also sheep, cashmere goats, some cattle	Tibetans supplied yaks as baggage animals for overland caravan trade; exchanged wool, skins, and milk with valley villagers and received barley in return
Andean Mountains	Llamas and alpacas	Andean pastoralists in a few places relied on their herds for a majority of their subsistence, supplemented with horticulture and hunting

were active in military affairs as well. (See Zooming In: Khutulun, page 477.) A thirteenth-century European visitor, the Franciscan friar Giovanni DiPlano Carpini, recorded his impressions of Mongol women:

> Girls and women ride and gallop as skillfully as men. We even saw them carrying quivers and bows, and the women can ride horses for as long as the men; they have shorter stirrups, handle horses very well, and mind all the property. [Mongol] women make everything: skin clothes, shoes, leggings, and everything made of leather. They drive carts and repair them, they load camels, and are quick and vigorous in all their tasks. They all wear trousers, and some of them shoot just like men.[2]

Certainly, literate observers from adjacent civilizations noticed and clearly disapproved of the freedom granted to pastoral women. Ancient Greek writers thought that the pastoralists with whom they were familiar were "women governed." To Han Kuan, a Chinese Confucian scholar in the first century B.C.E., China's northern pastoral neighbors "[made] no distinction between men and women."[3]

The most characteristic feature of pastoral societies was their mobility, as local environmental conditions largely dictated their patterns of movement. In some favorable regions, pastoralists maintained seasonal settlements, migrating, for instance, between highland pastures in the summer and less harsh lowland environments in the winter. Others lived more nomadic lives, moving their herds frequently in regular patterns to systematically follow the seasonal changes in vegetation and water supply. But even the most nomadic pastoralists were not homeless; they took their homes, often elaborate felt tents, with them. Whatever their patterns of movement, pastoralists shared a life based on turning grass, which people cannot eat, into usable food and energy through their animals.

Although pastoralists represented an alternative to the agricultural way of life that they disdained, they were almost always deeply connected to, and often dependent on, their agricultural neighbors. Few of these peoples could live solely from the products of their animals, and most of them actively sought access to the foodstuffs, manufactured goods, and luxury items available from the urban workshops and farming communities of nearby civilizations. Particularly among the pastoral peoples of inner Eurasia, this desire for the fruits of civilization periodically stimulated the creation of tribal confederations or states that could more effectively deal with the powerful agricultural societies on their borders. The Mongol Empire of

■ Connection

In what ways did pastoral societies interact with their agricultural neighbors?

The Scythians
An ancient horse-riding pastoral people during the second-wave era, the Scythians occupied a region in present-day Kazakhstan and southern Russia. Their pastoral way of life is apparent in this detail from an exquisite gold necklace from the fourth century B.C.E. (Historical Museum, Kiev, Ukraine/Photo © Boltin Picture Library/Bridgeman Images)

the thirteenth century was but the most recent and largest in a long line of such efforts, dating back to the first millennium B.C.E.

Constructing a large state among pastoralists was no easy task. Such societies generally lacked the surplus wealth needed to pay for the professional armies and bureaucracies that everywhere sustained the states and empires of agricultural civilizations. And the fierce independence of widely dispersed pastoral clans and tribes as well as their internal rivalries made any enduring political unity difficult to achieve. Nonetheless, charismatic leaders, such as Chinggis Khan, were periodically able to weld together a series of tribal alliances that for a time became powerful states. In doing so, they often employed the device of "fictive kinship," designating allies as blood relatives and treating them with a corresponding respect.

Despite their limited populations, such states had certain military advantages in confronting larger and more densely populated civilizations. They could draw on the horseback-riding and hunting skills of virtually the entire male population and some women as well. Easily transferred to the role of warrior, these skills, which were practiced from early childhood, were an integral part of inner Eurasian pastoral life. But what sustained these states was their ability to extract wealth, through raiding, trading, or extortion, from agricultural civilizations such as China, Persia, and Byzantium. As long as that wealth flowed into pastoral states, rulers could maintain the fragile alliances among fractious clans and tribes. When it was interrupted, however, those states often fragmented.

Pastoralists interacted with their agricultural neighbors not only economically and militarily but also culturally as they "became acquainted with and tried on for size all the world and universal religions."[4] At one time or another, Judaism, Buddhism, Islam, and several forms of Christianity all found a home somewhere among the pastoral peoples of inner Eurasia. So did Manichaeism, a religious tradition born in third-century Persia and combining elements of Zoroastrian, Christian, and Buddhist practice. Usually conversion was a top-down process as pastoral elites and rulers adopted a foreign religion for political purposes, sometimes changing religious allegiance as circumstances altered. Pastoral peoples, in short, did not inhabit a world totally apart from their agricultural and civilized neighbors.

Surely the most fundamental contribution of pastoralists to the larger human story was their mastery of environments unsuitable for agriculture. Through the creative use of their animals, they brought a version of the food-producing revolution and a substantial human presence to the arid grasslands and desert regions of Afro-Eurasia. As the pastoral peoples of the Inner Asian steppes learned the art of horseback riding, by roughly 1000 B.C.E., their societies changed dramatically. Now they could accumulate and tend larger herds of horses, sheep, and goats and move more rapidly over a much wider territory. New technologies, invented or adapted by pastoral societies, added to the mastery of their environment and spread widely across the Eurasian steppes, creating something of a common culture in this vast region. These innovations included complex horse harnesses, saddles with iron stirrups, a small compound bow that could be fired from horseback, various forms of armor, and new kinds of swords. Agricultural peoples were amazed at the centrality of the horse in pastoral life. As a Roman historian noted about the Huns, "From their horses, by day and night every one of that nation buys and sells, eats and drinks, and bowed over the narrow neck of the animal relaxes in a sleep so deep as to be accompanied by many dreams."[5]

Before the Mongols: Pastoralists in History

What enabled pastoral peoples to make their most visible entry onto the stage of world history was the military potential of horseback riding, and of camel riding somewhat later. Their mastery of mounted warfare made possible a long but intermittent series of pastoral empires across the steppes of inner Eurasia and parts of Africa. For 2,000 years, those states played a major role in Afro-Eurasian history and represented a standing challenge to and influence upon the agrarian civilizations on their borders.

One early large-scale pastoral empire was associated with the people known as the Xiongnu, who lived in the Mongolian steppes north of China (see Chapter 8). Provoked by Chinese penetration of their territory, the Xiongnu in the third and second centuries B.C.E. created a huge military confederacy that stretched from Manchuria deep into Central Asia. Under the charismatic leadership of Modun (r. 210–174 B.C.E.), the Xiongnu Empire effected a revolution in pastoral life. Earlier fragmented and egalitarian societies were now transformed into a far more centralized and hierarchical political system in which

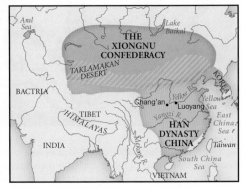

The Xiongnu Confederacy

power was concentrated in a divinely sanctioned ruler and differences between "junior" and "senior" clans became more prominent. "All the people who draw the bow have now become one family," declared Modun. Tribute, exacted from other pastoral peoples and from China itself, sustained the Xiongnu Empire and forced the Han dynasty emperor Wen to acknowledge, unhappily, the equality of people he regarded as barbarians. "Our two great nations," he declared, no doubt reluctantly, "the Han and the Xiongnu, stand side by side."[6]

Although it subsequently disintegrated under sustained Chinese counterattacks, the Xiongnu Empire created a model that later Turkic and Mongol empires emulated. Even without a powerful state, various nomadic or semi-nomadic peoples played a role in the collapse of the already-weakened Chinese and Roman empires and in the subsequent rebuilding of those civilizations (see Chapter 3).

It was during the era of third-wave civilizations (500–1500) that pastoral peoples made their most significant mark on the larger canvas of world history. Arabs, Berbers, Turks, and Mongols—all of them of pastoral origin—created the largest and most influential empires of that millennium. The most expansive religious tradition of the era, Islam, derived from a largely pastoral people, the Arabs, and was carried to new regions by another pastoral people, the Turks. In that millennium, most of the great civilizations of outer Eurasia—Byzantium, Persia, India, and China—had come under the control of previously pastoral people, at least for a time. But as

■ **Significance**
In what ways did the Xiongnu, Arabs, Turks, and Berbers make an impact on world history?

Seljuk Tiles
Among the artistic achievements of Turkic Muslims were lovely ceramic tiles used to decorate mosques, minarets, palaces, and other public spaces. They contained intricate geometric designs, images of trees and birds, and inscriptions from the Quran. This one, dating from the thirteenth century, was used in a Seljuk palace, built as a summer residence for the sultan in the city of Konya in what is now central Turkey. (© Images & Stories/Alamy)

pastoralists entered and shaped the arena of world history, they too were transformed by the experience.

The first and most dramatic of these incursions came from Arabs. In the Arabian Peninsula, the development of a reliable camel saddle somewhere between 500 and 100 B.C.E. enabled pastoral Bedouin (desert-dwelling) Arabs to fight effectively from atop their enormous beasts. With this new military advantage, they came to control the rich trade routes in incense running through Arabia. Even more important, these camel pastoralists served as the shock troops of Islamic expansion, providing many of the new religion's earliest followers and much of the military force that carved out the Arab Empire. Although intellectual and political leadership came from urban merchants and settled farming communities, the Arab Empire was in some respects a pastoralist creation that subsequently became the foundation of a new and distinctive civilization.

Even as the pastoral Arabs encroached on the world of Eurasian civilizations from the south, Turkic-speaking pastoralists were making inroads from the north. Never a single people, various Turkic-speaking clans and tribes migrated from their homeland in Mongolia and southern Siberia generally westward and entered the historical record as creators of a series of empires between 552 and 965 C.E., most of them lasting little more than a century. Like the Xiongnu Empire, they were fragile alliances of various tribes headed by a supreme ruler known as a *kaghan*, who was supported by a faithful corps of soldiers called "wolves," for the wolf was the mythical ancestor of Turkic peoples. From their base in the steppes, these Turkic states confronted the great civilizations to their south—China, Persia, Byzantium—alternately raiding them, allying with them against common enemies, trading with them, and extorting tribute payments from them. Turkic language and culture spread widely over much of Inner Asia, and elements of that culture entered the agrarian civilizations. In the courts of northern China, for example, yogurt thinned with water, a drink derived from the Turks, replaced for a time the traditional beverage of tea, and at least one Chinese poet wrote joyfully about the delights of snowy evenings in a felt tent.[7]

A major turning point in the history of the Turks occurred with their conversion to Islam between the tenth and fourteenth centuries. This extended process represented a major expansion of the faith and launched the Turks into a new role as the third major carrier of Islam, following the Arabs and the Persians. It also brought the Turks into an increasingly important position within the heartland of an established Islamic civilization as they migrated southward into the Middle East. There they served first as slave soldiers within the Abbasid caliphate, and then, as the caliphate declined, they increasingly took political and military power themselves. In the Seljuk Turkic Empire of the eleventh and twelfth centuries, centered in Persia and present-day Iraq, Turkic rulers began to claim the Muslim title of *sultan* (ruler) rather than the Turkic *kaghan*. Although the Abbasid caliph remained the formal ruler, real power was exercised by Turkic sultans.

Not only did Turkic peoples become Muslims themselves, but they carried Islam to new areas as well. Their invasions of northern India solidly planted Islam in that ancient civilization. In Anatolia, formerly ruled by Christian Byzantium, they brought both Islam and a massive infusion of Turkic culture, language, and people, even as they created the Ottoman Empire, which by 1500 became one of the great powers of Eurasia (see Chapter 12, page 516). In both places, Turkic dynasties governed and would continue to do so well into the modern era. Thus Turkic people, many of them at least, had transformed themselves from pastoralists to sedentary farmers, from creators of steppe empires to rulers of agrarian civilizations, and from polytheistic worshippers of their ancestors and various gods to followers and carriers of a monotheistic Islam.

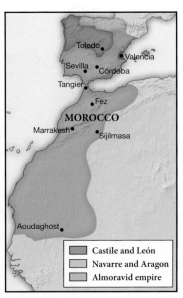

The Almoravid Empire

Broadly similar patterns prevailed in Africa as well. All across northern Africa and the Sahara, the introduction of the camel, probably during the first millennium B.C.E., gave rise to pastoral societies. Much like the Turkic-speaking pastoralists of Central Asia, many of these peoples later adopted Islam, but at least initially had little formal instruction in the religion. In the eleventh century C.E., a reform movement arose among the Sanhaja Berber pastoralists living in the western Sahara; they had only recently converted to Islam and were practicing it rather superficially. The movement was sparked by a scholar, Ibn Yasin, who returned from a pilgrimage to Mecca around 1039 seeking to purify the practice of the faith among his own people in line with orthodox principles. That religious movement soon became an expansive state, the Almoravid Empire, which incorporated a large part of northwestern Africa and in 1086 crossed into southern Spain, where it offered vigorous opposition to Christian efforts to conquer the region.

For a time, the Almoravid state enjoyed considerable prosperity, based on its control of much of the West African gold trade and the grain-producing Atlantic plains of Morocco. The Almoravids also brought to Morocco the sophisticated Islamic culture of southern Spain, still visible in the splendid architecture of the city of Marrakesh, for a time the capital of the Almoravid Empire. By the mid-twelfth century, that empire had been overrun by its longtime enemies, Berber farming people from the Atlas Mountains. But for roughly a century, the Almoravid movement represented an African pastoral people, who had converted to Islam, came into conflict with their agricultural neighbors, built a short-lived empire, and had a considerable impact on neighboring civilizations in both North Africa and Europe.

Breakout: The Mongol Empire

Of all the pastoral peoples who took a turn on the stage of world history, the Mongols made the most stunning entry. Their thirteenth-century breakout from Mongolia gave rise to the largest land-based empire in all of human history, stretching from the Pacific coast of Asia to Eastern Europe (see Map 11.1). This empire joined the pastoral peoples of the inner Eurasian steppes with the settled agricultural civilizations of outer Eurasia more extensively and more intimately than ever before. It also brought the major civilizations of Eurasia—Europe, China, and the Islamic world—into far more direct contact than in earlier times. Both the enormous destructiveness of the process and the networks of exchange and communication

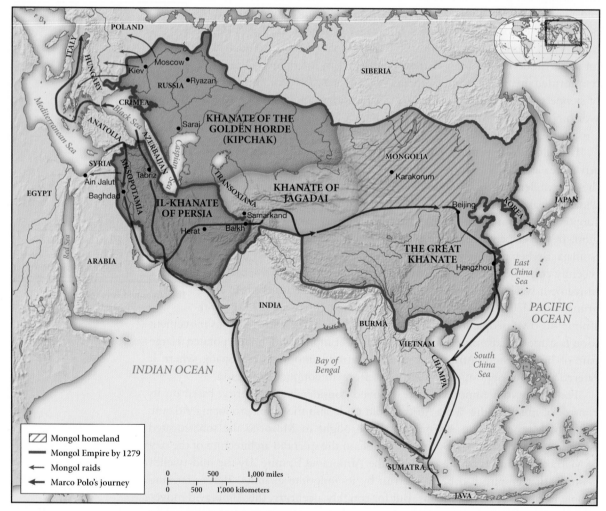

Map 11.1   The Mongol Empire

Encompassing much of Eurasia, the Mongol Empire was divided into four khanates after the death of Chinggis Khan.

that it spawned were the work of the Mongols, numbering only about 700,000 people. It was another of history's unlikely twists.

For all of its size and fearsome reputation, the Mongol Empire left a surprisingly modest cultural imprint on the world it had briefly governed. Unlike the Arabs, the Mongols bequeathed to the world no new language, religion, or civilization. Whereas Islam offered a common religious home for all converts—conquerors and conquered alike—the Mongols never tried to spread their own faith among subject peoples. Their religion centered on rituals invoking the ancestors, which were performed around the family hearth. Rulers sometimes consulted religious specialists, known as shamans, who might predict the future, offer sacrifices, and communicate with the spirit world, particularly with Tengri, the supreme sky god of the Mongols. There was little in this tradition to attract outsiders, and in any event the Mongols proved uninterested in religious imperialism.

The Mongols offered the majority of those they conquered little more than the status of defeated, subordinate, and exploited people, although people with skills were put to work in ways useful to Mongol authorities. Unlike the Turks, whose languages and culture flourish today in many places far from the Turkic homeland, Mongol culture remains confined largely to Mongolia. Furthermore, the Mongol Empire, following in the tradition of Xiongnu and Turkic state building, proved to be "the last, spectacular bloom of pastoral power in Inner Eurasia."[8] Some Mongols themselves became absorbed into the settled societies they conquered. After the decline and disintegration of the Mongol Empire, the tide turned against the pastoralists of inner Eurasia, who were increasingly swallowed up in the expanding Russian or Chinese empires. Nonetheless, while it lasted and for a few centuries thereafter, the Mongol Empire made an enormous impact throughout the entire Eurasian world.

From Temujin to Chinggis Khan: The Rise of the Mongol Empire

World historians are prone to focus attention on large-scale and long-term processes of change in explaining "what happened in history," but in understanding the rise of the Mongol Empire, most scholars have found themselves forced to look closely at the role of a single individual—Temujin (TEM-oo-chin) (1162–1227), later known as Chinggis Khan (universal ruler). The twelfth-century world into which he was born found the Mongols an unstable and fractious collection of tribes and clans, much reduced from a somewhat earlier and more powerful position in the shifting alliances in what is now Mongolia. "Everyone was feuding," declared a leading Mongol shaman. "Rather than sleep, they robbed each other of their possessions. . . . There was no respite, only battle. There was no affection, only mutual slaughter."[9]

The early life of Temujin showed few signs of a prominent future. The boy's father had been a minor chieftain of a noble clan, but he was murdered by tribal rivals before Temujin turned ten, and the family was soon deserted by other members of the clan. As social outcasts without livestock, Temujin's small family, headed

■ **Description**
Identify the major steps in the rise of the Mongol Empire.

by his resourceful mother, was forced to abandon pastoralism, living instead by hunting, fishing, and gathering wild foods. It was an enormous and humiliating drop in their social status. In these desperate circumstances, Temujin's remarkable character came into play. His personal magnetism and courage and his inclination to rely on trusted friends rather than ties of kinship allowed him to build up a small following and to ally with a more powerful tribal leader. This alliance received a boost from Chinese patrons, who were always eager to keep the pastoralists divided. Military victory over a rival tribe resulted in Temujin's recognition as a chief in his own right with a growing band of followers.

Temujin's rise to power within the complex tribal politics of Mongolia was a surprise to everyone. It took place amid shifting alliances and betrayals, a mounting string of military victories, the indecisiveness of his enemies, a reputation as a leader generous to friends and ruthless to enemies, and the incorporation of warriors from defeated tribes into his own forces. In 1206, a Mongol tribal assembly recognized Temujin as Chinggis Khan, supreme leader of a now unified Great Mongol Nation. (See Working with Evidence, Source 11.1, page 488.) It was a remarkable achievement, but one little noticed beyond the highland steppes of Mongolia. That would soon change.

The unification of the Mongol tribes raised an obvious question: what was Chinggis Khan to do with the powerful army he had assembled? Without a common task, the new and fragile unity of the Mongols would surely dissolve into quarrels and chaos; and without external resources to reward his followers, Chinggis Khan would be hard-pressed to maintain his supreme position. Both considerations pointed in a single direction—expansion, particularly toward China, long a source of great wealth for pastoral peoples.

In 1209, the first major attack on the settled agricultural societies south of Mongolia set in motion half a century of a Mongol world war, a series of military campaigns, massive killing, and empire building without precedent in world history. In the process, Chinggis Khan, followed by his sons and grandsons (Ogodei, Mongke, and Khubilai), constructed an empire that contained China, Korea, Central Asia, Russia, much of the Islamic Middle East, and parts of Eastern Europe (see Map 11.1, page 466). "In a flash," wrote a recent scholar, "the Mongol warriors would defeat every army, capture every fort, and bring down the walls of every city they encountered. Christians, Muslims, Buddhists, and Hindus would soon kneel before the dusty boots of illiterate young Mongol horsemen."[10]

Various setbacks marked the outer limits of the Mongol Empire—the Mongols' withdrawal from Eastern Europe (1242), their defeat at Ain Jalut in Palestine at the hands of Egyptian forces (1260), the failure of their invasion of Japan owing to typhoons, and the difficulty of penetrating the tropical jungles of Southeast Asia. But what an empire it was! How could a Mongol confederation, with a total population of less than 1 million people and few resources beyond their livestock, assemble an imperial structure of such staggering transcontinental dimensions? (See Zooming In: A Mongol Failure, page 470.)

Explaining the Mongol Moment

Like the Roman Empire but far more rapidly, the Mongol realm grew of its own momentum without any grand scheme or blueprint for world conquest. Each fresh victory brought new resources for making war and new threats or insecurities that seemed to require further expansion. As the empire took shape and certainly by the end of his life, Chinggis Khan had come to see his career in terms of a universal mission. "I have accomplished a great work," he declared, "uniting the whole world in one empire."[11] Thus the Mongol Empire acquired an ideology in the course of its construction.

What made this "great work" possible? The odds seemed overwhelming, for China alone outnumbered the Mongols 100 to 1 and possessed incomparably greater resources. Furthermore, the Mongols did not enjoy any technological superiority over their many adversaries. They did, however, enjoy the luck of good timing, for China was divided, having already lost control of its northern territory to the pastoral Jurchen people, while the decrepit Abbasid caliphate, once the center of the Islamic world, had shrunk to a fraction of its earlier size. But clearly, the key to the Mongols' success lay in their army. According to one scholar, "Mongol armies were simply better led, organized, and disciplined than those of their opponents."[12] In an effort to diminish a divisive tribalism, Chinggis Khan reorganized the entire social structure of the Mongols into military units of 10, 100, 1,000, and 10,000 warriors, an arrangement that allowed for effective command and control. Conquered tribes, especially, were broken up, and their members were scattered among these new units, which enrolled virtually all men and supplied the cavalry forces of Mongol armies. A highly prestigious imperial guard, also recruited across tribal lines, marked the further decline of the old tribalism as a social revolution, imposed from above, reshaped Mongol society.

An impressive discipline and loyalty to their leaders characterized Mongol military forces, and discipline was reinforced by the provision that should any members of a unit desert in battle, all were subject to the death penalty. More positively, loyalty was cemented by the leaders' willingness to share the hardships of their men. "I eat the same food and am dressed in the same rags as my humble herdsmen," wrote Chinggis Khan. "I am always in the forefront, and in battle I am never at the rear."[13] (See Working with Evidence,

A Mongol Warrior
Horseback-riding skills, honed in herding animals and adapted to military purposes, were central to Mongol conquests, as illustrated in this Ming dynasty Chinese painting of a mounted Mongol archer. (Victoria & Albert Museum, London, UK/Bridgeman Images)

A Mongol Failure: The Invasion of Japan

Japanese samurai attacking a Mongol warship.

The Mongols are best known for their remarkable military victories, which gave them one of the largest empires in history, but they experienced stunning defeats as well.[14] None was more dramatic than the failed invasion of Japan in 1281. The armada assembled by the Mongols for this campaign was one of the largest in history, comprising thousands of ships and as many as 140,000 sailors and soldiers. With little experience in naval warfare, the Mongols built their armada by drawing on the resources of their vassal state in Korea and their recently conquered subjects in China. But even with the aid of these seafaring peoples, this huge invasion fleet stretched the resources of the Mongols, who resorted to commuting the death sentences of criminals willing to serve in the fleet.

The invasion was the culmination of a deteriorating relationship between Japanese authorities and the Mongol ruler Khubilai Khan, grandson of Chinggis Khan and founder of the Chinese Yuan dynasty. In the 1260s,

Japan's government ignored the khan's demands that it become a vassal state of the Mongol Empire. In 1274, the khan dispatched a raiding force against Japan that briefly landed on the main Japanese island of Kyushu. This force both scouted a suitable invasion route and put pressure on the Japanese to accept Mongol demands. In the years that followed, tensions increased, especially when the Japanese summarily beheaded Mongol envoys sent to demand their submission.

Following the final conquest of China in 1279, the khan shifted his attention to subjugating Japan. The massive invasion fleet sailed from ports in Korea and southern China with plans to combine off the shores of Japan. The fleet from Korea arrived first and attacked the mainland without waiting for the Chinese fleet. The Mongols sought to establish a beachhead at the site where Mongol forces had briefly come ashore in 1274, but the

Source 11.2, page 490.) Such discipline and loyalty made possible the elaborate tactics of encirclement, retreat, and deception that proved decisive in many a battle. Furthermore, the enormous flow of wealth from conquered civilizations benefited all Mongols, though not equally. Even ordinary Mongols could now dress in linens and silks rather than hides and felt, could own slaves derived from the many prisoners of war, and had far greater opportunities to improve their social position in a constantly expanding empire.

To compensate for their own small population, the Mongols incorporated huge numbers of conquered peoples into their military forces. "People who lived in felt tents"—mostly Mongol and Turkic pastoralists—were conscripted en masse into the cavalry units of the Mongol army, while settled agricultural peoples supplied the infantry and artillery forces. As the Mongols penetrated major civilizations, with their walled cities and elaborate fortifications, they quickly acquired Chinese techniques and technology of siege warfare. Some 1,000 Chinese artillery crews, for

heavily outnumbered Japanese forces were waiting for them behind recently constructed defensive walls. Unable to establish a beachhead, the Mongol fleet anchored in the harbor, where it was attacked by groups of Japanese warriors, known as samurai, in small open boats, like the one depicted in a contemporary scroll recounting the battle (see photo opposite). In daring raids, often at night, the samurai boarded the much larger Mongol ships and engaged their crews in deadly close-quarters combat.

Under pressure, the Korean fleet withdrew and made its rendezvous with the Chinese fleet that had arrived in the waters off Japan. The combined forces then moved against another Japanese island, where they engaged in a fierce all-night sea battle that once again pitted the large seagoing ships of the Mongol armada against heavily outnumbered groups of samurai in small raiding boats. It was at this moment that a typhoon, named the *kamikaze*, or "divine wind," by the Japanese defenders, struck, destroying perhaps 30 percent of the Korean fleet and between 60 and 90 percent of the Chinese flotilla. In the aftermath, the Mongol commanders abandoned the invasion, leaving behind thousands of shipwrecked soldiers and sailors on the beaches. Such was the role of natural events in confounding human plans.

The defeat had little impact on Khubilai Khan, whose empire recovered quickly from the setback. But the khan never again turned his attentions to Japan, instead seeking to expand his empire elsewhere, including the islands of Southeast Asia, the target of another ambitious but unsuccessful naval expedition in the 1290s. In Japan, the Mongol invasion had a much greater long-term impact. The destruction of the Mongol fleet through what was perceived as divine intervention strengthened Japanese conceptions of their island nation as the *shinkoku*, or "land of the gods." Memories of triumph over the Mongols continued to resonate into the twentieth century. At the end of World War II, when Japan was again faced with foreign invasion, Japanese suicide pilots who sought to stop the Allied advance took the name *kamikazes*, evoking the memory of the typhoon that had turned back the Mongol invasion centuries earlier.

Question: How does the Mongols' military defeat at the hands of the Japanese shape your understanding of the Mongols and their empire?

example, took part in the Mongol invasion of distant Persia. Beyond military recruitment, Mongols demanded that their conquered people serve as laborers, building roads and bridges and ferrying supplies over long distances. Artisans, craftsmen, and skilled people generally were carefully identified, spared from massacre, and often sent to distant regions of the empire where their services were required. A French goldsmith, captured by Mongol forces in Hungary, wound up as a slave in the Mongol capital of Karakorum (kah-rah-KOR-um), where he constructed an elaborate silver fountain that dispensed wine and other intoxicating drinks.

A further element in the military effectiveness of Mongol forces lay in a growing reputation for a ruthless brutality and utter destructiveness. Chinggis Khan's policy was clear: "Whoever submits shall be spared, but those who resist, they shall be destroyed with their wives, children and dependents . . . so that the others who hear and see should fear and not act the same."[15] City after city was utterly destroyed, and enemy soldiers were passed out in lots to Mongol troops for execution, while women and skilled craftsmen were enslaved. Unskilled civilians served as human shields for attacks on the next city or were used as human fill in the moats surrounding those cities. (See Working with Evidence, Sources 11.3 and 11.4, pages 492 and 494.)

One scholar explained such policies in this way: "Extremely conscious of their small numbers and fearful of rebellion, Chinggis often chose to annihilate a region's entire population, if it appeared too troublesome to govern."[16] These policies also served as a form of psychological warfare, a practical inducement to surrender for those who knew of the Mongol terror. Historians continue to debate the extent and uniqueness of the Mongols' brutality, but their reputation for unwavering harshness proved a military asset.

Underlying the purely military dimensions of the Mongols' success was an impressive ability to mobilize both the human and material resources of their growing empire. Elaborate census taking allowed Mongol leaders to know what was available to them and made possible the systematic taxation of conquered people. An effective system of relay stations, about a day's ride apart, provided rapid communication across the empire and fostered trade as well. Marco Polo, the Venetian trader who traveled through Mongol domains in the thirteenth century, claimed that the Mongols maintained some 10,000 such stations, together with 200,000 horses available to authorized users. The beginnings of a centralized bureaucracy with various specialized offices took shape in the new capital of Karakorum. There scribes translated official decrees into the various languages of the empire, such as Persian, Uighur, Chinese, and Tibetan.

Other policies appealed to various groups among the conquered peoples of the empire. Interested in fostering commerce, Mongol rulers often offered merchants 10 percent or more above their asking price and allowed them the free use of the relay stations for transporting their goods. In administering the conquered regions, Mongols held the highest decision-making posts, but Chinese and Muslim officials held many advisory and lower-level positions in China and Persia respectively. In religious matters, the Mongols welcomed and supported many religious traditions—Buddhist, Christian, Muslim, Daoist—as long as they did not become the focus of political opposition. This policy of religious toleration allowed Muslims to seek converts among Mongol troops and afforded Christians much greater freedom than they had enjoyed under Muslim rule. Toward the end of his life, apparently feeling his approaching death, Chinggis Khan himself summoned a famous Daoist master from China and begged him to "communicate to me the means of preserving life." (See Working with Evidence, Source 11.2, page 490.) One of his successors, Mongke, arranged a debate among representatives of several religious faiths, after which he concluded: "Just as God gave different fingers to the hand, so has He given different ways to men."[17] Such economic, administrative, and religious policies provided some benefits and a place within the empire—albeit subordinate—for many of its conquered peoples.

SUMMING UP SO FAR

What accounts for the political and military success of the Mongols?

Encountering the Mongols: Comparing Three Cases

The Mongol moment in world history represented an enormous cultural encounter between pastoralists and the settled civilizations of Eurasia. Differences among those civilizations—Confucian China, Muslim Persia, Christian Russia—ensured considerable diversity as this encounter unfolded across a vast realm. The process of conquest, the length and nature of Mongol rule, the impact on local people, and the extent of Mongol assimilation into the cultures of the conquered—all this and more varied considerably across the Eurasian domains of the empire. The experiences of China, Persia, and Russia provide brief glimpses into several expressions of this massive clash of cultures.

China and the Mongols

Long the primary target for pastoral steppe dwellers in search of agrarian wealth, China proved the most difficult and extended of the Mongols' many conquests, lasting some seventy years, from 1209 to 1279. The invasion began in northern China, which had been ruled for several centuries by various dynasties of pastoral origin and was characterized by destruction and plunder on a massive scale. Southern China, under the control of the native Song dynasty, was a different story, for there the Mongols were far less violent and more concerned with accommodating the local population. Landowners, for example, were guaranteed their estates in exchange for their support or at least their neutrality. By whatever methods, the outcome was the unification of a divided China, a treasured ideal among educated Chinese. This achievement persuaded some of them that the Mongols had indeed been granted the Mandate of Heaven and, despite their foreign origins, were legitimate rulers. One highly educated Chinese scholar wrote a short biography of a recently deceased Mongol official, praising him for curtailing the violence of Mongol soldiers, offering leniency to rebels, and providing tax relief and food during a famine. In short, he was behaving like a good Chinese official.

Having acquired China, what were the Mongols to do with it? One possibility, apparently considered by the Great Khan Ogodei (ERG-uh-day) in the 1230s, was to exterminate everyone in northern China and turn the country into pastureland for Mongol herds. That suggestion, fortunately, was rejected in favor of extracting as much wealth as possible from the country's advanced civilization. Doing so meant some accommodation to Chinese culture and ways of governing, for the Mongols had no experience with the operation of a complex agrarian society.

That accommodation took many forms. The Mongols made use of Chinese administrative practices and techniques of taxation as well as their postal system. They gave themselves a Chinese dynastic title, the Yuan, suggesting a new beginning in Chinese history. They transferred their capital from Karakorum in Mongolia to what is now Beijing, building a wholly new capital city there known as Khanbalik, the "city of the khan." Thus the Mongols were now rooting themselves

■ **Change**

How did Mongol rule change China? In what ways were the Mongols changed by China?

Marco Polo and Khubilai Khan

In ruling China, the Mongols employed in high positions a number of Muslims and a few Europeans, such as Marco Polo, shown here kneeling before Khubilai Khan in a painting from the fifteenth century. (From *Livre des Merveilles du Monde*, ca. 1410–1412, Boucicaut Master [fl. 1390–1430], and workshop/Bibliothèque Nationale de France, Paris, France/Bridgeman Images)

solidly on the soil of a highly sophisticated civilization, well removed from their homeland on the steppes. Khubilai Khan (koo-buh-l'eye kahn), the grandson of Chinggis Khan and China's Mongol ruler from 1271 to 1294, ordered a set of Chinese-style ancestral tablets to honor his ancestors and posthumously awarded them Chinese names. Many of his policies evoked the values of a benevolent Chinese emperor as he improved roads, built canals, lowered some taxes, patronized scholars and artists, limited the death penalty and torture, supported peasant agriculture, and prohibited Mongols from grazing their animals on peasants' farmland. Mongol khans also made use of traditional Confucian rituals, supported the building of some Daoist temples, and were particularly attracted to a Tibetan form of Buddhism, which returned the favor with strong political support for the invaders.

Despite these accommodations, Mongol rule was still harsh, exploitative, foreign, and resented. Marco Polo, who was in China at the time, reported that some Mongol officials or their Muslim intermediaries treated Chinese "just like slaves," demanding bribes for services, ordering arbitrary executions, and seizing women at will—all of which generated outrage and hostility. The Mongols did not become Chinese, nor did they accommodate every aspect of Chinese culture. Deep inside the new capital, the royal family and court could continue to experience something of steppe life as their animals roamed freely in large open areas, planted with steppe grass. Many of the Mongol elite much preferred to live, eat, sleep, and give birth in the traditional tents that sprouted everywhere. In administering the country, the Mongols largely ignored the traditional Chinese examination system and relied heavily on foreigners, particularly Muslims from Central Asia and the Middle East, to serve as officials, while keeping the top decision-making posts for themselves. Few Mongols learned Chinese, and Mongol law discriminated against the Chinese, reserving for them the most severe punishments. Furthermore, the Mongols honored and supported merchants and artisans far more than Confucian bureaucrats had been inclined to do.

In social life, the Mongols forbade intermarriage and prohibited Chinese scholars from learning the Mongol script. Mongol women never adopted foot binding and scandalized the Chinese by mixing freely with men at official gatherings and riding to the hunt with their husbands. The Mongol ruler Khubilai Khan retained the Mongol tradition of relying heavily on female advisers, the chief of which was his favorite wife, Chabi. Ironically, she urged him to accommodate his Chinese subjects, forcefully and successfully opposing an early plan to turn Chinese farmland into pastureland. Unlike many Mongols, biased as they were against farming, Chabi recognized the advantages of agriculture and its ability to generate tax revenue. With a vision of turning Mongol rule into a lasting dynasty that might rank with the splendor of the Tang, she urged her husband to emulate the best practices of that earlier era of Chinese history.

However one assesses Mongol rule in China, it was relatively brief, lasting little more than a century. By the mid-fourteenth century, intense factionalism among the Mongols, rapidly rising prices, furious epidemics of the plague, and growing peasant rebellions combined to force the Mongols out of China. By 1368, rebel forces had triumphed, and thousands of Mongols returned to their homeland in the steppes. For several centuries, they remained a periodic threat to China, but during the Ming dynasty that followed, the memory of their often-brutal and alien rule stimulated a renewed commitment to Confucian values and restrictive gender practices and an effort to wipe out all traces of the Mongols' impact.

Persia and the Mongols

A second great civilization conquered by the Mongols was Islamic Persia. There the Mongol takeover was far more abrupt than the extended process of conquest in China. A first invasion (1219–1221), led by Chinggis Khan himself, was followed thirty years later by a second assault (1251–1258) under his grandson Hulegu (HE-luh-gee), who became the first il-khan (subordinate khan) of Persia. Although Persia had been repeatedly attacked, from the invasion of Alexander the Great to that of the Arabs, nothing prepared them for the Mongols. Before the Mongols, the most recent incursion had featured Turkic peoples, but they had been Muslims, recently converted, small in number, and seeking only acceptance within the Islamic world. The Mongols, however, were infidels in Muslim eyes, and their stunning victory was a profound shock to people accustomed to viewing history as the progressive expansion of Islamic rule. Furthermore, Mongol military victory brought in its wake a degree of ferocity and slaughter that had no parallel in Persian experience. (See Working with Evidence, Source 11.3, page 492, for a description of the Mongol seizure of the city of Bukhara.) The Persian historian Juvaini described it in fearful terms:

> Every town and every village has been several times subjected to pillage and massacre and has suffered this confusion for years so that even though there be generation and increase until the Resurrection the population will not attain to a tenth part of what it was before.[18]

■ Comparison

How was Mongol rule in Persia different from that in China?

The sacking of Baghdad in 1258, which put an end to the Abbasid caliphate, was accompanied by the massacre of more than 200,000 people, according to Hulegu himself.

Beyond this human catastrophe lay the damage to Persian and Iraqi agriculture and to those who tilled the soil. Heavy taxes, sometimes collected twenty or thirty times a year and often under torture or whipping, pushed large numbers of peasants off their land. Furthermore, the in-migration of pastoral Mongols, together with their immense herds of sheep and goats, turned much agricultural land into pasture and sometimes into desert. As a result, a fragile system of underground water channels that provided irrigation to the fields was neglected, and much good agricultural land was reduced to waste. Some sectors of the Persian economy gained, however. Wine production increased because the Mongols were fond of alcohol, and the Persian silk industry benefited from close contact with a Mongol-ruled China. In general, though, even more so than in China, Mongol rule in Persia represented "disaster on a grand and unparalleled scale."[19]

Nonetheless, the Mongols in Persia were themselves transformed far more than their counterparts in China. They made extensive use of the sophisticated Persian bureaucracy, leaving the greater part of government operations in Persian hands. During the reign of Ghazan (haz-ZAHN) (1295–1304), they made some efforts to repair the damage caused by earlier policies of ruthless exploitation by rebuilding damaged cities and repairing neglected irrigation works. Most important, the Mongols who conquered Persia became Muslims, following the lead of Ghazan, who converted to Islam in 1295. No such widespread conversion to the culture of the conquered occurred in China or in Christian Russia. Members of the court and Mongol elites learned at least some Persian, unlike most of their counterparts in China. A number of Mongols also turned to farming, abandoning their pastoral ways, while some married local people.

When the Mongol dynasty of Hulegu's descendants collapsed in the 1330s for lack of a suitable heir, the Mongols were not driven out of Persia as they had been from China. Rather, they and their Turkic allies simply disappeared, assimilated into Persian society. From a Persian point of view, the barbarians had been civilized, and Persians had successfully resisted cultural influence from their uncivilized conquerors. When the great Persian historian Rashid al-Din wrote his famous history of the Mongols, he apologized for providing information about women, generally unmentioned in Islamic writing, explaining that Mongols treated their women equally and included them in decisions of the court.[20] Now Persian rulers could return to their more patriarchal ways.

Khutulun, a Mongol Wrestler Princess

Born around 1260 into the extended family network of Chinggis Khan, Khutulun was the only girl among fourteen brothers.[21] Even among elite Mongol women, many of whom played important roles in public life, Khutulun was unique. Her father, Qaidu Khan, was the Mongol ruler of Central Asia and a bitter opponent of Khubilai Khan, the Mongol ruler of China who was trying to extend his

A Mongol woman riding with Chinggis Khan, as Khutulun rode with her father.

control over Central Asia. A large and well-built young woman, Khutulun excelled in horse riding, archery, and wrestling, outperforming her brothers. Winning fame as a wrestler in public competitions, she soon joined her father on the battlefield, was awarded a medallion of office normally reserved for men alone, and gained a reputation for being blessed of the gods. According to Marco Polo, during battle Khutulun would often seize one of the enemy, "as deftly as a hawk pounces on a bird," and carry him off to her father.

It was when she became of marriageable age that trouble began. She turned down the possibility of marrying a cousin who governed Mongol Persia, for this woman of the steppes had no desire to live as a secluded urban wife. In fact, she declared that she would only marry someone who could defeat her in wrestling. Many suitors tried, wagering 10, 100, or in one case 1,000 horses that they could defeat her. All of them failed, and, in the process, Khutulun accumulated a very substantial herd of horses.

Khutulun's extraordinary public life and her unwillingness to marry provided an opening for her enemies. Rumors circulated that she refused to marry because she was engaged in an incestuous relationship with her father. To put an end to such stories, Khutulun finally agreed to wed one of her father's followers without any wrestling

contest. Still, the decision was hers. As the Mongol chronicles put it, "She chose him herself for her husband."

Even after her marriage, Khutulun continued to campaign with Qaidu Khan, and together they protected the steppe lands of Central Asia from incorporation into Mongol-ruled China. In 1301, her father was wounded in battle and, shortly thereafter, died. Some accounts suggest that he tried to name Khutulun as khan in his place, but the resistance of her brothers nixed that plan. "You should mind your scissors and needles," declared her rivals. "What have you to do with kingship?" Khutulun herself supported one of her brothers as khan, while she remained at the head of the army. She died in 1306, though whether in battle or as the result of an assassination remains unclear.

In her public and military life and in her fierce independence about marriage, Khutulun reflected the relative freedom and influence of Mongol women, particularly of the elite class. In her preference for the open life of the steppes and in her resistance to the intrusion of Mongol-ruled China, she aligned with those who saw themselves as "true Mongols," in opposition to those who had come under the softening influence of neighboring Chinese or Persian civilizations. To this day, when Mongolian men wrestle, they wear a vest with an open chest in honor of Khutulun, ensuring that they are wrestling with other men rather than with a woman who might throw them to the ground.

Question: What does the life of Khutulun reveal about Mongol gender relationships?

photo: National Palace Museum, Taipei, Taiwan/Bridgeman Images

Mongol Rulers and Their Women
The wives of Mongol rulers exercised considerable influence at court. This fourteenth-century painting shows Chinggis Khan's fourth son, Tului, the ruler of the Mongol heartland after his father's death, with his Christian wife Sorgaqtani. After her husband's early death from alcoholism, she maneuvered her children, including Khubilai Khan, into powerful positions and strongly encouraged them in the direction of religious toleration. (By Rashid al-Din, *Djamil el Tawarak*, 15th century Persian illumination/ Bibliothèque Nationale de France, Paris, France/akg-images)

Russia and the Mongols

When the Mongol military machine rolled over Russia between 1237 and 1240, it encountered a relatively new third-wave civilization, located on the far eastern fringe of Christendom (see Chapter 10). Whatever political unity this new civilization of Kievan Rus had earlier enjoyed was now gone, and various independent princes proved unable to unite even in the face of the Mongol onslaught. Although they had interacted extensively with pastoral people of the steppes north of the Black Sea, Mongol ferocity was stunning. City after city fell to Mongol forces, which were now armed with the catapults and battering rams adopted from Chinese or Muslim sources. The slaughter that sometimes followed was described in horrific terms by Russian chroniclers, although twentieth-century historians often regard such accounts as exaggerated. (See Working with Evidence, Source 11.4, page 494, for one such account.) From the survivors and the cities that surrendered early, laborers and skilled craftsmen were deported to other Mongol lands or sold into slavery. A number of Russian crafts were so depleted of their workers that they did not recover for a century or more.

■ Comparison

What was distinctive about the Russian experience of Mongol rule?

If the violence of initial conquest bore similarities to the experiences of Persia, Russia's incorporation into the Mongol Empire was very different. To the Mongols, it was the Kipchak (KIP-chahk) Khanate, named after the Kipchak Turkic-speaking peoples north of the Caspian and Black seas, among whom the Mongols had settled. To the Russians, it was the "Khanate of the Golden Horde." By whatever name, the Mongols had conquered Russia, but they did not occupy it as they had China and Persia. Because there were no garrisoned cities, permanently stationed administrators, or Mongol settlers, the Russian experience of Mongol rule was quite different from that of conquered peoples elsewhere. From the Mongol point of view, Russia had little to offer. Its economy was not nearly so sophisticated or productive as that of more established civilizations; nor was it located on major international trade routes. It was simply not worth the expense of occupying. Furthermore, the availability of extensive steppe lands for pasturing their flocks north of the Black and Caspian seas meant that the Mongols could maintain their preferred pastoral way of life, while remaining in easy reach of Russian cities when the need arose to send further military expeditions. They could dominate and exploit Russia from the steppes.

And exploit they certainly did. Russian princes received appointment from the khan and were required to send substantial tribute to the Mongol capital at Sarai, located on the lower Volga River. A variety of additional taxes created a heavy burden, especially on the peasantry, while continuing border raids sent tens of thousands of Russians into slavery. The Mongol impact was highly uneven, however. Some Russian princes benefited considerably because they were able to manipulate their role as tribute collectors to grow wealthy. The Russian Orthodox Church likewise flourished under the Mongol policy of religious toleration, for it received exemption from many taxes. Nobles who participated in Mongol raids earned a share of the loot. Some cities, such as Kiev, resisted the Mongols and were devastated, while others collaborated and were left undamaged. Moscow in particular emerged as the primary collector of tribute for the Mongols, and its princes parlayed this position into a leading role as the nucleus of a renewed Russian state when Mongol domination receded in the fifteenth century.

Mongol Russia
This sixteenth-century painting depicts the Mongol burning of the Russian city of Ryazan in 1237. Similar destruction awaited many Russian towns that resisted the invaders. (Sovfoto/Universal Images Group/akg-images)

The absence of direct Mongol rule had implications for the Mongols themselves, for they were far less influenced by or assimilated within Russian cultures than their counterparts in China and Persia had been. The Mongols in China had turned themselves into a Chinese dynasty, with the khan as a Chinese emperor. Some learned calligraphy, and a few came to appreciate Chinese poetry. In Persia, the Mongols had converted to Islam, with some becoming farmers. Not so in Russia. There "the Mongols of the Golden Horde were still spending their days in the saddle and their nights in tents."[22] They could dominate Russia from the adjacent steppes without in any way adopting Russian culture. Even though they remained culturally separate from Christian Russians, eventually the Mongols assimilated to the culture and the Islamic faith of the Kipchak people of the steppes, and in the process they lost their distinct identity and became Kipchaks.

Despite this domination from a distance, "the impact of the Mongols on Russia was, if anything, greater than on China and Iran [Persia]," according to a leading scholar.[23] Russian princes, who were more or less left alone if they paid the required tribute and taxes, found it useful to adopt the Mongols' weapons, diplomatic rituals, court practices, taxation system, and military draft. Mongol policies facilitated, although not intentionally, the rise of Moscow as the core of a new Russian state, and that state made good use of the famous Mongol mounted courier service, which Marco Polo had praised so highly. Mongol policies also strengthened the hold of the Russian Orthodox Church and enabled it to penetrate the rural areas more fully than before. Some Russians, seeking to explain their country's economic backwardness and political autocracy in modern times, have held the Mongols responsible for both conditions, though most historians consider such views vastly exaggerated.

Divisions among the Mongols, the disruptive influence of plague, and the growing strength of the Russian state, centered now on the city of Moscow, enabled the Russians to break the Mongols' hold by the end of the fifteenth century. With the earlier demise of Mongol rule in China and Persia, and now in Russia, the Mongols had retreated from their brief but spectacular incursion into the civilizations of outer Eurasia. Nonetheless, they continued to periodically threaten these civilizations for several centuries, until their homelands were absorbed into the expanding Russian and Chinese empires. But the Mongol moment in world history was over.

The Mongol Empire as a Eurasian Network

During the third-wave millennium, Chinese culture and Buddhism provided a measure of integration among the peoples of East Asia; Christianity did the same for Europe, while the realm of Islam connected most of the lands in between. But it was the Mongol Empire, during the thirteenth and fourteenth centuries, that brought all of these regions into a single interacting network. It was a unique moment in world history and an important step toward the global integration of the modern era.

Toward a World Economy

The Mongols themselves did not produce much of value for distant markets, nor were they active traders. Nonetheless, they consistently promoted international commerce, largely so that they could tax it and thus extract wealth from more developed civilizations. The Great Khan Ogodei, for example, often paid well over the asking price to attract merchants to his capital of Karakorum. The Mongols also provided financial backing for caravans, introduced standardized weights and measures, and gave tax breaks to merchants.

In providing a relatively secure environment for merchants making the long and arduous journey across Central Asia between Europe and China, the Mongol Empire brought the two ends of the Eurasian world into closer contact than ever before and launched a new phase in the history of the Silk Roads. Marco Polo was only the most famous of many European merchants, mostly from Italian cities, who made their way to China through the Mongol Empire. So many traders attempted the journey that guidebooks circulated with much useful advice about the trip. Merchants returned with tales of rich lands and prosperous commercial opportunities, but what they described were long-established trading networks of which Europeans had been largely ignorant.

The Mongol trading circuit was a central element in an even larger commercial network that linked much of the Afro-Eurasian world in the thirteenth century (see Map 11.2). Mongol-ruled China was the fulcrum of this vast system, connecting the overland route through the Mongol Empire with the oceanic routes through the South China Sea and Indian Ocean.

■ **Connection**

What kinds of cross-cultural interactions did the Mongol Empire generate?

Diplomacy on a Eurasian Scale

Not only did the Mongol Empire facilitate long-distance commerce, but it also prompted diplomatic relationships from one end of Eurasia to the other. As their invasion of Russia spilled over into Eastern Europe, Mongol armies destroyed Polish, German, and Hungarian forces in 1241–1242 and seemed poised to march on Central and Western Europe. But the death of the Great Khan Ogodei required Mongol leaders to return to Mongolia, and Western Europe lacked adequate pasture for Mongol herds. Thus Western Europe was spared the trauma of conquest, but fearing the possible return of the Mongols, both the pope and European rulers dispatched delegations to the Mongol capital, mostly led by Franciscan friars. They hoped to learn something about Mongol intentions, to secure Mongol aid in the Christian crusade against Islam, and, if possible, to convert Mongols to Christianity.

These efforts were largely in vain, for no alliance or widespread conversion occurred. In fact, one of these missions came back with a letter for the pope from the Great Khan Guyuk, demanding that Europeans submit to him. "But if you should not believe our letters and the command of God nor hearken to our counsel," he warned, "then we shall know for certain that you wish to have war. After that we do not know what will happen."[24] Perhaps the most important outcome of these diplomatic probings was the useful information about lands to the east that European missions brought back. Those reports contributed to a dawning European awareness of a wider world, and they have certainly provided later historians with much useful information about the Mongols. Somewhat later, in 1287, the il-khanate of Persia sought an alliance with European powers to take Jerusalem and crush the forces of Islam, but the Persian Mongols' conversion to Islam soon put an end to any such anti-Muslim coalition.

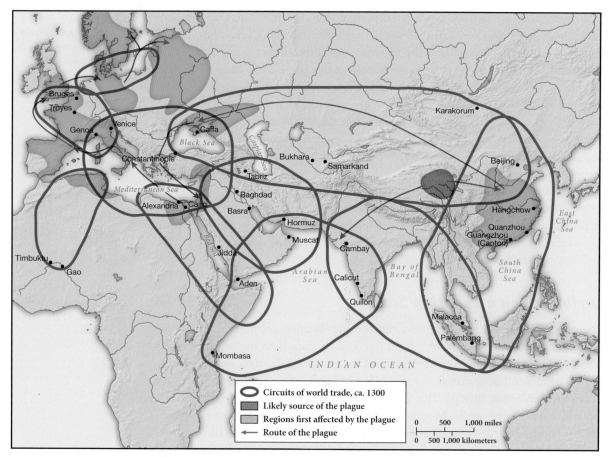

Map 11.2   Trade and Disease in the Fourteenth Century

The Mongol Empire played a major role in the commercial integration of the Eurasian world as well as in the spread of the plague across this vast area.

Within the Mongol Empire itself, close relationships developed between the courts of Persia and China. They regularly exchanged ambassadors, shared intelligence information, fostered trade between their regions, and sent skilled workers back and forth. Thus political authorities all across Eurasia engaged in diplomatic relationships with one another to an unprecedented degree.

Cultural Exchange in the Mongol Realm

Accompanying these transcontinental economic and political relationships was a substantial exchange of peoples and cultures. Mongol policy forcibly transferred many thousands of skilled craftsmen and educated people from their homelands to distant parts of the empire, while the Mongols' religious tolerance and support of merchants drew missionaries and traders from afar. The Mongol capital at Karakorum was a cosmopolitan city with places of worship for Buddhists, Daoists, Muslims, and Christians. Chinggis Khan and several other Mongol rulers married Christian women. Actors and musicians from China, wrestlers from Persia, and a jester from Byzantium provided entertainment for the Mongol court. Persian and Arab doctors and administrators were sent to China, while Chinese physicians and engineers found their skills in demand in the Islamic world.

This movement of people facilitated the exchange of ideas and techniques, a process actively encouraged by Mongol authorities. A great deal of Chinese technology and artistic conventions—such as painting, printing, gunpowder weapons, compass navigation, high-temperature furnaces, and medical techniques—flowed westward. Acupuncture, for example, was poorly received in the Middle East because it required too much bodily contact for Muslim taste, but Chinese techniques for diagnosing illness by taking the pulse of patients proved quite popular, as they involved minimal body contact. Muslim astronomers brought their skills and knowledge to China because Mongol authorities wanted "second opinions on the reading of heavenly signs and portents" and assistance in constructing the accurate calendars needed for ritual purposes.[25] Plants and crops likewise circulated within the Mongol domain. Lemons and carrots from the Middle East found a welcome reception in China, while the Persian il-khan Ghazan sent envoys to India, China, and elsewhere to seek "seeds of things which are unique in that land."[26]

Europeans arguably gained more than most from these exchanges, for they had long been cut off from the fruitful interchange with Asia, and in comparison to the Islamic and Chinese worlds, they were less technologically developed. Now they could reap the benefits of new technology, new crops, and new knowledge of a wider world. And almost alone among the peoples of Eurasia, they could do so without having suffered the devastating consequences of Mongol conquest. In these circumstances, some historians have argued, lay the roots of Europe's remarkable rise to global prominence in the centuries that followed.

The Plague: An Afro-Eurasian Pandemic

Any benefits derived from participation in Mongol networks of communication and exchange must be measured alongside the hemispheric catastrophe known as the "plague" or the "pestilence" and later called the Black Death. Originating most likely in China, the bacteria responsible for the disease, known as *Yersinia pestis*, spread across the trade routes of the vast Mongol Empire in the early fourteenth century (see Map 11.2, page 482). Carried by rodents and transmitted by fleas to humans, the plague erupted initially in 1331 in northeastern China and had reached the Middle East and Western Europe by 1347. One lurid but quite uncertain story has the Mongols using catapults to hurl corpses infected with the plague into the Genoese city of Caffa in the Crimea. In 1409, the plague reached East Africa, probably by way of the famous Chinese maritime expeditions that encompassed the Indian Ocean basin.

■ **Change**

Disease changes societies. How might this argument apply to the plague?

The disease itself was associated with swelling of the lymph nodes, most often in the groin; terrible headaches; high fever; and internal bleeding just below the skin. Infected people generally died within a few days. In the densely populated civilizations of China, the Islamic world, and Europe as well as in the steppe lands of the pastoralists, the plague claimed enormous numbers of human victims, causing a sharp contraction in Eurasian population for a century or more. Chroniclers reported rates of death that ranged from 50 to 90 percent of the affected population, depending on the time and place. A recent study suggests that about half of Europe's people perished during the initial outbreak of 1348–1350.[27] A fifteenth-century Egyptian historian wrote that within a month of the plague's arrival in 1349, "Cairo had become an abandoned desert. . . . Everywhere one heard lamentations and one could not pass by any house without being overwhelmed by the howling."[28] The Middle East generally had lost perhaps one-third of its population by the early fifteenth century.[29] The intense first wave of the plague was followed by periodic visitations over the next several centuries. However, other regions of the Eastern Hemisphere, especially India and sub-Saharan Africa, were much less affected, so the plague's impact varied significantly.

In those places where it struck hardest, the plague left thoughtful people grasping for language with which to describe a horror of such unprecedented dimensions. One Italian man, who had buried all five of his children with his own hands, wrote in 1348 that "so many have died that everyone believes it is the end of the world."[30] Another Italian, the Renaissance scholar Francesco Petrarch, was equally stunned by the impact of the Black Death; he wrote to a friend in 1349:

> When at any time has such a thing been seen or spoken of? Has what happened in these years ever been read about: empty houses, derelict cities, ruined estates, fields strewn with cadavers, a horrible and vast solitude encompassing the whole world? Consult historians, they are silent; ask physicians, they are stupefied; seek the answers from philosophers, they shrug their shoulders, furrow their brows, and with fingers pressed against their lips, bid you be silent. Will posterity believe these things, when we who have seen it can scarcely believe it?[31]

In the Islamic world, the famous historian Ibn Khaldun, who had lost both of his parents to the plague, also wrote about it in apocalyptic terms:

> Civilization in both the East and the West was visited by a destructive plague which devastated nations and caused populations to vanish. It swallowed up many of the good things of civilization and wiped them out. . . . It was as if the voice of existence had called out for oblivion and restriction, and the world responded to its call.[32]

Beyond its immediate devastation, the Black Death worked longer-term social changes in Europe, the region where the plague's impact has been most thoroughly studied. Labor shortages following the initial outburst provoked sharp conflict between scarce workers, who sought higher wages or better conditions, and the rich, who resisted those demands. A series of peasant revolts in the fourteenth century reflected this tension, which also undermined the practice of serfdom. That labor shortage also may have fostered a greater interest in technological innovation and created, at least for a time, more employment opportunities for women. Thus a resilient European civilization survived a cataclysm that had the power to destroy it. In a strange way, that catastrophe may have actually fostered its future growth.

Whatever its impact in particular places, the plague also had larger consequences. Ironically, that human disaster, born of the Mongol network, was a primary reason for the demise of that network in the fourteenth and fifteenth centuries. Population contracted, cities declined, and the volume of trade diminished all across the Mongol world. By 1350, the Mongol Empire itself was in disarray, and within a century the Mongols had lost control of Chinese, Persian, and Russian civilizations. The Central Asian trade route, so critical to the entire Afro-Eurasian world economy, largely closed.

This disruption of the Mongol-based land routes to the east, coupled with a desire to avoid Muslim intermediaries, provided incentives for Europeans to take to the sea in their continuing efforts to reach the riches of Asia. Their naval technology gave them military advantages on the seas, much as the Mongols' skill with the bow and their mobility on horseback gave these pastoralists a decisive edge in land battles. As Europeans penetrated Asian and Atlantic waters in the sixteenth century, they took on, in some ways, the role of the Mongols in organizing and fostering world trade and in creating a network of communication and exchange over an even larger area. Like the Mongols, Europeans were people on the periphery of the major established civilizations; they too were economically less developed in comparison to Chinese and Islamic civilizations. Both Mongols and Europeans were apt to forcibly plunder the wealthier civilizations they encountered, and European empire building in the Americas, like that of the Mongols in Eurasia, brought devastating disease and catastrophic population decline in its wake.[33] Europeans, of course, brought far more of their own culture and many more of their own people to the societies they conquered, as Christianity, European languages, settler societies, and Western science and technology took root within their empires. Although their imperial presence lasted far longer and operated on a much larger scale, European actions at the beginning of their global expansion bore some resemblance to those of their Mongol predecessors. They were, as one historian put it, "the Mongols of the seas."[34]

The Plague
This illustration depicts a European doctor visiting a patient with the plague. Notice that the doctor and others around the bedside cover their noses to prevent infection. During the Black Death, doctors were often criticized for refusing to treat dying patients, as they feared for their own lives.

REFLECTIONS

Changing Images of Pastoral Peoples

Historians frequently change their minds, and long-term consensus on most important matters has been difficult to achieve. For example, until recently, pastoralists generally received bad press in history books. Normally they entered the story only when they were threatening or destroying established civilizations. In presenting a largely negative image of pastoral peoples, historians were reflecting the long-held attitudes of literate elites in the civilizations of Eurasia. Fearing and usually despising such peoples, educated observers in China, the Middle East, and Europe often described them as bloodthirsty savages or barbarians, bringing only chaos and destruction in their wake. Han Kuan, a Chinese scholar of the first century B.C.E., described the Xiongnu people as "abandoned by Heaven . . . in foodless desert wastes, without proper houses, clothed in animal hides, eating their meat uncooked and drinking blood."[35] To the Christian Saint Jerome (340–420 C.E.), the Huns "filled the whole earth with slaughter and panic alike as they flitted hither and thither on their swift horses."[36] Almost a thousand years later, the famous Arab historian Ibn Khaldun described pastoralists in a very similar fashion: "It is their nature to plunder whatever other people possess."[37]

Because pastoral peoples generally did not have written languages, the sources available to historians came from less-than-unbiased observers in adjacent agricultural civilizations. Furthermore, in the long-running conflict across the farming/pastoral frontier, agricultural civilizations ultimately triumphed. Over the centuries, some pastoralist or semi-agricultural peoples, such as the Germanic tribes of Europe and the Arabs, created new civilizations. Others, such as the Turkic and Mongol peoples, took over existing civilizations or were encompassed within established agrarian empires. By the early twentieth century, and in most places much earlier, pastoral peoples everywhere had lost their former independence and had often shed their pastoral life as well. Since "winners" usually write history, the negative views of pastoralists held by agrarian civilizations normally prevailed.

Reflecting more inclusive contemporary values, historians in recent decades have sought to present a more balanced picture of pastoralists' role in world history, emphasizing what they created as well as what they destroyed. These historians have highlighted the achievements of herding peoples, such as their adaptation to inhospitable environments; their technological innovations; their development of horse-, camel-, or cattle-based cultures; their role in fostering cross-cultural exchange; and their state-building efforts.

A less critical or judgmental posture toward the Mongols may also owe something to the "total wars" and genocides of the twentieth century, in which the mass slaughter of civilians became a strategy to induce enemy surrender. During the cold war, the United States and the Soviet Union were prepared, apparently, to obliterate each other's entire population with nuclear weapons in response to an attack. In light of this recent history, Mongol massacres may appear a little less unique. Historians living in the glass houses of contemporary societies are perhaps more reluctant to cast stones at the Mongols. In understanding the Mongols, as in so much else, historians are shaped by the times and circumstances of their own lives as much as by "what really happened" in the past.

Second Thoughts

What's the Significance?

pastoralism, 458–65
Modun, 463
Xiongnu, 463
Turks, 463–65
Almoravid Empire, 465

Temujin/Chinggis Khan, 467–69
the Mongol world war, 469–72
Yuan dynasty China, 473–75
Khubilai Khan, 474–75

Hulegu, 475
Khutulun, 477
Kipchak Khanate/Golden Horde, 478–80
Black Death/plague, 483–85

Big Picture Questions

1. What accounts for the often-negative attitudes of settled societies toward the pastoral peoples living on their borders?
2. Why have historians often neglected pastoral peoples' role in world history? How would you assess the perspective of this chapter toward the Mongols? Does the chapter strike you as negative and critical of the Mongols, as bending over backward to portray them in a positive light, or as a balanced presentation?
3. In what different ways did Mongol rule affect the Islamic world, Russia, China, and Europe? In what respects did it foster Eurasian integration?
4. Why did the Mongol Empire last only a relatively short time?
5. **Looking Back:** In what ways did the Mongol Empire resemble previous empires (Arab, Roman, Chinese, or the Greek empire of Alexander, for example), and in what ways did it differ from them?

Next Steps: For Further Study

John Aberth, *The First Horseman: Disease in Human History* (2007). A global study of the history of disease, with a fine chapter on the Black Death.

Thomas Allsen, *Culture and Conquest in Mongol Eurasia* (2001). A history of cultural exchange within the Mongol realm, particularly between China and the Islamic world.

Thomas J. Barfield, *The Nomadic Alternative* (1993). An anthropological and historical survey of pastoral peoples on a global basis.

Carter Finley, *The Turks in World History* (2005). The evolution of Turkic-speaking people, from their nomadic origins to the twentieth century.

Jack Weatherford, *Genghis Khan and the Making of the Modern World* (2004). A lively, well-written, and balanced account of the world the Mongols made and the legacy they left for the future.

"Horseback Riding and Bronze Age Pastoralism in the Eurasian Steppes," http://www.youtube.com /watch?v=QapUGZ0ObjA. An illustrated lecture on the origins of pastoralism by David W. Anthony, a prominent scholar.

"The Mongols in World History," http://afe.easia.columbia.edu/mongols. A wonderful resource on the Mongols generally, with a particular focus on their impact in China.

WORKING WITH EVIDENCE

Perspectives on the Mongols

How did the Mongols understand themselves and the enormous empire they had created? How did the peoples who were forcibly incorporated within that empire or threatened by it view the Mongols? What did outsiders who encountered the Mongols notice about their ways of living? In studying the Mongol phenomenon, historians use documents that reflect both the Mongols' perception of themselves and the perspectives of others. The first two documents derive from Mongol sources, while the final three represent views from Persian, Russian, and European observers.

Sorting through these various perceptions of the Mongols raises questions about the kinds of understandings — or misunderstandings — that arise as culturally different peoples meet, especially under conditions of conquest. These documents also require reflection on the relative usefulness of sources that come from the Mongols themselves as well as those that derive from the victims of Mongol aggression.

Source 11.1
Mongol History from a Mongol Source

The major literary work to emerge from the Mongols themselves, widely known as *The Secret History of the Mongols*, was written a decade or two after the death in 1227 of Chinggis Khan. The unknown author of this work was clearly a contemporary of the Great Khan and likely a member of the royal household. The first selection discusses the Mongol practice of *anda*, a very close relationship between two unrelated men. The anda relationship of Temujin, the future Chinggis Khan, and his friend Jamugha was important in Temujin's rise to power, although they later broke with one another. The second selection from the *Secret History* describes the process by which Temujin was elevated to the rank of Chinggis Khan, the ruler of a united Mongol nation, while the third recounts the reflections of Ogodei, Chinggis Khan's son and successor, probably toward the end of his reign, which lasted from 1229 to 1241.

■ How would you describe the anda relationship?

■ What does the *Secret History* suggest about the nature of political authority and political relationships among the Mongols?

■ What did Ogodei regard as his greatest achievements and his most notable mistakes?

■ What evidence do these selections from the *Secret History* provide that the author was an insider?

The Secret History of the Mongols
ca. 1240

Anda: Temujin and Jamugha

Temujin and Jamugha pitched their tents in the Khorkonagh Valley. With their people united in one great camp, the two leaders decided they should renew their friendship, their pledge of anda. They remembered when they'd first made that pledge, and said, "We should love one another again."

That first time they'd met Temujin was eleven years old. . . . So Temujin and Jamugha said to each other: "We've heard the elders say, 'When two men become anda their lives become one, one will never desert the other and will always defend him.' This is the way we'll act from now on. We'll renew our old pledge and love each other forever."

Temujin took the golden belt he'd received in the spoils from Toghtoga's defeat and placed it around Anda Jamugha's waist. Then he led out the Merkid chief's warhorse, a light yellow mare with black mane and tail, and gave it to Anda Jamugha to ride. Jamugha took the golden belt he'd received in the spoils from Dayir Usun's defeat and placed it around the waist of Anda Temujin. Then he led out the whitish-tan warhorse of Dayir Usun and had Anda Temujin ride on it.

Before the cliffs of Khuldaghar in the Khorkonagh Valley, beneath the Great Branching Tree of the Mongol, they pledged their friendship and promised to love one another. They held a feast on the spot and there was great celebration. Temujin and Jamugha spent that night alone, sharing one blanket to cover them both. Temujin and Jamugha loved each other for one year, and when half of the second year had passed they agreed it was time to move camp. . . .

Temujin Becomes Chinggis Khan

Then they moved the whole camp to the shores of Blue Lake in the Gurelgu Mountains. Altan, Khuchar, and Sacha Beki conferred with each other there, and then said to Temujin: "We want you to be khan. Temujin, if you'll be our khan we'll search through the spoils for the beautiful women and virgins, for the great palace tents, . . . for the finest geldings and mares. We'll gather all these and bring them to you. When we go off to hunt for wild game, we'll go out first to drive them together for you to kill. We'll drive the wild animals of the steppe together so that their bellies are touching. We'll drive the wild game of the mountains together so that they stand leg to leg. If we disobey your command during battle, take away our possessions, our children, and wives. Leave us behind in the dust, cutting off our heads where we stand and letting them fall to the ground. If we disobey your counsel in peacetime, take away our tents and our goods, our wives, and our children. Leave us behind when you move, abandoned in the desert without a protector." Having given their word, having taken this oath, they proclaimed Temujin khan of the Mongol and gave him the name Chingis Khan. . . .

Reflections of Ogodei

Then Ogodei Khan spoke these words: "Since my father the Khan passed away and I came to sit on his great throne, what have I done? I went to war against the people of Cathay [China] and I destroyed them. For my second accomplishment I established a network of post stations so that my words are carried across the land with great speed. Another of my accomplishments has been to have my commanders dig wells in the desert so that there would be pasture and water for the people there. Lastly I placed spies and agents among all the people of the cities. In all directions I've brought peace to the Nation and the people. . . .

"Since the time of my father the Khan, I added these four accomplishments to all that he did. But also since my father passed away and I came to sit on his great throne with the burden of all the numerous people on my shoulders, I allowed myself to be conquered by wine. This was one of my mistakes. Another of my mistakes was to listen to a woman with no principles and because of her take away the daughters who belonged to my Uncle Odchigin. Even though I'm the Khan, the Lord of the Nation, I have no right to go against established principle, so this was my mistake.

"Another mistake was to secretly harm Dok-holkhu. If you ask, 'Why was this wrong?' I would

say that to secretly harm Dokholkhu, a man who had served his proper lord, my father the Khan, performing heroic deeds in his service, was a mistake. Now that I've done this, who'll perform heroic deeds in my service? Then my last mistake was to desire too much, to say to myself, 'I'm afraid that all the wild game born under Heaven will run off toward the land of my brothers.' So I ordered earthen walls to be built to keep the wild game from running away, but even as these walls were being built I heard my brothers speaking badly of me. I admit that I was wrong to do this. Since the time of my father the Khan I've added four accomplishments to all that he'd done and I've done four things which I admit were wrong."

Source: Paul Kahn, *The Secret History of the Mongols: The Origin of Chingis Khan* (San Francisco: North Point Press, 1984), 44–45, 48–49, 192–93.

Source 11.2
Chinggis Khan and Changchun

Source 11.2 begins with a remarkable letter that Chinggis Khan sent to the seventy-two-year-old Chinese Daoist master Changchun in 1219, requesting a personal meeting with the teacher.

- Why did Chinggis Khan seek a meeting with Changchun? Do you think he was satisfied with the outcome of that meeting?

- How does Chinggis Khan define his life's work? What is his image of himself?

- How would you describe the tone of Chinggis Khan's letter to Changchun? What does the letter suggest about Mongol attitudes toward the belief systems of conquered peoples?

- How do Sources 11.1 and 11.2 help explain the success of the Mongols' empire-building efforts?

- What core Mongol values do these documents suggest?

CHINGGIS KHAN
Letter to Changchun
1219

Heaven has abandoned China owing to its haughtiness and extravagant luxury. But I, living in the northern wilderness, have not inordinate passions. I hate luxury and exercise moderation. I have only one coat and one food. I eat the same food and am dressed in the same tatters as my humble herdsmen. I consider the people my children, and take an interest in talented men as if they were my brothers. . . . At military exercises I am always in the front, and in time of battle am never behind. In the space of seven years I have succeeded in accomplishing a great work, and uniting the whole world into one empire. I have not myself distinguished qualities. But the government of the [Chinese] is inconstant, and therefore Heaven assists me to obtain the throne. . . . All together have acknowledged my supremacy. It seems to me that since the remote time . . . such an empire has not been seen. . . . Since the time I came to the throne I have always taken to heart the ruling of my people; but I could not find worthy men to occupy [high offices]. . . . With respect to these circumstances I inquired, and heard that thou, master, hast penetrated the truth. . . . For a long time thou hast lived in the caverns of the rocks, and hast retired from the world; but to thee the people who have acquired sanctity repair, like clouds on the paths of the immortals, in innumerable multitudes. . . . But what shall I do? We are separated by mountains and plains of great extent, and I cannot meet thee. I can only descend from the throne and stand by the side. I have fasted and washed. I have ordered my adjutant . . . to prepare an escort and a cart for thee. Do not be afraid of the thousand *li* [a great distance]. I implore thee to move thy sainted steps. Do not think of the extent of the sandy desert. Commiserate the people in the present situation of affairs, or have pity upon me, and communicate to me the means of preserving life. I shall serve thee myself. I hope that at least thou wilt leave me a trifle of thy wisdom. Say only one word to me and I shall be happy.

[*After a long journey, Changchun arrived at the camp of Chinggis Khan, located in what is now Afghanistan. One of Changchun's disciples recorded what happened in their initial meeting.*]

[T]he master presented himself to the Emperor, who greeted him, and said: "You were invited by the other courts (the Kin and the Sung), but you refused. Now you have come to see me, having traversed a road of ten thousand li. I am much gratified." The master answered: "The wild man of the mountains came to see the emperor by order of your majesty; it was the will of Heaven." Chinghiz invited him to sit down, and ordered a meal to be set before him. After this he asked: "Sainted man, you have come from a great distance. Have you a medicine of immortality?" The master replied: "There are means for preserving life, but no medicines for immortality." Chinghiz lauded him for his sincerity and candour. By imperial order two tents were pitched for the master east of the emperor's tents. The emperor gave him the title of *shen sien* (the immortal).

Source: E. Bretschneider, *Mediaeval Researches from Eastern Asiatic Sources,* vol. 1 (London, 1875), 37–39, 86.

Source 11.3
The Conquest of Bukhara:
A Persian View

While Chinggis Khan was hosting Changchun, he was also personally leading Mongol forces into the lands of the Persian Empire, then ruled by the Turkic Khwarazmian dynasty. The thirteenth-century Persian historian Juvaini, himself a high official in the Mongol government of his homeland, wrote an account of the creation of the Mongol Empire titled *The History of the World Conqueror*. This excerpt from that work describes the conquest of the city of Bukhara, a major commercial and intellectual center of the Persian Islamic world.

■ What can we learn about the policies and strategies of the Mongols from Juvaini's account? What parts of this account seem most reliable?

■ How might you describe Juvaini's posture toward the Mongols? Keep in mind that he was working for them.

■ What aspects of Mongol behavior would be most offensive to Muslims?

■ How did Chinggis Khan justify his conquest of Bukhara?

JUVAINI
The History of the World Conqueror
1219

[C]hinggis Khan's] troops were more numerous than ants or locusts, being in their multitude beyond estimation or computation. Detachment after detachment arrived, each like a billowing sea, and encamped round about the town. At sunrise twenty thousand men from the Sultan's [Muslim ruler of Bukhara] auxiliary army issued forth from the citadel together with most of the inhabitants. . . . When these forces reached the banks of the Oxus, the patrols and advance parties of the Mongol army fell upon them and left no trace of them.

On the following day when from the reflection of the sun that plain seemed to be a tray filled with blood, the people of Bukhara opened their gates and closed the door of strife and battle. The imams and notables came on a deputation to Chingis-Khan, who entered to inspect the town and citadel. He rode into the Juma Mosque. . . . Chingis-Khan asked those present whether this was the palace of the Sultan; they replied it was the house of God. Then he too got down from his horse, and mounting two or three steps of the pulpit he exclaimed: "The countryside is empty of fodder, fill our horses' bellies." Whereupon they opened all the magazines in the town and began carrying off the grain. And they brought the cases in which the Qurans were kept out in the courtyard of the mosque, where they cast the Qurans right and left and turned the cases into mangers for their horses. After which they circulated cups and sent for the singing-girls of the town to sing and dance for them; while the Mongols raised their voices to the tunes of their own songs. Meanwhile, the imams, shaikhs, sayyids, doctors and scholars of the age kept watch over their horses in the stables. . . . After an hour or two Chingis-Khan arose to return to his camp. . . . [T]he leaves of the Quran were trampled beneath the dirt beneath their own feet and their horses' hooves.

When Chingis-Khan left the town he went to the festival muhalla and mounted the pulpit; and, the people having assembled, he asked which were wealthy amongst them. Two hundred and eighty persons were designated (a hundred and ninety of them being natives of the town and the rest strangers, i.e., ninety merchants from various places) and were led before him. He then began a speech, in which, after describing the resistance and treachery of the Sultan, he addressed them as follows: "O People! know that you have committed great sins, and that the great ones among you have committed these sins. If you ask me what proof I have for these words, I say it is because I am the punishment of God. If you had not committed these great sins, God would not have sent a punishment like me upon you." When he had finished speaking in this strain, he continued his discourse with words of admonition, saying, "There is no need to declare your property that is on the face of the earth; tell me of that which is in the belly of the earth." . . . [A]lthough not subjecting them to disgrace or humiliation, they began to exact money from these men; and when they delivered it up they did not torment them by excessive punishment or demanding what was beyond their power to pay.

Chingis-Khan had given orders for the Sultan's troops to be driven out of the interior of the town and the citadel. . . . [H]e now gave orders for all quarters of the town to be set on fire; and since the houses were built entirely out of wood, within several days the greater part of the town had been consumed, with the exception of the Juma mosque and some of the palaces, which were built with baked bricks. Then the people of Bukhara were driven against the citadel. And on either side the furnace of battle was heated. On the outside, mangonels [catapults] were erected, bows bent, and stones and arrows discharged, and, on the inside, . . . pots of naphtha [a flammable liquid] were set in motion. It was like a red hot furnace. . . . For days they fought in this manner; the garrison made sallies against the besiegers. . . . But finally they were reduced to the last extremity; resistance was no longer in their power; and they stood excused before God and man. The moat had been filled with animate and inanimate and raised up with levies and Bukharans; . . . their khans, leaders and notables, who were the chief men of the age and the favorites of the Sultan who in their glory would set their feet on the head of Heaven, now became captives of abasement and were drowned in the sea of annihilation. . . . Of the Qanqli [Turkic defenders of the city] no male was spared who stood higher than the butt of a whip and more than thirty thousand were counted amongst the slain; whilst their small children, the children of their nobles and their womenfolk, slender as the cypress, were sold to slavery.

When the town and the citadel had been purged of rebels and the walls and outworks levelled with the dust, the inhabitants of the town, men and women, ugly and beautiful, were driven out onto the field of the *musalla* [an open space outside of a mosque]. Chingis-Khan spared their lives, but the youths and full-grown men that were fit for such service were pressed into a levy for the attack on Samarqand and Dabusiya.

Source: Juvaini, *The History of the World Conqueror*, translated by John Boyle (Manchester: Manchester University Press, 1958), 103–6.

Source 11.4

A Russian View of the Mongols

In 1238, some nineteen years after their initial assault on Persia, Mongol forces began their conquest of Russia. Source 11.4 offers a Russian commentary on those events, drawn from *The Chronicle of Novgorod*, one of the major sources for the history of early Russia.

■ How did the Russian writer of the *Chronicle* account for what he saw as the disaster of the Mongol invasion?

■ Can you infer from the document any additional reasons for the Mongol success?

■ Beyond the conquest itself, what other aspects of Mongol rule offended the Russians?

■ To what extent was the Mongol conquest of Russia also a clash of cultures?

■ What similarities and differences do you notice between this account of Mongol conquest and that of Juvaini in Source 11.3?

The Chronicle of Novgorod
1238

That same year [1238] foreigners called Tartars [Mongols] came in countless numbers, like locusts, into the land of Ryazan, and on first coming they halted at the river Nukhla, and took it, and halted in camp there. And thence they sent their emissaries to the *Knyazes* [princes] of Ryazan, a sorceress and two men with her, demanding from them one-tenth of everything: of men and *Knyazes* and horses—of everything one-tenth. And the *Knyazes* of Ryazan . . . without letting them into their towns, went out to meet them to Voronazh. And the *Knyazes* said to them: "Only when none of us remain then all will be yours." . . . And the *Knyazes* of Ryazan sent to Yuri of Volodimir asking for help, or himself to come. But Yuri neither went himself nor listened to the request of the *Knyazes* of Ryazan, but he himself wished to make war separately. But it was too late to oppose the wrath of God. . . . Thus also did God before these men take from us our strength and put into us perplexity and thunder and dread and trembling for our sins. And then the pagan foreigners surrounded Ryazan and fenced it in with a stockade. . . . And the Tartars took the town on December 21, and they had advanced against it on the 16th of the same month. They likewise killed the *Knyaz* and *Knyaginya*, and men, women, and children, monks, nuns and priests, some by fire, some by the sword, and violated nuns, priests' wives, good women and girls in the presence of their mothers and sisters. But God saved the Bishop, for he had departed the same moment when the troops invested the town. And who, brethren, would not lament over this, among those of us left alive when they suffered this bitter and violent death? And we, indeed, having seen it, were terrified and wept with sighing day and night over our sins, while we sigh every day and night, taking thought for our possessions and for the hatred of brothers.

. . . The pagan and godless Tartars, then, having taken Ryazan, went to Volodimir. . . . And when the lawless ones had already come near and set up battering rams, and took the town and fired it on Friday . . . , the *Knyaz* and *Knyaginya* and *Vladyka*, seeing that the town was on fire and that the people were already perishing, some by fire and others by the sword, took refuge in the Church of the Holy Mother of God and shut themselves in the Sacristy. The pagans breaking down the doors, piled up wood and set fire to the sacred church; and slew all, thus they perished, giving up their souls to God. . . . And Rostov and Suzdal went each its own way. And the accursed ones having come thence took Moscow, Pereyaslavi, Yurev, Dmitrov, *Volok*, and Tver; there also they killed the son of Yaroslav. And thence the lawless ones came and invested Torzhok on the festival of the first Sunday in Lent. They fenced it all round with a fence as they had taken other towns, and here the accursed ones fought with battering rams for two weeks. And the people in the town were exhausted and from Novgorod there was no help for them; but already every man began to be in perplexity and terror. And so the pagans took the town, and slew all from the male sex even to the female, all the priests and the monks, and all stripped and reviled gave up their souls to the Lord in a bitter and a wretched death, on March 5 . . . Wednesday in Easter week.

Source: Robert Mitchell and Nevill Forbes, trans., *The Chronicle of Novgorod, 1016–1471* (New York: AMS Press, 1970; repr. from the edition of 1914, London), 81–83, 88.

Source 11.5
Mongol Women through European Eyes

Source 11.5 provides some insight into the roles of Mongol women and men through the eyes of a European observer, William of Rubruck (1220–1293). A Flemish Franciscan friar, William was one of several emissaries sent to the Mongol court by the pope and the king of France. The Mongols' invasion of Russia and their incursions into Central Europe looked ominous to many European leaders. They hoped that these diplomatic missions might lead to the conversion of the Mongols to Christianity, or perhaps to an alliance with the Mongols against Islam, or at least to some useful intelligence about Mongol intentions. While no agreements with the Mongols came from these missions, William of Rubruck left a detailed account of Mongol life in the mid-thirteenth century, which included observations about the domestic roles of men and women.

■ How does William of Rubruck portray the lives of Mongol women? What was the class background of the Mongol women he describes?

■ What do you think he would have found most upsetting about the position of women in Mongol society?

■ Based on this account, how might you compare the life of Mongol women to that of women in more established civilizations, such as China, Europe, or the Islamic world?

WILLIAM OF RUBRUCK
Journey to the Land of the Mongols
ca. 1255

The matrons (married women) make for themselves most beautiful (luggage) carts. . . . A single rich Mo'al or Tartar (Mongol) has quite one hundred or two hundred such carts with coffers. Baatu [grandson of Chinggis Khan] has twenty-six wives, each of whom has a large dwelling, exclusive of the other little ones which they set up after the big one, and which are like closets, in which the sewing girls live, and to each of these (large) dwellings are attached quite two hundred carts. And when they set up their houses, the first wife places her dwelling on the extreme west side, and after her the others according to their rank, so that the last wife will be in the extreme east; and there will be the distance of a stone's throw between the yurt of one wife and that of another. The *ordu* [residence] of a rich Mo'al seems like a large town, though there will be very few men in it.

When they have fixed their dwelling, the door turned to the south, they set up the couch of the master on the north side. The side for the women is always the east side . . . on the left of the house of the master, he sitting on his couch his face turned to the south. The side for the men is the west side . . . on the right. Men coming into the house would never hang up their bows on the side of the woman.

It is the duty of the women to drive the carts, get the dwellings on and off them, milk the cows, make butter and *gruit* [sour curd], and to dress and sew skins, which they do with a thread made of tendons. They divide the tendons into fine shreds, and then twist them into one long thread. They also sew the boots, the socks, and the clothing. They never wash clothes, for they say that God would be angered, and that it would thunder if they hung them up to dry. They will even beat those they find washing [their clothes]. Thunder they fear extraordinarily; and when it thunders they will turn out of their dwellings all strang-

ers, wrap themselves in black felt, and thus hide themselves till it has passed away. Furthermore, they never wash their bowls, but when the meat is cooked they rinse out the dish in which they are about to put it with some of the boiling broth from the kettle, which they pour back into it. They [the women] also make the felt and cover the houses.

The men make bows and arrows, manufacture stirrups and bits, make saddles, do the carpentering on their dwellings and the carts; they take care of the horses, milk the mares, churn the *cosmos* or mare's milk, make the skins in which it is put; they also look after the camels and load them. Both sexes look after the sheep and goats, sometimes the men, other times the women, milking them.

They dress skins with a thick mixture of sour ewe's milk and salt. When they want to wash their hands or head, they fill their mouths with water, which they let trickle onto their hands, and in this way they also wet their hair and wash their heads.

As to their marriages, you must know that no one among them has a wife unless he buys her; so it sometimes happens that girls are well past marriageable age before they marry, for their parents always keep them until they sell them. . . . Among them no widow marries, for the following reason: they believe that all who serve them in this life shall serve them in the next, so as regards a widow they believe that she will always return to her first husband after death. Hence this shameful custom prevails among them, that sometimes a son takes to wife all his father's wives, except his own mother; for the *ordu* of the father and mother always belongs to the youngest son, so it is he who must provide for all his father's wives . . . and if he wishes it, he uses them as wives, for he esteems not himself injured if they return to his father after death. When then anyone has made a bargain with another to take his daughter, the father of the girl gives a feast, and the girl flees to her relatives and hides there. Then the father says: "Here, my daughter is yours: take her wheresoever you find her." Then he searches for her with his friends till he finds her, and he must take her by force and carry her off with a semblance of violence to his house.

Source: *The Journey of William of Rubruck . . .*, translated from the Latin and edited, with an introductory notice, by William Woodville Rockhill (London: Hakluyt Society, 1900), chaps. 2, 7.

DOING HISTORY

Perspectives on the Mongols

1. **Assessing sources:** What are the strengths and limitations of these documents for understanding the Mongols? Taking the positions of their authors into account, what exaggerations, biases, or misunderstandings can you identify in these sources? What information seems credible, and what should be viewed more skeptically?

2. **Characterizing the Mongols:** Based on these documents and on the text of Chapter 11, write an essay assessing the Mongol moment in world history. How might you counteract the view of many that the Mongols were simply destructive barbarians? How do your own values affect your understanding of the Mongol moment?

3. **Considering values and practice:** How would you describe the core values of Mongol culture? (Consider the leaders' goals, their attitudes toward conquered peoples, the duties of rulers, the views of political authority, and the role of women.) To what extent were these values put into practice in acquiring and ruling the Mongols' huge empire? And in what ways were these values undermined or eroded as that empire took shape?

French painting, 19th century/Monastery of La Rabida, Huelva, Andalusia, Spain/Bridgeman Images

The Worlds of the Fifteenth Century

"Columbus was a perpetrator of genocide . . . , a slave trader, a thief, a pirate, and most certainly not a hero. To celebrate Columbus is to congratulate the process and history of the invasion."[1] This was the view of Winona LaDuke, president of the Indigenous Women's Network, on the occasion in 1992 of the 500th anniversary of Columbus's arrival in the Americas. Much of the commentary surrounding the event echoed the same themes, citing the history of death, slavery, racism, and exploitation that followed in the wake of Columbus's first voyage to what was for him an altogether New World. A century earlier, in 1892, the tone of celebration had been very different. A presidential proclamation cited Columbus as a brave "pioneer of progress and enlightenment" and instructed Americans to "express honor to the discoverer and their appreciation of the great achievements of four completed centuries of American life." The century that followed witnessed the erosion of Western dominance in the world and the discrediting of racism and imperialism and, with it, the reputation of Columbus.

This sharp reversal of opinion about Columbus provides a reminder that the past is as unpredictable as the future. Few Americans in 1892 could have guessed that their daring hero could emerge so tarnished only a century later. And few people living in 1492 could have imagined the enormous global processes set in motion by the voyage of Columbus's three small ships — the Atlantic slave trade, the decimation of the native peoples of the Americas, the massive growth of world population, the Industrial Revolution, and the growing prominence of Europeans on the world stage. None of these developments were even remotely foreseeable in 1492.

The Meeting of Two Worlds This nineteenth-century painting shows Columbus on his first voyage to the New World. He is reassuring his anxious sailors by pointing to the first sight of land. In light of its long-range consequences, this voyage represents a major turning point in world history.

Thus, in historical hindsight, that voyage of Columbus was arguably the single most important event of the fifteenth century. But it was not the only significant marker of that century. A Central Asian Turkic warrior named Timur launched the last major pastoral invasion of adjacent civilizations. Russia emerged from two centuries of Mongol rule to begin a huge empire-building project across northern Asia. A new European civilization was taking shape in the Renaissance. In 1405, an enormous Chinese fleet, dwarfing that of Columbus, set out across the entire Indian Ocean basin, only to voluntarily withdraw twenty-eight years later. The Islamic Ottoman Empire put a final end to Christian Byzantium with the conquest of Constantinople in 1453, even as Spanish Christians completed the "reconquest" of the Iberian Peninsula from the Muslims in 1492. And in the Americas, the Aztec and Inca empires gave a final and spectacular expression to Mesoamerican and Andean civilizations before they were both swallowed up in the burst of European imperialism that followed the arrival of Columbus.

Because the fifteenth century was a hinge of major historical change on many fronts, it provides an occasion for a bird's-eye view of the world through a kind of global tour. This excursion around the world will serve to briefly review the human saga thus far and to establish a baseline from which the enormous transformations of the centuries that followed might be measured. How, then, might we describe the world, and the worlds, of the fifteenth century?

SEEKING THE MAIN POINT

What predictions about the future might a global traveler in the fifteenth century have reasonably made?

The Shapes of Human Communities

One way to describe the world of the fifteenth century is to identify the various types of societies that it contained. Bands of hunters and gatherers, villages of agricultural peoples, newly emerging chiefdoms or small states, pastoral communities, established civilizations and empires—all of these social or political forms would have been apparent to a widely traveled visitor in the fifteenth century. Representing alternative ways of organizing human life, all of them were long established by the fifteenth century, but the balance among these distinctive kinds of societies in 1500 was quite different than it had been a thousand years earlier.

Paleolithic Persistence: Australia and North America

Despite millennia of agricultural advance, substantial areas of the world still hosted gathering and hunting societies, known to historians as Paleolithic (Old Stone Age) peoples. All of Australia, much of Siberia, the arctic coastlands, and parts of Africa and the Americas fell into this category. These peoples were not simply relics of a bygone age. They too had changed over time, though more slowly than their agricultural counterparts, and they too interacted with their neighbors. In short, they had a history, although most history books largely ignore them after the age of agri-

A MAP OF TIME

1345–1521	Aztec Empire in Mesoamerica
1368–1644	Ming dynasty in China
1370–1405	Conquests of Timur
15th century	Spread of Islam in Southeast Asia Civil war among Japanese warlords Rise of Hindu state of Vijayanagara in southern India European Renaissance Flourishing of African states of Ethiopia, Kongo, Benin, Zimbabwe
1405–1433	Chinese maritime voyages
1415	Beginning of Portuguese exploration of West African coast
1438–1533	Inca Empire along the Andes
1453	Ottoman seizure of Constantinople
1464–1591	Songhay Empire in West Africa
1492	Christian reconquest of Spain from Muslims completed; Columbus's first transatlantic voyage
1497–1520s	Portuguese entry into the Indian Ocean world
1501	Founding of Safavid Empire in Persia
1526	Founding of Mughal Empire in India

culture arrived. Nonetheless, this most ancient way of life still had a sizable and variable presence in the world of the fifteenth century.

Consider, for example, Australia. That continent's many separate groups, some 250 of them, still practiced a gathering and hunting way of life in the fifteenth century, a pattern that continued well after Europeans arrived in the late eighteenth century. Over many thousands of years, these people had assimilated various material items or cultural practices from outsiders—outrigger canoes, fishhooks, complex netting techniques, artistic styles, rituals, and mythological ideas—but despite the presence of farmers in nearby New Guinea, no agricultural practices penetrated the Australian mainland. Was it because large areas of Australia were unsuited for the kind of agriculture practiced in New Guinea? Or did the peoples of Australia, enjoying an environment of sufficient resources, simply see no need to change their way of life?

Despite the absence of agriculture, Australia's peoples had mastered and manipulated their environment, in part through the practice of "firestick farming," a pattern of deliberately set fires, which they described as "cleaning up the country."

■ **Comparison**

In what ways did the gathering and hunting people of Australia differ from those of the northwest coast of North America?

These controlled burns served to clear the underbrush, thus making hunting easier and encouraging the growth of certain plant and animal species. In addition, native Australians exchanged goods among themselves over distances of hundreds of miles, created elaborate mythologies and ritual practices, and developed sophisticated traditions of sculpture and rock painting. They accomplished all of this on the basis of an economy and technology rooted in the distant Paleolithic past.

A very different kind of gathering and hunting society flourished in the fifteenth century along the northwest coast of North America among the Chinookan, Tulalip, Skagit, and other peoples. With some 300 edible animal species and an abundance of salmon and other fish, this extraordinarily bounteous environment provided the foundation for what scholars sometimes call "complex" or "affluent" gathering and hunting cultures. What distinguished the northwest coast peoples from those of Australia were permanent village settlements with large and sturdy houses, considerable economic specialization, ranked societies that sometimes included slavery, chiefdoms dominated by powerful clan leaders or "big men," and extensive storage of food.

Although these and other gathering and hunting peoples persisted still in the fifteenth century, both their numbers and the area they inhabited had contracted greatly as the Agricultural Revolution unfolded across the planet. That relentless advance of the farming frontier continued in the centuries ahead as the Russian, Chinese, and European empires encompassed the lands of the remaining Paleolithic peoples. By the early twenty-first century, what was once the only human way of life had been reduced to minuscule pockets of people whose cultures seemed doomed to a final extinction.

Agricultural Village Societies: The Igbo and the Iroquois

Far more numerous than gatherers and hunters were those many peoples who, though fully agricultural, had avoided incorporation into larger empires or civilizations and had not developed their own city- or state-based societies. Living usually in small village-based communities and organized in terms of kinship relations, such people predominated during the fifteenth century in much of North America; in most of the tropical lowlands of South America and the Caribbean; in parts of the Amazon River basin, Southeast Asia, and Africa south of the equator; and throughout Pacific Oceania. Historians have largely relegated such societies to the periphery of world history, viewing them as marginal to the cities, states, and large-scale civilizations that predominate in most accounts of the global past. Viewed from within their own circles, though, these societies were at the center of things, each with its own history of migration, cultural transformation, social conflict, incorporation of new people, political rise and fall, and interaction with strangers. In short, they too changed as their histories took shape.

East of the Niger River in the heavily forested region of West Africa lay the lands of the Igbo (EE-boh) peoples. By the fifteenth century, their neighbors, the

■ **Change**
What kinds of changes were transforming the societies of the West African Igbo and the North American Iroquois as the fifteenth century unfolded?

Yoruba and Bini, had begun to develop small states and urban centers. But the Igbo, whose dense population and extensive trading networks might well have given rise to states, declined to follow suit. The deliberate Igbo preference was to reject the kingship and state-building efforts of their neighbors. They boasted on occasion that "the Igbo have no kings." Instead, they relied on other institutions to maintain social cohesion beyond the level of the village: title societies in which wealthy men received a series of prestigious ranks, women's associations, hereditary ritual experts serving as mediators, and a balance of power among kinship groups. It was a "stateless society," famously described in Chinua Achebe's *Things Fall Apart*, the most widely read novel to emerge from twentieth-century Africa.

But the Igbo peoples and their neighbors did not live in isolated, self-contained societies. They traded actively among themselves and with more distant peoples, such as the large African kingdom of Songhay (sahn-GEYE) far to the north. Cotton cloth, fish, copper and iron goods, decorative objects, and more drew neighboring peoples into networks of exchange. Common artistic traditions reflected a measure of cultural unity in a politically fragmented region, and all of these peoples seem to have changed from a matrilineal to a patrilineal system of tracing their descent. Little of this registered in the larger civilizations of the Afro-Eurasian world, but to the peoples of the West African forest during the fifteenth century, these processes were central to their history and their daily lives. Soon, however, all of them would be caught up in the transatlantic slave trade and would be changed substantially in the process.

Across the Atlantic in what is now central New York State, other agricultural village societies were also in the process of substantial change during the several centuries preceding their incorporation into European trading networks and empires. The Iroquois-speaking peoples of that region had only recently become fully agricultural, adopting maize- and bean-farming techniques that had originated centuries earlier in Mesoamerica. As this productive agriculture took hold by 1300 or so, the population grew, the size of settlements increased, and distinct peoples emerged. Frequent warfare also erupted among them. Some scholars have speculated that as agriculture, largely seen as women's work, became the primary economic activity, "warfare replaced successful food getting as the avenue to male prestige."[2]

Whatever caused it, this increased level of conflict among Iroquois peoples triggered a remarkable political innovation around the fifteenth century: a loose alliance or confederation among five Iroquois-speaking peoples—the Mohawk, Oneida, Onondaga, Cayuga, and Seneca. Based on an agreement known as the Great Law of Peace (see Map 12.5, page 523), the Five Nations, as they called themselves, agreed to settle their differences peacefully through a confederation council of clan leaders, some fifty of them altogether, who had the authority to adjudicate disputes and set reparation payments. Operating by consensus, the Iroquois League of Five

Igbo Art
Widely known for their masks, used in a variety of ritual and ceremonial occasions, the Igbo were also among the first to produce bronze castings using the "lost wax" method. This exquisite bronze pendant in the form of a human head derives from the Igbo Ukwu archeological site in eastern Nigeria and dates to the ninth century C.E. (The British Museum, London, UK/ Werner Forman/Art Resource, NY)

Nations effectively suppressed the blood feuds and tribal conflicts that had only recently been so widespread. It also coordinated their peoples' relationship with outsiders, including the Europeans, who arrived in growing numbers in the centuries after 1500.

The Iroquois League gave expression to values of limited government, social equality, and personal freedom, concepts that some European colonists found highly attractive. One British colonial administrator declared in 1749 that the Iroquois had "such absolute Notions of Liberty that they allow no Kind of Superiority of one over another, and banish all Servitude from their Territories."[3] Such equality extended to gender relationships, for among the Iroquois, descent was matrilineal (reckoned through the woman's line), married couples lived with the wife's family, and women controlled agriculture and property. While men were hunters, warriors, and the primary political officeholders, women selected and could depose those leaders.

Wherever they lived in 1500, over the next several centuries independent agricultural peoples such as the Iroquois and Igbo were increasingly encompassed in expanding economic networks and conquest empires based in Western Europe, Russia, China, or India. In this respect, they replicated the experience of many other village-based farming communities that had much earlier found themselves forcibly included in the powerful embrace of Egyptian, Mesopotamian, Roman, Indian, Chinese, and other civilizations.

Pastoral Peoples: Central Asia and West Africa

Pastoral peoples had long impinged more directly and dramatically on civilizations than did hunting and gathering or agricultural village societies. The Mongol incursion, along with the enormous empire to which it gave rise, was one in a long series of challenges from the steppes, but it was not quite the last. As the Mongol Empire disintegrated, a brief attempt to restore it occurred in the late fourteenth and early fifteenth centuries under the leadership of a Turkic warrior named Timur, born in what is now Uzbekistan and known in the West as Tamerlane (see Map 12.1, page 506).

■ **Significance**
What role did Central Asian and West African pastoralists play in their respective regions?

With a ferocity that matched or exceeded that of his model, Chinggis Khan, Timur's army of pastoralists brought immense devastation yet again to Russia, Persia, and India. Timur himself died in 1405, while preparing for an invasion of China. Conflicts among his successors prevented any lasting empire, although his descendants retained control of the area between Persia and Afghanistan for the rest of the fifteenth century. That state hosted a sophisticated elite culture, combining Turkic and Persian elements, particularly at its splendid capital of Samarkand, as its rulers patronized artists, poets, traders, and craftsmen. Timur's conquest proved to be the last great military success of pastoral peoples from Central Asia. In the centuries that followed, their homelands were swallowed up in the expanding Russian and Chinese empires, as the balance of power between steppe pastoralists of inner Eurasia and the civilizations of outer Eurasia turned decisively in favor of the latter.

In Africa, pastoral peoples stayed independent of established empires several centuries longer than those of Inner Asia, for not until the late nineteenth century were they incorporated into European colonial states. The experience of the Fulbe, West Africa's largest pastoral society, provides an example of an African herding people with a highly significant role in the fifteenth century and beyond. From their homeland in the western fringe of the Sahara along the upper Senegal River, the Fulbe had migrated gradually eastward in the centuries after 1000 C.E. (see Map 12.3, page 514). Unlike the pastoral peoples of Inner Asia, they generally lived in small communities among agricultural peoples and paid various grazing fees and taxes for the privilege of pasturing their cattle. Relations with their farming hosts often were tense because the Fulbe resented their subordination to agricultural peoples, whose way of life they despised. That sense of cultural superiority became even more pronounced as the Fulbe, in the course of their eastward movement, slowly adopted Islam. Some of them in fact dropped out of a pastoral life and settled in towns, where they became highly respected religious leaders. In the eighteenth and nineteenth centuries, the Fulbe were at the center of a wave of religiously based uprisings, or jihads, which greatly expanded the practice of Islam and gave rise to a series of new states, ruled by the Fulbe themselves.

Civilizations of the Fifteenth Century: Comparing China and Europe

Beyond the foraging, farming, and pastoral societies of the fifteenth-century world were its civilizations, those city-centered and state-based societies that were far larger and more densely populated, more powerful and innovative, and much more unequal in terms of class and gender than other forms of human community. Since the First Civilizations had emerged between 3500 and 1000 B.C.E., both the geographic space they encompassed and the number of people they embraced had grown substantially. By the fifteenth century, a considerable majority of the world's population lived within one or another of these civilizations, although most of these people no doubt identified more with local communities than with a larger civilization. What might an imaginary global traveler notice about the world's major civilizations in the fifteenth century?

Ming Dynasty China

Such a traveler might well begin his or her journey in China, heir to a long tradition of effective governance, Confucian and Daoist philosophy, a major Buddhist presence, sophisticated artistic achievements, and a highly productive economy. That civilization, however, had been greatly disrupted by a century of Mongol rule, and its population had been sharply reduced by the plague. During the Ming dynasty (1368–1644), however, China recovered (see Map 12.1). The early decades of that dynasty witnessed an effort to eliminate all signs of foreign rule, discouraging the use of Mongol names and dress, while promoting Confucian learning and orthodox

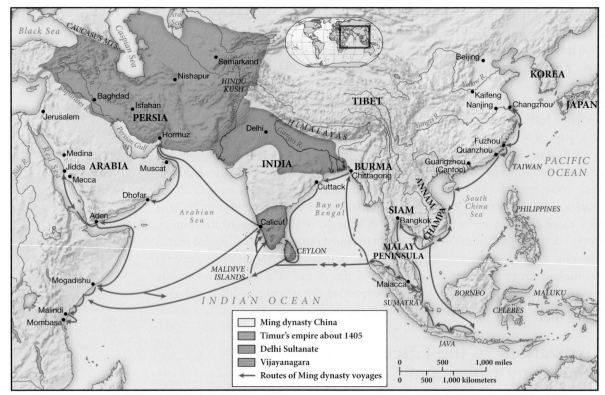

Map 12.1   Asia in the Fifteenth Century

The fifteenth century in Asia witnessed the massive Ming dynasty voyages into the Indian Ocean, the last major eruption of pastoral power in Timur's empire, and the flourishing of the maritime city of Malacca.

gender roles, based on earlier models from the Han, Tang, and Song dynasties. Emperor Yongle (YAHNG-leh) (r. 1402–1422) sponsored an enormous *Encyclopedia* of some 11,000 volumes. With contributions from more than 2,000 scholars, this work sought to summarize or compile all previous writing on history, geography, philosophy, ethics, government, and more. Yongle also relocated the capital to Beijing, ordered the building of a magnificent imperial residence known as the Forbidden City, and constructed the Temple of Heaven, where subsequent rulers performed Confucian-based rituals to ensure the well-being of Chinese society. Two empresses wrote instructions for female behavior, emphasizing traditional expectations after the disruptions of the previous century. Culturally speaking, China was looking to its past.

■ **Description**

How would you define the major achievements of Ming dynasty China?

Politically, the Ming dynasty reestablished the civil service examination system that had been neglected under Mongol rule and went on to create a highly centralized government. Power was concentrated in the hands of the emperor himself, while a cadre of eunuchs (castrated men) personally loyal to the emperor exercised great authority, much to the dismay of the official bureaucrats. The state acted vigorously to repair the damage of the Mongol years by restoring millions of acres to cultivation; rebuilding canals, reservoirs, and irrigation works; and planting, according to some estimates, a billion trees in an effort to reforest China. As a result, the economy rebounded, both international and domestic trade flourished, and the population grew. During the fifteenth century, China had recovered and was perhaps the best governed and most prosperous of the world's major civilizations.

China also undertook the largest and most impressive maritime expeditions the world had ever seen. Since the eleventh century, Chinese sailors and traders had been a major presence in the South China Sea and in Southeast Asian port cities, with much of this activity in private hands. But now, after decades of preparation, an enormous fleet, commissioned by Emperor Yongle himself, was launched in 1405, followed over the next twenty-eight years by six more such expeditions. On board more than 300 ships of the first voyage was a crew of some 27,000, including 180 physicians, hundreds of government officials, 5 astrologers, 7 high-ranking or grand eunuchs, carpenters, tailors, accountants, merchants, translators, cooks, and thousands of soldiers and sailors. Visiting many ports in Southeast Asia, Indonesia, India, Arabia, and East Africa, these fleets, captained by the Muslim eunuch Zheng He (JUHNG-huh), sought to enroll distant peoples and states in the Chinese tribute system (see Map 12.1). Dozens of rulers accompanied the fleets back to China, where they presented tribute, performed the required rituals of submission, and received in return abundant gifts, titles, and trading opportunities. Chinese officials were amused by some of the exotic products to be found abroad—ostriches, zebras, and giraffes, for example. Officially described as "bringing order to the world," Zheng He's expeditions served to establish Chinese power and prestige in the Indian Ocean and to exert Chinese control over foreign trade in the region. The Chinese, however, did not seek to conquer new territories, establish Chinese settlements, or spread their culture, though they did intervene in a number of local disputes. (See Zooming In: Zheng He, page 508.)

Temple of Heaven
Set in a forest of more than 650 acres, the Temple of Heaven was constructed in the early fifteenth century. In Chinese thinking, it was the primary place where Heaven and Earth met. From his residence in the Forbidden City, the Chinese emperor led a procession of thousands twice a year to this sacred site, where he offered sacrifices, implored the gods for a good harvest, and performed the rituals that maintained the cosmic balance. (Imaginechina for AP Images)

Zheng He,
China's Non-Chinese Admiral

At the helm of China's massive maritime expeditions in the early fifteenth century was a most unusual person named Zheng He.[4] Born in 1371 in the frontier region of Yunnan in southwestern China, his family roots were in Central Asia in what is now Uzbekistan. Both his father and grandfather were devout Muslims who had made the pilgrimage to Mecca. The family had also achieved local prominence as high officials serving the Mongol rulers of China for a century. Zheng He would surely have continued in this tradition had not a major turning point in China's history decisively altered the trajectory of his life.

Zheng He's birth, as it happened, coincided with the end of Mongol rule. His own father was killed resisting the forces of the new Ming dynasty that ousted the Mongols from Yunnan in 1382. Eleven-year-old Zheng He was taken prisoner along with hundreds of Mongols and their Muslim supporters. But young Zheng He lost more than his freedom; he also lost his male sex organs as he underwent castration, becoming a eunuch. The practice had a long history in China as well as in Chris-

Among the acquisitions of Zheng He's expeditions, none excited more interest in the Chinese court than an African giraffe.

tian and Islamic civilizations. During the 276 years of the Ming dynasty (1368–1644), some 1 million eunuchs served the Chinese emperor and members of the elite. A small number became powerful officials, especially at the central imperial court, where their utter dependence upon and loyalty to the emperor gained them the enduring hostility of the scholar-bureaucrats of China's civil service. Strangely enough, substantial numbers of Chinese men voluntarily became eunuchs, trading their manhood for the possibility of achieving power, prestige, and wealth.

After his castration, pure chance shaped Zheng He's life as he was assigned to Zhu Di, the fourth son of the reigning emperor, who was then establishing himself in the northern Chinese region around Beijing. Zheng He soon won the confidence of his master, and eventually the almost seven-foot-tall eunuch proved himself an effective military leader in various skirmishes against the Mongols

photo: *Tribute Giraffe with Attendant*, 1414, China, Ming Dynasty (1368–1644), Yongle Period (1403–1424), ink and color on silk/Gift of John T. Dorrance, 1977 (1977-42-1)/The Philadelphia Museum of Art/Art Resource, NY

The most surprising feature of these voyages was how abruptly and deliberately they were ended. After 1433, Chinese authorities simply stopped such expeditions and allowed this enormous and expensive fleet to deteriorate in port. "In less than a hundred years," wrote a recent historian of these voyages, "the greatest navy the world had ever known had ordered itself into extinction."[5] Part of the reason involved the death of the emperor Yongle, who had been the chief patron of the enterprise. Many high-ranking officials had long seen the expeditions as a waste of resources because China, they believed, was the self-sufficient "middle kingdom,"

and in the civil war that brought Zhu Di to power as the emperor Yongle in 1402. With his master as emperor, Zheng He served first as Grand Director of Palace Servants. Now he could don the prestigious red robe, rather than the blue one assigned to lower-ranking eunuchs. But soon Zheng He found himself with a far more ambitious assignment—commander of China's huge oceangoing fleet.

The seven voyages that Zheng He led between 1405 and 1433 have defined his role in Chinese and world history. But they also revealed something of the man himself. Clearly, he was not an explorer in the mold of Columbus, for he sailed in well-traveled waters and usually knew where he was going. While his journeys were largely peaceful, with no effort to establish colonies or control trade, on several occasions Zheng He used force to suppress piracy or to punish those who resisted Chinese overtures. Once he personally led 2,000 Chinese soldiers against a hostile ruler in the interior of Ceylon. He also had a keen eye for the kind of exotica that the imperial court found fascinating, returning to China with ostriches, zebras, lions, elephants, and a giraffe.

The voyages also disclose Zheng He's changing religious commitments. Born and raised a Muslim, he had not lived in a primarily Islamic setting since his capture at the age of eleven. Thus it is hardly surprising that he adopted the more eclectic posture toward religion common in China. During his third voyage in Ceylon, he erected a trilingual tablet recording lavish gifts and praise to the Buddha, to Allah, and to a local form of the Hindu deity Vishnu. He also apparently expressed some interest in a famous relic said to be a tooth of the Buddha. And Zheng He credited the success of his journeys to the Daoist goddess Tianfei, protector of sailors and seafarers.

To Zheng He, the voyages surely represented the essential meaning of his own life. In an inscription erected just prior to his last voyage, Zheng He summarized his achievements: "When we arrived at the foreign countries, barbarian kings who resisted transformation [by Chinese civilization] and were not respectful we captured alive, and bandit soldiers who looted and plundered recklessly we exterminated. Because of this, the sea routes became pure and peaceful and the foreign peoples could rely upon them and pursue their occupations in safety." But after his death, Zheng He vanished from the historical record, even as his country largely withdrew from the sea, and most Chinese forgot about the unusual man who had led those remarkable voyages. In the early twenty-first century, however, Zheng He has been resurrected as a potent symbol of China's growing global position and of its peaceful intentions. In such ways, the past is appropriated, and sometimes distorted, as it proves useful in the present.

Questions: How might you describe the arc of Zheng He's life? What were its major turning points? How did Zheng He's castration shape his life?

requiring little from the outside world. In their eyes, the real danger to China came from the north, where barbarians constantly threatened. Finally, they viewed the voyages as the project of the court eunuchs, whom these officials despised. Even as these voices of Chinese officialdom prevailed, private Chinese merchants and craftsmen continued to settle and trade in Japan, the Philippines, Taiwan, and Southeast Asia, but they did so without the support of their government. The Chinese state quite deliberately turned its back on what was surely within its reach—a large-scale maritime empire in the Indian Ocean basin.

European Comparisons: State Building and Cultural Renewal

At the other end of the Eurasian continent, similar processes of demographic recovery, political consolidation, cultural flowering, and overseas expansion were under way. Western Europe, having escaped Mongol conquest but devastated by the plague, began to regrow its population during the second half of the fifteenth century. As in China, the infrastructure of civilization proved a durable foundation for demographic and economic revival.

■ **Comparison**

What political and cultural differences stand out in the histories of fifteenth-century China and Western Europe? What similarities are apparent?

Politically too Europe joined China in continuing earlier patterns of state building. In China, however, this meant a unitary and centralized government that encompassed almost the whole of its civilization, while in Europe a decidedly fragmented system of many separate, independent, and highly competitive states made for a sharply divided Western civilization (see Map 12.2). Many of these states—Spain, Portugal, France, England, the city-states of Italy (Milan, Venice, and Florence), various German principalities—learned to tax their citizens more efficiently, to create more effective administrative structures, and to raise standing armies. A small Russian state centered on the city of Moscow also emerged in the fifteenth century as Mongol rule faded away. Much of this state building was driven by the needs of war, a frequent occurrence in such a fragmented and competitive political environment. England and France, for example, fought intermittently for more than a century in the Hundred Years' War (1337–1453) over rival claims to territory in France. Nothing remotely similar disturbed the internal life of Ming dynasty China.

A renewed cultural blossoming, known in European history as the Renaissance, likewise paralleled the revival of all things Confucian in Ming dynasty China. In Europe, however, that blossoming celebrated and reclaimed a classical Greco-Roman tradition that earlier had been lost or obscured. Beginning in the vibrant commercial cities of Italy between roughly 1350 and 1500, the Renaissance reflected the belief of the wealthy male elite that they were living in a wholly new era, far removed from the confined religious world of feudal Europe. Educated citizens of these cities sought inspiration in the art and literature of ancient Greece and Rome; they were "returning to the sources," as they put it. Their purpose was not so much to reconcile these works with the ideas of Christianity, as the twelfth- and thirteenth-century university scholars had done, but to use them as a cultural standard to imitate and then to surpass. The elite patronized great Renaissance artists such as Leonardo da Vinci, Michelangelo, and Raphael, whose paintings and sculptures were far more naturalistic, particularly in portraying the human body, than those of their medieval counterparts. Some of these artists looked to the Islamic world for standards of excellence, sophistication, and abundance. (See Working with Evidence: Islam and Renaissance Europe, page 536.)

Although religious themes remained prominent, Renaissance artists now included portraits and busts of well-known contemporary figures, scenes from ancient

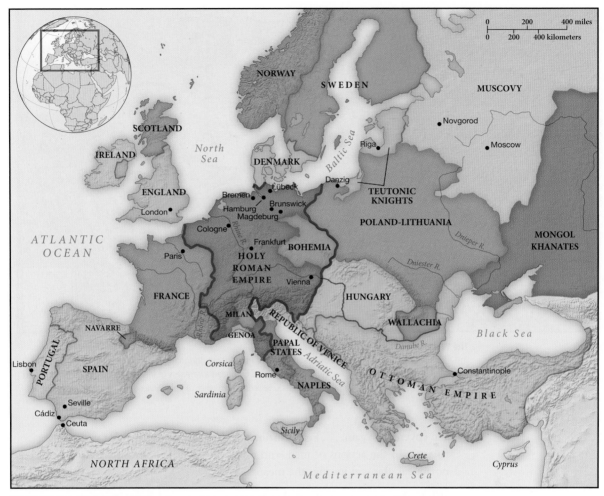

Map 12.2   Europe in 1500

By the end of the fifteenth century, Christian Europe had assumed its early modern political shape as a system of competing states threatened by an expanding Muslim Ottoman Empire.

mythology, and depictions of Islamic splendor. In the work of scholars, known as humanists, reflections on secular topics such as grammar, history, politics, poetry, rhetoric, and ethics complemented more religious matters. For example, Niccolò Machiavelli's (1469–1527) famous work *The Prince* was a prescription for political success based on the way politics actually operated in a highly competitive Italy of rival city-states rather than on idealistic and religiously based principles. To the question of whether a prince should be feared or loved, Machiavelli replied:

> One ought to be both feared and loved, but as it is difficult for the two to go together, it is much safer to be feared than loved. . . . For it may be said of men in general that they are ungrateful, voluble, dissemblers, anxious to avoid danger,

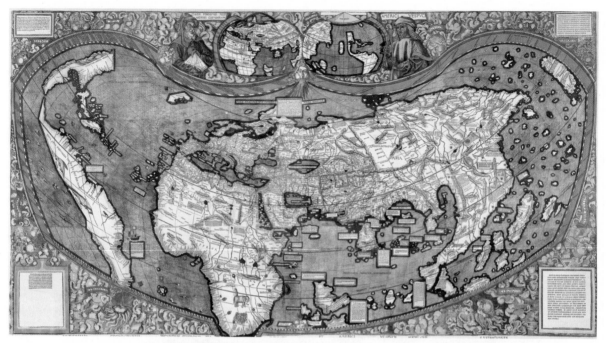

The Waldseemüller Map of 1507
Just fifteen years after Columbus landed in the Western Hemisphere, this map, which was created by the German cartographer Martin Waldseemüller, reflected a dawning European awareness of the planet's global dimensions and the location of the world's major landmasses. (bpk, Berlin/Staatsbibliothek zu Berlin, Stiftung Preussischer Kulturbesitz/Photo: Ruth Schacht/Art Resource, NY)

and covetous of gain. . . . Fear is maintained by dread of punishment which never fails. . . . In the actions of men, and especially of princes, from which there is no appeal, the end justifies the means.[6]

While the great majority of Renaissance writers and artists were men, among the remarkable exceptions to that rule was Christine de Pizan (1363–1430), the daughter of a Venetian official, who lived mostly in Paris. Her writings pushed against the misogyny of so many European thinkers of the time. In her *City of Ladies*, she mobilized numerous women from history, Christian and pagan alike, to demonstrate that women too could be active members of society and deserved an education equal to that of men. Aiding in the construction of this allegorical city is Lady Reason, who offers to assist Christine in dispelling her poor opinion of her own sex. "No matter which way I looked at it," she wrote, "I could find no evidence from my own experience to bear out such a negative view of female nature and habits. Even so . . . I could scarcely find a moral work by any author which didn't devote some chapter or paragraph to attacking the female sex."[7]

Heavily influenced by classical models, Renaissance figures were more interested in capturing the unique qualities of particular individuals and in describing the world as it was than in portraying or exploring eternal religious truths. In its focus on the affairs of this world, Renaissance culture reflected the urban bustle and commercial preoccupations of Italian cities. Its secular elements challenged the otherworldliness of Christian culture, and its individualism signaled the dawning of a more capitalist economy of private entrepreneurs. A new Europe was in the making, one more different from its own recent past than Ming dynasty China was from its pre-Mongol glory.

European Comparisons: Maritime Voyaging

A global traveler during the fifteenth century might be surprised to find that Europeans, like the Chinese, were also launching outward-bound maritime expeditions. Initiated in 1415 by the small country of Portugal, those voyages sailed ever farther down the west coast of Africa, supported by the state and blessed by the pope (see Map 12.3). As the century ended, two expeditions marked major breakthroughs, although few suspected it at the time. In 1492, Christopher Columbus, funded by Spain, Portugal's neighbor and rival, made his way west across the Atlantic hoping to arrive in the East and, in one of history's most consequential mistakes, ran into the Americas. Five years later, in 1497, Vasco da Gama launched a voyage that took him around the tip of South Africa, along the East African coast, and, with the help of a Muslim pilot, across the Indian Ocean to Calicut in southern India.

The differences between the Chinese and European oceangoing ventures were striking, most notably perhaps in terms of size. Columbus captained three ships and a crew of about 90, while da Gama had four ships, manned by perhaps 170 sailors. These were minuscule fleets compared to Zheng He's hundreds of ships and a crew in the many thousands. "All the ships of Columbus and da Gama combined," according to a recent account, "could have been stored on a single deck of a single vessel in the fleet that set sail under Zheng He."[8]

■ **Comparison**

In what ways did European maritime voyaging in the fifteenth century differ from that of China? What accounts for these differences?

Motivation as well as size differentiated the two ventures. Europeans were seeking the wealth of Africa and Asia — gold, spices, silk, and more. They also were in search of Christian converts and of possible Christian allies with whom to continue their long crusading struggle against threatening Muslim powers. China, by contrast, faced no equivalent power, needed no military allies in the Indian Ocean basin, and required little that these regions produced. Nor did China possess an impulse to convert foreigners to its culture or religion, as the Europeans surely did. Furthermore, the confident and overwhelmingly powerful Chinese fleet sought neither conquests nor colonies, while the Europeans soon tried to monopolize by force the commerce of the Indian Ocean and violently carved out huge empires in the Americas.

The most striking difference in these two cases lay in the sharp contrast between China's decisive ending of its voyages and the continuing, indeed escalating, European effort, which soon brought the world's oceans and growing numbers of the world's people under its control. This is why Zheng He's voyages were so long neglected in China's historical memory. They led nowhere, whereas the initial

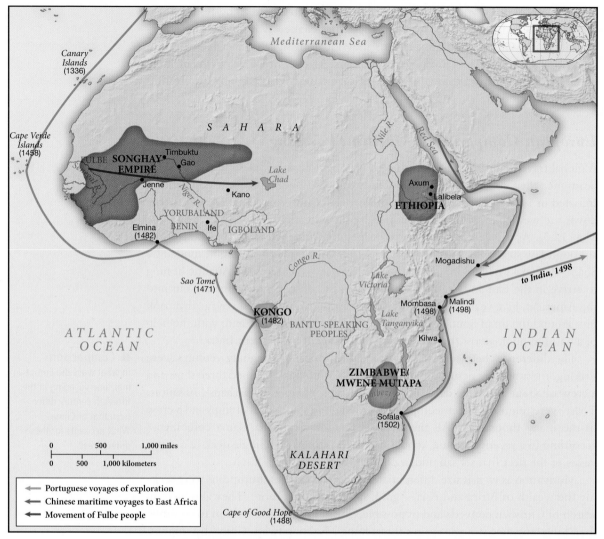

Map 12.3   Africa in the Fifteenth Century

By the fifteenth century, Africa was a virtual museum of political and cultural diversity, encompassing large empires, such as Songhay; smaller kingdoms, such as Kongo; city-states among the Yoruba, Hausa, and Swahili peoples; village-based societies without states at all, as among the Igbo; and pastoral peoples, such as the Fulbe. Both European and Chinese maritime expeditions touched on Africa during that century, even as Islam continued to find acceptance in the northern half of the continent.

European expeditions, so much smaller and less promising, were but the first steps on a journey to world power. But why did the Europeans continue a process that the Chinese had deliberately abandoned?

In the first place, Europe had no unified political authority with the power to order an end to its maritime outreach. Its system of competing states, so unlike

China's single unified empire, ensured that once begun, rivalry alone would drive the Europeans to the ends of the earth. Beyond this, much of Europe's elite had an interest in overseas expansion. Its budding merchant communities saw opportunity for profit; its competing monarchs eyed the revenue from taxing overseas trade or from seizing overseas resources; the Church foresaw the possibility of widespread conversion; impoverished nobles might imagine fame and fortune abroad. In China, by contrast, support for Zheng He's voyages was very shallow in official circles, and when the emperor Yongle passed from the scene, those opposed to the voyages prevailed within the politics of the court.

Finally, the Chinese were very much aware of their own antiquity, believed strongly in the absolute superiority of their culture, and felt with good reason that, should they desire something from abroad, others would bring it to them. Europeans too believed themselves unique, particularly in religious terms as the possessors of Christianity, the "one true religion." In material terms, though, they were seeking out the greater riches of the East, and they were highly conscious that Muslim power blocked easy access to these treasures and posed a military and religious threat to Europe itself. All of this propelled continuing European expansion in the centuries that followed.

The Chinese withdrawal from the Indian Ocean actually facilitated the European entry. It cleared the way for the Portuguese to penetrate the region, where they faced only the eventual naval power of the Ottomans. Had Vasco da Gama encountered Zheng He's massive fleet as his four small ships sailed into Asian waters in 1498, world history may well have taken quite a different turn. As it was, however, China's abandonment of oceanic voyaging and Europe's embrace of the seas marked different responses to a common problem that both civilizations shared— growing populations and land shortage. In the centuries that followed, China's rice-based agriculture was able to expand production internally by more intensive use of the land, while the country's territorial expansion was inland toward Central Asia. By contrast, Europe's agriculture, based on wheat and livestock, expanded primarily by acquiring new lands in overseas possessions, which were gained as a consequence of a commitment to oceanic expansion.

Civilizations of the Fifteenth Century: The Islamic World

Beyond the domains of Chinese and European civilization, our fifteenth-century global traveler would surely have been impressed with the transformations of the Islamic world. Stretching across much of Afro-Eurasia, the enormous realm of Islam experienced a set of remarkable changes during the fifteenth and early sixteenth centuries, as well as the continuation of earlier patterns. The most notable change lay in the political realm, for an Islamic civilization that had been severely fragmented since at least 900 now crystallized into four major states or empires (see Map 12.4). At the same time, a long-term process of conversion to Islam continued the cultural transformation of Afro-Eurasian societies both within and beyond these new states.

In the Islamic Heartland: The Ottoman and Safavid Empires

■ Comparison
What differences can you identify among the four major empires in the Islamic world of the fifteenth and sixteenth centuries?

The most impressive and enduring of the new Islamic states was the Ottoman Empire, which lasted in one form or another from the fourteenth to the early twentieth century. It was the creation of one of the many Turkic warrior groups that had migrated into Anatolia, slowly and sporadically, in the several centuries following 1000 C.E. By the mid-fifteenth century, these Ottoman Turks had already carved out a state that encompassed much of the Anatolian peninsula and had pushed deep into southeastern Europe (the Balkans), acquiring in the process a substantial Christian population. During the sixteenth century, the Ottoman Empire extended its control to much of the Middle East, coastal North Africa, the lands surrounding the Black Sea, and even farther into Eastern Europe.

The Ottoman Empire was a state of enormous significance in the world of the fifteenth century and beyond. In its huge territory, long duration, incorporation of many diverse peoples, and economic and cultural sophistication, it was one of the great empires of world history. In the fifteenth century, only Ming dynasty China and the Incas matched it in terms of wealth, power, and splendor. The empire represented the emergence of the Turks as the dominant people of the Islamic world, ruling now over many Arabs, who had initiated this new faith more than 800 years before. In adding "caliph" (successor to the Prophet) to their other titles, Ottoman sultans claimed the legacy of the earlier Abbasid Empire. They sought to bring a renewed unity to the Islamic world, while also serving as protector of the faith, the "strong sword of Islam."

The Ottoman Empire also represented a new phase in the long encounter between Christendom and the world of Islam. In the Crusades, Europeans had taken the aggressive initiative in that encounter, but the rise of the Ottoman Empire reversed their roles. The seizure of Constantinople in 1453 marked the final demise of Christian Byzantium and allowed Ottoman rulers to see themselves as successors to the Roman Empire. (See Zooming In: 1453 in Constantinople, page 518.) It also opened the way to further expansion in heartland Europe, and in 1529 a rapidly expanding Ottoman Empire laid siege to Vienna in the heart of Central Europe. The political and military expansion of Islam, at the expense of Christendom, seemed clearly under way. Many Europeans spoke fearfully of the "terror of the Turk."

In the neighboring Persian lands to the east of the Ottoman Empire, another Islamic state was also taking shape in the late fifteenth and early sixteenth centuries—the Safavid (SAH-fah-vihd) Empire. Its leadership was also Turkic, but in this case it had emerged from a Sufi religious order founded several centuries earlier by Safi al-Din (1252–1334). The long-term significance of the Safavid Empire, which was established in the decade following 1500, was its decision to forcibly

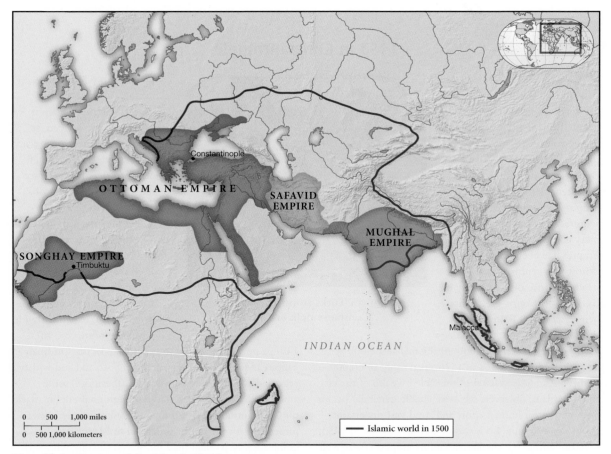

Map 12.4   Empires of the Islamic World

The most prominent political features of the vast Islamic world in the fifteenth and sixteenth centuries were four large states: the Songhay, Ottoman, Safavid, and Mughal empires.

impose a Shia version of Islam as the official religion of the state. Over time, this form of Islam gained popular support and came to define the unique identity of Persian (Iranian) culture.

This Shia empire also introduced a sharp divide into the political and religious life of heartland Islam, for almost all of Persia's neighbors practiced a Sunni form of the faith. For a century (1534–1639), periodic military conflict erupted between the Ottoman and Safavid empires, reflecting both territorial rivalry and sharp religious differences. In 1514, the Ottoman sultan wrote to the Safavid ruler in the most bitter of terms:

> You have denied the sanctity of divine law . . . you have deserted the path of salvation and the sacred commandments . . . you have opened to Muslims the gates of tyranny and oppression . . . you have raised the standard of irreligion

1453 in Constantinople

On May 29, 1453, forces of the Muslim Ottoman sultan Mehmed II seized control of the great Christian city of Constantinople, an event that marked the final end of the Roman/Byzantine Empire and the ascendency of the Ottoman Empire. In retrospect, this event acquired a certain air of inevitability about it, for the Byzantine Empire had been retreating for almost two centuries before the steady advance of the Ottomans. By 1453, that once-great empire, heir to all things Roman, had shrunk to little more than the city itself, with only some 50,000 inhabitants and 8,000 active defenders compared to a vast Ottoman army of 60,000 soldiers. And little was left of the fabled wealth of the city. But what later observers see as inevitable generally occurs only with great human effort and amid vast uncertainty about the outcome. So it was in Constantinople in 1453.

Constantine XI, the last Byzantine emperor, was well aware of the odds he faced. Yet his great city, protected by water on two sides and a great wall on a third, had repeatedly withstood many attacks and sieges. Furthermore, until the very end, he had hoped for assistance

Ottoman Turks storm the walls of Constantinople in 1453.

from Western Christians, even promising union with the Roman Church to obtain it. But no such help arrived, at least not in sufficient quantities to make a difference, though rumors of a fleet from Venice persisted. The internal problems of the Western powers as well as the long-standing hostility between Eastern Orthodoxy and Roman Catholicism ensured that Constantinople would meet its end alone.

On the Ottoman side, enormous effort was expended with no assurance of success. In 1451, a new sultan came to the throne of the Ottoman Empire, Mehmed II, only nineteen years old and widely regarded as not very promising. Furthermore, some among the court officials had reservations about an attack on Constantinople. But the young sultan seemed determined to gain the honor promised in Islamic prophesies going back to Muhammad himself to the one who conquered the city. Doing so could also rid him of a potential rival to the Ottoman throne, who had taken refuge in Constantinople.

photo: © ullstein bild/The Image Works

---

and heresy. . . . [Therefore] the *ulama* and our doctors have pronounced a sentence of death against you, perjurer and blasphemer.[9]

This Sunni/Shia hostility has continued to divide the Islamic world into the twenty-first century.

On the Frontiers of Islam: The Songhay and Mughal Empires

While the Ottoman and Safavid empires brought both a new political unity and a sharp division to the heartland of Islam, two other states performed a similar role on the expanding African and Asian frontiers of the faith. In the West African savan-

And so preparations began for an assault on the once-great city. The Ottomans assembled a huge fleet, gathered men and materials, and constructed a fortress to control access to Constantinople by water. In late 1452, Mehmed secured the services of a Hungarian master cannon builder named Orban, who constructed a number of huge cannons, one of which could hurl a 600-pound stone ball over a mile. These weapons subsequently had a devastating effect on the walls surrounding Constantinople. Interestingly enough, Orban had first offered his services to the Byzantine emperor, who simply could not afford to pay for this very expensive project.

In early April of 1453, the siege began, and it lasted for fifty-seven days. As required by Islamic law, Mehmed offered three times to spare the emperor and his people if they surrendered. Constantine apparently considered the offer seriously, but he finally refused, declaring, "We have all decided to die with our own free will." After weeks of furious bombardment, an ominous silence descended on May 28. Mehmed had declared a day of rest and prayer before the final assault the next day. That evening, the Byzantine emperor ordered a procession of icons and relics about the city and then entered the ancient Christian church of Hagia Sophia, seeking forgiveness for his sins and receiving Holy Communion.

And then, early the next day, the final assault began as Ottoman forces breached the walls of Constantinople and took the city. The Christians bravely defended their city, and Constantine discarded his royal regalia and died fighting like a common soldier. A later legend suggested that angels turned Constantine into marble and buried him in a nearby cave from which he would eventually reappear to retake the city for Christendom.

Islamic law required that soldiers be permitted three days of plundering the spoils, but Mehmed was reluctant, eager to spare the city he longed for as his capital. So he limited plundering to one day. Even so, the aftermath was terrible. According to a Christian eyewitness, "The enraged Turkish soldiers . . . gave no quarter. When they had massacred and there was no longer any resistance, they were intent on pillage and roamed through the town stealing, disrobing, pillaging, killing, raping, taking captive men, women, children, monks, priests."[10] When Mehmed himself entered the city, praying at the Christian altar of Hagia Sophia, he reportedly wept at seeing the destruction that had occurred.

Constantinople was now a Muslim city, capital of the Ottoman Empire, and Hagia Sophia became a mosque. A momentous change had occurred in the relationship between the world of Islam and that of Christendom.

Questions: What factors contributed to Mehmed's victory? Under what circumstances might a different outcome have been possible?

---

nas, the Songhay Empire rose in the second half of the fifteenth century. It was the most recent and the largest in a series of impressive states that operated at a crucial intersection of the trans-Saharan trade routes and that derived much of their revenue from taxing that commerce. Islam was a growing faith in Songhay but was limited largely to urban elites. This cultural divide within Songhay largely accounts for the religious behavior of its fifteenth-century monarch Sonni Ali (r. 1465–1492), who gave alms and fasted during Ramadan in proper Islamic style but also enjoyed a reputation as a magician and possessed a charm thought to render his soldiers invisible to their enemies. Nonetheless, Songhay had become a major center of Islamic learning and commerce by the early sixteenth century. A North African traveler known as Leo Africanus remarked on the city of Timbuktu:

Ottoman Janissaries
Originating in the fourteenth century, the Janissaries became the elite infantry force of the Ottoman Empire. Complete with uniforms, cash salaries, and marching music, they were the first standing army in the region since the days of the Roman Empire. When gunpowder technology became available, Janissary forces soon were armed with muskets, grenades, and handheld cannons. This Turkish miniature painting dates from the sixteenth century. (Turkish miniature, Topkapi Palace Library, Istanbul, Turkey/Album/Art Resource, NY)

> Here are great numbers of [Muslim] religious teachers, judges, scholars, and other learned persons who are bountifully maintained at the king's expense. Here too are brought various manuscripts or written books from Barbary [North Africa] which are sold for more money than any other merchandise. . . . Here are very rich merchants and to here journey continually large numbers of negroes who purchase here cloth from Barbary and Europe. . . . It is a wonder to see the quality of merchandise that is daily brought here and how costly and sumptuous everything is.[11]

See Working with Evidence, Source 7.3, page 318, for more from Leo Africanus about West Africa in the early sixteenth century. Sonni Ali's successor made the pilgrimage to Mecca and asked to be given the title "Caliph of the Land of the Blacks." Songhay then represented a substantial Islamic state on the African frontier of a still-expanding Muslim world. (See the photo on page 305 for manuscripts long preserved in Timbuktu.)

The Mughal (MOO-guhl) Empire in India bore similarities to Songhay, for both governed largely non-Muslim populations. Much as the Ottoman Empire initiated a new phase in the interaction of Islam and Christendom, so too did the Mughal Empire continue an ongoing encounter between Islamic and Hindu civilizations. Established in the early sixteenth century, the Mughal Empire was the creation of yet another Islamized Turkic group, which invaded India in 1526. Over the next century, the Mughals (a Persian term for Mongols) established unified control over most of the Indian peninsula, giving it a rare period of political unity and laying the foundation for subsequent British colonial rule. During its first 150 years, the Mughal Empire, a land of great wealth and imperial splendor, undertook a remarkable effort to blend many Hindu groups and a variety of Muslims into an effective partnership. The inclusive policies of the early Mughal emperors showed that Muslim rulers could accommodate their overwhelmingly Hindu subjects in somewhat the same fashion as Ottoman authorities provided religious autonomy for their Christian minority. In southernmost India, however, the distinctly Hindu kingdom of Vijayanagara flourished in the fifteenth century, even as it borrowed architectural styles from the Muslim states of northern India and sometimes employed Muslim mercenaries in its military forces.

Together these four Muslim empires—Ottoman, Safavid, Songhay, and Mughal—brought to the Islamic world a greater measure of political coherence, military power, economic prosperity, and cultural brilliance than it had known since the early centuries of Islam. This new energy, sometimes called a "second flowering of Islam," impelled the continuing spread of the faith to yet new regions. The most prominent of these was oceanic Southeast Asia, which for centuries had been intimately bound up in the world of Indian Ocean commerce, while borrowing elements of both Hindu and Buddhist traditions. By the fifteenth century, that trading network was largely in Muslim hands, and the demand for Southeast Asian spices was mounting as the Eurasian world recovered from the devastation of Mongol conquest and the plague. Growing numbers of Muslim traders, many of them from India, settled in Java and Sumatra, bringing their faith with them. Eager to attract those traders to their port cities, a number of Hindu or Buddhist rulers along the Malay Peninsula and in Indonesia converted to Islam, while transforming themselves into Muslim sultans and imposing Islamic law. Thus, unlike in the Middle East and India, where Islam was established in the wake of Arab or Turkic conquest, in Southeast Asia, as in West Africa, it was introduced by traveling merchants and solidified through the activities of Sufi holy men.

The rise of Malacca, strategically located on the waterway between Sumatra and Malaya, was a sign of the times (see Map 12.1, page 506). During the fifteenth century, it was transformed from a small fishing village to a major Muslim port city. A Portuguese visitor in 1512 observed that Malacca had "no equal in the world. . . . Commerce between different nations for a thousand leagues on every hand must come to Malacca."[12] That city also became a springboard for the spread of Islam throughout the region. In the eclectic style of Southeast Asian religious history, the Islam of Malacca demonstrated much blending with local and Hindu/Buddhist traditions, while the city itself, like many port towns, had a reputation for "rough behavior." An Arab Muslim pilot in the 1480s commented critically: "They have no culture at all. . . . You do not know whether they are Muslim or not."[13] Nonetheless, Malacca, like Timbuktu on the West African frontier of an expanding Islamic world, became a center for Islamic learning, and students from elsewhere in Southeast Asia were studying there in the fifteenth century. As the more central regions of Islam were consolidating politically, the frontier of the faith continued to move steadily outward.

SUMMING UP SO FAR

In what ways did the civilizations of China, Europe, and the Islamic world in the fifteenth century seem to be moving in the same direction, and in what respects were they diverging from one another?

Civilizations of the Fifteenth Century: The Americas

Across the Atlantic, centers of civilization had long flourished in Mesoamerica and in the Andes. The fifteenth century witnessed new, larger, and more politically unified expressions of those civilizations, embodied in the Aztec and Inca empires. Both were the work of previously marginal peoples who had forcibly taken over and absorbed older cultures, giving them new energy, and both were decimated in the sixteenth century at the hands of Spanish conquistadores and their diseases. To conclude this global tour of world civilizations, we will send our intrepid traveler to the Western Hemisphere for a brief look at these American civilizations (see Map 12.5).

The Aztec Empire

■ **Comparison**

What distinguished the Aztec and Inca empires from each other?

The empire known to history as the Aztec state was largely the work of the Mexica (meh-SHEEH-kah) people, a semi-nomadic group from northern Mexico who had migrated southward and by 1325 had established themselves on a small island in Lake Texcoco. Over the next century, the Mexica developed their military capacity, served as mercenaries for more powerful people, negotiated elite marriage alliances with them, and built up their own capital city of Tenochtitlán. In 1428, a Triple Alliance between the Mexica and two other nearby city-states launched a highly aggressive program of military conquest, which in less than 100 years brought more of Mesoamerica within a single political framework than ever before. Aztec authorities, eager to shed their rather undistinguished past, now claimed descent from earlier Mesoamerican peoples such as the Toltecs and Teotihuacán.

With a core population recently estimated at 5 to 6 million people, the Aztec Empire was a loosely structured and unstable conquest state that witnessed frequent rebellions by its subject peoples. Conquered peoples and cities were required to provide labor for Aztec projects and to regularly deliver to their Aztec rulers

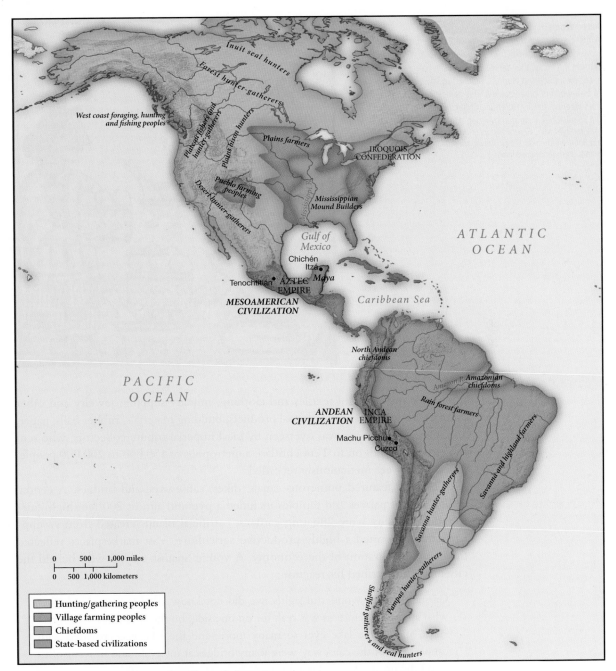

Map 12.5   The Americas in the Fifteenth Century

The Americas before Columbus represented a world almost completely separate from Afro-Eurasia. It featured similar kinds of societies, though with a different balance among them, but it largely lacked the pastoral economies that were so important in the Eastern Hemisphere.

Aztec Women
Within the home, Aztec women cooked, cleaned, spun and wove cloth, raised their children, and undertook ritual activities. Outside the home, they served as officials in palaces, priestesses in temples, traders in markets, teachers in schools, and members of craft workers' organizations. This domestic image comes from the sixteenth-century Florentine Codex, which was compiled by the Spanish but illustrated by Aztec artists. (Facsimile from Book IV of Florentine Codex, *General History of Things in New Spain*, 16th century, Mexico/Museo del Templo Mayor, Mexico City, Mexico/De Agostini Picture Library/Bridgeman Images)

impressive quantities of textiles and clothing, military supplies, jewelry and other luxuries, various foodstuffs, animal products, building materials, rubber balls, paper, and more. The process was overseen by local imperial tribute collectors, who sent the required goods on to Tenochtitlán, a metropolis of 150,000 to 200,000 people, where they were meticulously recorded.

That city featured numerous canals, dikes, causeways, and bridges. A central walled area of palaces and temples included a pyramid almost 200 feet high. Surrounding the city were "floating gardens," artificial islands created from swamplands that supported a highly productive agriculture. Vast marketplaces reflected the commercialization of the economy. A young Spanish soldier who beheld the city in 1519 described his reaction:

> Gazing on such wonderful sights, we did not know what to say, or whether what appeared before us was real, for on one side, on the land there were great cities, and in the lake ever so many more, and the lake was crowded with canoes, and in the causeway were many bridges at intervals, and in front of us stood the great city of Mexico.[14]

Beyond tribute from conquered peoples, ordinary trade, both local and long-distance, permeated Aztec domains. The extent of empire and rapid population growth stimulated the development of markets and the production of craft goods, particularly in the fifteenth century. Virtually every settlement, from the capital city to the smallest village, had a marketplace that hummed with activity during weekly market days. The largest was that of Tlatelolco, near the capital city, which stunned the Spanish with its huge size, its good order, and the immense range of goods available. Hernán Cortés, the Spanish conquistador who defeated the Aztecs, wrote that "every kind of merchandise such as can be met with in every land is for sale there, whether of food and victuals, or ornaments of gold and silver, or lead, brass, copper, tin, precious stones, bones, shells, snails and feathers."[15] Professional merchants, known as *pochteca*, were legally commoners, but their wealth, often exceeding that of the nobility, allowed them to rise in society and become "magnates of the land."

Among the "goods" that the pochteca obtained were slaves, many of whom were destined for sacrifice in the bloody rituals so central to Aztec religious life. Long a part of Mesoamerican and many other world cultures, human sacrifice assumed an unusually prominent role in Aztec public life and thought during the fifteenth century. Tlacaelel (1398–1480), who was for more than half a century a prominent official of the Aztec Empire, is often credited with crystallizing the ideology of state that gave human sacrifice such great importance.

■ **Description**
How did Aztec religious thinking support the empire?

In that cyclical understanding of the world, the sun, central to all life and identified with the Aztec patron deity Huitzilopochtli (wee-tsee-loh-pockt-lee), tended to lose its energy in a constant battle against encroaching darkness. Thus the Aztec world hovered always on the edge of catastrophe. To replenish its energy and thus postpone the descent into endless darkness, the sun required the life-giving force found in human blood. Because the gods had shed their blood ages ago in creating humankind, it was wholly proper for people to offer their own blood to nourish the gods in the present. The high calling of the Aztec state was to supply this blood, largely through its wars of expansion and from prisoners of war, who were destined for sacrifice. The victims were "those who have died for the god." The growth of the Aztec Empire therefore became the means for maintaining cosmic order and avoiding utter catastrophe. This ideology also shaped the techniques of Aztec warfare, which put a premium on capturing prisoners rather than on killing the enemy. As the empire grew, priests and rulers became mutually dependent, and "human sacrifices were carried out in the service of politics."[16] Massive sacrificial rituals, together with a display of great wealth, served to impress enemies, allies, and subjects alike with the immense power of the Aztecs and their gods.

Alongside these sacrificial rituals was a philosophical and poetic tradition of great beauty, much of which mused on the fragility and brevity of human life. Such an outlook characterized the work of Nezahualcoyotl (1402–1472), a poet and king of the city-state of Texcoco, which was part of the Aztec Empire:

> Truly do we live on Earth?
> Not forever on earth; only a little while here.
> Although it be jade, it will be broken.
> Although it be gold, it is crushed.
> Although it be a quetzal feather, it is torn asunder.
> Not forever on earth; only a little while here.[17]

The Inca Empire

While the Mexica were constructing an empire in Mesoamerica, a relatively small community of Quechua-speaking people, known to us as the Incas, was building the Western Hemisphere's largest imperial state along the entire spine of the Andes Mountains. Much as the Aztecs drew on the traditions of the Toltecs and Teotihuacán, the Incas incorporated the lands and cultures of earlier Andean civilizations: the Chavín, Moche, Wari, and Tiwanaku. The Inca Empire, however, was much larger than the Aztec state; it stretched some 2,500 miles along the Andes and contained perhaps 10 million subjects. Although the Aztec Empire controlled only part of the Mesoamerican cultural region, the Inca state encompassed practically the whole of Andean civilization during its short life in the fifteenth and early sixteenth centuries. In the speed of its creation and the extent of its territory, the Inca Empire bears some similarity to that of the Mongols.

Both the Aztec and Inca empires represent rags-to-riches stories in which quite modest and remotely located people very quickly created by military conquest the largest states ever witnessed in their respective regions, but the empires themselves were quite different. In the Aztec realm, the Mexica rulers largely left their conquered people alone, if the required tribute was forthcoming. No elaborate administrative system arose to integrate the conquered territories or to assimilate their people to Aztec culture.

The Incas, on the other hand, erected a rather more bureaucratic empire. At the top reigned the emperor, an absolute ruler regarded as divine, a descendant of the creator god Viracocha and the son of the sun god Inti. Each of the some eighty provinces in the empire had an Inca governor. In theory, the state owned all land and resources, though in practice state lands, known as "lands of the sun," existed alongside properties owned by temples, elites, and traditional communities. At least in the central regions of the empire, subjects were grouped into hierarchical units of 10, 50, 100, 500, 1,000, 5,000, and 10,000 people, each headed by local officials, who were appointed and supervised by an Inca governor or the emperor. A separate set of "inspectors" provided the imperial center with an independent check on provincial officials. Births, deaths, marriages, and other population data were carefully recorded on *quipus*, the knotted cords that served as an accounting device. A resettlement program moved one-quarter or more of the population to new locations, in part to disperse conquered and no doubt resentful people and sometimes to reward loyal followers with promising opportunities. Efforts at cultural integration required the leaders of conquered peoples to learn Quechua. Their sons were removed to the capital of Cuzco for instruction in Inca culture and language. Even now, millions of people from Ecuador to Chile still speak Quechua, and it is the official second language of Peru after Spanish.

But the sheer human variety of the Incas' enormous empire required great flexibility. In some places Inca rulers encountered bitter resistance; in others local elites were willing to accommodate Incas and thus benefit from their inclusion in the

■ **Description**
In what ways did Inca authorities seek to integrate their vast domains?

Machu Picchu
Machu Picchu, high in the Andes Mountains, was constructed by the Incas in the fifteenth century on a spot long held sacred by local people. Its 200 buildings stand at some 8,000 feet above sea level, making it a "city in the sky." It was probably a royal retreat or religious center, rather than serving administrative, commercial, or military purposes. The outside world became aware of Machu Picchu only in 1911, when it was discovered by a Yale University archeologist. (fStop/Superstock)

empire. Where centralized political systems already existed, Inca overlords could delegate control to native authorities. Elsewhere they had to construct an administrative system from scratch. Everywhere they sought to incorporate local people into the lower levels of the administrative hierarchy. While the Incas required their subject peoples to acknowledge major Inca deities, these peoples were then largely free to carry on their own religious traditions. The Inca Empire was a fluid system that varied greatly from place to place and over time. It depended as much on the posture of conquered peoples as on the demands and desires of Inca authorities.

Like the Aztec Empire, the Inca state represented an especially dense and extended network of economic relationships within the "American web," but these relationships took shape in quite a different fashion. Inca demands on their conquered people were expressed, not so much in terms of tribute, but as labor service, known as *mita*, which was required periodically of every household. What people produced at home usually stayed at home, but almost everyone also had to work for the state. Some labored on large state farms or on "sun farms," which supported temples and religious institutions; others herded, mined, served in the military, or toiled on state-directed construction projects.

Those with particular skills were put to work manufacturing textiles, metal goods, ceramics, and stonework. The most well-known of these specialists were the "chosen women," who were removed from their homes as young girls, trained in Inca ideology, and set to producing corn beer and cloth at state centers. Later they were given as wives to men of distinction or sent to serve as priestesses in various temples, where they were known as "wives of the Sun." In return for such labor services, Inca ideology, expressed in terms of family relationships, required the state to arrange elaborate feasts at which large quantities of food and drink were consumed and to provide food and other necessities when disaster struck. Thus the authority of the state penetrated and directed Inca society and economy far more than did that of the Aztecs. (See Working with Evidence, Source 13.4, page 596, for an early Spanish account of Inca governing practices.)

If the Inca and Aztec civilizations differed sharply in their political and economic arrangements, they resembled each other more closely in their gender systems. Both societies practiced what scholars call "gender parallelism," in which "women and men operate in two separate but equivalent spheres, each gender enjoying autonomy in its own sphere."[18]

In both Mesoamerican and Andean societies, such systems had emerged long before their incorporation into the Aztec and Inca empires. In the Andes, men reckoned their descent from their fathers and women from their mothers, while Mesoamericans had long viewed children as belonging equally to their mothers and fathers. Parallel religious cults for women and men likewise flourished in both societies. Inca men venerated the sun, while women worshipped the moon, with matching religious officials. In Aztec temples, both male and female priests presided over rituals dedicated to deities of both sexes. Particularly among the Incas, parallel hierarchies of male and female political officials governed the empire, while in Aztec society, women officials exercised local authority under a title that meant "female person in charge of people." Social roles were clearly defined and different for men and women, but the domestic concerns of women—childbirth, cooking, weaving, cleaning—were not regarded as inferior to the activities of men. Among the Aztecs, for example, sweeping was a powerful and sacred act with symbolic significance as "an act of purification and a preventative against evil elements penetrating the center of the Aztec universe, the home."[19] In the Andes, men broke the ground, women sowed, and both took part in the harvest.

This was gender complementarity, not gender equality. Men occupied the top positions in both political and religious life, and male infidelity was treated more lightly than was women's unfaithfulness. As the Inca and Aztec empires expanded, military life, limited to men, grew in prestige, perhaps skewing an earlier gender parallelism. The Incas in particular imposed a more rigidly patriarchal order on their subject peoples. In other ways, the new Aztec and Inca rulers adapted to the gender systems of the people they had conquered. Among the Aztecs, the tools of women's work, the broom and the weaving spindle, were ritualized as weapons; sweeping the home was believed to assist men at war; and childbirth was regarded by women as "our kind of war."[20] Inca rulers replicated the gender parallelism of their subjects at a higher level, as the *sapay Inca* (the Inca ruler) and the *coya* (his female consort) governed jointly, claiming descent respectively from the sun and the moon.

Webs of Connection

Few people in the fifteenth century lived in entirely separate and self-contained communities. Almost all were caught up, to one degree or another, in various and overlapping webs of influence, communication, and exchange.[21] Perhaps most obvious were the webs of empire, large-scale political systems that brought together a variety of culturally different people. Christians and Muslims encountered each other directly in the Ottoman Empire, as did Hindus and Muslims in the Mughal Empire. And no empire tried more diligently to integrate its diverse peoples than the fifteenth-century Incas.

Religion too linked far-flung peoples, and divided them as well. Christianity provided a common religious culture for peoples from England to Russia, although the great divide between Roman Catholicism and Eastern Orthodoxy endured, and in the sixteenth century the Protestant Reformation would shatter permanently the Christian unity of the Latin West. Although Buddhism had largely vanished from its South Asian homeland, it remained a link among China, Korea, Tibet, Japan, and parts of Southeast Asia, even as it splintered into a variety of sects and practices. More than either of these, Islam actively brought together its many peoples. In the hajj, the pilgrimage to Mecca, Africans, Arabs, Persians, Turks, Indians, and many others joined as one people as they rehearsed together the events that gave birth to their common faith. And yet divisions and conflicts persisted within the vast realm of Islam, as the violent hostility between the Sunni Ottoman Empire and the Shia Safavid Empire so vividly illustrates.

■ **Connection**

In what different ways did the peoples of the fifteenth century interact with one another?

Long-established patterns of trade among peoples occupying different environments and producing different goods were certainly much in evidence during the fifteenth century, as they had been for millennia. Hunting societies of Siberia funneled furs and other products of the forest into the Silk Road trading network traversing the civilizations of Eurasia. In the fifteenth century, some of the agricultural peoples in southern Nigeria were receiving horses brought overland from the drier regions of Africa to the north, where those animals flourished better. The Mississippi River in North America and the Orinoco and Amazon rivers in South America facilitated a canoe-borne commerce along those waterways. Coastal shipping in large seagoing canoes operated in the Caribbean and along the Pacific coast between Mexico and Peru. In Pacific Polynesia, the great voyaging networks across vast oceanic distances that had flourished especially since 1000 were in decline by 1500 or earlier, leading to the abandonment of a number of islands. Ecological devastation perhaps played a role, and some scholars believe that a cooling and fluctuating climate change known as the Little Ice Age created less favorable conditions

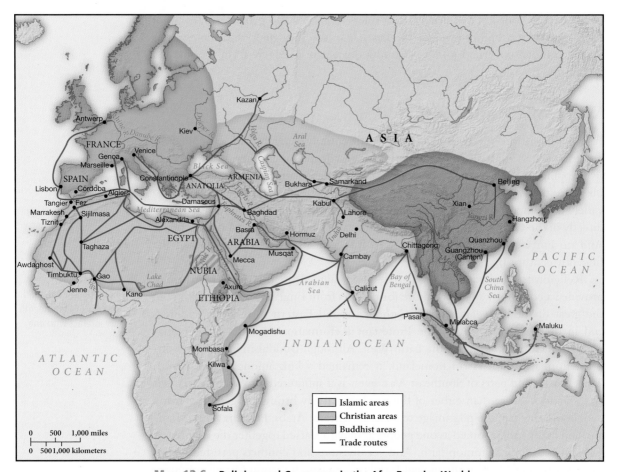

Map 12.6   Religion and Commerce in the Afro-Eurasian World

By the fifteenth century, the many distinct peoples and societies of the Eastern Hemisphere were linked to one another by ties of religion and commerce. Of course, most people were not directly involved in long-distance trade, and many people in areas shown as Buddhist or Islamic on the map practiced other religions. While much of India, for example, was ruled by Muslims, the majority of its people followed some form of Hinduism. And although Islam had spread to West Africa, that religion had not penetrated much beyond the urban centers of the region.

for inter-island exchange. The great long-distance trading patterns of the Afro-Eurasian world, in operation for a thousand years or more, continued in the fifteenth century, although the balance among them was changing (see Map 12.6). The Silk Road overland network, which had flourished under Mongol control in the thirteenth and fourteenth centuries, contracted in the fifteenth century as the Mongol Empire broke up and the devastation of the plague reduced demand for its products. The rise of the Ottoman Empire also blocked direct commercial contact between Europe and China, but oceanic trade from Japan, Korea, and China through the islands of Southeast Asia and across the Indian Ocean picked up considerably. Larger ships made it possible to trade in bulk goods such as grain as well as luxury products, while more sophisticated partnerships and credit mechanisms greased the wheels of commerce. A common Islamic culture over much of this vast region likewise smoothed the passage of goods among very different peoples, as it also did for the trans-Saharan trade.

A Preview of Coming Attractions: Looking Ahead to the Modern Era, 1500–2015

While ties of empire, culture, commerce, and disease surely linked many of the peoples in the world of the fifteenth century, none of those connections operated on a genuinely global scale. Although the densest webs of connection had been woven within the Afro-Eurasian zone of interaction, this huge region had no sustained ties with the Americas, and neither of them had sustained contact with the peoples of Pacific Oceania. That situation was about to change as Europeans in the sixteenth century and beyond forged a set of genuinely global relationships that generated sustained interaction among all of these regions. That huge process and the many outcomes that flowed from it marked the beginning of what world historians commonly call the modern age—the more than five centuries that followed the voyages of Columbus starting in 1492.

Over those five centuries, the previously separate worlds of Afro-Eurasia, the Americas, and Pacific Oceania became inextricably linked, with enormous consequences for everyone involved. Global empires, a global economy, global cultural exchanges, global migrations, global disease, global wars, and global environmental changes have made the past 500 years a unique phase in the human journey. Those webs of communication and exchange—the first defining feature of the modern era—have progressively deepened, so much so that by the end of the twentieth century few if any people lived beyond the cultural influences, economic ties, or political relationships of a globalized world.

Several centuries after the Columbian voyages, and clearly connected to them, a second distinctive feature of the modern era took shape: the emergence of a radically new kind of human society, first in Europe during the nineteenth century and then in various forms elsewhere in the world. The core feature of such societies was industrialization, with its sustained growth of technological innovation and its massive consumption of energy and raw materials. The human ability to create wealth made an enormous leap forward in a very short period of time, at least by world history standards. Accompanying this economic or industrial revolution was an equally distinctive and unprecedented jump in human numbers, a phenomenon that has affected not only human beings but also many other living species and the earth itself. (See Snapshot, page 532.)

Moreover, these modern societies were far more urbanized and much more commercialized than ever before, as more and more people began to work for wages, to produce for the market, and to buy the requirements of daily life rather

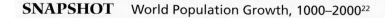

SNAPSHOT   World Population Growth, 1000–2000[22]

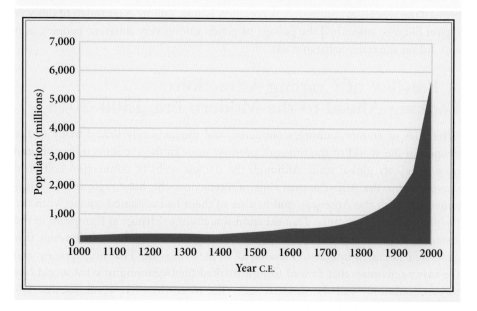

than growing or making those products for their own use. These societies gave prominence and power to holders of urban wealth—merchants, bankers, industrialists, educated professionals—at the expense of rural landowning elites, while simultaneously generating a substantial factory working class and diminishing the role of peasants and handicraft artisans.

Modern societies were generally governed by states that were more powerful and intrusive than earlier states and empires had been, and they offered more of their people an opportunity to play an active role in public and political life. Literacy in modern societies was far more widespread than ever before, while new national identities became increasingly prominent, competing with more local loyalties and with those of empire. To the mix of established religious ideas and folk traditions were now added the challenging outlook and values of modern science, with its secular emphasis on the ability of human rationality to know and manipulate the world. Modernity has usually meant a self-conscious awareness of living and thinking in new ways that deliberately departed from tradition.

This revolution of modernity, comparable in its pervasive consequences only to the Agricultural Revolution of some 10,000 years ago, introduced new divisions and new conflicts into the experience of humankind. The ancient tensions between rich and poor within particular societies were now paralleled by new economic inequalities among entire regions and civilizations and a much-altered global balance of power. The first societies to experience the modern transformation—those in Western Europe and North America—became both a threat and a source of envy to much of the rest of the world. As modern societies emerged and spread, they were enormously destructive of older patterns of human life, even as they gave rise to many new ways of living. Sorting out what was gained and what was lost during the modern transformation has been a persistent and highly controversial thread of human thought over the past several centuries.

A third defining feature of the last 500 years was the growing prominence of European peoples on the global stage. In ancient times, the European world, focused in the Mediterranean basin of Greek culture and the Roman Empire, was but one of several second-wave civilizations in the Eastern Hemisphere. After 500 C.E., Western Europe was something of a backwater, compared to the more prosperous and powerful civilizations of China and the Islamic world.

In the centuries following 1500, however, this western peninsula of the Eurasian continent became the most innovative, most prosperous, most powerful, most expansive, and most imitated part of the world. European empires spanned the globe. European peoples created new societies all across the Americas and as far away as South Africa, Australia, and New Zealand. Their languages were spoken and their Christian religion was widely practiced throughout the Americas and in parts of Asia and Africa. Their businessmen bought, sold, and produced goods around the world. It was among Europeans that the Scientific and Industrial Revolutions first took shape, with enormously powerful intellectual and economic consequences for the entire planet. The quintessentially modern ideas of liberalism, nationalism, feminism, and socialism all bore the imprint of their European origin. By the beginning of the twentieth century, Europeans or peoples of European descent exercised unprecedented influence and control over the earth's many other peoples, a wholly novel experience in human history.

For the rest of the world, growing European dominance posed a common challenge. Despite their many differences, the peoples of Asia, Africa, the Middle East, the Americas, and Pacific Oceania all found themselves confronted by powerful and intrusive Europeans. The impact of this intrusion and how various peoples responded to it—resistance, submission, acceptance, imitation, adaptation—represent critically important threads in the world history of the past five centuries.

REFLECTIONS

What If? Chance and Contingency in World History

Seeking meaning in the stories they tell, historians are inclined to look for deeply rooted or underlying causes for the events they recount. And yet, is it possible that, at least on occasion, historical change derives less from profound and long-term sources than from coincidence, chance, or the decisions of a few that might well have gone another way?

Consider, for example, the problem of explaining the rise of Europe to a position of global power in the modern era. What if the Great Khan Ogodei had not died in 1241, requiring the Mongol forces then poised for an assault on Germany to return to Mongolia? It is surely possible that Central and Western Europe might have been overrun by Mongol armies as so many other civilizations had been, a prospect that could have drastically altered the trajectory of European history. Or what if the Chinese had decided in 1433 to continue their huge maritime expeditions, creating an empire in the Indian Ocean basin and perhaps moving on to "discover" the Americas and Europe? Such a scenario suggests a wholly different future for world history than the one that in fact occurred. Or what if the forces of the Ottoman Empire had taken the besieged city of Vienna in 1529? Might they then have incorporated even larger parts of Europe into their expanding domain, requiring a halt to Europe's overseas empire-building enterprise?

None of this necessarily means that the rise of Europe was merely a fluke or an accident of history, but it does raise the issue of "contingency," the role of unforeseen or small events in the unfolding of the human story. An occasional "what if" approach to history reminds us that alternative possibilities existed in the past and that the only certainty about the future is that we will be surprised.

Second Thoughts

What's the Significance?

Big Picture Questions

1. Assume for the moment that the Chinese had not ended their maritime voyages in 1433. How might the subsequent development of world history have been different? What value is there in asking this kind of "what if" or counterfactual question?

2. How does this chapter distinguish among the various kinds of societies contained in the world of the fifteenth century? What other ways of categorizing the world's peoples might work as well or better?

3. What common patterns might you notice across the world of the fifteenth century? And what variations in the historical trajectories of various regions can you identify?

4. **Looking Back:** What would surprise a knowledgeable observer from 500 or 1000 C.E., were he or she to make a global tour in the fifteenth century? What features of that earlier world might still be recognizable?

Next Steps: For Further Study

Terence N. D'Altroy, *The Incas* (2002). A history of the Inca Empire that draws on recent archeological and historical research.

Edward L. Dreyer, *Zheng He: China and the Oceans in the Early Ming Dynasty* (2006). The most recent scholarly account of the Ming dynasty voyages.

Halil Inalcik and Donald Quataert, *An Economic and Social History of the Ottoman Empire, 1300–1914* (1994). A classic study of the Ottoman Empire.

Robin Kirkpatrick, *The European Renaissance, 1400–1600* (2002). A beautifully illustrated history of Renaissance culture as well as the social and economic life of the period.

Charles C. Mann, *1491: New Revelations of the Americas before Columbus* (2005). A review of Western Hemisphere societies and academic debates about their pre-Columbian history.

J. R. McNeill and William H. McNeill, *The Human Web* (2003). A succinct account of the evolving webs or relationships among human societies in world history.

Michael Smith, *The Aztecs* (2003). A history of the Aztec Empire, with an emphasis on the lives of ordinary people.

"Italian Renaissance," http://www.history.com/topics/italian-renaissance. A History channel presentation of the European Renaissance, with a number of brief videos.

"Ming Dynasty," http://www.metmuseum.org/toah/hd/ming/hd_ming.htm. A sample of Chinese art from the Ming dynasty from the collection of the Metropolitan Museum of Art.

WORKING WITH EVIDENCE

Islam and Renaissance Europe

The Renaissance era in Europe, roughly 1400 to 1600, represented the crystallization of a new civilization at the western end of Eurasia. In cultural terms, its writers and artists sought to link themselves to the legacy of the pre-Christian Greeks and Romans. But if Europeans were reaching back to their classical past, they were also reaching out—westward to the wholly new world of the Americas, southward to Africa, and eastward to Asia generally and the Islamic world in particular. The European Renaissance, in short, was shaped not only from within but also by its encounters with a wider world.

Interaction with the world of Islam was, of course, nothing new. Centuries of Muslim rule in Spain, the Crusades, and the expansion of the Ottoman Empire were markers in the long relationship of conflict, cooperation, and mutual influence between Christendom and the realm of Islam. Politically, that relationship was changing in the fifteenth century. The Christian reconquest of Spain from Muslim rule was completed by 1492. At the other end of the Mediterranean Sea, the Turkish Ottoman Empire was expanding into the previously Christian regions of the Balkans (southeastern Europe), seizing the ancient capital of the Byzantine Empire, Constantinople, in 1453, while becoming a major player in European international politics. Despite such conflicts, commerce flourished across political and religious divides. European bulk goods such as wool, timber, and glassware, along with silver and gold, were exchanged for high-value luxury goods from the Islamic world or funneled through it from farther east. These included spices, silks, carpets, tapestries, brocades, art objects, precious stones, gold, dyes, and pigments. In 1384, a Christian pilgrim from the Italian city of Florence wrote: "Really all of Christendom could be supplied for a year with the merchandise of Damascus."[23] And a fifteenth-century Italian nobleman said of Venice: "It seems as if all the world flocks here, and that human beings have concentrated there all their force for trading."[24]

The acquisition of such Eastern goods was important for elite Europeans as they sought to delineate and measure their emerging civilization. As that civilization began to take shape in the centuries after 1100 or so, it had drawn extensively on Arab or Muslim learning—in medicine, astronomy, philosophy, architecture, mathematics, business practices, and more. As early as the twelfth century, a Spanish priest and Latin translator of Arab texts wrote, "It

befits us to imitate the Arabs, for they are as it were our teachers and the pio-
neers." During the Renaissance centuries as well, according to a recent account,
"Europe began to define itself by purchasing and emulating the opulence and
cultured sophistication of the cities, merchants, scholars, and empires of the
Ottomans, Persians, and the Egyptian Mamluks." That engagement with the
Islamic world found various expressions in Renaissance art, as the images that
follow illustrate.

The year 1453 marked a watershed in the long relationship between
Christendom and the Islamic world, for it was in that year that the Ottoman
sultan Mehmed II decisively conquered the great Christian city of Constantinople, bringing the thousand-year history of Byzantium to an inglorious
end. To many Europeans, that event was a catastrophe and Mehmed was the
"terror of the world." On hearing the news, one Italian bishop, later to
become the pope, foresaw a dismal future for both the Church and Western civilization: "Who can doubt that the Turks will vent their wrath upon
the churches of God? . . . This will be a second death to Homer and a second
destruction of Plato." Others, however, saw opportunity. Less than a year after
that event, the northern Italian city of Venice signed a peace treaty with the
Ottoman sultan, declaring, "It is our intention to live in peace and friendship
with the Turkish emperor." Some even expressed admiration for the conquering Muslim ruler. George of Trebizond, a Greek-speaking Renaissance
scholar, described Mehmed as "a wise king and one who philosophizes about
the greatest matters."

For his part, Mehmed admired both classical and contemporary European
culture, even as his armies threatened European powers. This cosmopolitan
emperor employed Italian scholars to read to him from ancient Greek and
Roman literature, stocked his library with Western texts, and decorated the
walls of his palace with Renaissance-style frescoes. Seeing himself as heir to
Roman imperial authority, he now added "Caesar" to his other titles. Although
Islam generally prohibited the depiction of human figures, Mehmed's long
interest in caricatures and busts and his desire to celebrate his many conquests
led him to commission numerous medals by European artists, bearing his
image. In 1480, he also had his portrait painted by the leading artist of Venice, Gentile Bellini, who had been sent to the Ottoman court as a cultural
ambassador of his city.

Source 12.1 shows Bellini's portrait of the emperor sitting under a marble
arch, a symbol of triumph that evokes his dramatic conquest of Constantinople. The three golden crowns on the upper left and right likely represent
the lands recently acquired for the Ottoman Empire, and the inscription at the
bottom describes Mehmed as "Conqueror of the World." Not long after the
painting was made, Mehmed died, and shortly thereafter his son and successor sold it to Venetian merchants to help finance a large mosque complex.
Thus the portrait returned to Venice.

National Gallery, London, UK/Bridgeman Images

Source 12.1 Gentile Bellini, Portrait of Mehmed II

- What overall impression of the sultan does this portrait convey?

- Why might this Muslim ruler want his portrait painted by a Christian artist from Venice?

- Why might Bellini and the city government of Venice be willing — even eager — to undertake the assignment, less than thirty years after the Muslim conquest of Constantinople?

- The candelabra decorating the arch were a common feature in Venetian church architecture. Why might the sultan have agreed to this element of Christian symbolism in his portrait?

- What does the episode surrounding this portrait indicate about the relationship of Venice and the Ottoman Empire in the wake of the conquest of Constantinople?

Venice had long been the primary point of commercial contact between Europe and the East and the source of the much-desired luxury goods that its merchants obtained from Alexandria in Egypt. At that time, Muslim Egypt was ruled by the Mamluks, a warrior caste of slave origins, who had checked the westward advance of the Mongols in 1260 and had driven the last of the European Crusaders out of the Middle East in 1291. Venetian traders, however, were more interested in commerce than in religion and by the fifteenth century enjoyed a highly profitable relationship with the Mamluk rulers of Egypt and Syria, despite the periodic opposition of the pope and threats of excommunication. Thus it is not surprising that the Renaissance artists of Venice were prominent among those who reflected the influence of the Islamic world in their work. By the late fifteenth century, something of a fad for oriental themes surfaced in Venetian pictorial art.

Source 12.2, painted by an anonymous Venetian artist in 1511, expresses this intense interest in the Islamic world. The setting is Damascus in Syria, then ruled by the Egyptian Mamluk regime. The local Mamluk governor of the city, seated on a low platform with an elaborate headdress, is receiving an ambassador from Venice, shown in a red robe and standing in front of the governor. Behind him in black robes are other members of the Venetian delegation, while in the foreground various members of Damascus society— both officials and merchants—are distinguished from one another by variations in their turbans. Behind the wall lies the city of Damascus with its famous Umayyad mosque, formerly a Roman temple to Jupiter and later a Christian church, together with its three minarets. The city's lush gardens and its homes with wooden balconies and rooftop terraces complete the picture of urban Islam.

- What impressions of the city and its relationship with Venice does the artist seek to convey?

- How are the various social groups of Damascus distinguished from one another in this painting? What does the very precise visual description of these differences suggest about Venetian understanding of urban Mamluk society?

- What does the total absence of women suggest about their role in the public life of Damascus?

Louvre, Paris, France/Bridgeman Images

Source 12.2 The Venetian Ambassador Visits Damascus

■ How would you know that this is a Muslim city? What role, if any, does religion play in this depiction of the relationship between Christian Venice and Islamic Damascus?

Beyond political and commercial relationships, Europeans had long engaged with the Islamic world intellectually as well. Source 12.3 illustrates that engagement in a work by Girolamo da Cremona, a fifteenth-century Italian painter known for his "illuminations" of early printed books. Created in 1483 (only some forty years after the invention of the printing press in Europe), it served as the frontispiece for one of the first printed versions of Aristotle's writings, translated into Latin, along with commentaries by the twelfth-century Muslim scholar Ibn Rushd, better known in the West as Averroes.

Aristotle, of course, was the great Greek philosopher of the fourth century B.C.E. whose writings presented a systematic and rational view of the world, while commenting on practically every branch of knowledge. The legacy of Greek thought in general and Aristotle in particular passed into both the Christian and Islamic worlds. Ibn Rushd (1126–1198), who wrote voluminous commentaries on Aristotle's works and much else as well, lived in Muslim Spain, where he argued for the compatibility of Aristotelian philosophy and the religious perspectives of Islam. While that outlook faced growing

Source 12.3 Aristotle and Averroes

opposition in the Islamic world, Aristotle's writings found more fertile ground among European scholars in the new universities of the twelfth and thirteenth centuries, where they became the foundation of university curricula and nourished the growth of "natural philosophy." In large measure it was through translations of Ibn Rushd's Arabic commentaries on Aristotle that Europeans regained access to the thinking of that ancient philosopher. A long line of European scholars defined themselves as "Averroists."

The painting in Source 12.3 is presented as a parchment leaf, torn to disclose two worlds behind Aristotle's text. At the top in a rural setting, Aristotle, dressed in a blue robe, is speaking to Ibn Rushd, clad in a yellow robe with a round white turban. The bottom of the painting depicts the world of classical Greek mythology. The painted jewels, gems, and pearls testify to the great value placed on such illuminated and printed texts.

- What might the possession of such a book say about the social status, tastes, and outlook of its owner?

- What overall impression of Renaissance thinking about the classical world and the world of Islam does this painting convey?

- Notice the gestures of the two men at the top as well as the pen in Ibn Rushd's hand and the book at his feet. How might you describe the relationship between them?

- What made it possible for at least some European Christians of the Renaissance era to embrace both the pagan Aristotle and the Islamic Ibn Rushd?

Despite the fluid relationship of Renaissance Europe with the world of Islam, the Ottoman Empire, apparently expanding inexorably, was a growing threat to Christian Europe, and Islam was a false religion to many Christians. Those themes too found expression in the art of the Renaissance. Source 12.4 provides an example. Painted during the first decade of the sixteenth century by the Venetian artist Vittore Carpaccio, it reflects the popular "orientalist" style with its elaborate and exotic depiction of Eastern settings, buildings, and costumes. This particular painting was part of a series illustrating the life of Saint George, a legendary soldier-saint who rescued a Libyan princess, slew the dragon about to devour her, and by his courageous example converted a large number of pagans to Christianity. Earlier paintings in this series portrayed the killing of the dragon, while this one shows the conversion of the infidels to the "true faith."

The setting for Source 12.4 is Muslim-ruled Jerusalem, where the action focuses on Saint George, on the right, baptizing a bareheaded Muslim ruler and a woman (perhaps his wife). Several others await their turns below the steps, while a group of Mamluk musicians play in honor of the occasion.

By Vittore Carpaccio (ca. 1460–1523), 1501–1507/Scuola di San Giorgio degli Schiavoni, Venice, Italy/Giraudon/Bridgeman Images

Source 12.4 Saint George Baptizes the Pagans of Jerusalem

■ What posture toward the Islamic world does this painting represent? Does it convey resistance to Ottoman expansion, or does it hold out the hope for the peaceful conversion of that powerful empire?

■ What is the significance of the large Ottoman turban at the foot of the steps?

■ Why might the legend of Saint George provide a potent symbol for European interaction with the Islamic world in the circumstances of the early sixteenth century?

■ Compare this urban scene with that of Source 12.2. What common features do you notice? Apart from any religious meanings, what do these paintings suggest about Venetian interests in the Islamic world?

An even more vitriolic anti-Muslim sensibility had long circulated in Europe, based on the fear of Islamic power, the distortions growing out of the Crusades, and the perception of religious heresy. In the early fourteenth century, the Italian poet Dante, author of *The Divine Comedy*, placed Muhammad in the eighth circle of Hell, where the "sowers of discord" were punished and mutilated. To many Christians, Muhammad was a "false prophet," sometimes portrayed as drunk. Protestants such as Martin Luther on occasion equated their great enemy, the pope, with the Muslim "Turk," both of them leading people away from authentic religion.

The most infamous Renaissance example of hostility to Islam as a religion is displayed in Source 12.5, a fresco by the Italian artist Giovanni da Modena, painted on a church wall in the northern Italian city of Bologna in 1415. It was a small part of a much larger depiction of Hell, featuring a gigantic image of Satan devouring and excreting the damned, while many others endured horrific punishments. Among them was Muhammad—naked, bound to a rock, and tortured by a winged demon with long horns. It reflected common understandings of Muhammad as a religious heretic, a false prophet, and even the anti-Christ and therefore "hell-bound."

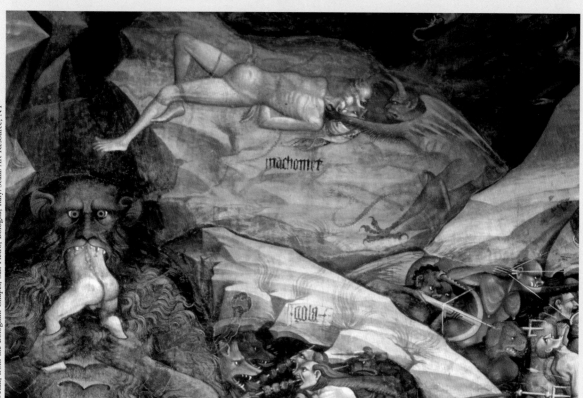

Detail, from the Bolognini Chapel, San Pietro, Bologna, Italy/Scala/Art Resource, NY

Source 12.5 Giovanni da Modena, Muhammad in Hell

▪ How does this fresco depict Hell? What does the larger context of the fresco as a whole suggest about Modena's view of Muhammad?

▪ How does this image differ from that of Source 12.4, particularly in its posture toward Islam?

▪ Italian Muslims have long objected to this image, noting that Islam portrays Jesus in a very positive light. In 2002 a radical group linked to al-Qaeda plotted unsuccessfully to blow up the church that housed this image in order to destroy the offending portrayal of their prophet. What particular objections do you imagine motivated Muslim opposition to this element of the fresco?

DOING HISTORY

Islam and Renaissance Europe

1. **Making comparisons:** What range of postures toward the Islamic world do these images convey? How might you account for the differences among them?

2. **Imagining reactions:** How might the artists who created the first four images respond to Source 12.5?

3. **Examining the content of visual sources:** While all of these images deal with the Islamic world, with what different aspects of that world are they concerned?

4. **Considering art and society:** In what ways were these images shaped by the concrete political, economic, and cultural conditions of Renaissance Europe? What role did the Islamic world play in the emerging identity of European civilization?

PART FOUR

THE EARLY MODERN WORLD

1450–1750

Contents

DEBATING THE CHARACTER OF AN ERA

For the sake of clarity and coherence, historians often characterize a particular period of time in a brief phrase—the age of First Civilizations, the age of empires, the era of revolutions, and so on. Though useful and even necessary, such capsule descriptions leave a lot out and vastly oversimplify what actually happened. Historical reality is always more messy, more complicated, and more uncertain than any shorthand label can convey. Such is surely the case when we examine the three centuries spanning the years from roughly 1450 to 1750.

An Early Modern Era?

Those three centuries, which are addressed in Chapters 13 through 15, are conventionally labeled as "the early modern era." In using this term, historians are suggesting that during these three centuries we can find some initial signs or markers of the modern world, such as those described at the end of Chapter 12: the beginnings of genuine globalization, elements of distinctly modern societies, and a growing European presence in world affairs.

The most obvious expression of globalization, of course, lay in the oceanic journeys of European explorers and the European conquest and colonial settlement of the Americas. The Atlantic slave trade linked Africa permanently to the Western Hemisphere, while the global silver trade allowed Europeans to use New World precious metals to buy their way into ancient Asian trade routes. The massive transfer of plants, animals, diseases, and people, known to historians as the Columbian exchange, created wholly new networks of interaction across both the Atlantic and Pacific oceans, with enormous global implications. Missionaries carried Christianity far beyond Europe, allowing it to become a genuinely world religion, with a presence in the Americas, China, Japan, the Philippines, and south-central Africa. Other threads in the emerging global web were also woven as Russians marched across Siberia to the Pacific, as China expanded deep into Inner Asia, and as the Ottoman Empire encompassed much of the Middle East, North Africa, and southeastern Europe (see Chapter 13).

Scattered signs of what later generations thought of as "modernity" appeared in various places around the world. The most obviously modern cultural development took place in Europe, where the Scientific Revolution transformed, at least for a few people, their view of the world, their approach to knowledge, and their understanding of traditional Christianity. Demographically, China,

Japan, India, and Europe experienced the beginnings of modern population growth as Eurasia recovered from the Black Death and Mongol wars and as the foods of the Americas—corn and potatoes, for example—provided nutrition to support larger numbers. World population more than doubled between 1400 and 1800 (from about 374 million to 968 million), even as the globalization of disease produced a demographic catastrophe in the Americas and the slave trade limited African population growth. More highly commercialized economies centered in large cities developed in various parts of Eurasia and the Americas. By the early eighteenth century, for example, Japan was one of the most urbanized societies in the world, with Edo (Tokyo) housing more than a million inhabitants and ranking as the world's largest city. In China, Southeast Asia, India, and across the Atlantic basin, more and more people found themselves, sometimes willingly and at other times involuntarily, producing for distant markets rather than for the use of their local communities.

Stronger and more cohesive states represented yet another global pattern as they incorporated various local societies into larger units while actively promoting trade, manufacturing, and a common culture within their borders. France, the Dutch Republic, Russia, Morocco, the Mughal Empire, Vietnam, Burma, Siam, and Japan all represent this kind of state.[1] Their military power likewise soared as the "gunpowder revolution" kicked in around the world. Thus large-scale empires proliferated across Asia and the Middle East, while various European powers carved out new domains in the Americas. Within these empires, human pressures on the land intensified as forests were felled, marshes drained, and the hunting grounds of foragers and the grazing lands of pastoralists were confiscated for farming or ranching.

A Late Agrarian Era?

All of these developments give some validity to the notion of an early modern era. But this is far from the whole story, and it may be misleading if it suggests that European world domination and more fully modern societies were a sure thing, an inevitable outgrowth of early modern developments. In fact, that future was far from clear in 1750.

Although Europeans ruled the Americas and controlled the world's sea routes, their political and military power in mainland Asia and Africa was very limited. Eighteenth-century China and Japan strictly controlled the European missionaries and merchants who operated in their societies, and African authorities frequently set the terms under which the slave trade was conducted. Islam, not Christianity, was the most rapidly spreading faith in much of Asia and Africa, and in 1750 Europe, India, and China were roughly comparable in their manufacturing output. In short, it was not obvious that Europeans would soon dominate the planet. Moreover, populations and economies had surged at various points in the past, only to fall back again in a cyclical pattern. Nothing guaranteed that the early modern surge would be any more lasting than the others.

Nor was there much to suggest that anything approaching modern industrial society was on the horizon. Animal and human muscles, wind, and water still provided almost all of the energy that powered human economies. Handicraft techniques of manufacturing had nowhere been displaced by factory-based production or steam power. Long-established elites, not middle-class upstarts, everywhere provided leadership and enjoyed the greatest privileges, while rural peasants, not urban workers, represented the primary social group in the lower classes. Kings and nobles, not parliaments and parties, governed. Female subordination was assumed to be natural almost everywhere. While the texture of patriarchy varied among cultures and fluctuated over time, nowhere had ideas of gender equality taken root. Modern society, with its promise of liberation from ancient inequalities and from mass poverty, hardly seemed around the corner.

Most of the world's peoples, in fact, continued to live in long-established ways, and their societies operated according to traditional principles. Kings ruled most of Europe, and male landowning aristocrats remained at the top of the social hierarchy. Another change in ruling dynasties occurred in China, while that huge country affirmed Confucian values and a social structure that privileged landowning and office-holding elites, all of them men. Most Indians practiced some form of Hinduism and owed their most fundamental loyalty to local castes, even as South Asia continued its centuries-long incorporation into the Islamic world. The realm of Islam maintained its central role in the Eastern Hemisphere as the Ottoman Empire revived the political fortunes of Islam, and the religion sustained its long-term expansion into Africa and Southeast Asia.

In short, for the majority of humankind, the three centuries between 1450 and 1750 marked less an entry into the modern era than the continuing development of older agrarian societies. It was as much a late agrarian era as an early modern age. Persistent patterns rooted in the past characterized that period, along with new departures and sprouts of modernity. And change was not always in the direction of what we now regard as "modern." In European, Islamic, and Chinese societies alike, some people urged a return to earlier ways of living and thinking rather than embracing what was new and untried. Although Europeans were increasingly prominent on the world stage, they certainly did not hold all the leading roles in the global drama of these three centuries.

From this mixture of what was new and what was old during the early modern era, the three chapters that follow highlight the changes. Chapter 13 turns the spotlight on the new empires of those three centuries—European, Middle Eastern, and Asian. New global patterns of long-distance trade in spices, sugar, silver, fur, and slaves represent the themes of Chapter 14. New cultural trends—both within the major religious traditions of the world and in the emergence of modern science—come together in Chapter 15. With the benefit of hindsight, we may see many of these developments as harbingers of a modern world to come, but from the viewpoint of 1700 or so, the future was open and uncertain, as it almost always is.

MAPPING PART FOUR

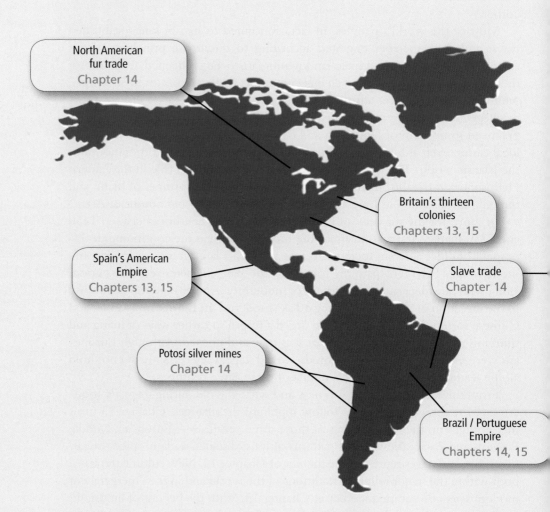

North American
fur trade
Chapter 14

Britain's thirteen
colonies
Chapters 13, 15

Spain's American
Empire
Chapters 13, 15

Slave trade
Chapter 14

Potosí silver mines
Chapter 14

Brazil / Portuguese
Empire
Chapters 14, 15

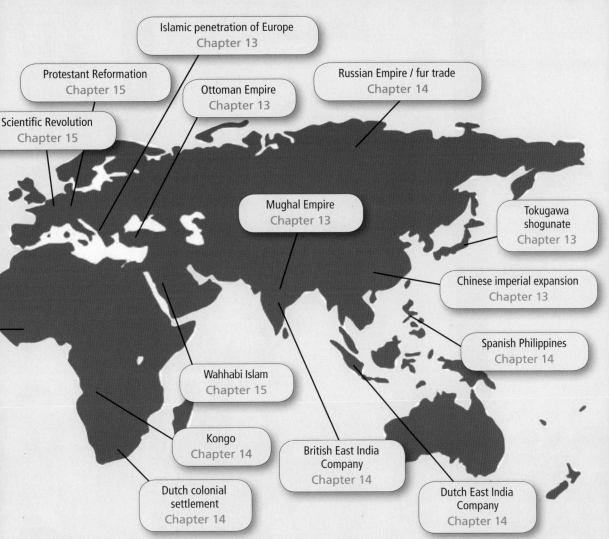

Islamic penetration of Europe
Chapter 13

Protestant Reformation
Chapter 15

Ottoman Empire
Chapter 13

Russian Empire / fur trade
Chapter 14

Scientific Revolution
Chapter 15

Mughal Empire
Chapter 13

Tokugawa
shogunate
Chapter 13

Chinese imperial expansion
Chapter 13

Spanish Philippines
Chapter 14

Wahhabi Islam
Chapter 15

Kongo
Chapter 14

British East India
Company
Chapter 14

Dutch colonial
settlement
Chapter 14

Dutch East India
Company
Chapter 14

Illustration from the *Padshahnama*, ca. 1630–1640 (bodycolour with gold on paper)/Royal Collection Trust © Her Majesty Queen Elizabeth II, 2014/Bridgeman Images

CHAPTER 13

Political Transformations

Empires and Encounters

1450–1750

"What he [Vladimir Putin] wants to do, you can just see the lust in his eyes, he wants to re-create the Russian empire, and this move on Crimea is his first step." So said U.S. senator Bill Nelson in March of 2014, referring to the Russian president's actions in seizing Crimea and in pressuring Ukraine to remain within a Russian sphere of influence. In reflecting on this very current political situation, the senator, and many others as well, invoked the Russian Empire, which had taken shape during the early modern era. In the same vein, commentators on the economic and political resurgence of twenty-first-century Turkey often refer to it as an effort "to rebuild the Ottoman Empire," likewise a creation of the early modern era.[1] In such ways, the memories of these earlier empires continue to shape understanding of current events and perhaps to inspire actions in the present as well.

As these comments imply, empire building has been largely discredited during the twentieth and twenty-first centuries, and "imperialist" has become a term of insult rather than a source of pride. How very different were the three centuries (1450–1750) of the early modern era, when empire building was a global process! In the Americas, the Aztec and Inca empires flourished before they were incorporated into the rival empires of the Spanish, Portuguese, British, French, and Dutch, constructed all across the Western Hemisphere. Within those imperial systems, vast transformations took place: old societies were destroyed, and new societies arose as Native Americans, Europeans, and Africans came into sustained contact with one another for the first time in world history.

The Mughal Empire   Among the most magnificent of the early modern empires was that of the Mughals in India. In this painting by an unknown Mughal artist, the seventeenth-century emperor Shah Jahan is holding a *durbar*, or ceremonial assembly, in the audience hall of his palace. The material splendor of the setting shows the immense wealth of the court, while the halo around Shah Jahan's head indicates the special spiritual grace or enlightenment associated with emperors.

It was a revolutionary encounter with implications that extended far beyond the Americas themselves.

But European empires in the Americas were not alone on the imperial stage of the early modern era. Across the immense expanse of Siberia, the Russians constructed what was then the world's largest territorial empire, making Russia an Asian as well as a European power. Qing (chihng) dynasty China penetrated deep into Inner Asia, doubling the size of the country while incorporating millions of non-Chinese people who practiced Islam, Buddhism, or animistic religions. On the South Asian peninsula, the Islamic Mughal Empire brought Hindus and Muslims into a closer relationship than ever before, sometimes quite peacefully and at other times with great conflict. In the Middle East, the Turkish Ottoman Empire reestablished something of the earlier political unity of heartland Islam and posed a serious military and religious threat to European Christendom.

Thus the early modern era was an age of empire. Within their borders, those empires mixed and mingled diverse peoples in a wide variety of ways. Those relationships represented a new stage in the globalization process and new arenas of cross-cultural encounter. The transformations they set in motion echo still in the twenty-first century.

SEEKING THE MAIN POINT

In what ways did European empires in the Americas resemble their Russian, Chinese, Mughal, and Ottoman counterparts, and in what respects were they different? Do you find the similarities or the differences more striking?

European Empires in the Americas

Among the early modern empires, those of Western Europe were distinctive because the conquered territories lay an ocean away from the imperial heartland, rather than adjacent to it. Following the breakthrough voyages of Columbus, the Spanish focused their empire-building efforts in the Caribbean and then, in the early sixteenth century, turned to the mainland, with stunning conquests of the powerful but fragile Aztec and Inca empires. Meanwhile, the Portuguese established themselves along the coast of present-day Brazil. In the early seventeenth century, the British, French, and Dutch launched colonial settlements along the eastern coast of North America. From these beginnings, Europeans extended their empires to encompass most of the Americas, at least nominally, by the mid-eighteenth century (see Map 13.1). It was a remarkable achievement. What had made it possible?

The European Advantage

■ Connection
What enabled Europeans to carve out huge empires an ocean away from their homelands?

Geography provides a starting point for explaining Europe's American empires. Countries on the Atlantic rim of Europe (Portugal, Spain, Britain, and France) were simply closer to the Americas than were any potential Asian competitors. Furthermore, the fixed winds of the Atlantic blew steadily in the same direction. Once these air currents were understood and mastered, they provided a far different maritime environment than the alternating monsoon winds of the Indian Ocean, in

A MAP OF TIME

1453	Ottoman conquest of Constantinople
1464–1591	Songhay Empire in West Africa
1480	Russia emerges from Mongol rule
1494	Treaty of Tordesillas divides the Americas between Spain and Portugal
1501	Safavid Empire established in Persia/Iran
1519–1521	Spanish conquest of Aztec Empire
1526	Mughal Empire established in India
1529	Ottoman siege of Vienna
1530s	First Portuguese plantations in Brazil
1532–1540	Spanish conquest of Inca Empire
1550	Russian expansion across Siberia begins
1565	Spanish takeover of Philippines begins
1607	Jamestown, Virginia: first permanent English settlement in Americas
1608	French colony established in Quebec
1680–1760	Chinese expansion into Inner Asia
1683	Second Ottoman siege of Vienna
After 1707	Fragmentation of Mughal Empire

which Asian powers had long operated. European innovations in mapmaking, navigation, sailing techniques, and ship design — building on earlier models from the Mediterranean, Indian Ocean, and Chinese regions — likewise enabled Europeans to penetrate the Atlantic Ocean. The enormously rich markets of the Indian Ocean world provided little incentive for its Chinese, Indian, or Muslim participants to venture much beyond their own waters.

Europeans, however, were powerfully motivated to do so. After 1200 or so, European elites were increasingly aware of their region's marginal position in the rich world of Eurasian commerce and were determined to gain access to that world. Once the Americas were discovered, windfalls of natural resources, including highly productive agricultural lands, drove further expansion, ultimately underpinning the long-term growth of the European economy into the nineteenth and twentieth centuries. Beyond these economic or ecological stimuli, rulers were driven by the enduring rivalries of competing states. The growing and relatively independent merchant class in a rapidly commercializing Europe sought direct access to Asian wealth

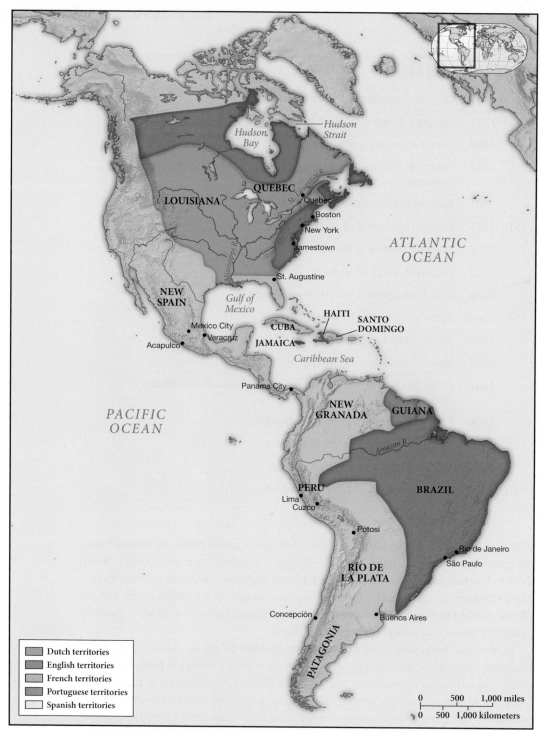

Map 13.1 European Colonial Empires in the Americas

By the beginning of the eighteenth century, European powers had laid claim to most of the Western Hemisphere. Their wars and rivalries during that century led to an expansion of Spanish and English claims, at the expense of the French.

to avoid the reliance on Muslim intermediaries that they found so distasteful. Impoverished nobles and commoners alike found opportunity for gaining wealth and status in the colonies. Missionaries and others were inspired by crusading zeal to enlarge the realm of Christendom. Persecuted minorities were in search of a new start in life. All of these compelling motives drove the relentlessly expanding imperial frontier in the Americas. Summarizing their intentions, one Spanish conquistador declared: "We came here to serve God and the King, and also to get rich."[2]

In carving out these empires, often against great odds and with great difficulty, Europeans nonetheless bore certain advantages, despite their distance from home. Their states and trading companies enabled the effective mobilization of both human and material resources. Their seafaring technology, built on Chinese and Islamic precedents, allowed them to cross the Atlantic with growing ease, transporting people and supplies across great distances. Their ironworking technology, gunpowder weapons, and horses initially had no parallel in the Americas, although many peoples subsequently acquired them.

Divisions within and between local societies provided allies for the determined European invaders. Various subject peoples of the Aztec Empire, for example, resented Mexica domination and willingly joined Hernán Cortés in the Spanish assault on that empire. In the final attack on the Aztec capital of Tenochtitlán, Cortés's forces contained fewer than 1,000 Spaniards and many times that number of Tlaxcalans, former subjects of the Aztecs. After their defeat, tens of thousands of Aztecs themselves joined Cortés as he carved out a Spanish Mesoamerican empire far larger than that of the Aztecs. (See Zooming In: Doña Marina, page 558.) Much of the Inca elite, according to a recent study, "actually welcomed the Spanish invaders as liberators and willingly settled down with them to share rule of Andean farmers and miners."[3] A violent dispute between two rival contenders for the Inca throne, the brothers Atahualpa and Huáscar, certainly helped the European invaders recruit allies to augment their own minimal forces. In short, Spanish military victories were not solely of their own making, but the product of alliances with local peoples, who supplied the bulk of the Europeans' conquering armies.

Perhaps the most significant of European advantages lay in their germs and diseases, with which Native Americans had no familiarity. Those diseases decimated society after society, sometimes in advance of the Europeans' actual arrival. In particular regions such as the Caribbean, Virginia, and New England, the rapid buildup of immigrant populations, coupled with the sharply diminished native numbers, allowed Europeans to actually outnumber local peoples within a few decades.

The Great Dying and the Little Ice Age

Whatever combination of factors explains the European acquisition of empires in the Americas, there is no doubting their global significance. Chief among the consequences was the demographic collapse of Native American societies. Although precise figures remain the subject of much debate, scholars generally agree that the

Doña Marina: Between Two Worlds

In her brief life, she was known variously as Malinal, Doña Marina, and La Malinche.[4] By whatever name, she was a woman who experienced the encounter of the Old World and the New in particularly intimate ways, even as she became a bridge between them. Born around 1505, Malinal was the daughter of an elite and cultured family in the borderlands between the Maya and Aztec cultures in what is now southern Mexico. Two dramatic events decisively shaped her life. The first occurred when her father died and her mother remarried, bearing a son to her new husband. To protect this boy's inheritance, Malinal's family sold her into slavery. Eventually, she came into the possession of a Maya chieftain in Tabasco on the Gulf of Mexico.

Here her second life-changing event took place in March 1519, when the Spanish conquistador Hernán Cortés landed his troops and inflicted a sharp military defeat on Tabasco. In the negotiations that followed, Tabasco authorities gave lavish gifts to the Spanish, including twenty women, one of whom was Malinal.

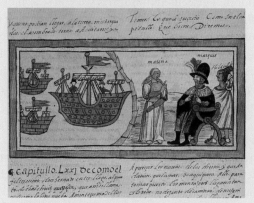

Doña Marina (center left) translating for Cortés.

Described by Bernal Díaz, one of Cortés's associates, as "good-looking, intelligent, and self-assured," the teenage Malinal soon found herself in service to Cortés himself. Since Spanish men were not supposed to touch non-Christian women, these newcomers were distributed among his officers, quickly baptized, and given Christian names. Thus Malinal became Doña Marina.

With a ready ear for languages and already fluent in Mayan and Nahuatl, the language of the Aztecs, Doña Marina soon picked up Spanish and quickly became indispensable to Cortés as an interpreter, cross-cultural broker, and strategist. She accompanied him on his march inland to the Aztec capital, Tenochtitlán, and on several occasions her language skills and cultural awareness allowed her to uncover spies and plots that might well have seriously impeded Cortés's defeat of the Aztec Empire. Díaz reported that "Doña Marina, who understood full well what was happening, told [Cortés] what

photo: Biblioteca Nacional Madrid/Giraudon/Bridgeman Images

pre-Columbian population of the Western Hemisphere was substantial, perhaps 60 to 80 million. The greatest concentrations of people lived in the Mesoamerican and Andean zones, which were dominated by the Aztec and Inca empires. Long isolation from the Afro-Eurasian world and the lack of most domesticated animals meant the absence of acquired immunities to Old World diseases such as smallpox, measles, typhus, influenza, malaria, and, later, yellow fever.

Therefore, when Native American peoples came into contact with these European and African diseases, they died in appalling numbers, in many cases losing up to 90 percent of the population. As one recent historian has noted, "It was as if the suffering these diseases had caused in Eurasia over the past millennia were concentrated into the span of decades."[5] The densely settled peoples of Caribbean islands

was going on." In the Aztec capital, where Cortés took the emperor Moctezuma captive, it fell to Doña Marina to persuade him to accept this humiliating position and surrender his wealth to the Spanish. Even Cortés, who was never very gracious with his praise for her, acknowledged that "after God, we owe this conquest of New Spain to Doña Marina." Aztecs soon came to see this young woman as the voice of Cortés, referring to her as La Malinche, a Spanish approximation of her original name. So paired did Cortés and La Malinche become in Aztec thinking that Cortés himself was often called "Malinche."

More than an interpreter for Cortés, Doña Marina also became his mistress and bore him a son. But after the initial conquest of Mexico was complete and he no longer needed her skills, Cortés married Doña Marina off to another Spanish conquistador, Juan Jaramillo, with whom she lived until her death, probably around 1530. Cortés did provide her with several pieces of land, one of which, ironically, had belonged to Moctezuma. Her son, however, was taken from her and raised in Spain.

In 1523, Doña Marina performed one final service for Cortés, accompanying him on a mission to Honduras to suppress a rebellion. There her personal life seemed to come full circle, for near her hometown she encountered her mother, who had sold her into slavery, and her half brother. Díaz reported that they "were very much afraid

of Doña Marina," thinking that they would surely be put to death by their now-powerful and well-connected relative. But in a replay of the biblical story of Joseph and his brothers, Doña Marina quickly reassured and forgave them, while granting them "many golden jewels and some clothes."

In the centuries since her death, Doña Marina has been highly controversial. For much of the colonial era, she was viewed positively as an ally of the Spanish. But after independence, some came to see her as a traitor to her own people, shunning her heritage and siding with the invaders. Still others have considered her as the mother of Mexico's mixed-race, or mestizo, culture. Should she be understood primarily as a victim or as a skillful survivor negotiating hard choices under difficult circumstances?

Whatever the judgments of later generations, Doña Marina herself seems to have made a clear choice to cast her lot with the Europeans. Even when Cortés had given her to another man, Doña Marina expressed no regret. According to Díaz, she declared, "Even if they were to make me mistress of all the provinces of New Spain, I would refuse the honor, for I would rather serve my husband and Cortés than anything else in the world."

Questions: How might you define the significance of Doña Marina's life? In what larger contexts might that life find a place?

---

virtually vanished within fifty years of Columbus's arrival. Central Mexico, with a population estimated at some 10 to 20 million before the Spanish conquest, declined to about 1 million by 1650. A native Nahuatl (nah-watl) account depicted the social breakdown that accompanied the smallpox pandemic: "A great many died from this plague, and many others died of hunger. They could not get up to search for food, and everyone else was too sick to care for them, so they starved to death in their beds."[6]

The situation was similar in Dutch and British territories of North America. A Dutch observer in New Netherland (later New York) reported in 1656 that "the Indians . . . affirm that before the arrival of the Christians, and before the small pox broke out amongst them, they were ten times as numerous as they are now, and that their population had been melted down by this disease, whereof nine-tenths of them have died."[7] To Governor Bradford of Plymouth colony (in present-day Massachusetts), such conditions represented the "good hand of God" at work, "sweeping away great multitudes of the natives . . . that he might make room for us."[8] Not until the late seventeenth century did native numbers begin to recuperate somewhat from this catastrophe, and even then, they did not recover everywhere.

As the Great Dying took hold in the Americas, it interacted with another natural phenomenon, this time one of genuinely global proportions. Known as the Little Ice Age, it was a period of unusually cool temperatures that spanned much of the early modern period, most prominently in the Northern Hemisphere. Scholars continue to debate its causes. Some have suggested a low point in sunspot activity, leading to less intense solar irradiation of the earth, while others have argued that the chief cause was volcanic eruptions, whose ash and gases blocked the sun's warming energy in the upper atmosphere. More recently, some scientists have linked the Little Ice Age to the demographic collapse in the Americas. The Great Dying, they argue, resulted in the desertion of large areas of Native American farmland and ended the traditional practices of forest management through burning in many regions. These changes sparked a resurgence of plant life, which in turn took large amounts of carbon dioxide, a greenhouse gas, out of the atmosphere, contributing to global cooling. Whatever the causes, shorter growing seasons and less hospitable weather conditions adversely affected food production in regions across the globe.

While the onset, duration, and effects of the Little Ice Age varied from region to region, the impact of a cooler climate reached its peak in many regions in the mid-seventeenth century, helping to spark what scholars term the General Crisis. Much of China, Europe, and North America experienced record or near-record cold winters during this period. Regions near the equator in the tropics and Southern Hemisphere also experienced extreme conditions and irregular rainfall, resulting, for instance, in the growth of the Sahara Desert. Wet, cold summers reduced harvests dramatically in Europe, while severe droughts ruined crops in many other regions, especially China, which suffered its worst years of drought in the previous five centuries between 1637 and 1641. Difficult weather conditions accentuated other stresses in societies, leading to widespread famines, epidemics, uprisings, and wars in which millions perished. Eurasia did not escape lightly from these stresses: the collapse of the Ming dynasty in China, nearly constant warfare in Europe, and civil war in Mughal India all occurred in the context of the General Crisis, which only fully subsided when more favorable weather patterns returned in the eighteenth century.

Nor were the Americas, already devastated by the Great Dying, spared the suffering that accompanied the Little Ice Age and the General Crisis of the seventeenth century. In central Mexico, heartland of the Aztec Empire and the center of Spanish colonial rule in the area, severe drought in the five years after 1639 sent the price of maize skyrocketing, left granaries empty and many people without water, and prompted an unsuccessful plot to declare Mexico's independence from Spain.

Continuing drought years in the decades that followed witnessed repeated public processions of the statue of Our Lady of Guadalupe, who had gained a reputation for producing rain. The Caribbean region during the 1640s experienced the opposite condition—torrential rains that accompanied more frequent El Niño weather patterns—which provided ideal conditions for the breeding of mosquitoes that carried both yellow fever and malaria. A Maya chronicle for 1648 noted, "There was bloody vomit and we began to die."[9]

Like the Great Dying, the General Crisis reminds us that climate often plays an important role in shaping human history. But it also reminds us that human activity—the importation of deadly diseases to the Americas, in this case—may also help shape the climate, and that this has been true long before the twenty-first century.

The Columbian Exchange

In sharply diminishing the population of the Americas, the Great Dying and the impact of the Little Ice Age created an acute labor shortage and certainly did make room for immigrant newcomers, both colonizing Europeans and enslaved Africans. Over the several centuries of the colonial era and beyond, various combinations of indigenous, European, and African peoples created entirely new societies in the Americas, largely replacing the many and varied cultures that had flourished before 1492. To those colonial societies, Europeans and Africans brought not only their germs and their people but also their plants and animals. Wheat, rice, sugarcane, grapes, and many garden vegetables and fruits, as well as numerous weeds, took hold in the Americas, where they transformed the landscape and made possible a recognizably European diet and way of life. Even more revolutionary were their animals—horses, pigs, cattle, goats, sheep—all of which were new to the Americas and multiplied spectacularly in an environment largely free of natural predators. These domesticated animals made possible the ranching economies and cowboy cultures of both North and South America. Horses also transformed many Native American societies, particularly in the North American West as settled farming peoples such

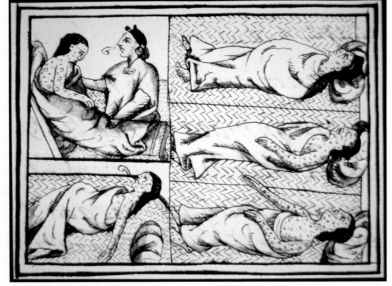

Disease and Death among the Aztecs
Smallpox, which accompanied the Spanish to the Americas, devastated native populations. This image, drawn by an Aztec artist and contained in the sixteenth-century *Florentine Codex*, illustrates the impact of the disease in Mesoamerica. (Private Collection/Peter Newark American Pictures/Bridgeman Images)

as the Pawnee abandoned their fields to hunt bison from horseback. In the process, women lost much of their earlier role as food producers as a male-dominated hunting and warrior culture emerged. Both environmentally and socially, these changes were nothing less than revolutionary.

■ Change
What large-scale trans-
formations did European
empires generate?

In the other direction, American food crops such as corn, potatoes, and cassava spread widely in the Eastern Hemisphere, where they provided the nutritional foundation for the immense population growth that became everywhere a hallmark of the modern era. In Europe, calories derived from corn and potatoes helped push human numbers from some 60 million in 1400 to 390 million in 1900. Those Amerindian crops later provided cheap and reasonably nutritious food for millions of industrial workers. Potatoes, especially, allowed Ireland's population to grow enormously and then condemned many of the Irish to starvation or emigration when an airborne fungus, also from the Americas, destroyed the crop in the mid-nineteenth century. In China, corn, peanuts, and especially sweet potatoes supplemented the traditional rice and wheat to sustain China's modern population explosion. By the early twentieth century, food plants of American origin represented about 20 percent of total Chinese food production. In Africa, corn took hold quickly and was used as a cheap food for the human cargoes of the transatlantic trade. Scholars have speculated that corn, together with peanuts and cassava, underwrote some of Africa's population growth and partially offset the population drain of the slave trade.

Beyond food crops, American stimulants such as tobacco and chocolate were soon used around the world. By the seventeenth century, how-to manuals instructed Chinese users on smoking techniques, and tobacco had become, in the words of one enamored Chinese poet, "the gentleman's companion, it warms my heart and leaves my mouth feeling like a divine furnace."[10] Tea from China and coffee from the Islamic world also spread globally, contributing to this worldwide biological exchange. Never before in human history had such a large-scale and consequential diffusion of plants and animals operated to remake the biological environment of the planet.

Furthermore, the societies that developed within the American colonies drove the processes of globalization and reshaped the world economy of the early modern era (see Chapter 14 for a more extended treatment). The silver mines of Mexico and Peru fueled both transatlantic and transpacific commerce, encouraged Spain's unsuccessful effort to dominate Europe, and enabled Europeans to buy the Chinese tea, silk, and porcelain that they valued so highly. The plantation owners of the tropical lowland regions needed workers and found them by the millions in Africa. The Atlantic slave trade, which brought these workers to the colonies, and the sugar and cotton trade, which distributed the fruits of their labor abroad, created a lasting link among Africa, Europe, and the Americas, while scattering peoples of African origin throughout the Western Hemisphere.

This enormous network of communication, migration, trade, disease, and the transfer of plants and animals, all generated by European colonial empires in the

Americas, has been dubbed the "Columbian exchange." It gave rise to something wholly new in world history: an interacting Atlantic world connecting four continents. Millions of years ago, the Eastern and Western hemispheres had physically drifted apart, and, ecologically speaking, they had remained largely apart. Now these two "old worlds" were joined, increasingly creating a single biological regime, a "new world" of global dimensions.

The long-term benefits of this Atlantic network were very unequally distributed. Western Europeans were clearly the dominant players in the Atlantic world, and their societies reaped the greatest rewards. Mountains of new information flooded into Europe, shaking up conventional understandings of the world and contributing to a revolutionary new way of thinking known as the Scientific Revolution. The wealth of the colonies—precious metals, natural resources, new food crops, slave labor, financial profits, colonial markets—provided one of the foundations on which Europe's Industrial Revolution was built. The colonies also provided an outlet for the rapidly growing population of European societies and represented an enormous extension of European civilization. In short, the colonial empires of the Americas greatly facilitated a changing global balance of power, which now thrust the previously marginal Western Europeans into an increasingly central and commanding role on the world stage. "Without a New World to deliver economic balance in the Old," concluded a prominent world historian, "Europe would have remained inferior, as ever, in wealth and power, to the great civilizations of Asia."[11]

Comparing Colonial Societies in the Americas

What the Europeans had encountered across the Atlantic was another "old world," but their actions surely gave rise to a "new world" in the Americas. Their colonial empires—Spanish, Portuguese, British, and French alike—did not simply conquer and govern established societies, but rather generated wholly new societies, born of the decimation of Native American populations and the introduction of European and African peoples, cultures, plants, and animals.

Furthermore, all the European rulers of these empires viewed their realms through the lens of the prevailing economic theory known as mercantilism. This view held that European governments served their countries' economic interests best by encouraging exports and accumulating bullion (precious metals such as silver and gold), believed to be the source of national prosperity. In this scheme of things, colonies provided closed markets for the manufactured goods of the "mother country" and, if they were lucky, supplied great quantities of bullion as well. Mercantilist thinking thus fueled European wars and colonial rivalries around the world in the early modern era. Particularly in Spanish America, however, it was a theory largely ignored or evaded in practice. Spain had few manufactured goods to sell, and piracy and smuggling allowed Spanish colonists to exchange goods with Spain's rivals.

But variations across the immense colonial world of the Western Hemisphere were at least as noticeable as these similarities. Some differences grew out of the societies of the colonizing power, such as the contrast between a semi-feudal and Catholic Spain and a more rapidly changing Protestant England. The kind of economy established in particular regions—settler-dominated agriculture, slave-based plantations, ranching, or mining—likewise influenced their development. So too did the character of the Native American cultures—the more densely populated and urbanized Mesoamerican and Andean civilizations differed greatly from the more sparsely populated rural villages of North America, for example.

Furthermore, women and men often experienced colonial intrusion in quite distinct ways. Beyond the common burdens of violent conquest, epidemic disease, and coerced labor, both Native American and enslaved African women had to cope with the additional demands made on them as females. Conquest was often accompanied by the transfer of women to the new colonial rulers. Cortés, for example, marked his alliance with the city of Tlaxcala (tlah-SKAH-lah) against the Aztecs by an exchange of gifts in which he received hundreds of female slaves and eight daughters of elite Tlaxcalan families, whom he distributed to his soldiers. And he commanded the Aztec ruler: "You are to deliver women with light skins, corn, chicken, eggs, and tortillas."[12]

Soon after conquest, many Spanish men married elite native women. It was a long-standing practice in Amerindian societies and was encouraged by both Spanish and indigenous male authorities as a means of cementing their new relationship. It was also advantageous for some of the women involved. One of Aztec emperor Moctezuma's daughters, who was mistress to Cortés and eventually married several other Spaniards, wound up with the largest landed estate in the valley of Mexico. Below this elite level of interaction, however, far more women experienced sexual violence and abuse. Rape accompanied conquest in many places, and dependent or enslaved women working under the control of European men frequently found themselves required to perform sexual services. This was tragedy and humiliation for native and enslaved men as well, for they were unable to protect their women from such abuse. Such variations in culture, policy, economy, and gender generated quite different colonial societies in several major regions of the Americas.

In the Lands of the Aztecs and the Incas

The Spanish conquest of the Aztec and Inca empires in the early sixteenth century gave Spain access to the most wealthy, urbanized, and densely populated regions of the Western Hemisphere. Within a century and well before the British had even begun their colonizing efforts in North America, the Spanish in Mexico and Peru had established nearly a dozen major cities; several impressive universities; hundreds of cathedrals, churches, and missions; an elaborate administrative bureaucracy; and a network of regulated international commerce.

The economic foundation for this emerging colonial society lay in commercial agriculture, much of it on large rural estates, and in silver and gold mining. In both

■ **Change**

What was the economic foundation of colonial rule in Mexico and Peru? How did it shape the kinds of societies that arose there?

cases, native peoples, rather than African slaves or European workers, provided most of the labor, despite their much-diminished numbers. Almost everywhere it was forced labor, often directly required by colonial authorities. In a legal system known as *encomienda*, the Spanish Crown granted to particular Spanish settlers a number of local native people from whom they could require labor, gold, or agricultural produce and to whom they owed "protection" and instruction in the Christian faith. It turned into an exploitative regime not far removed from slavery and was replaced by a similar system, *repartimiento*, with slightly more control by the Crown and Spanish officials. By the seventeenth century, the *hacienda* system had taken shape by which the owners of large estates directly employed native workers. With low wages, high taxes, and large debts to the landowners, the *peons* who worked these estates enjoyed little control over their lives or their livelihood.

On this economic base, a distinctive social order grew up, replicating something of the Spanish class and gender hierarchy while accommodating the racially and culturally different Indians and Africans as well as growing numbers of racially mixed people. At the top of this colonial society were the male Spanish settlers, who were politically and economically dominant and seeking to become a landed aristocracy. One Spanish official commented in 1619: "The Spaniards, from the able and rich to the humble and poor, all hold themselves to be lords and will not serve [do manual labor]."[13] Politically, they increasingly saw themselves not as colonials, but as residents of a Spanish kingdom, subject to the Spanish monarch, yet separate and distinct from Spain itself and deserving of a large measure of self-government. Therefore, they chafed under the heavy bureaucratic restrictions imposed by the Crown. "I obey but I do not enforce" was a slogan that reflected local authorities' resistance to orders from Spain.

But the Spanish minority, never more than 20 percent of the population, was itself a divided community. Descendants of the original conquistadores sought to protect their privileges against immigrant newcomers; Spaniards born in the Americas (*creoles*) resented the pretensions to superiority of those born in Spain (*peninsulares*); landowning Spaniards felt threatened by the growing wealth of commercial and mercantile groups practicing less prestigious occupations. Spanish missionaries and church authorities

Racial Mixing in Colonial Mexico

This eighteenth-century painting by the famous Zapotec artist Miguel Cabrera shows a Spanish man, a *mestiza* woman, and their child, who was labeled as *castiza*. By the twentieth century, such mixed-race people represented the majority of the population of Mexico, and cultural blending had become a central feature of the country's identity. (Museo de América, Madrid, Spain/Bridgeman Images)

were often sharply critical of how these settlers treated native peoples. While Spanish women shared the racial privileges of their husbands, they were clearly subordinate in gender terms, unable to hold public office and viewed as weak and in need of male protection. But they were also regarded as the "bearers of civilization," and through their capacity to produce legitimate children, they were the essential link for transmitting male wealth, honor, and status to future generations. This required strict control of their sexuality and a continuation of the Iberian obsession with "purity of blood." In Spain, that concern had focused on potential liaisons with Jews and Muslims; in the colonies, the alleged threat to female virtue derived from Native American and African men.

From a male viewpoint, the problem with Spanish women was that there were very few of them. This demographic fact led to the most distinctive feature of these new colonial societies in Mexico and Peru—the emergence of a *mestizo* (mehs-TEE-zoh), or mixed-race, population, initially the product of unions between Spanish men and Indian women. Rooted in the sexual imbalance among Spanish immigrants (seven men to one woman in early colonial Peru, for example), the emergence of a mestizo population was facilitated by the desire of many surviving Indian women for the relative security of life in a Spanish household, where they and their children would not be subject to the abuse and harsh demands made on native peoples. Over the 300 years of the colonial era, mestizo numbers grew substantially, becoming the majority of the population in Mexico sometime during the nineteenth century. Such mixed-race people were divided into dozens of separate groups known as *castas* (castes), based on their racial heritage and skin color.

Mestizos were largely Hispanic in culture, but Spaniards looked down on them during much of the colonial era, regarding them as illegitimate, for many were not born of "proper" marriages. Despite this attitude, their growing numbers and the economic usefulness of their men as artisans, clerks, supervisors of labor gangs, and lower-level officials in both church and state bureaucracies led to their recognition as a distinct social group. *Mestizas*, women of mixed racial background, worked as domestic servants or in their husbands' shops, wove cloth, and manufactured candles and cigars, in addition to performing domestic duties. A few became quite wealthy. An illiterate mestiza named Mencia Perez married successively two reasonably well-to-do Spanish men and upon their deaths took over their businesses, becoming in her own right a very rich woman by the 1590s. At that point, no one would have referred to her as a mestiza.[14] Particularly in Mexico, mestizo identity blurred the sense of sharp racial difference between Spanish and Indian peoples and became a major element in the identity of modern Mexico.

At the bottom of Mexican and Peruvian colonial societies were the indigenous peoples, known to Europeans as "Indians." Traumatized by the Great Dying, they were subject to gross abuse and exploitation as the primary labor force for the mines and estates of the Spanish Empire and were required to render tribute payments to their Spanish overlords. Their empires dismantled by Spanish conquest, their religions attacked by Spanish missionaries, and their diminished numbers forcibly relocated into larger settlements, many Indians gravitated toward the world of their conquerors. Many learned Spanish; converted to Christianity; moved to cities to work for wages; ate the meat of cows, chickens, and pigs; used plows and draft animals rather than traditional digging sticks; and took their many grievances to Spanish courts. Indian women endured some distinctive conditions as Spanish legal codes generally defined them as minors rather than responsible adults. As those codes took hold, Indian women were increasingly excluded from the courts or represented by their menfolk. This made it more difficult to maintain female property rights. In 1804, for example, a Maya legal petition identified eight men and ten women from a particular family as owners of a piece of land, but the Spanish translation omitted the women's names altogether.[15]

But much that was indigenous persisted. At the local level, Indian male authorities retained a measure of autonomy, and traditional markets operated regularly. Both Andean and Maya women continued to leave personal property to their female descendants. Maize, beans, and squash persisted as the major elements of Indian diets in Mexico. Christian saints in many places blended easily with specialized indigenous gods, while belief in magic, folk medicine, and communion with the dead remained strong. Memories of the past also endured. The Tupac Amaru revolt in Peru during 1780–1781 was made in the name of the last independent Inca emperor. In that revolt, the wife of the leader, Micaela Bastidas, was referred to as La Coya, the female Inca, evoking the parallel hierarchies of male and female officials who had earlier governed the Inca Empire (see Chapter 12, pages 528–29).

Thus Spaniards, mestizos, and Indians represented the major social categories in the colonial lands of what had been the Inca and Aztec empires, while African slaves and freemen were less numerous than elsewhere in the Americas. Despite the sharp divisions among these groups, some movement was possible. Indians who acquired an education, wealth, and some European culture might "pass" as mestizo. Likewise, more fortunate mestizo families might be accepted as Spaniards over time. Colonial Spanish America was a vast laboratory of ethnic mixing and cultural change. It was dominated by Europeans, to be sure, but with a rather more fluid and culturally blended society than in the racially rigid colonies of British North America.

Colonies of Sugar

Another and quite different kind of colonial society emerged in the lowland areas of Brazil, ruled by Portugal, and in the Spanish, British, French, and Dutch colonies in the Caribbean. These regions lacked the great civilizations of Mexico and Peru. Nor did they provide much mineral wealth until the Brazilian gold rush of the 1690s and the discovery of diamonds a little later. Still, Europeans found a very profitable substitute in sugar, which was much in demand in Europe, where it was used as a medicine, a spice, a sweetener, a preservative, and in sculptured forms as a decoration that indicated high status. Although commercial agriculture in the

Spanish Empire served a domestic market in its towns and mining camps, these sugar-based colonies produced almost exclusively for export, while importing their food and other necessities.

Large-scale sugar production had been pioneered by Arabs, who had introduced it in the Mediterranean. Europeans learned the technique and transferred it to their Atlantic island possessions and then to the Americas. For a century (1570–1670), Portuguese planters along the northeast coast of Brazil dominated the world market for sugar. Then the British, French, and Dutch turned their Caribbean territories into highly productive sugar-producing colonies, breaking the Portuguese and Brazilian monopoly.

Sugar decisively transformed Brazil and the Caribbean. Its production, which involved both growing the sugarcane and processing it into usable sugar, was very labor-intensive and could most profitably occur in a large-scale, almost industrial setting. It was perhaps the first modern industry in that it produced for an international and mass market, using capital and expertise from Europe, with production facilities located in the Americas. However, its most characteristic feature—the massive use of slave labor—was an ancient practice. In the absence of a Native American population, which had been almost totally wiped out in the Caribbean or had fled inland in Brazil, European sugarcane planters turned to Africa and the Atlantic slave trade for an alternative workforce. The vast majority of the African captives transported across the Atlantic, some 80 percent or more, ended up in Brazil and the Caribbean. (See Chapter 14 for a more extensive description of the Atlantic slave trade.)

Slaves worked on sugar-producing estates in horrendous conditions. The heat and fire from the cauldrons, which turned raw sugarcane into crystallized sugar, reminded many visitors of scenes from Hell. These conditions, combined with disease, generated a high death rate, perhaps 5 to 10 percent per year, which required plantation owners to constantly import fresh slaves. A Jesuit observer in 1580 aptly summarized the situation: "The work is great and many die."[16]

More male slaves than female slaves were imported from Africa into the sugar economies of the Americas, leading to major and persistent gender imbalances. Nonetheless, female slaves did play distinctive roles in these societies. Women made up about half of the field gangs that did the heavy work of planting and harvesting sugarcane. They were subject to the same brutal punishments and received the same rations as their male counterparts, though they were seldom permitted to undertake the more skilled labor inside the sugar mills. Women who worked in urban areas, mostly for white female owners, did domestic chores and were often hired out as laborers in various homes, shops, laundries, inns, and brothels. Discouraged from establishing stable families, women had to endure, often alone, the wrenching separation from their children that occurred when they were sold. Mary Prince, a Caribbean slave who wrote a brief account of her life, recalled the pain of families torn apart: "The great God above alone knows the thoughts of the poor slave's heart, and the bitter pains which follow such separations as these. All that we love taken away from us—oh, it is sad, sad! and sore to be borne!"[17]

■ **Comparison**

How did the plantation societies of Brazil and the Caribbean differ from those of southern colonies in British North America?

The extensive use of African slave labor gave these plantation colonies a very different ethnic and racial makeup than that of highland Spanish America, as the Snapshot on page 570 indicates. Thus, after three centuries of colonial rule, a substantial majority of Brazil's population was either partially or wholly of African descent. In the French Caribbean colony of Haiti in 1790, the corresponding figure was 93 percent.

As in Spanish America, a considerable amount of racial mixing took place in Brazil. Cross-racial unions accounted for only about 10 percent of all marriages in Brazil, but the use of concubines and informal liaisons among Indians, Africans, and Portuguese produced a substantial mixed-race population. From their ranks derived much of the urban skilled workforce and many of the supervisors in the sugar industry. *Mulattoes*, the product of Portuguese-African unions, predominated, but as many as forty separate and named groups, each indicating a different racial mixture, emerged in colonial Brazil.

The plantation complex of the Americas, based on African slavery, extended beyond the Caribbean and Brazil to encompass the southern colonies of British North America, where tobacco, cotton, rice, and indigo were major crops, but the social outcomes of these plantation colonies were quite different from those farther south. Because European women had joined the colonial migration to North

Plantation Life in the Caribbean
This painting from 1823 shows the use of slave labor on a plantation in Antigua, a British-ruled island in the Caribbean. Notice the overseer with a whip supervising the tilling and planting of the field. (*Breaking Up the Land, from Ten Views in the Island of Antigua, 1823, color engraving by William Clark [fl. 1823]/British Library, London, UK/© British Library Board. All Rights Reserved/Bridgeman Images*)

SNAPSHOT   Ethnic Composition of Colonial Societies
in Latin America (1825)[18]

	Highland Spanish America	Portuguese America (Brazil)
Europeans	18.2 percent	23.4 percent
Mixed-race	28.3 percent	17.8 percent
Africans	11.9 percent	49.8 percent
Native Americans	41.7 percent	9.1 percent

America at an early date, these colonies experienced less racial mixing and certainly demonstrated less willingness to recognize the offspring of such unions and accord them a place in society. A sharply defined racial system (with black Africans, "red" Native Americans, and white Europeans) evolved in North America, whereas both Portuguese and Spanish colonies acknowledged a wide variety of mixed-race groups.

Slavery too was different in North America than in the sugar colonies. By 1750 or so, slaves in what became the United States proved able to reproduce themselves, and by the time of the Civil War almost all North American slaves had been born in the New World. That was never the case in Latin America, where large-scale importation of new slaves continued well into the nineteenth century. Nonetheless, many more slaves were voluntarily set free by their owners in Brazil than in North America, and free blacks and mulattoes in Brazil had more economic opportunities than did their counterparts in the United States. At least a few among them found positions as political leaders, scholars, musicians, writers, and artists. Some were even hired as slave catchers.

Does this mean, then, that racism was absent in colonial Brazil? Certainly not, but it was different from racism in North America. For one thing, in North America, any African ancestry, no matter how small or distant, made a person "black"; in Brazil, a person of African and non-African ancestry was considered not black, but some other mixed-race category. Racial prejudice surely persisted, for white characteristics were prized more highly than black features, and people regarded as white had enormously greater privileges and opportunities than others. Nevertheless, skin color in Brazil, and in Latin America generally, was only one criterion of class status, and the perception of color changed with the educational or economic standing of individuals. A light-skinned mulatto who had acquired some wealth or education might well pass as a white. One curious visitor to Brazil was surprised to find a darker-skinned man serving as a local official. "Isn't the governor a mulatto?" inquired the visitor. "He was, but he isn't any more," was the reply. "How can a governor be a mulatto?"[19]

Settler Colonies in North America

Yet another distinctive type of colonial society emerged in the northern British colonies of New England, New York, and Pennsylvania. Because the British were the last of the European powers to establish a colonial presence in the Americas, a full century after Spain, they found that "only the dregs were left."[20] The lands they acquired were widely regarded in Europe as the unpromising leftovers of the New World, lacking the obvious wealth and sophisticated cultures of the Spanish possessions. Until at least the eighteenth century, these British colonies remained far less prominent on the world stage than those of Spain or Portugal.

The British settlers came from a more rapidly changing society than did those from an ardently Catholic, semi-feudal, authoritarian Spain. When Britain launched its colonial ventures in the seventeenth century, it had already experienced considerable conflict between Catholics and Protestants, the rise of a merchant capitalist class distinct from the nobility, and the emergence of Parliament as a check on the authority of kings. Although they brought much of their English culture with them, many of the British settlers—Puritans in Massachusetts and Quakers in Pennsylvania, for example—sought to escape aspects of an old European society rather than to re-create it, as was the case for most Spanish and Portuguese colonists. The easy availability of land and the outsider status of many British settlers made it even more difficult to follow the Spanish or Portuguese colonial pattern of sharp class hierarchies, large rural estates, and dependent laborers.

Thus men in Puritan New England became independent heads of family farms, a world away from Old England, where most land was owned by nobles and gentry and worked by servants, tenants, and paid laborers. But if men escaped the class restrictions of the old country, women were less able to avoid its gender limitations. While Puritan Christianity extolled the family and a woman's role as wife and mother, it reinforced largely unlimited male authority. "Since he is thy Husband," declared Boston minister Benjamin Wadsworth in 1712 to the colony's women, "God has made him the Head and set him above thee."[21] Women were prosecuted for the crime of "fornication" far more often than their male companions; the inheritance of daughters was substantially less than that of sons; few girls attended school; and while women were the majority of church members, they could never become ministers.

Furthermore, British settlers were far more numerous than their Spanish counterparts, outnumbering them five to one by 1750. This disparity was the most obvious distinguishing feature of the New England and middle Atlantic colonies. By the time of the American Revolution, some 90 percent or more of these colonies' populations were Europeans. Devastating diseases and a highly aggressive military policy had largely cleared the colonies of Native Americans, and their numbers, which were far smaller to start with than those of their Mesoamerican and Andean counterparts, did not rebound in subsequent centuries as they did in the lands of the Aztecs and the Incas. Moreover, slaves were not needed in an agricultural economy

■ **Comparison**

What distinguished the British settler colonies of North America from their counterparts in Latin America?

dominated by numerous small-scale independent farmers working their own land, although elite families, especially in urban areas, sometimes employed household slaves. These were almost pure settler colonies, without the racial mixing that was so prominent in Spanish and Portuguese territories.

Other differences likewise emerged. A largely Protestant England was far less interested in spreading Christianity among the remaining native peoples than were the large and well-funded missionary societies of Catholic Spain. Although religion loomed large in the North American colonies, the church and colonial state were not so intimately connected as they were in Latin America. The Protestant emphasis on reading the Bible for oneself led to a much greater mass literacy than in Latin America, where three centuries of church education still left some 95 percent of the population illiterate at independence. By contrast, well over 75 percent of white males in British North America were literate by the 1770s, although women's literacy rates were somewhat lower. Furthermore, British settler colonies evolved traditions of local self-government more extensively than in Latin America. Preferring to rely on joint stock companies or wealthy individuals operating under a royal charter, Britain had nothing resembling the elaborate imperial bureaucracy that governed Spanish colonies. For much of the seventeenth century, a prolonged power struggle between the English king and Parliament meant that the British government paid little attention to the internal affairs of the colonies. Therefore, elected colonial assemblies, seeing themselves as little parliaments defending "the rights of Englishmen," vigorously contested the prerogatives of royal governors sent to administer their affairs.

The grand irony of the modern history of the Americas lay in the reversal of long-established relationships between the northern and southern continents. For thousands of years, the major centers of wealth, power, commerce, and innovation lay in Mesoamerica and the Andes. That pattern continued for much of the colonial era, as the Spanish and Portuguese colonies seemed far more prosperous and successful than their British or French counterparts in North America. In the nineteenth and twentieth centuries, however, the balance shifted. What had once been the "dregs" of the colonial world became the United States, more politically stable, more democratic, more economically successful, and more internationally powerful than a divided, unstable, and much less prosperous Latin America.

SUMMING UP SO FAR

In what ways might European empire building in the Americas be understood as a single phenomenon? And in what respects should it be viewed as a set of distinct and separate processes?

The Steppes and Siberia: The Making of a Russian Empire

At the same time as Western Europeans were building their empires in the Americas, the Russian Empire, which subsequently became the world's largest state, was beginning to take shape. When Columbus crossed the Atlantic, a small Russian state centered on the city of Moscow was emerging from two centuries of Mongol rule. That state soon conquered a number of neighboring Russian-speaking cities and incorporated them into its expanding territory. Located on the remote, cold, and heavily forested eastern fringe of Christendom, it was perhaps an unlikely candidate for constructing one of the great empires of the modern era. And yet, over the next three centuries, it did precisely that, extending Russian domination over the vast tundra, forests, and grasslands of northern Asia that lay to the south and east of Moscow, all the way to the Pacific Ocean. Furthermore, Russians also expanded westward, bringing numerous Poles, Germans, Ukrainians, Belorussians, and Baltic peoples into the Russian Empire.

Russian attention was drawn first to the grasslands south and east of the Russian heartland, an area long inhabited by various nomadic pastoral peoples, who were organized into feuding tribes and clans and adjusting to the recent disappearance of the Mongol Empire. From the viewpoint of the emerging Russian state, the problem was security because these pastoral peoples, like the Mongols before them, frequently raided their agricultural Russian neighbors and sold many into slavery. To the east, across the vast expanse of Siberia, Russian motives were quite different, for the scattered peoples of its endless forests and tundra posed no threat to Russia. Numbering only some 220,000 in the seventeenth century and speaking more than 100 languages, they were mostly hunting, gathering, and herding people, living in small-scale societies and largely without access to gunpowder weapons. What drew the Russians across Siberia was opportunity—primarily the "soft gold" of fur-bearing animals, whose pelts were in great demand on the world market.

Whatever motives drove it, this enormous Russian Empire took shape in the three centuries between 1500 and 1800 (see Map 13.2). A growing line of wooden forts offered protection to frontier towns and trading centers as well as to mounting numbers of Russian farmers. Empire building was an extended process, involving the Russian state and its officials as well as a variety of private interests—merchants, hunters, peasants, churchmen, exiles, criminals, and adventurers. For the Russian migrants to these new eastern lands, the empire offered "economic and social improvements over what they had known at home—from more and better land to fewer lords and officials."[22] Political leaders and educated Russians generally defined the empire in grander terms: defending Russian frontiers; enhancing the power of the Russian state; and bringing Christianity, civilization, and enlightenment to savages. But what did that empire mean to those on its receiving end?

Experiencing the Russian Empire

First, of course, empire meant conquest. Although resistance was frequent, especially from nomadic peoples, in the long run Russian military might, based in modern weaponry and the organizational capacity of a state, brought both the steppes and Siberia under Russian control. Everywhere Russian authorities demanded an oath of allegiance by which native peoples swore "eternal submission to the grand tsar,"

■ Description
What motivated Russian empire building?

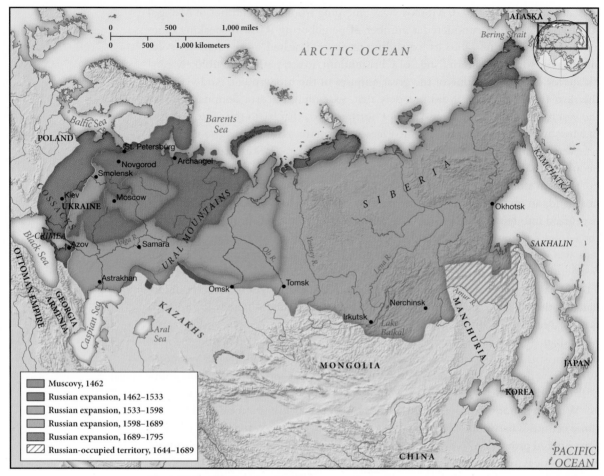

Map 13.2   The Russian Empire

From its beginnings as a small principality under Mongol control, Moscow became the center of a vast Russian Empire during the early modern era.

the monarch of the Russian Empire. They also demanded *yasak*, or "tribute," paid in cash or in kind. In Siberia, this meant enormous quantities of furs, especially the extremely valuable sable, which Siberian peoples were compelled to produce. As in the Americas, devastating epidemics accompanied conquest, particularly in the more remote regions of Siberia, where local people had little immunity to smallpox or measles. Also accompanying conquest was an intermittent pressure to convert to Christianity. Tax breaks, exemptions from paying tribute, and the promise of land or cash provided incentives for conversion, while the destruction of many mosques and the forced resettlement of Muslims added to the pressures. Yet the Russian state did not pursue conversion with the single-minded intensity that Spanish authorities exercised in Latin America, particularly if missionary activity threatened political and social stability. The empress Catherine the Great, for example, established religious tolerance for Muslims in the late eighteenth century and created a state agency to oversee Muslim affairs.

The most profoundly transforming feature of the Russian Empire was the influx of Russian settlers, whose numbers by the end of the eighteenth century had overwhelmed native peoples, giving their lands a distinctively Russian character. By 1720, some 700,000 Russians lived in Siberia, thus reducing the native Siberians to 30 percent of the total population, a proportion that dropped to 14 percent in the nineteenth century. The loss of hunting grounds and pasturelands to Russian agricultural settlers undermined long-standing economies and rendered local people dependent on Russian markets for grain, sugar, tea, tobacco, and alcohol. Pressures to encourage pastoralists to abandon their nomadic ways included the requirement to pay fees and to obtain permission to cross agricultural lands. Kazakh herders responded with outrage: "The grass and the water belong to Heaven, and why should we pay any fees?"[23] Intermarriage, prostitution, and sexual abuse resulted in some mixed-race offspring, but these were generally absorbed as Russians rather than identified as distinctive communities, as in Latin America.

Over the course of three centuries, both Siberia and the steppes were incorporated into the Russian state. Their native peoples were not driven into reservations or eradicated as in the Americas. Many of them, though, were Russified, adopting the Russian language and converting to Christianity, even as their traditional ways of life—hunting and herding—were much disrupted. The Russian Empire represented the final triumph of an agrarian civilization over the hunting societies of Siberia and over the pastoral peoples of the grasslands.

■ **Change**
How did the Russian Empire transform the life of its conquered people and of the Russian homeland itself?

The Cossacks
In the vanguard of Russian expansion across Siberia were the Cossacks, bands of fiercely independent warriors consisting of peasants who had escaped serfdom as well as criminals and other adventurers. Here the sixteenth-century Cossack warrior Yermak is shown leading his troops. (De Agostini Picture Library/akg-images)

Russians and Empire

If the empire transformed the conquered peoples, it also fundamentally changed Russia itself. Within an increasingly multiethnic empire, Russians diminished as a proportion of the overall population, although they remained politically dominant. Among the growing number of non-Russians in the empire, Slavic-speaking Ukrainians and Belorussians predominated, while the vast territories of Siberia and the steppes housed numerous separate peoples, but with quite small populations.[24] The wealth of empire—rich agricultural lands, valuable furs, mineral deposits—played a major role in making Russia one of the great powers of Europe by the eighteenth century, and it has enjoyed that position ever since.

Unlike its expansion to the east, Russia's westward movement occurred in the context of military rivalries with the major powers of the region—the Ottoman Empire, Poland, Sweden, Lithuania, Prussia, and Austria. During the late seventeenth and eighteenth centuries, Russia acquired substantial territories in the Baltic region, Poland, and Ukraine. This contact with Europe also fostered an awareness of Russia's backwardness relative to Europe and prompted an extensive program of westernization, particularly under the leadership of Peter the Great (r. 1689–1725). His massive efforts included vast administrative changes, the enlargement and modernization of Russian military forces, a new educational system for the sons of noblemen, and dozens of manufacturing enterprises. Russian nobles were instructed to dress in European styles and to shave their sacred and much-revered beards. The newly created capital city of St. Petersburg was to be Russia's "window on the West." One of Peter's successors, Catherine the Great (r. 1762–1796), followed up with further efforts to Europeanize Russian cultural and intellectual life, viewing herself as part of the European Enlightenment. Thus Russians were the first of many peoples to measure themselves against the West and to mount major "catch-up" efforts.

But this European-oriented and Christian state had also become an Asian power, bumping up against China, India, Persia, and the Ottoman Empire. It was on the front lines of the encounter between Christendom and the world of Islam. This straddling of Asia and Europe was the source of a long-standing identity problem that has troubled educated Russians for 300 years. Was Russia a backward European country, destined to follow the lead of more highly developed Western European societies? Or was it different, uniquely Slavic or even Asian, shaped by its Mongol legacy and its status as an Asian power? It is a question that Russians have not completely answered even in the twenty-first century. Either way, the very size of that empire, bordering on virtually all of the great agrarian civilizations of outer Eurasia, turned Russia, like many empires before it, into a highly militarized state, "a society organized for continuous war," according to one scholar.[25] It also reinforced the highly autocratic character of the Russian Empire because such a huge state arguably required a powerful monarchy to hold its vast domains and highly diverse peoples together.

Clearly, the Russians had created an empire, similar to those of Western Europe in terms of conquest, settlement, exploitation, religious conversion, and feelings of superiority. Nonetheless, the Russians had acquired their empire under different circumstances than did the Western Europeans. The Spanish and the British had conquered and colonized the New World, an ocean away and wholly unknown to them before 1492. They acquired those empires only after establishing themselves as distinct European states. The Russians, on the other hand, absorbed adjacent territories, and they did so at the same time that a modern Russian state was taking shape. "The British had an empire," wrote historian Geoffrey Hosking. "Russia *was* an empire."[26] Perhaps this helps explain the unique longevity of the Russian Empire. Whereas the Spanish, Portuguese, and British colonies in the Americas long ago achieved independence, the Russian Empire remained intact until the collapse of the Soviet Union in 1991. So thorough was Russian colonization that Siberia and much of the steppes remain still an integral part of the Russian state

Asian Empires

Even as West Europeans were building their empires in the Americas and the Russians were expanding across Siberia, other imperial projects were likewise under way. The Chinese pushed deep into central Eurasia; Turko-Mongol invaders from Central Asia created the Mughal Empire, bringing much of Hindu South Asia within a single Muslim-ruled political system; and the Ottoman Empire brought Muslim rule to a largely Christian population in southeastern Europe and Turkish rule to largely Arab populations in North Africa and the Middle East. None of these empires had the global reach or worldwide impact of Europe's American colonies; they were regional rather than global in scope. Nor did they have the same devastating and transforming impact on their conquered peoples, for those peoples were not being exposed to new diseases. Nothing remotely approaching the catastrophic population collapse of Native American peoples occurred in these Asian empires. Moreover, the process of building these empires did not transform the imperial homeland as fundamentally as did the wealth of the Americas and to a lesser extent Siberia for European imperial powers. Nonetheless, these expanding Asian empires reflected the energies and vitality of their respective civilizations in the early modern era, and they gave rise to profoundly important cross-cultural encounters, with legacies that echoed for many centuries.

Making China an Empire

In the fifteenth century, China had declined an opportunity to construct a maritime empire in the Indian Ocean, as Zheng He's massive fleet was withdrawn and left to wither away (see Chapter 12, pages 507–9). In the seventeenth and eighteenth centuries, however, China built another kind of empire on its northern and western frontiers that vastly enlarged the territorial size of the country and incorporated a number of non-Chinese peoples. Undertaking this enormous project of imperial expansion was China's Qing, or Manchu, dynasty (1644–1912). Strangely enough, the Qing dynasty was itself of foreign and nomadic origin, hailing from Manchuria, north of the Great Wall. Having conquered China, the Qing rulers sought to maintain their ethnic distinctiveness by forbidding intermarriage between themselves and the Chinese. Nonetheless, their ruling elites also mastered the Chinese language and Confucian teachings and used Chinese bureaucratic techniques to govern the empire. Perhaps because they were foreigners, Qing rulers went to great lengths to reinforce traditional Confucian gender roles, honoring men who were loyal sons, officials, and philanthropists and women who demonstrated loyalty to their spouses by resisting rape or remaining chaste as widows.

For many centuries, the Chinese had interacted with the nomadic peoples, who inhabited the dry and lightly populated regions now known as Mongolia, Xinjiang, and Tibet. Trade, tribute, and warfare ensured that these ecologically and culturally different worlds were well known to each other, quite unlike the New World "discoveries" of the Europeans. Chinese authority in the area had been intermittent and actively resisted. Then, in the early modern era, Qing dynasty China undertook an eighty-year military effort (1680–1760) that brought these huge regions solidly under Chinese control. It was largely security concerns, rather than economic need, that motivated this aggressive posture. During the late seventeenth century, the creation of a substantial state among the western Mongols, known as the Zunghars, revived Chinese memories of an earlier Mongol conquest. As in so many other cases, Chinese expansion was viewed as a defensive necessity. The eastward movement of the Russian Empire likewise appeared potentially threatening, but this

■ Description

What were the distinctive features of Chinese empire building in the early modern era?

Chinese Conquests in Central Asia
Painted by the Chinese artist Jin Tingbiao in the mid-eighteenth century, this image portrays Machang, a leading warrior involved in the westward extension of the Chinese empire. The painting was commissioned by the emperor himself and served to honor the bravery of Machang. (Pictures from History/CPA Media)

danger was resolved diplomatically, rather than militarily, in the Treaty of Nerchinsk (1689), which marked the boundary between Russia and China.

Although undertaken by the non-Chinese Manchus, the Qing dynasty campaigns against the Mongols marked the evolution of China into a Central Asian empire. The Chinese, however, have seldom thought of themselves as an imperial power. Rather, they spoke of the "unification" of the peoples of central Eurasia within a Chinese state. Nonetheless, historians have seen many similarities between Chinese expansion and other cases of early modern empire building, while noting some clear differences as well.

Clearly the Qing dynasty takeover of central Eurasia was a conquest, making use of China's more powerful military technology and greater resources. Furthermore, the area was ruled separately from the rest of China through a new office called the Court of Colonial Affairs. Like other colonial powers, the Chinese made active use of local notables—Mongol aristocrats, Muslim officials, Buddhist leaders—as they attempted to govern the region as inexpensively as possible. Sometimes these native officials abused their authority, demanding extra taxes or labor service from local people and thus earning their hostility. In places, those officials imitated Chinese ways by wearing peacock feathers, decorating their hats with gold buttons, or adopting a Manchu hairstyle that was much resented by many Chinese who were forced to wear it.

More generally, however, Chinese or Qing officials did not seek to assimilate local people into Chinese culture and showed considerable respect for the Mongolian, Tibetan, and Muslim cultures of the region. People of noble rank, Buddhist monks, and those associated with monasteries were excused from the taxes and labor service required of ordinary people. Nor was the area flooded with Chinese settlers. In parts of Mongolia, for example, Qing authorities sharply restricted the entry of Chinese merchants and other immigrants in an effort to preserve the area as a source of recruitment for the Chinese military. They feared that the "soft" and civilized Chinese ways might erode the fighting spirit of the Mongols.

The long-term significance of this new Chinese imperial state was tremendous. It greatly expanded the territory of China and added a small but important minority of non-Chinese people to the empire's vast population (see Map 13.3). The borders of contemporary China are essentially those created during the Qing dynasty. Some of those peoples, particularly those in Tibet and Xinjiang, have retained their older identities and in recent decades have actively sought greater autonomy or even independence from China.

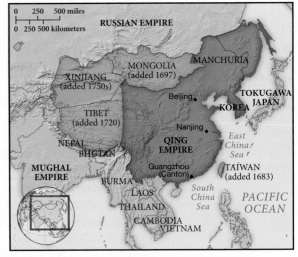

Map 13.3   China's Qing Dynasty Empire

After many centuries of intermittent expansion into Central Asia, the Qing dynasty brought this vast region firmly within the Chinese empire.

Even more important, Chinese conquests, together with the expansion of the Russian Empire, utterly transformed Central Asia. For centuries, that region had been the cosmopolitan crossroads of Eurasia, hosting the Silk Road trading network, welcoming all the major world religions, and generating an enduring encounter between the nomads of the steppes and the farmers of settled agricultural regions. Now under Russian or Chinese rule, it became the backward and impoverished region known to nineteenth- and twentieth-century observers. Land-based commerce across Eurasia increasingly took a backseat to oceanic trade. Indebted Mongolian nobles lost their land to Chinese merchants, while nomads, no longer able to herd their animals freely, fled to urban areas, where many were reduced to begging. The incorporation of inner Eurasia into the Russian and Chinese empires "eliminated permanently as a major actor on the historical stage the nomadic pastoralists, who had been the strongest alternative to settled agricultural society since the second millennium B.C.E."[27] It was the end of a long era.

Muslims and Hindus in the Mughal Empire

If the creation of a Chinese imperial state in the early modern era provoked a final clash of nomadic pastoralists and settled farmers, India's Mughal Empire hosted a different kind of encounter—a further phase in the long interaction of Islamic and Hindu cultures in South Asia. That empire was the product of Central Asian warriors, who were Muslims in religion and Turkic in culture and who claimed descent from Chinggis Khan and Timur (see Chapters 11 and 12). Their brutal conquests in the sixteenth century provided India with a rare period of relative political unity (1526–1707), as Mughal emperors exercised a fragile control over a diverse and fragmented subcontinent, which had long been divided into a bewildering variety of small states, principalities, tribes, castes, sects, and ethno-linguistic groups.

■ **Change**
How did Mughal attitudes and policies toward Hindus change from the time of Akbar to that of Aurangzeb?

The central division within Mughal India was religious. The ruling dynasty and perhaps 20 percent of the population were Muslims; most of the rest practiced some form of Hinduism. Mughal India's most famous emperor, Akbar (r. 1556–1605), clearly recognized this fundamental reality and acted deliberately to accommodate the Hindu majority. After conquering the warrior-based and Hindu Rajputs of northwestern India, Akbar married several of their princesses but did not require them to convert to Islam. He incorporated a substantial number of Hindus into the political-military elite of the empire and supported the building of Hindu temples as well as mosques, palaces, and forts. (See Working with Evidence, Source 13.1, page 590.) But Akbar acted to soften some Hindu restrictions on women, encouraging the remarriage of widows, discouraging child marriages and *sati* (the practice in which a widow followed her husband to death by throwing herself on his funeral pyre), and persuading merchants to set aside special market days for women so as to moderate their seclusion in the home. Nur Jahan, the twentieth and favorite wife of Emperor Jahangir (r. 1605–1627), was widely regarded as the power behind the throne of her alcohol- and opium-addicted husband, giving audiences to visiting dignitaries, consulting with ministers, and even having a coin issued in her name.

In directly religious matters, Akbar imposed a policy of toleration, deliberately restraining the more militantly Islamic *ulama* (religious scholars) and removing the special tax (*jizya*) on non-Muslims. He constructed a special House of Worship where he presided over intellectual discussion with representatives of many religions — Muslim, Hindu, Christian, Buddhist, Jewish, Jain, and Zoroastrian. His son Jahangir wrote proudly of his father: "He associated with the good of every race and creed and persuasion. . . . The professors of various faiths had room in the broad expanse of his incomparable sway."[28] Akbar went so far as to create his own state cult, a religious faith aimed at the Mughal elite, drawing on Islam, Hinduism, and Zoroastrianism and emphasizing loyalty to the emperor himself. The overall style of the Mughal Empire was that of a blended elite culture in which both Hindus and various Muslim groups could feel comfortable. Thus Persian artists and writers were welcomed into the empire, and the Hindu epic *Ramayana* was translated into Persian, while various Persian classics appeared in Hindi and Sanskrit. In short, Akbar and his immediate successors downplayed a distinctly Islamic identity for the Mughal Empire in favor of a cosmopolitan and hybrid Indian-Persian-Turkic culture.

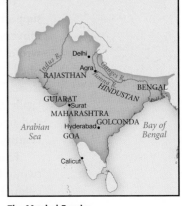

The Mughal Empire

Such policies fostered sharp opposition among some Muslims. The philosopher Shaykh Ahmad Sirhindi (1564–1624), claiming to be a "renewer" of authentic Islam in his time, strongly objected to this cultural synthesis. The worship of saints, the sacrifice of animals, and support for Hindu religious festivals all represented impure intrusions of Sufi Islam or Hinduism that needed to be rooted out. In Sirhindi's view, it was primarily women who had introduced these deviations: "Because of their utter stupidity women pray to stones and idols and ask for their help. This practice is common, especially when small pox strikes, and there is hardly a woman who is not involved in this polytheistic practice. Women participate in the holidays of Hindus and Jews. They celebrate Diwali [a major Hindu festival] and send their sisters and daughters presents similar to those exchanged by the infidels."[29] It was therefore the duty of Muslim rulers to impose the sharia (Islamic law), to enforce the jizya, and to remove non-Muslims from high office.

This strain of Muslim thinking found a champion in the emperor Aurangzeb (ow-rang-ZEHB) (r. 1658–1707), who reversed Akbar's policy of accommodation and sought to impose Islamic supremacy. While Akbar had discouraged the Hindu practice of sati, Aurangzeb forbade it outright. Music and dance were now banned at court, and previously tolerated vices such as gambling, drinking, prostitution, and narcotics were actively suppressed. Dancing girls were ordered to get married or leave the empire altogether. Some Hindu temples were destroyed, and the jizya was reimposed. "Censors of public morals," posted to large cities, enforced Islamic law.

Aurangzeb's religious policies, combined with intolerable demands for taxes to support his many wars of expansion, antagonized Hindus and prompted various movements of opposition to the Mughals. "Your subjects are trampled underfoot," wrote one anonymous protester. "Every province of your empire is impoverished. . . . God is the God of all mankind, not the God of Mussalmans [Muslims] alone."[30] These opposition movements, some of them self-consciously Hindu, fatally fractured the Mughal Empire, especially after Aurangzeb's death in 1707, and opened the way for a British takeover in the second half of the eighteenth century.

Thus the Mughal Empire was the site of a highly significant encounter between two of the world's great religious traditions. It began with an experiment in multicultural empire building and ended in growing antagonism between Hindus and Muslims. In the centuries that followed, both elements of the Mughal experience would be repeated.

Muslims and Christians in the Ottoman Empire

Like the Mughal state, the Ottoman Empire was also the creation of Turkic warrior groups, whose aggressive raiding of agricultural civilization was now legitimized in Islamic terms. Beginning around 1300 from a base area in northwestern Anatolia, these Ottoman Turks over the next three centuries swept over much of the Middle East, North Africa, and southeastern Europe to create the Islamic world's most significant empire (see Map 13.4). During those centuries, the Ottoman state was transformed from a small frontier principality to a prosperous, powerful, cosmopolitan empire, heir both to the Byzantine Empire and to leadership within the Islamic world. Its sultan combined the roles of a Turkic warrior prince, a Muslim caliph, and a conquering emperor, bearing the "strong sword of Islam" and serving as chief defender of the faith.

Gaining such an empire transformed Turkish social life as well. The relative independence of Central Asian pastoral women, their open association with men, and their political influence in society all diminished as the Turks adopted Islam, beginning in the tenth century, and later acquired an empire in the heartland of ancient and patriarchal Mediterranean civilizations. Now elite Turkish women found themselves secluded and often veiled; slave women from the Caucasus Mountains and the Sudan grew more numerous; official imperial censuses did not count women; and orthodox Muslim reformers sought to restrict women's religious gatherings.

And yet within the new constraints of a settled Islamic empire, Turkish women retained something of the social power they had enjoyed in pastoral societies. From around 1550 to 1650, women of the royal court had such an influence in political matters that their critics referred to the "sultanate of women." Islamic law permitted women important property rights, which enabled some to become quite

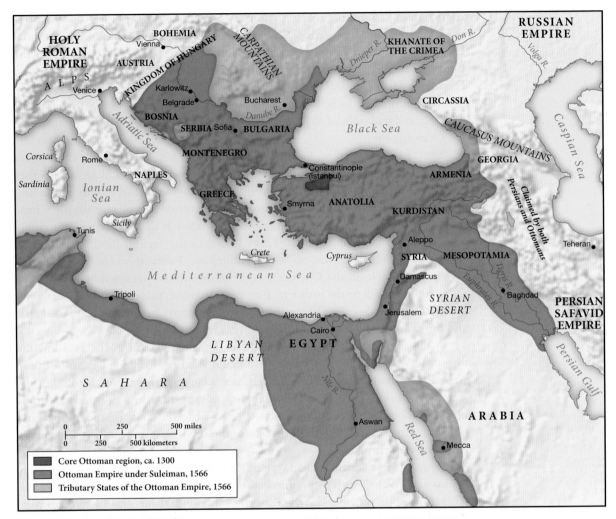

Map 13.4   The Ottoman Empire

At its high point in the mid-sixteenth century, the Ottoman Empire encompassed a vast diversity of peoples; straddled Europe, Africa, and Asia; and battled both the Austrian and Safavid empires.

wealthy, endowing religious and charitable institutions. Many women actively used the Ottoman courts to protect their legal rights in matters of marriage, divorce, and inheritance, sometimes representing themselves or acting as agents for female relatives. In 1717, the wife of an English ambassador to the Ottoman Empire compared the lives of Turkish and European women, declaring, "'Tis very easy to see that they have more liberty than we have."[31]

Within the Islamic world, the Ottoman Empire represented the growing prominence of Turkic people, for their empire now incorporated a large number of

■ **Significance**

In what ways was the Ottoman Empire important for Europe in the early modern era?

Arabs, among whom the religion had been born. The responsibility and the prestige of protecting Mecca, Medina, and Jerusalem—the holy cities of Islam—now fell to the Ottoman Empire. A century-long conflict (1534–1639) between the Ottoman Empire, espousing the Sunni version of Islam, and the Persian Safavid Empire, holding fast to the Shia form of the faith, expressed a deep and enduring division within the Islamic world. Nonetheless, Persian culture, especially its poetry, painting, and traditions of imperial splendor, occupied a prominent position among the Ottoman elite.

The Ottoman Empire, like its Mughal counterpart, was the site of a highly significant cross-cultural encounter in the early modern era, adding yet another chapter to the long-running story of interaction between the Islamic world and Christendom. As the Ottoman Empire expanded across Anatolia, its mostly Christian population converted in large numbers to Islam as the Byzantine state visibly weakened and large numbers of Turks settled in the region. By 1500, some 90 percent of Anatolia's inhabitants were Muslims and Turkic speakers. The climax of this Turkic assault on the Christian world of Byzantium occurred in 1453, when Constantinople fell to the invaders. Renamed Istanbul, that splendid Christian city became the capital of the Ottoman Empire. Byzantium, heir to the glory of Rome and the guardian of Orthodox Christianity, was no more.

In the empire's southeastern European domains, known as the Balkans, the Ottoman encounter with Christian peoples unfolded quite differently than it had in Anatolia. In the Balkans, Muslims ruled over a large Christian population, but the scarcity of Turkish settlers and the willingness of the Ottoman authorities to accommodate the region's Christian churches led to far fewer conversions. By the early sixteenth century, only about 19 percent of the area's people were Muslims, and 81 percent were Christians.

Many of these Christians had welcomed Ottoman conquest because taxes were lighter and oppression less pronounced than under their former Christian rulers. Christian communities such as the Eastern Orthodox and Armenian Churches were granted considerable autonomy in regulating their internal social, religious, educational, and charitable affairs. Nonetheless, many Christian and Jewish women appealed legal cases dealing with marriage and inheritance to Muslim courts, where their property rights were greater. A substantial number of Christian men—Balkan landlords, Greek merchants, government officials, and high-ranking clergy—became part of the Ottoman elite, sometimes without converting to Islam. Jewish refugees, fleeing Christian persecution in a Spain recently "liberated" from Islamic rule, likewise found greater opportunity in the Ottoman Empire, where they became prominent in trade and banking circles. In these ways, Ottoman dealings with the Christian and Jewish populations of their empire broadly resembled Akbar's policies toward the Hindu majority of Mughal India. In another way, however, Turkish rule bore heavily on Christians. Through a process known as the *devshirme* (devv-shirr-MEH) (the collecting or gathering), Ottoman authorities siphoned off

many thousands of young boys from Christian families into the service of the state. (See Zooming In: Devshirme, page 586.)

Even though Ottoman authorities were relatively tolerant toward Christians within their borders, the empire itself represented an enormous threat to Christendom generally. The seizure of Constantinople, the conquest of the Balkans, Ottoman naval power in the Mediterranean, and the siege of Vienna in 1529 and again in 1683 raised anew "the specter of a Muslim takeover of all of Europe."[32] (See Working with Evidence, Source 13.2, page 593.) One European ambassador reported fearfully in 1555 from the court of the Turkish ruler Suleiman:

> He tramples the soil of Hungary with 200,000 horses, he is at the very gates of Austria, threatens the rest of Germany, and brings in his train all the nations that extend from our borders to those of Persia.[33]

Indeed, the "terror of the Turk" inspired fear across much of Europe and placed Christendom on the defensive, even as Europeans were expanding aggressively across the Atlantic and into the Indian Ocean.

The Ottoman Siege of Vienna, 1683

In this late seventeenth-century painting by the Flemish artist Frans Geffels, the last Ottoman incursion into the Austrian Empire is pushed back with French and Polish help, marking the end of a serious Muslim threat to Christian Europe. (Wien Museum Karlsplatz, Vienna, Austria/Erich Lessing/Art Resource, NY)

Devshirme: The "Gathering" of Christian Boys in the Ottoman Empire

Every few years, Ottoman official recruiters descended on rural Christian villages in the Balkan provinces of the empire, mostly among Serbs, Greeks, and Albanians. There they required the village priest to present the birth records of the village and to assemble boys of about ten to eighteen years of age. Then they selected a certain number of these boys, dressed them in red uniforms, and marched them off to Constantinople. Once the boys arrived, they were circumcised, converted to Islam, given a Muslim name, and enrolled in a long training program to prepare them for administrative or military positions within the Ottoman government.

Ottoman officials selecting Christian boys, in red, for the devshirme.

This was the *devshirme*, or "gathering," of Christian boys, a distinctive practice that began in the mid- to late fourteenth century when the rapid expansion of the Ottoman Empire required more soldiers and officials. It extended a much older Islamic tradition of using prisoners captured in war as slave soldiers. The devshirme enabled the sultan to create a cadre of civil and military officials personally loyal to and dependent upon him,

thus avoiding reliance on the Turkish nobility. Boys with the greatest potential received a prestigious education, lasting some fourteen years, in Arabic, Turkish, and Persian languages; mathematics; Islamic studies; horsemanship; weaponry; and more. They were tracked into civil administrative careers, often in the palace itself. Others entered a rigorous training for military service and generally ended up in the Janissary corps, an elite military unit responsible directly to the sultan.

Technically, the devshirme recruits were slaves, but they were quite different from ordinary purchased slaves. They were absorbed into Ottoman society in distinctive and privileged roles, and some of them were able to rise to very prominent positions, including that of grand vizier, the chief adviser to the sultan himself. One such official recalled that he was taken "weeping and in distress," but also reported with some pride that "a shepherd may be [transported] to a sultan's domain."[34]

photo: From the "Suleymanname" (Mss Hazine, 1517 f. 31v.), 1558 (ink and gold leaf on vellum)/Topkapi Palace Museum, Istanbul, Turkey/Bridgeman Images

But the Ottoman encounter with Christian Europe spawned admiration and cooperation as well as fear and trembling. Italian Renaissance artists portrayed the splendor of the Islamic world. (See Working with Evidence, Chapter 12, page 536.) The sixteenth-century French philosopher Jean Bodin praised the religious tolerance of the Ottoman sultan in contrast to Christian intolerance: "The King of the Turks who rules over a great part of Europe safeguards the rites of religion as well as any prince in this world. Yet he constrains no-one, but on the contrary permits everyone to live as his conscience dictates."[35] The French government on occasion found it useful to ally with the Ottoman Empire against their common enemy of Habsburg Austria, while European merchants willingly violated a papal ban on selling firearms to the Turks. Cultural encounter involved more than conflict.

So prestigious were such positions—or so desperate were impoverished Christians—that some Christian families voluntarily offered their sons to the recruiters, and some free Muslim families schemed to get their children into the exalted ranks of the devshirme.

Yet there is little doubt that the devshirme system brought great suffering to the empire's Christian subjects and was widely hated and resisted. In 1395, an Eastern Orthodox metropolitan, or archbishop, named Isidore Glabas from Thessaloniki in Greece delivered a scathing public sermon denouncing the practice, no doubt reflecting the views of his parishioners. "My eyes are filled with tears and can no longer bear to see my beloved ones," he began. Then he outlined the various ways that the devshirme brought grief to his people: their children were "forced to change over to alien customs and to become a vessel of barbaric garb, speech, impiety, and other contaminations, all in a moment." His words reflected the Greeks' view of Turks as "barbarians" and their fear that their children might be subjected to castration as eunuchs or exposed to the homosexuality widely regarded as a part of Janissary life. Furthermore, according to the archbishop, the devshirme threatened the continuity of family life, for a father "will not have his son to send him to his grave in fitting manner." And who, he asked, would not "lament his son because a free child becomes a slave?" Worst of all, in the archbishop's view, was the danger to the immortal soul of a Christian boy who was circumcised and converted to Islam, for "he is shamefully separated from God and has become miserably entangled with the devil, and in the end will be sent to darkness and hell with the demons."[36]

It was no wonder then that Ottoman Christians deployed many strategies to avoid the devshirme. Some communities required their boys to formally marry at a very young age; parish priests might conveniently lose names from the parish registries; families sometimes fled to avoid the recruiters; Eastern Orthodox Christians on occasion appealed to the pope or to Catholic military orders for help, "lest we lose our children." On several occasions, villagers murdered the recruiters and many times sought to bribe them.

By the mid-seventeenth century, the devshirme system had been largely abandoned, as recruitment to these positions was opened to free Muslim Turks. But the memory lingered well into the twentieth century as an irritant in the conflicted relations of Greeks and Turks. A song recently sung in northern Greece recalled the memory: "Be Dammed, Emperor, thrice be dammed. . . . You catch and shackle the old and the archpriests, in order to take the children as janissaries. Their parents weep, their sisters and brothers, too."[37]

Questions: How might you summarize the origins and outcomes of the devshirme system? How does this practice alter your understanding of slavery?

REFLECTIONS

The Centrality of Context in World History

World history is, to put it mildly, a big subject. To teachers and students alike, it can easily seem overwhelming in its detail. And yet the central task of world history is *not* the inclusion of endless facts or particular cases. It is rather to establish contexts or frameworks within which carefully selected facts and cases take on new meaning. In world history, every event, every process, every historical figure, and every culture, society, or civilization gain significance from their incorporation into some larger context or framework. Contextual thinking is central to world history.

The broad outlines of European colonization in the Americas are familiar to most American and European students. And yet, when that story is set in the context of other empire-building projects of the early modern era, it takes on new and different meanings. Such a context helps to counter any remaining Eurocentrism in our thinking about the past by reminding us that Western Europe was not the only center of vitality and expansion and that the interaction of culturally different peoples, so characteristic of the modern age, derived from multiple sources. How often do we notice that a European Christendom creating empires across the Atlantic was also the victim of Ottoman imperial expansion in the Balkans?

This kind of contextualizing also allows us to see more clearly the distinctive features of European empires as we view them in the mirror of other imperial creations. The Chinese, Mughal, and Ottoman empires continued older patterns of historical development, while those of Europe represented something wholly new in human history — an interacting Atlantic world of Europe, Africa, and the Americas. Furthermore, the European empires had a far greater impact on the peoples they incorporated than did other empires. Nowhere else did empire building generate such a catastrophic population collapse as in the Americas. Nor did Asian empires foster the kind of slave-based societies and transcontinental trade in slaves that were among the chief outcomes of Europe's American colonies. Finally, Europe was enriched and transformed by its American possessions far more than China and the Ottomans were by their territorial acquisitions. Europeans gained enormous new biological resources from their empires — corn, potatoes, tomatoes, chocolate, tobacco, timber, and much more — as well as enormous wealth in the form of gold, silver, and land.

Should we need a motto for world history, consider this one: in world history, nothing stands alone; context is everything.

Second Thoughts

What's the Significance?

Big Picture Questions

1. The experience of empire for conquered peoples was broadly similar whoever their rulers were. Does the material in this chapter support or challenge this idea?

2. In thinking about the similarities and differences among the empires of the early modern era, what categories of comparison might be most useful to consider?

3. Have a look at the maps in this chapter with an eye to the areas of the world that were not incorporated into a major empire. Pick one or more of them and do a little research as to what was happening there in the early modern era.

4. **Looking Back:** Compared to the world of the fifteenth century, what new patterns of development are visible in the empire-building projects of the centuries that followed?

Next Steps: For Further Study

Jane Burbank and Frederick Cooper, *Empires in World History* (2010). Chapters 5–7 of this recent work describe and compare the empires of the early modern world.

Jorge Canizares-Esguerra and Erik R. Seeman, eds., *The Atlantic in Global History* (2007). A collection of essays that treats the Atlantic basin as a single interacting region.

Alfred W. Crosby, *The Columbian Voyages, the Columbian Exchange, and Their Historians* (1987). A brief and classic account of changing understandings of Columbus and his global impact.

John Kicza, *Resilient Cultures: America's Native Peoples Confront European Colonization, 1500–1800* (2003). An account of European colonization in the Americas that casts the native peoples as active agents rather than passive victims.

Charles C. Mann, *1493: Uncovering the New World Columbus Created* (2011). A global account of the Columbian exchange that presents contemporary scholarship in a very accessible fashion.

Peter Perdue, *China Marches West: The Qing Conquest of Central Eurasia* (2005). Describes how China became an empire as it incorporated the non-Chinese people of Central Asia.

Willard Sutherland, *Taming the Wild Fields: Colonization and Empire on the Russian Steppe* (2004). An up-to-date account of Russian expansion in the steppes.

"Discover the Ottomans," http://www.theottomans.org/english/index.asp. A series of essays and images that traces the history of the Ottoman Empire over six centuries.

"1492: An Ongoing Voyage," http://www.ibiblio.org/expo/1492.exhibit/Intro.html. An interactive Web site based on an exhibit from the Library of Congress that provides a rich context for exploring the meaning of Columbus and his voyages.

State Building in the Early Modern Era

The empires of the early modern era were the projects of states, though these states often made use of various private groups—missionaries, settlers, merchants, mercenaries—to achieve the goals of empire. Such imperial states—Mughal India, the Ottoman Empire, France, and the Inca Empire, for example—were invariably headed by kings or emperors who were the source of ultimate political authority in their lands. Each of those rulers sought to govern societies divided by religion, region, ethnicity, or class.

During the three centuries between 1450 and 1750, all of these states, and a number of non-imperial states as well, moved toward greater political integration and centralization. In all of them, more effective central bureaucracies curtailed, though never eliminated, entrenched local interests; royal courts became more elaborate; and the role of monarchs grew more prominent. The growth of empire accompanied this process of political integration, and perhaps helped cause it. However, efforts at state building differed considerably across the early modern world, depending on variations in historical backgrounds, the particular problems and circumstances that each state faced, the cultural basis of political authority, and the policies that individual leaders followed.

The documents that follow allow us to examine this state-building effort in several distinct settings. Two of them were written by monarchs themselves and two by outside observers. What similarities and variations in this process of state building can you notice as you study the documents? How did these early modern states differ from the states of later centuries or those of today? To what extent was government personal rather than institutional? In what ways was power exercised—through coercion and violence, through accommodation with established elites, through the operation of new bureaucratic structures, or by persuading people that the central authority was in fact legitimate?

Source 13.1

The Memoirs of Emperor Jahangir

The peoples of India had only rarely experienced a political system that encompassed most of the subcontinent. Its vast ethnic and cultural diversity and the division between its Hindu and Muslim peoples usually generated a fragmented political order of many competing states and principalities. But in the early modern era, the Mughal Empire gave to South Asia a rare period of substantial political unity. Source 13.1 offer excerpts from the memoirs of Jahangir, who ruled the Mughal state from 1605 to 1627, following the reign of his more famous father Akbar (see pages 580–81). Written in Persian, the literary language of the eastern Islamic world, Jahangir's account of his reign followed the tradition of earlier Mughal emperors in noting major events of his lifetime, but it departed from that tradition in reflecting personally on art, politics, family life, and more.

- ▪ Why do you think Jahangir mounted such an elaborate coronation celebration for himself?

- ▪ In what ways did Jahangir seek to ensure the effective authority of the state he led?

- ▪ In what ways was Jahangir a distinctly Muslim ruler? In what respects did he and his father depart from Islamic principles?

- ▪ Based on these selections, what concrete problems of governance can you infer were facing Jahangir?

JAHANGIR

Memoirs

1605–1627

At the age of thirty-eight, I became Emperor. . . . As at the very instant that I seated myself on the throne, the sun rose from the horizon; I accepted this as the omen of victory, and as indicating a reign of unvarying prosperity. Hence I assumed the titles of . . . the world-subduing emperor, the world-subduing king.

On this occasion I made use of the throne prepared by my father, and enriched at an expense without parallel for the celebration of the festival of the new year. . . . Having thus seated myself on the throne of my expectations and wishes, I caused also the imperial crown, which my father had caused to be made after the manner of that which was worn by the great kings of Persia, to be brought before me, and then, in the presence of the whole assembled Emirs, having placed it on my brows, as an omen auspicious to the stability and happiness of my reign, kept it there for the space of a full astronomical hour. . . .

For forty days and forty nights I caused the . . . great imperial state drum, to strike up, without ceasing, the strains of joy and triumph; and . . . around my throne, the ground was spread by my directions with the most costly brocades and gold embroidered carpets. Censers [containers for burning incense] of gold and silver were disposed in different directions for the purpose of burning odoriferous drugs, and nearly three thousand camphorated wax lights . . . illuminated the scene from night till morning. Numbers of blooming youths, beautiful as young Joseph in the pavilions of Egypt, clad in dresses of the most costly materials . . . awaited my commands, rank after rank, and in attitude most respectful. And finally, the Emirs of the empire . . . covered from head to foot in gold and jewels, and shoulder to shoulder, stood round in brilliant array, also waiting for the commands of their sovereign. For forty days and forty nights did I keep open to the world these scenes of festivity and splendor, furnishing altogether an example of imperial magnificence seldom paralleled in this stage of earthly existence. . . .

I instituted . . . special regulations . . . as rules of conduct, never to be deviated from in their respective stations.

1. I remitted [canceled] altogether to my subjects three sources of revenue taxes or duties. . . .

2. I directed, when the district lay waste or destitute of inhabitants, that towns should be built. . . . I charged the Jaguir-daurs [local rulers granted a certain territory by the emperor], or feudatories of the empire, in such deserted places to erect mosques and substantial . . . stations for the accommodation of travelers, in order to render the district once more an inhabited country, and that wayfaring men might again be able to pass and repass in safety.

3. Merchants traveling through the country were not to have their bales or packages of any kind opened without their consent. But when they were perfectly willing to dispose of any article of merchandise, purchasers were permitted to deal with them, without, however, offering any species of molestation. . . .

5. No person was permitted either to make or sell either wine or any other kind of intoxicating liquor. I undertook to institute this regulation, although it is sufficiently notorious that I have myself the strongest inclination for wine, in which from the age of sixteen I have liberally indulged. . . .

6. No person [official] was permitted to take up his abode obtrusively in the dwelling of any subject of my realm. . . .

7. No person was to suffer, for any offense, the loss of a nose or ear. If the crime were theft, the offender was to be scourged with thorns, or deterred from further transgression by an attestation on the Koran.

8. [High officials] were prohibited from possessing themselves by violence of the lands of the subject, or from cultivating them on their own account. . . .

10. The governors in all the principal cities were directed to establish infirmaries or hospitals, with competent medical aid for the relief of the sick. . . .

11. During the month of my birth . . . the use of all animal food was prohibited both in town and country; and at equidistant periods throughout the year a day was set apart, on which all slaughtering of animals was strictly forbidden.

[H]aving on one occasion asked my father [Akbar] the reason why he had forbidden any one to prevent or interfere with the building of these haunts of idolatry [Hindu temples], his reply was in the following terms: "My dear child," said he, "I find myself a powerful monarch, the shadow of God upon earth. I have seen that he bestows the blessings of his gracious providence upon all his creatures without distinction. Ill should I discharge the duties of my exalted station, were I to withhold my compassion and indulgence from any of those entrusted to my charge. With all of the human race, with all of God's creatures, I am at peace: why then should I permit myself, under any consideration, to be the cause of molestation or aggression to any one? Besides, are not five parts in six of mankind either Hindus or aliens to the faith; and were I to be governed by motives of the kind suggested in your inquiry, what alternative can I have but to put them all to death! I have thought it therefore my wisest plan to let these men alone. Neither is it to be forgotten, that the class of whom we are speaking . . . are usefully engaged, either in the pursuits of science or the arts, or of improvements for the benefit of mankind, and have in numerous instances arrived at the highest distinctions in the state, there being, indeed, to be found in this city men of every description, and of every religion on the face of the earth."

Source: *The Memoirs of the Emperor Jahangir*, translated from the Persian by Major David Price (London: Oriental Translation Committee, 1829), 1–3, 5–8, 15.

Source 13.2

An Outsider's View of the Ottoman Empire

Under Suleiman I (r. 1520–1566), the Ottoman Empire reached its greatest territorial extent and perhaps its golden age in terms of culture and economy (see Map 13.4, page 583). A helpful window into the life of this most powerful of Muslim states comes from the writings of Ogier Ghiselin de Busbecq, a Flemish nobleman who served as a diplomat for the Austrian Empire, which then felt under great threat from Ottoman expansion into Central Europe. Busbecq's letters to a friend, excerpted in Source 13.2, present his view of the Ottoman court and his reflections on Ottoman military power.

■ How do you think Busbecq's outsider status shaped his perceptions of Ottoman political and military life? To what extent does his role as a foreigner enhance or undermine the usefulness of his account for historians?

■ How did he define the differences between the Ottoman Empire and Austria? What do you think he hoped to accomplish by highlighting these differences?

■ What sources of Ottoman political authority are apparent in Busbecq's account?

■ What potential problems of the Ottoman Empire does this document imply or state?

OGIER GHISELIN DE BUSBECQ

The Turkish Letters

1555–1562

On his [Suleiman's] arrival we were admitted to an audience. . . . His air [attitude], was by no means gracious, and his face wore a stern, though dignified, expression. On entering we were separately conducted into the royal presence by the chamberlains, who grasped our arms. This has been the Turkish fashion of admitting people to the Sovereign ever since a Croat, in order to avenge the death of his master . . . asked Amurath [an earlier Sultan] for an audience, and took advantage of it to slay him. After having gone through a pretense of kissing his hand, we were conducted backward to the wall opposite his seat, care being taken that we should never turn our backs on him. . . .

The Sultan's hall was crowded with people, among whom were several officers of high rank. Besides these there were all the troopers of the Imperial guard and a large force of Janissaries; but there was not in all that great assembly a single man who owed his position to aught save his valor and his merit. No distinction is attached to birth among the Turks. . . . In making his appointments the Sultan pays no regard to any pretensions on the score of wealth or rank, nor does he take into consideration recommendations or popularity. . . . It is by merit that men rise in the service, a system which ensures that posts should only be assigned to the competent. . . . Those who receive the highest offices from the Sultan are for the most part the sons of shepherds or herdsmen, and so far from being ashamed of their parentage, they actually glory in it, and consider it a matter of boasting that they owe nothing to the accident of birth. . . .

Among the Turks, therefore, honors, high posts, and judgeships are the rewards of great ability and good service. If a man be dishonest, or lazy, or careless, he remains at the bottom of the ladder, an object of contempt; for such qualities there are no honors in Turkey! This is the reason that they are successful in their undertakings, that they lord it over others, and are daily extending the bounds of their empire. These are not our ideas, with us [Europeans] there is no opening left for merit; birth is the standard for everything; the prestige of birth is the sole key to advancement in the public service. . . .

[T]ake your stand by my side, and look at the sea of turbaned heads, each wrapped in twisted folds of the whitest silk; look at those marvelously handsome dresses of every kind and every color; time would fail me to tell how all around is glittering with gold, with silver, with purple, with silk, and with velvet; words cannot convey an adequate idea of that strange and wondrous sight: it was the most beautiful spectacle I ever saw.

With all this luxury, great simplicity and economy are combined; every man's dress, whatever his position may be, is of the same pattern; no fringes or useless points are sewn on, as is the case with us, appendages which cost a great deal of money, and are worn out in three days. . . . I was greatly struck with the silence and order that prevailed in this great crowd. There were no cries, no hum of voices, the usual accompaniments of a motley gathering, neither was there any jostling; without the slightest disturbance each man took his proper place according to his rank. . . .

On leaving the assembly we had a fresh treat in the sight of the household cavalry returning to their quarters; the men were mounted on splendid horses, excellently groomed, and gorgeously accoutred. And so we left the royal presence, taking with us but little hope of a successful issue to our embassy.

The Turkish monarch going to war takes with him over 40,000 camels and nearly as many baggage mules, of which a great part, when he is invading Persia, are loaded with rice and other kinds of grain. . . . The invading army carefully abstains from encroaching on its magazines [supplies] at the outset. . . . The Sultan's magazines are opened, and a ration just sufficient to sustain life is daily weighed out to the Janissaries and other troops of the royal household.

From this you will see that it is the patience, self-denial, and thrift of the Turkish soldier that enable him to face the most trying circumstances. . . . What a contrast to our men! Christian soldiers on a campaign refuse to put up with their ordinary food, and call for thrushes, beccaficos [small birds], and such like dainty dishes! If these are not supplied they grow mutinous and work their own ruin; and, if they are supplied, they are ruined all the same. For each man is his own worst enemy, and has no foe more deadly than his own intemperance, which is sure to kill him, if the enemy be not quick.

It makes me shudder to think of what the result of a struggle between such different systems must be; one of us must prevail and the other be destroyed. . . . On their side is the vast wealth of their empire, unimpaired resources, experience and practice in arms, a veteran soldiery, an uninterrupted series of victories, readiness to endure hardships, union, order, discipline, thrift, and watchfulness. On ours are found an empty exchequer, luxurious habits, exhausted resources, broken spirits, a raw and insubordinate soldiery, and greedy generals; there is no regard for discipline, license runs riot, the men indulge in drunkenness and debauchery, and, worst of all, the enemy are accustomed to victory, we, to defeat. Can we doubt what the result must be? The only obstacle is Persia, whose position on his rear forces the invader to take precautions. The fear of Persia gives us a respite, but it is only for a time. When he has secured himself in that quarter, he will fall upon us with all the resources of the East. How ill prepared we are to meet such an attack it is not for me to say.

[*In the following passage, Busbecq reflects on a major problem of the Ottoman state, succession to the throne.*]

The sons of Turkish Sultans are in the most wretched position in the world, for, as soon as one of them succeeds his father, the rest are doomed to certain death. The Turk can endure no rival to the throne, and, indeed, the conduct of the Janissaries renders it impossible for the new Sultan to spare his brothers; for if one of them survives, the Janissaries are forever asking largesses. If these are refused, forthwith the cry is heard, "Long live the brother!" "God preserve the brother!"—a tolerably broad hint that they intend to place him on the throne. So that the Turkish Sultans are compelled to celebrate their succession by imbruing their hands in the blood of their nearest relatives.

Source: Charles Thornton Forester and F. H. Blackburne Daniell, *The Life and Letters of Ogier Ghiselin de Busbecq* (London: C. Kegan Paul, 1881), 114–15, 152–56, 219–22.

Source 13.3
French State Building and Louis XIV

Like their counterparts in the Middle East and Asia, a number of European states in the early modern era also pursued the twin projects of imperial expansion abroad and political integration at home. But consolidating central authority was a long and difficult task. Obstacles to the ambitions of kings in Europe were many—the absence of an effective transportation and communication infrastructure; the difficulty of acquiring information about the population and resources; the entrenched interests of privileged groups such as the nobility, church, town councils, and guilds; and the division between Catholics and Protestants.

Perhaps the most well-known example of such European state-building efforts is that of France under the rule of Louis XIV (r. 1643–1715). Louis and other European monarchs, such as those in Spain and Russia, operated under a set of assumptions known as absolutism, which held that kings ruled by "divine right" and could legitimately claim sole and uncontested authority in their realms. Louis's famous dictum *"L'état, c'est moi"* ("I am the state") summed up the absolutist ideal. Source 13.3 illustrates at least one way in which Louis attempted to realize this ideal.

Written by Louis himself, this document focuses on the importance of "spectacle" and public display in solidifying the exalted role of the monarch. The "carousel" described here was an extravagant pageant, held in Paris in June 1662. It featured various exotic animals, slaves, princes, and nobles arrayed in fantastic costumes representing distant lands, as well as many equestrian competitions. Unifying this disparate assembly was King Louis himself, dressed as a Roman emperor, while on the shields of the nobles was that grand symbol of the monarchy, the sun.

- What posture does Louis take toward his subjects in this document?

- How does he understand the role of spectacle in general and the carousel in particular?

- What does the choice of the sun as a royal symbol suggest about Louis's conception of his role in the French state and empire?

LOUIS XIV

Memoirs

1670

It was necessary to conserve and cultivate with care all that which, without diminishing the authority and the respect due to me, linked me by bonds of affection to my peoples and above all to the people of rank, so as to make them see by this very means that it was neither aversion for them nor affected severity, nor harshness of spirit, but simply reason and duty, that made me more reserved and more exact toward them in other matters. That sharing of pleasures, which gives people at court a respectable familiarity with us, touches them and charms them more than can be expressed. The common people, on the other hand, are delighted by shows in which, at bottom, we always have the aim of pleasing them; and all our subjects, in general, are delighted to see that we like what they like, or what they excel in. By this means we hold on to their hearts and their minds, sometimes more strongly perhaps than by recompenses and gifts; and with regard to foreigners, in a state they see flourishing and well ordered, that which is spent on expenses and which could be called superfluous, makes a very favorable impression on them, of magnificence, of power, of grandeur. . . .

The carousel, which has furnished me the subject of these reflections, had only been conceived at first as a light amusement; but little by little, we were carried away, and it became a spectacle that was fairly grand and magnificent, both in the number of exercises, and by the novelty of the costumes and the variety of the [heraldic] devices. It was

then that I began to employ the one that I have always kept since and which you see in so many places . . . it ought to represent in some way the duties of a prince, and constantly encourage me to fulfill them. For the device they chose the sun, which . . . is the most noble of all, and which, by its quality of being unique, by the brilliance that surrounds it, by the light that it communicates to the other stars which form for it a kind of court, by the just and equal share that the different climates of the world receive of this light, by the good it does in all places, ceaselessly producing as it does, in every sphere of life, joy and activity, by its unhindered movement, in which it nevertheless always appears calm, by its constant and invariable course, from which it never departs nor wavers, is the most striking and beautiful image of a great monarch.

Those who saw me governing with a good deal of ease and without being confused by anything, in all the numerous attentions that royalty demands, persuaded me to add the earth's globe, and for motto, *nec pluribus impar* (not unequal to many things): by which they meant something that flattered the aspirations of a young king, namely that, being sufficient to so many things, I would doubtless be capable of governing other empires, just as the sun was capable of lighting up other worlds if they were exposed to its rays.

Source: Robert Campbell, *Louis XIV* (London: Longmans, 1993), 117–18.

Source 13.4

An Outsider's View of the Inca Empire

Pedro de Cieza de León (1520–1554), a Spanish chronicler of the Inca Empire of the early sixteenth century, came to the Americas as a boy at the age of thirteen. For the next seventeen years, Cieza took part as a soldier in a number of expeditions that established Spanish rule in various parts of South America. Along the way, he collected a great deal of information, especially about the Inca Empire, which he began to publish on his return to Spain in 1550. Despite a very limited education, Cieza wrote a series of works that have become a major source for historians about the workings of the Inca Empire and about the Spanish conquest of that land. The selection that follows focuses on the techniques that the Incas used to govern their huge empire.

- How would you describe Cieza's posture toward the Inca Empire? What in particular did he seem to appreciate about it?

- Based on this account, what difficulties did the Inca rulers face in governing their large and diverse realm?

- What policies or practices did the Inca authorities follow in seeking to integrate their empire?

- Some modern observers have described the Inca Empire as "totalitarian" or "socialist." Do such terms seem appropriate? How else might you describe the Inca state?

- How does Cieza's relationship to the Inca Empire compare to that of Busbecq to the Ottoman Empire?

PEDRO DE CIEZA DE LEÓN

Chronicles of the Incas

ca. 1550

The Incas had the seat of their empire in the city of Cuzco, where the laws were given and the captains set out to make war. . . . As soon as one of these large provinces was conquered, ten or twelve thousand of the men and their wives, or six thousand, or the number decided upon were ordered to leave and remove themselves from it. These were transferred to another town or province of the same climate and nature as that which they left. . . . And they had another device to keep the natives from hating them, and this was that they never divested the natural chieftains of their power. If it so happened that one of them committed a crime or in some way deserved to be stripped of his power, it was vested in his sons or brothers, and all were ordered to obey them. . . .

One of the things most to be envied in these rulers is how well they knew to conquer such vast lands. . . .

[T]hey entered many lands without war, and the soldiers who accompanied the Inca were ordered to do no damage or harm, robbery or violence. If there was a shortage of food in the province, he ordered supplies brought in from other regions so that those newly won to his service would not find his rule and acquaintance irksome. . . .

In many others, where they entered by war and force of arms, they ordered that the crops and houses of the enemy be spared. . . . But in the end the Incas always came out victorious, and when they had vanquished the others, they did not do them further harm, but released those they had taken prisoner, if there were any, and restored the booty, and put them back in possession of their property and rule, exhorting them not to be foolish and try to compete with his royal majesty nor abandon his friendship, but to be his friends as their neighbors were. And saying this, he gave them a number of beautiful women and fine pieces of wool or gold. . . .

They never deprived the native chieftains of their rule. They were all ordered to worship the sun as God, but they were not prohibited from observing their own religions and customs. . . .

It is told for a fact of the rulers of this kingdom that in the days of their rule they [the Incas] had their representatives in the capitals of all the provinces. . . . They served as head of the provinces or regions, and from every so many leagues around the tributes were brought to one of these capitals. . . . This was so well organized that there was not a village that did not know where it was to send its tribute. In all these capitals the Incas had temples of the sun, mints, and many silversmiths who did nothing but work rich pieces of gold or fair vessels of silver. . . . The tribute paid by each of these districts where the capital was situated, and that turned over by the natives, whether gold, silver, clothing, arms, and all else they gave, was entered in the accounts of the [*quipu-*] *camayocs*, who kept the quipus and did everything ordered by the governor in the matter of finding the soldiers or supplying whomever the Inca ordered, or making delivery to Cuzco; but when they came from the city of Cuzco to go over the accounts, or they were ordered to go to Cuzco to give an accounting, the accountants themselves gave it by the quipus, or went to give it where there could be no fraud, but everything had to come out right. Few years went by in which an accounting of all these things was not made. . . .

When the Incas set out to visit their kingdom, it is told that they traveled with great pomp, riding in rich litters set upon smooth, long poles of the finest wood and adorned with gold and silver. . . .

So many people came to see his passing that all the hills and slopes seemed covered with them, and all called down blessings upon him. . . .

He [the Inca] traveled four leagues each day, or as much as he wished; he stopped wherever he liked to inquire into the state of his kingdom; he willingly listened to those who came to him with complaints, righting wrongs and punishing those who had committed an injustice. . . .

[T]hese rulers, as the best measure, ordered and decreed, with severe punishment for failure to obey, that all the natives of their empire should know

and understand the language of Cuzco, both they and their women. . . . This was carried out so faithfully that in the space of a very few years a single tongue was known and used in an extension of more than 1,200 leagues; yet, even though this language was employed, they all spoke their own [languages], which were so numerous that if I were to list them it would not be credited. . . .

[The Inca] appointed those whose duty it was to punish wrongdoers, and to this end they were always traveling about the country. The Incas took such care to see that justice was meted out that nobody ventured to commit a felony or theft. This was to deal with thieves, ravishers of women, or conspirators against the Inca; however, there were many provinces that warred on one another, and the Incas were not wholly able to prevent this. By the river [Huatanay] that runs through Cuzco justice was executed on those who were caught or brought in as prisoners from some other place. There they had their heads cut off, or were put to death in some other manner which they chose. Mutiny and conspiracy were severely punished, and, above all, those who were thieves and known as such; even their wives and children were despised and considered to be tarred with the same brush. . . .

[I]n each of the many provinces there were many storehouses filled with supplies and other needful things; thus, in times of war, wherever the armies went they draw upon the contents of these storehouses, without ever touching the supplies of their confederates or laying a finger on what they had in their settlements. And when there was no war, all this stock of supplies and food was divided up among the poor and the widows. These poor were the aged, or the lame, crippled, or paralyzed, or those afflicted with some other diseases. . . . If there came a lean year, the storehouses were opened and the provinces were lent what they needed in the way of supplies; then, in a year of abundance, they paid back all they had received.

Source: *The Incas of Pedro de Cieza de León*, translated by Harriet de Onis (Norman: University of Oklahoma Press, 1959), 56–57, 158–60, 165–73, 177–78.

DOING HISTORY

State Building in the Early Modern Era

1. **Making comparisons:** To what extent did these four early modern states face similar problems and devise similar solutions? How did they differ? In particular, how did the rulers of these states deal with subordinates? How did they use violence? What challenges to imperial authority did they face?

2. **Assessing spectacle:** In what different ways was spectacle, royal splendor, or public display evident in the documents? How would you define the purpose of such display? How effective do you think spectacle has been in consolidating state authority?

3. **Distinguishing power and authority:** Some scholars have made a distinction between "power," the ability of a state to coerce its subjects into some required behavior, and "authority," the ability of a state to persuade its subjects to do its bidding voluntarily by convincing them that it is proper, right, or natural to do so. What examples of power and authority can you find in these documents? How were power and authority related? What are the advantages and disadvantages of each, from the viewpoint of ambitious rulers?

4. **Comparing past and present:** It is important to recognize that early modern states differed in many ways from twentieth- or twenty-first-century states. How would you define those differences? Consider, among other things, the personal role of the ruler, the use of violence, the means of establishing authority, and the extent to which the state could shape the lives of its citizens.

5. **Comparing insiders' and outsiders' accounts:** What differences do you notice between the two passages written by monarchs themselves and the two composed by foreign observers? What advantages and limitations do these two types of sources offer to historians seeking to use them as evidence?

Slave Merchant in Gorée Island, Senegal, from *Encyclopédie des Voyages*, engraved by L. F. Labrousse, 1796/Bibliothèque des Arts Décoratifs, Paris, France/Archives Charmet/Bridgeman Images

Economic Transformations

Commerce and Consequence

1450–1750

"I have come full circle back to my destiny: from Africa to America and back to Africa. I could hear the cries and wails of my ancestors. I weep with them and for them."[1] This is what an African American woman from Atlanta wrote in 2002 in the guest book of the Cape Coast Castle, one of the many ports of embarkation for slaves located along the coast of Ghana in West Africa. There she no doubt saw the whips and leg irons used to discipline the captured Africans as well as the windowless dungeons in which hundreds were crammed while waiting for the ships that would carry them across the Atlantic to the Americas. Almost certainly she also caught sight of the infamous "gate of no return," through which the captives departed to their new life as slaves.

This visitor's emotional encounter with the legacy of the Atlantic slave trade reminds us of the enormous significance of this commerce in human beings for the early modern world and of its continuing echoes even in the twenty-first century. The slave trade, however, was only one component of those international networks of exchange that shaped human interactions during the centuries between 1450 and 1750. Europeans now smashed their way into the ancient spice trade of the Indian Ocean, developing new relationships with Asian societies as a result. Silver, obtained from mines in Spanish America, enriched Western Europe, even as much of it made its way to China, where it allowed Europeans to participate more fully in the rich commerce of East Asia. Furs from North America and Siberia found a ready market in Europe and China, while the hunting and trapping of those fur-bearing animals transformed

The Atlantic Slave Trade This eighteenth-century French engraving shows the sale of slaves at Gorée, a major slave-trading port in what is now Dakar in Senegal. A European merchant and an African authority figure negotiate the arrangement, while the shackled victims themselves wait for their fate to be decided.

both natural environments and human societies. Despite their growing prominence in long-distance exchange, Europeans were far from the only actors in early modern commerce. Southeast Asians, Chinese, Indians, Armenians, Arabs, Africans, and Native Americans likewise played major roles in the making of the world economy during the early modern era.

Thus commerce joined empire as the twin creators of a global network during these centuries. Together they gave rise to new relationships, disrupted old patterns, brought distant peoples into contact with one another, enriched some, and impoverished or enslaved others. They also generated new ways of expressing status, as the Working with Evidence feature on pages 634–41 illustrates. From the various "old worlds" of the premodern era, a single "new world" emerged—slowly, amid much suffering, and accompanied by growing inequalities. What was gained and what was lost in the transformations born of global commerce have been the subject of great controversy ever since.

> **SEEKING THE MAIN POINT**
>
> In what different ways did global commerce transform human societies and the lives of individuals during the early modern era?

Europeans and Asian Commerce

Schoolchildren everywhere know that European empires in the Western Hemisphere grew out of an accident—Columbus's unknowing encounter with the Americas—and that new colonial societies and new commercial connections across the Atlantic were the result. In Asia, it was a very different story. The voyage (1497–1499) of the Portuguese mariner Vasco da Gama, in which Europeans sailed to India for the first time, was certainly no accident. It was the outcome of a deliberate, systematic, century-long Portuguese effort to explore a sea route to the East, by creeping slowly down the West African coast, around the tip of South Africa, up the East African coast, and finally across the Indian Ocean to Calicut in southern India in 1498. There Europeans encountered an ancient and rich network of commerce that stretched from East Africa to China. They were certainly aware of the wealth of that commercial network, but largely ignorant of its workings.

■ **Causation**
What drove European involvement in the world of Asian commerce?

The most immediate motivation for this massive effort was the desire for tropical spices—cinnamon, nutmeg, mace, cloves, and, above all, pepper—which were widely used as condiments and preservatives and were sometimes regarded as aphrodisiacs. A fifteenth-century English book declared: "Pepper [from Java] is black and has a good smack, And every man doth buy it."[2] Other products of the East, such as Chinese silk, Indian cottons, rhubarb for medicinal purposes, emeralds, rubies, and sapphires, were also in great demand.

Underlying this growing interest in Asia was the more general recovery of European civilization following the disaster of the Black Death in the early fourteenth century. During the fifteenth century, Europe's population was growing again, and its national monarchies—in Spain, Portugal, England, and France—were learning how to tax their subjects more effectively and to build substantial military forces equipped with gunpowder weapons. Its cities were growing too. Some of them—

A MAP OF TIME

Early 15th century	Beginning of Portuguese voyages along the coast of West Africa
1440s	First European export of slaves from West Africa
1492	Columbus reaches the Americas
1497	Vasco da Gama reaches India
1545	Founding of Potosí as silver mining town in Bolivia
1565	Beginning of Spanish takeover of the Philippines
1570s	Beginning of silver shipments from Mexico to Manila
17th century	Russian conquest of Siberia
1601–1602	British and Dutch East India companies established in Asia
18th century	Peak of the transatlantic slave trade
1750s	British begin military conquest of India

in England, the Netherlands, and northern Italy, for example—were becoming centers of international commerce, giving birth to economies based on market exchange, private ownership, and the accumulation of capital for further investment.

For many centuries, Eastern goods had trickled into the Mediterranean through the Middle East from the Indian Ocean commercial network. From the viewpoint of an increasingly dynamic Europe, several major problems accompanied this pattern of trade. First, of course, the source of supply for these much-desired goods lay solidly in Muslim hands. Most immediately, Muslim Egypt was the primary point of transfer into the Mediterranean basin and its European Christian customers. The Italian commercial city of Venice largely monopolized the European trade in Eastern goods, annually sending convoys of ships to Alexandria in Egypt. Venetians resented the Muslim monopoly on Indian Ocean trade, and other European powers disliked relying on Venice as well as on Muslims. Circumventing these monopolies was yet another impetus—both religious and political—for the Portuguese to attempt a sea route to India that bypassed both Venetian and Muslim intermediaries. In addition, many Europeans of the time were persuaded that a mysterious Christian monarch, known as Prester John, ruled somewhere in Asia or Africa. Joining with his mythical kingdom to continue the Crusades and combat a common Islamic enemy was likewise a goal of the Portuguese voyages.

A further problem for Europeans lay in paying for Eastern goods. Few products of an economically less developed Europe were attractive in Eastern markets. Thus Europeans were required to pay cash—gold or silver—for Asian spices or textiles.

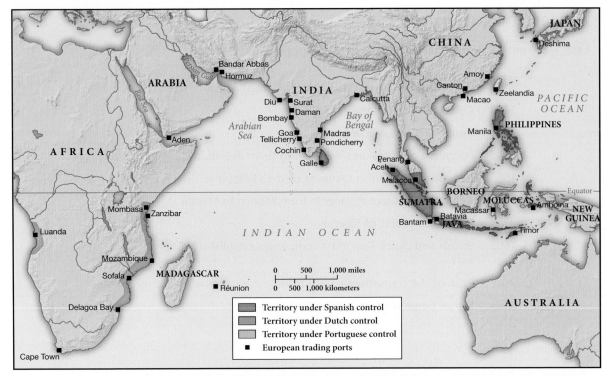

Map 14.1   Europeans in Asia in the Early Modern Era

The early modern era witnessed only very limited territorial control by Europeans in Asia. Trade, rather than empire, was the chief concern of the Western newcomers, who were not, in any event, a serious military threat to major Asian states.

This persistent trade deficit contributed much to the intense desire for precious metals that attracted early modern European explorers, traders, and conquerors. Portuguese voyages along the West African coast, for example, were seeking direct access to African goldfields. The enormously rich silver deposits of Mexico and Bolivia provided at least a temporary solution to this persistent European problem.

First the Portuguese and then the Spanish, French, Dutch, and British found their way into the ancient Asian world of Indian Ocean commerce (see Map 14.1). How they behaved in that world and what they created there differed considerably among the various European countries, but collectively they contributed much to the new regime of globalized trade.

A Portuguese Empire of Commerce

The arena of Indian Ocean commerce into which Vasco da Gama and his Portuguese successors sailed was a world away from anything they had known. It was vast, both in geographic extent and in the diversity of those who participated in it. East Africans, Arabs, Persians, Indians, Malays, Chinese, and others traded freely.

Most of them were Muslims, though hailing from many separate communities, but Hindus, Buddhists, Christians, Jews, and Chinese likewise had a role in this commercial network. Had the Portuguese sought simply to participate in peaceful trading, they certainly could have done so, but it was quickly apparent that European trade goods were crude and unattractive in Asian markets and that Europeans would be unable to compete effectively. Moreover, the Portuguese soon learned that most Indian Ocean merchant ships were not heavily armed and certainly lacked the onboard cannons that Portuguese ships carried. Since the withdrawal of the Chinese fleet from the Indian Ocean early in the fifteenth century, no major power was in a position to dominate the sea lanes, and the many smaller-scale merchants generally traded openly, although piracy was sometimes a problem.

Given these conditions, the Portuguese saw an opening, for their ships could outgun and outmaneuver competing naval forces, while their onboard cannons could devastate coastal fortifications. Although their overall economy lagged behind that of Asian producers, Europeans had more than caught up in the critical area of naval technology and naval warfare. This military advantage enabled the Portuguese to quickly establish fortified bases at several key locations within the Indian Ocean world—Mombasa in East Africa, Hormuz at the entrance to the Persian Gulf, Goa on the west coast of India, Malacca in Southeast Asia, and Macao on the south coast of China. With the exception of Macao, which had been obtained through bribery and negotiations with Chinese authorities, these Portuguese bases were obtained forcibly against small and weak states. In Mombasa, for example, the commander of a Portuguese fleet responded to local resistance in 1505 by burning and sacking the city, killing some 1,500 people, and seizing large quantities of cotton and silk textiles and carpets. The king of Mombasa wrote a warning to a neighboring city:

■ **Connection**
To what extent did the Portuguese realize their own goals in the Indian Ocean?

> This is to inform you that a great lord has passed through the town, burning it and laying it waste. He came to the town in such strength and was of such a cruelty that he spared neither man nor woman, or old nor young—nay, not even the smallest child. . . . Nor can I ascertain nor estimate what wealth they have taken from the town.[3]

What the Portuguese created in the Indian Ocean is commonly known as a "trading post empire," for they aimed to control commerce, not large territories or populations, and to do so by force of arms rather than by economic competition. Seeking to monopolize the spice trade, the Portuguese king grandly titled himself "Lord of the Conquest, Navigation, and Commerce of Ethiopia, Arabia, Persia, and India." Portuguese authorities in the East tried to require all merchant vessels to purchase a *cartaz*, or pass, and to pay duties of 6 to 10 percent on their cargoes. They partially blocked the traditional Red Sea route to the Mediterranean and for a century or so monopolized the highly profitable route around Africa to Europe. Even so, they never succeeded in controlling much more than half of the spice trade to Europe.

The Spice Trade
For thousands of years, spices were a major trade item in the Indian Ocean commercial network, as this fifteenth-century French depiction of the gathering of pepper in southern India illustrates. In the early modern era, Europeans gained direct access to this ancient network for the first time. (From the *Livres des Merveilles du Monde*, ca. 1410–1412, by Master Boucicaut [fl. 1390–1430] and workshop/Bibliothèque Nationale, Paris, France /Archives Charmet/Bridgeman Images)

Failing to dominate Indian Ocean commerce as they had hoped, the Portuguese gradually assimilated themselves to its ancient patterns. They became heavily involved in carrying Asian goods to Asian ports, selling their shipping services because they were largely unable to sell their goods. Even in their major settlements, the Portuguese were outnumbered by Asian traders, and many married Asian women. Hundreds of Portuguese escaped the control of their government altogether and settled in Asian or African ports, where they learned local languages, sometimes converted to Islam, and became simply one more group in the diverse trading culture of the East.

By 1600, the Portuguese trading post empire was in steep decline. This small European country was overextended, and rising Asian states such as Japan, Burma, Mughal India, Persia, and the sultanate of Oman actively resisted Portuguese commercial control. Unwilling to accept a dominant Portuguese role in the Indian Ocean, other European countries also gradually contested Portugal's efforts to monopolize the rich spice trade to Europe.

Spain and the Philippines

Spain was the first to challenge Portugal's position. As precious and profitable spices began to arrive in Europe on Portuguese ships in the early sixteenth century, the Spanish soon realized that they were behind in the race to gain access to the riches of the East. In an effort to catch up, they established themselves on what became the Philippine Islands, named after the Spanish king Philip II. The Spanish first encountered the region during the famous round-the-world voyage (1519–1521) of Ferdinand Magellan, a Portuguese mariner sailing on behalf of the Spanish Crown. There they found an archipelago of islands, thousands of them, occupied by culturally diverse peoples and organized in small and highly competitive chiefdoms. One of the local chiefs later told the Spanish: "There is no king and no sole authority in this land; but everyone holds his own view and opinion, and does as he prefers."[4] Some were involved in tribute trade with China, and a small number of Chinese settlers lived in the port towns. Nonetheless, the region was of little interest to the governments of China and Japan, the major powers in the area.

These conditions—proximity to China and the spice islands, small and militarily weak societies, the absence of competing claims—encouraged the Spanish to establish outright colonial rule on the islands, rather than to imitate a Portuguese-style trading post empire. Accomplished largely from Spanish Mexico, conquest and colonization involved small-scale military operations, gunpowder weapons, local alliances, gifts and favors to chiefs, and the pageantry of Catholic ritual, all of which contributed to a relatively easy and often-bloodless Spanish takeover of the islands in the century or so after 1565. They remained a Spanish colonial territory until the end of the nineteenth century, when the United States assumed control following the Spanish-American War of 1898.

Accompanying Spanish rule was a major missionary effort, which turned Filipino society into the only major outpost of Christianity in Asia. That effort also opened up a new front in the long encounter of Christendom and Islam, for on the southern island of Mindanao, Islam was gaining strength and provided an ideology of resistance to Spanish encroachment for 300 years. Indeed, Mindanao remains a contested part of the Philippines into the twenty-first century.

Beyond the missionary enterprise, other features of Spanish colonial practice in the Americas found expression in the Philippines. People living in scattered settlements were persuaded or forced to relocate into more concentrated Christian communities. Tribute, taxes, and unpaid labor became part of ordinary life. Large landed estates emerged, owned by Spanish settlers, Catholic religious orders, or prominent Filipinos. Women who had played major roles as ritual specialists, healers, and midwives were now displaced by male Spanish priests, and the ceremonial instruments of these women were deliberately defiled and disgraced. Short-lived revolts and flight to interior mountains were among the Filipino responses to colonial oppression.

Yet others fled to Manila, the new capital of the colonial Philippines. By 1600, it had become a flourishing and culturally diverse city of more than 40,000 inhabitants and was home to many Spanish settlers and officials and growing numbers of Filipino migrants. Its rising prosperity also attracted some 3,000 Japanese and more than 20,000 Chinese. Serving as traders, artisans, and sailors, the Chinese in particular became an essential element in the Spanish colony's growing economic

■ **Comparison**

How did the Portuguese, Spanish, Dutch, and British initiatives in Asia differ from one another?

relationship with China; however, their economic prominence and their resistance to conversion earned them Spanish hostility and clearly discriminatory treatment. Periodic Chinese revolts, followed by expulsions and massacres, were the result. On one occasion in 1603, the Spanish killed about 20,000 people, nearly the entire Chinese population of the island.

The East India Companies

Far more important than the Spanish as European competitors for the spice trade were the Dutch and English, both of whom entered Indian Ocean commerce in the early seventeenth century. Together they quickly overtook and displaced the Portuguese, often by force, even as they competed vigorously with each other as well. These rising Northern European powers were both militarily and economically stronger than the Portuguese. During the sixteenth century, the Dutch had become a highly commercialized and urbanized society, and their business skills and maritime shipping operations were the envy of Europe. Around 1600, both the British and the Dutch, unlike the Portuguese, organized their Indian Ocean ventures through private trading companies, which were able to raise money and share risks among a substantial number of merchant investors. The British East India Company and the Dutch East India Company received charters from their respective governments granting them trading monopolies and the power to make war and to govern conquered peoples. Thus they established their own parallel and competing trading post empires, with the Dutch focused on the islands of Indonesia and the English on India. Somewhat later, a French company also established settlements in the Indian Ocean basin.

■ **Change**
To what extent did the British and Dutch trading companies change the societies they encountered in Asia?

Operating in a region of fragmented and weak political authority, the Dutch acted to control not only the shipping of cloves, cinnamon, nutmeg, and mace but also their production. With much bloodshed, the Dutch seized control of a number of small spice-producing islands, forcing their people to sell only to the Dutch and destroying the crops of those who refused. On the Banda Islands, famous for their nutmeg, the Dutch killed, enslaved, or left to starve virtually the entire population of some 15,000 people and then replaced them with Dutch planters, using a slave labor force to produce the nutmeg crop. One Indonesian sultan asked a Dutch commander, "Do you believe that God has preserved for your trade alone islands which lie so far from your homeland?"[5] Apparently the Dutch did. And for a time in the seventeenth century, they were able to monopolize the trade in nutmeg, mace, and cloves and to sell these spices in Europe and India at fourteen to seventeen times the price they paid in Indonesia.[6] While Dutch profits soared, the local economy of the Spice Islands was shattered, and their people were impoverished.

The Dutch East India Company also established itself briefly on the large island of Taiwan, off the coast of southern China, between 1624 and 1662, hoping to produce deerskins, rice, and sugar for export. Finding the local people unwilling to take part in commercial agriculture, the Dutch opened the island to large-scale

Chinese immigration. Thus, under a regime of Dutch and Chinese "co-colonization," Taiwan became ethnically Chinese. Later in the century, Chinese forces expelled the Dutch, bringing Taiwan into China politically as well. And so Taiwan emerged as a site of intersection between European and Chinese expansion in the early modern era.[7]

The British East India Company operated differently from its Dutch counterpart. Less well financed and less commercially sophisticated, the British were largely excluded from the rich Spice Islands by the Dutch monopoly. Thus they fell back on India, where they established three major trading settlements during the seventeenth century: Bombay (now Mumbai), on India's west coast, and Calcutta and Madras, on the east coast. Although British naval forces soon gained control of the Arabian Sea and the Persian Gulf, largely replacing the Portuguese, on land they were no match for the powerful Mughal Empire, which ruled most of the Indian subcontinent. Therefore, the British were unable to practice "trade by warfare," as the Dutch did in Indonesia.[8] Rather, they secured their trading bases with the permission of Mughal authorities or local rulers, with substantial payments and bribes as the price of admission to the Indian market. When some independent English traders plundered a Mughal ship in 1636, local authorities detained British East India Company officials for two months and forced them to pay a whopping fine. Although pepper and other spices remained important in British trade, British merchants came to focus much more heavily on Indian cotton textiles, which were becoming widely popular in England and its American colonies. Hundreds of villages in the interior of southern India became specialized producers for this British market.

Like the Portuguese before them, both the Dutch and English became heavily involved in trade within Asia. The profits from this "carrying trade" enabled them to purchase Asian goods without paying for them in gold or silver from Europe. Dutch and English traders also began to deal in bulk goods for a mass market—pepper, textiles, and later, tea and coffee—rather than just luxury goods for an elite market. In the second half of the eighteenth century, both the Dutch and British trading post empires slowly evolved into a more conventional form of colonial domination, in which the British came to rule India and the Dutch controlled Indonesia.

A European View of Asian Commerce
The various East India companies (British, French, and Dutch) represented the major vehicle for European commerce in Asia during the early modern era. This wall painting, dating from 1778 and titled *The East Offering Its Riches to Britannia*, hung in the main offices of the British East India Company. (*The East Offering Its Riches to Britannia*, by Roma Spiridione [d. 1787]/British Library, London, UK/© British Library Board. All Rights Reserved/ Bridgeman Images)

Asians and Asian Commerce

The attention of historians often falls disproportionately on what is new. Although European commerce in the Indian Ocean and the South China Sea certainly qualifies as "something new," the European presence was far less significant in Asia than it was in the Americas or Africa during these centuries. European political control was limited to the Philippines, parts of Java, and a few of the Spice Islands. The small Southeast Asian state of Siam was able to expel the French in 1688, outraged by their aggressive religious efforts at conversion and their plotting to extend French influence. To the great powers of Asia — Mughal India, China, and Japan — Europeans represented no real military threat and played minor roles in their large and prosperous economies. Japan provides a fascinating case study in the ability of major Asian powers to control the European intruders.

When Portuguese traders and missionaries first arrived in that island nation in the mid-sixteenth century, soon followed by Spanish, Dutch, and English merchants, Japan was plagued by endemic conflict among numerous feudal lords, known as *daimyo*, each with his own cadre of *samurai* warriors. In these circumstances, the European newcomers found a hospitable welcome, for their military technology, shipbuilding skills, geographic knowledge, commercial opportunities, and even religious ideas proved useful or attractive to various elements in Japan's fractious and competitive society. The second half of the sixteenth century, for example, witnessed the growth of a substantial Christian movement, with some 300,000 converts and a Japanese-led church organization.

By the early seventeenth century, however, a series of remarkable military figures had unified Japan politically, under the leadership of a supreme military commander known as the *shogun*, who hailed from the Tokugawa clan. With the end of Japan's civil wars, successive shoguns came to view Europeans as a threat to the country's newly established unity rather than an opportunity. They therefore expelled Christian missionaries and violently suppressed the practice of Christianity. This policy included the execution, often under torture, of some sixty-two missionaries and thousands of Japanese converts. Shogunate authorities also forbade Japanese from traveling abroad and banned most European traders altogether, permitting only the Dutch, who appeared less interested in spreading Christianity, to trade at a single site. Thus, for two centuries (1650–1850), Japanese authorities of the Tokugawa shogunate largely closed their country off from the emerging world of European commerce, although they maintained their trading ties to China, Korea, and Southeast Asia.

In the early seventeenth century, a large number of Japanese traders began to operate in Southeast Asia, where they behaved much like the newly arriving Europeans, frequently using force in support of their commercial interests. But unlike European states, the Japanese government of the Tokugawa shogunate explicitly disavowed any responsibility for or connection with these Japanese merchants. In one of many letters to rulers of Southeast Asian states, the Tokugawa shogun wrote to officials in Cambodia in 1610: "Merchants from my country [Japan] go to several places in your country [Cambodia] as well as Cochinchina and Champa [Vietnam]. There they become cruel and ferocious. . . . These men cause terrible damage. . . . They commit crimes and cause suffering. . . . Their offenses are extremely serious. Please punish them immediately according to the laws of your country. It is not necessary to have any reservations in this regard."[9] Thus Japanese merchants lacked the kind of support from their government that European merchants consistently received, but they did not refrain from trading in Southeast Asia.

Nor did other Asian merchants disappear from the Indian Ocean, despite European naval dominance. Arab, Indian, Chinese, Javanese, Malay, Vietnamese, and other traders benefited from the upsurge in seaborne commerce. Resident communities of Chinese merchants inhabited many Southeast Asian port cities and dominated the growing spice trade between that region and China. Southeast Asian merchants, many of them women, continued a long tradition of involvement in international trade. Malay proverbs from the sixteenth century, for example, encouraged "teaching daughters how to calculate and make a profit."[10] Overland trade within Asia remained wholly in Asian hands and grew considerably. Christian merchants from Armenia were particularly active in the commerce linking Europe, the Middle East, and Central Asia. Tens of thousands of Indian merchants and moneylenders, mostly Hindus representing sophisticated family firms, lived throughout Central Asia, Persia, and Russia, thus connecting this vast region to markets in India. These international Asian commercial networks, equivalent in their commercial sophistication to those of Europe, continued to operate successfully even as Europeans militarized the seaborne commerce of the Indian Ocean.

Within India, large and wealthy family firms, such as the one headed by Vijri Vora during the seventeenth century, were able to monopolize the buying and selling of particular products, such as pepper or coral, and thus dictate terms and prices to the European trading companies. "He knoweth that wee must sell," complained one English trader about Vora, "and so beats us downe till we come to his owne rates." Furthermore, Vora was often the only source of loans for the cash-strapped Europeans, forcing them to pay interest rates as high as 12 to 18 percent annually. Despite their resentments, Europeans had little choice, because "none but Virji Vora hath moneye to lend or will lend."[11]

Silver and Global Commerce

Even more than the spice trade of Eurasia, it was the silver trade that gave birth to a genuinely global network of exchange (see Map 14.2). As one historian put it, silver "went round the world and made the world go round."[12] The mid-sixteenth-century discovery of silver deposits in Bolivia, and simultaneously in Japan, suddenly provided a vastly increased supply of that precious metal. Spanish America alone produced perhaps 85 percent of the world's silver during the early modern era. Spain's sole Asian colony, the Philippines, provided a critical link in

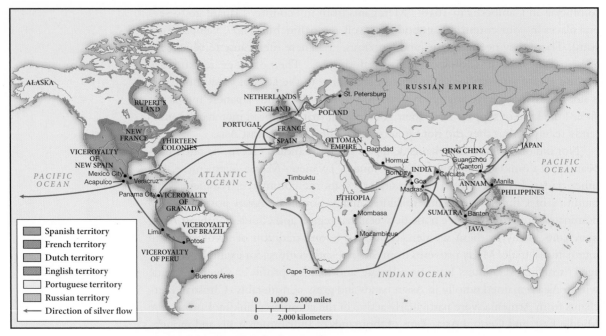

Map 14.2   The Global Silver Trade

Silver was one of the first major commodities to be exchanged on a genuinely global scale.

this emerging network of global commerce. Manila, the colonial capital of the Philippines, was the destination of annual Spanish shipments of silver, which were drawn from the rich mines of Bolivia, transported initially to Acapulco in Mexico, and from there shipped across the Pacific to the Philippines. This trade was the first direct and sustained link between the Americas and Asia, and it initiated a web of Pacific commerce that grew steadily over the centuries.

At the heart of that Pacific web, and of early modern global commerce generally, was China's huge economy, especially its growing demand for silver. In the 1570s, Chinese authorities consolidated a variety of tax levies into a single tax, which its huge population was now required to pay in silver. This sudden new demand for the white metal caused its value to skyrocket. It meant that foreigners with silver could now purchase far more of China's silks and porcelains than before.

This demand set silver in motion around the world, with the bulk of the world's silver supply winding up in China and much of the rest elsewhere in Asia. The routes by which this "silver drain" operated were numerous. Chinese, Portuguese, and Dutch traders flocked to Manila to sell Chinese goods in exchange for silver. European ships carried Japanese silver to China. Much of the silver shipped across the Atlantic to Spain was spent in Europe generally and then used to pay for the Asian goods that the French, British, and Dutch so greatly desired. Silver paid for some African slaves and for spices in Southeast Asia. The standard Spanish silver

■ **Connection**

What was the significance of the silver trade in the early modern era of world history?

coin, known as a "piece of eight," was used by merchants in North America, Europe, India, Russia, and West Africa as a medium of exchange. By 1600, it circulated widely in southern China. A Portuguese merchant in 1621 noted that silver "wanders throughout all the world . . . before flocking to China, where it remains as if at its natural center."[13]

In its global journeys, silver transformed much that it touched, and nowhere more profoundly than at Potosí, the site of a huge silver-mining operation in what is now Bolivia. (See Zooming In: Potosí, page 614.) In Spain itself, which was the initial destination for much of Latin America's silver, the precious metal vastly enriched the Crown, making Spain the envy of its European rivals during the sixteenth century. Spanish rulers could now pursue military and political ambitions in both Europe and the Americas far beyond the country's own resource base. "New World mines," concluded several prominent historians, "supported the Spanish empire."[14] Nonetheless, this vast infusion of wealth did not fundamentally transform the Spanish economy, because it generated more inflation of prices than real economic growth. A rigid economy laced with monopolies and regulations, an aristocratic class that preferred leisure to enterprise, and a crusading insistence on religious uniformity all prevented the Spanish from using their silver windfall in a productive fashion. When the value of silver dropped in the early seventeenth century, Spain lost its earlier position as the dominant Western European power. More generally, the flood of American silver that circulated in Europe drove prices higher, further impoverished many, stimulated uprisings across the continent, and, together with the Little Ice Age of global cooling, contributed to what historians sometimes call a "General Crisis" of upheaval and instability in the seventeenth century. (For a broader discussion of the General Crisis, see Chapter 13, page 560.)

Japan, another major source of silver production in the sixteenth century, did better. Its military rulers, the Tokugawa shoguns, used silver-generated profits to defeat hundreds of rival feudal lords and unify the country. Unlike their Spanish counterparts, the shoguns allied with the country's vigorous domestic merchant class to develop a market-based economy and to invest heavily in agricultural and industrial enterprises. Japanese state and local authorities alike acted vigorously to protect and renew Japan's dwindling forests, while millions of families in the eighteenth century took steps to have fewer children by practicing late marriages, contraception, abortion, and infanticide. The outcome was the dramatic slowing of Japan's population growth, the easing of an impending ecological crisis, and a flourishing, highly commercialized economy. These were the foundations for Japan's remarkable nineteenth-century Industrial Revolution.

In China, silver deepened the already-substantial commercialization of the country's economy. To obtain the silver needed to pay their taxes, more and more people had to sell something—either their labor or their products. Communities that devoted themselves to growing mulberry trees, on which silkworms fed, had to buy their rice from other regions. Thus the Chinese economy became more

Potosí, a Mountain of Silver

The mines of Potosí.

China's insatiable demand for silver during the early modern period drove global commerce, transforming the economies and societies of far distant lands. Perhaps nowhere did the silver trade have a greater impact than at Cerro de Potosí, a mountain located in a barren and remote stretch of Andean highlands, ten weeks' travel by mule from Lima, Peru. In 1545, Spanish prospectors discovered the richest deposit of silver in history at Potosí, and within a few decades this single mountain was producing over half of the silver mined in the world each year. At its foot, the city of Potosí grew rapidly. "New people arrive by the hour, attracted by the smell of silver," commented a Spanish observer in the 1570s. Within just a few decades, Potosí's population had reached 160,000 people, making it the largest city in the Americas and equivalent in size to London, Amsterdam, or Seville.

The silver was mined and processed at great human and environmental cost. The Spanish authorities forced Native American villages across a wide region of the Andes to supply workers for the mines, with as many as 14,000 to 16,000 at a time laboring in horrendous conditions. A Spanish priest observed, "Once inside, they spend the whole week in there without emerging, working with tallow candles. They are in great danger inside there, for one very small stone that falls injures or kills anyone it strikes. If 20 healthy Indians enter on Monday, half may emerge crippled on Saturday."[15] Work aboveground, often undertaken by slaves of African descent, was also dangerous because extracting silver from the mined ore required mixing it with the toxic metal mercury. Many thousands died. Mortality rates were so high that some families held funeral

regionally specialized. Particularly in southern China, this surging economic growth resulted in the loss of about half the area's forest cover as more and more land was devoted to cash crops. No Japanese-style conservation program emerged to address this growing problem. An eighteenth-century Chinese poet, Wang Dayue, gave voice to the fears that this ecological transformation generated:

Rarer, too, their timber grew, and rarer still and rarer
As the hills resembled heads now shaven clean of hair.
For the first time, too, moreover, they felt an anxious mood
That all their daily logging might not furnish them with fuel.[16]

China's role in the silver trade is a useful reminder of Asian centrality in the world economy of the early modern era. Its large and prosperous population,

services for men drafted to work in the mines before they embarked for Potosí. Beyond the human cost, the environment suffered as well when highly intensive mining techniques deforested the region and poisoned and eroded the soil.

Although some indigenous merchants, muleteers, and chiefs were enriched by mining, much of the wealth generated flowed to the Europeans who owned the mines and to the Spanish government, which impounded one-fifth of the silver as well as collecting other taxes and duties. European elites in Potosí lived in luxury, with all the goods of Europe and Asia at their disposal. Merchants brought to Potosí French hats, Venetian glass, German swords, Persian carpets, Southeast Asian spices, and Chinese porcelain and silks. Potosí also imported almost all of its basic needs because the dry, cold region was unable to support the city. Pack trains of llamas brought large quantities of foodstuffs, cloth, and other necessities from Ecuador, Peru, Chile, and Argentina. By the early seventeenth century, the economies of many regions in Spanish South America were structured to supply this huge mining operation.

While the mines caused much suffering, the silver-fueled economy of Potosí also offered opportunity to groups beyond the mine-owning European elite, not least to women. To earn a few pesos for the household, Spanish women might rent out buildings they owned for commercial purposes or send their slaves into the streets as small-scale traders. Less well-to-do Spanish women often ran stores, pawnshops, bakeries, and taverns. Indian and *mestiza* women likewise opened businesses that provided the city with beverages, food, clothing, and credit. The wealth created a hive of commercial activity in this otherwise-barren backwater.

But the silver that created Potosí also caused its decline. After a century of intensive mining, all that remained were lower-quality ores that were difficult to extract from the ground. This led the mines to shut down. By 1800, Potosí, which had once rivaled the largest cities in Europe, was just a shadow of its former self. The history of this remote region of the Andes reminds us of the profound and often-conflicting results of world trade during the early modern period. While many suffered in the hellish conditions of the mines, others grew wealthy off the demand for silver.

Question: What can Potosí tell us about the consequences of global trade in the early modern period?

increasingly operating within a silver-based economy, fueled global commerce, vastly increasing the quantity of goods exchanged and the geographic range of world trade. Despite their obvious physical presence in the Americas, Africa, and Asia, economically speaking Europeans were essentially middlemen, funneling American silver to Asia and competing with one another for a place in the rich markets of the East. The productivity of the Chinese economy was evident in Spanish America, where cheap and well-made Chinese goods easily outsold those of Spain. In 1594, the Spanish viceroy of Peru observed that "a man can clothe his wife in Chinese silks for [25 pesos], whereas he could not provide her with clothing of Spanish silks with 200 pesos."[17] Indian cotton textiles likewise outsold European woolen or linen textiles in the seventeenth century to such an extent that French laws in 1717 prohibited the wearing of Indian cotton or Chinese silk clothing as a means of protecting French industry.

"The World Hunt": Fur in Global Commerce

In the early modern era, furs joined silver, textiles, and spices as major items of global commerce.[18] Their production had an important environmental impact as well as serious implications for the human societies that generated and consumed them. Furs, of course, had long provided warmth and conveyed status in colder regions of the world, but the integration of North America and of northern Asia (Siberia) into a larger world economy vastly increased their significance in global trade.

■ **Change**

Describe the impact of the fur trade on North American native societies.

By 1500, European population growth and agricultural expansion had sharply diminished the supply of fur-bearing animals, such as beaver, rabbits, sable, marten, and deer. Furthermore, much of the early modern era witnessed a period of cooling temperatures and harsh winters, known as the Little Ice Age, which may well have increased the demand for furs. "The weather is bitterly cold and everyone is in furs although we are almost in July," observed a surprised visitor from Venice while in London in 1604.[19] These conditions pushed prices higher. The cost of a good-quality beaver pelt, for example, quadrupled in France between 1558 and 1611. This price increase translated into strong economic incentives for European traders to tap the immense wealth of fur-bearing animals found in North America. At the same time, the collapse of Native American populations in North America caused by the Great Dying led to the regrowth of forest habitats for fur-bearing animals and deer herds.

Like other aspects of imperial expansion, the fur trade was a highly competitive enterprise. The French were most prominent in the St. Lawrence valley, around the Great Lakes, and later along the Mississippi River; British traders pushed into the Hudson Bay region; and the Dutch focused their attention along the Hudson River in what is now New York. They were frequently rivals for the great prize of North American furs. In the southern colonies of British North America, deerskins by the hundreds of thousands found a ready market in England's leather industry (see Map 14.3).

Only a few Europeans directly engaged in commercial trapping or hunting. They usually waited for Indians to bring the furs or skins initially to their coastal settlements and later to their fortified trading posts in the interior of North America. European merchants paid for the furs with a variety of trade goods, including guns, blankets, metal tools, rum, and brandy, amid much ceremony, haggling over prices, and ritualized gift giving. Native Americans represented a cheap labor force in this international commercial effort, but they were not a directly coerced labor force.

Over the three centuries of the early modern era, enormous quantities of furs and deerskins found their way to Europe, where they considerably enhanced the standard of living in those cold climates. The environmental price was paid in the Americas, and it was high. A consistent demand for beaver hats led to the near extinction of that industrious animal in much of North America by the early nineteenth century and with it the degradation or loss of many wetland habitats. Other

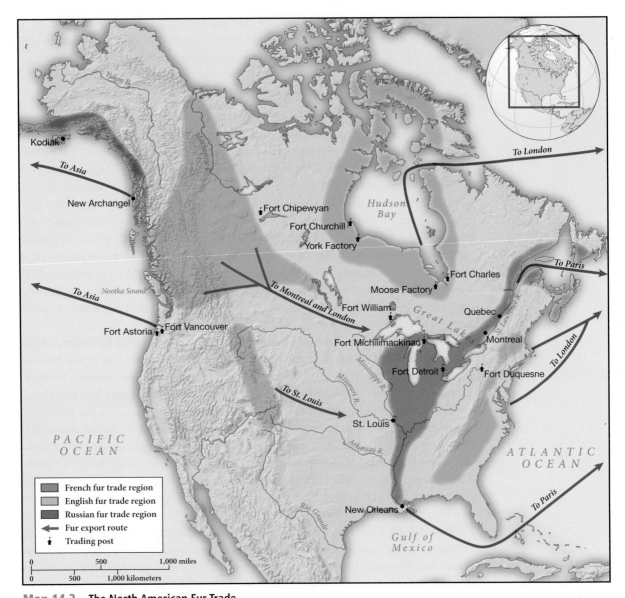

Map 14.3 The North American Fur Trade

North America, as well as Russian Siberia, funneled an apparently endless supply of furs into the circuits of global trade during the early modern era.

fur-bearing species were also seriously depleted as the trade moved inexorably westward. By the 1760s, hunters in southeastern British colonies took about 500,000 deer every year, seriously diminishing the deer population of the region. As early as 1642, Miantonomo, a chief of the New England Narragansett people, spoke of the environmental consequences of English colonialism:

> You know our fathers had plenty of deer and skins and our plains were full of game and turkeys, and our coves and rivers were full of fish. But, brothers, since these Englishmen have seized our country, they have cut down the grass with scythes, and the trees with axes. Their cows and horses eat up the grass, and their hogs spoil our bed of clams; and finally we shall all starve to death.[20]

For the Native American peoples who hunted, trapped, processed, and transported these products, the fur trade bore various benefits, particularly at the beginning. The Hurons, for example, who lived on the northern shores of Lakes Erie and Ontario in the early seventeenth century, annually exchanged some 20,000 to 30,000 pelts, mostly beaver, and in return received copper pots, metal axes, knives, cloth, firearms, and alcohol. Many of these items were of real value, which strengthened the Hurons in their relationships with neighboring peoples. These goods also enhanced the authority of Huron chiefs by providing them with gifts to distribute among their followers. At least initially, competition among Europeans ensured that Native American leaders could negotiate reasonable prices for their goods. Furthermore, their important role in the lucrative fur trade protected them for a time from the kind of extermination, enslavement, or displacement that was the fate of native peoples in Portuguese Brazil.

Nothing, however, protected them against the diseases carried by Europeans. In the 1630s and 1640s, to cite only one example of many, about half of the Hurons perished from influenza, smallpox, and other European-borne diseases. Furthermore, the fur trade generated warfare beyond anything previously known. Competition among Native American societies became more intense as the economic stakes grew higher. Catastrophic population declines owing to disease stimulated "mourning wars," designed to capture people who could be assimilated into much-diminished societies. A century of French-British rivalry for North America (1664–1763) forced Native American societies to take sides, to fight, and to die in these European imperial conflicts. Firearms, of course, made warfare far more deadly than before.

Beyond the fur trade, many Native American peoples sought actively to take advantage of the new commercial economy now impinging upon them. The Iroquois, for example, began to sell new products such as ginseng root, much in demand in China as a medicine. They also rented land to Europeans, worked for wages in various European enterprises, and started to use currency, when barter was ineffective. But as they became enmeshed in these commercial relationships, Native Americans grew dependent on European trade goods. Among the Algonquians, for example, iron tools and cooking pots replaced those of stone, wood, or bone; gunpowder weapons took the place of bows and arrows; European textiles proved more attractive than traditional beaver and deerskin clothing; and flint and steel were found to be more effective for starting fires than wooden drills. A wide range of traditional crafts were thus lost, while the native peoples did not gain a corresponding ability to manufacture the new items for themselves. Enthusiasm for these imported goods and continued European demands for furs and skins frequently eroded the customary restraint that characterized traditional hunting practices, resulting in the depletion of many species. One European observer wrote of the Creek Indians: "[They] wage eternal war against deer and bear . . . which is indeed carried to an unreasonable and perhaps criminal excess, since the white people have dazzled their senses with foreign superfluities."[21]

Alongside germs and guns, yet another highly destructive European import was alcohol—rum and brandy, in particular. Whiskey, a locally produced grain-based alcohol, only added to the problem. With no prior experience of alcohol and little time to adjust to its easy availability, these drinks "hit Indian societies with explosive force."[22] Binge drinking, violence among young men, promiscuity, and addiction followed in many places. In 1753, Iroquois leaders complained bitterly to European authorities in Pennsylvania: "These wicked Whiskey Sellers, when they have once got the Indians in liquor, make them sell their very clothes from their backs. . . . If this practice be continued, we must be inevitably ruined."[23] In short, it was not so much the fur trade itself that decimated Native American societies, but all that accompanied it—disease, dependence, guns, alcohol, and the growing encroachment of European colonial empires.

All of this had particular implications for women. A substantial number of native women married European traders according to the "custom of the country"—with no sanction from civil or church authorities. Such marriages eased the difficulties of this cross-cultural exchange, providing traders with guides, interpreters, and negotiators. But sometimes these women were left abandoned when their husbands returned to Europe. More generally, the fur trade enhanced the position of men in their societies since hunting or trapping animals was normally a male occupation. Among the Ojibwa, a gathering and hunting people in the northern Great Lakes region, women had traditionally acquired economic power by creating

Fur and the Russians
This colored engraving shows a sixteenth-century Russian ambassador and his contingent arriving at the court of the Holy Roman Emperor and bearing gifts of animal pelts, the richest fruit of the expanding Russian Empire. (Contemporary color line engraving, 1576/The Granger Collection, NYC—All rights reserved)

food, utensils, clothing, and decorations from the hides and flesh of the animals that their husbands caught. With the fur trade in full operation, women spent more time processing those furs for sale than in producing household items, some of which were now available for purchase from Europeans. And so, as one scholar put it, "women lost authority and prestige." At the same time, however, women generated and controlled the trade in wild rice and maple syrup, both essential to the livelihood of European traders.[24] Thus the fur trade offered women a mix of opportunities and liabilities.

Paralleling the North American fur trade was the one simultaneously taking shape within a rapidly expanding Russian Empire, which became a major source of furs for Western Europe, China, and the Ottoman Empire. The profitability of that trade in furs was the chief incentive for Russia's rapid expansion during the sixteenth and seventeenth centuries across Siberia, where the "soft gold" of fur-bearing animals was abundant. The international sale of furs greatly enriched the Russian state as well as many private merchants, trappers, and hunters. Here the silver trade and the fur trade intersected, as Europeans paid for Russian furs largely with American gold and silver.

■ **Comparison**

How did the North American and Siberian fur trades differ from each other? What did they have in common?

The consequences for native Siberians were similar to those in North America as disease took its toll, as indigenous people became dependent on Russian goods, as the settler frontier encroached on native lands, and as many species of fur-bearing mammals were seriously depleted. In several ways, however, the Russian fur trade was unique. Whereas several European nations competed in North America and generally obtained their furs through commercial negotiations with Indian societies, no such competition accompanied Russian expansion across Siberia. Russian authorities imposed a tax or tribute, payable in furs, on every able-bodied Siberian male between eighteen and fifty years of age. To enforce the payment, they took hostages from Siberian societies, with death as a possible outcome if the required furs were not forthcoming. A further difference lay in the large-scale presence of private Russian hunters and trappers, who competed directly with their Siberian counterparts.

SUMMING UP SO FAR

What differences can you identify in the operation and impact of the spice, silver, and fur trades?

Commerce in People: The Atlantic Slave Trade

Of all the commercial ties that linked the early modern world into a global network of exchange, none had more profound or enduring human consequences than the Atlantic slave trade. Between 1500 and 1866, this trade in human beings took an estimated 12.5 million people from African societies, shipped them across the Atlantic in the infamous Middle Passage, and deposited some 10.7 million of them in the Americas, where they lived out their often-brief lives as slaves. About 1.8 million (14.4 percent) died during the transatlantic crossing, while countless others perished in the process of capture and transport to the African coast.[25] (See Map 14.4.)

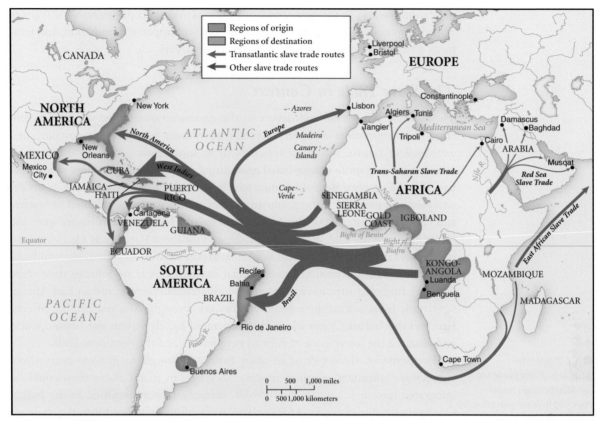

Map 14.4   The Atlantic Slave Trade

Stimulated by the plantation complex of the Americas, the Atlantic slave trade represented an enormous extension of the ancient practice of people owning and selling other people.

Beyond the multitude of individual tragedies that it spawned—capture and sale, displacement from home cultures, forced labor, beatings and brandings, broken families—the Atlantic slave trade transformed all of its participants. Within Africa itself, that commerce thoroughly disrupted some societies, strengthened others, and corrupted many. Elites often enriched themselves, while the slaves, of course, were victimized almost beyond imagination.

In the Americas, the slave trade added a substantial African presence to the mix of European and Native American peoples. This African diaspora (the global spread of African peoples) injected into these new societies issues of race that endure still in the twenty-first century. It also introduced elements of African culture, such as religious ideas, musical and artistic traditions, and cuisine, into the making of American cultures. The profits from the slave trade and the forced labor of African slaves certainly enriched European and Euro-American societies, even as the practice of slavery contributed much to the racial stereotypes of European peoples. Finally, slavery became a metaphor for many kinds of social oppression, quite different from plantation slavery, in the centuries that followed. Workers protested the slavery of wage labor, colonized people rejected the slavery of imperial domination, and feminists sometimes defined patriarchy as a form of slavery.

The Slave Trade in Context

The Atlantic slave trade and slavery in the Americas represented the most recent large-scale expression of a very widespread human practice—the owning and exchange of human beings. It was present in some early gathering and hunting societies, among some village-based agricultural peoples, and in pastoral communities. But the practice flourished most widely in civilizations where it was generally accepted as a perfectly normal human enterprise and was closely linked to warfare and capture. Before 1500, the Mediterranean and Indian Ocean basins were the major arenas of the Old World slave trade, and southern Russia was a major source of slaves. Many African societies likewise both practiced slavery themselves and sold slaves into these international commercial networks. A trans-Saharan slave trade had long funneled African captives into Mediterranean slavery, and an East African slave trade from at least the seventh century C.E. brought Africans into the Middle East and the Indian Ocean basin. Both operated largely within the Islamic world and initiated the movement of African peoples beyond the continent itself.

■ **Comparison**

What was distinctive about the Atlantic slave trade? What did it share with other patterns of slave owning and slave trading?

Furthermore, slavery came in many forms. Although slaves were everywhere vulnerable "outsiders" to their masters' societies, in many places they could be integrated into their owners' households, lineages, or communities. In the Indian Ocean world, for example, African slaves were often assimilated into the societies of their owners and lost the sense of a distinctive identity that was so prominent in North America. In some places, children inherited the slave status of their parents; elsewhere those children were free persons. Within the Islamic world, where most slaves worked in domestic settings, the preference was for female slaves by a two-to-one margin, while the later Atlantic slave trade, which funneled captives into plantation labor, favored males by a similar margin. Not all slaves, however, occupied degraded positions. Some in the Islamic world acquired prominent military or political status. Most slaves in the premodern world worked in their owners' households, farms, or shops, with smaller numbers laboring in large-scale agricultural or industrial enterprises.

The slavery that emerged in the Americas was distinctive in several ways. One was simply the immense size of the traffic in slaves and its centrality to the economies of colonial America. Furthermore, this New World slavery was largely based on plantation agriculture and treated slaves as a form of dehumanized property, lacking any rights in the society of their owners. Slave status throughout the Americas was inherited across generations, and there was little hope of eventual freedom for the vast majority. Nowhere else, with the possible exception of ancient Greece, was widespread slavery associated with societies that affirmed values of human freedom and equality. Perhaps most distinctive was the racial dimension: Atlantic slavery came to be identified wholly with Africa and with "blackness." How did this exceptional form of slavery emerge?

The origins of Atlantic slavery clearly lie in the Mediterranean world and with that now-common sweetener known as sugar. Until the Crusades, Europeans knew nothing of sugar and relied on honey and fruits to sweeten their bland diets. However, as they learned from the Arabs about sugarcane and the laborious techniques for producing usable sugar, Europeans established sugar-producing plantations within the Mediterranean and later on various islands off the coast of West Africa. It was a "modern" industry, perhaps the first one, in that it required huge capital investment, substantial technology, an almost factory-like discipline among workers, and a mass market of consumers. The immense difficulty and danger of the work, the limitations attached to serf labor, and the general absence of wageworkers all pointed to slavery as a source of labor for sugar plantations.

Initially, Slavic-speaking peoples from the Black Sea region furnished the bulk of the slaves for Mediterranean plantations, so much so that "Slav" became the basis for the word "slave" in many European languages. In 1453, however, when the Ottoman Turks seized Constantinople, the supply of Slavic slaves was effectively cut off. At the same time, Portuguese mariners were exploring the coast of West Africa; they were looking primarily for gold, but they also found there an alternative source of slaves available for sale. Thus, when sugar, and later tobacco and cotton, plantations took hold in the Americas, Europeans had already established links to a West African source of supply. They also now had religious justification for their actions, for in 1452 the pope formally granted to the kings of Spain and Portugal "full and free permission to invade, search out, capture, and subjugate the Saracens [Muslims] and pagans and any other unbelievers . . . and to reduce their persons into perpetual slavery."[26] Largely through a process of elimination, Africa became the primary source of slave labor for the plantation economies of the Americas. Slavic peoples were no longer available; Native Americans quickly perished from European diseases; marginal Europeans were Christians and therefore supposedly exempt from slavery; and European indentured servants, who agreed to work for a fixed period in return for transportation, food, and shelter, were expensive and temporary. Africans, on the other hand, were skilled farmers; they had some immunity to both tropical and European diseases; they were not Christians; they were, relatively speaking, close at hand; and they were readily available in substantial numbers through African-operated commercial networks.

Moreover, Africans were black. The precise relationship between slavery and European racism has long been a much-debated subject. Historian David Brion Davis has suggested the controversial view that "racial stereotypes were transmitted, along with black slavery itself, from Muslims to Christians."[27] For many centuries, Muslims had drawn on sub-Saharan Africa as one source of slaves and in the process had developed a form of racism. The fourteenth-century Tunisian scholar

■ **Causation**
What explains the rise of the Atlantic slave trade?

Ibn Khaldun wrote that black people were "submissive to slavery, because Negroes have little that is essentially human and have attributes that are quite similar to those of dumb animals."[28]

Other scholars find the origins of racism within European culture itself. For the English, argues historian Audrey Smedley, the process of conquering Ireland had generated by the sixteenth century a view of the Irish as "rude, beastly, ignorant, cruel, and unruly infidels," perceptions that were then transferred to Africans enslaved on English sugar plantations of the West Indies.[29] Whether Europeans borrowed such images of Africans from their Muslim neighbors or developed them independently, slavery and racism soon went hand in hand. "Europeans were better able to tolerate their brutal exploitation of Africans," writes a prominent world historian, "by imagining that these Africans were an inferior race, or better still, not even human."[30]

The Slave Trade in Practice

The European demand for slaves was clearly the chief cause of this tragic commerce, and from the point of sale on the African coast to the massive use of slave labor on American plantations, the entire enterprise was in European hands. Within Africa itself, however, a different picture emerges, for over the four centuries of the Atlantic slave trade, European demand elicited an African supply. A few early efforts by the Portuguese at slave raiding along the West African coast convinced Europeans that such efforts were unwise and unnecessary, for African societies were quite capable of defending themselves against European intrusion, and many were willing to sell their slaves peacefully. Furthermore, Europeans died like flies when they entered the interior because they lacked immunities to common tropical diseases. Thus the slave trade quickly came to operate largely with Europeans waiting on the coast, either on their ships or in fortified settlements, to purchase slaves from African merchants and political elites. Certainly, Europeans tried to exploit African rivalries to obtain slaves at the lowest possible cost, and the firearms they funneled into West Africa may well have increased the warfare from which so many slaves were derived. But from the point of initial capture to sale on the coast, the entire enterprise was normally in African hands. Almost nowhere did Europeans attempt outright military conquest; instead they generally dealt as equals with local African authorities.

■ **Connection**

What roles did Europeans and Africans play in the unfolding of the Atlantic slave trade?

An arrogant agent of the British Royal Africa Company in the 1680s learned the hard way who was in control when he spoke improperly to the king of Niumi, a small state in what is now Gambia. The company's records describe what happened next:

> [O]ne of the grandees [of the king], by name Sambalama, taught him better manners by reaching him a box on the ears, which beat off his hat, and a few thumps on the back, and seizing him . . . and several others, who together with the agent were taken and put into the king's pound and stayed there three or four days till their ransom was brought, value five hundred bars.[31]

In exchange for slaves, African sellers sought both European and Indian textiles, cowrie shells (widely used as money in West Africa), European metal goods, firearms and gunpowder, tobacco and alcohol, and various decorative items such as beads. Europeans purchased some of these items—cowrie shells and Indian textiles, for example—with silver mined in the Americas. Thus the slave trade connected with commerce in silver and textiles as it became part of an emerging worldwide network of exchange. Issues about the precise mix of goods African authorities desired, about the number and quality of slaves to be purchased, and always about the price of everything were settled in endless negotiation. Most of the time, a leading historian concluded, the slave trade took place "not unlike international trade anywhere in the world of the period."[32]

For the slaves themselves—seized in the interior, often sold several times on the harrowing journey to the coast, sometimes branded, and held in squalid slave dungeons while awaiting transportation to the New World—it was anything but a normal commercial transaction. One European engaged in the trade noted that "the negroes are so willful and loath to leave their own country, that they have often leap'd out of the canoes, boat, and ship, into the sea, and kept under water till they were drowned, to avoid being taken up and saved by our boats."[33]

Over the four centuries of the slave trade, millions of Africans underwent such experiences, but their numbers varied considerably over time. During the sixteenth century, slave exports from Africa averaged fewer than 3,000 annually. In those years, the Portuguese were at least as much interested in African gold, spices, and textiles. Furthermore, as in Asia, they became involved in transporting African goods, including slaves, from one African port to another, thus becoming the "truck drivers" of coastal West African commerce.[34] In the seventeenth century, the pace picked up as the slave trade became highly competitive, with the

The Middle Passage
This mid-nineteenth-century painting of slaves held belowdecks on a Spanish slave ship illustrates the horrendous conditions of the transatlantic voyage, a journey experienced by many millions of captured Africans. (Watercolor by Lt. Francis Meinelli, British Royal Navy/The Granger Collection, NYC—All rights reserved)

British, Dutch, and French contesting the earlier Portuguese monopoly. The century and a half between 1700 and 1850 marked the high point of the slave trade as the plantation economies of the Americas boomed. (See Snapshot, opposite.)

Where did these Africans come from, and where did they go? Geographically, the slave trade drew mainly on the societies of West and South-Central Africa, from present-day Mauritania in the north to Angola in the south. Initially focused on the coastal regions, the slave trade progressively penetrated into the interior as the demand for slaves picked up. Socially, slaves were mostly drawn from various marginal groups in African societies—prisoners of war, criminals, debtors, people who had been "pawned" during times of difficulty. Thus Africans did not generally sell "their own people" into slavery. Divided into hundreds of separate, usually small-scale, and often rival communities—cities, kingdoms, microstates, clans, and villages—the various peoples of West Africa had no concept of an "African" identity. Those whom they captured and sold were normally outsiders, vulnerable people who lacked the protection of membership in an established community. When short-term economic or political advantage could be gained, such people were sold. In this respect, the Atlantic slave trade was little different from the experience of enslavement elsewhere in the world.

The destination of enslaved Africans, half a world away in the Americas, was very different. The vast majority wound up in Brazil or the Caribbean, where the labor demands of the plantation economy were most intense. Smaller numbers found themselves in North America, mainland Spanish America, or in Europe itself. Their journey across the Atlantic was horrendous, with the Middle Passage having an overall mortality rate of more than 14 percent.

Enslaved Africans frequently resisted their fates in a variety of ways. About 10 percent of the transatlantic voyages experienced a major rebellion by desperate captives, and resistance continued in the Americas, taking a range of forms from surreptitious slowdowns of work to outright rebellion. One common act was to flee. Many who escaped joined free communities of former slaves known as maroon societies, which were founded in remote regions, especially in South America and the Caribbean. The largest such settlement was Palmares in Brazil, which endured for most of the seventeenth century, housing 10,000 or more people, mostly of African descent but also including Native Americans, mestizos, and renegade whites. While slave owners feared wide-scale slave rebellions, these were rare, and even small-scale rebellions were usually crushed with great brutality. It was only with the Haitian Revolution of the 1790s that a full-scale slave revolt brought lasting freedom for its participants.

Consequences: The Impact of the Slave Trade in Africa

From the viewpoint of world history, the chief outcome of the slave trade lay in the new transregional linkages that it generated as Africa became a permanent part of an interacting Atlantic world. Millions of its people were now compelled to make

SNAPSHOT   The Slave Trade in Numbers (1501–1866)[35]

The Rise and Decline of the Slave Trade

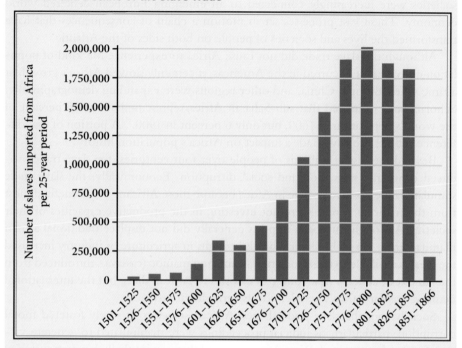

The Destinations of Slaves

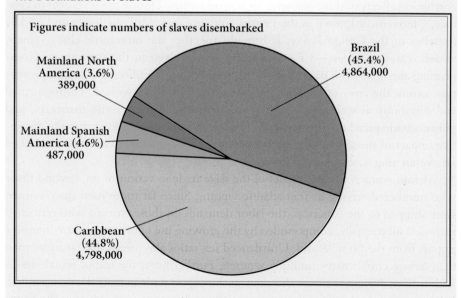

Figures indicate numbers of slaves disembarked

Mainland North America (3.6%) 389,000

Brazil (45.4%) 4,864,000

Mainland Spanish America (4.6%) 487,000

Caribbean (44.8%) 4,798,000

their lives in the Americas, where they made an enormous impact both demo-graphically and economically. Until the nineteenth century, they outnumbered European immigrants to the Americas by three or four to one, and West African societies were increasingly connected to an emerging European-centered world economy. These vast processes set in motion a chain of consequences that have transformed the lives and societies of people on both sides of the Atlantic.

■ **Change**

In what different ways did the Atlantic slave trade transform African societies?

Although the slave trade did not cause Africa to experience the kind of popu-lation collapse that occurred in the Americas, it certainly slowed Africa's growth at a time when Europe, China, and other regions were expanding demographically. Scholars have estimated that sub-Saharan Africa represented about 18 percent of the world's population in 1600, but only 6 percent in 1900.[36] A portion of that dif-ference reflects the slave trade's impact on Africa's population history.

Beyond the loss of millions of people over four centuries, the slave trade pro-duced economic stagnation and social disruption. Economically, the slave trade stimulated little positive change in Africa because those Africans who benefited most from the traffic in people were not investing in the productive capacities of their societies. Although European imports generally did not displace traditional artisan manufacturing, no technological breakthroughs in agriculture or industry increased the wealth available to these societies. Maize and manioc (cassava), introduced from the Americas, added a new source of calories to African diets, but the international demand was for Africa's people, not its agricultural products.

Socially too, the slave trade shaped African societies. It surely fostered moral corruption, particularly as judicial proceedings were manipulated to generate vic-tims for the slave trade. A West African legend that cowrie shells, a major currency of the slave trade, grew on corpses of the slaves was a symbolic recognition of the corrupting effects of this commerce in human beings. During the seventeenth cen-tury, a movement known as the Lemba cult appeared along the lower and middle stretches of the Congo River. It brought together the mercantile elite—chiefs, traders, caravan leaders—of a region heavily involved in the slave trade. Com-plaining about stomach pains, breathing problems, and sterility, they sought protec-tion against the envy of the poor and the sorcery that it provoked. Through ritual and ceremony as well as efforts to control markets, arrange elite marriages, and police a widespread trading network, Lemba officials sought to counter the disrup-tive impact of the slave trade and to maintain elite privileges in an area that lacked an overarching state authority.

African women felt the impact of the slave trade in various ways, beyond those who numbered among its transatlantic victims. Since far more men than women were shipped to the Americas, the labor demands on those women who remained increased substantially, compounded by the growing use of cassava, a labor-intensive import from the New World. Unbalanced sex ratios also meant that far more men than before could marry multiple women. Furthermore, the use of female slaves within West African societies also grew as the export trade in male slaves expanded. Retaining female slaves for their own use allowed warriors and nobles in the Senegambia region to distinguish themselves more clearly from ordinary peasants. In the Kongo, female slaves provided a source of dependent laborers for the plantations that sustained the lifestyle of urban elites. A European merchant on the Gold Coast in the late eighteenth century observed that every free man had at least one or two slaves.

For much smaller numbers of women, the slave trade provided an opportunity to exercise power and accumulate wealth. In the Senegambia region, where women had long been involved in politics and commerce, marriage to European traders offered advantage to both partners. For European male merchants, as for fur traders in North America, such marriages afforded access to African-operated commercial networks as well as the comforts of domestic life. Some of the women involved in these cross-cultural marriages, known as *signares*, became quite wealthy, operating their own trading empires, employing large numbers of female slaves, and acquiring elaborate houses, jewelry, and fashionable clothing.

Furthermore, the state-building enterprises that often accompanied the slave trade in West Africa offered yet other opportunities to a few women. As the Kingdom of Dahomey (deh-HOH-mee) expanded during the eighteenth century, the royal palace, housing thousands of women and presided over by a powerful Queen Mother, served to integrate the diverse regions of the state. Each lineage was required to send a daughter to the palace even as well-to-do families sent additional girls to increase their influence at court. In the Kingdom of Kongo, women held lower-level administrative positions, the head wife of a nobleman exercised authority over hundreds of junior wives and slaves, and women served on the council that advised the monarch. The neighboring region of Matamba was known for its female rulers, most notably the powerful Queen Nzinga (1626–1663), who guided the state amid the complexities and intrigues of various European and African rivalries and gained a reputation for her resistance to Portuguese imperialism.

Within particular African societies, the impact of the slave trade differed considerably from place to place and over time. Many small-scale kinship-based societies, lacking the protection of a strong state, were thoroughly disrupted by raids from more powerful neighbors, and insecurity was pervasive. Oral traditions in southern Ghana, for example, reported that "there was no rest in the land," that people went about in groups rather than alone, and that mothers kept their children inside when European ships appeared.[37] Some larger kingdoms such as Kongo and Oyo slowly disintegrated as access to trading opportunities and firearms enabled outlying regions to establish their independence. (For an account of one young man's journey to slavery and back, see Zooming In: Ayuba Suleiman Diallo, page 630.)

However, African authorities also sought to take advantage of the new commercial opportunities and to manage the slave trade in their own interests. The Kingdom of Benin, in the forest area of present-day Nigeria, successfully avoided a deep involvement in the trade while diversifying the exports with which it purchased European firearms and other goods. As early as 1516, its ruler began to

Ayuba Suleiman Diallo:
To Slavery and Back

February 1730 found Ayuba Suleiman Diallo, less than thirty years of age, living between the Gambia and Senegal rivers in West Africa among the Fulbe-speaking people.[38] Like his father, a prominent Islamic scholar and teacher, Ayuba was a Muslim who was literate in Arabic, a prayer leader in the local mosque, and a *hafiz*, someone who had memorized the entire Quran. He was also husband to two wives and father to four children. Now his father sent the young man on an errand. He was to take several of their many slaves to a location some 200 miles away, where an English trading ship had anchored, and exchange them for paper and other goods. The paper was especially important, for his father's income depended on inscribing passages from the Quran on small slips of paper and selling them as protective charms.

To put it mildly, things did not go as planned. Unable to reach an agreement with the English merchant Captain

Ayuba Suleiman Diallo.

Stephen Pike, Ayuba traveled farther south and traded his slaves for a number of cows in the land of the Mandinka people. Well beyond the safety of his own country, he was in dangerous territory. As he and his companions stopped to rest on the journey home, they were seized, their heads were shaved, and they were sold as slaves to the very same Captain Pike. Although Ayuba was able to send a message to his father asking to be ransomed in exchange for some of their slaves, the ship sailed before a reply was received. And so Ayuba, along with 168 other slaves, both men and women, headed for the British American colony of Maryland, where 150 of them arrived alive.

Sold to a local planter, Ayuba was immediately sent to the tobacco fields, but when he became ill from this heavy and unaccustomed work, his owner assigned him

photo: By William Hoare of Bath (1707–1792), 1733, oil on canvas/photo © Christie's Images/Bridgeman Images

restrict the slave trade and soon forbade the export of male slaves altogether, a ban that lasted until the early eighteenth century. By then, the ruler's authority over outlying areas had declined, and the country's major exports of pepper and cotton cloth had lost out to Asian and then European competition. In these circumstances, Benin felt compelled to resume limited participation in the slave trade. The neighboring kingdom of Dahomey, on the other hand, turned to a vigorous involvement in the slave trade in the early eighteenth century under strict royal control. The army conducted annual slave raids, and the government soon came to depend on the trade for its essential revenues. The slave trade in Dahomey became the chief business of the state and remained so until well into the nineteenth century.

the less arduous and more familiar task of tending cattle. Alone with the cattle, Ayuba was able to withdraw into a nearby forest to pray, but he was spotted by a young white boy who mocked him and threw dirt in his face. Sometime later, no doubt in despair, Ayuba ran away, but he was soon captured and housed in the county jail, located in the back room of a tavern. There he became something of a local curiosity and attracted the attention of a lawyer named Thomas Bluett. When Ayuba refused wine, wrote a few lines in Arabic, and mentioned "Allah" and "Muhammad," Bluett realized that he was "no common slave." After locating an old slave who could translate for him, Bluett became fascinated by Ayuba's story, and he initiated a process that took both of them to England in 1733, where philanthropists purchased Ayuba's freedom.

Ayuba's reception in England was amazing. Now fluent in English, Ayuba was received by the English royal family and various members of the nobility, hosted by leading scholars, and entertained by wealthy merchants, eager to tap his knowledge of economic conditions in West Africa. The prominent artist William Hoare painted his portrait, complete with a small Quran hanging from his neck.

In 1734, he finally set off for home, loaded with gifts from his English friends. There he encountered, quite by chance, the same Mandinka men who had sold him only a few years before. Francis Moore, a European trader accompanying Ayuba, wrote that he "fell into a most terrible passion and was for killing them" and was restrained from doing so only with difficulty. He arrived in his hometown to find that his father had recently died. His wives and children, however, were all alive and welcomed him warmly. One of his wives had remarried, believing him gone forever, but her new husband readily gave way, and Ayuba resumed his place of prominence in his own community until his death in 1773.

He also resumed his life as a slave owner. Selling some of the gifts he had acquired in England, he purchased a woman slave and two horses soon after his arrival back in West Africa. According to Moore, he "spoke always very handsomely of the English," and he continued his association with the Royal African Company, the primary English trading firm in West Africa, in their rivalry with French traders.[39] The last mention of Ayuba in the records of that company noted that he was seeking compensation for the loss of two slaves and a watch, probably the one given him in England by Queen Caroline.

Questions: What might you infer about Ayuba's own view of slavery and the slave trade? What insights or questions about the slave trade does his remarkable story suggest?

Economic Globalization — Then and Now

The study of history reminds us of two quite contradictory truths. One is that our lives in the present bear remarkable similarities to those of people long ago. We are perhaps not so unique as we might think. The other is that our lives are very different from theirs and that things have changed substantially. This chapter about global commerce — long-distance trade in spices and textiles, silver and gold, beaver pelts and deerskins, slaves and sugar — provides both perspectives.

If we are accustomed to thinking about globalization as a product of the late twentieth century, early modern world history provides a corrective. Those three centuries reveal much that is familiar to people of the twenty-first century—the global circulation of goods; an international currency; production for a world market; the growing economic role of the West on the global stage; private enterprise, such as the British and Dutch East India companies, operating on a world scale; national governments eager to support their merchants in a highly competitive environment. By the eighteenth century, many Europeans dined from Chinese porcelain dishes called "china," wore Indian-made cotton textiles, and drank chocolate from Mexico, tea from China, and coffee from Yemen while sweetening these beverages with sugar from the Caribbean or Brazil. The millions who worked to produce these goods, whether slave or free, were operating in a world economy. Some industries were thoroughly international. New England rum producers, for example, depended on molasses imported from the Caribbean, while the West Indian sugar industry used African labor and European equipment to produce for a global market.

Nonetheless, early modern economic globalization was a far cry from that of the twentieth century. The most obvious differences, perhaps, were scale and speed. By 2000, immensely more goods circulated internationally, and far more people produced for and depended on the world market than was the case even in 1750. Back-and-forth communications between England and India that took eighteen months in the eighteenth century could be accomplished in an hour by telegraph in the late nineteenth century and almost instantaneously via the Internet in the late twentieth century. Moreover, by 1900 globalization was firmly centered in the economies of Europe and North America. In the early modern era, by contrast, Asia in general and China in particular remained major engines of the world economy, despite the emerging presence of Europeans around the world. By the end of the twentieth century, the booming economies of Turkey, Brazil, India, and China suggested at least a partial return to that earlier pattern.

Early modern globalization differed in still other ways from that of the contemporary world. Economic life then was primarily preindustrial: it was still powered by human and animal muscles, wind, and water and lacked the enormous productive capacity that accompanied the later technological breakthrough of the steam engine and the Industrial Revolution. Finally, the dawning of a genuinely global economy in the early modern era was tied unapologetically to empire building and to slavery, both of which had been discredited by the late twentieth century. Slavery lost its legitimacy during the nineteenth century, and formal territorial empires largely disappeared in the twentieth. Most people during the early modern era would have been surprised to learn that a global economy, as it turned out, could function effectively without either of these long-standing practices.

Second Thoughts

What's the Significance?

Indian Ocean commercial network, 604–6
trading post empire, 605
Philippines (Spanish), 606–8
British/Dutch East India companies, 608–9
Tokugawa shogunate, 610–11
"silver drain," 611–15

Potosí, 613–15
"soft gold," 616–20
African diaspora, 626–30
Benin/Dahomey, 629–30
Ayuba Suleiman Diallo, 630–31

Big Picture Questions

1. To what extent did Europeans transform earlier patterns of commerce, and in what ways did they assimilate into those older patterns?
2. How should we distribute the moral responsibility for the Atlantic slave trade? Is this an appropriate task for historians?
3. What lasting legacies of early modern globalization are evident in the twenty-first century? Pay particular attention to the legacies of the slave trade.
4. **Looking Back:** Asians, Africans, and Native Americans experienced early modern European expansion in quite different ways. Based on Chapters 13 and 14, how might you describe and explain those differences? In what respects were they active agents in the historical process rather than simply victims of European actions?

Next Steps: For Further Study

Glenn J. Ames, *The Globe Encompassed: The Age of European Discovery, 1500–1700* (2007). An up-to-date survey of European expansion in the early modern era.

Andre Gunder Frank, *ReOrient: Global Economy in the Asian Age* (1998). An account of the early modern world economy that highlights the centrality of Asia.

Erik Gilbert and Jonathan Reynolds, *Trading Tastes: Commodity and Cultural Exchange to 1750* (2006). A world historical perspective on transcontinental and transoceanic commerce.

David Northrup, ed., *The Atlantic Slave Trade* (2002). A fine collection of essays about the origins, practice, impact, and abolition of Atlantic slavery.

John Richards, *The Endless Frontier* (2003). Explores the ecological consequences of early modern commerce.

John K. Thornton, *A Cultural History of the Atlantic World, 1250–1820* (2012). A recent account of the intersection of European, African, and Native American people by a highly respected historian.

"Atlantic Slave Trade and Slave Life in the Americas: A Visual Record," http://hitchcock.itc.virginia.edu /Slavery/index.php. An immense collection of maps and images, illustrating the slave trade and the life of slaves in the Americas.

"The Spice of Life: Pepper, the Master Spice," https://www.youtube.com/watch?v=NuZujx-LMfg. A BBC film that presents the history of pepper, so central to the spice trade of the early modern era.

WORKING WITH EVIDENCE

Exchange and Status in the Early Modern World

In many cultures across many centuries, the possession of scarce foreign goods has served not only to meet practical needs and desires but also to convey status. For centuries, Chinese silk signified rank, position, or prestige across much of Eurasia. Pepper and other spices from South and Southeast Asia likewise appealed to elite Romans and Chinese, eager to demonstrate their elevated position in society. In the late twentieth century, American blue jeans were much in demand among Russian young people who sought to display their independence from an oppressive communist regime, while Americans who could afford a German Porsche or an Italian Ferrari acquired an image of sophistication or glamour, setting them apart from others.

As global commerce expanded in the early modern era, so too did the exchange of foods, fashions, finery, and more. Already in 1500, according to a recent study, "it would be possible for a person in the Persian Gulf to wear cotton cloth from India while eating a bowl of rice also from India while sitting under a roof made of timber imported from East Africa. As he finished the rice he would see a Chinese character—the bowl itself came from China."[40] In the centuries that followed, growing numbers of people all across the world, particularly in elite social circles, had access to luxury goods from far away with which they could display, and perhaps enhance, their status. Some of these goods—sugar, pepper, tobacco, tea, and Indian cotton textiles, for example—gradually dropped in price, becoming more widely available. The images that follow illustrate this relationship between global trade and the display of status during the several centuries after 1500.

More than the peoples of other major civilizations, Europeans in the early modern era embraced the goods of the world. They had long been fascinated by and impressed with the wealth and splendor of Asia, which Marco Polo had described in the early fourteenth century after returning from his famous sojourn in China. Now in the early modern era, Western Europe was increasingly at the hub of a growing network of global commerce with access to products from around the world. Tea, porcelain, and silk from China; cotton textiles and spices from India and Southeast Asia; sugar, chocolate, and tobacco from the Americas; coffee from the Middle East—all of this and much more flooded into Europe. By the eighteenth century, a fascination for things Chinese had seized the elite classes of Europe—Chinese textiles, porcelains, tea, wallpaper, furniture, gardens, and artistic styles. The son of King George II of England built a "Mandarin yacht" resembling a Chinese pleasure boat to sail on a large artificial lake near London.

Source 14.1, which shows a German painting from the early eighteenth century, illustrates the growing popularity of tea as a beverage of choice in Europe as well as Chinese teacups. Long popular in China and Japan, tea made its entry into Europe in the sixteenth century aboard Portuguese ships. Initially, it was extremely expensive and limited to the very wealthy, but the price dropped as the supply increased, and by the eighteenth century it was widely consumed in Europe. Chinese teacups without handles also became popular and arrived packed in tea or rice via European merchant vessels. Like many other porcelains, these teacups had been created by Chinese artisans

Staatliche Schloesser und Gaerton, Karlsruhe, Germany/Erich Lessing/Art Resource, NY

Source 14.1 Tea and Porcelain in Europe

specifically for a European market. Those sitting on the table in the fore-ground of the image were manufactured in China between 1662 and 1722. Notice the practice of pouring the tea into the saucer to cool it.

■ What foreign trade items can you identify in this painting?

■ Note the European house on the teacup at the bottom left. What does this indicate about the willingness of the Chinese to cater to the tastes of European customers?

■ From what social class do you think the woman in the image comes?

■ How might you explain the great European interest in Chinese products and styles during the eighteenth century? Why might their possession have suggested status?

Like tea from China and coffee from Ethiopia, chocolate from Meso-america also became an elite beverage and an indicator of high status in Europe during the early modern era. It was the Olmecs, the Maya, and the Aztecs who first discovered how to process the seeds of the cacao tree into a choco-late drink. After the Spanish conquest of the Aztec Empire, that drink was introduced into Spain, where it became highly fashionable in court and aris-tocratic circles. And from Spain it spread to much of the rest of Europe, also limited to the elite social classes, who could afford to purchase this expensive import. Not until the Industrial Revolution made it possible to produce solid chocolate candy for mass consumption did this Mesoamerican acquisition become more widely available. Unlike tobacco and coffee, however, choco-late did not take hold in the Islamic world or China until more recent times.

A part of the larger Columbian exchange, chocolate in Europe lost the religious or ritual associations with which the Aztecs had invested it, becom-ing a medicine, sometimes an aphrodisiac, and in general a recreational bev-erage. Hernán Cortés, the Spanish conqueror of the Aztecs, described choco-late as "the divine drink which builds up resistance and fights fatigue" and reported, "A cup of this precious drink permits a man to walk for a whole day without food."[41] After some debate, the Church approved it as a nutri-tional substitute during times of fasting, when taking solid food was forbid-den. Europeans also innovated with the beverage, adding sugar, cinnamon, and other spices, and later milk. With ingredients from the Americas and Asia, some of them produced by African slave labor, chocolate illustrated the process by which Europe was becoming the center of an emerging world economy.

Source 14.2, a painted tile panel from the early eighteenth century, shows a *chocolatada*, or "chocolate party," in Valencia, Spain. Notice the saucer, or *mancerina*, also a European innovation, for drinking chocolate without spill-ing it.

Museu de Ceramica, Barcelona, Spain/Album/Art Resource, NY

Source 14.2 A Chocolate Party in Spain

- What marks this event as an upper–class occasion?
- What steps in the preparation of the chocolate drink can you observe in the image?
- Why do you think Europeans embraced a practice of people they regarded as uncivilized, bloodthirsty, and savage? What does this suggest about the process of cultural borrowing?

Europeans, of course, were not the only people to embrace foreign tastes newly available in the early modern era. Tobacco and coffee, like tea, soon found a growing range of consumers all across Eurasia. Originating in the Americas, tobacco smoking spread quickly to Europe and Asia. Well before 1700, it had become perhaps the first global recreation. In the Ottoman Empire, as elsewhere, it provoked strenuous opposition on the grounds that it was an intoxicant, like wine, and was associated with unwholesome and promiscuous behavior. It was also associated with coffee, which had entered the Ottoman Empire in the sixteenth century from its place of origin in Ethiopia and Yemen. Coffee too encountered considerable opposition, partly because it was consumed in the new social arena of the coffeehouse. To moralists and other critics, the coffeehouse was a "refuge of Satan," which drew people away from the mosques even as it drew together all different classes. Authorities suspected that coffeehouses were places of political intrigue. None of this stopped the spread of either tobacco or coffee, and the coffeehouse, in the Ottoman Empire and in Europe, came to embody a new "public culture of fun" as it wore away at earlier religious restrictions on the enjoyment of life.[42]

Source 14.3 is a sixteenth-century miniature painting depicting a Turkish coffeehouse in the Ottoman Empire.

■ What activities can you identify in the painting?

■ Would you read this painting as critical of the coffeehouse, as celebrating it, or as a neutral description? Notice that the musicians and those playing board games at the bottom were engaged in activities considered rather disreputable. How would you describe the general demeanor of the men in the coffeehouse?

■ Notice the cups that the patrons are using and those stacked in the upper right. Do they look similar to those shown in Source 14.1? Certainly Ottoman elites by the sixteenth century preferred Chinese porcelain to that manufactured within their own empire.

The emerging colonial societies of Spanish and Portuguese America gave rise to a wide variety of recognized mixed-race groups known as *castas*, or "castes," defined in terms of the precise mixture of Native American, European, and African ancestry that an individual possessed. While this system slotted people into a hierarchical social order defined by race and heritage, it did allow for some social mobility. If individuals managed to acquire some education, land, or money, they might gain in social prestige and even pass as members of a more highly favored category (see Chapter 13, pages 565–67). Adopting the dress and lifestyle of higher-ranking groups could facilitate this process.

Source 14.4 shows a woman of Indian ancestry and a man of African/Indian descent as well as their child, who is categorized as a *loba*, or "wolf." It comes from a series of "casta paintings" created in eighteenth-century Mexico by the well-known Zapotec artist Miguel Cabrera to depict some eighteen or more mixed-race couples and their children, each with a distinct designation. The woman in this image is wearing a lovely *huipil*, a traditional Maya tunic or blouse, while the man is dressed in a European-style waistcoat, vest, and lace shirt, while holding a black tricorne hat, widely popular in Europe during the seventeenth and eighteenth centuries. Interest in such

Source 14.3 An Ottoman Coffeehouse

De Chino cambujo y d India ; Loba

Source 14.4 Clothing and Status in Colonial Mexico

paintings reflected both a Spanish fascination with race and a more general European concern with classification, which was characteristic of eighteenth-century scientific thinking.

■ What indications of status ambition or upward mobility can you identify in this image? Keep in mind that status here is associated with race and gender as well as the possession of foreign products.

■ Why do you think the woman is shown in more traditional costume, while the man is portrayed in European dress?

■ Notice the porcelain items at the bottom right. Where might they have come from?

■ In what cultural tradition do you think this couple raised their daughter? What problems might they have experienced in the process?

DOING HISTORY

Exchange and Status in the Early Modern World

1. **Analyzing the display of status:** In what different ways did the possession of foreign objects convey status in the early modern world? Toward whom were these various claims of status directed? Notice the difference between the display of status in public and private settings.

2. **Noticing gender differences:** In what ways are men and women portrayed in these visual sources? Why might women be absent in Sources 14.2 and 14.3?

3. **Exploring the functions of trade:** How might you use these images to support the idea that trade served more than economic needs?

4. **Raising questions about cultural borrowing:** What issues about cross-cultural borrowing do these visual sources suggest?

5. **Evaluating images as evidence:** What are the strengths and limitations of visual sources as a means of understanding the relationship of trade and status in the early modern era? What other kinds of sources would be useful for pursuing this theme?

National Palace, Mexico City, Mexico/The Art Archive at Art Resource, NY

CHAPTER 15

Cultural Transformations

Religion and Science
1450–1750

Nigerian pastor Daniel Ajayi-Adeniran is a missionary to the United States, with his mission field in the Bronx. The church he represents, the Redeemed Christian Church of God, began in Nigeria in 1952. It has acquired millions of members in Nigeria and boasts a missionary network with a presence in 100 countries. According to its leader, the church was "made in heaven, assembled in Nigeria, exported to the world." And the Redeemed Church of God is not alone. As secularism and materialism born of the Scientific Revolution and modern life have eroded religious faith in the West, many believers in Asia, Africa, and Latin America have felt called to reinvigorate a declining Christianity in Europe and North America. In a remarkable reversal of an earlier pattern, they now seek to "re-evangelize" the West, from which they originally received the faith. After all, more than 60 percent of the world's professing Christians now live outside Europe and North America, and, within the United States, one in six Catholic diocesan priests and one in three seminary students are foreign-born. For example, hundreds of Filipino priests, nuns, and lay workers now serve churches in the West. "We couldn't just throw up our hands and see these churches turned into nightclubs or mosques," declared Tokunboh Adeyemo, another Nigerian church leader seeking to minister to an "increasingly godless West."[1]

The early modern era of world history gave birth to two intersecting cultural trends that continue to play out in the twenty-first century. The first was the spread of Christianity to Asians, Africans, and Native Americans, some of whom now seem to be returning the favor. The second was the emergence of a modern scientific outlook, which sharply challenged Western Christianity even as it too acquired a global presence.

The Virgin of Guadalupe   According to Mexican tradition, a dark-skinned Virgin Mary appeared to an indigenous peasant named Juan Diego in 1531, an apparition reflected in this Mexican painting from 1720. Belief in the Virgin of Guadalupe represented the incorporation of Catholicism into the emerging culture and identity of Mexico.

And so, alongside new empires and new patterns of commerce, the early modern centuries also witnessed novel cultural transformations that likewise connected distant peoples. Riding the currents of European empire building and commercial expansion, Christianity was established solidly in the Americas and the Philippines; far more modestly in Siberia, China, Japan, and India; and hardly at all within the vast and still-growing domains of Islam. A cultural tradition largely limited to Europe in 1500 now became a genuine world religion, spawning a multitude of cultural encounters. While this ancient faith was spreading, a new understanding of the universe and a new approach to knowledge were taking shape among European thinkers of the Scientific Revolution, giving rise to another kind of cultural encounter—that between science and religion. Science was a new and competing worldview, and for some it became almost a new religion. In time, it grew into a defining feature of global modernity, achieving a worldwide acceptance that exceeded that of Christianity or any other religious tradition.

Although Europeans were central players in the globalization of Christianity and the emergence of modern science, they did not act alone in the cultural transformations of the early modern era. Asian, African, and Native American peoples largely determined how Christianity would be accepted, rejected, or transformed as it entered new cultural environments. Science emerged within an international and not simply a European context, and it met varying receptions in different parts of the world. Islam continued a long pattern of religious expansion and renewal, even as Christianity began to compete with it as a world religion. Buddhism maintained its hold in much of East Asia, as did Hinduism in South Asia and numerous smaller-scale religious traditions in Africa. And Europeans themselves were certainly affected by the many "new worlds" that they now encountered. The cultural interactions of the early modern era, in short, did not take place on a one-way street.

SEEKING THE MAIN POINT

To what extent did the cultural changes of the early modern world derive from cross-cultural interaction? And to what extent did they grow from within particular societies or civilizations?

The Globalization of Christianity

Despite its Middle Eastern origins and its earlier presence in many parts of the Afro-Asian world, Christianity was largely limited to Europe at the beginning of the early modern era. In 1500, the world of Christendom stretched from Spain and England in the west to Russia in the east, with small and beleaguered communities of various kinds in Egypt, Ethiopia, southern India, and Central Asia. Internally, the Christian world was seriously divided between the Roman Catholics of Western and Central Europe and the Eastern Orthodox of Eastern Europe and Russia. Externally, it was very much on the defensive against an expansive Islam. Muslims had ousted Christian Crusaders from their toeholds in the Holy Land by 1300, and with the Ottoman seizure of Constantinople in 1453, they had captured the prestigious capital of Eastern Orthodoxy. The Ottoman siege of Vienna in 1529 marked a Muslim advance into the heart of Central Europe. Except in Spain and Sicily,

A MAP OF TIME

1453	Ottoman conquest of Constantinople
1469–1539	Life of Guru Nanak; beginning of Sikh tradition
1472–1529	Life of Wang Yangming in China
1498–1547	Life of Mirabai, bhakti poet of India
1517	Luther's Ninety-Five Theses; beginning of Protestant Reformation
1543	Publication of Copernicus's masterwork about a sun-centered universe
1545–1563	Council of Trent
1560s	Taki Onqoy movement in Peru
1582–1610	Matteo Ricci in China
1598	Edict of Nantes proclaiming religious toleration in France
Early 17th century	European missionaries expelled from Japan
1618–1648	Thirty Years' War in Europe
1642–1727	Life of Isaac Newton; culmination of European Scientific Revolution
18th century	European Enlightenment
Early 18th century	Missionaries lost favor in the Chinese court
1740–1818	Wahhabi movement of Islamic reform in Arabia

which had recently been reclaimed for Christendom after centuries of Muslim rule, the future, it must have seemed, lay with Islam rather than Christianity.

Western Christendom Fragmented: The Protestant Reformation

As if these were not troubles enough, in the early sixteenth century the Protestant Reformation shattered the unity of Roman Catholic Christianity, which for the previous 1,000 years had provided the cultural and organizational foundation of an emerging Western European civilization. The Reformation began in 1517 when a German priest, Martin Luther (1483–1546), publicly invited debate about various abuses within the Roman Catholic Church by issuing a document, known as the Ninety-Five Theses, allegedly nailing it to the door of a church in Wittenberg. In itself, this was nothing new, for many people were critical of the luxurious life of the popes, the corruption and immorality of some clergy, the Church's selling of

The Protestant Reformation
An engraving of Martin Luther nailing his Ninety-Five Theses to the door of the Wittenberg castle church in 1517, thus launching the Protestant Reformation. (Photo © Tarker/ Bridgeman Images)

indulgences (said to remove the penalties for sin), and other aspects of church life and practice.

■ **Change**
In what ways did the Protestant Reformation transform European society, culture, and politics?

What made Luther's protest potentially revolutionary, however, was its theological basis. A troubled and brooding man anxious about his relationship with God, Luther had recently come to a new understanding of salvation: he believed that it came through faith alone. Neither the good works of the sinner nor the sacraments of the Church had any bearing on the eternal destiny of the soul, for faith was a free gift of God, graciously granted to his needy and undeserving people. To Luther, the source of these beliefs, and of religious authority in general, was not the teaching of the Church, but the Bible alone, interpreted according to the individual's conscience. All of this challenged the authority of the Church and called into question the special position of the clerical hierarchy and of the pope in particular. In sixteenth-century Europe, this was the stuff of revolution. (See the Snapshot, opposite, for a brief summary of Catholic and Protestant differences.)

Contrary to Luther's original intentions, his ideas provoked a massive schism within the world of Catholic Christendom, for they came to express a variety of political, economic, and social tensions as well as religious differences. Some kings and princes, many of whom had long disputed the political authority of the pope, found in these ideas a justification for their own independence and an opportunity to gain the lands and taxes previously held by the Church. In the Protestant idea

SNAPSHOT Catholic/Protestant Differences in the Sixteenth Century

	Catholic	Protestant
Religious authority	Pope and church hierarchy	The Bible, as interpreted by individual Christians
Role of the pope	Ultimate authority in faith and doctrine	Authority of the pope denied
Ordination of clergy	Apostolic succession: direct line between original apostles and all subsequently ordained clergy	Apostolic succession denied; ordination by individual congregations or denominations
Salvation	Importance of church sacraments as channels of God's grace	Importance of faith alone; God's grace is freely and directly granted to believers
Status of Mary	Highly prominent, ranking just below Jesus; provides constant intercession for believers	Less prominent; Mary's intercession on behalf of the faithful denied
Prayer	To God, but often through or with Mary and saints	To God alone; no role for Mary and saints
Holy Communion	Transubstantiation: bread and wine become the actual body and blood of Christ	Transubstantiation denied; bread and wine have a spiritual or symbolic significance
Role of clergy	Priests are generally celibate; sharp distinction between priests and laypeople; priests are mediators between God and humankind	Ministers may marry; priesthood of all believers; clergy have different functions (to preach, administer sacraments) but no distinct spiritual status
Role of saints	Prominent spiritual exemplars and intermediaries between God and humankind	Generally disdained as a source of idolatry; saints refer to all Christians

that all vocations were of equal merit, middle-class urban dwellers found a new religious legitimacy for their growing role in society, since the Roman Catholic Church was associated in their eyes with the rural and feudal world of aristocratic privilege. For common people, who were offended by the corruption and luxurious living of some bishops, abbots, and popes, the new religious ideas served to express their opposition to the entire social order, particularly in a series of German peasant revolts in the 1520s. Although large numbers of women were attracted to Protestantism, Reformation teachings and practices did not offer them a substantially greater role in the church or society. In Protestant-dominated areas, the veneration of Mary and female saints ended, leaving the male Christ figure as the sole

Map 15.1
Reformation Europe in the Sixteenth Century

The rise of Protestantism added yet another set of religious divisions, both within and between states, to the world of Christendom, which was already sharply divided between the Roman Catholic Church and the Eastern Orthodox Church.

Protestant dominant
Some Protestant influence
Catholic
Eastern Orthodox Christian
— Boundary of the Holy Roman Empire

object of worship. Protestant opposition to celibacy and monastic life closed the convents, which had offered some women an alternative to marriage. Nor were Protestants (except the Quakers) any more willing than Catholics to offer women an official role within their churches. The importance that Protestants gave to reading the Bible for oneself stimulated education and literacy for women, but given the emphasis on women as wives and mothers subject to male supervision, they had little opportunity to use that education outside of the family.

Reformation thinking spread quickly both within and beyond Germany, thanks in large measure to the recent invention of the printing press. Luther's many pamphlets and his translation of the New Testament into German were soon widely available. "God has appointed the [printing] Press to preach, whose voice the pope is never able to stop," declared one Reformation leader.[2] As the movement spread to France, Switzerland, England, and elsewhere, it also splintered, amoeba-like, into a variety of competing Protestant churches—Lutheran, Calvinist, Anglican, Quaker, Anabaptist—many of which subsequently subdivided, producing a bewildering array of Protestant denominations. Each was distinctive, but none gave allegiance to Rome or the pope.

Thus to the sharp class divisions and the fractured political system of Europe was now added the potent brew of religious difference, operating both within and between states (see Map 15.1). For more than thirty years (1562–1598), French society was torn by violence between Catholics and the Protestant minority known as Huguenots (HYOO-guh-naht). On a single day, August 24, 1572, Catholic mobs in Paris massacred some 3,000 Huguenots, and thousands more perished in provincial towns in the weeks that followed. Finally, a war-weary monarch, Henry IV, issued the Edict of Nantes (nahnt) in 1598, granting a substantial measure of religious toleration to French Protestants, though with the intention that they would soon return to the Catholic Church. The culmination of European religious conflict took shape in the Thirty Years' War (1618–1648), a Catholic–Protestant struggle that began in the Holy Roman Empire but eventually engulfed most of Europe. It was a horrendously destructive war, during which, scholars estimate, between 15 and 30 percent of the German population perished from violence, famine, or disease. Finally, the Peace of Westphalia (1648) brought the conflict to an end, with some reshuffling of boundaries and an agreement that each state was sovereign, authorized to control religious affairs within its own territory. Whatever religious unity Catholic Europe had once enjoyed was now permanently splintered.

The Protestant breakaway, combined with reformist tendencies within the Catholic Church itself, provoked a Catholic Reformation, or Counter-Reformation. In the Council of Trent (1545–1563), Catholics clarified and reaffirmed their unique doctrines and practices, such as the authority of the pope, priestly celibacy, the veneration of saints and relics, and the importance of church tradition and good works, all of which Protestants had rejected. Moreover, they set about correcting the abuses and corruption that had stimulated the Protestant movement by placing a new emphasis on the education of priests and their supervision by bishops. A crackdown on dissidents included the censorship of books, fines, exile, penitence, and occasionally the burning of heretics. Renewed attention was given to individual spirituality and personal piety. New religious orders, such as the Society of Jesus (Jesuits), provided a dedicated brotherhood of priests committed to the renewal of the Catholic Church and its extension abroad.

Although the Reformation was profoundly religious, it encouraged a skeptical attitude toward authority and tradition, for it had, after all, successfully challenged the immense prestige and power of the pope and the established Church. Protestant

Map 15.2
The Globalization of Christianity

The growing Christian presence in Asia, Africa, and especially the Americas, combined with older centers of that faith, gave the religion derived from Jesus a global dimension during the early modern era.

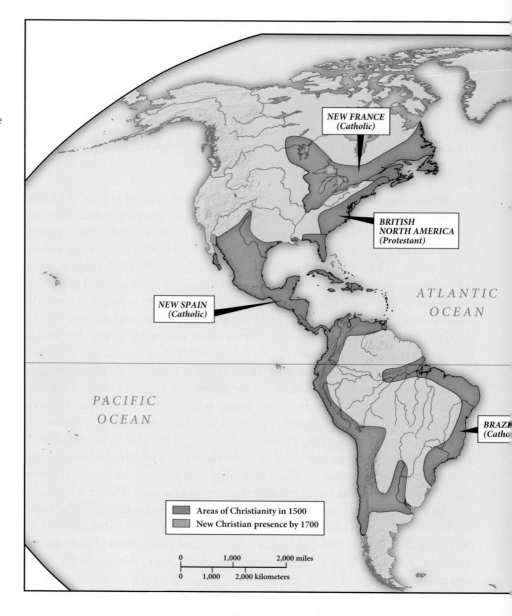

NEW FRANCE
(Catholic)

BRITISH
NORTH AMERICA
(Protestant)

NEW SPAIN
(Catholic)

ATLANTIC
OCEAN

PACIFIC
OCEAN

BRAZI
(Catho

Amazon R.

■ Areas of Christianity in 1500
■ New Christian presence by 1700

```
0         1,000        2,000 miles
0    1,000    2,000 kilometers
```

reformers fostered religious individualism, as people were now encouraged to read and interpret the scriptures for themselves and to seek salvation without the mediation of the Church. In the centuries that followed, some people turned that skepticism and the habit of thinking independently against all conventional religion. Thus the Protestant Reformation opened some space for new directions in European intellectual life.

In short, it was a more highly fragmented but also a renewed and revitalized Christianity that established itself around the world in the several centuries after 1500 (see Map 15.2).

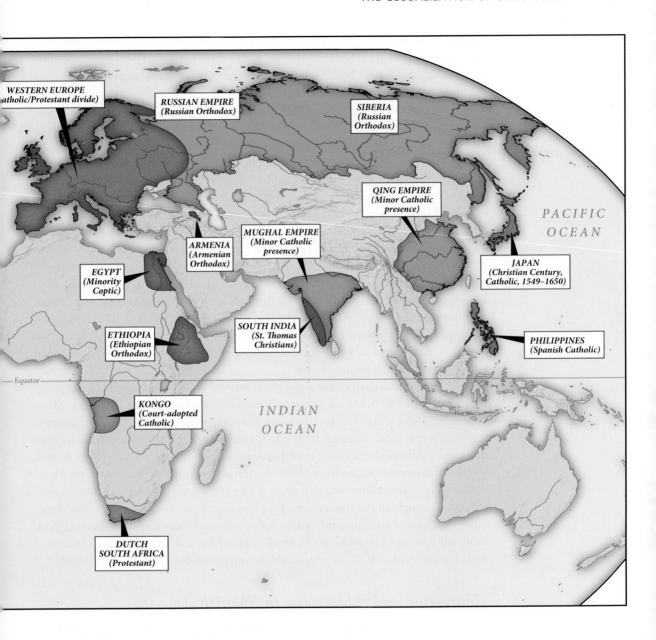

WESTERN EUROPE
(Catholic/Protestant divide)

RUSSIAN EMPIRE
(Russian Orthodox)

SIBERIA
(Russian Orthodox)

QING EMPIRE
(Minor Catholic presence)

ARMENIA
(Armenian Orthodox)

MUGHAL EMPIRE
(Minor Catholic presence)

JAPAN
(Christian Century, Catholic, 1549–1650)

EGYPT
(Minority Coptic)

ETHIOPIA
(Ethiopian Orthodox)

SOUTH INDIA
(St. Thomas Christians)

PHILIPPINES
(Spanish Catholic)

KONGO
(Court-adopted Catholic)

PACIFIC OCEAN

INDIAN OCEAN

Equator

DUTCH SOUTH AFRICA
(Protestant)

Christianity Outward Bound

Christianity motivated European political and economic expansion and also benefited from it. The resolutely Catholic Spanish and Portuguese both viewed their movement overseas as a continuation of a long crusading tradition, which only recently had completed the liberation of their countries from Muslim control. When Vasco da Gama's small fleet landed in India in 1498, local authorities understandably asked, "What brought you hither?" The reply: they had come "in search of Christians and of spices."[3] Likewise, Columbus, upon arriving in the Americas, expressed the no doubt sincere hope that the people "might become Christians," even as he promised his Spanish patrons an abundant harvest of gold, spice, cotton, aloe wood, and slaves.[4] Neither man sensed any contradiction or hypocrisy in this blending of religious and material concerns.

■ Connection

How was European imperial expansion related to the spread of Christianity?

If religion drove and justified European ventures abroad, it is difficult to imagine the globalization of Christianity (see Map 15.2) without the support of empire. Colonial settlers and traders, of course, brought their faith with them and sought to replicate it in their newly conquered homelands. New England Puritans, for example, planted a distinctive Protestant version of Christianity in North America, with an emphasis on education, moral purity, personal conversion, civic responsibility, and little tolerance for competing expressions of the faith. They did not show much interest in converting native peoples but sought rather to push them out of their ancestral territories. It was missionaries, mostly Catholic, who actively spread the Christian message beyond European communities. Organized in missionary orders such as the Dominicans, Franciscans, and Jesuits, Portuguese missionaries took the lead in Africa and Asia, while Spanish and French missionaries were most prominent in the Americas. Missionaries of the Russian Orthodox Church likewise accompanied the expansion of the Russian Empire across Siberia, where priests and monks ministered to Russian settlers and trappers, who often donated their first sable furs to a church or monastery.

Missionaries had their greatest success in Spanish America and in the Philippines, areas that shared two critical elements beyond their colonization by Spain. Most important, perhaps, was an overwhelming European presence, experienced variously as military conquest, colonial settlement, missionary activity, forced labor, social disruption, and disease. Surely it must have seemed as if the old gods had been bested and that any possible future lay with the powerful religion of the European invaders. A second common factor was the absence of a literate world religion in these two regions. Throughout the modern era, peoples solidly rooted in Confucian, Buddhist, Hindu, or Islamic traditions proved far more resistant to the Christian message than those who practiced more localized, small-scale, orally based religions. (See Working with Evidence, page 679, for images illustrating the global spread of Christianity.)

Conversion and Adaptation in Spanish America

Spanish America and China illustrate the difference between those societies in which Christianity became widely practiced and those that largely rejected it. Both cases, however, represent major cultural encounters of a kind that was becoming more frequent as European expansion brought the Christian faith to distant peoples with very different cultural traditions.

■ Connection

In what ways was European Christianity assimilated into the Native American cultures of Spanish America?

The decisive conquest of the Aztec and Inca empires and all that followed from it—disease, population collapse, loss of land to Europeans, forced labor, resettlement into more compact villages—created a setting in which the religion of the victors took hold in Spanish American colonies. Europeans saw their political and military success as a demonstration of the power of the Christian God. Native American peoples generally agreed, and by 1700 or earlier the vast majority had been baptized and saw themselves in some respects as Christians. After all, other conquerors such as the Aztecs and the Incas had always imposed their gods in some fashion on defeated peoples. So it made sense, both practically and spiritually, to affiliate with the Europeans' God, saints, rites, and rituals. Many millions accepted baptism, contributed to the construction of village churches, attended services, and embraced images of saints. Despite the prominence of the Virgin Mary as a religious figure across Latin America, the cost of conversion was high, especially for women. Many women, who had long served as priests, shamans, or ritual specialists, had no corresponding role in a Catholic church, led by an all-male clergy. And, with a few exceptions, convent life, which had provided some outlet for female authority and education in Catholic Europe, was reserved largely for Spanish women in the Americas. (See Zooming In: Úrsula de Jesús, page 654, for an exception.)

Earlier conquerors had made no attempt to eradicate local deities and religious practices. The flexibility and inclusiveness of Mesoamerican and Andean religions had made it possible for subject people to accommodate the gods of their new rulers while maintaining their own traditions. But Europeans were different. They claimed an exclusive religious truth and sought the utter destruction of local gods and everything associated with them. Operating within a Spanish colonial regime that actively encouraged conversion, missionaries often proceeded by persuasion and patient teaching. At times, though, their frustration with the persistence of "idolatry, superstition,

Andean Christianity
In 1753, Marcos Zapata, a native Peruvian artist trained in European techniques, painted this rendering of Jesus' Last Supper with his disciples, which included a number of Andean elements. The central dish on the table was a roasted guinea pig, a traditional sacrificial animal, while a local fermented corn drink called *chicha* was also part of the meal. Side dishes featured pomegranates, a Eurasian fruit brought to Peru by the Columbian exchange symbolizing the passion of Christ. At the bottom right, looking away from Jesus while grasping a money bag, is the figure of Judas, painted, some say, to resemble Francisco Pizarro, the Spanish conqueror of the Inca Empire. (© Yadid Levy/age fotostock)

Úrsula de Jesús, an Afro-Peruvian Slave and Christian Visionary

Úrsula de Jesús was born in the prosperous Spanish colonial city of Lima, Peru, in 1606, the daughter of a slave mother. Thus she entered life at the lowest rung of Spanish colonial society. But among enslaved people, Úrsula was fortunate. Her mother's owner was a wealthy aristocratic woman, and at age eight Úrsula was sent to live in the home of another elite woman with a reputation for piety and religious visions. Five years later, Úrsula accompanied a third woman into the Convent of Santa Clara, where she spent the rest of her life. There Úrsula found a place for herself in the world of colonial Peru and Latin American Christianity—but not easily or immediately.[5]

For the next quarter of a century, Úrsula was one of more than a hundred slaves in the convent, where she attended to the personal needs of her mistress and participated in communal labor—cooking, cleaning, and attending the sick. In the convent, as in the larger society, Úrsula was at the bottom of the social ladder as nuns, novices, and *doñadas* (religious laywomen) all

A wealthy white Peruvian woman and her African slave.

enjoyed a higher status. But the wealth of her mistress or perhaps her own day labor allowed her to dress well and to elevate herself above common slaves. She later noted that she went about "beautifully adorned from head to toe." She recalled, "I used to wear fancy clothes and parade about the choir."

The year 1642 marked a dramatic turning point in Úrsula's life, when she almost fell into a deep well. Crediting her deliverance from certain death to the Virgin of Carmen, Úrsula turned decisively away from her earlier vain and self-centered ways and embraced an ever-deepening spirituality. She sold her lovely clothes, devoted every spare moment to prayer, and sought out the most onerous tasks such as caring for contagious patients and washing soiled garments. She took to whipping herself twice daily, wearing a coarse and painful hair shirt, and placing a crown of thorns beneath her hair. In Catholic

and error" boiled over into violent campaigns designed to uproot old religions once and for all. In 1535, the bishop of Mexico proudly claimed that he had destroyed 500 pagan shrines and 20,000 idols. During the seventeenth and early eighteenth centuries, church authorities in the Andean region periodically launched movements of "extirpation," designed to fatally undermine native religion. They destroyed religious images and ritual objects, publicly urinated on native "idols," desecrated the remains of ancestors, flogged "idolaters," and held religious trials and "processions of shame" aimed at humiliating offenders.

It is hardly surprising that such aggressive action generated resistance. Writing around 1600, the native Peruvian nobleman Guaman Poma de Ayala commented on the posture of native women toward Christianity: "They do not confess; they

religious thinking of the time, such "mortification" of the body served to enhance identification with Jesus' suffering.

Úrsula's new religious fervor incurred the displeasure of her mistress, who felt neglected by her slave. By 1645, a deeply unhappy Úrsula determined to leave the convent and find a new owner. Then one of the nuns, hoping to retain her pious services, purchased Úrsula's freedom. Nonetheless, Úrsula chose to stay in the convent as a *doñada*. Doing so represented a modest elevation in her social status, an opportunity to pursue her spiritual life with fewer restrictions, and a measure of social and economic security.

Still, she continued to perform the same exhausting tasks she had as a slave and complained frequently about them. "I was up to my ears with cooking and other things," she confided to her diary, "desiring only to be in the mountains where there are no people." Even as she struggled with the restrictions of her position in the convent, Úrsula enhanced her reputation as a "servant of God," a woman of extraordinary devotion and humility, and as a visionary and a mystic.

In her diary, Úrsula recounted numerous direct encounters with God, Jesus, Mary, and with dead souls seeking her intervention to shorten their time in the purifying fires of purgatory. These visions frequently reflected the tensions of class, race, and position within the convent and in the larger society. Several priests, suffering in purgatory for their sexual sins, luxurious living, and mistreatment of slaves, appealed to Úrsula. So too did nuns who had been lax in their spiritual practices or placed their business interests above their religious duties. Úrsula had a special concern for the female slaves and servants who asked for her intercession. One feared becoming an "orphan" in purgatory with no one to remember her. Another confessed to a lesbian love affair with a nun. Although Úrsula once questioned "whether black women went to heaven," it was later revealed to her as an abode of "great harmony," but not of social equality, for "everyone had their place . . . in accordance with their standing and the obligations of their class." By the end of her life, however, Úrsula was able to affirm the spiritual equality of all. "In memory, understanding, and will," she declared, "they [blacks and whites] are all one."

When Úrsula died in 1666, a prominent nun confirmed that she had entered Heaven directly, with no intervening time in purgatory. Her funeral was attended by many high officials of both state and church, and she was buried beneath the chapel of the convent she had served.

Question: To what extent did Úrsula shape her own life, and in what way was it shaped by larger historical forces?

do not attend catechism classes . . . nor do they go to mass. . . . And resuming their ancient customs and idolatry, they do not want to serve God or the crown."[6] Occasionally, overt resistance erupted. One such example was the religious revivalist movement in central Peru in the 1560s, known as Taki Onqoy (dancing sickness). Possessed by the spirits of local gods, or *huacas*, traveling dancers and teachers predicted that an alliance of Andean deities would soon overcome the Christian God, inflict the intruding Europeans with the same diseases that they had brought to the Americas, and restore the world of the Andes to an imagined earlier harmony. They called on native peoples to cut off all contact with the Spanish, to reject Christian worship, and to return to traditional practices. "The world has turned about," one member declared, "and this time God and the Spaniards [will be] defeated and all the Spaniards killed and their cities drowned; and the sea will rise and overwhelm them, so that there will remain no memory of them."[7]

More common than such frontal attacks on Christianity, which colonial authorities quickly smashed, were efforts at blending two religious traditions, reinterpreting Christian practices within an Andean framework, and incorporating local elements into an emerging Andean Christianity. Even female dancers in the Taki Onqoy movement sometimes took the names of Christian saints, seeking to appropriate for themselves the religious power of Christian figures. Within Andean Christian communities, women might offer the blood of a llama to strengthen a village church or make a cloth covering for the Virgin Mary and a shirt for an image of a huaca with the same material. Although the state cults of the Incas faded away, missionary attacks did not succeed in eliminating the influence of local huacas. Images and holy sites might be destroyed, but the souls of the huacas remained, and their representatives gained prestige. One resilient Andean resident inquired of a Jesuit missionary: "Father, are you tired of taking our idols from us? Take away that mountain if you can, since that is the God I worship."[8]

In Mexico as well, an immigrant Christianity was assimilated into patterns of local culture. Parishes were organized largely around precolonial towns or regions. Churches built on or near the sites of old temples became the focus of community identity. *Cofradias*, church-based associations of laypeople, organized community processions and festivals and made provisions for proper funerals and burials for their members. Central to an emerging Mexican Christianity were the saints who closely paralleled the functions of precolonial gods. Saints were imagined as parents of the local community and the true owners of its land, and their images were paraded through the streets on the occasion of great feasts and were collected by individual households. Mexico's Virgin of Guadalupe neatly combined both Mesoamerican and Spanish notions of Divine Motherhood (see the chapter-opening photo on page 642). Although parish priests were almost always Spanish, the *fiscal*, or leader of the church staff, was a native Christian of great local prestige, who carried on the traditions and role of earlier religious specialists.

Throughout the colonial period and beyond, many Mexican Christians also took part in rituals derived from the past, with little sense of incompatibility with Christian practice. Incantations to various gods for good fortune in hunting, farming, or healing; sacrifices of self-bleeding; offerings to the sun; divination; the use of hallucinogenic drugs—all of these practices provided spiritual assistance in those areas of everyday life not directly addressed by Christian rites. Conversely, these practices also showed signs of Christian influence. Wax candles, normally used in Christian services, might now appear in front of a stone image of a precolonial god. The anger of a neglected saint, rather than that of a traditional god, might explain someone's illness and require offerings, celebration, or a new covering to regain his or her favor. In such ways did Christianity take root in the new cultural environments of Spanish America, but it was a distinctly Andean or Mexican Christianity, not merely a copy of the Spanish version.

An Asian Comparison: China and the Jesuits

The Chinese encounter with Christianity was very different from that of Native Americans in Spain's New World empire. The most obvious difference was the political context. The peoples of Spanish America had been defeated, their societies thoroughly disrupted, and their cultural confidence sorely shaken. China, on the other hand, encountered European Christianity between the sixteenth and eighteenth centuries during the powerful and prosperous Ming (1368–1644) and Qing (1644–1912) dynasties. Although the transition between these two dynasties occasioned several decades of internal conflict, at no point was China's political independence or cultural integrity threatened by the handful of European missionaries and traders working there.

The reality of a strong, independent, confident China required a different missionary strategy, for Europeans needed the permission of Chinese authorities to operate in the country. Whereas Spanish missionaries working in a colonial setting sought primarily to convert the masses, the leading missionary order in China, the Jesuits, took deliberate aim at the official Chinese elite. Following the example of their most famous missionary, Matteo Ricci (in China 1582–1610), many Jesuits learned Chinese, became thoroughly acquainted with classical Confucian texts, and dressed like Chinese scholars. Initially, they downplayed their mission to convert and instead emphasized their interest in exchanging ideas and learning from China's ancient culture. As highly educated men, the Jesuits carried the recent secular knowledge of Europe—science, technology, geography, mapmaking—to an audience of curious Chinese scholars. In presenting Christian teachings, Jesuits were at pains to be respectful of Chinese culture, pointing out parallels between Confucianism and Christianity rather than portraying it as something new and foreign. They chose to define Chinese rituals honoring the emperor or venerating ancestors as secular or civil observances rather than as religious practices that had to be abandoned. Such efforts to accommodate Chinese culture contrast sharply with the frontal attacks on Native American religions in the Spanish Empire undertaken by many missionaries.

The religious and cultural outcomes of the missionary enterprise likewise differed greatly in the two regions. Nothing approaching mass conversion to Christianity took place in China, as it had in Latin America. During the sixteenth and seventeenth centuries, a modest number of Chinese scholars and officials did become Christians, attracted by the personal lives of the missionaries, by their interest in Western science, and by the moral certainty that Christianity offered. Jesuit missionaries found favor for a time at the Chinese imperial court, where their mathematical, astronomical, technological, and mapmaking skills rendered them useful. For more than a century, they were appointed to head the Chinese Bureau of Astronomy. Among ordinary people, Christianity spread very modestly amid tales of miracles attributed to the Christian God, while missionary teachings about "eternal life" sounded to some like Daoist prescriptions for immortality. At most, though,

■ **Comparison**

Why were missionary efforts to spread Christianity so much less successful in China than in Spanish America?

Jesuits in China

In this seventeenth-century Dutch engraving, two Jesuit missionaries hold a map of China. Their mapmaking skills were among the reasons that the Jesuits were initially welcomed among the educated elite of that country. (Frontispiece [engraving] from *China Monumentis* by Athanasius Kircher, 1667/Private Collection/Bridgeman Images)

missionary efforts over the course of some 250 years (1550–1800) resulted in 200,000 to 300,000 converts, a minuscule number in a Chinese population approaching 300 million by 1800. What explains the very limited acceptance of Christianity in early modern China?

Fundamentally, the missionaries offered little that the Chinese really wanted. Confucianism for the elites and Buddhism, Daoism, and a multitude of Chinese gods and spirits at the local level adequately supplied the spiritual needs of most Chinese. Furthermore, it became increasingly clear that Christianity was an all-or-nothing faith that required converts to abandon much of traditional Chinese culture. Christian monogamy, for example, seemed to require Chinese men to put away their concubines. What would happen to these deserted women?

By the early eighteenth century, the papacy and competing missionary orders came to oppose the Jesuit policy of accommodation. The pope claimed authority over Chinese Christians and declared that sacrifices to Confucius and the veneration of ancestors were "idolatry" and thus forbidden to Christians. The pope's pronouncements represented an unacceptable challenge to the authority of the emperor and an affront to Chinese culture. In 1715, an outraged Emperor Kangxi wrote:

> I ask myself how these uncultivated Westerners dare to speak of the great precepts of China. . . . [T]heir doctrine is of the same kind as the little heresies of the Buddhist and Taoist monks. . . . These are the greatest absurdities that have ever been seen. As from now I forbid the Westerners to spread their doctrine in China; that will spare us a lot of trouble.[9]

This represented a major turning point in the relationship of Christian missionaries and Chinese society. Many were subsequently expelled, and missionaries lost favor at court.

In other ways as well, missionaries played into the hands of their Chinese opponents. Their willingness to work under the Manchurian Qing dynasty, which came to power in 1644, discredited them with those Chinese scholars who viewed the Qing as uncivilized foreigners and their rule in China as disgraceful and illegitimate. Missionaries' reputation as miracle workers further damaged their standing as men of science and rationality, for elite Chinese often regarded miracles and supernatural religion as superstitions, fit only for the uneducated masses. Some viewed the Christian ritual of Holy Communion as a kind of cannibalism. Others came to see missionaries as potentially subversive, for various Christian groups met in secret, and such religious sects had often provided the basis for peasant rebellion. Nor did it escape Chinese notice that European Christians had taken over the Philippines and that their warships were active in the Indian Ocean. Perhaps the missionaries, with their great interest in maps, were spies for these aggressive foreigners. All of this contributed to the general failure of Christianity to secure a prominent presence in China.

Persistence and Change in Afro-Asian Cultural Traditions

Although Europeans were central players in the globalization of Christianity, theirs was not the only expanding or transformed culture of the early modern era. African religious ideas and practices, for example, accompanied slaves to the Americas. Common African forms of religious revelation—divination, dream interpretation, visions, spirit possession—found a place in the Africanized versions of Christianity that emerged in the New World. Europeans frequently perceived these practices as evidence of sorcery, witchcraft, or even devil worship and tried to suppress them. Nonetheless, syncretic (blended) religions such as Vodou in Haiti, Santeria in Cuba, and Candomblé and Macumba in Brazil persisted. They derived from various West African traditions and featured drumming, ritual dancing, animal sacrifice, and spirit possession. Over time, they incorporated Christian beliefs and practices such as church attendance, the search for salvation, and the use of candles and crucifixes and often identified their various spirits or deities with Catholic saints.

Expansion and Renewal in the Islamic World

The early modern era likewise witnessed the continuation of the "long march of Islam" across the Afro-Asian world. In sub-Saharan Africa, in the eastern and western wings of India, and in Central and Southeast Asia, the expansion of the Islamic frontier, a process already a thousand years in the making, extended farther still. Conversion to Islam generally did not mean a sudden abandonment of old religious practices in favor of the new. Rather, it was more often a matter of "assimilating Islamic rituals, cosmologies, and literatures into . . . local religious systems."[10]

Continued Islamization was not usually the product of conquering armies and expanding empires. It depended instead on wandering Muslim holy men or Sufis, Islamic scholars, and itinerant traders, none of whom posed a threat to local rulers. In fact, such people often were useful to those rulers and their village communities.

■ **Explanation**
What accounts for the continued spread of Islam in the early modern era and for the emergence of reform or renewal movements within the Islamic world?

They offered literacy in Arabic, established informal schools, provided protective charms containing passages from the Quran, served as advisers to local authorities and healers to the sick, often intermarried with local people, and generally did not insist that new converts give up their older practices. What they offered, in short, was connection to the wider, prestigious, prosperous world of Islam. Islamization extended modestly even to the Americas, where enslaved African Muslims practiced their faith in North America, particularly in Brazil, where Muslims led a number of slave revolts in the early nineteenth century. (See Zooming In: Ayuba Suleiman Diallo in Chapter 14, page 630.)

The islands of Southeast Asia illustrate the diversity of belief and practice that accompanied the spread of Islam in the early modern era. During the seventeenth century in Aceh, a Muslim sultanate on the northern tip of Sumatra, authorities sought to enforce the dietary codes and almsgiving practices of Islamic law. After four successive women ruled the area in the late seventeenth century, women were forbidden from exercising political power. On Muslim Java, however, numerous women served in royal courts, and women throughout Indonesia continued their longtime role as buyers and sellers in local markets. Among ordinary Javanese, traditional animistic practices of spirit worship coexisted easily with a tolerant and accommodating Islam, while merchants often embraced a more orthodox version of the religion in line with Middle Eastern traditions.

To such orthodox Muslims, religious syncretism, which accompanied Islamization almost everywhere, became increasingly offensive, even heretical. Such sentiments played an important role in movements of religious renewal and reform that emerged throughout the vast Islamic world of the eighteenth century. The leaders of such movements sharply criticized those practices that departed from earlier patterns established by Muhammad and from the authority of the Quran. For example, in India, which was governed by the Muslim Mughal Empire, religious resistance to official policies that accommodated Hindus found concrete expression during the reign of the emperor Aurangzeb (r. 1658–1707) (see Chapter 13, page 581). A series of religious wars in West Africa during the eighteenth and early nineteenth centuries took aim at corrupt Islamic practices and the rulers, Muslim and non-Muslim alike, who permitted them. In Southeast and Central Asia, tension grew between practitioners of localized and blended versions of Islam and those who sought to purify such practices in the name of a more authentic and universal faith.

The most well-known and widely visible of these Islamic renewal movements took place during the mid-eighteenth century in Arabia itself, where the religion had been born more than 1,000 years earlier. This movement originated in the teachings of the Islamic scholar Muhammad Ibn Abd al-Wahhab (1703–1792). The growing difficulties of the Islamic world, such as the weakening of the Ottoman Empire, were directly related, he argued, to deviations from the pure faith of early Islam. Al-Wahhab was particularly upset by common religious practices in central Arabia that seemed to him idolatry—the widespread veneration of Sufi saints and their tombs, the adoration of natural sites, and even the respect paid to Muhammad's tomb at Medina. All of this was a dilution of the absolute monotheism of authentic Islam.

The Wahhabi movement took a new turn in the 1740s when it received the political backing of Muhammad Ibn Saud, a local ruler who found al-Wahhab's ideas compelling. With Ibn Saud's support, the religious movement became an expansive state in central Arabia. Within that state, offending tombs were razed; "idols" were eliminated; books on logic were destroyed; the use of tobacco, hashish, and musical instruments was forbidden; and certain taxes not authorized by religious teaching were abolished.

Al-Wahhab's ideas about the role of women have attracted considerable attention in light of the highly restrictive practices of Wahhabi Islam in contemporary Saudi Arabia. He did on one occasion reluctantly authorize the stoning of a woman who persisted in an adulterous sexual relationship after numerous warnings, but more generally he emphasized the rights of women within a patriarchal Islamic framework. These included the right to consent to and stipulate conditions for a marriage, to control her dowry, to divorce, and to engage in commerce. Such rights, long embedded in Islamic law, had apparently been forgotten or ignored in eighteenth-century Arabia. Furthermore, he did not insist on head-to-toe covering of women in public and allowed for the mixing of unrelated men and women for business or medical purposes.

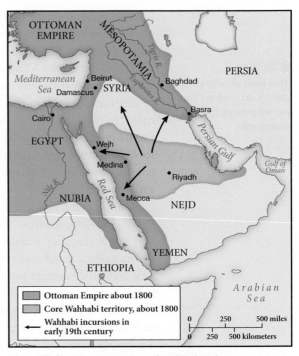

Map 15.3   The Expansion of Wahhabi Islam
From its base in central Arabia, the Wahhabi movement represented a challenge to the Ottoman Empire, while its ideas subsequently spread widely within the Islamic world.

By the early nineteenth century, this new reformist state encompassed much of central Arabia, with Mecca itself coming under Wahhabi control in 1803 (see Map 15.3). Although an Egyptian army broke the power of the Wahhabis in 1818, the movement's influence continued to spread across the Islamic world. Together with the ongoing expansion of the religion, these movements of reform and renewal signaled the continuing cultural vitality of the "abode of Islam," even as the European presence on the world stage assumed larger dimensions. In the nineteenth and twentieth centuries, such movements persisted and became associated with resistance to the political, military, and cultural intrusion of the European West into the affairs of the Islamic world.

China: New Directions in an Old Tradition

Neither China nor India experienced cultural or religious change as dramatic as that of the Reformation in Europe, nor did Confucian or Hindu cultures during the early modern era spread widely, as did Christianity and Islam. Nonetheless, neither of these traditions remained static. As in Christian Europe, challenges to established orthodoxies in China and India emerged as commercial and urban life, as well as political change, fostered new thinking.

■ Change
What kinds of cultural changes occurred in China and India during the early modern era?

China during the Ming and Qing dynasties continued to operate broadly within a Confucian framework, enriched now by the insights of Buddhism and Daoism to generate a system of thought called Neo-Confucianism. Chinese Ming dynasty rulers, in their aversion to the despised Mongols, embraced and actively supported this native Confucian tradition, whereas the foreign Manchu or Qing rulers did so to woo Chinese intellectuals to support the new dynasty. Within this context, a considerable amount of controversy, debate, and new thinking emerged during the early modern era.

During late Ming times, for example, the influential thinker Wang Yangming (1472–1529) argued that "intuitive moral knowledge exists in people . . . even robbers know that they should not rob."[11] Thus anyone could achieve a virtuous life by introspection and contemplation, without the extended education, study of classical texts, and constant striving for improvement that traditional Confucianism prescribed for an elite class of "gentlemen." Such ideas figured prominently among Confucian scholars of the sixteenth century, although critics later contended that such thinking promoted an excessive individualism. They also argued that Wang Yangming's ideas had undermined the Ming dynasty and contributed to China's conquest by the foreign Manchus. Some Chinese Buddhists as well sought to make their religion more accessible to ordinary people, by suggesting that laypeople at home could undertake practices similar to those performed by monks in monasteries. Withdrawal from the world was not necessary for enlightenment. This kind of moral or religious individualism bore some similarity to the thinking of Martin Luther, who argued that individuals could seek salvation by "faith alone," without the assistance of a priestly hierarchy.

Another new direction in Chinese elite culture took shape in a movement known as *kaozheng*, or "research based on evidence." Intended to "seek truth from facts," kaozheng was critical of the unfounded speculation of conventional Confucian philosophy and instead emphasized the importance of verification, precision, accuracy, and rigorous analysis in all fields of inquiry. During the late Ming years, this emphasis generated works dealing with agriculture, medicine, pharmacology, botany, craft techniques, and more. In the Qing era, kaozheng was associated with the recovery and critical analysis of ancient historical documents, which sometimes led to sharp criticism of Neo-Confucian orthodoxy. It was a genuinely scientific approach to knowledge, but it was applied more to the study of the past than to the natural world of astronomy, physics, or anatomy, which was the focus in the West.

While such matters occupied the intellectual elite of China, in the cities a lively popular culture emerged among the less educated. For city-dwellers, plays, paintings, short stories, and especially novels provided diversion and entertainment that were a step up from what could be found in teahouses and wineshops. Numerous "how-to" painting manuals allowed a larger public to participate in this favorite

Chinese art form. Even though Confucian scholars disdained popular fiction, a vigorous printing industry responded to the growing demand for exciting novels. The most famous was Cao Xueqin's mid-eighteenth-century novel *The Dream of the Red Chamber*, a huge book that contained 120 chapters and some 400 characters, most of them women. It explored the social life of an eighteenth-century elite family with connections to the Chinese court.

India: Bridging the Hindu/Muslim Divide

In a largely Hindu India, ruled by the Muslim Mughal Empire, several significant cultural departures took shape in the early modern era that brought Hindus and Muslims together in new forms of religious expression. At the level of elite culture, the Mughal ruler Akbar formulated a state cult that combined elements of Islam, Hinduism, and Zoroastrianism (see Chapter 13, page 581). The Mughal court also embraced Renaissance Christian art, and soon murals featuring Jesus, Mary, and Christian saints appeared on the walls of palaces, garden pavilions, and harems. The court also commissioned a prominent Sufi spiritual master to compose an illustrated book describing various Hindu yoga postures. Intended to bring this Hindu tradition into Islamic Sufi practice, the book, known as the *Ocean of Life*, portrayed some of the yogis in a Christ-like fashion.

Within popular culture, the flourishing of a devotional form of Hinduism known as *bhakti* also bridged the gulf separating Hindu and Muslim. Through songs, prayers, dances, poetry, and rituals, devotees sought to achieve union with one or another of India's many deities. Appealing especially to women, the bhakti movement provided an avenue for social criticism. Its practitioners often set aside caste distinctions and disregarded the detailed rituals of the Brahmin priests in favor of direct contact with the Divine. This emphasis had much in common with mystical Sufi forms of Islam and helped blur the distinction between these two traditions in India.

Among the most beloved of bhakti poets was Mirabai (1498–1547), a high-caste woman from northern India who abandoned her upper-class family and conventional Hindu practice. Upon her husband's death, tradition asserts, she declined to burn herself on his funeral pyre (a practice known as *sati*). She further offended caste restrictions by

Guru Nanak
This painting shows a seated Guru Nanak, the founder of Sikhism, disputing with four kneeling Hindu holy men. (British Library, London, UK/© British Library Board. All Rights Reserved/Robena/Art Resource, NY)

taking as her guru (religious teacher) an old untouchable shoemaker. To visit him, she apparently tied her saris together and climbed down the castle walls at night. Then she would wash his aged feet and drink the water from these ablutions. Much of her poetry deals with her yearning for union with Krishna, a Hindu deity she regarded as her husband, lover, and lord. She wrote:

> What I paid was my social body, my town body, my family body, and all my inherited jewels. Mirabai says: The Dark One [Krishna] is my husband now.[12]

Yet another major cultural change that blended Islam and Hinduism emerged with the growth of Sikhism as a new and distinctive religious tradition in the Punjab region of northern India. Its founder, Guru Nanak (1469–1539), had been involved in the bhakti movement but came to believe that "there is no Hindu; there is no Muslim; only God." His teachings and those of subsequent gurus also generally ignored caste distinctions and untouchability and ended the seclusion of women, while proclaiming the "brotherhood of all mankind" as well as the essential equality of men and women. Drawing converts from Punjabi peasants and merchants, both Muslim and Hindu, the Sikhs gradually became a separate religious community. They developed their own sacred book, known as the Guru Granth (teacher book); created a central place of worship and pilgrimage in the Golden Temple of Amritsar; and prescribed certain dress requirements for men, including keeping hair and beards uncut, wearing a turban, and carrying a short sword. During the seventeenth century, Sikhs encountered hostility from both the Mughal Empire and some of their Hindu neighbors. In response, Sikhism evolved from a peaceful religious movement, blending Hindu and Muslim elements, into a militant community whose military skills were highly valued by the British when they took over India in the late eighteenth century.

SUMMING UP SO FAR

In what ways did religious changes in Asia and the Middle East parallel those in Europe, and in what ways were they different?

A New Way of Thinking: The Birth of Modern Science

While some Europeans were actively attempting to spread the Christian faith to distant corners of the world, others were nurturing an understanding of the cosmos at least partially at odds with traditional Christian teaching. These were the makers of Europe's Scientific Revolution, a vast intellectual and cultural transformation that took place between the mid-sixteenth and early eighteenth centuries. These men of science would no longer rely on the external authority of the Bible, the Church, the speculations of ancient philosophers, or the received wisdom of cultural tradition. For them, knowledge would be acquired through rational inquiry based on evidence, the product of human minds alone. Those who created this revolution—Copernicus from Poland, Galileo from Italy, Descartes from France,

Newton from England, and many others—saw themselves as departing radically from older ways of thinking. "The old rubbish must be thrown away," wrote a seventeenth-century English scientist. "These are the days that must lay a new Foundation of a more magnificent Philosophy."[13]

The long-term significance of the Scientific Revolution can hardly be overestimated. Within early modern Europe, it fundamentally altered ideas about the place of humankind within the cosmos and sharply challenged both the teachings and the authority of the Church. Over the past several centuries, it has substantially eroded religious belief and practice in the West, particularly among the well educated. When applied to the affairs of human society, scientific ways of thinking challenged ancient social hierarchies and political systems and played a role in the revolutionary upheavals of the modern era. But science was also used to legitimize racial and gender inequalities, giving new support to old ideas about the natural inferiority of women and enslaved people. When married to the technological innovations of the Industrial Revolution, science fostered both the marvels of modern production and the horrors of modern means of destruction. By the twentieth century, science had become so widespread that it largely lost its association with European culture and became the chief marker of global modernity. Like Buddhism, Christianity, and Islam, modern science became a universal worldview, open to all who could accept its premises and its techniques.

The Question of Origins: Why Europe?

Why did the breakthrough of the Scientific Revolution occur first in Europe and during the early modern era? The realm of Islam, after all, had generated the most advanced science in the world during the centuries between 800 and 1400. Arab scholars could boast of remarkable achievements in mathematics, astronomy, optics, and medicine, and their libraries far exceeded those of Europe.[14] And what of China? Its elite culture of Confucianism was both sophisticated and secular, less burdened by religious dogma than that of the Christian or Islamic worlds; its technological accomplishments and economic growth were unmatched anywhere in the several centuries after 1000. In neither civilization, however, did these achievements lead to the kind of intellectual innovation that occurred in Europe.

Europe's historical development as a reinvigorated and fragmented civilization arguably gave rise to conditions particularly favorable to the scientific enterprise. By the twelfth and thirteenth centuries, Europeans had evolved a legal system that guaranteed a measure of independence for a variety of institutions—the Church, towns and cities, guilds, professional associations, and universities. This legal revolution was based on the idea of a "corporation," a collective group of people that was treated as a unit, a legal person, with certain rights to regulate and control its own members.

Most important for the development of science in the West was the autonomy of its emerging universities. By 1215, the University of Paris was recognized as a

■ **Comparison**
Why did the Scientific Revolution occur in Europe rather than in China or the Islamic world?

"corporation of masters and scholars," which could admit and expel students, establish courses of instruction, and grant a "license to teach" to its faculty. Such universities—for example, in Paris, Bologna, Oxford, Cambridge, and Salamanca—became "neutral zones of intellectual autonomy" in which scholars could pursue their studies in relative freedom from the dictates of church or state authorities. Within them, the study of the natural order began to slowly separate itself from philosophy and theology and to gain a distinct identity. Their curricula featured "a basically scientific core of readings and lectures" that drew heavily on the writings of the Greek thinker Aristotle, which had only recently become available to Western Europeans. Most of the major figures in the Scientific Revolution had been trained in and were affiliated with these universities.

In the Islamic world, by contrast, science was patronized by a variety of local authorities, but it occurred largely outside the formal system of higher education. Within colleges known as madrassas, Quranic studies and religious law held the central place, whereas philosophy and natural science were viewed with great suspicion. To religious scholars, the Quran held all wisdom, and scientific thinking might well challenge it. An earlier openness to free inquiry and religious toleration was increasingly replaced by a disdain for scientific and philosophical inquiry, for it seemed to lead only to uncertainty and confusion. "May God protect us from useless knowledge" was a saying that reflected this outlook. Nor did Chinese authorities permit independent institutions of higher learning in which scholars could conduct their studies in relative freedom. Instead, Chinese education focused on preparing for a rigidly defined set of civil service examinations and emphasized the humanistic and moral texts of classical Confucianism. "The pursuit of scientific subjects," one recent historian concluded, "was thereby relegated to the margins of Chinese society."[15]

Beyond its distinctive institutional development, Western Europe was in a position to draw extensively on the knowledge of other cultures, especially that of the Islamic world. Arab medical texts, astronomical research, and translations of Greek classics played a major role in the birth of European natural philosophy (as science was then called) between 1000 and 1500. Then, in the sixteenth through the eighteenth centuries, Europeans found themselves at the center of a massive new exchange of information as they became aware of lands, peoples, plants, animals, societies, and religions from around the world. This tidal wave of new knowledge, uniquely available to Europeans, shook up older ways of thinking and opened the way to new conceptions of the world. The sixteenth-century Italian doctor, mathematician, and writer Girolamo Cardano (1501–1576) clearly expressed this sense of wonderment: "The most unusual [circumstance of my life] is that I was born in this century in which the whole world became known; whereas the ancients were familiar with but a little more than a third part of it." He worried, however, that amid this explosion of knowledge, "certainties will be exchanged for uncertainties."[16] It was precisely those uncertainties—skepticism about established views—that provided such a fertile cultural ground for the emergence of modern science.

The Reformation too contributed to that cultural climate in its challenge to authority, its encouragement of mass literacy, and its affirmation of secular professions.

Science as Cultural Revolution

Before the Scientific Revolution, educated Europeans held a view of the world that derived from Aristotle, perhaps the greatest of the ancient Greek philosophers, and from Ptolemy, a Greco-Egyptian mathematician and astronomer who lived in Alexandria during the second century C.E. To medieval European thinkers, the earth was stationary and at the center of the universe, and around it revolved the sun, moon, and stars embedded in ten spheres of transparent crystal. This understanding coincided well with the religious outlook of the Catholic Church because the attention of the entire universe was centered on the earth and its human inhabitants, among whom God's plan for salvation unfolded. It was a universe of divine purpose, with angels guiding the hierarchically arranged heavenly bodies along their way while God watched over the whole from his realm beyond the spheres. The Scientific Revolution was revolutionary because it fundamentally challenged this understanding of the universe.

The initial breakthrough in the Scientific Revolution came from the Polish mathematician and astronomer Nicolaus Copernicus, whose famous book *On the Revolutions of the Heavenly Spheres* was published in the year of his death, 1543. Its essential argument was that "at the middle of all things lies the sun" and that the earth, like the other planets, revolved around it. Thus the earth was no longer unique or at the obvious center of God's attention.

■ **Change**
What was revolutionary about the Scientific Revolution?

Other European scientists built on Copernicus's central insight, and some even argued that other inhabited worlds and other kinds of humans existed. Less speculatively, in the early seventeenth century Johannes Kepler, a German mathematician, showed that the planets followed elliptical orbits, undermining the ancient belief that they moved in perfect circles. The Italian Galileo (gal-uh-LAY-oh) developed an improved telescope, with which he made many observations that undermined established understandings of the cosmos. (See Zooming In: Galileo and the Telescope, page 668.) Some thinkers began to discuss the notion of an unlimited universe in which humankind occupied a mere speck of dust in an unimaginable vastness. The French mathematician and philosopher Blaise Pascal (1623–1662) perhaps spoke for many when he wrote, "The eternal silence of infinite space frightens me."[17]

The culmination of the Scientific Revolution came in the work of Sir Isaac Newton (1642–1727), the Englishman who formulated the modern laws of motion and mechanics, which remained unchallenged until the twentieth century. At the core of Newton's thinking was the concept of universal gravitation. "All bodies whatsoever," Newton declared, "are endowed with a principle of mutual gravitation."[18] Here was the grand unifying idea of early modern science. The radical implication of this view was that the heavens and the earth, long regarded as separate and distinct spheres, were not so different after all, for the motion of a cannonball

Galileo and the Telescope: Reflecting on Science and Religion

The Scientific Revolution was predicated on the idea that knowledge of how the universe worked was acquired through a combination of careful observations, controlled experiments, and the formulation of general laws, expressed in mathematical terms. New scientific instruments capable of making precise empirical observations underpinned some of the most important break-

Galileo on trial.

throughs of the period. Perhaps no single invention produced more dramatic discoveries than the telescope, the first of which were produced in the early seventeenth century by Dutch eyeglass makers.

The impact of new instruments depended on how scientists employed them. In the case of the telescope, it was the brilliant Italian mathematician and astronomer Galileo Galilei (1564–1642) who unlocked its potential when he used it to observe the night sky. Within months of creating his own telescope, which improved on earlier designs, Galileo made a series of discoveries that put into question well-established understandings of the cosmos. He observed craters on the moon and sunspots, or blemishes, moving across the face of the sun, which challenged the traditional notion that no imperfection or change

marred the heavenly bodies. Moreover, his discovery of the moons of Jupiter and many new stars suggested a cosmos far larger than the finite universe of traditional astronomy. In 1610, Galileo published his remarkable findings in a book titled *The Starry Messenger*, where he emphasized time and again that his precise observations provided irrefutable evidence of a cosmos unlike that described by traditional authorities. "With the aid of the telescope," he argued, "this has been scrutinized so directly and with such ocular certainty that all the disputes which have vexed the philosophers through so many ages have been resolved, and we are at last freed from wordy debates about it."[19]

Galileo's empirical evidence transformed the debate over the nature of the cosmos. His dramatic and unexpected discoveries were readily grasped, and with the aid of a telescope anyone could confirm their veracity. His initial findings were heralded by many in the scientific community, including Christoph Clavius, the Church's leading astronomer in Rome. Galileo's findings led him

photo: *Trial of Galileo*, 1633, oil on canvas, Italian/Private Collection/Bridgeman Images

or the falling of an apple obeyed the same natural laws that governed the orbiting planets.

By the time Newton died, a revolutionary new understanding of the physical universe had emerged among educated Europeans: the universe was no longer propelled by supernatural forces but functioned on its own according to scientific principles that could be described mathematically. Articulating this view, Kepler wrote, "The machine of the universe is not similar to a divine animated being but similar to a clock."[20] Furthermore, it was a machine that regulated itself, requiring neither God nor angels to account for its normal operation. Knowledge of that universe could be obtained through human reason alone—by observation, deduction, and experimentation—without the aid of ancient authorities or divine reve-

to conclude that Copernicus (1473–1543), an earlier astronomer and mathematician, had been correct when he had advanced the theory that the sun rather than the earth was at the center of the solar system. But Galileo's evidence could not definitively prove Copernicus's theory to the satisfaction of critics, leading Galileo to study other phenomena, such as the tides, that could provide further evidence that the earth was in motion.

When the Church condemned Copernicus's theory in 1616, it remained silent on Galileo's astronomical observations, instead warning him to refrain from teaching or promoting Copernicus's ideas. Ultimately, though, Galileo came into conflict with church authorities when in 1629 he published, with what he thought was the consent of the Church, the *Dialogue Concerning the Two Chief World Systems*, a work sympathetic to Copernicus's sun-centric system. In 1632, Galileo was tried by the Roman Inquisition, an ecclesiastical court charged with maintaining orthodoxy, and convicted of teaching doctrines against the express orders of the Church. He recanted his beliefs and at the age of sixty-nine was sentenced to house arrest.

Although Galileo was formally convicted of disobeying the Church's order to remain silent on the issue of Copernicus's theory, the question most fundamentally at stake in the trial was "What does it mean, 'to know something'?"[21] This question of the relationship between scientific knowledge, primarily concerned with how the universe works, and other forms of "knowledge," derived from divine revelation or mystical experience, has persisted in the West. Over 350 years after the trial, Pope John Paul II spoke of Galileo's conviction in a public speech in 1992, declaring it a "sad misunderstanding" that belongs to the past, but one with ongoing resonance because "the underlying problems of this case concern both the nature of science and the message of faith." Addressing the central question of what it means to know something, the pope declared scientific and religious knowledge to be compatible: "There exist two realms of knowledge, one which has its source in Revelation and one which reason can discover by its own power. . . . The distinction between the two realms of knowledge ought not to be understood as opposition. . . . The methodologies proper to each make it possible to bring out different aspects of reality."[22]

Strangely enough, Galileo himself had expressed something similar centuries earlier. "Nor is God," he wrote, "any less excellently revealed in Nature's actions than in the sacred statements of the Bible."[23] Finding the place of new scientific knowledge in a constellation of older wisdom traditions proved a fraught but highly significant development in the emergence of the modern world.

Question: What can Galileo's discoveries with his telescope and his conviction by the Inquisition tell us about the Scientific Revolution?

lation. The French philosopher René Descartes (day-KAHRT) resolved "to seek no other knowledge than that which I might find within myself, or perhaps in the book of nature."[24]

Like the physical universe, the human body also lost some of its mystery. The careful dissections of cadavers and animals enabled doctors and scientists to describe the human body with much greater accuracy and to understand the circulation of the blood throughout the body. The heart was no longer the mysterious center of the body's heat and the seat of its passions; instead it was just another machine, a complex muscle that functioned as a pump.

The movers and shakers of this enormous cultural transformation were almost entirely male. European women, after all, had been largely excluded from the

The Telescope
Johannes Hevelius, an astronomer of German Lutheran background living in what is now Poland, constructed extraordinarily long telescopes in the mid-seventeenth century with which he observed sunspots, charted the surface of the moon, and discovered several comets. Such telescopes played a central role in transforming understandings of the universe during the Scientific Revolution. (© World History Archive/Alamy)

universities where much of the new science was discussed. A few aristocratic women, however, had the leisure and connections to participate informally in the scientific networks of their male relatives. Through her marriage to the Duke of Newcastle, Margaret Cavendish (1623–1673) joined in conversations with a circle of "natural philosophers," wrote six scientific texts, and was the only seventeenth-century English woman to attend a session of the Royal Society of London, created to foster scientific learning. In Germany, a number of women took part in astronomical work as assistants to their husbands or brothers. Maria Winkelman, for example, discovered a previously unknown comet, though her husband took credit for it. After his death, she sought to continue his work in the Berlin Academy of Sciences but was refused on the grounds that "mouths would gape" if a woman held such a position.

Much of this scientific thinking developed in the face of strenuous opposition from the Catholic Church, for both its teachings and its authority were under attack. The Italian philosopher Giordano Bruno, proclaiming an infinite universe and many worlds, was burned at the stake in 1600, and Galileo was compelled by the Church to publicly renounce his belief that the earth moved around an orbit and rotated on its axis.

But scholars have sometimes exaggerated the conflict of science and religion, casting it in military terms as an almost unbroken war. None of the early scientists rejected Christianity. Copernicus in fact published his famous book with the support of several leading Catholic churchmen and dedicated it to the pope. After all, several earlier Catholic writers had proposed the idea of the earth in motion. He more likely feared the criticism of fellow scientists than that of the church hierarchy. Galileo himself proclaimed the compatibility of science and faith, and his lack of diplomacy in dealing with church leaders was at least in part responsible for his quarrel with the Church.[25] Newton was a serious biblical scholar and saw no inherent contradiction between his ideas and belief in God. "This most beautiful system of the sun, planets, and comets," he declared, "could only proceed from the counsel and dominion of an intelligent Being."[26] Thus the Church gradually accommodated as well as resisted the new ideas, largely by compartmentalizing them. Science might prevail in its limited sphere of describing the physical universe, but religion was still the arbiter of truth about those ultimate questions concerning human salvation, righteous behavior, and the larger purposes of life.

Science and Enlightenment

Initially limited to a small handful of scholars, the ideas of the Scientific Revolution spread to a wider European public during the eighteenth century. That process was aided by novel techniques of printing and bookmaking, by a popular press, by growing literacy, and by a host of scientific societies. Moreover, the new approach to knowledge—rooted in human reason, skeptical of authority, expressed in natural laws—was now applied to human affairs, not just to the physical universe. The Scottish professor Adam Smith (1723–1790), for example, formulated laws that accounted for the operation of the economy and that, if followed, he believed, would generate inevitably favorable results for society. Growing numbers of people believed that the long-term outcome of scientific development would be "enlightenment," a term that has come to define the eighteenth century in European history. If human reason could discover the laws that governed the universe, surely it could uncover ways in which humankind might govern itself more effectively.

"What is Enlightenment?" asked the prominent German intellectual Immanuel Kant (1724–1804). "It is man's emergence from his self-imposed . . . inability to use one's own understanding without another's guidance. . . . Dare to know! 'Have the courage to use your own understanding' is therefore the motto of the enlightenment."[27] Although they often disagreed sharply with one another, European Enlightenment thinkers shared this belief in the power of knowledge to transform human society. They also shared a satirical, critical style, a commitment to open-mindedness and inquiry, and in various degrees a hostility to established political and religious authority. Many took aim at arbitrary governments, the "divine right of kings," and the aristocratic privileges of European society. The English philosopher John Locke (1632–1704) offered principles for constructing a constitutional government, a contract between rulers and ruled that was created by human ingenuity rather than divinely prescribed. Much of Enlightenment thinking was directed against the superstition, ignorance, and corruption of established religion. In his *Treatise on Toleration*, the French writer Voltaire (1694–1778) reflected the outlook of the Scientific Revolution as he commented sarcastically on religious intolerance:

■ **Change**
In what ways did the Enlightenment challenge older patterns of European thinking?

> This little globe, nothing more than a point, rolls in space like so many other globes; we are lost in its immensity. Man, some five feet tall, is surely a very small part of the universe. One of these imperceptible beings says to some of his neighbors in Arabia or Africa: "Listen to me, for the God of all these worlds has enlightened me; there are nine hundred million little ants like us on the earth, but only my anthill is beloved of God; He will hold all others in horror through all eternity; only mine will be blessed, the others will be eternally wretched."[28]

Voltaire's own faith, like that of many others among the "enlightened," was deism. Deists believed in a rather abstract and remote Deity, sometimes compared to a clockmaker, who had created the world, but not in a personal God who intervened

The Philosophers of the Enlightenment
This painting shows the French philosopher Voltaire with a group of intellectual luminaries at the summer palace of the Prussian king Frederick II. Such literary gatherings, sometimes called salons, were places of lively conversation among mostly male participants and came to be seen as emblematic of the European Enlightenment. (Painting by Adolph Menzel [1815–1905], 1850/© akg-images/The Image Works)

in history or tampered with natural law. Others became *pantheists*, who believed that God and nature were identical. Here was a conception of religion shaped by the outlook of science. Sometimes called "natural religion," it was devoid of mystery, revelation, ritual, and spiritual practice, while proclaiming a God that could be "proven" by human rationality, logic, and the techniques of scientific inquiry. In this view, all else was superstition. Among the most radical of such thinkers were the several Dutchmen who wrote the *Treatise of Three Imposters*, which claimed that Moses, Jesus, and Muhammad were fraudulent impostors who based their teachings on "the ignorance of Peoples [and] resolved to keep them in it."[29]

Prominent among the debates spawned by the Enlightenment was the question of women's nature, their role in society, and the education most appropriate for them. Although well-to-do Parisian women hosted in their elegant salons many gatherings of the largely male Enlightenment figures, most of those men were anything but ardent feminists. The male editors of the famous *Encyclopédie*, a vast compendium of Enlightenment thought, included very few essays by women. One of the male authors expressed a common view: "[Women] constitute the principal ornament of the world. . . . May they, through submissive discretion and . . . artless cleverness, spur us [men] on to virtue." In his treatise *Emile*, Jean-Jacques Rousseau described women as fundamentally different from and inferior to men and urged that "the whole education of women ought to be relative to men."

Such views were sharply contested by any number of other Enlightenment figures—men and women alike. The *Journal des Dames* (Ladies Journal), founded in Paris in 1759, aggressively defended women. "If we have not been raised up in the sciences as you have," declared Madame Beaulmer, the *Journal*'s first editor, "it is you [men] who are the guilty ones; for have you not always abused . . . the bodily strength that nature has given you?"[30] The philosopher Condorcet looked forward to the "complete destruction of those prejudices that have established an inequality of rights between the sexes." And in 1792, the British writer Mary Wollstonecraft directly confronted Rousseau's view of women and their education: "What nonsense! . . . Til women are more rationally educated, the progress of human virtue and improvement in knowledge must receive continual checks." Thus was initiated a debate that echoed throughout the centuries that followed.

Though solidly rooted in Europe, Enlightenment thought was influenced by the growing global awareness of its major thinkers. Voltaire, for example, idealized China as an empire governed by an elite of secular scholars selected for their talent, which stood in sharp contrast to continental Europe, where aristocratic birth and military prowess were far more important. The example of Confucianism—supposedly secular, moral, rational, and tolerant—encouraged Enlightenment thinkers to imagine a future for European civilization without the kind of supernatural religion that they found so offensive in the Christian West.

The central theme of the Enlightenment—and what made it potentially revolutionary—was the idea of progress. Human society was not fixed by tradition or divine command but could be changed, and improved, by human action guided by reason. No one expressed this soaring confidence in human possibility more clearly than the French thinker the Marquis de Condorcet (1743–1794), who boldly declared that "the perfectibility of humanity is indefinite." Belief in progress was a sharp departure from much of premodern social thinking, and it inspired those who later made the great revolutions of the modern era in the Americas, France, Russia, China, and elsewhere. Born of the Scientific Revolution, that was the faith of the Enlightenment. For some, it was virtually a new religion.

The age of the Enlightenment, however, also witnessed a reaction against too much reliance on human reason. Jean-Jacques Rousseau (1712–1778) minimized the importance of book learning for the education of children and prescribed instead an immersion in nature, which taught self-reliance and generosity rather than the greed and envy fostered by "civilization." The Romantic movement in art and literature appealed to emotion, intuition, passion, and imagination rather than cold reason and scientific learning. Religious awakenings—complete with fiery sermons, public repentance, and intense personal experience of sin and redemption—shook Protestant Europe and North America in the eighteenth and early nineteenth centuries. The Methodist movement—with its emphasis on Bible study, confession of sins, fasting, enthusiastic preaching, and resistance to worldly pleasures—was a case in point.

Various forms of "enlightened religion" also arose in the early modern centuries, reflecting the influence of Enlightenment thinking. Quakers, for example, emphasized tolerance, an absence of hierarchy and ostentation, a benevolent God, and an "inner light" available to all people. Unitarians denied the Trinity, original sin, predestination, and the divinity of Jesus, but honored him as a great teacher and a moral prophet. Later, in the nineteenth century, proponents of the "social gospel" saw the essence of Christianity not in personal salvation but in ethical behavior. Science and the Enlightenment surely challenged religion, and for some they eroded religious belief and practice. Just as surely, though, religion persisted, adapted, and revived for many others.

Looking Ahead: Science in the Nineteenth Century and Beyond

The perspectives of the Enlightenment were challenged not only by romanticism and religious "enthusiasm" but also by the continued development of European science itself. This remarkable phenomenon justifies a brief look ahead at several scientific developments in the nineteenth and twentieth centuries.

■ **Change**

How did nineteenth-century developments in the sciences challenge the faith of the Enlightenment?

Modern science was a cumulative and self-critical enterprise, which in the nineteenth century and later was applied to new domains of human inquiry in ways that undermined some of the assumptions of the Enlightenment. In the realm of biology, for example, Charles Darwin (1809–1882) laid out a complex argument that all life was in constant change, that an endless and competitive struggle for survival over millions of years constantly generated new species of plants and animals, while casting others into extinction. Human beings were not excluded from this vast process, for they too were the work of evolution operating through natural selection. Darwin's famous books *The Origin of Species* (1859) and *The Descent of Man* (1871) were threatening to many traditional Christian believers, perhaps more so than Copernicus's ideas about a sun-centered universe had been several centuries earlier.

At the same time, Karl Marx (1818–1883) articulated a view of human history that likewise emphasized change and struggle. Conflicting social classes—slave owners and slaves, nobles and peasants, capitalists and workers—successively drove the process of historical transformation. Although he was describing the evolution of human civilization, Marx saw himself as a scientist. He based his theories on extensive historical research; like Newton and Darwin, he sought to formulate general laws that would explain events in a rational way. Nor did he believe in heavenly intervention, chance, or the divinely endowed powers of kings. The coming of socialism, in this view, was not simply a good idea; it was inscribed in the laws of historical development. (See Working with Evidence, Source 17.1, page 776.)

Like the intellectuals of the Enlightenment, Darwin and Marx believed strongly in progress, but in their thinking, conflict and struggle rather than reason and education were the motors of progress. The Enlightenment image of the thoughtful, rational, and independent individual was fading. Individuals—plant, animal, and human alike—were now viewed as enmeshed in vast systems of biological, economic, and social conflict.

The work of the Viennese doctor Sigmund Freud (1856–1939) applied scientific techniques to the operation of the human mind and emotions and in doing so cast further doubt on Enlightenment conceptions of human rationality. At the core of each person, Freud argued, lay primal impulses toward sexuality and aggression, which were only barely held in check by the thin veneer of social conscience derived from civilization. Our neuroses arose from the ceaseless struggle between our irrational drives and the claims of conscience. This too was a far cry from the Enlightenment conception of the human condition.

And in the twentieth century, developments in physics, such as relativity and quantum theory, called into question some of the established verities of the Newtonian view of the world, particularly at the subatomic level and at speeds approaching that of light. In this new physics, time is relative to the position of the observer; space can warp and light can bend; matter and energy are equivalent; black holes and dark matter abound; and probability, not certain prediction, is the best that scientists can hope for. None of this was even on the horizon of those who made the original Scientific Revolution in the early modern era.

European Science beyond the West

In the long run, the achievements of the Scientific Revolution spread globally, becoming the most widely sought-after product of European culture and far more desired than Christianity, democracy, socialism, or Western literature. In the early modern era, however, interest in European scientific thinking within major Asian societies was both modest and selective. The telescope provides an example. Invented in early seventeenth-century Europe and endlessly improved in the centuries that followed, the telescope provoked enormous excitement in European scientific circles. It made possible any number of astronomical discoveries, including the rugged surface of the moon, the moons of Jupiter, the rings of Saturn, and the phases of Venus. "We are here . . . on fire with these things," wrote an English astronomer in 1610.[31] Soon the telescope was available in China, Mughal India, and the Ottoman Empire. But in none of these places did it evoke much interest or evolve into the kind of "discovery machine" that it was rapidly becoming in Europe.

In China, Qing dynasty emperors and scholars were most interested in European techniques, derived largely from Jesuit missionaries, for predicting eclipses, reforming the calendar, and making accurate maps of the empire. European medicine, however, was of little importance for Chinese physicians before the nineteenth century. But the reputation of the Jesuits suffered when it became apparent in the 1760s that for two centuries the missionaries had withheld information about Copernican views of a sun-centered solar system because those ideas had been condemned by the Church. Nonetheless, European science had a substantial impact on

■ **Connection**
In what ways was European science received in the major civilizations of Asia in the early modern era?

a number of Chinese scholars as it seemed compatible with the data-based kaozheng movement, described by one participant as "an ant-like accumulation of facts."[32] European mathematics was of particular interest to kaozheng researchers who were exploring the history of Chinese mathematics. To convince their skeptical colleagues that the barbarian Europeans had something to offer in this field, some Chinese scholars argued that European mathematics had in fact grown out of much earlier Chinese ideas and could therefore be adopted with comfort.[33] In such ways, early modern Chinese thinkers selectively assimilated Western science very much on their own terms.[34]

Although Japanese authorities largely closed their country off from the West in the early seventeenth century (see Chapter 14), one window remained open. Alone among Europeans, the Dutch were permitted to trade in Japan at a single location near Nagasaki, but not until 1720 did the Japanese lift the ban on importing Western books. Then a number of European texts in medicine, astronomy, geography, mathematics, and other disciplines were translated and studied by a small group of Japanese scholars. They were especially impressed with Western anatomical studies, for in Japan dissection was work fit only for outcasts. Returning from an autopsy conducted by Dutch physicians in the mid-eighteenth century, several Japanese observers reflected on their experience: "We remarked to each other how amazing the autopsy had been, and how inexcusable it had been for us to be ignorant of the anatomical structure of the human body."[35] Nonetheless, this small center of "Dutch learning," as it was called, remained isolated amid a pervasive Confucian-based culture. Not until the mid-nineteenth century, when Japan was forcibly opened to Western penetration, would European-style science assume a prominent place in Japanese culture.

Like China and Japan, the Ottoman Empire in the sixteenth and seventeenth centuries was an independent, powerful, successful society whose intellectual elites saw no need for a wholesale embrace of things European. Ottoman scholars were conscious of the rich tradition of Muslim astronomy and chose not to translate the works of major European scientists such as Copernicus, Kepler, or Newton, although they were broadly aware of European scientific achievements by 1650. Insofar as they were interested in these developments, it was for their practical usefulness in making maps and calendars rather than for their larger philosophical implications. In any event, the notion of a sun-centered solar system did not cause the kind of upset that it did in Europe.

More broadly, theoretical science of any kind—Muslim or European—faced an uphill struggle in the face of a conservative Islamic educational system. In 1580, for example, a highly sophisticated astronomical observatory was dismantled under pressure from conservative religious scholars and teachers, who interpreted an outbreak of the plague as God's disapproval with those who sought to understand his secrets. As in Japan, the systematic embrace of Western science would have to await the nineteenth century, when the Ottoman Empire was under far more intense European pressure and reform seemed more necessary.

REFLECTIONS

Cultural Borrowing and Its Hazards

Ideas are important in human history. They shape the mental or cultural worlds that people everywhere inhabit, and they often influence behavior as well. Many of the ideas developed or introduced during the early modern era have had enormous and continuing significance in the centuries that followed. The Western Hemisphere was solidly incorporated into Christendom. A Wahhabi version of Islam remains the official faith of Saudi Arabia into the twenty-first century and has influenced many contemporary Islamic revival movements, including al-Qaeda. Modern science and the associated notions of progress have become for many people something approaching a new religion.

Accompanying the development of these ideas has been a great deal of cultural borrowing. Filipinos, Siberians, and many Native American peoples borrowed elements of Christianity from Europeans. Numerous Asian and African peoples borrowed Islam from the Arabs. North Indian Sikhs drew on both Hindu and Muslim teachings. Europeans borrowed scientific and medical ideas from the Islamic world and subsequently contributed their own rich scientific thinking to the entire planet.

In virtually every case, though, borrowing was selective rather than wholesale, even when it took place under conditions of foreign domination or colonial rule. Many peoples who appropriated Christianity or Islam certainly did not accept the rigid exclusivity and ardent monotheism of more orthodox versions of those faiths. Elite Chinese were far more interested in European mapmaking and mathematics than in Western medicine, while Japanese scholars became fascinated with the anatomical work of the Dutch. Neither, however, adopted Christianity in a widespread manner.

Borrowing was frequently the occasion for serious conflict. Some objected to much borrowing at all, particularly when it occurred under conditions of foreign domination or foreign threat. Thus members of the Taki Onqoy movement in Peru sought to wipe out Spanish influence and control, while Chinese and Japanese authorities clamped down firmly on European missionaries, even as they maintained some interest in European technological and scientific skills. Another kind of conflict derived from the efforts to control the terms of cultural borrowing. For example, European missionaries and Muslim reformers alike sought to root out "idolatry" among native converts.

To ease the tensions of cultural borrowing, efforts to "domesticate" foreign ideas and practices proliferated. Thus the Jesuits in China tried to point out similarities between Christianity and Confucianism, and Native American converts identified Christian saints with their own gods and spirits. By the late seventeenth century, some local churches in central Mexico had come to associate Catholicism less with the Spanish than with ancient pre-Aztec communities and beliefs that were now, supposedly, restored to their rightful position.

The pace of global cultural borrowing and its associated tensions stepped up even more as Europe's modern transformation unfolded in the nineteenth century and as its imperial reach extended and deepened around the world.

Second Thoughts

What's the Significance?

Big Picture Questions

1. Why did Christianity take hold in some places more than in others?
2. In what ways was the missionary message of Christianity shaped by the cultures of Asian and American peoples?
3. In what ways did the spread of Christianity, Islam, and modern science give rise to culturally based conflicts?
4. **Looking Back:** Based on Chapters 13 through 15, how might you challenge a Eurocentric understanding of the early modern era while acknowledging the growing role of Europeans on the global stage?

Next Steps: For Further Study

Natana J. Delong-Bas, *Wahhabi Islam: From Revival and Reform to Global Jihad* (2004). A careful study of the origins of Wahhabi Islam and its subsequent development.

Patricia Buckley Ebrey et al., *East Asia: A Cultural, Social, and Political History* (2005). A broad survey by major scholars in the field.

Geoffrey C. Gunn, *First Globalization: The Eurasian Exchange, 1500–1800* (2003). Explores the two-way exchange of ideas between Europe and Asia in the early modern era.

Toby E. Huff, *The Rise of Early Modern Science* (2003). A fascinating and controversial explanation as to why modern science arose in the West rather than in China or the Islamic world.

Úrsula de Jesús, *The Souls of Purgatory: The Spiritual Diary of a Seventeenth-Century Afro-Peruvian Mystic* (2004). A scholarly introduction by Nancy E. van Deusen places Úrsula in a broader context.

Diarmaid MacCulloch, *Christianity: The First Three Thousand Years* (2009). A masterful exploration of global Christianity with extensive coverage of the early modern era.

Deva Sobel, *A More Perfect Heaven: How Copernicus Revolutionized the Cosmos* (2011). A fascinating account of a major breakthrough in the Scientific Revolution.

"Christianity: A History of 'Dark Continents,' " http://vimeo.com/15944175.

Internet Modern History Sourcebook, "The Scientific Revolution," http://www.fordham.edu/halsall/mod/modsbook09.html. A collection of primary-source documents dealing with the breakthrough to modern science in Europe.

WORKING WITH EVIDENCE

Global Christianity in the Early Modern Era

During the early modern centuries, the world of European Christendom, long divided between its Roman Catholic and Eastern Orthodox branches, underwent two major transformations. First, the Reformation sharply divided Western Christendom into bitterly hostile Protestant and Catholic halves. And while that process was unfolding in Europe, missionaries— mostly Roman Catholic—rode the tide of European expansion to establish the faith in the Americas and parts of Africa and Asia. In those places, native converts sometimes imitated European patterns and at other times adapted the new religion to their own cultural traditions. Furthermore, smaller but ancient Christian communities persisted in Ethiopia, Armenia, Egypt, southern India, and elsewhere. Thus the Christian world of the early modern era was far more globalized and much more varied than before 1500. That variety found expression in both art and architecture, as the sources that follow illustrate.

Some of the differences between Protestant and Catholic Christianity become apparent in the interiors of their churches. To Martin Luther, the founder of Protestant Christianity, elaborate church interiors, with their many sculptures and paintings, represented a spiritual danger, for he feared that the wealthy few who endowed such images would come to believe that they were buying their way into Heaven rather than relying on God's grace. "It would be better," he wrote, "if we gave less to the churches and altars, . . . and more to the needy."[36] John Calvin, the prominent French-born Protestant theologian, went even further, declaring that "God forbade . . . the making of any images representing him."[37]

Behind such statements lay different understandings of the church building. While Roman Catholics generally saw a church as a temple or "house of God," sacred because it is where God dwells on earth, Protestants viewed churches more as meetinghouses, gathering places for a congregation. They were not sacred in themselves as places, but only on account of the worship that occurred within them.[38] Furthermore, to Protestants, images of the saints were an invitation to idolatry. Acting on such ideas, Protestants in various places stripped older churches of the offending images, decapitated statues, and sometimes ritually burned statues and paintings at the stake. The new

Interior of the Choir of St. Bavo's Church at Haarlem, 1660 (oil on panel), by Pieter Jansz Saenredam (1597–1665)/Worcester Art Museum, Massachusetts, USA/Bridgeman Images

Source 15.1 Interior of a Dutch Reformed Church

churches they created were often quite different from their Catholic counterparts. Source 15.1, a painting by the seventeenth-century Dutch artist Pieter Saenredam, portrays the interior of a Dutch Reformed (Protestant) church in the city of Haarlem.

Roman Catholic response to the Reformation took shape in the Catholic Reformation, or Counter-Reformation (see page 649). That vigorous movement found expression in a style of church architecture known as Baroque, which emerged powerfully in Catholic Europe as well as in the Spanish and Portuguese colonies of Latin America during the seventeenth and eighteenth centuries. The interiors of such churches were ornately adorned with paintings, ceiling frescoes, and statues, depicting Jesus on the cross, the Virgin and child, numerous saints, and biblical stories. The exuberant art of these church interiors appealed to the senses, seeking to provoke an emotional response of mystery, awe, and grandeur while kindling the faith of the worshippers and binding them firmly to the Catholic Church in the face of Protestant competition. Source 15.2 is a photograph of the interior of the Pilgrimage Church of Mariazell, located in present-day Austria. A church site since the twelfth century, the building was enlarged and refurbished in Baroque style in the seventeenth century.

Erich Lessing/Art Resource, NY

Source 15.2 Catholic Baroque, Interior of Pilgrimage Church, Mariazell, Austria

■ What obvious differences do you notice between these two church interiors? What kind of emotional responses would each of them have evoked?

■ In what ways do these church interiors reflect differences between Protestant and Catholic theology? (See Snapshot, page 647.)

■ How might Protestants and Catholics have reacted upon entering each other's churches?

■ Keep in mind that Source 15.1 is a painting. Why do you think the artist showed the people disproportionately small?

Throughout Latin America, Christianity was established in the context of European conquest and colonial rule (see pages 652–56). As the new faith took hold across the region, it incorporated much that was of European origin, as the construction of many large and ornate Baroque churches illustrates. But local communities also sought to blend this European Catholic Christianity with religious symbols and concepts drawn from their own traditions in a process that historians call syncretism. In the Andes, for example, Inca religion featured a supreme creator god (Viracocha); a sun god (Inti), regarded as the creator of the Inca people; a moon goddess (Killa), who was the wife of Inti and was attended by an order of priestesses; and an earth mother goddess (Pachamama), associated with mountain peaks and fertility. Those religious figures found their way into Andean understanding of Christianity, as Source 15.3 illustrates.

Painted around 1740 by an unknown artist, this striking image shows the Virgin Mary placed within the "rich mountain" of Potosí in Bolivia, from which the Spanish had extracted so much silver (see Chapter 14, page 614). Thus Christianity was visually expressed in an Andean tradition that viewed mountains as the embodiment of the gods. A number of smaller figures within the mountain represent the native miners whose labor had enriched their colonial rulers. A somewhat larger figure at the bottom of the mountain is an Inca ruler dressed in royal garb receiving tribute from his people. At the bottom left are the pope and a cardinal, while on the right stand the Habsburg emperor Charles V and perhaps his wife.

■ What is Mary's relationship to the heavenly beings standing above her (God the Father on the right; the dove, symbolizing the Holy Spirit, in the center; and Jesus on the left) as well as to the miners at work in the mountain? What is the significance of the crown above her head and her outstretched arms?

■ The European figures at the bottom are shown in a posture of prayer or thanksgiving. What might the artist have been trying to convey? How would you interpret the relative size of the European and Andean figures?

■ Why do you think the artist placed Mary actually inside the mountain rather than on it, while depicting her dress in a mountain-like form?

Museo de la Casa de la Mondea, Potosí, Bolivia/Gilles Mermet/akg-images

15.3 Cultural Blending in Andean Christianity

- What marks this painting and the one on page 653 as examples of syncretism?

- Do you read these two images from the Andes as subversive of the colonial order or as supportive of it? Do you think the artist who painted Source 15.3 was a European or a Native American Christian?

In China, unlike in Latin America, Christian missionaries operated in a setting wholly outside of European political control, bringing their faith to a powerful and proud civilization, long dominant in eastern Asia, where Confucianism, Daoism, and Buddhism had for many centuries mixed and mingled. The outcome of those missionary efforts was far more modest and much less successful than in the Americas. Nonetheless, in China too the tendency toward syncretism was evident. Jesuit missionaries themselves sought to present the Christian message within a Chinese cultural context to the intellectual and political elites who were their primary target audience. And Chinese Christians often transposed the new religion into more familiar cultural concepts. European critics of the Jesuit approach, however, feared that syncretism watered down the Christian message and risked losing its distinctive character.

Source 15.4 provides an example of Christianity becoming Chinese.[39] In the early seventeenth century, the Jesuits published several books in the Chinese language describing the life of Christ and illustrated them with a series of woodblock prints created by Chinese artists affiliated with the Jesuits. Although they were clearly modeled on European images, those prints cast Christian

Roma, ARSI, Jap. Sin I 43

Source 15.4 Making Christianity Chinese

figures into an altogether Chinese setting. The print in Source 15.4 portrays the familiar biblical story of the Annunciation, when an angel informs Mary that she will be the mother of Jesus. The house and furniture shown in the print suggest the dwelling of a wealthy Chinese scholar. The reading table in front of Mary was a common item in the homes of the literary elite of the time. The view from the window shows a seascape, mountains in the distance, a lone tree, and a "scholar's rock"—all of which were common features in Chinese landscape painting. The clouds that appear at the angel's feet and around the shaft of light shining on Mary are identical to those associated with sacred Buddhist and Daoist figures. To Chinese eyes, the angel might well appear as a Buddhist bodhisattva, while Mary may resemble a Ming dynasty noblewoman or perhaps Kuanyin, the Chinese Buddhist goddess of mercy and compassion.

- What specifically Chinese elements can you identify in this image?

- To whom might this image have been directed?

- How might educated Chinese have responded to this image?

- The European engraving on which this Chinese print was modeled included in the background the scene of Jesus' crucifixion. Why might the Chinese artist have chosen to omit that scene from his image?

- How would European critics of the Jesuits' approach to missionary work have reacted to this image? To what extent has the basic message of Catholic Christianity been retained or altered in this Chinese cultural setting?

As Chinese emperors welcomed Jesuit missionaries at court, so too did the rulers of Mughal India during the time of Akbar (r. 1556–1605) and Jahangir (r. 1605–1627). But while Chinese elite circles received the Jesuits for their scientific skills, especially in astronomy, the Mughal court seemed more interested in the religious and artistic achievements of European civilization. Akbar invited the Jesuits to take part in cross-religious discussions that included Muslim, Hindu, Jain, and Zoroastrian scholars. Furthermore, the Mughal emperors eagerly embraced the art of late Renaissance Europe, which the Jesuits provided to them, much of it devotional and distinctly Christian. Mughal artists quickly learned to paint in the European style, and soon murals featuring Jesus, Mary, and Christian saints appeared on the walls of palaces, garden pavilions, and harems of the Mughal court, while miniature paintings adorned books, albums, and jewelry.

In religious terms, however, the Jesuit efforts were "a fantastic and extravagant failure,"[40] for these Muslim rulers of India were not in the least interested in abandoning Islam for the Christian faith, and few conversions of any kind occurred. Akbar and Jahangir, however, were cosmopolitan connoisseurs of art, which they collected, reproduced, and displayed. European religious art also had propaganda value in enhancing their status. Jesus and Mary, after all, had a prominent place within Islam. Jesus was seen both as an earlier prophet and as a mystical figure, similar to the Sufi masters who were so important in Indian Islam. Mughal paintings, pairing the adult Jesus and Mary side by side, were placed above the imperial throne as well as on the emperor's jewelry and his official seal, suggesting an identification of Jesus and a semi-divine emperor. That the mothers of both Akbar and Jahangir were named Mary only added to the appeal. Thus Akbar and Jahangir sought to incorporate European-style Christian art into their efforts to create a blended and tolerant religious culture for the elites of their vast and diverse realm. It was a culture that drew on Islam, Hinduism, Zoroastrianism, and Christianity.

But as Catholic devotional art was reworked by Mughal artists, it was also subtly changed. Source 15.5 shows an early seventeenth-century depiction of the Holy Family painted by an Indian artist.

The Free Library of Philadelphia/Bridgeman Images

Source 15.5 Christian Art at the Mughal Court

■ Why do you think that this Mughal painter portrayed Mary and Joseph as rather distinguished and educated persons rather than as the humble carpenter and his peasant wife, as in so many European images? Why might he have placed the family in rather palatial surroundings instead of a stable?

■ How do you imagine European missionaries responded to this representation of the Holy Family?

■ How might more orthodox Muslims have reacted to the larger project of creating a blended religion making use of elements from many traditions?

■ What similarities can you identify between this Indian image and the Chinese print in Source 15.4? Pay attention to the setting, the clothing, the class status of the human figures, and the scenes outside the windows.

DOING HISTORY

Global Christianity in the Early Modern Era

1. **Making comparisons:** What common Christian elements can you identify in these visual sources? What differences in the expression of Christianity can you define?

2. **Considering Mary:** The Catholic Christian tradition as it developed in Latin America, China, and India as well as Europe assigned a very important role to representations of the Virgin Mary. Why might such images of Mary have been so widely appealing? But in what ways does the image of the Holy Mother differ in Sources 15.3, 15.4, and 15.5? In what ways were those images adapted to the distinctive cultures in which they were created?

3. **Pondering syncretism:** From a missionary viewpoint, develop arguments for and against religious syncretism using these visual sources as points of reference.

4. **Considering visual sources as evidence:** What are the strengths and limitations of these visual sources, as opposed to texts, as historians seek to understand the globalization of Christianity in the early modern era? What other visual sources might be useful?

PART FIVE

THE EUROPEAN MOMENT IN WORLD HISTORY

1750–1914

Contents

EUROPEAN CENTRALITY AND THE PROBLEM OF EUROCENTRISM

During the century and a half between 1750 and 1914, sometimes referred to as the "long nineteenth century," two new and related phenomena held center stage in the global history of humankind and represent the major themes of the four chapters that follow. The first of these, explored in Chapters 16 and 17, was the creation of a new kind of human society, commonly called "modern." It emerged from the intersection of the Scientific, French, and Industrial Revolutions, all of which took shape initially in Western Europe. Those societies generated many of the transformative ideas that have guided human behavior over the past several centuries: that movement toward social equality and the end of poverty was possible; that ordinary people might participate in political life; that nations might trump empires; that women could be equal to men; that slavery was no longer necessary.

The second theme of this long nineteenth century, which is addressed in Chapters 18 and 19, was the growing ability of these modern societies to exercise enormous power and influence over the rest of humankind. In some places, this occurred within expanding European empires, such as those that governed India, Southeast Asia, Africa, and Pacific Oceania. Elsewhere, it took place through less formal means—economic penetration, military intervention, diplomatic pressure, missionary activity—in states that remained officially independent, such as China, Japan, the Ottoman Empire, and various countries in Latin America.

Together, these two phenomena thrust Western Europe, and to a lesser extent North America, into a new and far more prominent role in world history than ever before. While various regions had experienced sprouts of modernity during the "early modern" centuries, it was in Western European societies that these novel ways of living emerged most fully. Those societies, and their North American offspring, also came to exercise a wholly unprecedented role in world affairs, as they achieved, collectively, something approaching global dominance by the early twentieth century.

But if Europeans were moving toward dominance over other peoples, they were also leading a human intervention in the natural order of unprecedented dimensions, largely the product of industrialization. The demand for raw materials to supply new factories and to feed their workers drove developments

MAPPING PART FIVE

U.S. westward
expansion
Chapters 17, 18

Women's rights
Chapter 16

American Revolution
Chapter 16

Haitian Revolution
Chapter 16

Mexican Revolution
Chapter 17

Abolition of slavery
Chapter 16

Latin American independence
and industrialization
Chapters 16, 17

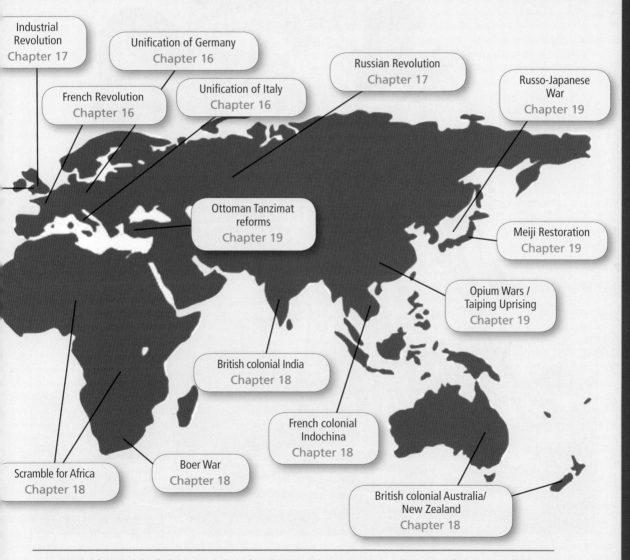

Industrial Revolution
Chapter 17

Unification of Germany
Chapter 16

Russian Revolution
Chapter 17

Russo-Japanese War
Chapter 19

French Revolution
Chapter 16

Unification of Italy
Chapter 16

Ottoman Tanzimat reforms
Chapter 19

Meiji Restoration
Chapter 19

Opium Wars / Taiping Uprising
Chapter 19

British colonial India
Chapter 18

French colonial Indochina
Chapter 18

Scramble for Africa
Chapter 18

Boer War
Chapter 18

British colonial Australia/ New Zealand
Chapter 18

Vive le Roi, Vive la Nation.

Jsavois ben Qu'jaurions not tour.

Atlantic Revolutions, Global Echoes

1750–1914

The Haitian earthquake of January 2010 not only devastated an already-impoverished country but also reawakened issues deriving from that country's revolution against slavery and French colonial rule, which finally succeeded in 1804. Twenty-one years later, the French government demanded from Haiti a payment of 150 million gold francs in compensation for the loss of its richest colony and its "property" in slaves. With French warships hovering offshore, Haitian authorities agreed. To make the heavy payments, even after they were somewhat reduced, Haiti took out major loans from French, German, and North American banks. Repaying those loans, finally accomplished only in 1947, represented a huge drain on the country's budget, costing 80 percent of the government's revenue in 1915. In 2010, with the country in ruins, an international petition signed by over 100 prominent people called on the French government to repay some $17 billion, effectively returning the "independence debt" extorted from Haiti 185 years earlier. While the French government dismissed those claims, the issue provided a reminder of the continuing echoes of events from an earlier age of revolution.

The Haitian Revolution was part of and linked to a much larger set of upheavals that shook both sides of the Atlantic world between 1775 and 1825. Haitians had drawn inspiration from the earlier North American and French revolutions, even as their successful overthrow of French rule helped shape the Latin American independence struggles that followed. These four closely related upheavals reflect the new connections among Europe, Africa,

---

Revolution and the Reversal of Class Roles Three French female figures, representing from right to left the clergy, nobility, and commoners (Third Estate), show the reversal of class roles that the revolution generated. Now the commoner rides on the back of the noblewoman and is shown in a dominant position over the nun.

SEEKING THE MAIN POINT

What were the most important outcomes of the Atlantic revolutions, both immediately and in the century that followed?

North America, and South America, which took shape in the wake of Columbus's voyages and the European conquests that followed. Together, they launched a new chapter in the history of the Atlantic world, while the echoes of those revolutions reverberated in the larger world.

Atlantic Revolutions in a Global Context

Writing to a friend in 1772, before any of the Atlantic revolutions had occurred, the French intellectual Voltaire asked, "My dear philosopher, doesn't this appear to you to be the century of revolutions?"[1] He was certainly on target, and not only for the European/Atlantic world. From the early eighteenth century to the mid-nineteenth, many parts of the world witnessed political and social upheaval, leading some historians to think in terms of a "world crisis" or "converging revolutions." By the 1730s, the Safavid dynasty that had ruled Persia (now Iran) for several centuries had completely collapsed, even as the powerful Mughal Empire governing India also fragmented. About the same time, the Wahhabi movement in Arabia seriously threatened the Ottoman Empire, and its religious ideals informed major political upheavals in Central Asia and elsewhere (see Chapter 15, pages 659–61). The Russian Empire under Catherine the Great experienced a series of peasant uprisings, most notably one led by the Cossack commander Pugachev in 1773–1774, which briefly proclaimed the end of serfdom before that rebellion was crushed. China too in the late eighteenth and early nineteenth centuries hosted a number of popular though unsuccessful rebellions, a prelude perhaps to the huge Taiping revolution of 1850–1864. Beginning in the early nineteenth century, a wave of Islamic revolutions shook West Africa, while in southern Africa a series of wars and migrations known as the *mfecane* (the breaking or crushing) involved widespread and violent disruptions as well as the creation of new states and societies.

Thus the Atlantic revolutions in North America, France, Haiti, and Latin America took place within a larger global framework. Like many of the other upheavals, they too occurred in the context of expensive wars, weakening states, and destabilizing processes of commercialization. But compared to upheavals elsewhere, the Atlantic revolutions were distinctive in various ways. The costly wars that strained European imperial states—Britain, France, and Spain in particular—were global rather than regional. In the so-called Seven Years' War (1754–1763), Britain and France joined battle in North America, the Caribbean, West Africa, and South Asia. The expenses of those conflicts prompted the British to levy additional taxes on their North American colonies and the French monarchy to seek new revenue from its landowners. These actions contributed to the launching of the North American and French revolutions, respectively.

Furthermore, the Atlantic revolutions were distinctive in that they were closely connected to one another. The American revolutionary leader Thomas Jefferson

A MAP OF TIME

1775–1787	North American Revolution
1780s	Beginnings of antislavery movement
1789–1799	French Revolution
1791–1804	Haitian Revolution
1793–1794	Execution of Louis XVI; the Terror in France
1799–1814	Reign of Napoleon
1807	End of slave trade in British Empire
1808–1825	Latin American wars of independence
1810–1811	Hidalgo-Morelos rebellion in Mexico
1822	Brazil gains independence from Portugal
1848	Women's Rights Convention, Seneca Falls, New York
1861	Emancipation of serfs in Russia
1861–1865	Civil War and abolition of slavery in United States
1870–1871	Unification of Germany and Italy
1886–1888	Cuba and Brazil abolish slavery
1920	Women gain the vote in United States

was the U.S. ambassador to France on the eve of the French Revolution. While there, he provided advice and encouragement to French reformers and revolutionaries. Simón Bolívar, a leading figure in Spanish American struggles for independence, twice visited Haiti, where he received military aid from the first black government in the Americas.

Beyond such direct connections, the various Atlantic revolutionaries shared a set of common ideas. The Atlantic basin had become a world of intellectual and cultural exchange as well as one of commercial and biological interaction. The ideas that animated the Atlantic revolutions derived from the European Enlightenment and were shared across the ocean in newspapers, books, and pamphlets. At the heart of these ideas was the radical notion that human political and social arrangements could be engineered, and improved, by human action. Thus conventional and long-established ways of living and thinking—the divine right of kings, state control of trade, aristocratic privilege, the authority of a single church—were no longer sacrosanct and came under repeated attack. New ideas of liberty, equality, free trade, religious tolerance, republicanism, and human rationality were in the air. Politically, the core notion was "popular sovereignty," which meant that the authority to govern derived from the people rather than from God or from established tradition. As the Englishman John Locke (1632–1704) had argued, the "social contract" between ruler and ruled should last only as long as it served the people well. In short, it was both possible and desirable to start over in the construction of human communities. In the late eighteenth and early nineteenth centuries, these ideas were largely limited to the Atlantic world. While all of the Atlantic revolutions involved the elimination of monarchs, at least temporarily, across Asia and the Middle East such republican political systems were virtually inconceivable until much later. There the only solution to a bad monarch was a new and better one.

■ **Causation**

In what ways did the ideas of the Enlightenment contribute to the Atlantic revolutions?

In the world of the Atlantic revolutions, ideas born of the Enlightenment generated endless controversy. Were liberty and equality compatible? What kind of government—unitary and centralized or federal and decentralized—best ensured freedom? And how far should liberty be extended? Except in Haiti, the chief beneficiaries of these revolutions were propertied white men of the "middling classes." Although women, slaves, Native Americans, and men without property did not gain much from these revolutions, the ideas that accompanied those upheavals gave them ammunition for the future. Because their overall thrust was to extend political rights further than ever before, these Atlantic movements have often been referred to as "democratic revolutions."

A final distinctive feature of the Atlantic revolutions lies in their immense global impact, extending well beyond the Atlantic world. The armies of revolutionary France, for example, invaded Egypt, Germany, Poland, and Russia, carrying seeds of change. The ideals that animated these Atlantic revolutions inspired efforts in many countries to abolish slavery, to extend the right to vote, to develop constitutions, and to secure greater equality for women. Nationalism, perhaps the most potent ideology of the modern era, was nurtured in the Atlantic revolutions and shaped much of nineteenth- and twentieth-century world history. The ideas of human equality articulated in these revolutions later found expression in feminist, socialist, and communist movements. The Universal Declaration of Human Rights, adopted by the United Nations in 1948, echoed and amplified those principles while providing the basis for any number of subsequent protests against oppression, tyranny, and deprivation. In 1989, a number of Chinese students, fleeing the suppression of a democracy movement in their own country, marched at the head of a huge parade in Paris, celebrating the bicentennial of the French Revolution. And in 2011, the Middle Eastern uprisings known as the Arab Spring initially prompted numerous comparisons with the French Revolution. The Atlantic revolutions had a long reach.

Comparing Atlantic Revolutions

Despite their common political vocabulary and a broadly democratic character, the Atlantic revolutions differed substantially from one another. They were triggered by different circumstances, expressed quite different social and political tensions, and varied considerably in their outcomes. Liberty, noted Simón Bolívar, "is a suc-culent morsel, but one difficult to digest."[2] "Digesting liberty" occurred in quite distinct ways in the various sites of the Atlantic revolutions.

The North American Revolution, 1775–1787

Every schoolchild in the United States learns early that the American Revolution was a struggle for independence from oppressive British rule. That struggle was launched with the Declaration of Independence in 1776, resulted in an unlikely military victory by 1781, and generated a federal constitution in 1787, joining thir-teen formerly separate colonies into a new nation (see Map 16.1). It was the first in a series of upheavals that rocked the Atlantic world and beyond in the century that followed. But was it a genuine revolution? What, precisely, did it change?

By effecting a break with Britain, the American Revolution marked a decisive political change, but in other ways it was, strangely enough, a conservative move-ment, because it originated in an effort to preserve the existing liberties of the colo-nies rather than to create new ones. For much of the seventeenth and eighteenth centuries, the British colonies in North America enjoyed a considerable degree of local autonomy, as the British government was embroiled in its own internal con-flicts and various European wars. Furthermore, Britain's West Indian colonies seemed more profitable and of greater significance than those of North America. In these circumstances, local elected assemblies in North America, dominated by the wealth-ier property-owning settlers, achieved something close to self-government. Colo-nists came to regard such autonomy as a birthright and part of their English heritage. Thus, until the mid-eighteenth century, almost no one in the colonies thought of breaking away from England because participation in the British Empire provided many advantages—protection in war, access to British markets, and confirmation of the settlers' continuing identity as "Englishmen"—and few drawbacks.

There were, however, real differences between Englishmen in England and those in the North American colonies. Within the colonies, English settlers had developed societies described by a leading historian as "the most radical in the con-temporary Western world." Certainly class distinctions were real and visible, and a small class of wealthy "gentlemen"—the Adamses, Washingtons, Jeffersons, and Hancocks—wore powdered wigs, imitated the latest European styles, were promi-nent in political life, and were generally accorded deference by ordinary people. But the ready availability of land following the dispossession of Native Americans, the scarcity of people, and the absence of both a titled nobility and a single estab-lished church meant that social life was far more open than in Europe. No legal distinctions differentiated clergy, aristocracy, and commoners, as they did in France. All free men enjoyed the same status before the law, a situation that excluded black slaves and, in some ways, white women as well. These conditions made for less poverty, more economic opportunity, fewer social differences, and easier relation-ships among the classes than in Europe. The famous economist Adam Smith observed

■ **Change**

What was revolutionary about the American Revo-lution, and what was not?

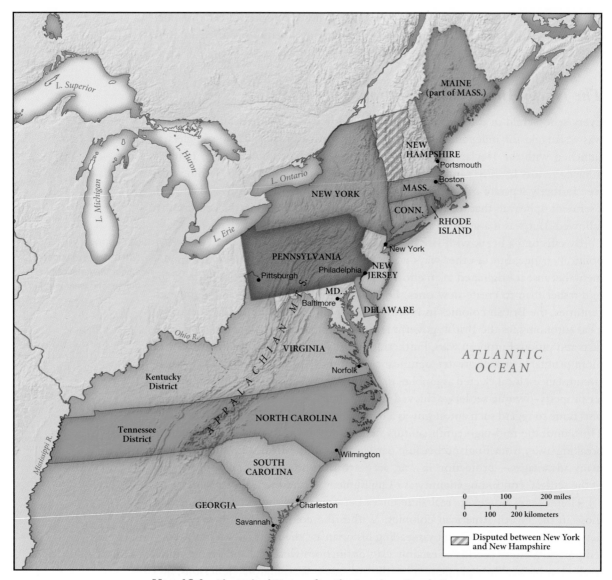

Map 16.1   The United States after the American Revolution

The union of the thirteen British colonies in North America created the embryonic United States, shown here in 1788. Over the past two centuries and more of anticolonial struggles, it was the only example of separate colonies joining together after independence to form a larger and enduring nation.

that British colonists were "republican in their manners . . . and their government" well before their independence from England.[3]

Thus the American Revolution grew not from social tensions within the colonies, but from a rather sudden and unexpected effort by the British government to tighten its control over the colonies and to extract more revenue from them. As

Britain's global struggle with France drained its treasury and ran up its national debt, British authorities, beginning in the 1760s, looked to America to make good these losses. Abandoning its neglectful oversight of the colonies, Britain began to act like a genuine imperial power, imposing a variety of new taxes and tariffs on the colonies without their consent, for they were not represented in the British Parliament. Many of the colonists were infuriated, because such measures challenged their economic interests, their established traditions of local autonomy, and their identity as true Englishmen. Armed with the ideas of the Enlightenment—popular sovereignty, natural rights, the consent of the governed—they went to war, and by 1781 they had prevailed, with considerable aid from the French, who were only too pleased to harm the interests of their British rivals.

What was revolutionary about the American experience was not so much the revolution itself but the kind of society that had already emerged within the colonies. Independence from Britain was not accompanied by any wholesale social transformation. Rather, the revolution accelerated the established democratic tendencies of the colonial societies. Political authority remained largely in the hands of existing elites who had led the revolution, although property requirements for voting were lowered and more white men of modest means, such as small farmers and urban artisans, were elected to state legislatures.

This widening of political participation gradually eroded the power of traditional gentlemen, but no women or people of color shared in these gains. Land was not seized from its owners, except in the case of pro-British loyalists who had fled the country. Although slavery was gradually abolished in the northern states, where it counted for little, it remained firmly entrenched in the southern states, where it counted for much. Chief Justice John Marshall later gave voice to this conservative understanding of the American Revolution: "All contracts and rights, respecting property, remained unchanged by the Revolution."[4] In the century that followed independence, the United States did become the world's most democratic country, but this development was less the direct product of the revolution and more the gradual working out in a reformist fashion of earlier practices and the principles of equality announced in the Declaration of Independence.

Nonetheless, many American patriots felt passionately that they were creating "a new order for the ages." James Madison in the *Federalist Papers* made the point clearly: "We pursued a new and more noble course . . . and accomplished a revolution that has no parallel in the annals of human society." Supporters abroad agreed. On the eve of the French Revolution, a Paris newspaper proclaimed that the United States was "the hope and model of the human race."[5] In both cases, they were referring primarily to the political ideas and practices of the new country. The American Revolution, after all, initiated the political dismantling of Europe's New World empires. The "right to revolution," proclaimed in the Declaration of Independence and made effective only in a great struggle, inspired revolutionaries and nationalists from Simón Bolívar in nineteenth-century Latin America to Ho Chi Minh in twentieth-century Vietnam. Moreover, the new U.S. Constitution—with its Bill of Rights, checks and balances, separation of church and state, and federalism—was one of the first sustained efforts to put the political ideas of the Enlightenment into practice. That document, and the ideas that it embraced, echoed repeatedly in the political upheavals of the century that followed.

The French Revolution, 1789–1815

Act Two in the drama of the Atlantic revolutions took place in France, beginning in 1789, although it was closely connected to Act One in North America. Thousands of French soldiers had provided assistance to the American colonists and now returned home full of republican enthusiasm. Thomas Jefferson, the U.S. ambassador in Paris, reported that France "has been awakened by our revolution."[6] More immediately, the French government, which had generously aided the Americans in an effort to undermine its British rivals, was teetering on the brink of bankruptcy and had long sought reforms that would modernize the tax system and make it more equitable. In a desperate effort to raise taxes against the opposition of the privileged classes, the French king, Louis XVI, had called into session an ancient representative body, the Estates General. It consisted of male representatives of the three "estates," or legal orders, of prerevolutionary France: the clergy, the nobility, and the commoners. The first two estates comprised about 2 percent of the population, and the Third Estate included everyone else. When that body convened in 1789, representatives of the Third Estate soon organized themselves as the National Assembly, claiming the sole authority to make laws for the country. A few weeks later, they drew up the Declaration of the Rights of Man and Citizen, which forthrightly declared that "men are born and remain free and equal in rights." These actions, unprecedented and illegal in the *ancien régime* (the old regime), launched the French Revolution and radicalized many of the participants in the National Assembly.

■ **Comparison**

How did the French Revolution differ from the American Revolution?

The French Revolution was quite different from its North American predecessor. Whereas the American Revolution expressed the tensions of a colonial relationship with a distant imperial power, the French insurrection was driven by sharp conflicts within French society. Members of the titled nobility—privileged, prestigious, and wealthy—resented and resisted the monarchy's efforts to subject them to new taxes. Educated middle-class men such as doctors, lawyers, lower-level officials, and merchants were growing in numbers and sometimes in wealth and were offended by the remaining privileges of the aristocracy, from which they were excluded. Ordinary urban men and women, many of whose incomes had declined for a generation, were hit particularly hard in the late 1780s by the rapidly rising price of bread and widespread unemployment. Peasants in the countryside, though largely free of serfdom, were subject to hated dues imposed by their landlords, taxes from the state, obligations to the Church, and the requirement to work without pay on public roads. As Enlightenment ideas penetrated French society, more and more people, mostly in the Third Estate but also including some priests and nobles, found a language with which to articulate these grievances. The famous French